RUMINATIONS OF AN ORTHOPAEDIST

Reflection on a changing discipline

Augusto Sarmiento, MD

Publisher: Augusto Sarmiento MD

Copyright © 2017 by Augusto Sarmiento MD.
ISBN: 978-0-9989257-3-8

All rights reserved. No part of this book may be reproduced in whole or in part without written permission from the publisher, except by reviewer who may quote excerpts in connection with a review in its newspaper, magazine, journal or electronic publication.

Neither the authors nor publisher can be held responsible for any loss or claim arising out of the use or misuse, of the suggestions made or implied.

Cover photo credit to: Einhard Scheimplug

Dedication

I dedicate this book to those seeking improved patient care, dream of a better future and are willing to question traditions and fashionable, unproven practices of the moment.

ACKNOWLEDGMENT

It is important to me to make clear to the readers of this book, that the entire text was written thirteen years ago. The publisher had edited and printed my book, in English as well as in Spanish, but suddenly withdrew his long-held position and cancelled its release to the public. In his statement to me, he clearly said they had recently found out his Company was not the appropriate vehicle for the completion of this type of project. Since no other reason was given, I let the readers discern why the publisher would spend so much effort to edit and print the book, and then stop abruptly.

Recently, as I was going over old documents, and once again reading the book, it occurred to me that its publication was probably a good idea, despite the fact time had taken care of modifying some of my views I had originally expressed. Some in a mild way, others in a radical and opposite direction. Such changes, I concluded, did not call for apologies, since they were honest acknowledgements of a logical evolution of my ideas. We all know that at the end of the day all ideas die, often to be replaced by new ones. Furthermore, I realized that many of the events and circumstances that had originally led me to write the book had remained unchanged. With that in mind, I elected not to clarify those changes and to allow the publication to take place without explanations. Reading the text as a history of rapid evolution might prove to be a learning experience.

PREFACE

"In every civilization its most impressive period seems to precede death by only a moment. Like the woods of autumn, life defies death in a glorious pageantry of colors."

Reinhold Neibuhr.

It is widely accepted that the United Sates is facing a "healthcare crisis" that has created an unprecedented level of discomfort at various levels of society. The issues surrounding the "crisis" are many and complex. It is, therefore, ludicrous to pretend that there is an easy explanation for the current unhappiness in all quarters. In my opinion, however, the deterioration of professionalism within the medical profession is an important factor, which unfortunately has received little attention in the debate. Organized medicine seems unwilling or unable to indulge in the necessary self-criticism that the situation requires; it finds itself on the defensive, giving its critics a clear advantage.

The relativism that dominates our society to a perhaps unpresented degree has effectively extended its tentacles into medicine in a rapid manner. Some of the traditional tenets that governed medicine for many a generation are vanishing. The "hunger for more" that characterizes our capitalist ethos applies to medicine as well. Everything is right, therefore there is nothing really wrong. To many, medicine is just another business where the methods used by the business community equally apply. Through a Faustian bargain we elected to sell out for the sake of profit. Any moral deviation no longer brings any stigma whatsoever.

There is no doubt that the scientific and technical revolution that began a few decades ago resulted in major improvements in medicine. However, such benefits have inadvertently created unanticipated problems. The use and abuse of those developments are an integral part of the genesis of the situation we face today.

The comments and statements I make throughout the text are primarily limited to my own orthopaedic discipline. This limitation should not suggest unawareness of the inescapable subordination to the rest of the medical profession or to society as a whole. A resolution of many of the difficulties Orthopaedics is confronting cannot and should not be addressed in isolation. However, I am not qualified to delve into discussions that encompass the whole spectrum. However, on several occasions I ventured into territories and subjects with which I lack the necessary knowledge and expertise. I hope to be forgiven for such intrusion.

The viability of medicine depends heavily on the ability of its practitioners to maintain the highest possible level of constant learning. Since continuing education of the orthopaedist is now virtually under the control of the pharmaceutical and surgical implant manufacturing industry, any hope that change in many existing trends and patterns may be unattainable. Organized medicine and academic institutions have elected to "get in bed" with industry in order to reap the economic benefits that such marriage provides them. We have lacked the intestinal fortitude and commitment to excellence required to offset the trend.

Our subordination to the awesome economic and social influence of industry seems to have been the consummation of a Faustian bargain that called for compromising moral values in return for financial rewards. The well-entrenched power of industry is likely to remain immovable, and in the process medicine will drift into moral degradation.

Though medicine in general is rapidly removing myths and preconceived notions about the nature of illness and disease, a trend that Hippocrates started over two millennia ago, but has not as yet completed the necessary "cleansing." Old erroneous dogmas are often replaced with new but equally erroneous ones. In Orthopaedic Surgery, this is to a great extend due to the fact that the mechanical approach to musculoskeletal disease has significantly displaced the biological one.

Over the years I have expressed concern over a number of metaphysical issues confronting our profession and have, to the best of my ability, tried to bring those concerns to the attention of my peers. I use this book to dwell on some of those issues as well. They touch on themes such as the very nature of our profession, its relationship with other disciplines within medicine, ethics and values, professionalism, education, research, sub-specialization, certificates of additional competency, academic medicine, resident education, health care reform, socio-economic changes, death and suffering, organized orthopaedics and its changing directions, the orthopaedic-industrial complex and many others.

I think that since I had the opportunity to practice my profession during explosive years of change and witnessed them at close range, I have a degree of understanding of those changes that younger generations may not have. I entered orthopaedics the year the polio vaccine was invented and the proliferation of potent antibiotics took place. I witnessed the advent of sophisticated means of fracture osteosynthesis; the correction of scoliosis and fusion of the spine with metallic instrumentation; the invention of the arthroscope; the successful performance of total joint arthroplasty; the spectacular contributions of imaging technology and many others. Now I expect to be witness to the loudly heralded era which promises to eradicate disease through genetic engineering means; an era, which, despite its promises may not become a reality in this or the next few generations.

I observed the appearance of sub-specialties and the continued fragmentation of orthopaedics into a multitude of separate disciplines; the erosion of our profession from outside forces and the loss of territory to others such as neuro-surgeons, physiatrists, podiatrists, plastic surgeons, rheumatologists, emergency room doctors, general surgeons, general practitioners, chiropractors, physician assistants, nurse practitioners, and many others. I experienced at close range the practicing orthopaedists' attitudinal changes brought about by the birth of Medicare and Medicaid, the commercialization of medicine and the resulting greed of some of its practitioners; the government intrusions into the lives of physicians; the disturbing effects of Managed Care, and the myriad of societal changes that inevitably altered the practice of medicine.

The fact that I had the opportunity to be involved not only in the practice of orthopaedics, but also had a major involvement in education, may have provided me with a more panoramic view of the evolution of the profession. For over thirty consecutive years I participated in the scientific program of the Academy. I served for twenty years as professor and chairman of two major orthopaedic residency programs: the University of Miami and the University of Southern California, the latter then the largest training program in the United States. In addition, I was involved in administrative and educational matters within subspecialty societies, having been a founding member of the Hip Society and the International Hip Society and served as president of the former. I was elected to the Board of Directors of the Academy and served in that capacity for eight years, and as its president for one year.

I feel this background justifies my voicing opinions, without expectation that all of them will be found to be correct, but without fear of criticism if proven wrong. I do not worry about the fact that one day every opinion I have rendered in this book will be found wanting, but so will the opinions of others, which I have dared to question.

These are some of the reasons that prompted me to write this book. A book that is not the typical medical publication we have on the shelves of our libraries. In it, I simply identify subjects familiar to me, where I think there is or should be controversy. I voice personal opinions and criticism; and raise questions in a manner, which will hopefully provoke thought, particularly, among the young readers.

Contrary to the practice of including references to information published in professional texts, I have elected to limit them to publications in which I was the principal author or had served as co-author because of my involvement in the effort. Embarking on a project that required precise quotation of references of others' work would have been a major undertaking, which I was not willing to assume.

I have divided the text into three sections which reflect the areas where I have had the greatest experience: I: TRAUMA, II: THE HIP JOINT: Fractures and Reconstructive Surgery, and III: MISCELLANEOUS. The latter section includes comments on a variety of subjects of philosophical, political or administrative nature. The Addendum contains a few published articles dealing with subjects of a political/academic nature, which should shed light into my overall personal attitudes toward a changing discipline.

SECTION 1 TRAUMA

A. Achilles Tendon Rupture
   Acromio-clavicular dislocation
   Amputations:
   Lower extremity
   Below-the knee amputation
   Skin Flaps
   The Fibula
   Nerves and Vessels
   Contractures
   Immediate post-operative fitting
   Syme's amputation
   Above-the knee amputation
   Upper Extremity
   Immediate post-operative fitting
   Angulation in Fractures
   Medial Malleolus Fractures
   Lateral Malleolus Fractures
   Tri-malleolar Fractures

B. Bracing (Fractures).   See FEMORAL, FOREARM, TIBIA, ULNA Fractures

C. Capitellum Fractures
   Children's Fractures
   Clavicle Fractures
   Collateral Ligaments (Knee)
   Colles' fractures
   Compartment Syndromes
   Cruciate Ligament Injuries

D. Deltoid Ligament Injuries
   Dislocation of the Shoulder (See Shoulder Dislocation)
   Dislocation of the tibia-fibular joint

E. Electrical Stimulation

F. Fat Embolism
   Femoral Head Fractures
   Femoral Neck Fractures
   Femoral Shaft Fractures
   Fibular Fractures
   Forearm Fractures
   Fracture Healing

G. Galeazzi Fractures
   Gunshot wounds (Fractures)

- H. Humeral Head Fractures
  Humeral Shaft Fractures

- I. Ilizarof Technique
  Incongruity
  Interlocking Nailing of Femoral Shaft Fractures (See FEMUR)
  Interlocking Nailing of Tibial Fractures
  Intertrochanteric Fractures
  Intraarticular Fractures of the Humerus (Distal)

- M. Malrotation (Fractures)
  Medial epycondyle Fractures
  Meniscus Injuries, Repair and Transplants
  Metacarpal Fractures

- N. Non Union

- O. Olecranon Fractures
  Open Fractures

- P. Patella Fractures
  Periosteum in Fracture Healing (See FRACTURE HEALING)
  Peripheral Nerve Injuries
  Peroneal Tendons Dislocation
  Plafond Fractures
  Plica

- R. Radial Head Fractures
  Radial Nerve Palsy
  Radio-Ulnar Joint (Distal)

- S. Shortening in Fractures
  Shoulder Dislocation
  Shoulder Sub-luxation
  Spinal Cord Injuries
  Synostosis

- T. Talus Fractures
  Tibia Condylar Fractures
  Tibial Plafond Fractures
  Tibial Shaft Fractures

- U. Ulnar Fractures

SECTION II   THE HIP JOINT: FRACTURES AND RECONSTRUCTIVE SURGERY

- A. Acetabular Fractures
  Acetabular Orientation (Total Hips)
  Acetabular osteotomy
  Age and Total Hips
  Avascular Necrosis

- B. Bilateral Total Hips
  Bio-degradable Materials
  Bipolar Prostheses

- C. Capsulectomy in Hip Osteoarthritis
  Carbon Composites in Total Hips

- D. Dislocations
  Dislocation of Total Hips

- E. Endoprostheses

- F. Femoral Head Fractures
  Femoral Neck Fractures
  Fusion

- G. Graft (Acetabulum. Total Hip)

- H. Heterotopic Bone
  Hybrid Total Hips

- I. Infection in Total Hips
  Intertrochanteric Fractures
  Isoelastic Total Hip Prostheses

- L. Labrum (Acetabulum)
  Laminar Air Flow Systems
  Length discrepancy (Total Hip surgery)
  Lysis

- M. Metal backed Acetabular Cups in Total Hip Surgery
  Metal on Metal Total Hips
  Minimally Invasive total hip replacement
  Modular Components

- N. Non-cemented Total Hips (See Press-Fit Implants)

- O. Osteoarthritis
  Osteoarthritis (Destructive)
  Osteotomy in the Treatment of Osteoarthritis of the Hip

P. Plugging the Medullary Canal
    Pre-coated Total Hips
    Press-Fit Implants
    Pressurization of Cement
    Progress in Total Hip Surgery
    Pulmonary embolism (See THROMBOEMBOLIC DISEASE)

R. Rehabilitation of Total Hip Patients. (See rehabilitation Section III)
    Revision Surgery without Trochanteric Osteotomy

T. Thromboembolic Disease
    Titanium in Total Hip Surgery
    Total Hip Surgery: Factors predictive of Success
    Varus deformity in hip fractures
    Vascular Injury in Total Hip Surgery

W. Wear
    Wires (broken)
    Wound Closure and Dressing

SECTION III MISCELLANEOUS

- A. Advertising
  Alternative Medicine
  American Academy of Orthopaedic Surgeons
  A.O.
  Association for the Rational Treatment of Fractures (ARTOF)
  Arthritis and Osteoporosis Programs
  Arthroscopy

- B. Back Pain
  Bone grafts and Substitutes

- C. Cartilage Transplants
  Certificates of Additional Qualifications (CAQ)
  Chondromalacia
  Complications in Surgery
  Criticizing colleagues

- E. Erosion of Orthopaedics
  Ethics in Medicine

- F. Fellowships in Orthopaedics
  For-profit Hospitals
  Fragmentation of Orthopaedics

- G. Gait Analysis
  Grand Rounds
  Greed

- H. Health Care Reform
  Hemiplegia

- I. Industry and Orthopaedics
  Interviewing prospective Residents
  Intra-articular osteochondromas

- J. Journals and other publications

- L. Litigation

- M. Magnetic resonance Imaging (MRI)

- N. Nursing Homes

- O. Objectivity
  Osteoarthritis (See Osteoarthritis, Section II, THE HIP JOINT)

Outcome Studies

P. Physical Therapy
Podiatry
Professionalism

R. Registries
Rehabilitation
Research
Royalties
Running and exercising

S. Setting Limits
Spondilolysthesis
Sports Medicine
Statistics
Sub-specialties in Orthopaedics

T. Teaching
Tendon Transfers
Traumatology
Tuberculosis

REFERENCES

ADDENDA

SECTION I

TRAUMA

SECTION I - TRAUMA

A

ACHILLES TENDON RUPTURES

Much debate has centered on the issue of whether ruptured Achilles tendons should be treated surgically or non-surgically. I do not believe we have found a definitive answer. There are strong advocates for both approaches.

I suspect that a more uniform agreement could be reached if we were to be more specific in describing the pathology. Most surgeons would agree that an individual with a rupture that demonstrates major separation between the two ends should have the defect managed by surgical means. This situation, however, is not always the rule. In many instances the separation between the fragments is not great and the gap can be overcome to a significant degree by plantar-flexion of the ankle. Since it is virtually impossible to prevent healing of tissues, spontaneous repair should take place. "Nature abhors the void", said John Hunter nearly two hundred years ago. Perhaps paraphrasing Hunter, Alan Apley, from England, when asked why broken bones heal replied, "Because they are broken."

It is believed by some that surgery always allows patients to return to normal activities sooner than they do with non-surgical treatment. The data thus far has not convincingly proven that point. It is also said by some that the non-surgical treatment leaves a residual weakness of plantar-flexion. I agree this is true in many instances, but not in all instances. The same is true when surgical treatment is carried out.

In sports medicine circles one hears claims that patients treated surgically can return sooner to athletic activities. How much sooner? Have any scientific comparative studies been conducted to prove the point? Or simply anecdotal observations? Are those "improved results" based perhaps on conclusions drawn from having catered more carefully to the surgically treated patients? George Bernard Shaw, the famous Irish philosopher/play writer, commented in his Pygmalion (better known as My Fair Lady), "The difference between a lady and a flower girl is the way we treat them."

That surgery is more convenient to the patient since casting is not necessary is true to some extent. However, what is the big problem that a light cast or heavy dressing creates? Immediate full, unprotected weight bearing on the injured extremity is not permitted regardless of the surgical or nonsurgical method used to treat the lesion.

Re-rupture is not unheard of from either method. However, surgery is associated with complications not possible from the non-operative method, such as skin dehiscence, (with or without associated infection), which is not infrequent following surgery. When this happens, the ultimate recovery is seriously delayed and the final result is often less than ideal.

The argument that healing takes place more rapidly when surgery is performed flies in the face of biological facts. Surgical exploration and re-approximation of the severed ends in itself retards healing, particularly if running sutures are used, since sutures strangle local circulation. The tighter the suture the greater the strangulation. If the suture is of the running type, it is logical to assume that the deprivation of circulation (without which healing cannot occur) extends throughout the entire suture line. Mother Nature, however, is wise and most resourceful. Sooner or later it manages to bring new vessels into the avascular area and overcomes the iatrogenically created tissue necrosis.

Rigid immobilization of the ankle following the application of the cast used with non-operative care is not necessary. Slight motion of the ankle allows tensile stresses to take place at the defect site. Those stresses encourage faster healing. It is not universally realized, though very well documented, that collagen tissues develop tensile strength faster when subjected to tension during the healing process. In such an environment their fibers organize sooner in a mature form. A phenomenon similar to the one that occurs in fractures where rigid immobilization delays healing and produces a weaker callus; but where motion at the fracture site encourages osteogenesis [115, 122].

There is data regarding the strength of healing according to the location of the lesion. Most believe that the worst scenario is an avulsion of the tendon from the os calcis. In this instance surgical fixation is usually the treatment of choice. Our animal laboratory data indicated that there is minimal difference in the strength of repaired structures between those that take place through the tendon mass and those at the musculo-tendon junction [34].

ACROMIO-CLAVICULAR DISLOCATION

Though it is logical to assume that properly restored congruity of any dislocated joint is the ideal situation, there are practical considerations that indicate that compromises and acceptance of the pathology may often be desirable.

A partially dislocated or incompletely reduced acromio-clavicular joint is more likely to result in chronic pain and late osteo-arthritic changes, than a completely dislocated joint. Pain is not a problem under the latter circumstance since in the absence of cartilage contact with bone or cartilage, articular damage and secondary synovitis do not develop. This is frequently seen in patients with congenital dislocation of the hip who remain free of pain longer than those who suffer from sub-luxation.

I believe there is little residual impairment of function of the shoulder in patients with untreated dislocated acromio-clavicular joints. I would not venture to say that the latter comment necessarily applies to all athletes. I have seen, however, people who continued to engage in athletic activities very effectively in spite of their dislocated AC joints. For the average person, the unreduced dislocation is an option providing the residual deformity is not a strong cosmetic deterrent. Obese or very muscular individuals are not likely to notice the deformity produced by the dislocation. The inevitable scar that surgery permanently creates can be more troublesome to some people, particularly if the scar becomes sensitive.

A number of surgical and non-surgical therapeutic approaches have been used over the years. Pinning with K wires is probably the most common method at this time. It does not guarantee, however, that arthritic changes will not develop in the future, particularly if the reduction is not anatomical or cannot be maintained. The closed reduction does not address the issue of a displaced, rupture or damage of the fibro-cartilage/like meniscus, normally found in the joint. I further suspect that the passage of the

SECTION I - TRAUMA

wires through the opposing articular surfaces deposits particles of bone and cartilage into the closed space. This "foreign" material can cause permanent damage since the synovial tissues react to its presence.

We investigated the amount of bone and cartilage that is generated when drilling of wires and screws through joints is performed. I was impressed by the large amount of material left behind. Obviously, it was much greater in the case of the screws. What prompted me to do the study was my reaction to the advocacy of someone who holds tarso-metatarsal joints with screws in the treatment of Lisfranc dislocations, and has them removed a few months later. The proponent of the method maintained that the "screwed" and rigidly immobilized joints would return to normal once the screws are removed at a later date. I still have serious reservation regarding the validity of his argument. A few months of rigid immobilization of a joint, where cartilage and bone "graft" have been deposited, are likely to produce irreversible stiffness and arthritic changes.

We have assumed that in all acromio-clavicular dislocations, regardless of the degree of separation between the two bones, there is a complete rupture of the trapezoid and conoid ligaments. It is a logical assumption, but not always necessarily true, even though the trapezoid and conoid ligaments are not very elastic. The fact that "high riding" of the dislocated clavicle is not always present gives some credence to the argument. This phenomenon can be explained if we consider the direction of the dislocation. If the clavicle is dislocated superiorly, it is logical to assume that rupture of the supporting ligaments takes place. However, if the clavicle is displaced inferiorly, there is no tension on the trapezoid and conoid ligaments.

Frequently, the two ligaments calcify when injured, stripped form the bone or ruptured, probably due to the resulting lower ph in the area. That calcification is not always observed following dislocated acromio-clavicular joints, gives some credibility to the belief that complete rupture is not always present. MRI studies in a large number of patients should answer the question once and for all.

I am surprised that the technique of fixation of the dislocated joint with a screw driven through the clavicle into the coracoid process is not frequently used. Bosworth, form New York, described the technique almost a half a century ago. As a resident I had the opportunity to observe the clinical results from the procedure, and was very impressed. Subsequently, I performed a few such procedures. The screw, however, must be removed a few weeks later, since if left in place for too long a period of time if breaks from fatigue. The procedure is not a panacea, since sub-luxation can take place after removal of the screw. Apparently, the torn tissues, immobilized by the metallic appliance, permanently lose their tensile properties.

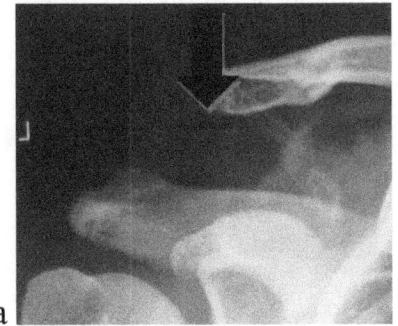
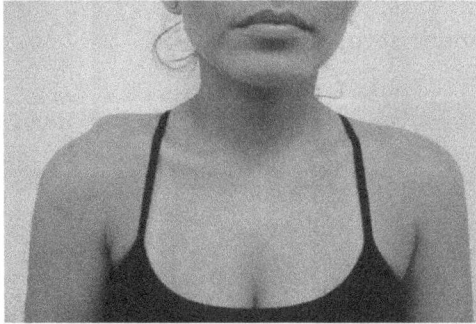

SECTION I - TRAUMA

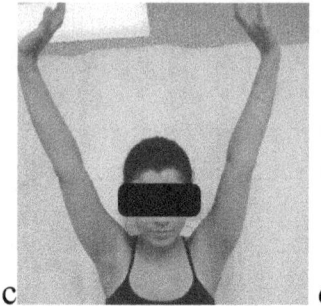 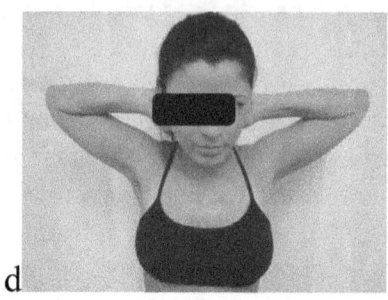 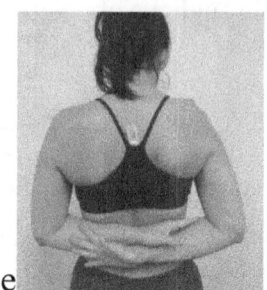

a) Radiological view of dislocated A.C joint. b-e: Notice the mild protuberance at the level of the dislocation. The twenty-two year old patient demonstrates the range of motion of her asymptomatic shoulder six months after the initial injury.

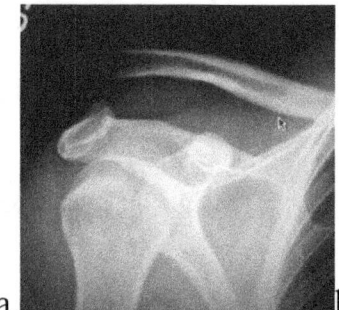 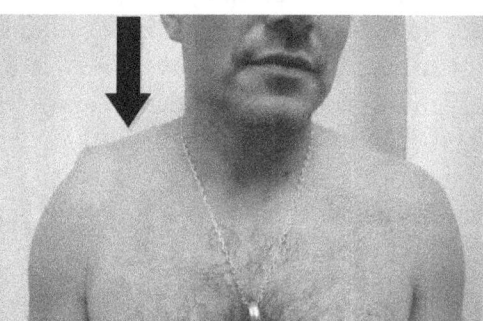 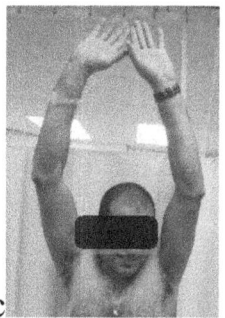

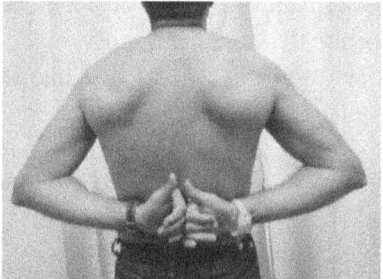

a) Radiograph of the dislocated right A.C joint.
b—d) :Notice the mild deformity at the level of the dislocation, and the range of motion of the asymptomatic shoulder.

SECTION I - TRAUMA

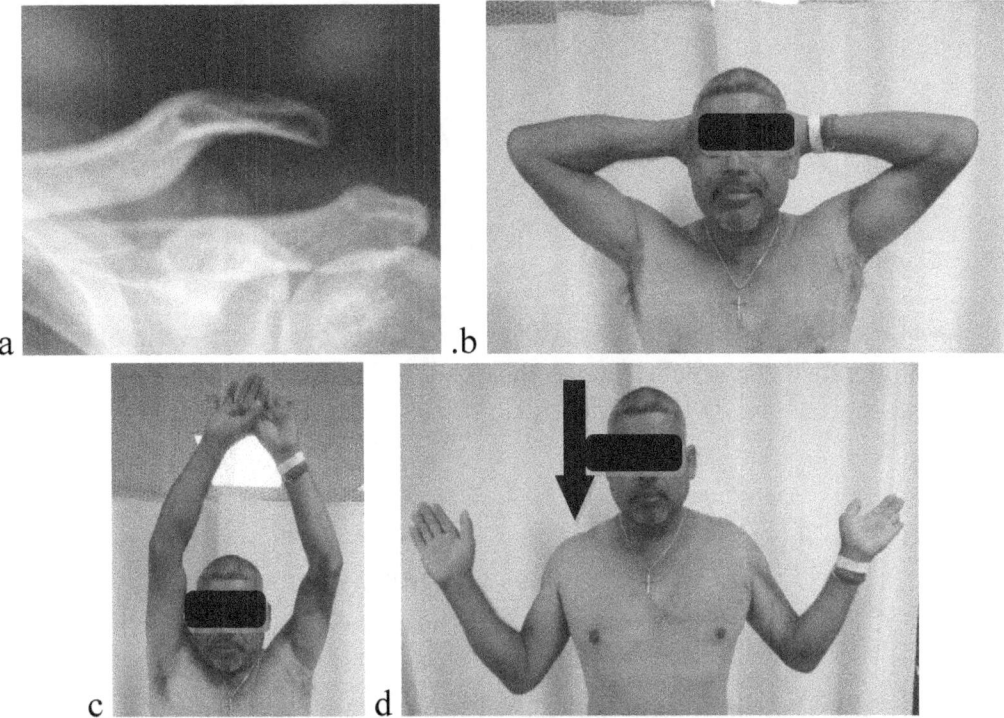

a) Radiograph of the dislocated A.C. joint of a fifty-four year old carpenter, obtained three months after the initial insult. b-d. Patient demonstrates the range of motion of his asymptomatic shoulder. .

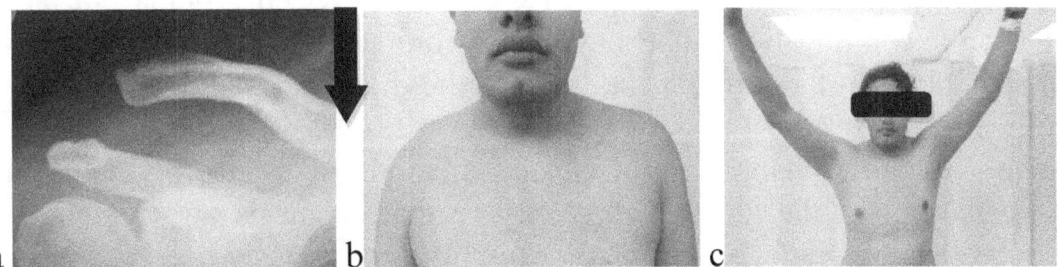

a) Radiograph of dislocated A.C. joint. b) Notice the mild deformity at the level of the dislocation, and the range of shoulder elevation seven weeks after the initial nonjury. .

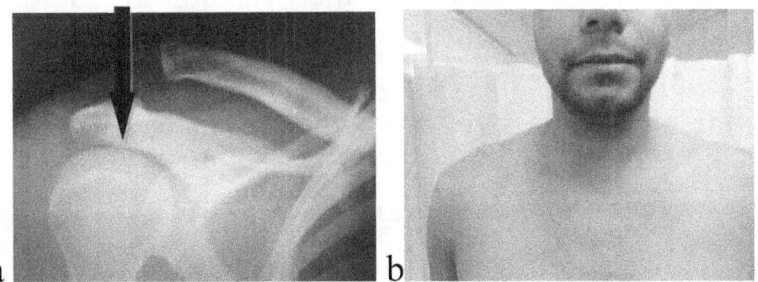

SECTION I - TRAUMA

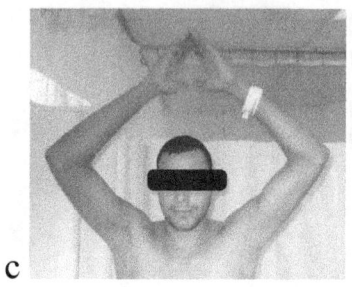
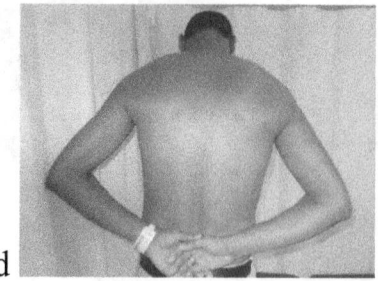

a) Radiograph of the dislocated right A.C. joint of a twenty-eight year old laborer. b-d: Notice the minimal protuberance at the level of the dislocation. Patient demonstrates the range of motion of his asymptomatic shoulder nine weeks after the injury.

DISCUSSION

The observations have made are based entirely on personal experiences. Long-term follow-up of these patients was difficult due primarily to their poor education and economic factors.

It is likely that the empirical data I have presented might support my argument that conservative treatmet has a major place in the management of dislocated acomio-clavicular dislocations. The functional results can be anticipated to be acceptable in most instances; the deformity the dislocation leaves behing is usually cosmetically acceptable; true secondary osteoarthitis is not likely since contact between articular surfaces is no longer present; the complications that may occur from surgery are avoided; the surgical scar is more visible than the lump at the level of the dislolction; and the overall cost of care is significantly reduced.

Surgical modalities remain the preferred methods of treatment in the instances where the displacemt of the clavicle is so severe that cosmesis and function may be compromized. If such high degrees of displacemnnt is erroneously accepted and painful symptoms develop, the distal end of the clavicle may be exised and held at a lower level, using the fascial sling-supported technique.

It is reasonable to ponder on the wisdom of subjecting patients to surgical interventions not likely to give better clinical resuts, when the main "benefit" from them may be the radiological appearance of the injured structures. *Primu non nocere,* still remais the sacred code of medicine. If despite the presence of a chronic dislocation, the patient is asymptomatic and the function of the shoulder is good, what is the "problem" reconstructive surgery proposes to addres?

SECTION I - TRAUMA

REFERENCES

1. Evaluation of the coracoclavicular reconstruction using LARS artificial ligament in acute acromio clavicular joint dislocation. Lu N, Zhu L, Ye T, Chen A, Jiang X, Zhang Z, Zhu Q, Guo Q, Yang D. *Knee Surg Sports Traumatol Arthrosc.* 2013 Jun 30.

2. Management of acute acromio clavicular joint dislocations: current concepts. Tauber M. *Arch Orthop Trauma Surg.* 2013 Jul;133(7):985-95.

3. Surgical treatment of acromio clavicular dislocation with LARS artificial ligament. Giannotti S, Dell'osso G, Bugelli G, Cazzella N, Guido G. *Eur. J Orthop Surg Traumatol.* 2012 Oct 30.

4. Current concepts in the treatment of acromio clavicular joint dislocations. Beitzel K, Cote MP, Apostolakos J, Solovyova O, Judson CH, Ziegler CG, Edgar CM, Imhoff AB, Arciero RA, Mazzocca AD. *Arthroscopy.* 2013 Feb;29(2):387-97.

5. Clavicular bone tunnel malposition leads to early failures in acromio-clavicular ligament reconstruction. Cook JB, Shaha JS, Rowles DJ, Bottoni CR, Shaha SH, Tokish JM. *Am J Sports Med.* 2013 Jan;41 (1):142-8.

SECTION I - TRAUMA

AMPUTATIONS - LOWER EXTREMITY

Orthopedic surgeons in the United States, seem to have lost interest in amputation surgery and rehabilitation of the amputee. Others professionals have moved forward and taken over this important segment of surgery. This happened when arthroscopy, total joint replacement and other more glamorous and financially rewarding procedures came into the picture in the 1970s and 1980s.

Salvage

To the surgical profession amputation still seems to represent an admission of defeat. This explains why we try to stubbornly save limbs in situations when it is already obvious that attempts to salvage the extremity are doomed. This is often the case in the management of severe peripheral vascular disease where vascular reconstruction is likely to fail, particularly in the diabetic patients; as well as in major injuries associated with extensive soft and bone tissue pathology with nerve damage [160].

Patients in the latter group, as a result of multiple procedures aimed at preserving the extremity, are left eventually with partially anaesthetic limbs and stiff joints that make function difficult and painful. I believe these people are better off as below-the-knee amputees. Those with peripheral vascular disease, who are subjected to multiple surgical procedures aimed at saving the extremity, often end up losing their legs at an above the knee level. Since they are usually older people, their chances of achieving functional ambulation are then minimal. An earlier amputation a few inches below the knee, while the skin is still normal, gives them a good chance to function well [49, 50, 90, 91, 95, 100]

Below-the-knee amputation

Amputation surgery should not be taken lightly. It is not the type of surgery that can be done without special care of the soft and bony tissues and still expect good results. The idea of letting junior residents perform amputations without supervision has precluded many patients from gratifying rehabilitation. Below-the-knee amputation is not a very disabling condition. Most people, regardless of age or underlying disease, can learn to function after being fit with a prosthetic appliance. Older above-the-knee amputees, on the other hand, find it impossible to walk with the heavy and unstable prosthesis. This is true even with modern lighter appliances that are more stable. These patients lack the ability to coordinate their motions, maintain balance and control the prostheses. Almost without exception, they refuse to use them once they find out that a wheel chair is a better, safer and most practical means of locomotion [52]

SECTION I - TRAUMA

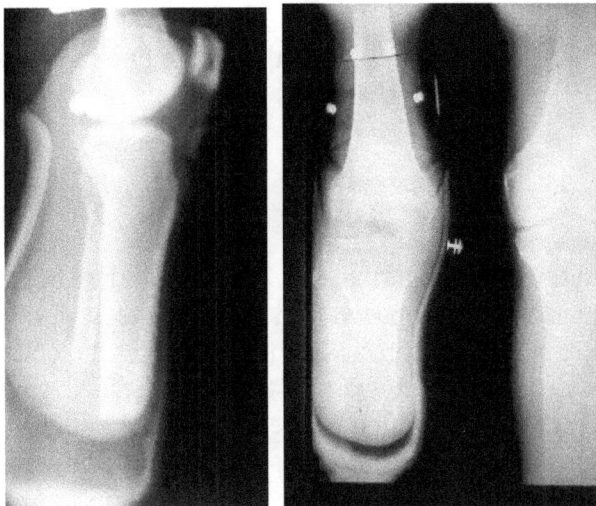

A) Well-fit B.K. stump.   B) A poorly fit B.K. stump. Notice the air pocket distally.

Technique

The skin flaps

Most amputations are performed in civilian practice either for diabetic gangrene or atherosclerosis. In the former condition, there is macro as well as microangiopathy. Diabetic patients, during below-the-knee amputation surgery, often demonstrate that the major anterior and posterior arteries bleed upon their severance and require ligation. This is not always the case when amputation is performed for atherosclerosis alone. The major vessels may not bleed when cut. This finding in itself is not a contraindication for amputation at that level. If the skin bleeds, even if the muscles show poor bleeding, the amputation can be successfully performed in most cases. If the skin bleeds it should heal after its ends are approximated. The chances are that these patients have been walking without circulation through the major vessels for quite some time. The ischemic pain experienced during ambulation came from muscles, which after the amputation are no longer used to the same degree.

A very short below-the-knee stump is better than the longest above-the-knee stump. Too long a stump, however, is not good. Often, skin abrasions develop when the amputation is performed a couple of inches above the ankle. It is best to sever the bone at the level where the muscle mass of the gastro-soleus begins to thin out. Dissecting the skin from the underlying tissues is a bad practice. The skin incision should include from the outset a portion of muscle mass.

The skin flaps need not have a significant length difference. The long posterior flap, which is often recommended, is not, in my opinion, better than flaps where their length is almost equal, the posterior one being only slightly longer. When a long posterior flap is created, the suture line ends up being located over the anterior, sharp end of the bone. The skin may become adherent to the bone making it prone to breakdown from pressure or tension. Furthermore, though it is true that the posterior flap is more vascular than the anterior one, a very long flap does not have as much vascularity as a shorter one. The vascular supply of the posterior flap is best preserved if it is shorter.

SECTION I - TRAUMA

When the two flaps are of equal length the suture line fall mid-line under the stump and therefore is less likely to be traumatized by the sharp end of the tibia [90]

The fibula

It has been traditionally taught that the fibula should be severed at a level much higher than the tibia. This tradition came from the observation that amputees who had their fibula severed at the same level of the tibia often experienced abrasion of the skin over the end of the fibula, as a result of the "bell clapping" and lateral swing of the stump against the prosthesis during gait. This was a good explanation, however, it no longer applies to the amputee wearing a PTB appliance. Previously, B.K. amputees were fit with wooden appliances that did not fit the stump tightly, making room for the stump to "bell clap". The PTB prosthesis, because of its total contact with the stump prevents the lateral swing. In my opinion, the fibula should be severed at the same level of the tibia in order to create a more square stump that not only provides a larger area of contact with the skin and increases proprioception, but also enhances rotary stability [95].

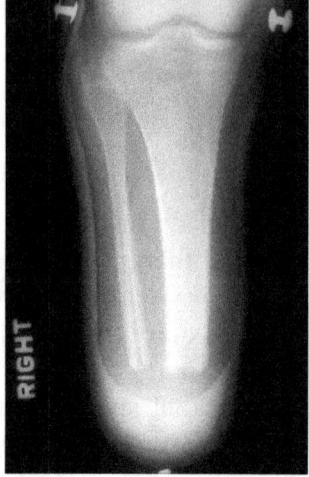

Below-the-knee stump with the tibia and fibula severed at the same level.

Nerves and vessels

The major nerves need not be pulled down forcefully and severed high. This traction maneuver might do harm to nerve fibers at a higher level. I think is best to gently pull on the nerves before sectioning them. They will retract sufficiently to ensure their ultimate location into the muscle belly where a neuroma at the end of the nerve will inevitably form. The neuroma remains asymptomatic as long as it is not irritated.

Contractures

Flexion contractures of below-the-knee stumps are more common than extension contractures and less disabling if their degrees are not major. A mild flexion contracture can be easily fitted with a PTB prosthesis with minimal difficulty. After all, the socket is normally built in flexion to allow weight-bearing distribution over the patellar tendon and tibial condyles. Function in the presence of an extension contracture is more difficult. This is why it is desirable to splint the stump in extension for only a few days after surgery and then initiate motion.

The pain that necessarily develops following surgery is partially relieved by flexion of the stump and, therefore, patients unconsciously seek that position. However, if maintained for too long a period of time it produces a flexion contracture, which may be difficult to correct once it is well established.

The immediate post-operative dressing, cast or temporary prosthesis

There is little doubt in my mind that the post-operative dressing is extremely important in the management of the amputee. In the early 1960's Marian Weiss, from Poland, popularized the concept of immediate post-surgical prosthetic fitting. I embraced the method with great enthusiasm and suspect I was the first individual to use it in the United States. I first learned about it when I heard, in New York, a physiatrist, who had just attended a meeting in Europe comment that a Polish surgeon had given a short paper on the subject. It was the first time that Weiss had spoken about it outside his country.

Immediately after my return to Miami from the trip to New York, I fit the first below-the-knee amputee with plaster prosthesis upon closure of the skin, and attached a pylon and a rubber foot. Not knowing the details of the method used by Weiss, I assumed that he had molded a plaster that resembled the PTB prosthesis. Therefore, the prosthesis I made was shaped in that manner. It was not until several months later that I found out that Weiss had simply applied a long leg cast that extended to the groin and, therefore, immobilized the knee joint. I continued to fit amputees with PTB-like casts and never saw the need to immobilize the knee joint [95, 96, 99].

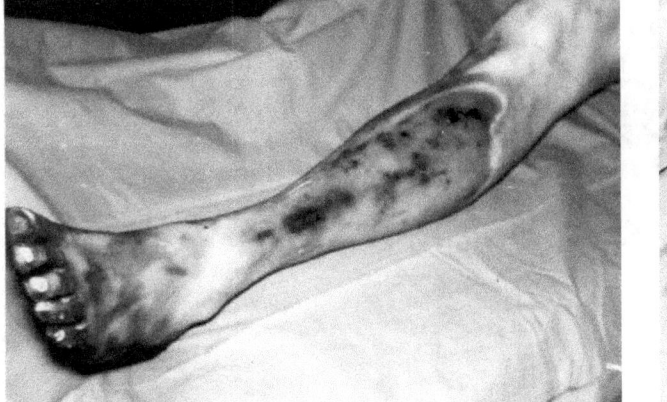 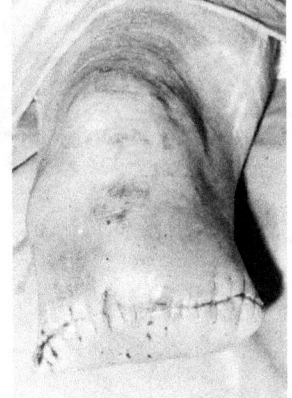

b and c. Well-demarcated gangrene (a), which made possible successful healing of below the knee amputation (b) Temporary plaster prosthesis applied after surgery (c).

SECTION I - TRAUMA

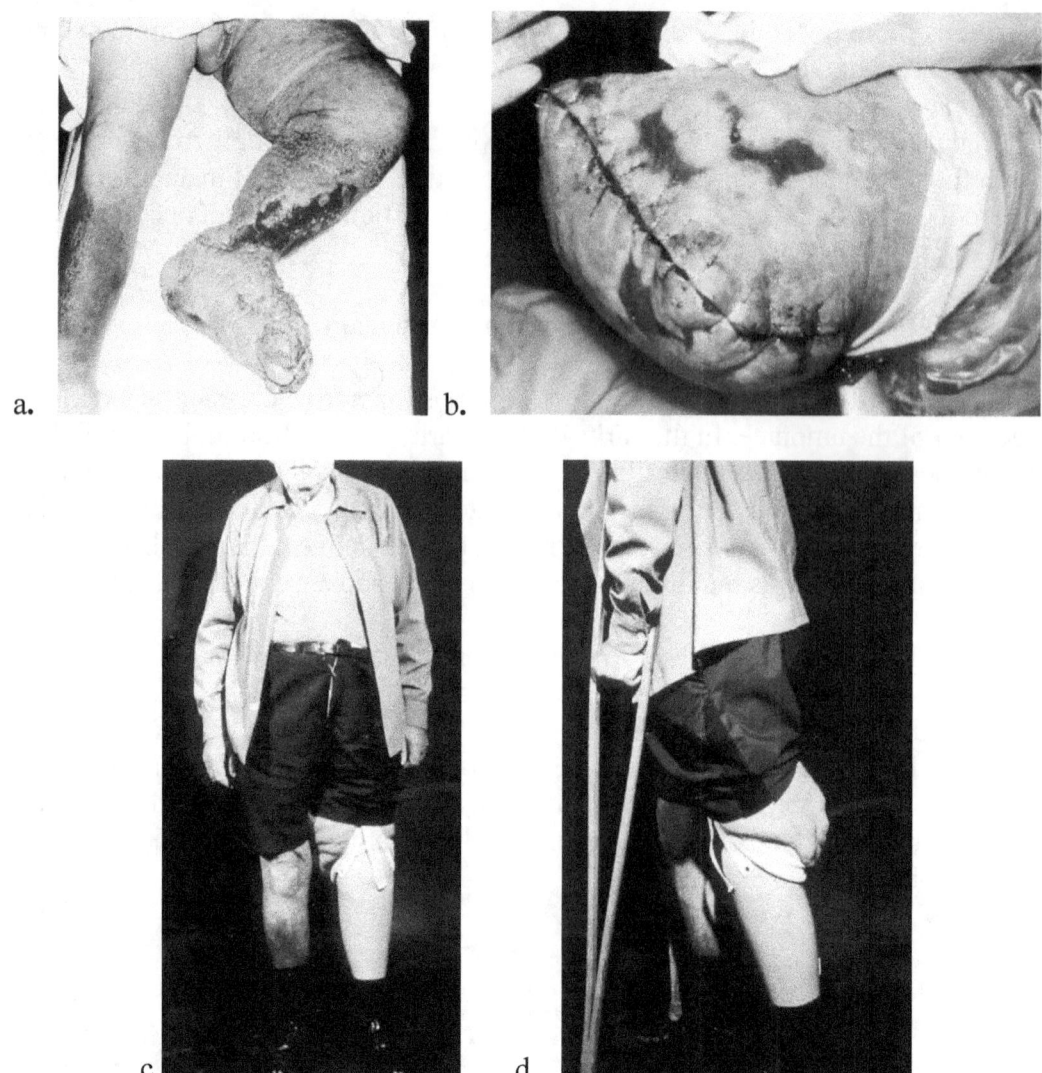

(a through d) Complication from chronic lymphedema treated by amputation below the knee followed by immediate prosthetic fitting.

SECTION I - TRAUMA

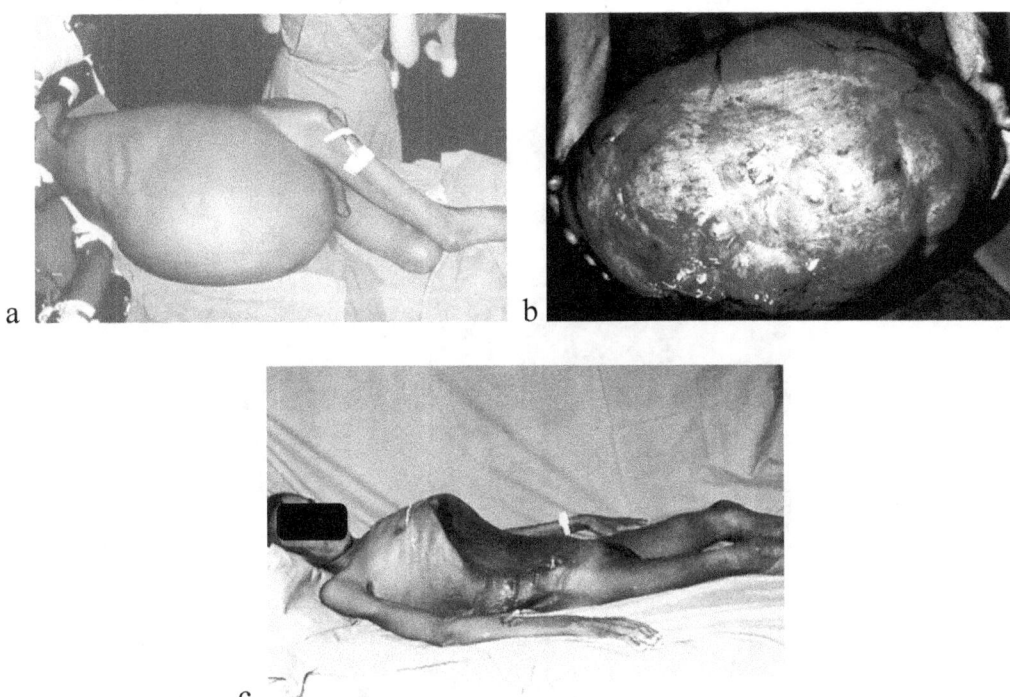

a through c. Slow-growing kidney cyst that was removed after bilateral below-the-knee amputation was performed. Immediate prosthetic fitting was carried out.

A few months after we began to experiment with the new technique, we held one of our post-graduate seminars dealing with amputation surgery and prosthetics. At that meeting we showed several amputees who had received their prostheses immediately following the amputation. Doctor Ernest Burgess, from Seattle, visited us during the course of the meeting and witnessed for the first time the immediate fitting. He was on his way to Poland to visit Doctor Weiss. After his return to the States he became a strong spokesman for the system.

The results we obtained were most gratifying and we continued to use the technique of immediate fitting for a long time. We learned eventually that complications could occur and found out that patients with severe vascular disease, particularly diabetics with additional neurological deficit, were prone to develop pressure sores over the stump. After comparing a group of amputees fitted immediately after surgery with prosthesis with a group where only a rigid cast was used in surgery but without the prosthetic component, we observed that the results were equal as far as survival of the stump was concerned. We concluded that the main value of the technique was the compression of the tissues and the careful surgery rather than the immediate weight bearing ambulation. This conclusion does not in any way negate the merits of immediate prosthetic fitting. When appropriately used in patients without advanced neurological deficit the physical and emotional advantages of the method are enormous [95, 98].

The Syme's amputation

The Syme's amputation provides a very good stump. Its length and preservation of the heel pad are distinct advantages. I performed many such amputations and felt at one time that it had a major place also in the management of the geriatric amputee. Early on I modified the surgical technique by shaving the malleoli so the narrower distal stump could make possible the construction of a windowless, cosmetic prosthesis.

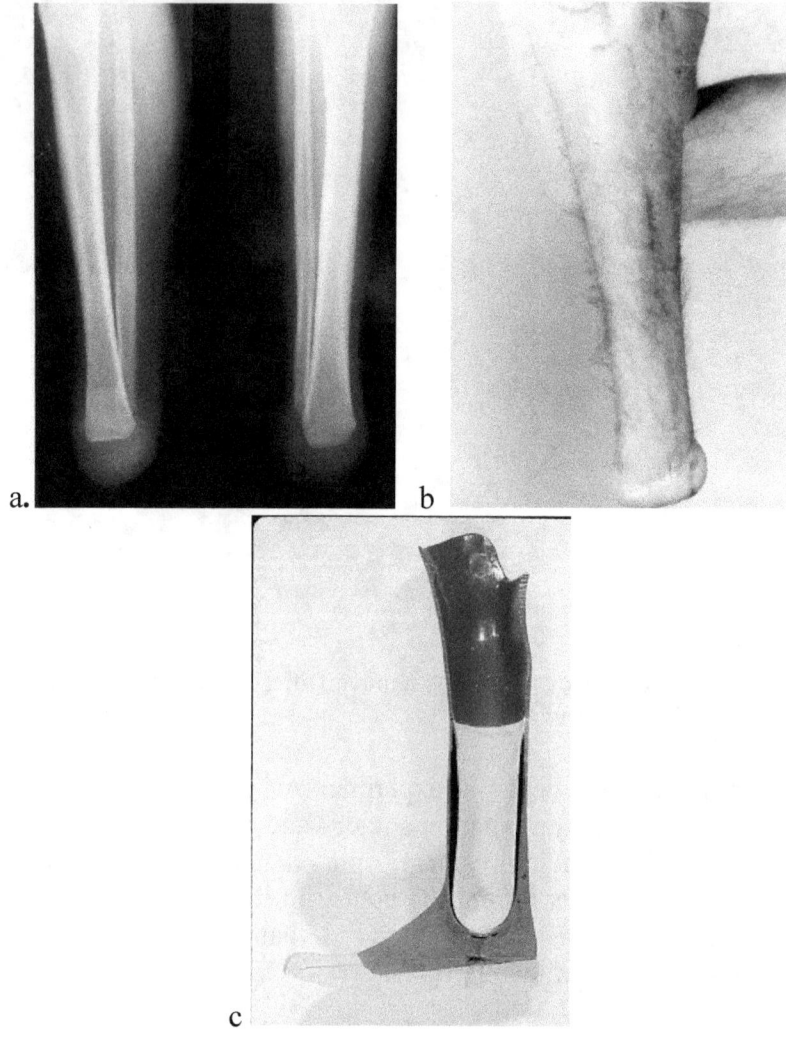

a, b and c. The modified Symes stump with the shaven malleoni (a and b) that makes possible the construction of a windowless prostheis. ©Cross section of the prosthesis illustrating the expandable inner wall.

SECTION I - TRAUMA

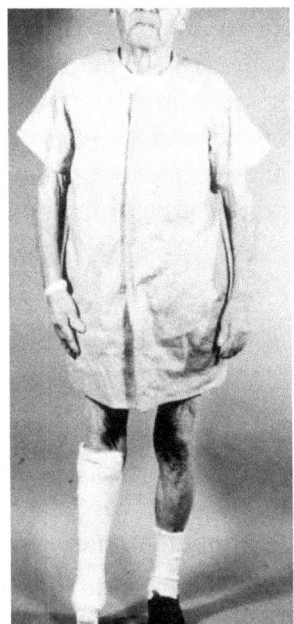 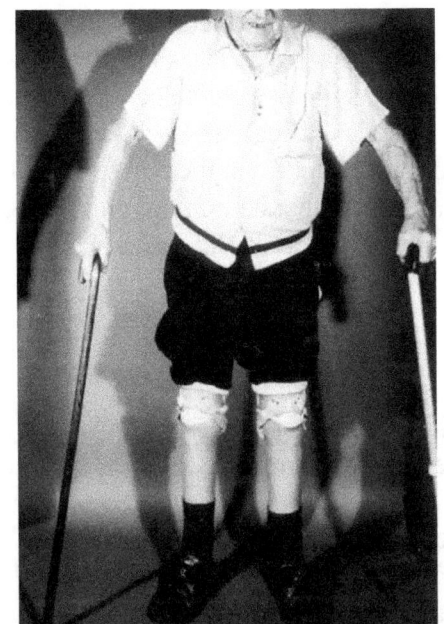

a, b. Diabetic patient, who immediately following a modified Symes' amputation was fit with a well molded plaster of paris cast (a). The patient eventually became a bilateral amputee and was managed in a similar way (b).

Though, the initial results were satisfactory, I eventually concluded that the advantages of the Syme's amputation were out-weighed by its disadvantages, particularly in the case of the elderly dysvascular amputee. The need for early re-amputation was high and the amputee's function was comparable to that of the below the knee ones [86, 105]. The increased success with more distal leg amputations has reduced the need for Syme's amputations.

The fact remains that a high percentage of diabetics who lose one extremity, regardless of how carefully their metabolic disease is controlled, require amputation of the opposite limb within a few years. The high figures given by Jansen, from Denmark, in the early sixties have been lowered only minimally. "Death by installments" was the term used by someone to illustrate that the amputation is simply a component of the progressive nature of the debilitating disease.

I first discussed our modification to the Syme's amputation and prosthesis during the course of our first post-graduate seminar in Miami Beach in December of 1964. We illustrated our experiences by bringing to the stage several amputees who had been managed in the new fashion. As part of the faculty of the Symposium was Richard Masset, from Los Angeles. Among the other experts were Cameron Hall, also from Los Angeles, Clinton Compere, from Chicago, Herbert Pedersen, from Michigan, Tom Aitkin, from Michigan, Newton McCollough Jr., from Orlando and many others. During the ensuing discussion, Masset expressed strong criticism of the proposed modification and indicated that others in the past had attempted to modify the original procedure and had failed.

A couple of years later Masset published an article describing a modification to the Syme's operation and prosthesis, identical to the one he had been shown in Miami and which he had so strongly criticized. He did not bother to give credit to us for the original change and made it sound as if he had conceived the whole idea on his own.

Of course, I was annoyed by his lack of integrity, but elected not to make an issue of it. I did, however, sent him a copy of the audiotape I had made of his remarks during the Miami course. I had recorded the entire symposium. When I ran into him some time later we greeted each other as if nothing had ever happened. Fifteen years later, when I moved to Los Angeles to serve as chairman of the Department of Orthopaedics at the University of Southern California, where Masset held a clinical faculty appointment, I heard others comment on several occasions about Masset's successful modification of the Syme's amputation. C'est la vie.

Above-the-knee amputation

In spite of progress made in prosthetics in the last few decades the consistent rehabilitation of the elderly above-the-knee amputee remains elusive. The loss of the knee joint is a major blow. Weeks and even months of intensive efforts to reach a practical level of function are very often met with disappointment. The weight of the appliance (even though lighter today) and the muscular control necessary to walk often become insurmountable obstacles. Most people who lose a leg above the knee in the late stages of life, end-up depending on a wheel chairs for all types of locomotion [49, 50, 52, 91, 95].

Newton McCollough III, with whom I was long associated, found out that bilateral below-the-knee elderly amputees are more likely to succeed in the use of prostheses than unilateral amputees in the same age bracket [49, 52].

AMPUTATION - UPPER EXTREMITY

The consequences of the loss of the elbow joint in upper extremity amputation surgery are similar to the loss of the knee in the lower extremity. Prosthetic rehabilitation of the below-the-elbow amputee is gratifying in most instances; above-he elbow amputees are more difficult to rehabilitate.

As in the case of the lower extremity, a very short below-the-elbow stump is better than the longest above-the-elbow stump.

A very high percentage of above-the-elbow amputees, particularly if older at the time of the amputation, often end-up abandoning the use of the prosthesis, as they find it difficult to use it in a practical manner. The opposite is true for the below-the-elbow amputee who with very few exceptions functions extremely well. Excellent cosmetic appliances are in vogue today, increasing therefore the social acceptability of the amputee. Power operated prostheses have further contributed significantly to the function of the amputee.

The younger the patient is at the time of the amputation the better the functional prognosis. In the case of the congenital amputee, fitting of a mitten within the first few months of life is most desirable. An articulated artificial hand should be given to the child before the first birthday. The same is true for the lower extremity congenital amputee. The old belief that congenital amputees should not receive prosthesis until they reached seven or ten years of age was a grave mistake.

Immediate post-operative fitting

My experience with immediate fitting of upper extremities is limited. However, to the best of my knowledge, I performed the first such procedure. Our report was the first one in the world literature [97]. It took place when I applied an articulated prosthesis on a twenty five year old man who had been bitten by a rattlesnake a few years earlier, leaving him with a severely deformed and disabled two-digit hand.

We disarticulated the wrist and immediately afterwards applied a plaster prosthesis with a hook as a terminal device. Within twenty-four hours, he was able to operate the terminal device and a few days later, he had mastered most activities of daily living. Less than four weeks later he received the permanent prosthesis (a and b)

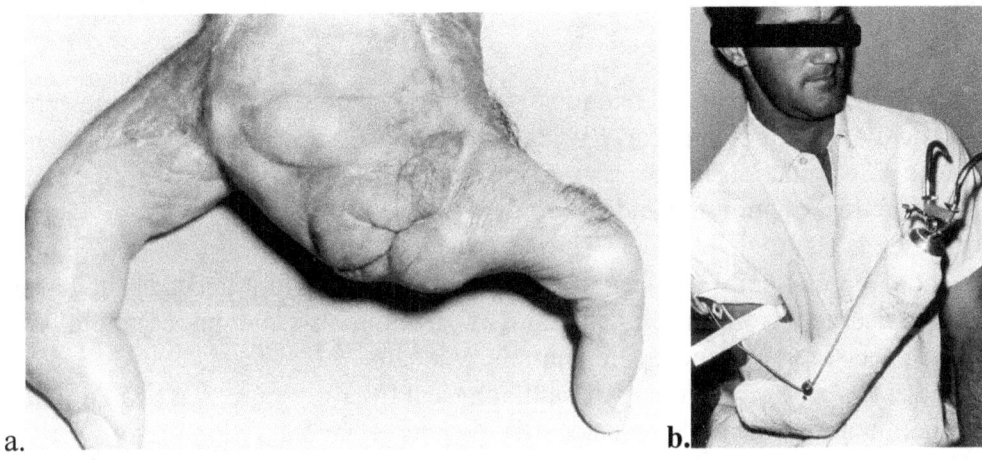

a and b. Residual deformity from rattlesnake bite (a) Temporary prosthesis applied in the operating room (b).

I had the opportunity to present this man, shortly after the amputation, to a group of hand surgeons attending a meeting of the American College of Surgeons in Miami. I first showed them photos of the "lobster" hand, where three digits were missing and function was very limited. The hand surgeons discussed the various therapeutic options. The more widely supported one was the transplantation of the great toe to the hand. Once the discussion was over, I brought the patient into the auditorium. He had been amputated only a few days earlier. The temporary prosthesis, made of plaster of Paris, was bloody. He then reached into his back pocket, produced his wallet and proceeded to remove form it his several credit cards using the metallic hook. It was an entertaining and educational experience.

The second patient sustained an above-the-elbow amputation when his hand was caught in a meat-grinding machine. Immediately after completing the amputation, we applied the temporary articulated prosthesis. He was a relatively young man who needed prosthesis in order to continue working as a butcher. He did well and returned to work. A few months later, he was admitted to the hospital after having his normal extremity caught also in a meat-grinding machine. I was out of town at the time so a conventional dressing was used. A few weeks later, he was fitted with an above-the-elbow prosthesis. I lost track of him after that.

SECTION I - TRAUMA

ANGULATION IN FRACTURES

In recent years, through improved technologies, it has become possible to obtain good alignment, rotation, or length in most long bone fractures. Plate osteosynthesis and intramedullary mailing are credited for this major improvement. Unfortunately, many have been led to believe that any deviation from the normal is a complication that cannot and should not be accepted under any circumstances. They reason that if the technique exists to restore normalcy it must be used. This pervasive philosophy has permeated the whole of orthopaedic surgery in an unprecedented manner. It is so great, that, in my opinion, it threatens the viability of orthopaedics as a scientific discipline and its conversion into a technical trade. Thinking and reasoning in biological terms has become outdated: and at the sight of a fracture many orthopaedists no longer ask, "what is the best treatment for this patient" but, "what operation does this fracture need" [135, 140, 154, 158].

The correction of mild deviations is claimed to be necessary because otherwise all sort of late adverse sequella eventually appear. Evidence to support that claim is never presented, simply because it does not exist. Angulation in the case of long bone fractures is one of those changes in anatomy that attracts a great deal of attention and is frequently used to justify surgery.

The subject of angular deformity has fascinated me for nearly four decades and has prompted me not only to carefully observe it from the clinical point of view but also to conduct laboratory studies that we have published in peer-review orthopaedic journals [17, 42, 66, 68, 73, 134, 168, 176].

I have never seen a patient with a diaphyseal tibial fracture that healed with less than 15 degrees of angulation in any plane develop osteoarthritis later. I have asked numerous orthopaedic surgeons who deal with arthritis of the knee or ankle if they see patients who required artificial replacement or fusion of either joint as a result of a diaphyseal, extra-articular fracture that healed within those degrees of angulation. The answer has been consistently NO. (a,b,c and a, b,c,d and a, b).

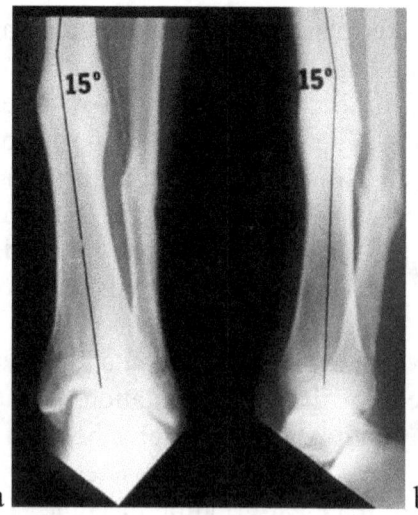
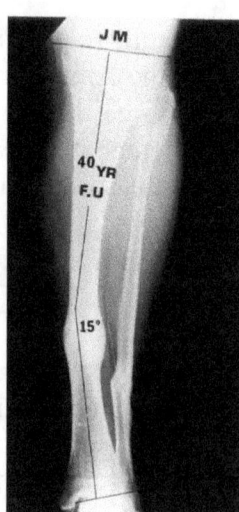

SECTION I - TRAUMA

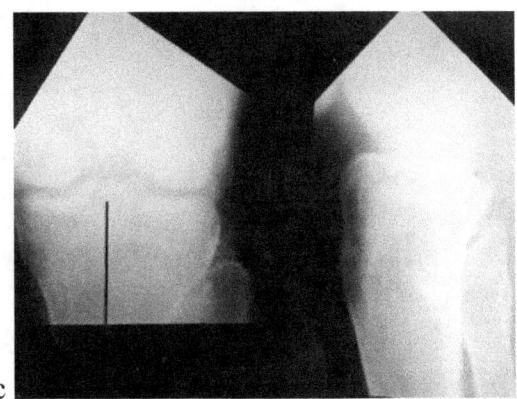

a through c Forty-year-old tibial fracture that healed with 15 degrees of valgus and recurvatum deformity. The adjacent joints were normal and asymptomatic.

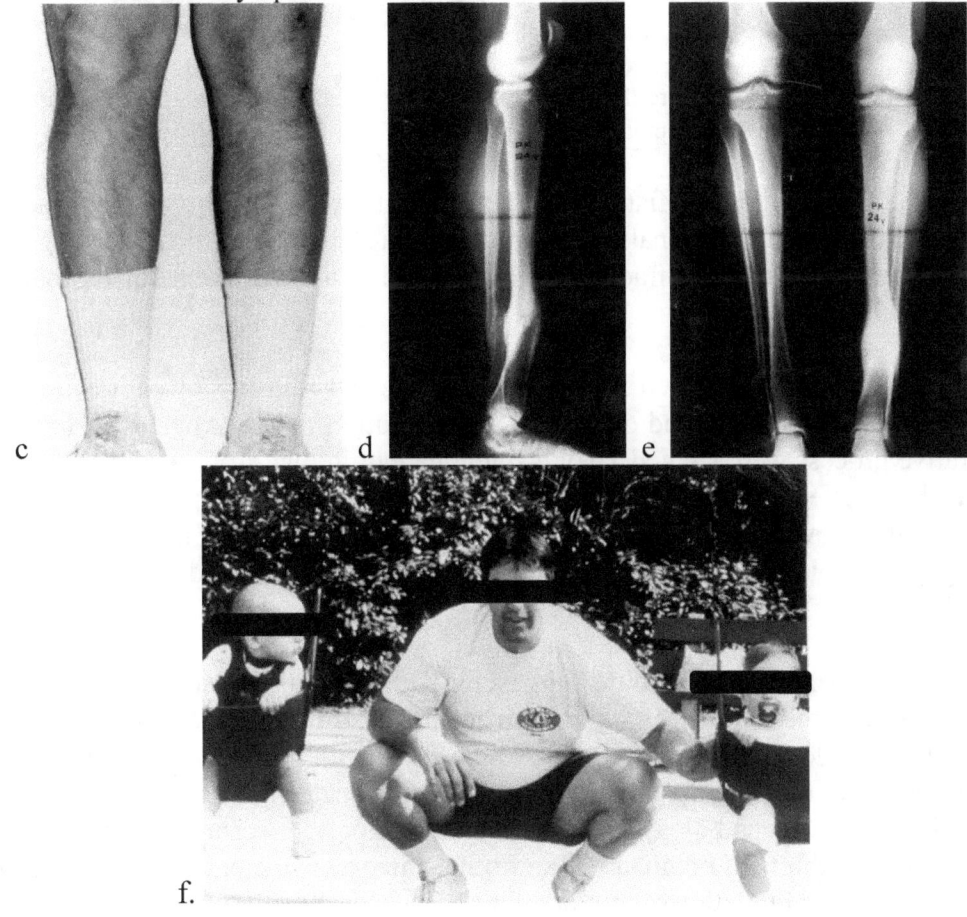

a through f. Twenty-four year old fracture. Despite the angular deformity, the adjacent joints are normal. He is my daughter's husband and the youngsters are my grandchildren.

SECTION I - TRAUMA

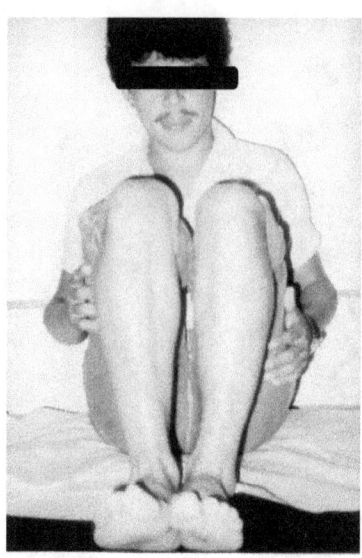 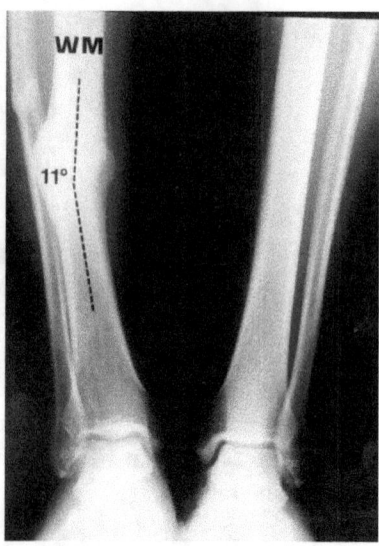

1a and b. Diaphyseal tibial fracture that healed with 11 degrees of varus angulation. Patient is asymptomatic and the deformity is cosmetically acceptable.

At the Universities of Miami and Southern California, the universities where I treated thousands of tibial fractures with functional braces and often accepted some residual angulation, I never saw a patient with an extra-articular fracture return for additional treatment for osteoarthritis of the knee or ankle.

Once, Donald Wiss, then my associate, reviewed a group of over one hundred ankle fusions performed within a given period of time at our institution in Los Angeles. The injuries that led to the degenerative process were studied. Not a single patient in that group had had a diaphyseal fracture that healed with imperfect alignment. Others have documented similar experiences. Among them Deitz, from the University of Iowa, who published a very well documented article based on a large number of patients with diaphyseal tibial fractures that healed with angulation and found no evidence of osteoarthritis for a period of follow-up as long as thirty years.

A few papers in the literature suggesting late osteoarthritis following diaphyseal angulation did not report on the mechanism of injury, particularly a differentiation between fractures produced by twisting or direct blow injuries, versus those associated with vertical impaction i.e. a fall from a height or the pressure of the foot against the dash board upon impact. These studies have not proven the absence of initial intra-articular pathology or presented any history concerning the method of treatment initially rendered, the length of immobilization and other important factors. Kristiansen, for example, clearly showed that pain and limitation of motion of the ankle was directly related to the length of immobilization in cast.

The argument that mild tibial angulation may affect the subtalar joint is also invalid. The clinical evidence is not there. The sub-talar and mid-tarsal joints respond readily to minor alteration in tibial alignment reducing, therefore, any possible harmful changes in pressure distribution. We conducted extensive laboratory studies to determine the effects of angulation in the knee, ankle, and sub-talar joints and demonstrated that tibial angulation of less than ten degrees represents only minor increases in contact stresses on the articular cartilage of the joints. A recurvatum deformity of the tibia produces the highest contact stresses among the various deformities [68, 176].

A debate has raged for a long time as to which of the two main coronal deviations - varus or valgus- is more important in regards to the possibility of late arthritic changes. In my opinion, there is very little difference from the point of view of cartilage stress concentration, as indicated above. I prefer, however, a minor varus deformity to a valgus one, in spite of the fact that varus motion in the sub-talar joint is greater than the valgus one. I prefer it from the cosmetic point of view. A five-degree varus angulation is usually difficult to recognize under visual inspection. A valgus deformity is more easily detectable particularly in the female patient who has (as most women have) slight valgus alignment of their knees. An additional valgus deformity at the level of the tibial fracture exaggerates the pre-existing valgus and might make it more noticeable. People with large or flabby legs camouflage deformities more effectively. [150, 151]

Despite the abundance of evidence to justify the claim that mild deformities are inconsequential from the clinical, physiological, and cosmetic points of view, a large segment of the orthopaedic community continues to accept the false belief that they need complete prevention or correction. At times, I am appalled by our lack of objectivity and common sense. Some argue that the reluctance to accept deviations from the normal is the fear of litigation. Though I am keenly aware that there are patients and attorneys willing and ready to pursue the legal route for trivial reasons, our system of law, imperfect as it is, almost guarantees that justice usually prevails. The time, embarrassment and efforts that the litigation process demand are significant, however, not enough to justify our surrendering our earned independence of judgment and professional rights.

ANKLE FRACTURES

Medial malleolus Fractures

Internal fixation of medial malleolar fractures has been a common procedure in the armamentarium of the orthopaedist since the inception of fracture surgery. It was assumed by many that anatomical reduction of this fracture was very important and even necessary. Less attention was paid to fractures of the lateral malleolus, which was often allowed to heal without surgery.

Many isolated fractures of the medial malleolus can be handled very effectively by plaster immobilization. Very few publications in recent years have dealt with non-surgical management of medial malleolar fractures. Recently, however, several papers have been published or delivered, indicating that the results from nonsurgical care of medial malleolar fractures are equal, if not better, that those obtained with open osteosynthesis. These reports, however, are rarely quoted.

Performing surgery for malleolar fractures has become a knee jerk reaction, brought about by the pervasive belief that all fractures are best treated surgically. The argument that healing takes place more rapidly when surgery is performed flies in the face of biologically data. Though this premise may apply to some metaphyseal fractures, a sweeping generalization of the concept does not fly in light of the biological evidence. Diaphyseal fractures heal faster and better in the absence of immobilization. That surgery is more convenient to the patient since casting is not necessary may be true to some extent. However, what is the big problem that a light cast or heavy dressing creates? Immediate full weight

SECTION I - TRAUMA

bearing on the injured extremity is not possible, for reasons of pain and residual instability, regardless of the surgical or nonsurgical method used to treat the fracture

Open reduction of the medial malleolar fracture is usually easily carried out. There are times when the fragment is either too small or there is too much comminution, and attempts to restore bony continuity between the main body of the tibia and the remnants of the malleolus are futile. Under those circumstances, it is best to leave the fracture alone and to allow the tissues to heal through a natural process

The medial malleolus does not seem to play the major stabilizing process we have been led to believe. I have seen a small number of patients who "lost" the malleolus at the time of the accident, but returned to normal function without it. On one occasion, the family of a patient with an open malleolar fracture brought me the fragment they had retrieved from the pavement at the site of the accident. They wanted me to re-implant it.

To support my premise that the medial malleolus is not that important for normal function of the ankle, one needs only look at the function of patients who develop a nonunion of the malleulus. They do not develop instability, and pain at the nonunion site is virtually unheard of. The more distal the fracture is, and the smaller and more rotated the fragment is, the more likely it is to experience non-union. The reasons given for this phenomenon have been the distraction between the fragments created by the "pull" of the deltoid ligament or the intra-articular nature of the fracture. I question the two explanations on the grounds that the deltoid ligament does not "pull" the malleolus distally. Other fractures around ligaments do not suffer the same fate with the same frequency. The fact that the fracture is intra-articular does not preclude healing. Does synovial fluid inhibit osteogenesis? I do not think so.

Hoping to find an anatomo/physiological answer, I dissected a few medial malleoli form cadaver specimens. What I found under the microscope was an absence of cambium in the periosteum at that level. Could that be an explanation? .

I have no illusions that the nonsurgical treatment of medial malleolar fractures will soon become a well-accepted therapeutic approach. Only if orthopaedist in underdeveloped country were given the opportunity (and we were to pay attention to their reports) that a realistic approach to the management of these fractures would occur. Those surgeons, in the absence of Western technology, treat all fractures by nonsurgical means. To believe that all their patients end up with results unacceptable by people in more "sophisticated societies" is a reflection of our ignorance and unawareness of the facts and lives in other places.

The fact that surgery is more convenient to the surgeon, more profitable to the surgeons and hospital, and the effective propaganda machine that recommends surgery for every musculoskeletal condition, guarantees the perpetuation of the status quo. Only if a change in the attitudes of the surgeons (an unlikely development) or a more rational method of reimbursement were to be established, could bring about a change. A change that applies not only to the subject at hand but also throughout the whole of medicine.

SECTION I - TRAUMA

Lateral Malleolus Fractures

Internal fixation of lateral malleolus fractures is a procedure, which did not become popular until relatively recently. In years past, only the medial and posterior malleolus received surgical attention. It was the observations made by the late Bernard Weber, from Switzerland that changed that tradition. He illustrated, quite convincingly, that the lateral aspect of the ankle deserved greater attention and recommended routine open reduction and anatomical reduction. He emphasized that even minimal displacement could alter the mechanics of the joint.

His radical conclusion needs to be balanced with reality. Millions of people with lateral malleolar fractures have been treated without surgery and most of them had some residual, incomplete reduction of the fragments. Many of them did well and never developed arthritic changes, suggesting that anatomical reduction is not always indispensable. The question remains: when can the fractured lateral malleolus are allowed to heal without anatomical reduction. How much incongruity of the tibia-fibula-talus joint is compatible with a good clinical and radiographic result?

The reading of studies published by others and my own anecdotal observations supports my opinion. If the separation is not significant (perhaps no more than three millimeters) and the medial malleolus is intact, plaster immobilization will likely render a good result. Otherwise, open reduction may be the treatment of choice.

Some would argue that if any doubt exists about the precise degree of displacement that can be accepted, why not operate in all of them. The procedure, after all, is associated with low morbidity and the subsequent rehabilitation is rather uncomplicated. There is merit in that argument. However, complications from surgery can and sometimes do occur. Elderly patients, particularly those afflicted with peripheral vascular disease and especially those with diabetes, are known to experience skin dehiscence with some frequency. Anesthesia complications, though rare have been reported. Infection is not unheard of and when it happens may produce irreversible damage to the ankle joint. Surgical fusion then becomes the only solution.

If the surgeon understands the patho-physiology of ankle fractures; the mechanics that govern their prognosis; and is familiar and skillful in the performance of the operation, the surgical intervention can be justified with greater ease. The problem is that almost nobody is ever going to admit that he or she is not familiar with the operation and skillful to perform it. I recall that on one occasion, when I was moderating a panel discussion one of the speakers made the statement that the surgical operation he had described should be performed only by the "above average" orthopaedist. As soon as I got a chance to address the audience I asked for a show of hands. I wanted to see how many in attendance considered themselves "below-average" orthopaedist. No hands went up. Food for thought.

The tri-malleolar fracture

Since in recent years the orthopaedic community has been led to believe that any bone that is fractured needs to be "fixed" surgically, few posterior malleoli escape the blade. However, many of these fractures do not require surgery and accept with impunity mild degrees of incongruity. Small gaps are filled with functional fibro-cartilage. Mild step-off deformities do not lead to late degenerative

SECTION I - TRAUMA

changes in the absence of instability [38, 41]. Certainly, these fractures can be technically reduced, but such a surgical exercise should be carried out only when surgery is clearly indicated. The existence of a technique is not in itself an indication for its use. As in the case of internal fixation of other malleolar fractures, complications from surgery can occur, and the anatomical reduction is not a guarantee that the possible sequella of intra-articular fractures are eliminated.

Often it is possible to reduce the degree of displacement of the displaced posterior malleolus by dorsi-flexion of the ankle through a mechanism of ligamentotaxis. Within a few days of stabilization in that position, the fracture becomes stable enough to permit decreasing the degree of dorsi-flexion of the ankle. It is commonly believed that fractures that involve more than one third of the articular surface necessarily require surgical treatment. Though this may be true, where is the evidence that more that one-third is the magic figure? If this degree of involvement creates chronic instability, then I would concur with the advanced premise.

I do not believe that the acceptance of minor incongruity, per se, in these fractures leads to "clinical" osteoarthritis. I emphasize "clinical" because is the only kind of osteoarthritis that matters. Radiological changes that are not associated with clinical symptoms are not a problem. Mild degenerative changes are not uncommon following any intraarticular fracture, regardless of the method of treatment used. It is also important to keep in mind that oftentimes the cartilage is permanently damaged at the time of the initial insult, and therefore anatomical reapproximation of oseo-cartilaginous fragments does not restore viability. Furthermore, perfect restoration of congruency is not always obtainable, leaving some incongruity behind.

B

BONE GRAFT SUBSTITUTES

The idea of using bone substitutes has been around for some time. However, attempts to successfully use them have been, for the most part, unrewarding. In the late 1950, a product called Ostomer, received a great deal of attention and it was welcome with great enthusiasm. A bone glue was injected at the site of a fresh fracture, or a nonunion. The material would polymerize within a few minutes and render the defect so stable that full weight bearing would be possible immediately. The material would eventually resorb, but by that time the fracture would have healed spontaneously.

The clinical results were demonstrated on live television. Patients with broken tibias, who had surgery a few hours earlier, were seen walking unassisted. The orthopaedic community and the public in general, celebrated a development worthy of a Nobel Prize. The excitement was overwhelming. At that time I was a senior resident in orthopaedics at the University of Miami, and therefore I had the opportunity to be involved in the use of Ostomer.

Indeed, the initial experiences were thrilling. However, within a very short time the complications became evident. The surgical wounds drained, the fractures did not heal and the foreign material had to be removed. These bad experiences, repeated across the country, put an end to further efforts to find a material that would do what Ostomer had promised to do. It was most unfortunate that orthopedists were allowed to use Ostomer before the original investigators had tried it before its general release.

Marshal Urist, a most reputable scientist, had not, to the best of my knowledge, started the investigations that led to his eventual discovery of BMP (Bone Morphogenic Protein). With enthusiasm, comparable to that expressed after the introduction of Ostomer, the description of the property of BMP rough a wave of hope toward the resolution of the ubiquitous nonunion.

I had an opportunity to know Doctor Urist fairly well. I visited his laboratories a number of times, even though we were working at different and competitive institutions. He was at UCLA and I was at USC, both in Los Angeles. His laboratory findings were most impressive. There was no doubt in my mind at that time that soon clinical experience would give BMP a permanent place in the care of nonunions, and eventually in the management of acute fractures. Who would resist the temptation to use a product that would expedite the healing of bone? [101]

Fortunately, Doctor Urist was a cautious investigator. He never made claims that the laboratory findings could be immediately reproduced in the clinical arena. Others, however, failed to recognize Urists's conservatism and jumped into the use of BMP without hesitation. Their less than satisfactory results brought about skepticism and doubts about the value of the protein.

Thirty years have elapsed since BMP was first discovered. In my opinion, we are no further along in seeing its application as a valuable ingredient in the management of nonunions, let alone in the care of acute fractures. The myriad of bone substitutes available on the market, based on the concept of bone inductive substances has failed the clinical test. The data presented thus far is not strong enough to declare a final victory.

A number of reputable investigator are pursuing the task of finding an answer to the slow progress in making BMP (in its many forms) the great adjunct it promised to be. Others, however, are investigators conducting studies, simply to allow the industrial concerns to continue the sales of the many pastes, glues, sheets or granules, allegedly possessing magic osteoinductive and osteoconductive properties. A number of orthopedists, functioning as peddlers for industry, travel the world lecturing on the subject. Needless to say, the "rep" of the respective firm precedes their entrance in the auditorium.

SECTION I - TRAUMA

Consistently, the speaker distributes elegant brochures that contain reprints of various papers published in peer-review journals as well as in "though-away" medical magazines. Then, they flash on the screen the worn-out photographs of artificially created bone defects in a variety of animals. The pictures depict the surgical defect filled with new bone in an impressive manner. The clinical studies they present are, in almost all instances, mediocre to say the least. No control studies are shown, and no mention is made of the number of variables that exist in the evaluation of nonunions.

The impressionable residents, or practitioners, listening to the presentations, only remember the pretty pictures of the experimental animals without paying attention to the weakness of the clinical data. They do not stop to consider the tremendous differences that exist between a pathological condition in the human and the clean, surgically produced ostectomy in a healthy animal. The healthy animal has healthy tissues at the time of surgery; its muscles and other tissues are normal. In the human with a nonunion, the local situation is quite different: the ends of the bone are usually sclerotic and poorly vascularized; the soft tissue surrounding the pathological site are also dysvascular; and the scarring of the soft tissues in equally poor condition.

Under such different circumstances, it is naive to believe that a bone graft substitute can produce the desired results. One can use in this scenario the words of Claude Bernard, the famous French scientists, when arguing with the even more famous French giant Louis Pasteur, "N"est pas the microbe, c'est le milieu" (It is not the bacteria that matters, it is the environment). My argument does not answer the question as to why the bone enhancing substances do not accelerate bone healing when applied to fresh injuries, which obviously do not suffer chronic, adverse local conditions. Maybe we are being told that attempts to improve on the systems developed by nature over tens of thousands of years of evolution cannot be manipulated very easily through "modern" technology.

I suspect that sooner or later (most likely later) bone-enhancing materials will be produced. However, we must be realistic in many respects. One is the fact that the research that needs to be conducted in this area is very expensive. Industry has put millions of dollars into the effort and thus far has been able, through marketing techniques, convinced the orthopaedic profession that the current products work. This is obviously not he case, and therefore, sooner or later, (probably sooner) orthopaedists will stop using the products. That means that the profit made by the industrial concerns will be seriously reduced. Industry will stop the support of further research in this area and move in another direction. Another good example of the unsatisfactory method we have in place for the conduct of research: if a research project does not produce immediate results, and profit is not generated overnight, the financial support is discontinued.

SECTION I - TRAUMA

C

CAPITELLUM FRACTURES

Fractures of the capitellum are not common and their treatment remains controversial. Currently, since the perception exists that any and all fracture must be "fixed" surgery is the only popular approach. However, we must recognize that there are times when anatomic reduction is not achievable because of extensive comminution of the fragments, and attempts to put together those intra-articular fragments often leaves a marked degree of incongruity. In addition, because of the "impact" nature of the injury the articular cartilage may be irreparably damaged at the time of his initial insult.

I had an opportunity to treat a number of capitellum fractures before open reduction and internal fixation became "mandatory'. When the fractures were comminuted I excised the fragments. The results, I believe, were satisfactory for the most part. It is a procedure more likely to render good clinical results than excision of the radial head. It does not result in elbow instability and cannot compromise the proximal or distal radio-ulna articulation. The intact interosseous membrane, probably, made the latter complication impossible [17, 76, 161].

Immobilization of the elbow or forearm following the surgical excision is not necessary. The gradual use of the extremity, beginning almost immediately after disappearance of acute symptoms can be introduced with impunity.

I recently noticed while looking at arthroscopy "movies" of the radial head that the last few proximal millimeters of the radial head seem to be made of articular cartilage suggesting that the radial head rotates 260 degrees over the ulna. This cartilaginous coverage needs an explanation. Is it possible that a surface of hyaline cartilage remains normal throughout a lifetime never being in contact with an opposing hyaline cartilage surface? Perhaps it is a situation similar to the knee joint where contact of some portions of articular cartilage never touch opposing cartilaginous surfaces. This being the case, what can we do with the revered theory that articular cartilage needs to be intermittently compressed in order to maintain is physical and physiological properties?

CHILDREN: Fractures

It is difficult for me to properly appreciate the recent surgical trend in the management of fractures in children. I pause before I criticize it because I still have clear recollection of the difficulties I encountered some years ago in convincing others at the Los Angeles county/University of Southern California (USC) residency program that skeletal pinning of humeral supracondylar fractures had earned a place in the armamentarium of the surgeon. I was confronted with powerful evidence to support traction as being the safest method. With time we all learned that when properly performed, pinning is a very effective treatment, with important financial implications.

Now I see an epidemic of surgery in the management of femoral, tibial and forearm fractures in children. I anticipate it will extend to fractures of the humerus and other bones as well. Only time,

SECTION I - TRAUMA

supported by reliable clinical and economic data will put a brake on the trend and find a logical balance between the various treatment modalities.

It appears logical that technology successfully used with adults, should also be made applicable to the child. However, in the process the effort may have gone too far, too quickly. Beautiful examples of successfully treated femoral fractures, using intramedullary nails are being flashed on screens around the world. At the sight of such views, residents in training salivate heavily. They see themselves forever free of the tedious labor of arranging traction apparatus or wrapping plaster of Paris. The profuse salivation is shared by the manufactures of orthopaedic implants who see before them huge business opportunities.

The "gurus" of the new method are recommending that all femoral fractures in children, six years and older, be managed with closed nailing. They report a "very low" incidence of avascular necrosis, and have assured us that this major complication can be avoided by appropriately entering the femoral shaft laterally to the trochanteric fossa. It makes sense. They shrug their shoulders and pay no attention to the also "low incidence" of valgus deformity, produced from damage to the greater trochanteric apophysis. Even less important to them is the frequently found two-centimeter residual discrepancy in the length of the extremities. The important thing is to be able to thread the nail into the narrow canal.

The most powerful argument given to support the surgical treatment is that in modern time's mothers no longer have to stay home with their injured children since they had chosen, or were forced to work. If a child is injured and is treated with a spica cast that is applied within a few days of the injury, the mother must be absent from work during the child's recovery. Logically, if the child's home confinement is not required, the mother is able to continue working.

The fact remains that following intramedullary nailing the young patients do not immediately become independent. Their discharge from the hospital is not possible in all instances within 24 or 48 hours after surgery. According to recent reports, the average hospital stay is of five days. Ambulation does not begin in the hospital for many of the children. They are given return appointments for one or two weeks later, at which time ambulation begins. At home many of them need assistance, which in our society is usually provided by the mother. I suspect those mothers will have to stay home until the children are sufficiently recovered to return to school. To assume the mothers leave the children at home alone, while they go to work is ludicrous. The same situation exists when the child is in a spica cast or brace. So what are the real superior gains that justify the anesthetic, surgical and skeletal risks?

I once made the comment that it was not necessarily an undesirable feature to have the working mothers be forced to stay home during the child's recovery. It could be a good fringe benefit. The time at home with their injured children could be used by the mothers to provide love and affection during times of pain and suffering.

Forearm fractures in children, with few exemptions, have long been successfully treated by non-surgical means. The remodeling that takes place following the acceptance of mild angular deformities is remarkable. Even in adults, a few degrees of angular deformity are associated with only minimal, and often inconspicuous functional impairment. I need to see better evidence before I accept the premise that plating or nailing of forearm fractures in children is a better therapeutic approach. (See FOREARM FRACTURES)

SECTION I - TRAUMA

As I witness the enthusiasts for the surgical treatment of fractures in children, I ask myself what is it that prompts the advocates of surgery to feel that way. I suspect that some do it because they are seriously seeking means to improve the care of patients and willing to sail on new and uncharted waters. Others probably do it hoping to gain recognition among their academic peers. Others prefer the surgical treatment because it generates higher revenues for themselves. This is how it is in many other areas of orthopaedics. Pediatric orthopaedists cannot be that much different from the rest of us.

If the surgical pattern continues, and I suspect it will, we are going to witness an unprecedented number of complications. The cost of surgical care is not lower than the nonsurgical on. There is already some data to indicate that the cost of care is the same in both groups... However, since reimbursement to the orthopaedists is higher with surgical treatment at this time, it is logical to anticipate that it soon will be lowered when third party payers face the problem of increased costs to them. ! This is another step toward to the specter of the day when physicians will be salaried employees and whose income will be fixed regardless of the types of surgical or nonsurgical procedures performed!

SECTION I - TRAUMA

CLAVICLE FRACTURES

Who would have thought, even a few years ago, that a debate could possibly take place regarding whether or not clavicle fractures should be treated surgically on a routine basis. We have always considered such fractures, with the exception of open ones resulting from very high energy, and severely displaced fractures located in the distal third, as being simple problems that readily respond to conservative measures. That is no longer the case. Proponents of surgical intervention in all fracture are passionately saying that even clavicle fractures are best managed with intramedullary nails or plate fixation.

I first learned about this fledgling trend a few years ago, during a visit to a trauma center in Germany. I had been invited to participate in a course dealing with skeletal trauma, during which time I had the opportunity to spend some time with a young trauma surgeon who took me around the hospital and with whom I discussed the philosophy and practices at his institution. He stated to me that all fractures treated in his facility were managed surgically. Reluctant to accept such sweeping statement, I probed into the matter further. It turned out that he was right since even all metacarpal fractures, displaced or non-displaced, were treated surgically. The same was true, according to him, for distal radial fractures. He did acknowledge, however, that "once in a while" very elderly patients with non-displaced Colles' fractures were treated with splints. Expecting to hear that there were some exceptions, I asked if clavicle fractures were also treated surgically. He responded that with greater and greater frequency they were approaching them with intramedullary nailing. When I said to him that I was having difficulty justifying such a practice he proceeded to lecture me on attitudinal changes that had taken place in his country. He stated that patients no longer accept the lump that non-surgically treated clavicle fractures may produce after they heal I remarked to him that I was "really" amazed to see how human behavior had changed so dramatically in such a short period of time. Accelerated Darwinian evolution, I said, must be responsible for such a narcissistic reaction to a minimal and usually unrecognizable deviation from the normal. Probably, unaware of the hidden criticism I was expressing, he proceeded to inform me that the only problem they were still having was finding an easy way to remove the nail after fracture union.

. I wonder if it ever occurred to him to ask a woman -likely to enjoy wearing dresses that expose the shoulders- whether she preferred a lump difficult to identify with a naked eye or a scar visible at all times.

What a wonderful example, I thought, of the dangers of unchecked technology. Many seem to think that if a technique exists for the treatment of a condition, then it should be used under all circumstances. The fact that many fractures do not require surgery does not matter to them. The existing techniques must be used. I suspect that surgeons who operate on clavicular fractures are paid a great deal more than the ones who use traditional conservative treatments and who, without any doubt, encounter fewer complications. Should we call this progress?

It was difficult for me to fully understand why such a practice had gained popularity in Germany, the country that first established the socialist system of health care; and where every citizen receives free medical care and most physicians are salaried. However, that is not true for all surgeons since those, like the professors, often make enormous amounts of money taking care of patients with additional private insurance. Perhaps their examples are followed by the students, who either because of enforced or voluntary loyalty follow their mentors dicta, or stop thinking about what they do and simply imitate others. We do that also in the United States as well. Residents, once in private practice, do what they saw

SECTION I - TRAUMA

their mentors do during their training. They are often deprived of the opportunity to learn from others outside the tight nucleus of full-time faculty... [140, 154, 158]

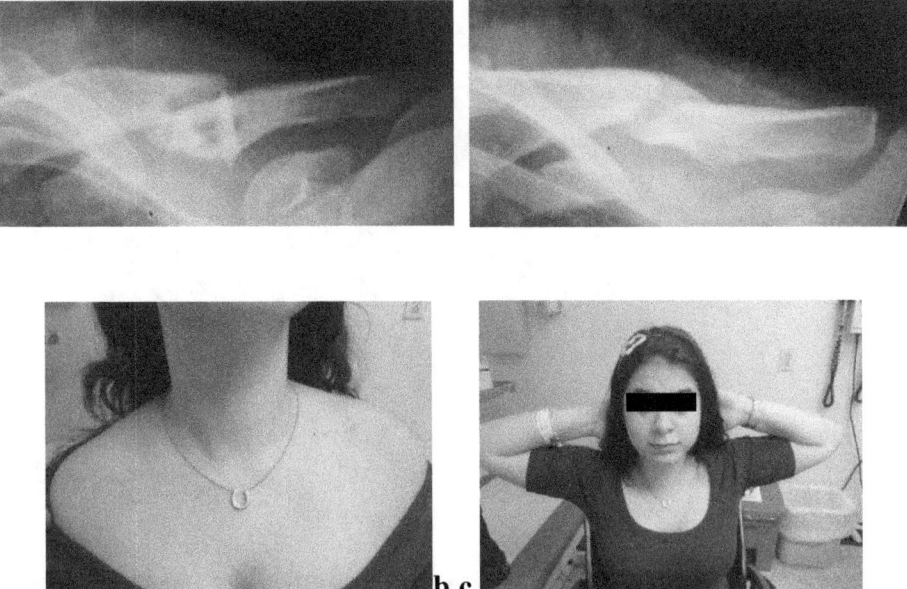

The patient demonstrating the range of motion of her shoulders ten weeks after the initial insult.

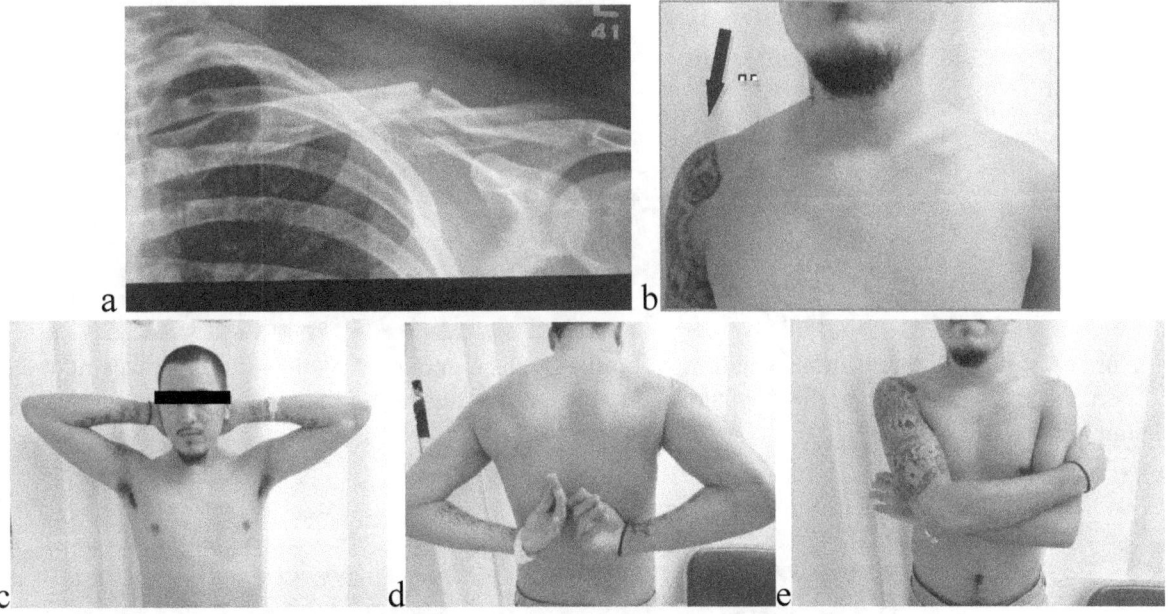

a) Radiograph obtained eight weeks after the initial injury. b-e) Clinical appearance and range of motion of the virtually asymptomatic shoulder at that time. No evidence of bony union has yet taken place.

SECTION I - TRAUMA

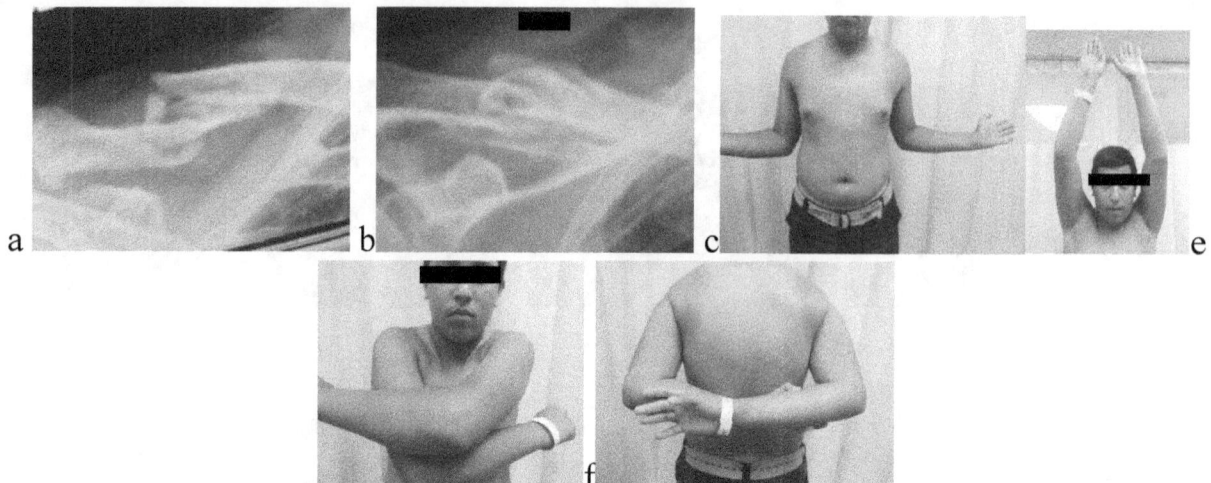

a and b) Radiographs of initial fracture and the healing shown at two and one-half months later. c-f. Patient demonstrates the range of motion of his asymptomatic shoulders at that time.

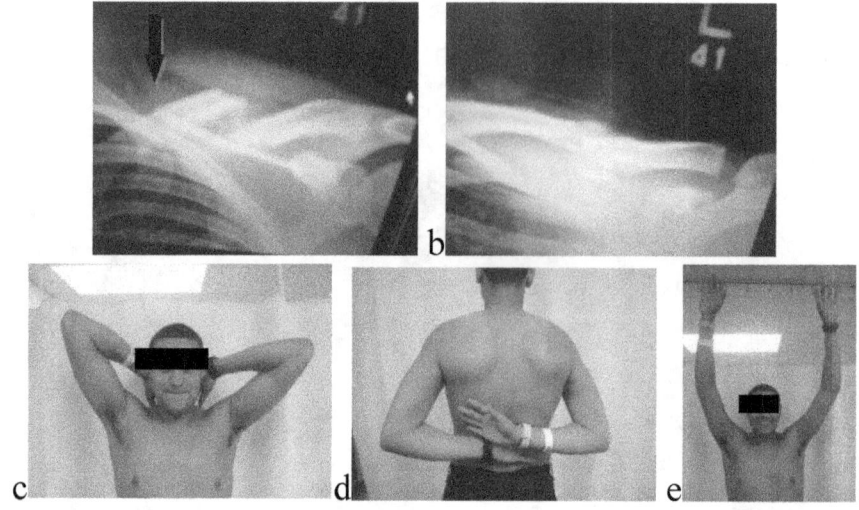

a and b) Initial and three and one-half month radiographs demonstrating the initial displacement and the spontaneous realignment to the fragments. c-f) Patient demonstrating the range of motion of his asymptomatic shoulder.

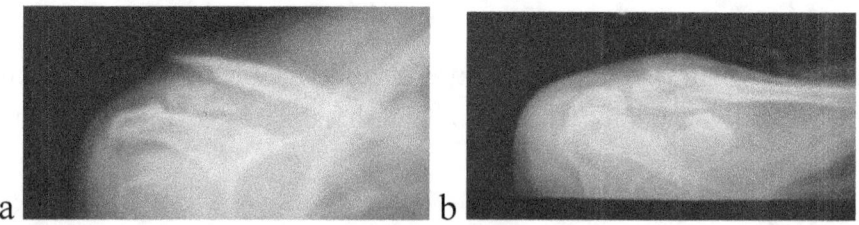

a and b) Radiographs of the initial injury and two and two and a half months later.

SECTION I - TRAUMA

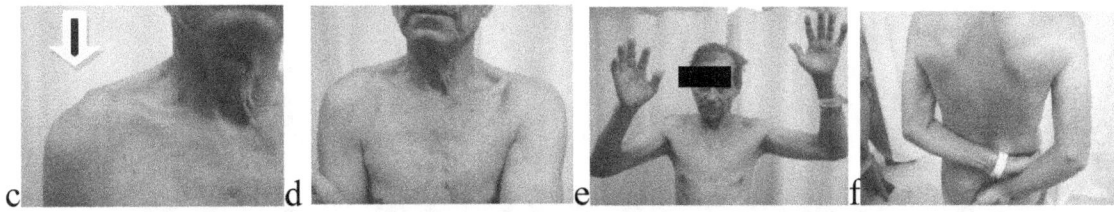

c-f.) Patient demonstrates the range of motion of his asymptomatic shoulder at that time.

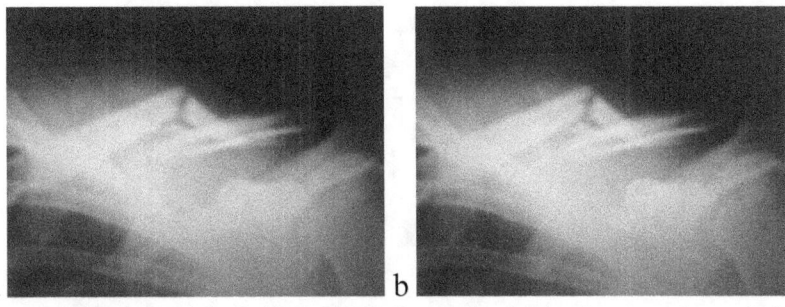

a) Radiograph taken on the day of the injury. b) Radiograph obtained two and one-half months later. No radiological evidence of healing can be detected.

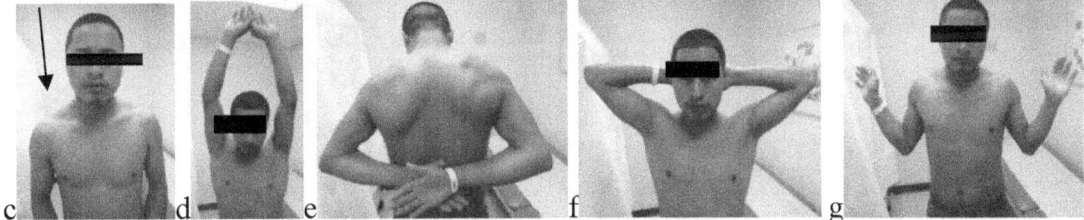

c-g) Patient demonstrate he range of motion of his asymptomatic shoulders at that time.

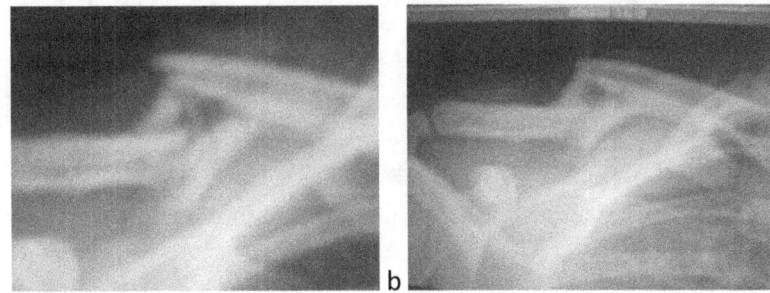

a) Radiograph taken on the day of the injury. b) Radiograph obtained three and one-half months later. Notice the presence of early peripheral callus.

SECTION I - TRAUMA

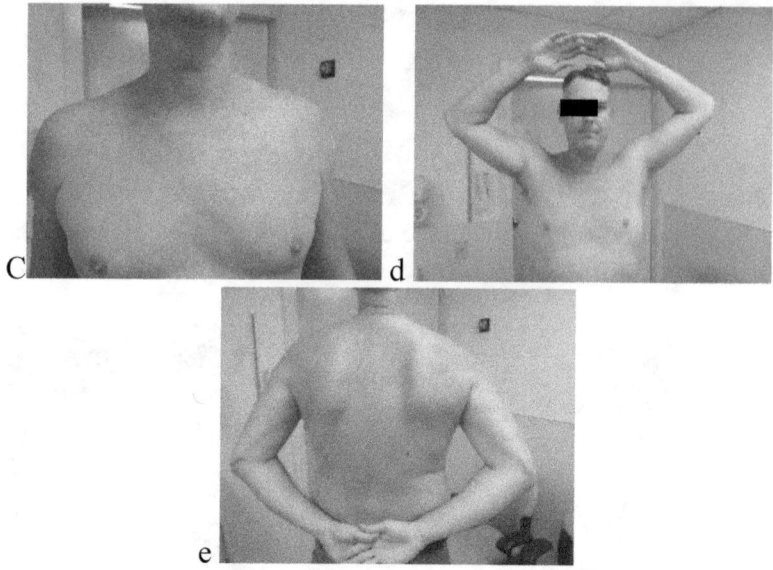

Patient demonstrates the range of motion of his asymptomatic shoulder at that time.

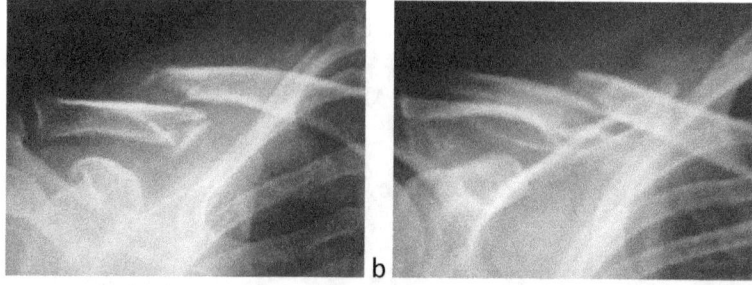

a) Radiograph taken on the day of the injury. b) Radiograph obtained two months later. Notice the apparent improvement in the alignment of the fragments. Peripheral callus is not visible.

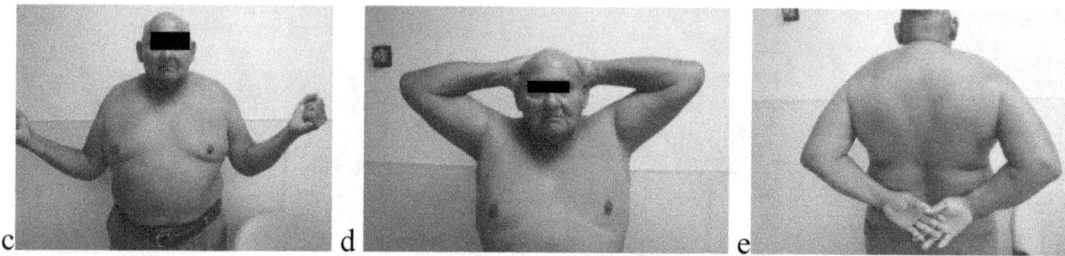

c-) Patient demonstrates the range of motion of his shoulders at that time.

DISCUSSION

Fractures of the clavicle were long considered benign fractures in most instances and treated by simple, nonsurgical methods. Recently, interest has been expressed in some quarters for the surgical approach. Several reports dealing with patients treated with plating or intramedullary fixation have suggested a high rate of union and good functional performance.

SECTION I - TRAUMA

Trying to support the surgical approach, some have reported an unacceptable percentage of nonunions and patient dissatisfaction with the conservative treatment, such as a nonunion rate of 15% and patient "unhappiness" in over 25 % of patients. I cannot claim expertise on the subject, but the first reading of such terrible results shocked me because they contradicted the traditional practice of the orthopaedic community as well as my own personal and vicariously obtained views. During the past decade I presided over a trauma clinic at Jackson Memorial Hospital, the main teaching hospital for the University of Miami. I suspect that not a single month went by without my seeing at least one patient with a clavicle fracture. Among that large number of patients, there were a few whose fractures had been treated surgically by the staff of the Department of Orthopaedics. Both groups had patients who demonstrated good as well as poor clinical result. However, my reaction to the surgical approach was not as positive I wanted it to be. There were times when I felt surgery was the most logical and best approach. In many other instances, I questioned the wisdom of the treatment given to them, since I believed that good clinical and radiological results would have taken place if the conservative approach had been used. It appeared that the decisions for surgery had been made by what the staff considered "unacceptable" degrees of displacement of the fragment or shortening of the bone.

I have arrived at the conclusion that the overall "epidemic' of unnecessary orthopaedic surgery was aggravated by economic considerations imposed on the orthopaedic discipline by hospitals, the implant manufacturing industry, and to a great extent the profession itself. The economic benefits these parties gain from the preference of surgical versus non-surgical treatments is enormous. Wishing to improve one's financial status is not in itself wrong, but using devious means to attain this goal, while sacrificing moral and ethical precepts, is inexcusable.

It would be unfair to indict the entire orthopaedic discipline of being motivated to too high a degree by economic concerns. There are many surgeons who firmly believe in providing the best possible care to their patients without deviating from ethical norms. I suspect that must surgeons promoting the surgical approach are motivated by their innate desire to have their results known by others, while others from a loss of objectivity, and the rest in order to continue to receive money and other perks from the manufactures of the implants.

It is difficult to predict the outcome of the present situation. Either irrefutable evidence in support of surgery will increase or economic concerns will force a more realistic approach.

SECTION I - TRAUMA

COLLATERAL LIGAMENTS (KNEE)

In so-called sports medical centers, injuries to the collateral ligaments of the knee represent a large percentage of the patients treated. Some years ago their surgical repair was the virtually universally accepted method of treatment. Then, various publications in the medical literature began to cast serious doubts on the need for surgical repair of the damaged ligaments. Bracing became popular. Currently we have noticed a renewed trend toward surgery. The revelations that the MRI has exposed have helped the reassessment of the role of surgery. The emphasis has shifted once again toward the need for anatomical repair.

I do not doubt the majority of the commonly seen torn medial collateral ligaments can be successfully treated by non-surgical means. I do remain skeptical, however, as to the true role played by the braces popularly used in their care. I cannot see how a brace that compresses the soft tissues of the thigh and calf can possibly provide immobilization to torn structures whether surgically repaired or not. If a valgus or varus force is introduced to the knee the proximal and distal portions of the brace sink into the soft tissues of the thigh and calf until the force is dissipated. The sinking of the brace means that a collateral ligament also shares the force. The only way to prevent stresses on the ligament would be if the cuffs of the brace had pins that penetrate into the femur and tibia! That obviously is not a suggestion but a statement of fact. The resulting immobilization would do more harm than good.

I became aware of the false rationale behind joint stabilizing knee braces when we conducted experimental work in amputated cadaver specimens we were using in the study of condylar fractures of the tibia. Loren L. Latta, PhD, director of orthopaedic research at the University of Miami, a very good friend and long-time associate, showed me how much the femoral stump of the specimen could travel within the soft tissues in either valgus or varus according to the forces applied.

I suspect that braces used in the care of surgically or non-surgically treated knee collateral ligaments help only as a reminder to the patients of the need to avoid major stresses to the joint.

COLLES' FRACTURES

The few recent reports, anecdotal for the most part, indicating that arthritis is a common sequella of Colles fractures, became, to some, an official excuse for their treatment by surgical means. I suspected the epidemic of surgery would soon spread when I first read the first such report a few years ago. Though the authors attempted to indicate that only certain distal fractures should be treated surgically, subsequent presentations at meetings clearly showed that they are, for all practical purposes, operating on virtually all of them.

I have seen the bills submitted by a group of popular hand surgeons in my community, that make you wondered how they can manage to sleep at night without their consciences keeping them awake. The surgical bill is not only more than twice the one normally submitted for the traditional closed treatment of the fracture, but also the post-operative care exceeds it. Three months of daily physical therapy (in their office, of course) is the rule. Needless to say, every physical therapy modality is billed separately.

SECTION I - TRAUMA

A new bill is sent for the surgical removal of the plate and screws, as well as for the few weeks or months of the subsequent physical therapy.

To some extent our journals have been guilty of assisting in the spread of the epidemic of unnecessary surgery, by not requesting from the authors of those publications data comparing results between various closed and opened treatment modalities. One such article appeared in the Journal of Bone and Joint Surgery not too long ago. The authors were from overseas. They simply compared two surgical treatments and concluded that one was better than the other. The incidence of arthritis was one of their criteria used. Radiological arthritis, that is. Not a word was said about any possible comparison with results obtained by others, using nonsurgical modalities.

It is interesting to note that currently the most common malpractice litigation against orthopaedic surgeons in South Florida relates to wrist fractures. Failure to perform surgery resulting in mild deformity is the reason for the litigation. This is one instance that proves that the epidemic of malpractice against orthopaedist has been often provoked by the profession's blind obsession with surgery and the alleged restoration of anatomy. If we were honest enough to admit that a mild residual deformity is not a complication but simple an inconsequential deviation from the normal, the number of malpractice suits would be reduced dramatically. Wishful thinking. A great deal of profit is made from the abuse of surgery and unnecessary physical therapy.

Fractures of the distal radius attracted my attention in my younger days when I asked myself why was it that sometimes, after what appeared to be a good reduction of the fracture, subsequent x-rays showed a return to the initial mal-position of the fragments.

It was not weight bearing on the painful hand that did it. All the patient had done was to follow instructions concerning active motion of the fingers and elevation of the swollen extremity. Muscle forces had to be responsible for the re-dislocation of the fragments.

I proceeded to conduct studies to identify the culprit. Using the ubiquitous medical students as Guinea pigs, I proceeded to identify the action of the various muscular structures around the wrist when active use of the fingers took place, and the arm, surrounded by a heavy cast, was actively elevated. We placed electromyography needles over the flexors and extensors of the wrist and fingers as well as the biceps, triceps and brachio-radialis muscles. Under those circumstances, above and below elbow casts were applied holding the forearm in pronation first and then in supination, and the wrist in the traditional mild volar and ulnar deviation position. The students were then asked to exercise their fingers and to actively elevate the immobilized arm.

The electromyographic readings were most interesting. Needless to say, the flexors and extensor were active when the fingers were actively moved. The biceps was moderately active, as expected, when the forearm was in pronation, but maximally when immobilized in supination. All this was detected when the students were simply doing the finger exercises and arm elevation that patients with Colles' fractures are encouraged to carry out. When the students were asked to close the fist we noticed that the brachio-radialis was significantly active when finger motion and elevation took place but only when the forearm was in the classical position of pronation. When the forearm was in supination the contracture of the brachio-radialis was minimal or non-existent [86].

SECTION I - TRAUMA

This prompted me to suspect that the brachio-radialis was capable of displacing a reduced but unstable fracture of the distal radius. Its attachment to the distal fragment of the Colles' fracture can re-create the typical deformity of dorsal deviation, shortening of the radius and radial deviation of the small distal fragment [86]. (Fig. 9)

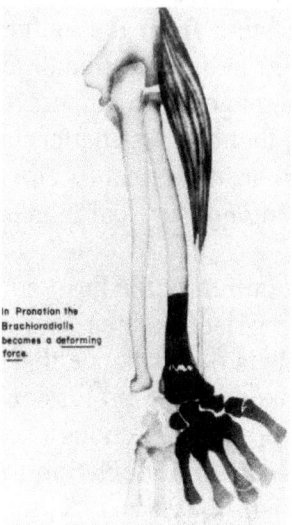

The brachio-radialis muscle upon contracting produces the typical Colles deformity.

Having observed those findings in non-injured people we repeated the study in patients with distal radial fractures. The findings were exactly the same and the changes were monitored under fluoroscopy. A well reduced comminuted fracture or one with an oblique geometry would show loss of reduction when the forearm was in pronation as soon as the brachio-radialis was electrically stimulated. The three typical components of the fracture were readily reproduced..

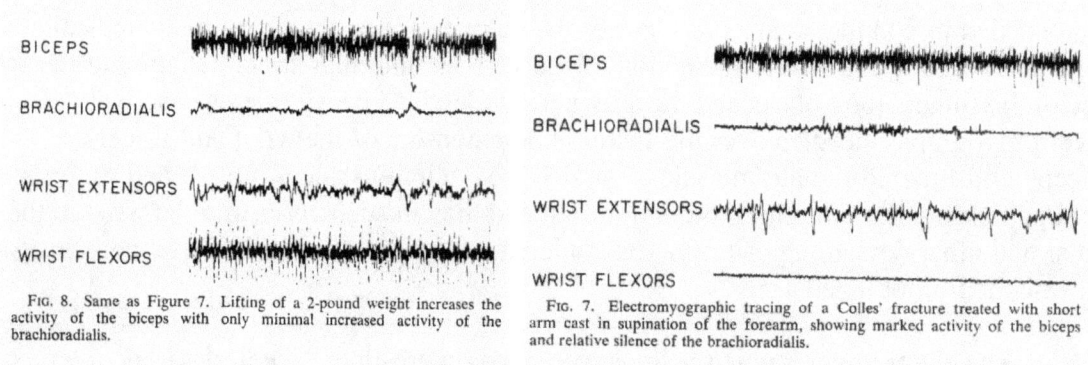

FIG. 8. Same as Figure 7. Lifting of a 2-pound weight increases the activity of the biceps with only minimal increased activity of the brachioradialis.

FIG. 7. Electromyographic tracing of a Colles' fracture treated with short arm cast in supination of the forearm, showing marked activity of the biceps and relative silence of the brachioradialis.

Fig. Electromyography tracing depicting the role of the various muscle about the wrist
.

SECTION I - TRAUMA

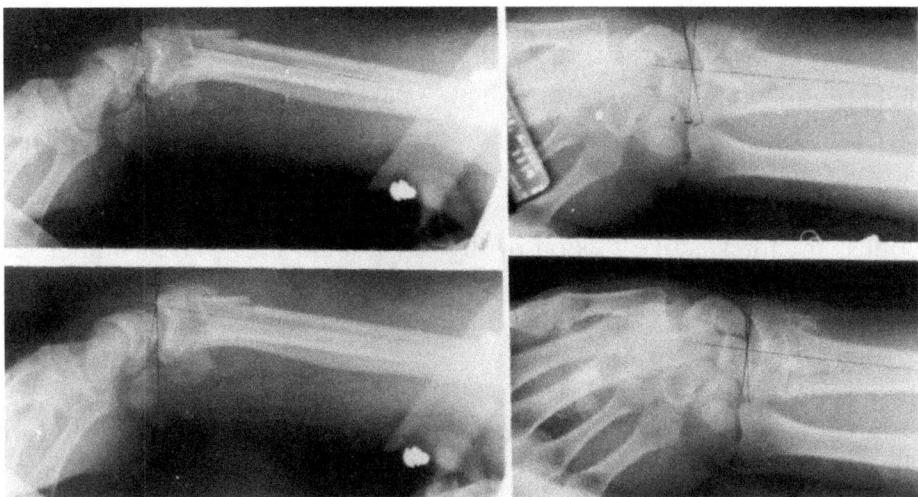

Fig. The top views demonstrate the relationship between the fragments prior to electrical stimulation of the brachioradialis muscles. Bottom pictures taken after electrical stimulation of the muscle. Notice the recurrence of deformity.

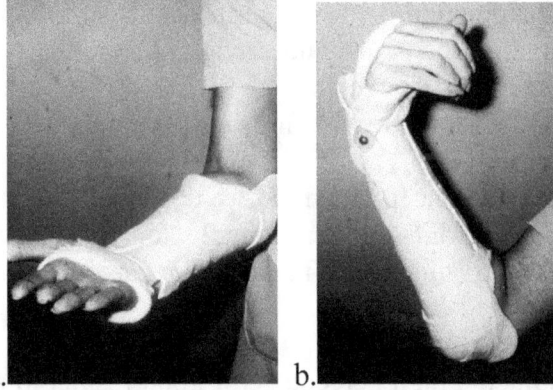

Fig. a and b. The Colles brace permits limited motion of the elbow, normal volar flexion; but prevents prono-supination and dorsi-flexion and ulnar and radial deviation of the wrist.

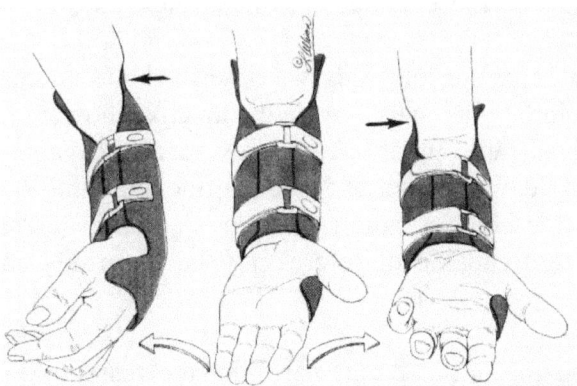

Fig. Schematic drawing of the Colles brace and its function.

The conclusion from those laboratory studies suggested that contrary to long-standing popular belief, the typical Colles' fracture should be stabilized in supination of the forearm and not in pronation. Pronation creates an environment conducive to loss of reduction. Cognizant of the newly found facts, we surmised that the cast used in the treatment of these fractures had to extend above the elbow and be critically molded to effectively prevent prono-supination. Furthermore we concluded that the forearm could be held in supination without immobilizing the elbow by molding a cast in a manner that resembled the Munster prosthesis worn by the very short below-the-elbow amputee. This prosthesis allows the amputee to flex and extend the elbow while keeping the prosthesis stable over the stump. The close molding of the prosthesis over the condyles of the humerus makes that possible. I suspected that in the case of Colles' fractures active flexion of the wrist could take place without fear of recurrence of the deformity, since contracture of the wrist and fingers' flexors would help maintain the position of volar flexion of the distal fragment. Extension, however, must be prevented.

The position of supination has the added advantage of ensuring that permanent loss of supination of the forearm does not develop. This statement does not imply that pronation should be compromised. Both motions are important but loss of the last few degrees of pronation are easily and inconspicuously compensated by shoulder flexion, abduction and internal rotation. Amputees use this mechanism to compensate for their lack of pronation. A comparable inconspicuous compensatory mechanism for the lack of supination does not exist. [29]

The position of supination of the forearm results in a better reduction of a dislocation or subluxation of the distal radio-ulnar joint and recognition of the not so uncommonly associated lunate dissociation, which is more easily recognized when x-rays are taken with the forearm in supination. Pronation makes accurate reading of wrist films more difficult.

With those ideas and concepts in mind we designed a plastic brace that would permit flexion of the elbow, limit its extension while allowing free flexion of wrist and fingers flexion and extension (Fig. 12 a, b, c). The clinical and radiographic results were carefully documented and subsequently reported. [111, 121, 150]

The report illustrated a high percentage of good results in regards to loss of reduction and rapid return to function. Our results were critically compared with those reported by a number of other investigators, leading us to conclude that the ultimate functional performance of patients treated by closed methods were comparable to those achieved from surgical plating. [163]

In order to best carry out the study we described a new classification for distal radial fractures, which we thought, would be practical. I made the mistake, however, of not paying sufficient attention to the condition of the distal radio-ulnar joint and eventually I came to recognize that dislocation of that joint is probably the single most important factor influencing the stability of the reduction. Even though we had concluded that the brachio-radialis muscle is a major deforming force, all the muscles crossing the fracture and wrist are capable of re-creating the deformity in the presence of distal radio-ulnar instability.

After publishing the initial report narrating the results obtained with the treatment of Colles' fractures with braces as described above, we conducted a prospective study comparing the results of bracing with forearm in supination versus the forearm in pronation. The data indicated that stable extra-articular non-displaced (Type I) and extra-articular non-displaced fractures (Type II) did equally as well regardless of the position of the forearm. Intra-articular, non-displaced fractures (Type III) demonstrated comparable findings. However, intra-articular, displaced fractures (Type IV) showed significantly better results when the forearm was stabilized in supination (FIG. 13 a, b, c and 14 a, b, c, d). This finding

SECTION I - TRAUMA

further supported the important role played by the brachio-radialis muscle. and we more carefully considered the condition of the distal radio-ulnar joint we would have concluded that in intra-articular fractures loss of reduction is very difficult if not impossible to prevent with casts or braces if the joint was dislocated at the time of the injury. In light of that information I believe that fixation, either with pins, plates or external fixators is the preferred treatment in those fractures.

FUNCTIONAL RESULTS

		EXCELLENT GOOD	FAIR POOR
TYPE I:	SUPINATION	86% (6/7)	14% (1/7)
	PRONATION	100% (5/5)	0%
TYPE II:	SUPINATION	100% (13/13)	0%
	PRONATION	94% (17/18)	6% (1/18)
TYPE III:	SUPINATION	100% (10/10)	0%
	PRONATION	88% (7/8)	12% (1/8)

ANATOMICAL RESULTS

ALL DISPLACED FRACTURES

(TYPES II & IV)

	SUPINATION	PRONATION
EXCELLENT OR GOOD	85%	53%
FAIR OR POOR	15%	47%

Fig. Table indicating the improved clinical and radiographic results obtained when the forearm is held in a relaxed attitude of supination

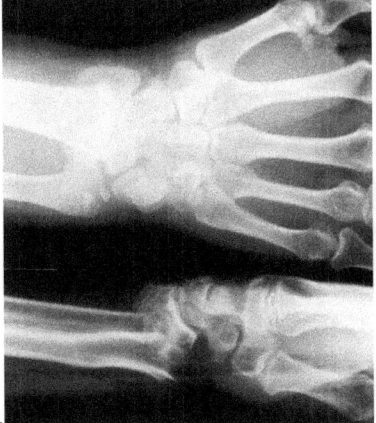
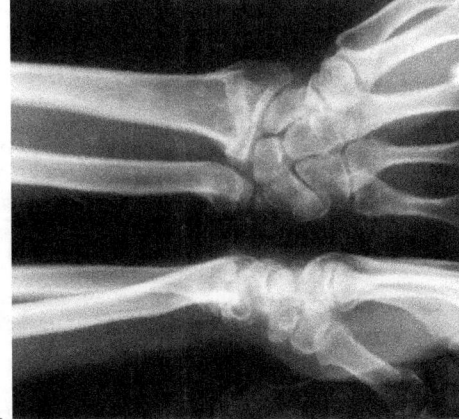

Fig. a and b. Displaced extra-articular fracture managed with a functional brace in supination.

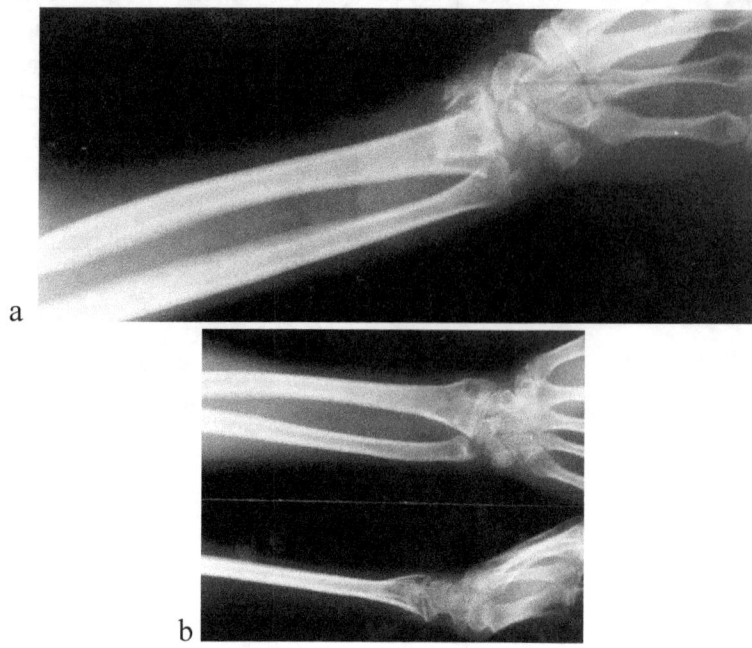

Fig. a nd b. Comminuted intraarticular fracture without dislocation of the radio-ulnar joint treated with a functional brace in supination.

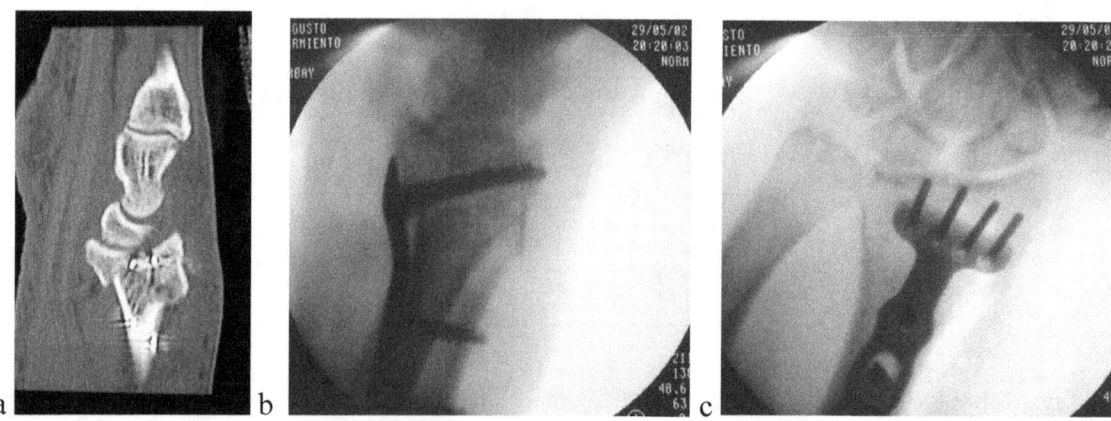

Fig a, b and c. Radiographs of the author's fractured right wrist initially treated with multiple pins. The fragments readily displaced. A volar plate was then used and a good reduction and function were obtained. Noticed the scaphoid-lunate sub-luxation.

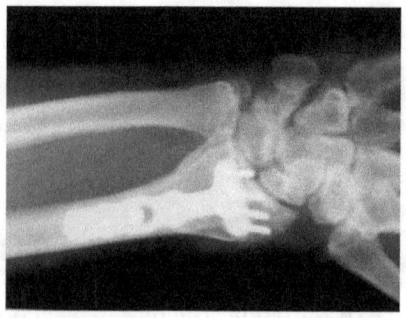

Fig. Radiograph obtained one year after surgery. Notice the mild incongruity. The scapho-lunate subluxaation improved spontaneously, and the wrist remains asymptomatic. .

It was not until I had already reported on the theory that supination of the forearm was more desirable that I learned that John Fahey, of Illinois, had made the same recommendation a few years earlier. As soon as obtained that information I contacted him and apologized for not having given him credit for the concept. We corresponded and discussed the issue at hand. The fact that he had not based his treatment on the possible role of the brachio-radialis muscle, somewhat assuaged by concern about the possibility of being accused of plagiarism. Apparently, we came to the same conclusion for different reasons.

I acknowledge internal fixation of distal radial fractures is the treatment of choice for many intraarticular fractures. However, the suggestion that all distal fractures of the radius are best treated by surgical means cannot be justified. Plate fixation is often associated with complications that may be serious. Infection can be a catastrophic event resulting either in non-union of the fracture, a destroyed, stiff and painful joint and or massive scarring of tendons and muscles, leaving behind a severely functionless hand and wrist. Even in the absence of infection, permanent limitation of motion is frequently encountered and expensive physical therapy needs to be administered for prolonged periods of time. Dorsiflexion is the motion most likely to be compromised. Nerve injuries and tendon ruptures are also possible complications. Removal of intact or broken implants is sometimes required to correct problems or to prevent some of them.

External Fixators are effective in the management of those fractures likely to render poor results when treated by non-surgical means. However, their use must be judiciously carried out. Pin track infections are common and sometimes they do not respond readily to non-surgical treatment. Stiffness of the wrist and fingers is a common finding that requires prolonged therapy before improvement becomes evident. Fixators that allow wrist motion are better, but do not necessarily prevent prolonged wrist stiffness.

Recently, the proponents of internal or external fixation have loudly emphasized the need to restore anatomical congruity of the fractured articular cartilage. However, the fact remains that clinical osteoarthritis of the wrist following Colles' fractures is rare. Colles himself recognized that fact and wrote about it.

While it is logical to assume that restored congruity is desirable and cosmetically better as far as the x-rays are concerned, there is, not as yet, solid data to justify the categorical statement that the risks involved with surgery are fully justified in order to prevent joint degeneration. As far as I am concerned the existing data is too soft. There is no evidence that incongruity leads to osteoarthritis in all instances or that elimination of incongruity in crushed articular cartilage precludes subsequent degenerative changes. We must also be realistic. Surgical attempts to anatomically put together multiple, small comminuted fragments of cartilage and sub-chondral bone are futile in most instances. Many gaps are impossible to fill. The pretty appearance of the post-operative x-rays does not tell the whole story.

Since impaction forces produce most Colles fractures, the possibility of permanent damage of the articular cartilage taking place at the time of the initial insult must be kept in mind. This might explain why long term radiographs show arthritic changes in many such fractures, regardless of the type of treatment initially rendered.

I suspect that years from now, someone looking at long term clinical results comparing those obtained from plated or externally fixed fractures and the ones treated non-surgically and with residual imperfect congruity, will find out that a difference between the two groups does not exist.

I used to tell our residents that if they wanted to see long-term results from Colles' fractures they should visit nursing homes where they were likely to see dozens of elderly people with deformed but totally asymptomatic wrists. Many of those joints if x-rayed would indicate that the original fractures had been intra-articular. Many of them probably had x-ray changes.

Intra-articular fractures with joint instability are the ones more likely to develop symptomatic pathology. We made that observation many years ago after experiences with intra-articular fractures of the proximal tibia we were treating with functional braces applied shortly after the initial injury. More recently we conducted experimental laboratory studies, which indicated that minor incongruity without instability does not lead to osteo-arthritic changes.[38] However, if incongruity is associated with joint instability rapid regeneration of the joint is readily seen.[41] We all have seen x-rays indicating articular damage in the absence of symptoms.[44] In general, it is not mild incongruity that matters in the treatment of any intraarticular fracture, but instability and limitation of motion. These latter two circumstances play different roles through probably different mechanism. In some joints, limitation of motion is the main culprit, in others instability.

I envision the dysplastic acetabulum being subjected to instability problems, and setting the stage for degenerative changes; in the distal tibio-talar joint, where instability is less likely on account of the mortise limitation of motion is probably a major contributing cause of osteoarthritis following a fracture.

COMPARTMENT SYNDROMES

A compartment syndrome is a complication that any orthopaedist who deals with fractures fears the most. It can be devastating. Much progress has been made over the years in understanding its patho-physiology and treatment. Routine measurement of muscle compartment pressures and early surgical intervention have helped prevent many unfortunate events.

The increased popularity of closed intra-medullary nailing of tibial fractures has, in my opinion, increased the frequency of the syndrome, because it is impossible to apply powerful traction to a swollen extremity without changing the geometry of the broken leg, and therefore without increasing muscle compartments pressures.

When a tibial fracture occurs the limb shortens bleeding around the fracture follows. This bleeding increases pressure on the surrounding musculature. The shortening of the fractures bone, however, helps in reducing the increased pressures by allowing more room for the collecting blood. If the bleeding is not severe or tamponade stops it, and the pressure is stabilized. However, if under those circumstances of increased pressure, still of a degree not necessarily dangerous, the geometry of the limb is suddenly changed, the muscle pressure necessarily increases. The geometrical change of the fracture leg, from oblong to conical is inevitable associated with increased soft tissue pressure. This increased pressure, brought about by the change in geometry is further increased by bleeding created by the reaming of the medullary canal. It can be sufficient to convert a potential compartment syndrome into a full-blown one.

Similarly, but to a lesser degree, a similar iatrogenic mechanism can be created when a fracture is treated by closed reduction, particularly if followed by the application of a tightly applied Plaster of Paris cast.

We demonstrated in cadaver specimens the above observations [150] which make me think that perhaps immediate nailing of acute fractures may not be always desirable. A period of pre-operative observation may be preferable.

Once a compartment syndrome develops, prompt surgical intervention is necessary. What is still open to question is whether a limb with a well-established compartment syndrome for more than twenty-four or forty-eight hours benefits from the extensive surgery necessary for acute compartment syndromes. I suspect that surgery may do more harm than good. The necrotic tissues, incapable of recovery, once exposed to the environment become a fertile medium for infection. A major complication.

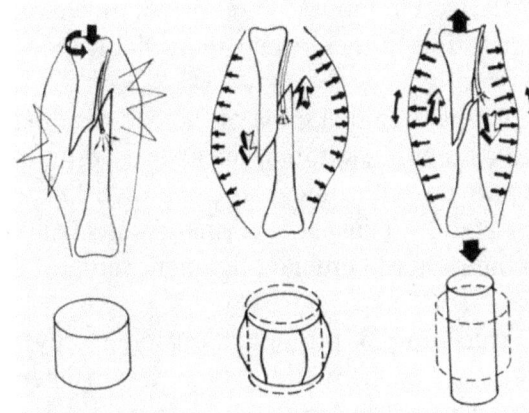

Fig. The geometry of the leg changes when the fracture occurs. If the shortening is manually corrected the compartment pressure increases.

CRUCIATE LIGAMENT INJURIES

During my residency day I attended some of the University of South Carolina football games with Austin More in Columbia, SC. With some frequency, we left the stadium to go directly to the operating room to "fix" torn knee ligaments of young athletes. Torn cruciate ligaments were the most common injuries he treated. He felt that early repair of the injured ligaments gave the best results. All this happened many years before the arthroscope was invented. The history of unsuccessful attempts to surgically repair cruciate ligaments goes back to the 17th. Century, long before the advent of anesthesia.

Austin Moore usually repaired or reconstructed the torn anterior cruciate ligament using the semitendinosus tendon, pretty much the same way it is done today through the arthroscope. He emphasized how important it was to place the tendon in the right position and under tension. The same ritual we hear today on the debate as to whether the repair of the torn ligament should be done individually to every trunk of the structure or jointly; and at what angle and where, precisely, the tendon or allograft should be placed. I heard from him that the tension on the ligament is supposed to be "very important".

SECTION I - TRAUMA

As a resident and later as young practitioner of the art of surgery I memorized the various techniques of cruciate ligament repair and the best way to immobilize the joint post-operatively, and for how long. As I hear my colleagues today passionately argue the merits of new procedures, I cannot help but wonder if the problem of torn cruciate ligaments will ever be resolved. I have serious reservations about the alleged "progress" that has occurred in this area in recent years. I wonder if the improvements made will in any way lessen the late development of degenerative osteoarthritis. I also question the belief that in the short run, patients treated with modern techniques do better than those people treated with old techniques did some thirty or forty years ago. When I express this view before an audience of "sport medicine doctors" I am immediately told, "Unequivocally those treated with modern, new techniques do best.

I have seen many "successfully" reconstructed cruciate ligaments demonstrate knee instability when subjected to critical clinical testing a few years down the road. This instability probably leads to late osteoarthritic changes Tendons, used to replace or reinforce a torn cruciate ligament have been known to undergo changes that often lead to failure. Their initial mechanical properties deteriorate with time and their incomplete revascularization further affects their viability.

It is argued with great passion that most of the bad results in the "old days" were primarily due to the prolonged post-operative immobilization of the knee. I admit that immobilization delays the regaining of motion of the joint. However, with time, most operated knees regain most, if not all, the necessary motion to function appropriately. ." I suspect the final results from modern techniques have not improved that much; the solution to the ruptured cruciate ligament remains elusive.

I also question the true value of prolonged muscle strengthening exercises of the quadriceps and hamstrings following surgical reconstruction, and the insistence that they become hypertrophied. Allegedly, the hypertrophied muscles "protect" the repaired ligaments. In order to gain hypertrophy months of expensive, "supervised" rehabilitation is prescribed. This practice flies in the face of basic physiology: Striated muscles do not function like the myocardium where the law of all-or-none applies. The force of the contraction of striated muscle is dependent on the demands imposed on it. One does not need a hypertrophied quadriceps muscle to walk in a normal fashion. If one wants to run or jump, a more powerful muscle contraction would be necessary. If the knee joint were to depend on hypertrophied muscles to gains stability, it would be necessary for the individual patient to consciously contract his muscles with every step, something that is impossible to do. In addition, it would become essential to maintain the muscle hypertrophy for the remaining of the patient's life. Another impossibility! Emphasis on the need to hypertrophy the hamstring muscles probably does more harm than good, particularly when the repaired ligament is the posterior one, since the contraction of these muscles encourages posterior subluxation of the knee.

As far as placing the greatest possible tension at the suture line, some thought should be given to observations made by Albright, from the University of Iowa, who found out that patients whose ligaments had been sutured under great tension did not do as well as those where less tension was applied. I heard him make that statement at a meeting in his institution.

These facts remind me of an experience I had with a resident in our program at USC. He was, and still is, a very muscular man who regularly exercised and lifted weights. His arm musculature was most impressive. One day, as we scrubbed in preparation for surgery, I noticed him contracting his biceps and admiring its bulge on the mirror. I turned around and said, "Richard, you have a very powerful biceps. What do you think of mine?" I assume that out of respect and fear of offending me he responded,

SECTION I - TRAUMA

"Well, not very good, kind of small". Then I said, "Richard, look at my arm closely again. I want you to remember what you have seen for a long time because your arms will one day look like mine. I had arms like yours when I was your age. Aging is inevitable and along with it comes a loss of muscle mass that you cannot prevent no matter how much you exercise".

Even physical fitness freaks when they age, end up looking like their contemporaries who never lifted anything heavier than a bottle of beer. I saw Richard again a few years later still looking young and athletic. I felt his biceps and they were as hard as a rock. I told him that some years from now I wanted him to pay me a visit at the nursing home where I will be waiting to die, to have him remind me of the bet we made in happier years.

D

DELTOID LIGAMENT INJURIES

The debate concerning the management of torn deltoid ligaments of the ankle seemed to have abated when the orthopaedic community came to the conclusion that their surgical repair was unnecessary. However, the popular growth of sports medicine and the routine use of MRI studies in soft tissue pathology have renewed interest in the surgical approach.

Is there, however, any evidence that surgery is better than conservative treatment? I do not think so. Anyone who has explored torn deltoid ligaments knows that very often approximation of the torn ends cannot be accomplished, and that all the surgeon can do is comb the strands of ligament into a more appealing position. Mother Nature takes care of healing the damaged structure, a process that takes place whether or not surgery is performed.

When ankle dysostosis is present and cannot be corrected manually, the possibility exists that one end of the torn ligament has folded into the joint. In this instance surgical treatment is necessary. However, the condition most likely to create an uncorrectable synostosis is the entrapment of the posterior tibial tendon between the talus and the medial malleolus. This occurs only in severe injuries associated with a dislocation that was manually corrected. Needless to say such pathology is only correctable by surgical means.

The surgeon must be aware of the possibility of entrapment of cartilaginous or osteo-cartilagenous fragments arising from fractures of either the talus or distal tibia. If present and definitely proven to be caught between the articular surfaces they should be excised. Otherwise they can be left alone anticipating their eventual resorption or their harmless permanent presence.

In the typical case of an isolated tear, a cast that holds the ankle in a position of neutral dorsiflexion with a few degrees of inversion of the subtalar joint is sufficient to ensure a satisfactory result

Since the MIR has found such an ubiquitous presence in the life of the orthopaedist, the discovery of anything other than normal structures has lead surgeons to approach any defects or changes as pathological findings in need to arthroscopic surgical intervention. I do not know to what extend this practice is motivated by financial profit and how much is an honest fear of accepting anything that is not seen under normal circumstances. One day we will know.

DISLOCATION OF THE PROXIMAL TIBIO-FIBULA JOINT

Very little has been said about this traumatic condition; it is as if it did not exist. Though uncommon, it is seen in association with a small number of tibial fractures. Failure to recognize the pathology may lead to undesirable consequences. Painful arthritic changes may be a sequella. The pull of the biceps tendon on the head of the fibula results in repeated abnormal motion of he fibula against the tibia, perpetuating the painful symptoms. I assume that the stability of the knee must be compromised, since the lateral collateral ligament also attaches to the dislocated fibular head. In any event the dislocated joint needs to be reduced and the reduction maintained.

The presence of a dislocated proximal tibia-fibular joint should be suspected whenever the tibial fracture, with an otherwise intact fibular shaft, shows overriding of the fragments and therefore, shortening of the extremity. A fractured tibia with an intact fibula cannot experience shortening unless the tibia-fibular joint is dislocated. Similarly, the presence of an abducted proximal tibial fragment, in the case of the tibial fracture with an intact fibula, indicates that the tibia-fibular joint is dislocated. Fractures of the tibia without an associated fibular fracture, if they are to show any angulation, and they usually do, can be only of a varus nature. If the deformity is of valgus nature, the fibula must be dislocated. [19, 123, 129, 138, 158, 144, 152, 156]

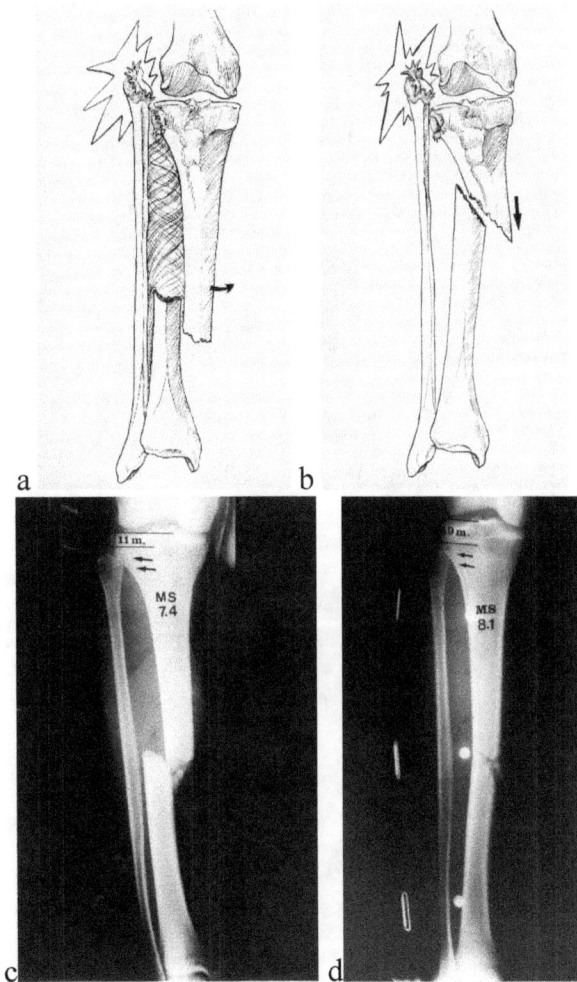

Fig. Schematic drawing of fractured tibia with a dislocated proximal fibula.(a). A closed reduction restored the tibia-fibular joint (b and c) An abducted proximal tibial fragment, showing a valgus deformity, is diagnostic of an associated dislocated fibular joint (d).

In the case of a transverse tibial fracture with an associated tibia-fibular dislocation, reduction of the tibia fracture often spontaneously reduces the dislocation. When the tibia fracture is axially unstable and reduced by traction and subsequent stabilization in a cast or brace, the introduction of weight bearing can readily result in loss of reduction of the reduced dislocation. Mechanically restored length cannot be maintained underweight bearing conditions [33, 70, 138, 144, 147] In order to ensure maintenance of reduction, the reduced fibula must be stabilized with a wire until healing of the torn ligaments takes place. I suspect that in some instances a residual degree of instability remains, giving rise to chronic pain in the area. Whether or not this is a permanent or transient condition I do not know.

E

ELECTRICAL STIMULATION

I should not be discussing this topic because my understanding of and my experience with it are very limited. The results reported in the literature range from very good to extremely poor. This subject is a very good example of how the premature commercialization of a good concept can lead to its demise. "Black boxes" claiming miraculous cures were widely marketed and sold across the land at a furious pace a few years ago. In the hands of many orthopaedists the results were less than satisfactory, either because the method was not good or because it was implemented without a clear understanding of the appropriate methodology or for the wrong indications.

It is impossible to dismiss the fact that piezo-electricity exists and that it probably plays a role in bone repair. This role is not completely clear yet and might never be. The original enthusiasm of the early investigators has dwindled and some of its pioneers have either died or retired.

At this time, adding electrical stimulation in the care of acute fractures is probably nonsense. I doubt we can make an acute fracture heal faster than nature intended. To prescribe it routinely following bone grafting procedures is probably nothing more than an unnecessary added expense. It is like hoping that one day human gestation will be shortened to three months.

Recently, I listened to a paper dealing with a prospective comparative study of electrical stimulation in acute fractures of the distal radius. The investigator reported that while treating approximately fifteen patients, he had found that those patients who received electrical stimulation had healed their fractures one week faster than the control group. He had examined the patients every week. He based the definition of healing on the grounds of absence of pain when the area was digitally compressed, and the radiological presence of "mature trabeculae" bridging the fracture site.

I raised questions about the reliability of the criteria and asked how the investigator had been able to tell within one week period of time that the "immature" trabeculae had become "mature". How had he measured the pressure applied to the fractured bone? and how did he know that the identical pressure had been applied every week over the same exact area?

I suspect that electrical stimulation in the management of acute fractures is at this time nothing more than a useless gimmick that benefits only the manufactures of the expensive products, and increases the cost of medical care.. Electrical stimulation in the care of acute fractures is only one of the many borderline quackery treatments that have gained so much popularity in recent years. I have asked if we are destined to rehash all the methodologists used in medieval days when hot irons, leaches, copper bracelets were used for the treatment of melancholy, heart disease, ulcers, tumors, kidney disease and other conditions.

F

FAT EMBOLISM

We dread the situation when a patient suffering from some type of musculoskeletal condition develops signs of fat embolism, since we know that the condition may be fatal. A number of measures to treat the syndrome have been advocated over the years. I am not qualified to comments on the merits of the various approaches. All I know is that the management of this complication is more successful today that it was a few decades ago. Much we owe to John Border, from Buffalo, New York for his sound studies and observations. From him we learned about possible etiologies of the syndrome and the role that respiratory and digestive factors play in its development.

My interest in the subject began in the early seventies while working with Tomas Kallos, an anesthesiologist at the University of Miami. He closely monitored patients of mine, on whom I was performing total hip surgery. Prior to beginning the surgical intervention he placed catheters into the major vessels leading to or leaving the heart. He was not the first one to notice that at the time of insertion of the cement and prosthesis into the medullary canal there was an audible "gurgle" coming from the vicinity of the heart. The sound was easily detected through the stethoscope. He identified, however, the large amount of bone marrow fat that flows into the systemic circulation at the time of injection of the cement and prosthesis in the medullary canal. In spite of that, patients did not develop symptoms or signs of fat embolism. Intrigued, he took the project to the animal laboratory, where he carried out a procedure similar to the cemented prosthetic replacement. His findings reproduced the ones observed in the human situation: the experimental animals did not show any of the clinical symptoms or findings of fat embolism.

He was able to create the syndrome by making the animals hypo-volemic prior to the injection of the cement. When the animals were subsequently sacrificed and studied, there was evidence of massive amounts of fat in organs such as the brain [44]. If the animals were maintained normo-volemic no complications occurred.

From his experiences we learned that appropriate oxygenation and maintenance of blood volume are essential for the prevention of the intra-operative fat embolism that leads to the clinical syndrome.

I have extrapolated from the total hip replacement observations to trauma. It has been said that early surgical stabilization of fractures of long bones reduces the incidence of fat embolism. The proponents of this approach argue that the early fixation either with plates or intra-medullary nails stops the leakage of medullary fat into the systemic circulation.

I find the argument lacking common sense. The nailing of a femur brings a massive shower of fat into the systemic circulation, even greater that the one experienced immediately following the original insult. Theoretically, the nailing should make matters worse. However, patients do better. I submit that they do better, not because the amount of released fat has been reduced but because the patient, prior to and throughout the surgical procedure, is maintained normo-volemic and properly oxygenated by the anesthesiologist. He wants to be certain that the patient's hemoglobin is within normal limits, transfuses and provides him, or her, with additional oxygen and blood transfusion.

The patient with a femoral fracture who is kept in traction is likely to lose blood into the tissues around the fracture bone and continues to do so for a period of time until tamponade occurs or spontaneous hemostasis takes place. It is during this relatively early period of time of progressive hypo-volemia that the patient develops the symptoms and signs of fat embolism. The early nailing prevents the undesirable environment.

===

FEMORAL HEAD FRACTURES. (See Femoral Head Fractures. Section II, The HIP)

FEMORAL NECK FRACTURES. See Femoral Neck Fractures. Section II. The HIP.

===

FEMORAL SHAFT FRACTURES

In the spring of 1978 I visited Hamburg, Germany hoping to learn firsthand from Doctor Hempel the technique of closed intramedullary nailing of intertrochanteric fractures of the femur. During my visit to the city we visited the Kuntscher Museum viewing his various devices. It was a very gratifying experience. It gave me a better understanding of the contribution that the German surgeon had made during his prolific career.

I noticed with interest that he had, at one time or another, designed different nails for fractures at different levels of the femur: the intertrochanteric, sub-trochanteric, diaphyseal and distal metaphyseal regions. That night, as I discussed the experience with a resident of ours who was spending a year with Harald Tscherne in Hanover, it occurred to me that a single nail could be developed to meet the demands of fractures at all levels. On a napkin I drew pictures of this "universal" nail. Full of enthusiasm I approached the clinical and laboratory team in our department at USC and received unanimous support for pursuing the idea further.

I approached the manufacturing industry. Biomet, showed great desire to sponsor the project and gave us funds to carry out a sophisticated, careful approach to the design of such a "universal" nail for the femur as well as interlocking nails for the tibia and humerus. We spent several years on the project, which eventually culminated in the manufacture and release of the nails in a Titanium alloy, known in commercial circles as the Uniflex Nail. [20, 55, 61, 65, 72, 130]

I was, at that time, deeply involved in the use of Titanium alloy totals hip prostheses and had experienced good results with them. (See TITANIUM PROSTHESES)

By the time we completed the long and careful investigations, another manufacturing company came out with a "Universal" nail, which precluded the identification of our nail in that manner. "A secret" in the laboratory is an oxymoron.

SECTION I - TRAUMA

We began to use the nails in large numbers, however, shortly afterwards I left USC to preside over the orthopaedic department at the Health Care International Center, in Glasgow, Scotland. Because of silly, juvenile and selfish internal politics in the USC environment, the institution failed to capitalize on the potential of the nails and the fact that we had been the first ones to scientifically study the topic.

Over the years, as a result of my unhappy experiences with Titanium hip prostheses I have developed serious misgivings about the material and have concluded that its use as implants in the body may not be desirable. The softness of the material and, therefore, its sensitivity to scratching predisposes to the release of metal debris. Debris that in the case of the total hip may lead to the initiation of third party wear and the generation of polyethylene debris that produces bone lysis. [10, 56, 67, 59, 69, 71, 74, 141]

In the case of the interlocking Titanium nail a similar debris problem may develop. The interlocking screws can easily scratch the nail and produce fretting corrosion. The metal debris from the corrosion can lead to metallosis with consequences not yet known. (See TITANIUM HIP PROSTHESES)

Recent work, particularly that of Professor Patrick Case, in Bristol England, has demonstrated chromosomal abnormalities associated with metal debris (See METAL ON METAL HIP PROSTHESES).

There is little I can say about femoral shaft fractures, other than interlocking nails have revolutionized in a most positive way the management of these fractures. Early in my orthopaedic career we used the open nailing technique, which in those days was limited to fractures of the isthmus. High and low metaphyseal fractures were managed with traction or plates. [47, 48] The interlocking nail enlarged the indications for nailing to the point that at this time there are relatively few femoral fractures that cannot be treated surgically.

This approach, unfortunately, is not available to all orthopaedists throughout the world because of the high cost of the instrumentation. In many regions the non-surgical treatment remains the treatment of choice. I have said "regions" rather than "countries" because I suspect that in every country there are facilities where the infrastructure of the hospital and the training of the surgeons who perform the operation exist. When that is the case, it is often only the financially "well-off" who benefit from the surgical treatment. The others get their femoral fractures treated in traction.

Shortly after I conceived the idea of treating diaphyseal tibial fractures with functional braces, I thought the same approach could be extended to femoral fractures. After all, the below-the-knee cast for the tibial fracture had been inspired by the PTB prosthesis of the below-the-knee amputee. It was logical for me to assume that a brace molded and designed like an above-the-knee prosthesis would adequately stabilize a fracture of the femur

The prosthesis-inspired brace would theoretically allow the weight of the body to be shared by the ischial tuberosity and the soft tissue of the thigh, without shortening of the extremity occurring. With great enthusiasm and elan I began to treat femoral fractures in that manner and eventually reported on my experiences with 250 fractures. [103, 150]. However, it did not take long for me to realize that the results were inconsistent. Distal femoral fractures, for the most part, did well but those located proximally showed a tendency to develop varus deformities. The higher the fracture the more severe the deformity. The varus angulation was a common development, even in instances where early callus had already developed.

SECTION I - TRAUMA

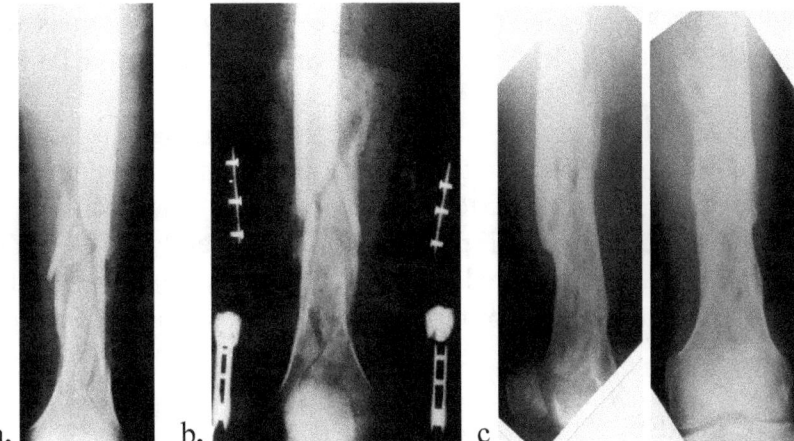

Fig. a, b and c. Comminuted fracture of the distal femur treated with functional bracing.

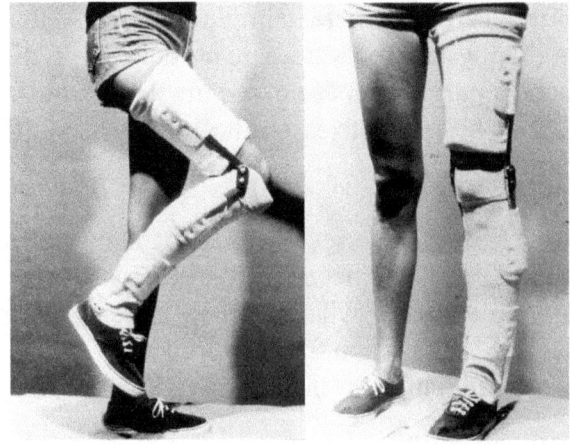

Fig. Functional brace for distal femoral fractures.

In spite of the disappointing results, I learned important lessons and gained a better understanding of the behavior of femoral shaft fractures under a non-surgical functional environment. Bracing makes possible the safe management of certain distal diaphyseal and metaphyseal fractures; shortens the hospitalization time; ensures a high rate of union; reduces the sequella of immobilization; and eliminates the possibility of anaesthetic and surgical complications.

Bracing requires a period of stabilization in traction that varies according to the type of fracture and the initial shortening. The greater the initial soft tissue damage, the greater the initial shortening of the extremity. The shortening corrected with traction has a tendency to recur when the traction is discontinued if sufficient intrinsic stability has not been achieved. Therefore the greater the initial shortening, the longer the period of traction stabilization. As a rule, oblique or comminuted distal femoral fractures that display minimal initial shortening do not require more than two or three weeks of traction. During that period of time, passive motion of the knee, with the assistance of pulleys, should be carried out. However, it is very likely that the degree of knee motion gained will be temporarily lost as soon as the brace is applied. The motion is regained with continued use of the extremity. Transverse fractures, where opposition between the fragments is present, are the ones that demonstrate the greatest tendency toward angulation. The same phenomenon has been observed with transverse fractures of the forearm, humerus and tibia (See FOREARM FRACTURES and TIBIAL SHAFT FRACTURES).

Though most femoral fractures have a tendency to angulate into varus, as it is the case with humeral fractures, it is not uncommon to see distal femoral fractures develop a valgus deformity during the traction period. This is usually due to excessive traction. Under tension, the rather inelastic ilio-tibial band creates the valgus deformity. This phenomenon is frequently observed during closed nailing of distal femoral fractures. In an attempt to reduce the fracture and regain length, the iliotibial band resists the force of the traction and a valgus deformity develops. Relaxation of traction often solves the problem.

FIBULA FRACTURES

Fractures of the fibula are, in general, simple fractures. However, on a number of occasions they can present problems. A diaphyseal fibula fracture produced by a direct force against the bone is a benign condition that for all practical purposes does not require treatment. A cast does not influence the outcome of the fracture. The cast at best might lessen the initial discomfort. The fracture becomes relatively asymptomatic within a few weeks.

I do not know why fibular fractures heal faster than tibial fractures. The argument that it has a better blood supply than the tibia is not necessarily true. Even if its medullary blood supply were better, which I question, there is no evidence whatsoever to indicate that the medullary blood supply of long bones is important in fracture repair when the fracture is not rigidly immobilized. In the absence of rigid fixation it is the peripheral circulation that plays a major role in osteogenesis (See FRACTURE HEALING).

To a great extent the fibula is a cortical structure with little bone marrow. It is superficially located and lacks the muscular coverage that other long bones have. Therefore, it is not necessarily correct to assume that muscle coverage is very important in fracture healing. The ulna, clavicle, ribs, metacarpals and phalanges are bones that testify against the desirability of muscle coverage. There must be other reasons to explain the rapid and rather consistent healing of diaphyseal fibular fractures.

The high fracture of the fibula that often accompanies an ankle dyastasis, known as the Maisoneuve fracture, can be a problematic fracture that requires correction of the ankle pathology in order to ensure a satisfactory result. It is assumed that in this fracture-subluxation situation the interosseous membrane is completely torn from the ankle to the upper part of the leg. This is not necessarily true. Loren Latta's studies on the interosseous membrane documented the fact that the membrane, that runs from a medial to lateral and from a proximal to distal direction at a twenty degree angle, can experience significant stretching without damaging its fibers if the stretching takes place along the grain of its fibers. However, if the membrane's fibers are stretched against the grain of its fibers, as in the case of a fracture that depicts initial shortening, damage to its integrity takes place more easily. If there is shortening as well as marked separation between the two bones, the damage to the interosseous membrane is the greater
[36, 108, 123, 129]

We have not been able to find any difference in the speed of healing of tibial fractures in relation to the level of the fibular fracture. In segmental fibular fractures it is common to see the middle fragment displace proximally. It is likely that the dorsiflexors that insert on that fragment bring the bone proximally upon their contraction.

FOREARM FRACTURES

No orthopaedist practicing in a developed nation in the world would question at this time that fractures of both bones of the forearm in the adult are best treated by means of plate fixation. This is the party line that has been held virtually unchallenged for several decades. The surgery is easy to perform and the complication rate is relatively small. The simplicity of the surgical procedure seems to outweigh its possible disadvantages. However, plating is not free from problems. Post-operative infection, though rare, occurs from time to time. Once an infection develops it is often difficult to overcome it and residual limitation of prono-supination is the rule. Synostosis between the two bones is not unheard of and it may leave a significant disability. Fractures above or below the plate are common, and fractures following removal pale removal occur frequently.

My enthusiasm with functional braces for tibial fractures in the early 1960's prompted me to attempt bracing of forearm fractures. We had already proven beyond any doubt, that immobilization of joints above and below a fracture was not a prerequisite for uneventful healing. For generations the practice of orthopaedics was predicated on that premise, as well as on the one that says that immobilization of fractured bones is also important for their uncomplicated healing. Our experiences with tibial fractures had debunked those undocumented dogmas.

My first patient was a taxi driver who appeared in the emergency room with displaced oblique fractures of both bones at the junction of the middle and distal thirds of the diaphysis. I proceeded to manipulate the fracture under anesthesia and stabilized the arm in an above-the-elbow cast. When the patient came back for follow-up a few days later the position of the fractured fragments had remained acceptable. I replaced the long arm cast with a below-the-elbow cast, firmly molded in a relaxed attitude of supination. The proximal end of the cast extended over the condyles of the humerus and olecranon but left the anterior aspect open in order to permit flexion of the elbow. Extension was limited by the olecranon extension of the cast. The distal cast was connected with a metal joint to a strip of plaster that I had wrapped around the palm and dorsum of the hand. The patient was able to flex his elbow through functional range, freely move his wrist and fingers, but the molded cast prevented his prono-supination with extensions over the humeral condyles.

The patient went home with instruction to return one week later. However, he never returned. Unsuccessfully, I tried to locate him. I assumed he had left town or had sought care at another institution. Not knowing the outcome, I abandoned further efforts to study the subject of functional bracing of fractures of both bones of the forearm.

A year later I flagged a taxi at the Miami airport and instructed the driver to take me home. Suddenly I realized that the driver was the man with the fractured forearm who never came back for follow-up. I re-introduced myself and tried to obtain a history. He informed that after a few weeks following the application of the brace his arm felt "pretty good", so much that he felt that additional visits to the doctor were not necessary. When the pain completely disappeared, he removed the brace himself and started to use his arm as normally as he could. I told him I wanted to have an x-ray of his arm taken that night. Rather than driving me home we went to the hospital, where I obtained x-rays and measured the range of motion of his various joints. There was full range of painless motion of all joints except for the last few degrees of pronation. He was unaware of the loss since he was inconspicuously compensating with rotation of the shoulder. He had been driving his taxicab for several months without any difficulty. The x-rays, however, showed the fractures healed with significant malalignment.

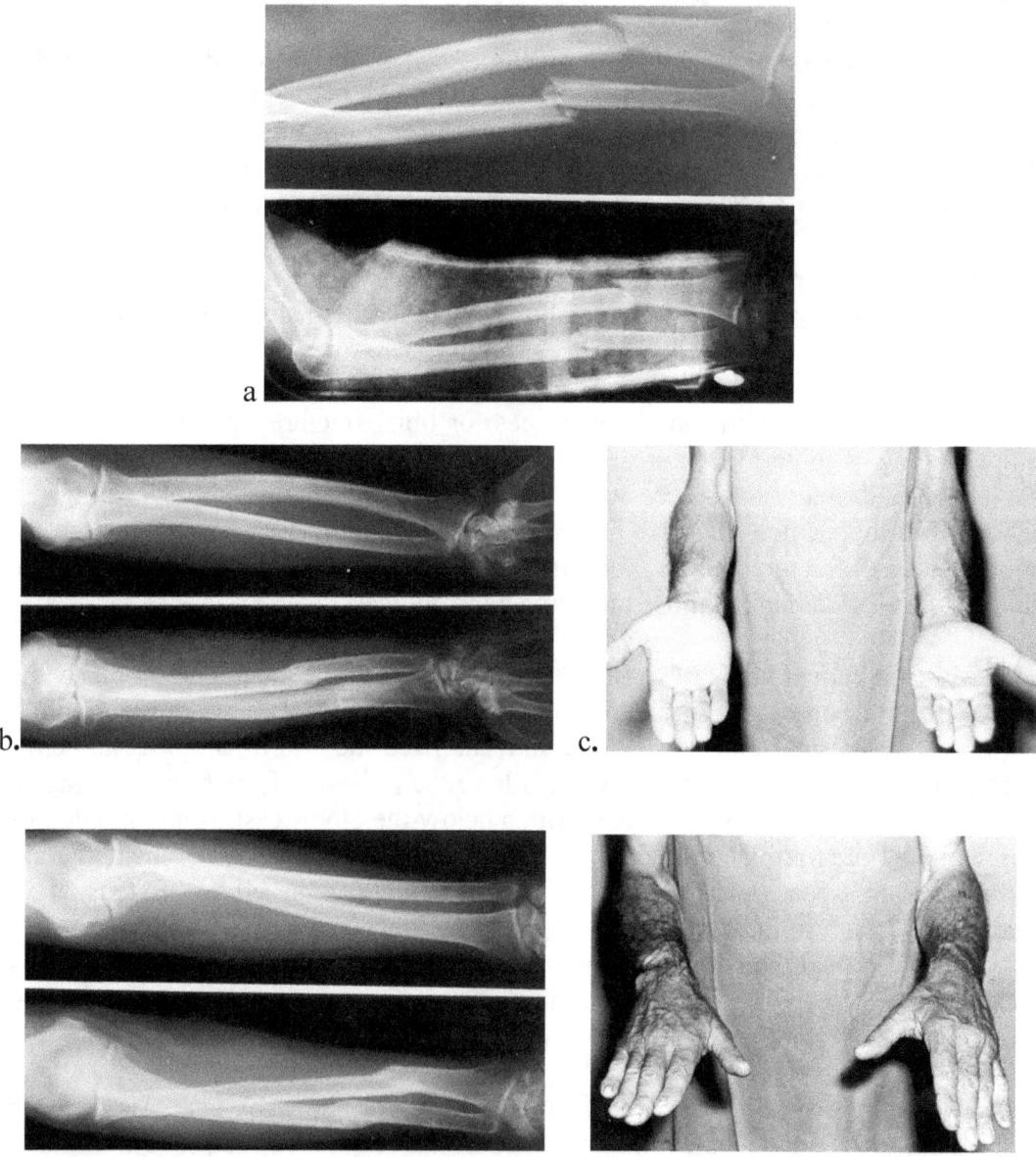

Fig. a through c. Closed oblique fractures of both bones of the forearm. Despite the angular deformity the patient had a very good cosmetic and functional result.

SECTION I - TRAUMA

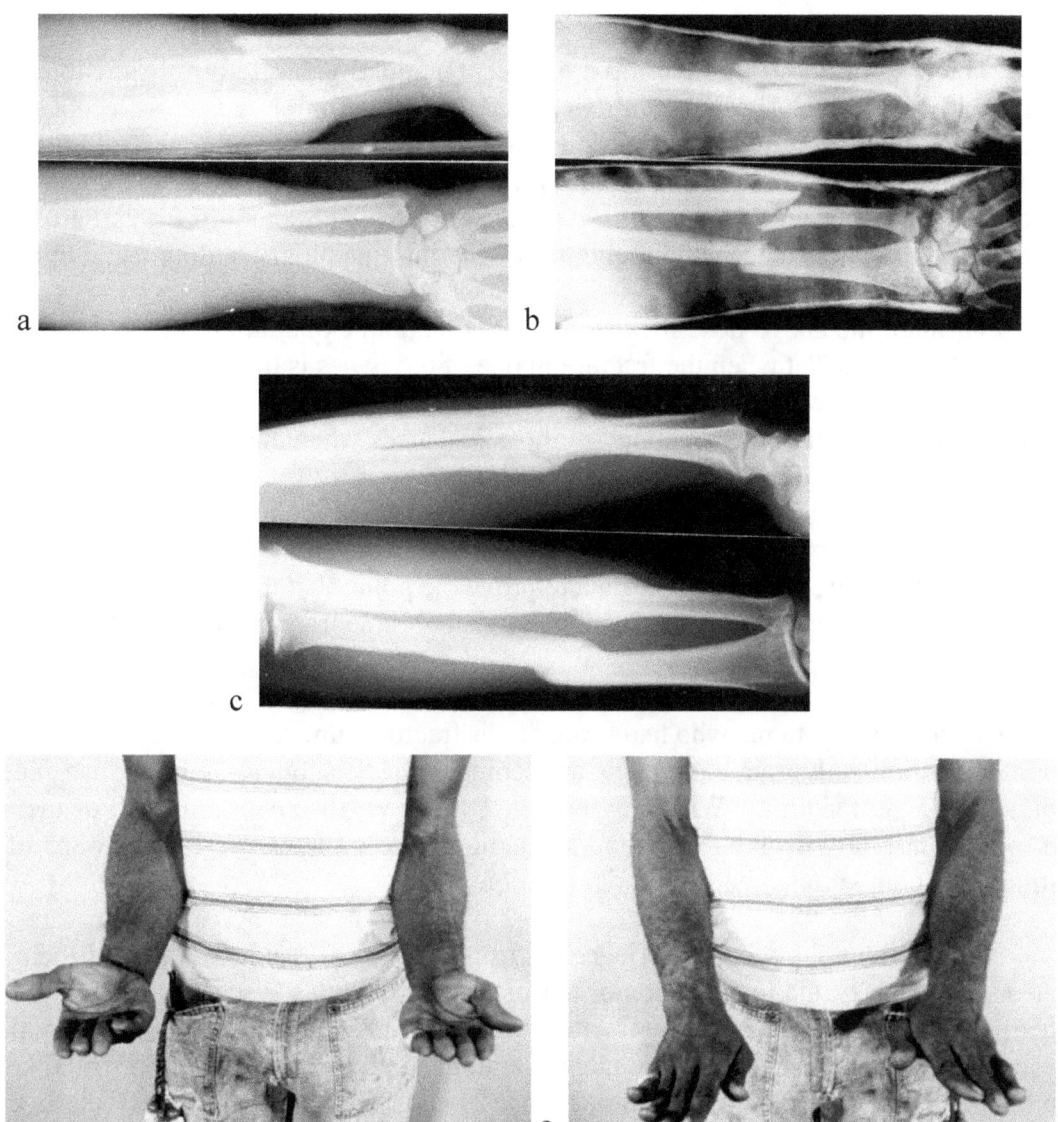

Fig. a through e. Oblique fractures of both bones of the forearm treated with functional brace. Functional result was satisfactory.

This experience was enormously interesting to me. The experience with the first patient was repeated dozens of times. However, the clinical experiences were not consistently good. We found that reduction of the fractures was not always maintained, necessitating some times more than one manipulation.

We went to work on the project and conducted cadaver studies in an effort to correlate angulation with physical impairment. The laboratory studies were very informative. We learned that for every degree of malrotation of the fragments there is a loss of one degree of prono-supination. We also learned that angular deformity as great as ten degrees produces only minimal limitation of prono-supination [134].

We also carried out a comparison between the range of motion of patients with established deformities and the limitation of motion detected in cadavers with similar deformities [112, 161].

SECTION I - TRAUMA

The bottom line is that the forearm accepts mild angular deformities without noticeable clinical impairment of function. Therefore, bracing of certain forearm fractures is an acceptable treatment option. Others have duplicated our experiences in other countries, where the cost of surgical treatment is an important factor. Doctors Eduardo Gilliardi and Sergio Villaverde, from Montevideo, reported their results at a recent meeting of the Latin America Orthopedic Society in Lima, Peru. They also reported most gratifying experiences with bracing following intramedullary nailing using thin Kirschner wires.

Through the above-described studies we found an explanation for the loss of reduction in some fractures. It appears that when the fracture in one of the bones is transverse and in the other bone oblique or comminuted, the reduction is difficult to maintain and the bones angulate toward the unstable fracture. The best clinical results were obtained in those instances when anatomical reduction was not attempted as in the case of overriding comminuted or oblique fractures [134, 150]. In retrospect, I have concluded that our obsession with anatomical reduction of fractures of both bones of the forearm was a mistake. If we had we accepted overriding of fragments, without panicking about a few degrees of angulation, we would have been able to say, with adequate data to prove the point, that transverse fractures of both bones of the forearm are best treated by internal fixation, but that oblique fractures not always require internal fixation.

Once, we reviewed our experiences with surgical plating of fractures of both bones of the forearm and selected twenty patients who had healed their fractures uneventfully. Using a machine that recorded prono-supination only and eliminated any compensatory shoulder motion, we measured the prono-supination of the forearm. With only two exceptions we discovered that all of them had a permanent loss of the last few degrees of prono-supination. The patients were not aware of the loss as they instinctively compensated with shoulder rotation

I was discussing these experiences in front a group of residents. One of them, who had recently joined the program, said to me, "Doctor Sarmiento, with all due respect I disagree with you. I broke my forearm a few years ago and had the fractures plated. Today I have no limitation of motion at all". "Well", I responded, "You may be one of the rare exceptions. Let me examine your arms. Take off your shirt and stand here". I placed his elbows against his chest and asked him to maintain them in that position. I then put pencils in his clenched fists. He then pronated and supinated his forearms. Lo and behold he lacked the last 8 degrees of pronation and was unaware of the loss!

Achievement of anatomical reduction and maintenance of reduction in a cast is extremely difficult in many instances. The experiences of the Uruguayans with the use of thin Kirschner wires, have reinforced by long held believe that the reported failure rate of intramedullary fixation of forearm fractures is due to the mistaken believe that the nail should rigidly immobilize the fragments. Immobilization is not needed; quite the contrary, it encourages nonunion. In the early 1980s Steve Ross, a member of our faculty at USC, attempted to develop a thin flexible IM nail that did not immobilize he fractured fragments but simply maintained their alignment. Unfortunately he abandoned the project.

SECTION I - TRAUMA

FRACTURE HEALING

There is very little we know about fracture healing despite the volumes of literature on the subject. I am convinced that many of the theories dealing with the mechanism of fracture healing or means to achieve healing rest on weak grounds. Some are no more scientific than the popular ones of antiquity.

I will touch only on a few of the most popular ideas; the ones that have been best accepted by the orthopaedic community and therefore govern the practice of fracture care.

In early days it was thought that open fractures experienced non-union because the "humors" that make fractures heal were lost through the open wound. That theory presupposed that those "humors", retained inside of the body in closed fractures, were responsible for osteogenesis. This old theory was slightly modified in more recent days by making the fracture hematoma responsible for the production of callus. The hematoma took the place of the "humors".

There is no scientific evidence to support the concept that the hematoma is an active participant in the healing process, let alone the most responsible factor for osteogenesis. Quite the contrary, if one observes the histology of fracture healing and follows the normal course of events, the hematoma appears to be a hindrance rather than a benefit. The hematoma is resorbed and is never converted into bone. The space occupied by the hematoma is eventually filled with cartilage in the process of ossification.

Recently we have been made aware that growth factors are found in blood cells, especially in the platelets. This implies that the larger the hematoma the greater the number of cells endowed with bone forming potentials. Therefore one can deduce that in order to expedite healing, blood obtained from a forearm vein and injected into the hematoma would make the fracture heal faster. The problem is that various investigators have documented that this approach has been proven ineffective in experimental animals. Furthermore others have found no difference in the healing of fractures that had the hematoma aspirated versus those where the hematoma was left intact.

Another extrapolation to negate the theory of hematoma participation can me made by observing that fractures that exhibit greater separation between the fragments, and therefore have a greater hematoma, heal more slowly than those with less displacement and a smaller accompanying hematoma.

It has been long believed that the periosteum plays a very important role in the healing of fractures. Histological slides have always shown new bone, apparently generated by the periosteum, bridging the fracture gap. This is difficult to deny. However, this new bone is observed only in fractures that had not been immobilized. The absence of peripheral callus in rigidly immobilized fractures has been noticed by all and it constituted the foundations upon the philosophy of the AO was built. They used that finding to support the value of rigid immobilization and called the healing "primary callus" [35, 36, 115, 122, 124]

If the periosteum is responsible for fracture repair, why does it fail to form bone when there is no motion at the fracture site? This is the case regardless of the absence of stripping of the periosteum from the bone, either when a plate is used, while exercising care not to touch it except over the area where the plate rests, or when the fracture is rigidly immobilized with external fixators that do not come close to the fracture site.

The idea that the periosteum is primarily responsible for fracture healing has been based on the knowledge that it plays a major role in the circumferential growth of the bone. Furthermore, we have long believed that open fractures associated with significant stripping of the periosteum and soft tissues are more likely to undergo non-union. This experience has given credence to the important role of the periosteum in fracture healing. I still suspect that capillaries arising from the surrounding soft tissues are probably more important than those coming from the periosteum. Bone probably does not heal itself; vessels from the surrounding tissues heal it.

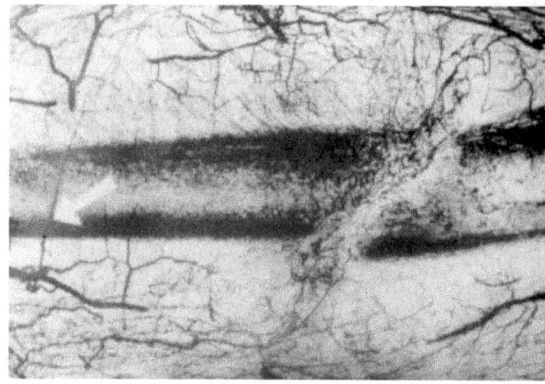

Fig. Angiogram of healing fracture suggesting that arterioles advance toward the fracture site from the surrounding soft tissue structures and the newly formed collagen band bridging the fractured fragments. Photograph from an old German text.

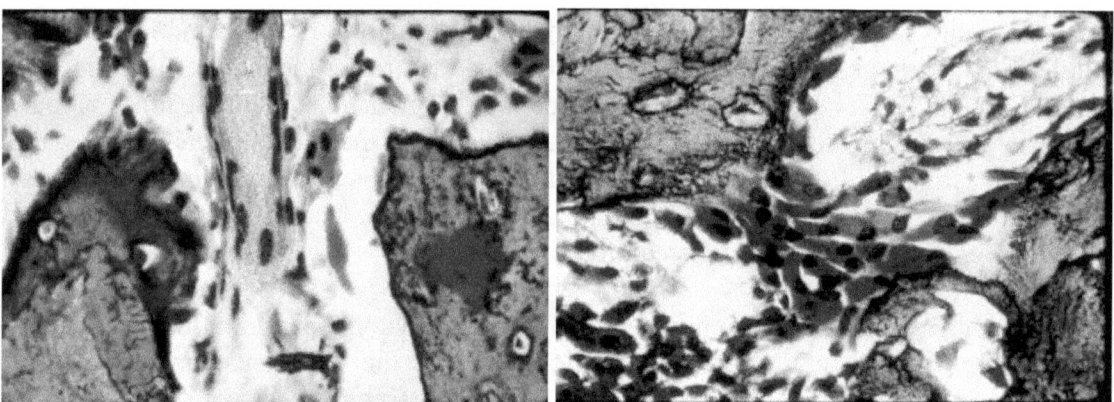

Fig. a and b. Perithelial and/or endothelial cells undergo metaplasia and become osteoblasts. The greater the number of capillary at the fracture site the larger the number of osteoblasts.

Another popular theory to explain the process of fracture healing is that immobilization enhances osteogenesis. This unsubstantiated belief flies in the face of overwhelming evidence to the contrary; and the animal kingdom is the most vivid example. Anthropologists have long recognized that nonunions are extremely rare among large animals. Malunions are common but nonunions are not [15, 122, 124, 150, 151]. (See AO).

The argument is often given that nonunion did not develop in animals with broken bones because predators disposed of the lame before the fractures had a chance to unite. No doubt that was the case in many instances. However there is ample evidence demonstrating that, for example, in many primate societies once a member of the group suffers a fracture, others protect the unfortunate one from being attacked by predators. The broken bones heal even though with deformities. It is also true that human skeletons of primitive men, recovered during excavations, seldom if ever, demonstrate nonunion. The chances are that we do not see nonunions in men of earlier years because if the fractures were closed they healed, or if open, they died from infection. When amputation surgery was perfected the ablation procedure became the treatment of choice.

I have long thought that the concept of the value of immobilization in fracture healing has been with us since time immemorial. I picture primitive men finding out that the pain from a broken bone was alleviated when the limb was held immobile either with bamboo splints, sand boxes or other rudimentary methods. The broken limb was less painful as long as the "immobilizing" devices were kept in place. Over the days or weeks they must have noticed that the pain had been replaced with discomfort and eventually all symptoms had disappeared. At that time they returned to using the injured limb in a gradual fashion.

I assume this experience led to the belief that immobilization was necessary for fracture healing. This "dogma" gained continued credence in modern times when plaster of Paris was introduced. In order to avoid any motion at the fracture site, incorporation of joints above and below a fracture became the rule. Later, when internal fixation became a reality, the dream of achieving perfect immobilization was crystallized. Motion at the fracture site became the enemy; an enemy that needed to be fought at all cost.

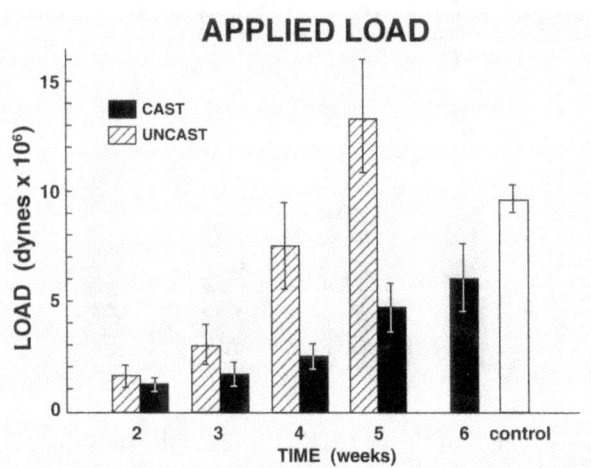

Fig. Bargraph demonstrating the weaker callus that bridges rigidly immobilized fractures.

The conclusion was made that if immobilization was necessary for fracture healing, the more secure the immobilization was the better the physiological environment. That explains why the AO perfected the original ideas of the Danis, a Flemish surgeon, who first spoke about the value of rigid fixation. The AO principles of rigid immobilization and interfragmentary fixation governed the thinking and practice in fracture care for nearly four decades. It was thought to constitute advancement from the preaching of the founders of modern Western orthopaedics, best exemplified by the long honored dictum enunciated by Robert Jones, "maintain broken bones immobilized, uninterruptedly until healing is complete".

The AO adhered rigidly to the principle of rigid immobilization until the late 1990's when they first acknowledged that some motion at the fracture site was desirable for osteogenesis.

SECTION I - TRAUMA

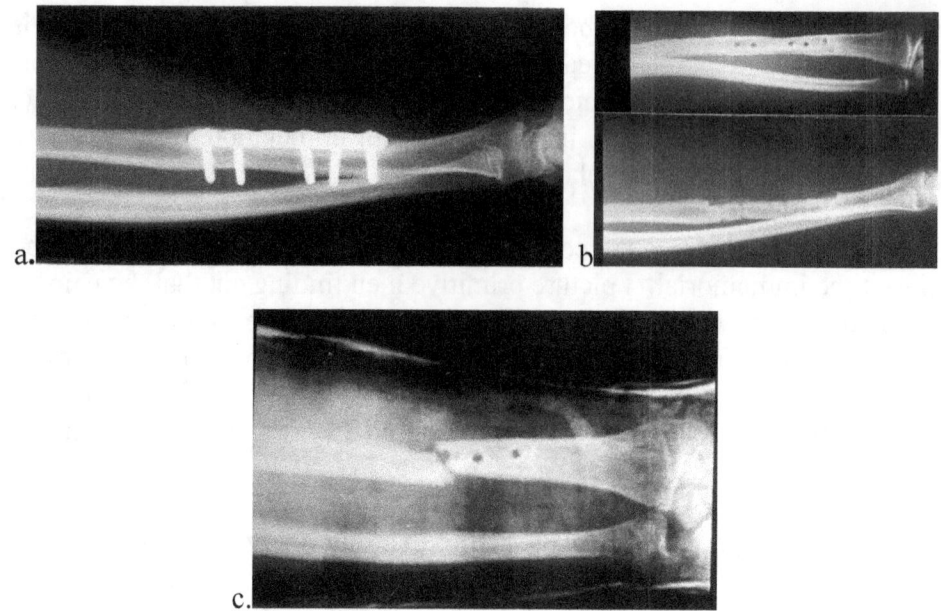

Fig. a through c. Fracture of the radius treated with a plate. Notice bony atrophy and refracture.

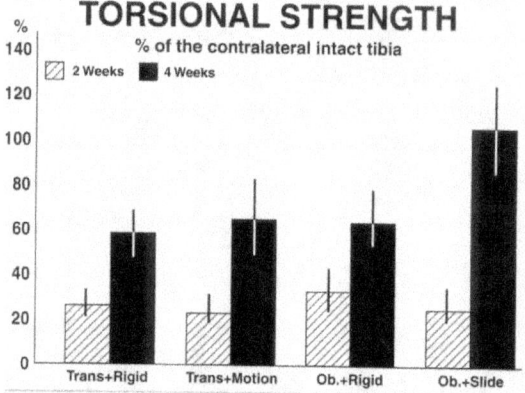

Fig. Illustration of greater torsional strength of the callus that bridges the most axially unstable fracture.

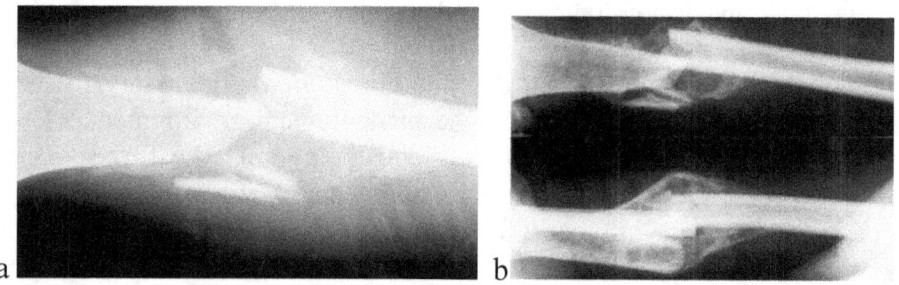

SECTION I - TRAUMA

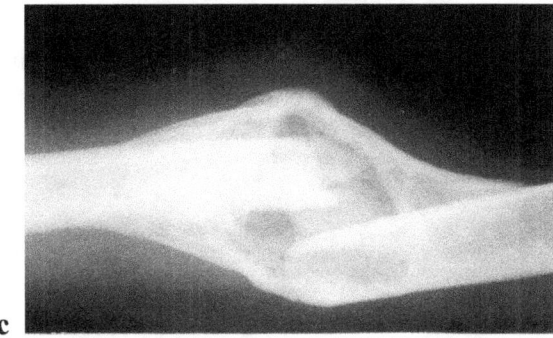

Fig a, b and c. Femoral fracture treated in traction and early passive exercises because major surgical contraindications. Notice the early development of peripheral callus

It is impossible to deny that some motion at the fracture site is beneficial to osteogenesis. With my associates, Loren L. Latta, in Miami, and San Yong, in Los Angeles, we conducted investigations, which unequivocally demonstrated the salutary effects of motion at the fracture site and illustrated the disadvantages of immobilization. The quality of the callus that forms in the presence of motion in diaphyseal fractures is greatly superior to the one that bridges rigidly immobilized fractures. [45, 78, 79, 115, 122] Others have conducted similar studies and have arrived at the same conclusions. Among then is the team at Oxford University under the direction of Professor John Kenwright.

For reasons I cannot clearly understand, motion at the fracture site brings about a cascade of metabolic, thermic, chemical, electric and mechanical phenomena that results in an invasion of capillaries into the fracture site. The endothelial and perithelial cells of those capillaries undergo metaplasia and become osteoblasts. Does that motion constitute an irritant capable of causing inflammation and a resulting capillary invasion? This could be a logical explanation. Scientific documentation is, however, lacking

More recently we have seen the introduction of a variety of techniques aimed at expediting the healing of fractures and to bring about a cure for pseudoarthrosis. At this time we are being inundated with a plethora of gimmicks to be used, not only for the care of non-unions but in the management of fresh fractures. Powders, jells, sponges that are supposed to carry miraculous osteogenic properties are advertised in the most vigorous way. They even claim that the artificial method is better than the one put together by the Great Creator. According to them we will soon be able to make fractures heal faster. With ultrasound waves, percussion or magnetism the bones are alleged to heal in shorter and shorter periods of time. The advocates of the various systems may prove themselves correct in making those claims, and there is early evidence to support some of their ideas.

At one end of the spectrum our society seems obsessed with the idea of prolonging our life span by preaching the benefits of exercise, special diets, natural foods, vitamins, hormones, and a number of other gimmicks. We have accepted with few questions why prolonging life is so important since aging, with all its disadvantages, cannot at this time be prevented. Is it better to live to the age of 100 years, full of arthritis and mental impairment and a burden on family and society, than at the age of 80, still physically and mentally independent?

SECTION I - TRAUMA

There seems no be no end to our desire to expedite events in all areas. Soon, somebody will be working on a way to shorten the period of gestation to three months. If some animals can do it so should we. Instant gratification is no longer good enough, it takes too long.

SECTION I - TRAUMA

G

GALEAZZI FRACTURES

Most people define the Galeazzi fracture as an isolated fracture of the distal third of the radius. However, this is this is not what the Italian surgeon had in mind. To him it was a fracture of the distal third of the radius, associated with a dislocation of the distal radio-ulnar joint.

When I first conceived the idea of using braces in the treatment of fractures, I experimented with forearm fractures as well. [92, 112]. Not only fractures of both bones but also isolated fractures of the ulna and radius. Those experiences provided us with a better understanding of the behavior of fractures in general. The most important piece of information I learned was that contrary to popular believe, the forearm tolerates very well mild angular deformities that have no clinical significance. (See FOREARM FRACTURES).

A true Galeazzi fracture should not be treated with a brace, since this fracture requires, regardless of its level, anatomic reduction of the dislocated joint.. Otherwise, wrist pain arising from the radio-ulnar joint results in chronic wrist pain. What my experiences with bracing indicated was that many isolated radial fractures, not associated with distal radial-ulnar pathology, may be treated by nonsurgical means in anticipation of union and acceptable subsequent function (see FOREARM FRACTURES)

Supported with the enthusiasm and talent of my associate Tillman Moore, we conducted clinical and laboratory experiments regarding the Galeazzi fracture and made some interesting observations.[76] Displaced fractures of the distal third of the radius produced in cadaver specimens were subjected to vertical loading. The behavior of the fragments and distal radio-ulnar joint was observed radiologically. In those instances where the distal radio-ulnar joint was intact the displacement of the fragments was minimal. When the radio-ulnar ligament was sectioned the vertical displacement was greater but moderate. When in addition to the severance of the ligament the interosseous membrane was stripped from the wrist to the level of the fracture the shortening was significant.

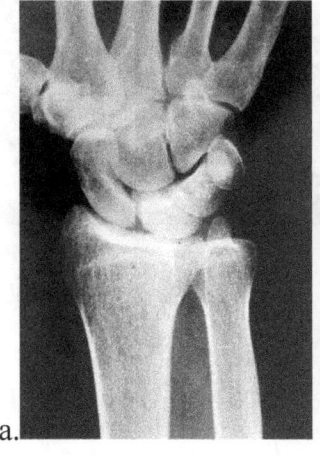
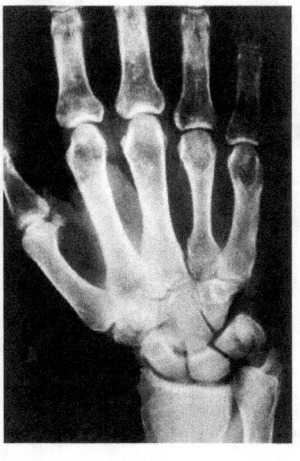
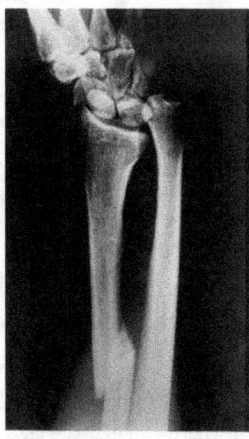

SECTION I - TRAUMA

Fig. a through c. experimentally produced Galleazi fracture leaving, however, an intact radio-ulnar ligament Twenty-five pounds of vertical loading was applied. Notice the minimal subluxation of the joint (a). When the radio-ulnar ligament was surgically section dislocation of the joint was observed (b). Severe dislocation was observed when in addition the interosseous membrane was section (c).

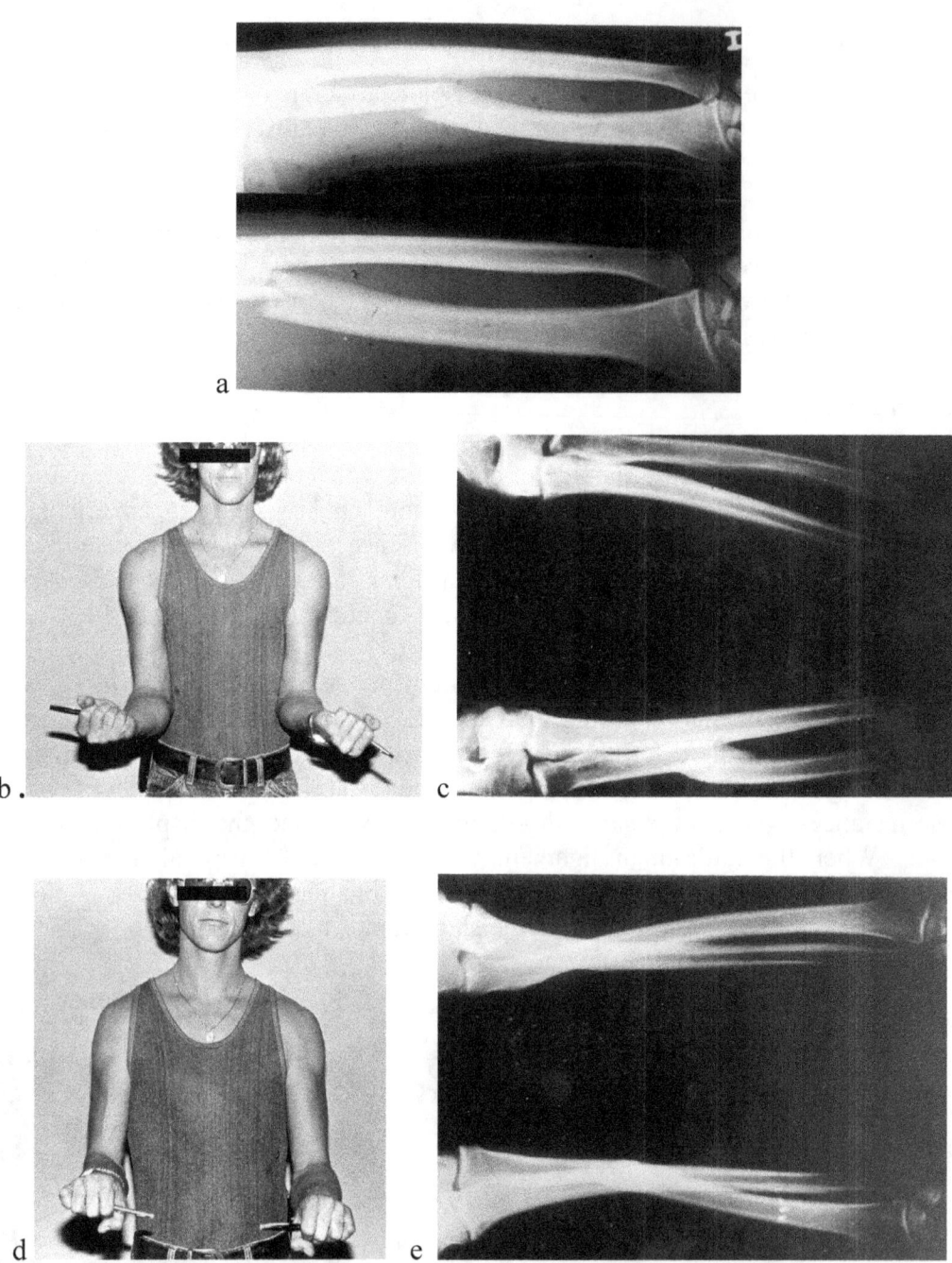

Fig. Isolated fracture of the radial shaft, the result of a direct blow. The distal radial joint is intact (a). Despite the "malalignment" the functional result is very good (b, c d,e).

These observations were supported with clinical and radiological evaluation of patients who had sustained isolated radial fractures that we had treated with braces. The few patients with true Galeazzi fractures that received braces had been mistakenly assumed not to have distal joint pathology. They served, however, to best appreciate the phenomena we were trying to identify. [13]

In summary, I think it is safe to state that isolated fractures of the radius, at any level, that are produced from a fall on the outstretched hand, almost always have an associated distal radio-ulnar pathology. They are best treated by surgical means that ensure maintenance of anatomical reduction. This reduction, however, not always guarantees a normal wrist since failure of the ligament to heal may result in joint instability and associated pain.

Isolated fractures of the radius, which are the result of direct blows on the forearm, do not have pathology at the distal radio-ulnar joint. If their original displacement is minimal, damage to the distal joint and interosseous membrane is not present. The alignment obtained by closed reduction and bracing is maintained. However, if the original displacement of the fragments is significant, due to the high energy that produced the fracture, one may assume that the interosseous membrane was damaged.

In essence, the place for non-surgical treatment of isolated radial fractures is very limited and should be reserved only for those fractures where absence of pathology in the distal joint and interosseous membrane can be confirmed. If I have discussed the subject is because any information on the biology of fractures should not be ignored. Perhaps one of these days this information may be useful since we might be able to determine with accuracy the condition of the soft tissues in the entire forearm with the use of MRI studies.

GUNSHOT WOUNDS (Fractures)

Since most of my academic career was spent working in county-supported teaching hospitals in Miami and Los Angeles, I had many opportunities to closely observe the behavior of fractures produced by firearms. Early in my professional life, when inner-city violence was not nearly as rampant as it is today and the weapons of choice sent lower velocity bullets, the general practice was to surgically debride the wound with no closure of the extended incision and to stabilize the fracture with either a cast or external fixators. The complication rate was relatively high as infection was always a possibility and nonunion a likely sequella.

At one time we estimated that on any given day there were three or four patients with fractures produced by bullets admitted to the orthopaedic service at the LAC/USC Medical Center in Los Angeles. We never knew precisely the number of patients admitted to other surgical services, but it was staggering. Needless to say, we encountered great difficulty in scheduling our patients for surgery because of the preference given to gunshot wounds to the chest, abdomen, head etc.

We documented that the average time that took for a patient with an open fracture of the tibia to reach the operating room, after being admitted through the emergency room, was twenty-six hours. That being the case, it meant that patients who sustained low velocity bullet wounds waited the longest because their wounds were usually very small.

In effect we ended-up cleaning the wounds produced by low velocity projectiles in the emergency room, initiating intravenous antibiotic therapy and stabilizing the fractured limbs in splints. Eventually, and for all practical purposes, most of these fractures were treated routinely without surgery. We discovered that the complication rate was very low, since infection rarely developed and union took place almost as consistently as it did in similar closed fractures. That became our official protocol. [129, 131, 138]

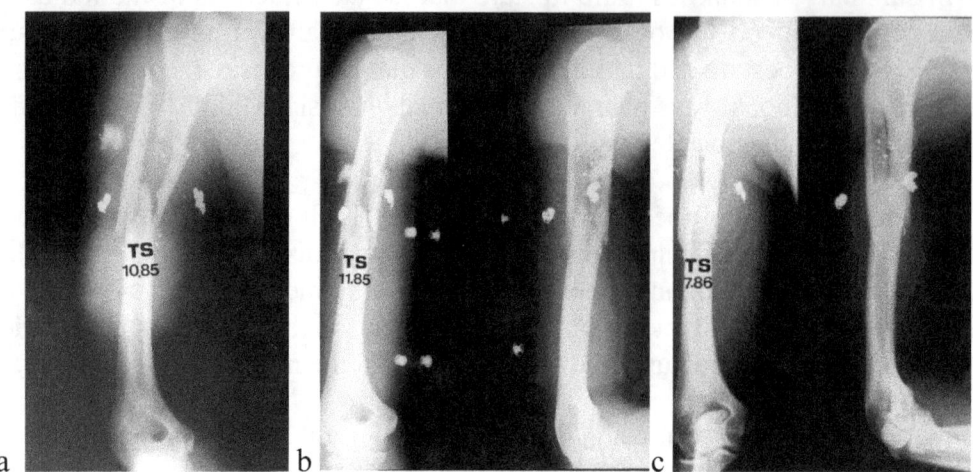

Fig. a, b, and c. Comminuted fracture of the humeral diaphysis produced by a low-velocity projectile. Treated with a functional brace. The fracture healed uneventfully.

I have surmised that low-velocity bullet produced fractures experience major bone damage because of their frequently comminuted nature. However, the associated soft tissue damage is probably relatively minor. Fractures produced, for example, in vehicular accidents may appear to have less or comparable bony damage, but the soft tissue damage is usually greater. These fractures are more likely to experience slower healing, proving the point that soft tissues heal fractured bones and that bones themselves are, to a great extent, innocent bystanders in their own reparative process. The peripheral callus that forms around fractures not rigidly immobilized is the product of endoplasmic metaplasia of the endothelial or perithelial cells of the capillaries that invade the fracture when motion at the fracture site takes place. [150, 151]

H

HUMERAL HEAD FRACTURES

Whenever a high fracture of the proximal end of the humerus occurs, the circulation of the humeral head is thought to be jeopardized. The risk of avascular necrosis becomes a possibility. The fear of this complication and the difficulties encountered in surgically re-positioning the fragments in an anatomical position, has given credence to the popular belief that primary prosthetic replacement should be the treatment of choice for three and four fragment fractures. No doubt, there is a place for such a modality, but a realistic assessment of the outcome of non-surgical management is needed.

In most cases, three-fragment fractures are not likely to develop avascular necrosis. In the absence of anatomic reduction, the functional results can be and often are acceptable, particularly in the older people, who are indeed the ones most likely to sustain this type of fracture. Some objective comparisons between surgical and non-surgical treatments have indicated that the non-surgical approach renders the best results. This is not readily accepted by those who believe that a good clinical result is not possible unless anatomic alignment is obtained by surgical means and immobilization of the fragments is achieved. Nothing could be further from the truth.

In the process of performing surgery and dissecting soft tissues, damage to the blood supply can occur and in the process produce avascular necrosis. Limitation of motion of the shoulder is likely to be found in the older age group regardless of the method of treatment used. However, in this age group, the limitation of motion is usually more severe in the surgical group. The risk of infection is a consideration when surgery is performed. An infected shoulder can be, and usually is, a major complication that almost always results in a joint with very poor function.

In the three fragment fracture, treated without surgery, passive exercises of the shoulder can be initiated early and in that manner ensure that the ultimate limitation of motion is reduced.

Not long ago I lectured in one of the poorest countries in Latin America. Traveling with me was a very distinguished shoulder surgeon from the United States. He delivered several papers discussing various shoulder fractures and other related pathology. One of his lectures dealt with fractures of the humeral head, during which he discussed the technique of primary prosthetic replacement and its good results. In the audience there were approximately 200 orthopaedists from various parts of the country. My colleague asked for a show of hands from those who performed shoulder arthroplasties. Not a single hand went up. They acknowledged that in most instances their patients had a residual limitation of motion but that most of them eventually were very satisfied with their functioned results. Obviously, they did not have to cope with the problem of infection.

Our reaction to such experiences is to dismiss very cavalierly the experiences of those in developing countries, and to assume that their results would not be acceptable in our country since our "sophistication and expectations" are so much higher. This attitude should be tempered with reality. We know that there are regions of the world where certain surgical procedures cannot be carried out. However, the fact remains that pain is pain everywhere in the world and so is limitation of motion. If technical constraints in a given area prohibit the performance of a certain surgical procedure, but if the clinical results obtained with less sophisticated methods are acceptable, we should be more willing to accept that there are other ways to effectively treat many conditions. Furthermore, there is much we can learn from orthopaedists practicing in less privileged parts of the world.

Four-fragment fractures of the humeral head are difficult to manage by surgical means. Avascular necrosis is likely to occur. Prosthetic replacement is at this time the preferred treatment. Nonetheless, these fractures are frequently seen in the elderly who have become osteoporotic and who are feeble. Many of them have diabetes. Surgery under those circumstances is frequently associated with complications. Despite of the performance of the prosthetic replacement in the most appropriate manner, the ultimate range of motion is limited. If the four-fragment fracture in those individuals is treated with a sling and graduated passive, and later, active exercises, the residual pain and limitation of motion are not disabling to many of them.

HUMERUS SHAFT FRACTURES

During the last few years of the twentieth century a trend developed toward closed nailing of humeral diaphyseal fractures. A trend was brought about in part by the success obtained from the nailing of femoral and tibial fractures, and probably more importantly by Industry's vision of additional marketing opportunities.

I set the stage for the discussion of the subject in this manner simply because there is no evidence that the humeral shaft fracture has been begging for solutions to problems associated with its management by traditional closed means. In the case of the femoral fracture there is no doubt that a better way to treat those fractures was needed, since all the orthopaedist had available was casting and traction. Those methods of treatment were expensive. A prolonged period of bed rest was necessary, residual joint stiffness was a sequella upon healing of the fracture and deformities were not uncommon. [16, 131, 150, 151, 155, 157].

None of those problems can be identified on a large scale with diaphyseal humeral fractures. These fractures, with few exceptions, heal well when treated with casts or braces. In the case of the closed fracture, hospitalization is rarely necessary, non-union is infrequent and deformity of clinical significance is only rarely a recognizable sequella.

Even some of the most influential advocates of plate fixation of diaphyseal fractures had been lukewarm at suggesting routine internal fixation, and had acknowledged a high incidence of complications from the use of plate osteosynthesis. They had noticed that radial nerve injury following surgery is quite common; that post-operative infection can be a very significant complication; and that non-union is more likely to occur. .

Though non-union can occur with cast treatment, its incidence is very low. There are situations where casting or bracing is also associated with the risk of non-union. This is particularly true in transverse fractures accompanied with a significant amount of soft tissue damage, manifested by distraction between the fragments. Longitudinal distraction between fragments, if seen in association with nerve palsy, can be an ominous sign, a precursor of nonunion. Therefore, in this instance, early surgical

SECTION I - TRAUMA

intervention is probably the treatment of choice. I do not know whether plating or external fixation is the preferred method of treatment.

The use of the hanging cast in the treatment of humeral shaft fractures was the first instance where the old precept of immobilization of joints above and below a fracture was violated. I recall that prior to the introduction of the hanging cast, humeral fractures were treated with heavy spica casts that incorporated the chest and the entire upper extremity. Various positions of the arm were recommended in order to offset the alleged deforming forces that produce angular deformities.

This mistaken belief still persists. Many textbooks refer to the pull of the deltoid, the pectoralis major and other muscles creating angular deformities. I don't believe there is any scientific basis to justify that claim. In order for a muscle to create a deformity it must contract. Following a fracture of the humerus, neither the deltoid nor the pectoralis muscle goes into a state of spasticity. Quite the contrary, they remains flaccid for a long time.

I first noticed this while I was studying the role of the gluteus medius and minimus muscles in the creation of varus deformity in intertrochanteric fractures (See VARUS DEFORMITY IN HIP FRACTURES).

I came upon the idea of bracing humeral shaft fractures after developing bracing techniques for the management of tibial, femoral and forearm fractures. I had convinced myself that in all those instances immobilization of joints adjacent to the fractures was unnecessary and that the special molding of the casts and braces could prevent angular deformities. With time, many of my original beliefs changed as further laboratory and clinical experiences shed light into the various issues. (See FRACTURE HEALING, TIBIAL FRACTURES, SHORTENING, ANGULATION).

I am confident that we have been able to gather sufficient information to make it possible to state, with some degree of authority, that the overwhelming majority of closed fractures of the humeral shaft can be successfully treated with adjustable sleeves that permit complete freedom of motion of all the joints in the injured extremity. In one of our reports dealing with 650 humeral diaphyseal fractures we encountered a nonunion rate among the closed fractures of only 1,5%. [142]

Protected, passive motion of the shoulder may be introduced almost immediately after the initial injury. The brace, which may be applied within the first or second week, provides compression of the soft tissues in such a manner that comfort is rapidly achieved. The compression of the soft tissues covering the fractured bone stiffen that segment of the body; provide stability to the fragments; and improve the malalignment created at the time of the injury. In addition, the fact that the sleeve eventually allows the patient to fully extend the elbow and to swing of the arm during ambulation in a normal fashion, spontaneous correction of angulation frequently takes place.

We conceived a simple design to appropriately explain the role of compression of the soft tissues in the creation of a stiff structure around the fractured bone. We wrapped a thin membrane around a slice of meat that we had previously rolled over two wooden sticks joined by a single axis joint. Needless to say, without the surrounding membrane, the structure would bend at the level of the single axis joint. However, when wrapped with the tightly applied membrane, some force was required to bend the structure. We had created a "sausage like" composite. Loren Latta, who had built the simple design and studied the results scientifically, elected to refer to this phenomenon as the "hot dog principle". [151]

SECTION I - TRAUMA

Our data have indicated that valgus angulation rarely occurs in humeral shaft fractures. On the other hand, varus angulation is common.[155, 157] The varus deformity is more common in large-breasted women, because the apex of the large breast functions as a fulcrum. The use of the sleeve is likely to eliminate the fulcrum since the fractured arm does not rest over the breast and falls behind during the erect position.

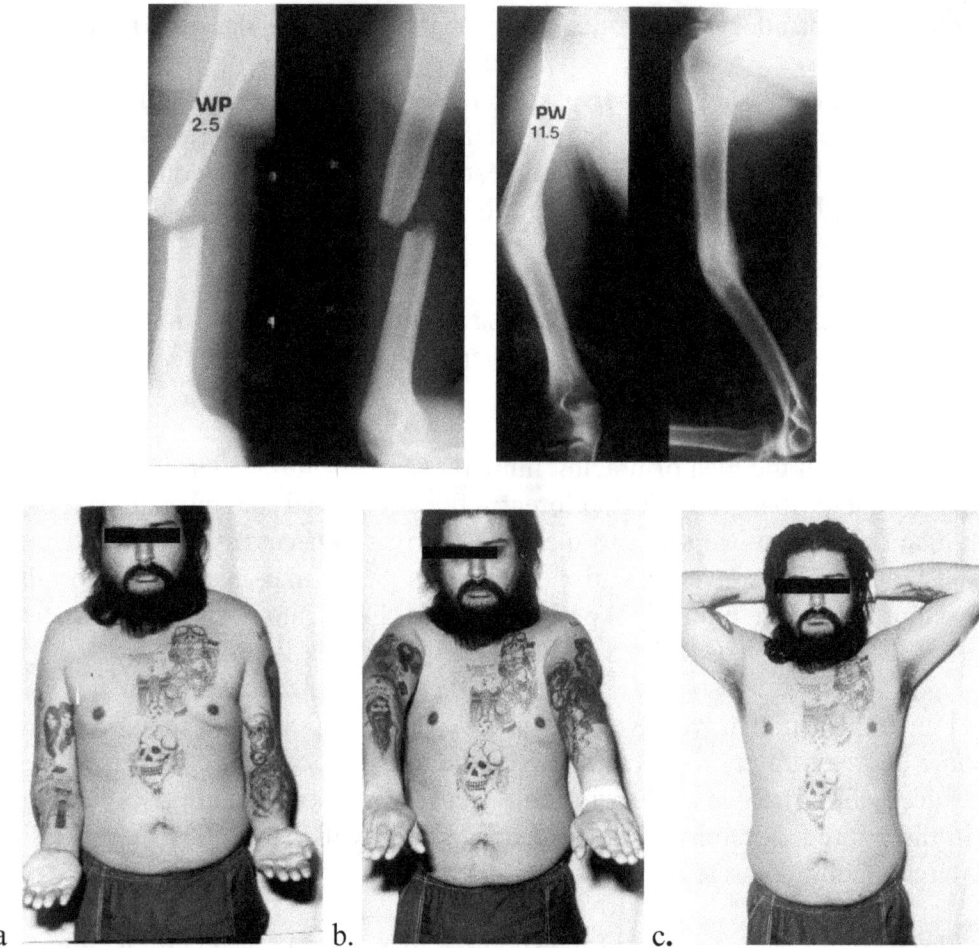

Fig. a through e. A distracted fracture of the humeral shaft treated with a functional brace. The patient abandoned the prescribed treatment and developed a severe angular deformity. The Ccsmetic and functional results were satisfactory.

SECTION I - TRAUMA

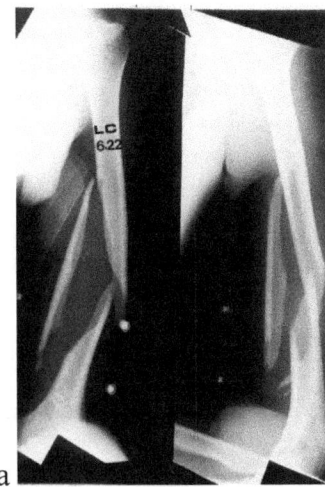 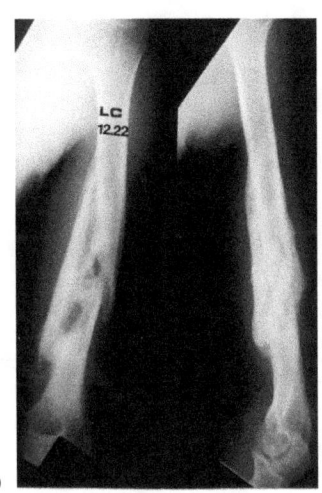 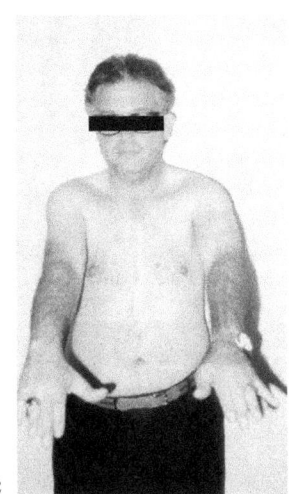

Fig. a through c. Comminuted humeral shaft fracture treated with a functional brace. Notice the residual loss of the "carrying angle."

Angular deformities, which are frequently present when functional bracing is used as the method of treatment, are rarely a problem either physiologically or cosmetically. The humerus tolerates deformity very well. Twenty degrees of varus are rarely noticeable under casual inspection. The loss of the carrying-angle, usually greater in the female, does not constitute a cosmetic impairment or a functional disability. It is simply an inconsequential deviation from the normal.

Varus deformity can occur when the patient leans on the elbow of the fractured extremity. This deformity is more likely to take place if the fracture is transverse and non-displaced. In the case of the oblique or comminuted fracture, vertical forces produce pistoning of the fragments without permanent angulation. Elastic pistoning is likely to have an osteogenic effect (See FRACTURE HEALING, SHORTENING).

The fact that serious rotary deformities are rarely observed in humeral shaft fractures treated with sleeves that cover only a portion of the diaphysis is puzzling. We have extrapolated that a possible explanation for this finding can be made on a physiologic basis: When the shoulder is internally rotated in the sling, the distal fragment must rotate internally in relation to the proximal one. However, the rotation of the bony fragments is associated with a coiling of the muscles that are attached to the bony structures. Therefore, when the muscles contract, a re-coiling takes place restoring the relationship between the humeral fragments. The muscles likely to be most involved are the biceps, brachialis and triceps. Flexion and extension of the elbow produced by those muscles create the uncoiling of the bony fragments.

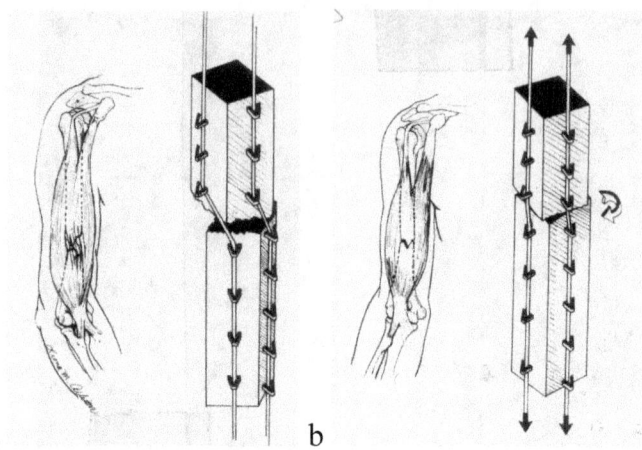

Fig.. Suspected mechanism of prevention of rotary deformity. The contraction of the flexors and extensor of the elbow uncoil the initial deformity.

Radial palsy is frequently a complication from humeral shaft fractures. In our most recent report on 650 fractures, we acknowledge an incidence of 11%. [155] We indicated that, in the case of closed fractures, a radial palsy that develops at the time of the injury recovers spontaneously in most instances. If the palsy appears later on, the prognosis is guarded suggesting that the nerve may have been entrapped in the callus or subsequently damaged by the bony fragments. In this latter instance early surgical intervention must be considered. Since entrapment is a rare complication, a period of observation before carrying out surgery is justifiable.

Some have expressed criticism about keeping patients under observation following radial palsy that appears immediately after the initial insult that produced a closed fracture. I insist, however, that if more than 98% of those situations result in spontaneous recovery, it is unnecessary to intervene surgically. I realize that it is troublesome to see patients not experiencing prompt recovery, but the question needs to be asked: what is it to be gained from surgical exploration? Doing surgery to find a contused nerve in the process of recovery does not expedite the recovery, it simply coverts a closed fracture an open one. Electromyography studies can be conducted from time to time to determine whether or not healing is taking place. After a couple of months of absolutely no clinical evidence of improvement surgical exploration is justified. If the nerve is found to be transected its repair can be carried out. It is very doubtful that the delay in repair will have any harmful effects. Quite the contrary, it is possible that the prognosis may be improved by virtue of the fact that after that period of time the pathophysiologic formation of the neuroma and glioma at the end of the severed nerves will be more easily identified.

SECTION I - TRAUMA

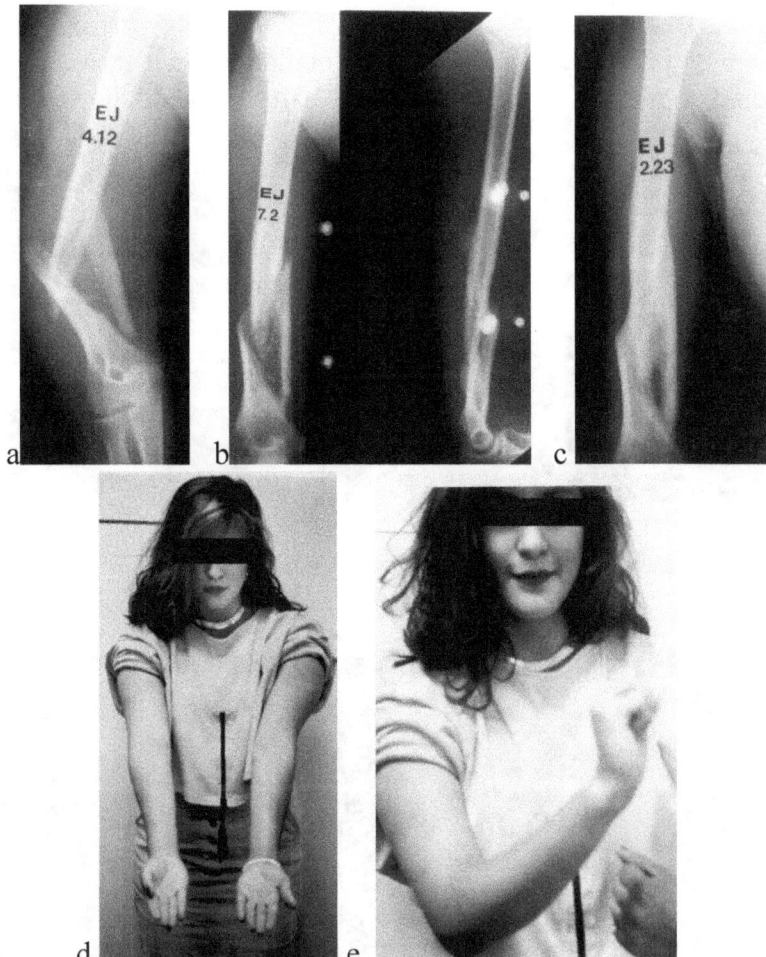

Fig. a through f. Comminuted fracture of the distal humeral diaphysis. Notice the usually present medial butterfly fragment and varus angular deformity (a). Compression of the soft tissues by the brace and the weight of the extremity restored good alignment of the fragments (b). The fracture healed (c,d). The radial palsy improved spontaneously and the overall aesthetic appearance of the injured extremity was very satisfactory (e and f)

I suspect MRI studies can tell us with some precision the type of damage incurred to nerves. A transection is readily recognized.

In the case of open fractures associated with nerve palsy, particularly those the result of high-energy injury, early exploration of the nerve is indicated. The prognosis from surgical anastomosis is good when dealing with the radial nerve but guarded when the medial or ulnar nerves are involved.

At the time of complete healing of humeral diaphysis fractures there is usually a residual limitation of motion of the shoulder, particularly in regards to external rotation. However, in most instances there is spontaneous recovery of motion following the use of the extremity. [155, 157] I personally believe that early, supervised physical therapy aimed at regaining early motion can be counterproductive. Active elevation or abduction of the arm prior to the presence of intrinsic stability at the fracture site may lead to angular deformity. The long and heavy lever arm formed by the distal humeral fragment and the forearm and hand prevails over the shorter and lighter lever arm made by the proximal fragment. Passive exercises of the pendulum type are the only exercises recommended to patients with humeral fractures during the period that precedes the formation of moderately stiff callus. Active exercises should be limited to the elbow joint. I have seen humeral nonunions, which were the result of attempts to regain motion too soon. Patients do better if they simply carry out pendulum exercises.

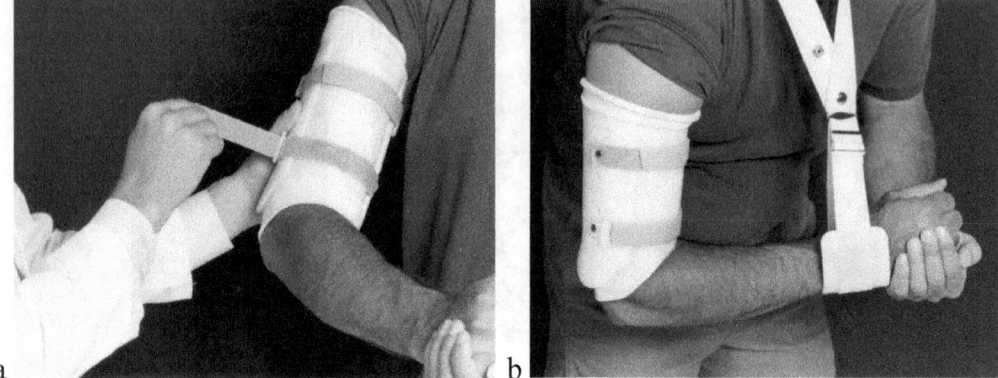

Fig. a and b. The prefabricated humeral fracture brace, which is adjustable in order to assure continued compression of the surrounding soft tissues.

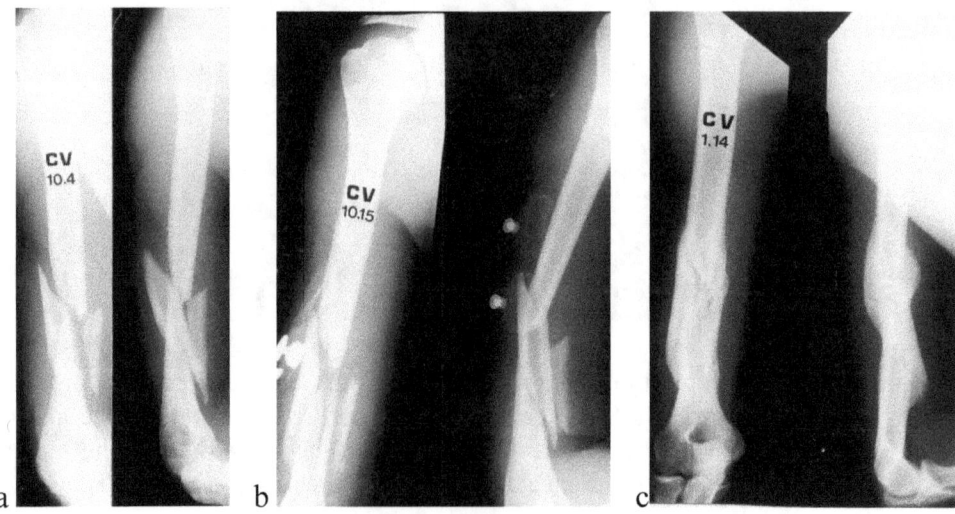

Fig. a through c. Comminuted fracture of the humeral diaphysis treated with a functional brace. Notice the good alignment of the fragments and the abundant peripheral callus.

I stated at the beginning of this discussion that it was difficult to justify the routine use of intramedullary nailing of diaphyseal humeral fractures in view of the fact that most of them heal rapidly within a short time. My experiences have indicated a non-union rate of 1.5% in closed fractures treated with functional braces. In open fractures the non-union rate was of 5%. This suggests that routine nailing cannot be justified unless it renders better results. This is, however, not the case at this time. The non-union rate from surgery is greater; the incidence of nerve injury is significantly higher and additional problems such as rotator cuff damage are frequent. Whether nailing is indicated as the treatment of choice in open fractures, has not been determined. I am inclined to believe at this time, that in the case of the open fracture with extensive soft tissue damage, external fixation is the treatment of choice.

SECTION I - TRAUMA

It is popularly believed that the polytraumatized patients require internal fixation of all their fractures. Though I agree that internal fixation has a greater place in the care of these patients, I hold reservations about its use in all instances. I have seen many patients with multiple fractures do very well being treated by non-surgical means. A patient with ipsilateral closed fractures of the femur and humeral shaft can, in most instances, be well treated with closed intramedullary nailing of the femur and functional bracing of the humeral fracture. As long as the patient can be made ambulatory- a prerequisite for functional humeral bracing – ambulation with the aid of one crutch is possible as the patient has his arm stabilized in a functional brace. The same is true for patients who have fractures of the homers and tibia. If the tibial fracture is one that can be appropriately treated with a brace, both fractures can be treated successfully without surgery. I am not in any way dismissing the possibility of treating those fractures by open means. I have seen very good results with that approach. I simply question the radical view that "all fractures" in the polytraumatized patient require surgery. Extreme views at either end are wrong. The patient with multiple organ injuries is the one that benefits the most from early surgical stabilization of his fractures since the chances are that ambulation will not be possible for a long period of time (See PULMONARY EMBOLISM).

SECTION I - TRAUMA

I

ILIZAROF TECHNIQUE

The technique of bone lengthening and correction of angular bony abnormalities described by Ilizarof in the Soviet Union has been enormously helpful. It is now possible to correct shortening of extremities to degrees that previously were considered unattainable and dangerous to attempt.

I had he opportunity to hear Ilizarof present his experiences in the late 1970's in Lecco, Italy, allegedly on his first trip outside his country. Dean McEwen, from Delaware and I were invited by the State Department to hear his presentations first hand.

I must admit that the experience was unforgettable. Ilizarof, using slides, showed a packed auditorium impressive examples of his results. He illustrated correction of non-unions associated with deformities that ordinarily we would have treated by primary amputation of the limb. He had lengthened extremities with congenital or post-traumatic conditions of grotesque degrees. He successfully managed to obtain union of congenital pseudo-arthrosis of the tibia that no one had ever succeeded in curing. All this in the remote Siberian city of Kurgan.

The concept fascinated me so much that I purchased the entire Ilizarof instrumentation that day. I brought it to the United Sates and did my best to encourage my associates, responsible for the trauma service, to use it. My efforts were futile. Now the procedure is being performed by many orthopaedists around the world with success.

Ever since the moment I heard Ilizarof presents his results, I was intrigued by the rationale he gave for the effectiveness of his distraction osteogenesis theory. Others had achieved various degrees of success in lengthening shortened extremities with a variety of gadgets. They had observed new bone filling the gap but had also realized that the amount of shortening to be overcome was limited and that the quality of the new bone remained inferior for a very long time.

What Ilizarof demonstrated was the possibility of gaining greater degrees of length and the more rapid maturation of the bone at the distraction level. I readily noticed from his presentation, as well as from the number of patients shown to us by the Italian surgeons, that a great emphasis was placed on initiating weight bearing ambulation shortly after the performance of the surgical procedure. When performed in the upper extremity active exercises and early use of the arm musculature was part of the post-operative protocol.

As a result of this observation, I was prompted to ask Ilizarof if he had thought about the possible value of motion at the fracture site, which was provoked by weight bearing and muscle activity. Since my conversation with him required a translator, I used the accordion as an example to describe the motions I suspected took place at the osteotomy and non-union sites. The translator responded that the "professor" had not understood the question. It is possible I did not word the question correctly or that Ilizarof had not paid attention to my suggested mechanism.

SECTION I - TRAUMA

Over the years I have come to conclude that the accordion motion that definitely occurs with the Ilizarof system is the key to its success. Obviously, is not immobilization. The distraction osteogenesis theory, in my opinion, loses a great deal of credence in the absence of intermittent compression and distraction. The fact that his results were obtained with the use of very thin bicycle spoke wires, gives further support to my views that stress and motion at the "fracture" site are essential for success.

SECTION I - TRAUMA

INCONGRUITY

The thought that any post-traumatic incongruity in articular surfaces is unacceptable has dominated the thinking of orthopaedists for a very long time, particularly since internal fixation of fractures became a reality. It is a logical feeling and a very difficult one to argue against. Who in his right mind would suggest that an incongruous joint is preferable?

To some, the issue was settled long ago with a simple, primal answer: incongruity is evil and every possible effort must be made to correct it. However, is this an intelligent and scientific answer? It is not. We all have seen incongruous surfaces that never developed osteoarthritic changes. Also, instances where anatomically restored congruity was followed by early degeneration of the joint.

So where does the truth lie and how can we determine whether or not incongruity may be accepted? How much? in what joints? And under what circumstances?

A reasonable amount of clinical and experimental work has been conducted to elucidate those issues. The findings are interesting, but still inconclusive. The names of Lansinger, from Sweden, Kristensen, from Denmark first come to mind. They conducted long term follow up reviews of patients whose intraarticular fractures of the knee and ankle had healed with a significant degree of incongruity. Some of the investigators demonstrated absence of arthritic changes in patients followed for as long as thirty years after the initial insult. Lansinger stated that as much as one-centimeter step-off in the tibial condyles was compatible with good clinical results.

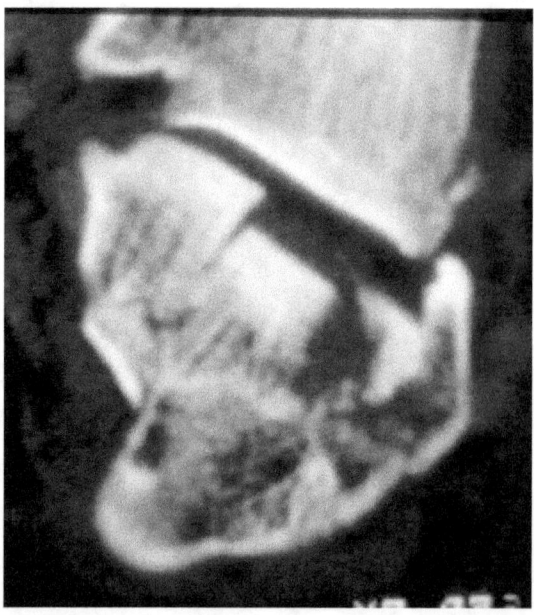

Fig A comminuted intraarticular fracture of the tibiotalar joint. The impaction nature of the fracture may have damaged the cartilage to the point that surgical anatomical reapproximation of the fragments will not prevent later arthritic changes.

As a result of my long-standing interest in the subject, we also studied the issue in our laboratories. Our work was done in experimental rabbits and the findings were most interesting. Doctor Adolfo Llinas, from Colombia, a fellow in our laboratories, presided over the investigation. We created step-off deformities on the condyles of the femur. The depth of the step-off was arbitrarily designed to be comparable the one most commonly seen in intraarticular tibial condylar fracture in the human. [38]

The animals were divided into three groups: the first was immobilized in a long leg cast; the second was not immobilized and allowed to run freely in the cage; and the third one was subjected to continuous passive motion of the operated joint.

The immobilized knees rapidly developed arthritic changes; the other two did not. There was no difference in the histological or anatomical results between the two groups of non-immobilized animals. In other words, continues passive motion did not make matters any better. The important thing was weight bearing and motion.

Under the microscope we demonstrated the presence of a tongue-like new cartilage extending from the high side of the step-off to the low side without arthritic changes developing. (Fig.   ).

Additional work was done by George Lovasz, from Hungary, also a research fellow in our laboratories. He added instability to the incongruous surface in the animal model by sectioning the cruciate ligaments of the knee. He concluded that incongruity, within the limits established in our original studies, was not important, but that added instability led to arthritic changes within a relatively short period of time. [41]

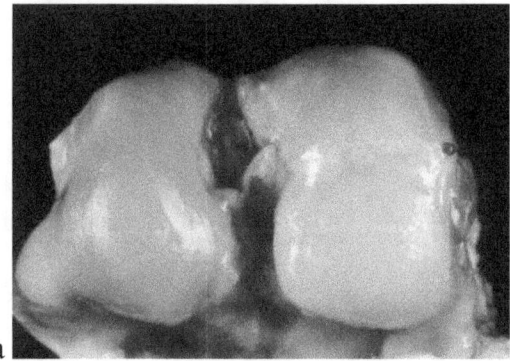 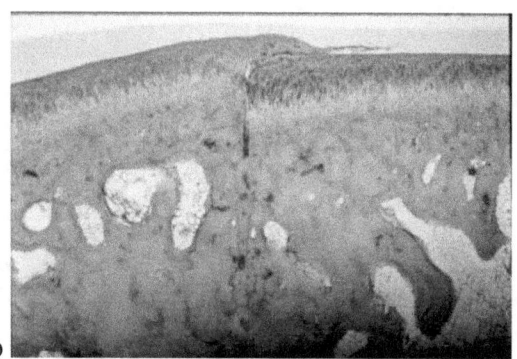

Fig. a and b.   Experimental work demonstrating the fact that step-off incongruity of articular cartilage, in the absence of instability, experiences spontaneous remodeling.

Their laboratory findings gave further credence to my anecdotal, undocumented perception that significant incongruity may be tolerated in many instances and that associated instability encourages degeneration. I first made that observation during experimental clinical studies I was conducting in patients with intraarticular knee fractures treated with functional braces. [19]

Many in the past have observed the absence of late arthritic changes in incongruous joints. The intraarticular fracture of the distal radius is a good example. Clinical arthritic changes are rarely seen, except in those instances where there is associated instability or when the fracture is the result of a severe impaction force. In this latter case, it is likely that initial irreparable pathological damage to the articular cartilage took place at the time of the traumatic event.

SECTION I - TRAUMA

Fractures of the acetabulum have also illustrated the point that not all of them develop arthritic changes when some incongruity was present and left unreduced. Joel Matta, of Los Angeles, recently studied the long term follow-up of acetabular fractures and seems to have concluded that some degree of incongruity is compatible with good clinical results if the fracture was located in certain areas of the dome of the acetabulum. Those areas are the ones less likely to create instability. He did, however, concluded that, in general, acetabular fractures that are anatomically reduced have a better prognosis. (See ACETABULAR FRACTURES)

It is my opinion that surgical repositioning of comminuted articular fragments can produce additional damage to an already damaged cartilage. I believe that the surgical dissection may further devascularize the sub-chondral bone. In addition, there is also strong experimental evidence that impact-fractures may produce severe and permanent damage to the cartilage. In other words, surgical reduction of intraarticular fractures produced through an impaction mechanism may not improve the final outcome. The reduction of devitalized fragments offers no benefits.

SECTION I - TRAUMA

INTERLOCKING NAILING OF TIBIAL FRACTURES

The success of interlocking nailing of femoral fractures promptly resulted in exploring the possibility of using similar techniques in the management of tibial fractures. The success has been so great that today it has become the treatment of choice for many such fractures. In closed tibial fractures associated with significant soft tissue damage and initial major shortening and displacement IM nailing is the preferred treatment. I question, however, the wide extension of the method, at this time, to the treatment of low energy fractures of the tibia for the following reasons:

The procedure is not free of complications. Infection is rare but it has been reported to range between 1 and 5%. If the infection migrates down the shaft, management of the complication becomes a difficult and often unrewarding task.

In the process of applying traction to the extremity and then reaming the medullary canal we demonstrated, in cadaver specimens, with mechanically produced fractures, that the muscle compartments of the leg experience significant elevation of pressure. We actually reproduced the mechanism of the classical compartment syndrome picture. This is easily explained in mechanical terms. When a fracture of the tibia occurs, bleeding takes place around the fracture. The leg shortens at the time of the injury to a degree determined by the severity of soft tissue damage. The girth of the extremity at that level increases to accommodate the bleeding. Fortunately, tamponade eventually stops the bleeding but by that time the compartmental pressures are elevated. In most instances the increase in pressure is not high enough to produce a compartment syndrome. However, if under those circumstances traction is applied to the leg, its geometry changes and is forced to obtain the conical shape of the normal leg. This cannot take place without increasing the muscle compartment pressures. If in addition closed reaming of the medullary canal is done, the added bleeding and reamed material from the medullary canal produce further elevation of pressure (See COMPARTMENT SNDROMES).

Since interlocking nails are usually inserted after applying traction to the fractured extremity, gaps between comminuted fragments are often increased. The interlocking screws perpetuate that separation until healing takes place. However, because of the gap there is greater axial instability at the fracture site. Weight bearing under those circumstances takes place at the screw-nail interface. This explains the high incidence of screw fracture, as high as 15 to 20 per cent at this time. Removal of the broken screws can be an impossible task due to galling corrosion between the mail and the screws, a problem more likely to happen when the softer Titanium metal is used. Bending or breaking of the nail is not infrequent and when this complication occurs the removal of the damaged nail becomes a major surgical undertaking. A broken nail is difficult to remove but a bent one can become an impossible task unless the fracture nails is surgically visually exposed and its two ends removed separately (Fig. 35).

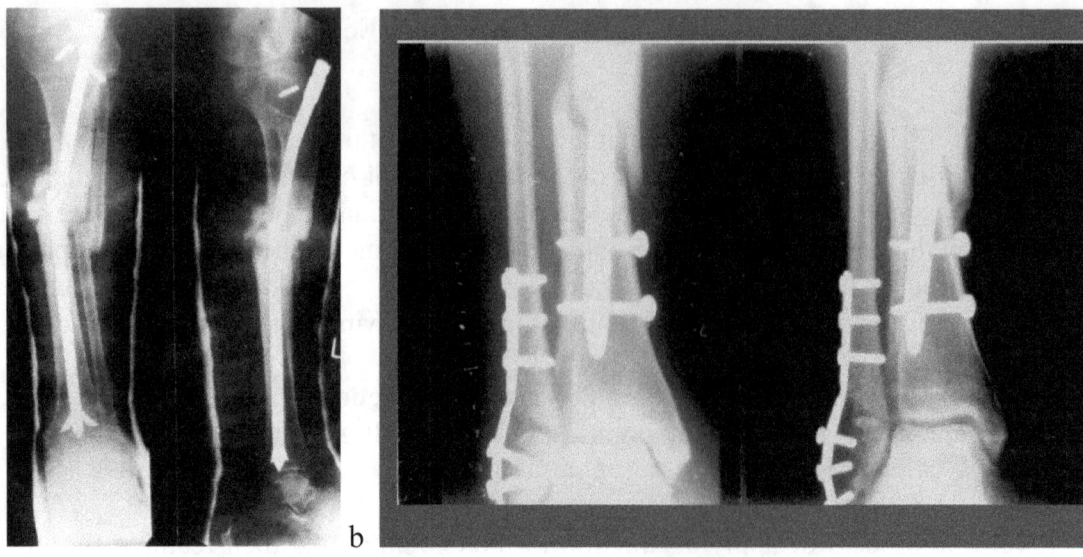

Fig. a. Complications from interlocking tibial nailing. A Broken nail. (b). Mild Varus angulation after breakage of screws.

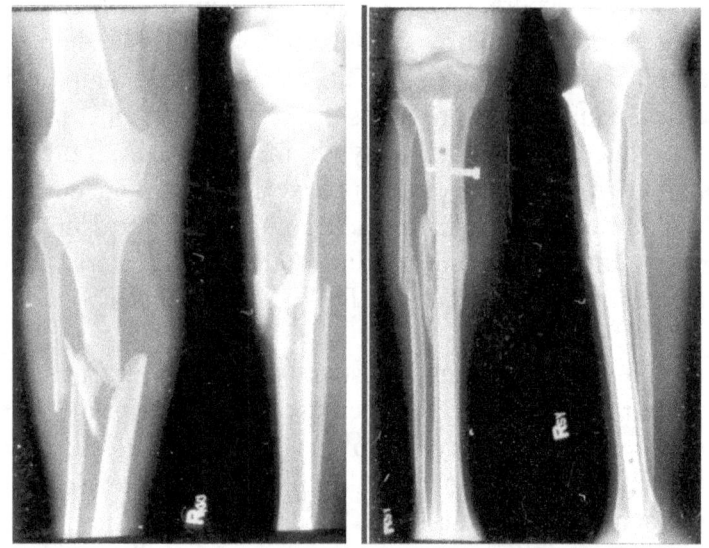

Fig. a and b. Successful result from nailing of displaced, shortened tibial fracture.

Knee pain is a very common complication. Keating and Court-Brown, from Edinburgh, and many others who have significant experience with intramedullary nailing of fractures, have reported that approximately 80 percent of patients with tibial fractures treated with intramedullary nails experience pain at the site of entrance of the nail. They further stated that removal of the nail relieves the pain only in approximately 50 percent of the patients. A report from Jarvinen, from Finland, indicated that the problem of knee pain is the same, regardless of the type or location of the skin incision.

Intramedullary nailing of the tibia does not, as it is commonly believed, expedite healing or the ability to ambulate without pain and external support. Though it is not difficult to find patients who following nailing of a tibial fracture are able to ambulate without discomfort at the fracture site, and do it without the need of external support at six or eight weeks after surgery, similar examples can be found among patients who had comparable fractures which are treated with casts or braces. However, most patients, regardless of the modality of treatment used, are not capable of reaching that degree of function and performance in such a short period of time. Most require between 12 and 18 weeks. It is my impression that patients with transverse fractures, which are anatomically reduced, require, in general, a longer period of time to get rid of pain at the fracture site and radiologically they heal more slowly. Even though our data did not indicate a significant difference in the speed of healing between the three most common types of fractures transverse, oblique and comminuted [129, 138, 156], our animal laboratory studies have proven convincingly that oblique fractures heal faster and develop a callus stronger that that seen in transverse fractures [78] (See TIBIAL SHAFT FRACTURES).

It is not appropriate to ignore the cost of fracture care. The cost of surgical treatment of tibial fractures is high and, therefore, it behooves us to pay attention to this issue. A second hospital admission for removal of the nail or broken screws adds to the overall cost. If the advantages of surgery are evident in all instances, the additional cost must be ignored. Those advantages are not found in the majority of closed diaphyseal fractures. Therefore, I believe at this time that I.M. nailing of tibial fractures should be reserved for open fractures and for closed ones, only in those instances where the initial shortening is unacceptable, an adequate alignment cannot be obtained, or for polytraumatized patients.

SECTION I - TRAUMA

INTRA-ARTICULAR FRACTURES OF THE HUMERUS (DISTAL)

My first assignment as a senior resident at the University of Miami was to review and report on the treatment of intra-articular fractures of the distal humerus. I looked forward to the opportunity because I had been interested in the subject for some time and had strongly advocated open reduction and internal fixation. I had performed a few such procedures, using a posterior approach, combined with olecranon osteotomy.

I compared the results obtained from open versus closed treatment. Much to may surprise, I found out that the functional results from the two groups were virtually identical. Most patients functioned with elbows that averaged a permanent loss of extension of 15 to 20 degrees and another 15 degrees of lack of flexion. It did not matter whether the elbow had been immobilized for a short period of time. Physical therapy had no effect on the final range of motion. The only finding that appeared to me to have some mild influence was the gender and race of the patients. Male patients had greater limitation of motion. Dark complexion people also experienced greater loss of motion. This observation may be invalid since the number of patients in the series was too small.

Prior to my review, my enthusiasm with the surgical approach was so great that I suggested to the chief of orthopaedics that we perform one such procedure and film the surgery. The surgery was carried out on a patient with a three-fragment fracture. The intervention went well. We submitted an application for presentation of the film at the next meeting of the Academy of Orthopaedic Surgeons. The film was accepted for presentation. The showing of the movie was cancelled later, when we found out that the range of motion the patient had finally attained was limited in the last twenty degrees of extension and the last 20 degrees of flexion.

Based on a most unhappy personal experience, I have long felt that an infected opened reduction of an intra-articular distal humeral fracture is one of the most catastrophic complications an orthopaedist can experience. The patient in question was a man in his fifties who could be classified as an alcoholic. I performed an open reduction of his comminuted humerus and obtained what I thought was a good and stable reduction. On the night of the surgery he experienced the symptoms of *delirium tremens;* fell to the ground and displaced the fragments. A deep infection ensued, which ultimately required removal of the metallic fixation since by that time it had ceased to provide stability. The ultimate result was an elbow that had the motion of a universal joint. He used a brace that locked the elbow at 90 degrees of flexion. A surgical fusion was ruled out because of the history of infection and the patient's reluctance to have additional surgery. The surgical fusion would have been difficult to carry out and the outcome probably unsatisfactory. Today, a total elbow arthroplasty would be an alternative.

For reasons not clear to me, the elbow tolerates incongruous articular surfaces better than many other joints. This explains why healed, intra-articular distal humeral fractures are not, in many instances, associated with pain.

Recent reports in the literature have indicated high success with total elbow arthroplasty as the primary treatment of these fractures in the elderly. Though I appreciate the potential advantages of the arthroplasty procedure, I remain, at this time, somewhat skeptical about its long-term success. It is, however, an attractive alternative.

SECTION I - TRAUMA

M

MALROTATION: (Tibial fractures)

Most axially unstable tibial fractures, i.e. oblique, spiral and comminuted, experience rotation of the distal fragment in relation to the proximal one at the time of the initial injury. The tendency of the leg to lie in an external rotation attitude during recumbence explains the fact that most initial rotational abnormalities are of the external rotation type. At the time of reduction or stabilization of the extremity in either a cast, nail or splint, an initially unrecognized rotary deformity is created or perpetuated. A permanent external rotary deformity of fifteen degrees may be cosmetically unacceptable particularly if the patient had, prior to the fracture, a mild internal tibial torsion. Rotary deformities of ten degrees or less are usually unrecognizable. It is important to have both legs exposed during the initial and subsequent application of splints, casts or braces in order to prevent unacceptable deformities.

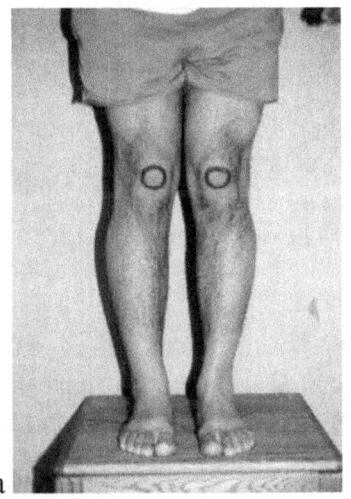
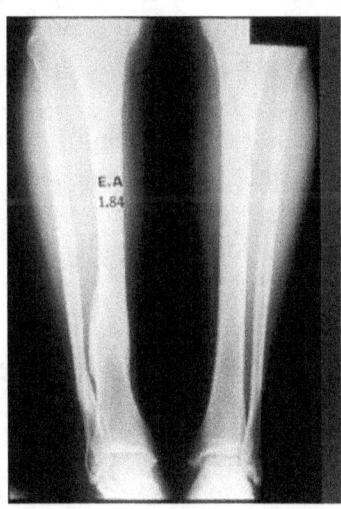

Fig. Malrotation of healed tibial fracture (a). Notice the widened space between the tibia and fibula proximally (b).

The surgeon should try do duplicate the shape of the non-fractured extremity when dealing with the fractured one. This applies not only to malrotation but also to angulation in any plane. Measuring rotational deformity following tibial fractures is not simple when the deformity is mild. X-rays of the entire leg and observation of the relationship between the tibia and the fibula can be helpful. Normally, the fibula is located postero-laterally to the tibia. Therefore a true antero-posterior x-ray of the leg shows the proximal fibula partially hidden behind the tibia. If the x-ray is taken with the leg in internal rotation the space between the tibia and fibula increase. If externally rotated, the space decreases. This information is helpful in assessing rotary deformities.

Fractures of the tibia with an intact fibula are often associated with a varus angulation of the tibia. The shorter tibial fragment is the one most likely to angulate into varus. The angulation is commonly associated with an internal rotation of the tibia. Since correction of the varus deformity is virtually impossible in the presence of an intact fibula, the appearance of the tibial varus deformity can be improved by externally rotating the distal leg.

We have conducted laboratory studies in both cadavers and patients, which indicated that the originally obtained rotational and angular alignment of the fractured tibia treated with below-the-knee functional braces can be maintained, providing their fit is appropriately maintained. During heel strike an elastic external rotation motion between the fragments occurs but the original relationship between the fragments returns during the swing phase and during rest. The same things occur in relation to mild angular deformities and to shortening. [139]

MEDIAL EPICONDYLE FRACTURES

Fractures of the medial epicondyles of the humerus are one of those fractures, which are instinctively approached surgically. What is the evidence to support such a practice? The fact that internal fixation is a simple procedure, is not a good enough answer.

One should not make sweeping, all-inclusive statements. A simple isolated minimally displaced fracture of the epicondyle is not the same as a severely displaced fracture associated with a dislocated elbow. The instability that the latter pathology is likely to create may justify the surgical intervention. The same is not true for the simple fractures. They heal either with bony tissues or through a fibro-cartilaginous bridge that renders the elbow stable.

Why then routinely subject patients to the possibility of complications? Internal fixation, despite its simplicity, has been reported as being associated in a certain number of instances with ulnar nerve pathology. The nerve may be inadvertently pierced, the groove through which the nerve glides narrowed, or scarring of the surrounding might take place.

SECTION I - TRAUMA

MENISCUS INJURIES, REPAIR AND GRAFTS

At this time, it is difficult to refute the argument that complete meniscectomy is likely to produce late degenerative changes in the knee joint. The evidence is very strong. What we do not understand yet is why it happens. To explain the phenomenon strictly on mechanical bases, as we seem to do instinctively in regards to most problems in orthopaedics, may not be the perfect answer. Some biological alteration may be also responsible for the arthritic changes. Otherwise, how does one explain that not all meniscectomized knee joints develop osteoarthritis?

It has been argued that the alignment of the knee joint determines the degree of change in stress distribution and therefore the subsequent arthritic changes. Supporters of this argument have said that lateral meniscectomy in patients with valgus knees are the most likely ones to result in arthritic problems; and that the excised lateral meniscus, in people with valgus knees, give the worst results. Though this is probably true, I have seen a few patients with valgus knees who had a lateral meniscus excised as long as fifty years earlier, who did not have any symptoms of degenerative joint disease. Some of them were significant obese. It is more likely that what determines the bad outcome from meniscectomy may be an associated joint instability produced by recognized or unrecognized associated cruciate or collateral ligament injury.

Based on the recognized incidence of late osteoarthritis following meniscectomy partial meniscectomy has become the preferred treatment for torn menisci. Things looked pretty good until recently. Longer follow-up is beginning to demonstrate that radiological signs of osteoarthritis also develop following partial meniscectomy. This finding supports my view that there is something else that we have not been able to identify yet, which is responsible for the no so infrequent development of degeneration. The fact that people who had their menisci excised a copile of generations ago did not have the benefit of MRI studies does not allow us to state categorically that associated pathology, i.e. torn cruciate ligaments may be the real culprit in the later degeneration.

The technique of stapling or suturing torn menisci was developed relatively recently. Nonetheless, a number of manufacturing companies have already produced their special products. There is no final verdict as yet regarding the value of the technique. I suspect the technique may not prove to be effective in a long-term basis because the contact of articular cartilage against a foreign body may lead to degenerative changes. Theoretically, biodegradable sutures might prove to be better. However, if the repaired meniscus does not heal prior to resorption of the material, the tear might reappear. (See BIO-DEGRADABLE MATERIALS).

Much progress has been made in recent years in the area of surgical replacement of damaged menisci. The field is rich with opportunities, and early reports suggest a promising future for meniscal replacement. Replacement of menisci, either partially or completely, using allograph implants or artificial materials, have not yet withstood the test of time. New, experimental bovine grafts have attracted some attention but serious questions remain. How will they age? What will the cumulative stresses do to the material? Will possible debris in the joint precipitate harmful chemical reactions? Though I believe that further progress in this area will be made, I am not going to hold my breath. Success, in my opinion, is still in the very distant future, even with further understanding of growth factors and their clinical applications.

SECTION I - TRAUMA

METACARPAL FRACTURES

At a meeting of the Orthopedic Fracture Association a young orthopaedist reported on his laboratory studies on metacarpal fractures, which had led him to conclude that even two to three millimeters of shortening would have undesirable consequences. He had taken critical measures of the pull required for the flexors and extensor tendons to reach normal levels according to various millimeters of shortening.

I gathered from listening to his presentation that he may have been one of the many who believes that the third digit is longer than the other four, because its metacarpal is longer than the adjacent ones. He never thought the reason for the discrepancy rested on its longer phalanges.

This is how standards of care are defined with great frequency these days. Ridiculous reports and heavy marketing by industry determine the "most appropriate" way to take care of our patients.

The young man's argument does not fly in the face of overwhelming evidence that metacarpal fractures, in varying degrees, tolerate minor shortening, angulation and malrotation, and that the results from the non-surgical treatment of most metacarpal fracture are good. This does not mean that certain fractures are not best treated surgically, which is certainly the case. But to claim that all of them need surgery is outrageous. Unfortunately, many surgeons at this time treat surgically all metacarpal fractures. These patients are then subjected to "intensive, supervised" physical and occupational therapy for to prolonged periods of time. Not infrequently in the doctor's office. Such an approach has increased the cost of fracture care significantly. I doubt very much that patients are better off because of the surgical treatment; only the surgeons, therapists, and the manufacturers of the internal fixation can claim any benefits.

Low energy oblique fractures of the last four metacarpals experience very little shortening at the time of the initial injury. The intact inter-metacarpal ligaments prevent greater shortening through a tethering mechanism. Angulation is in most instances controlled by the molding of a cast and mild residual angulation is acceptable clinically and cosmetically.

It is said, and rightly so, that the fifth metacarpal tolerates well as much as 45 degrees of angulation. What is gained from carrying out plate fixation of fractures that readily heal without surgery and simply leave an inconsequential minor "lump" over the dorsum of the hand particularly if the angular deformity can be brought to very reasonable degrees?

As a rule, malrotation is correctable by splinting more than one digit so the normal non-fractured digit or digits, maintaining in that manner acceptable alignment of the fragments. Needless to say, injuries that result in major initial deformities require surgical intervention.

I heard a very distinguished hand surgeon comment on the need for internal fixation of phalangeal and metacarpal fractures in order to obtain the most desirable degree of range of motion and to expedite fracture healing. I wonder where he gained his information. We know that rigidly immobilized diaphyseal fractures heal more slowly than those not immobilized and the strength of the callus in the former group is much weaker. [115, 122] Also, that metacarpal and phalangeal fractures that undergo stripping of soft tissues from the bone require a much longer period of time before joints regain the maximum recovery of

SECTION I - TRAUMA

function. Adhesion of tendons to the bone is common and joint stiffness requires a long time to improve; sometimes a permanent limitation of motion can be identified.

A mild loss of motion of the fingers is often inconsequential, since full range of motion of interphalageal joints is rarely if ever necessary. I think that the only time when full flexion is present is during bare-knuckled boxing or pounding on a desk in anger. The holding of even small diameter objects precludes full range of flexion.

Metacarpal and phalangeal fractures are good examples to refute the long-held myth that fractures heal faster if surrounded by large muscle masses, such as the femur and humerus. Muscles, with exception of interosseous and lumbricals do not surround these small bones.

SECTION I - TRAUMA

N

NON-UNION- TIBIA

For a number of years I made it habit to introduce myself to the curator of whatever museum I happened to visit, and to inquire as to the frequency of non-union in prehistoric days as well as in more recent, though extinct, civilizations. The answer was always the same. Non-union of fractures is a very rare finding. Malunion, on the other hand is not uncommon. This applied to both man as well as other animals. One must conclude that nonunion is a condition found primarily in advanced civilization.

The assumption is logical. In the "old days" many people who sustained open fractures did not survive the infection which was likely to develop. The smell and presence of blood must also have attracted predators who disposed of the injured. The latter explanation applies more readily to the animal in the wild. However, it is a proven fact that certain species of primates upon the injury of one of its members surround the victim and protect it until the fracture heals. Bony deformities are common among those animals but, once again, non-union is quite uncommon.

Why non-union develops in a closed diaphyseal fracture, remains an unanswered question. Why is it that two virtually identical fractures, produced through the same mechanism and at similar levels, you may see one fracture heal rapidly and the other heal slowly or not at all? Much speculation has centered on the topic but, to the best of my knowledge, no clear answers have come forward.

A popular though unscientific explanation for the cause of nonunion is that too much motion at the fracture site is responsible for the it. Where is the data to prove this myth? The incidence of non-union is greater from plating of fractures than from casting or bracing. Boehler's work in Austria and that of Dehne, Brown and Burkhalter in the United States military disproves that theory. Their treatment of tibial fractures with above-the-knee casts and immediate ambulation was associated with a very low incidence of nonunion. My experiences with a below-the-knee functional cast or brace in closed tibial fractures demonstrated a nonunion rate of less than 1.5%.

No one would question that ambulation in a long or short cast or brace is associated with greater motion at the fracture site. The conclusion that must be made from these observations is that motion at the fracture site favors osteogenesis[35, 36, 78, 138, 147].

If motion at the fracture site were evil, clavicular fractures would never heal with slings. Rib fractures would not heal without paralyzing the diaphragm and intercostal muscles until union took place. This argument usually gets the rebuttal that ribs and clavicle are different, and some go as far as saying that their proximity to the heart gives those bone special reparative powers. I suspect that people advancing these archaic views believe that thunder and lightning are an expression of God's wrath and that the sun rotates around the earth every day.

Having had the opportunity to observe the behavior of a very large number of long bone fractures treated with braces that did not preclude motion at the fracture site, I made it a project to find out how non-unions would respond in an environment that did not curtail motion at the fracture site. We performed an ostectomy of the fibula (which increased the motion at the nonunion site) and then applied

SECTION I - TRAUMA

braces to tibial delayed unions and to non-unions. We found out that contrary to expectations, in many instances well-established delayed unions and non-unions went to uneventful healing. [150]

How could that be? How was it possible that increasing motion between the ununited fragments resulted in healing? The matter was investigated in greater detail and some clinical conclusions were drawn.

In most instances we performed an ostectomy of the fibula approximately one inch distally or proximally to the non-union site. I had known of others, who in the past had used osteotomies or ostectomies in the management of nonunion but not of ambulating those patients in below the knee braces that permit free motion of the knee and ankle joints. A few years later, however, it was brought to my attention that Smith, from Philadelphia, in the latter part of the 19th century, had published an article describing his results treating non unions of long bones with "prostheses" which resembled our modern braces. Allegedly, Smith had a patient with a recalcitrant non-union of the femur, which he had planned to treat by amputating the limb. The patient, however, refused the ablation procedure. Under those circumstances Smith fitted the patient with a "prosthesis". Much to his amazement the non-union eventually healed.

Subsequently, he treated other patients suffering from the same condition with comparable satisfactory results. Smith's findings did nothing but increase my interest in the project.

My enthusiasm with the "new method" of treatment somewhat blinded me, and I began to use braces indiscriminately in infected as well as non-infected non-unions. In one instance, I attempted the method on a young man with an infected nonunion that had also sustained a spinal cord injury that had left him with a partially paralyzed and insensitive limb. I ended up performing and amputation. A few other failures also called for amputation surgery.

I noticed quite early that even in those unsuccessful instances where surgery and bone grafting became necessary, the period of ambulation with the removable braces had improved the condition of the extremity. Perhaps it created an environment more conducive to successful bone grafting. The atrophied musculature of the limb, the dry and scaly skin of the leg and the stiffness of the adjacent joints were much improved.

In order to use this method of treatment, either as a permanent solution or as a temporary step, it is necessary to have an extremity that does not have a major angular deformity. Weight bearing in the presence of major angulation is likely to result in increased deformity and problems with the surrounding skin. We also noticed that infected fractures demonstrated increased drainage following the initiation of weight bearing ambulation. In the first patient with an infected non-union the additional drainage was so profuse that I came close to discontinuing the method. After a few days the drainage decreased and eventually completely disappeared (Fig. 42, a,b,c., 43 a,b,c., 44 a, b,c. and 45 a, b, c, d.).

What explanation can we offer to shed some light into the subject? How can an infected non-union go to spontaneous healing by increasing the instability at the nonunion site? Perhaps it is possible that the "new injury", produced by the ostectomy and the trauma inflicted to the area by the increased motion at the non-union site are enough to create a mechanical, thermic and vascular environment conducive to osteogenesis.

SECTION I - TRAUMA

The length of treatment for these patients was long. However, it should be noted that during that period of time, most patients were able to function quite independently. Many walked eventually without crutches while awaiting healing. They maintained good hygiene of their extremity, bathed and changed socks on a daily basis. Surgeons in a hurry to see faster results may dismiss this treatment modality and they may be correct in taking that position. I cannot help but remember a European who once said to me that Americans had invented instant gratification but ended up abandoning it because it took too long.

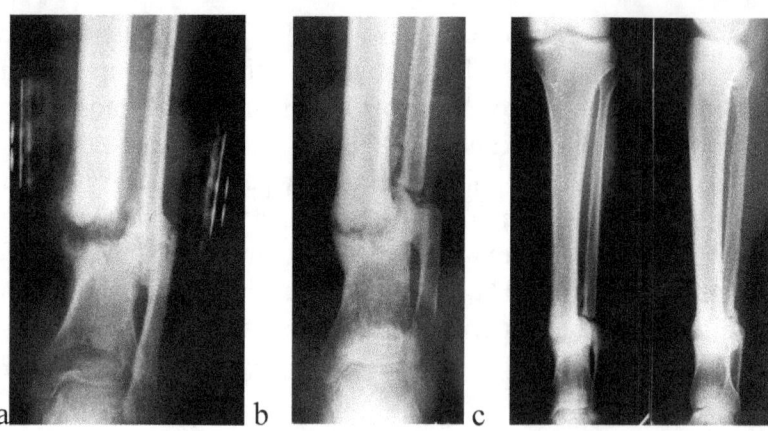

Fig. a, b and c. Septic nonunion of distal tibial fracture treated with a fibula ostectomy and a functional brace.

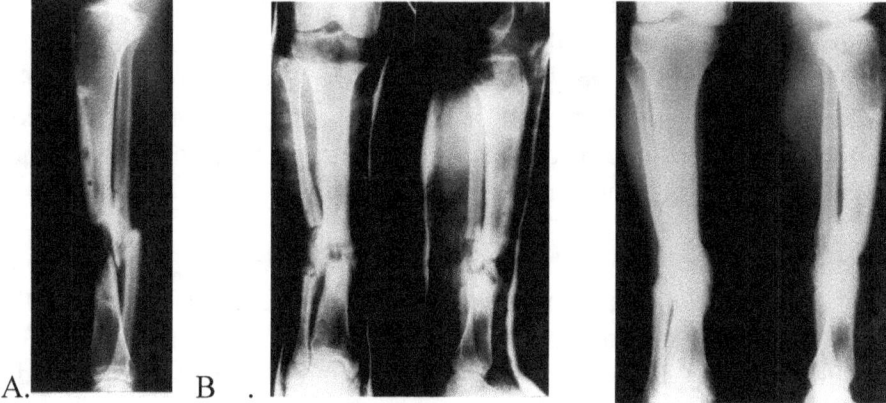

Fig. a, b and c. Nonunited fracture of the tibia previously subjected to several surgical procedures. A fibula ostectomy and bone grafting were followed by the application of a below-the-knee functional brace.

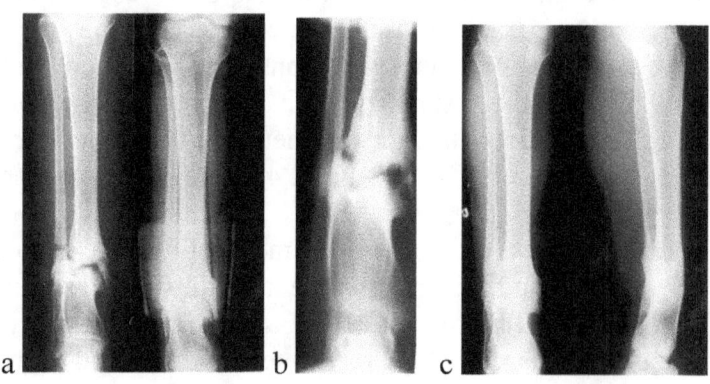

SECTION I - TRAUMA

Fig. a, b and c. Nonunion treated with ostectomy of the fibula and functional brace. Notice the resulting nonunion of the fibula.

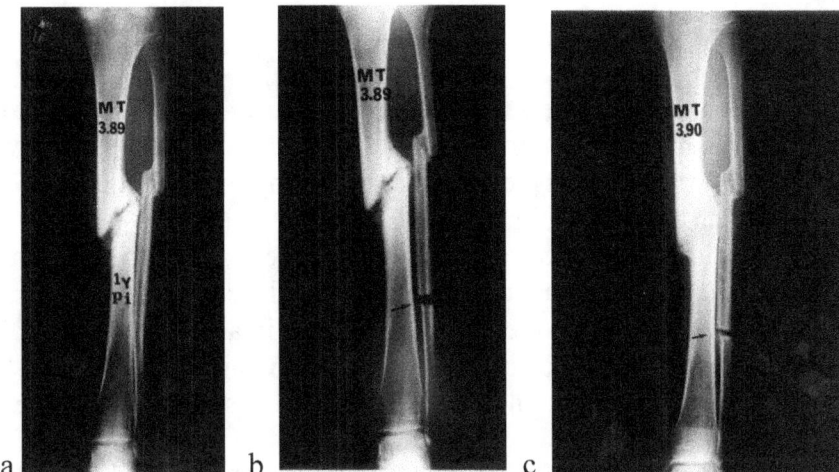

Fig. a, b and c. Nonunited tibial fracture successfully treated with a fibular ostectomy and a functional brace.

I do not propose that functional bracing with or without additional surgery is the treatment of choice under all circumstances. However, the lessons we learned from it should not be ignored. These clinical observations should provoke some reassessment of our tradition belief in immobilization in fracture non-union care.

A number of surgical and non-surgical procedures have been recommended for the treatment of delayed and fracture non-union. I believe there is probably a place for each one of them. Electrical stimulation, until now, has failed to prove its value on a consistent basis. (See ELECTRICAL STIMULATION).

Other treatment methods to stimulate fracture healing are currently being heralded as the final answer for non-union. As in the case of electrical stimulation, the desire to profit from the new "gimmicks" will destroy whatever potential value they may have had. The only practical effect those methods have had is the increased cost of care.

BMP (Bone Morphogenic Protein), described by Marshal Urist in 1979, was heralded as a major discovery, and indeed it was. However, 30 years later, despite important additional discoveries, locally applied BMP has failed to produce the anticipated clinical results. Industry has enthusiastically and aggressively produced a plethora of "bone forming" products, which are being widely used by the orthopaedic community. Sponges, pastes and a multitude of ingenious designs are effectively marketed. Though I have seen the impressive results obtained in experimental animals, I have not as yet seen well documented clinical studies demonstrating their efficacy. I have the uncomfortable feeling that the current products are nothing more than a passing fancy, and it will be a long time before biologically produced materials prove themselves useful.

O

OLECRANON: (Fractures)

Since the technology necessary to "fix" fractures is available and we instinctively prefer anatomical restoration, most olecranon fractures are treated surgically, either with screws, tension bands or plates. The results are good for the most part with any of these methods. However, removal of the fixation device is often necessary either because if fails in itself or because of painful irritation of the overlying tissues. Neither union nor healing without infection can be guaranteed. Limitation of motion of the elbow may also be a complication, particularly if the surgeon is not comfortable with the stability achieved at the time of surgery and then holds the elbow in a cast or splint for several weeks. The elbow is notorious for its ready tendency to become "stiff" following immobilization, particularly if surgery has been performed. Permanent limitation of extension in the last 10 to 15 degrees is not uncommon.

. If in spite of the lack of anatomical reduction is not always achieved many patients do well. This is, because the articular cartilage of the trochlea and olecranon tolerate incongruity to a degree probably greater than many other major joints.

Excision of the olecranon is a viable option in the treatment of certain fractures, particularly when they are comminuted, since attempts to anatomically reduce them are often unsuccessful. Following excision of the olecranon, function of the elbow is usually very good. Weakness of extension, if present, is not clinically significant and in most instances there should be no residual limitation of elbow flexion.

There has been much speculation on the amount of elecranon that can be safely removed without creating instability. I believe that as long as the powerful medial collateral ligaments are intact, 50 per cent of its body can be safely excised. Heresy, some would argue. It would be nice, however, if they were able to talk to some of the "old timers" and have them tell them of their experiences with excision.

It would also benefit them if there were to talk to physicians practicing in underdeveloped countries where surgery is not available to most citizens. They will "shock" the inquiring physicians by their statement that in most instances the victims of these fractures eventually return to work and carry out normal functional lives.

OPEN FRACTURES

It is of great interest to observe that open fractures, even in the absence of infection, seem to heal more slowly than closed ones. Some have said that the loss of the hematoma is the main cause of delayed union. This answer does not stand careful scrutiny. Where is the evidence that the hematoma possesses osteogenic powers? If it did, we should be injecting autologous blood into the fracture site of closed as well as open fractures. That in open fractures the periosteum is damaged more extensively? This may be true in some instances but not in others. An open tibial fracture, sustained from a direct blow with an object may not displace the fragments very much and therefore produce minimal damage to the periosteum. Displacement of fragments is more likely to detach periosteum and other soft tissues from the bone in the case of a closed spiral fracture produced by a twisting mechanism and then angulated from

SECTION I - TRAUMA

the weight of the body. The simple open fracture, even under these circumstances, is the one more likely to demonstrate slower healing.

Furthermore, there is no specific proof to support the theory that the periosteum plays a major role in fracture healing. The periosteum is an important structure in the development and growth of normal bone but its degree of participation in fracture healing, in my opinion, is still debatable. If it plays a major role in the production of callus, why a diaphyseal fracture treated by means of rigid external fixation or a plate, very careful placed in order to limit periosteal damage, does not show periosteal activity? (See FRACTURE HEALING).

The discovery of antiseptic agents and later of antibiotics changed the management of open fractures in a radical way. Most open fractures today can be treated without having to resort to ablation surgery. This does not mean that open fractures are no longer a problem because, indeed, they can be.

Technology has improved the care of open fractures and therefore it is customary today to make every attempt possible to save the injured limb. This pattern, however, needs to be broken from time to time. Open fractures, which I usually refer to as "partial amputations" rather than fractures, if severe enough, may leave patients with a disability greater than that produced by an amputation. In the lower extremity, open fractures associated with major nerve injury often result in limbs which are virtually useless. The residual anaesthetic foot, the partially paralyzed leg, stiff joints and painful extremity can have devastating consequences. If pain is of the causalgic type the problem is magnified manifold.

It has been well documented that patients with severely injured extremities, who are subjected to multiple procedures over a long period time and eventually end up having an amputation are prone to suffer from phantom pain. This condition is often extremely difficult to treat. A number of people have become addicted to narcotics or have committed suicide as a result of the intolerable pain.

I suspect that not enough amputations are performed in the early management of severe open fractures. If the knee joint can be preserved, an amputation is functionally better than a limb that is partially anaesthetic, partially paralyzed, stiff and associated with a severe limp. A below-the-knee amputee, in most instances, even with a very short stump can function very well and walk with minimal or no limp within a very short time after the amputation is performed. [160] (See AMPUTATIONS).

Not only the lay community, but members of the medical profession as well, still consider amputation an enormous tragedy. Though I do not wish to minimize the magnitude of the event, I insist that with modern prosthetic appliances, below-the-knee amputees are not significantly disabled. In addition, for too long we have exaggerated the psychological problems associate with amputations. If properly managed, below-the-knee amputees adjust into society quite rapidly and perform the majority of the tasks required in their lives. (See AMPUTATIONS).

We are by nature very reluctant to admit defeat when treating patients. Having to amputate a limb of an individual suffering from traumatic injuries, we usually consider a personal defeat. Therefore, we go to extremes to save limbs, regardless of the fact that often the patients are better off as amputees.

At this moment intramedullary fixation of open fractures of the tibia and femur is being carried out with increasing frequency and enthusiasm. The reported results are most encouraging. I suspect that external fixators are preferable in very severe fractures with extensive soft tissue damage. No matter how

SECTION I - TRAUMA

unphysiological external fixators are and how they are " instruments of the devil and non-union making machines", as I have called them in the past, they have a useful place in the care of open fractures. The use of new and powerful antibiotics and imaging technology have made possible the good results.

Also contributing to higher success in the care of open fractures has been the advances in soft tissue coverage techniques. This "plastic surgery" contribution has been very salutary, but has diminished the role of the orthopaedist in the care of open fractures. However, in doing so it has, perhaps, enhanced the cooperation between the two medical disciplines. I resent, however, the loss of this important territory to others. There is no reason why the orthopaedist should not know how to handle soft tissues as well as bones. It troubles me to see orthopaedic residents, when presented with a major open fracture, get on the phone to summon the help of a plastic surgeon. The orthopaedist does the mechanical fixation of the fracture and the plastic surgeon does the sophisticated work. This relationship does not speak well for the sophistication of our profession.

Our complete dependency on the plastic surgeon for the management of associated soft tissue pathology in open fracture care has made us forget an important lesson from the past: coverage of exposed bone is not essential for uneventful healing of fractures. "Nature abhors the void", said John Hunter nearly two hundred years ago but that lesson no longer impresses us. Healing by "secondary intention" is not necessarily evil. The spontaneous healing of skin over the exposed bone can also provide excellent results in many instances.

There is still some minor controversy regarding whether coverage of open wounds should be done as soon as possible or after a period of time. Most reports favor the former. What is not often mentioned is that major full thickness skin grafts are not always successful, and when successful can be very unsightly

To the best of my knowledge Trueta made the most significant break-through in the treatment of open fractures in modern times. He was a surgeon from Barcelona, who during the Spanish Civil War in the 1030's found it necessary to emigrate to England. There he became the professor and chief of orthopaedics at Oxford University. It was during that war that he noticed that soldiers with open fractures healed their fractures by cleansing and debridement of the wound and stabilization in casts without any attempts being made to surgically close the wound. The British establishment dismissed his results until experiences during the Second World War proved Trueta's ideas to be correct. As the Second World War began to affect the British troops, it became obvious that closure of the skin over a fractured bone led to complications. Ever since then, and throughout every military conflict, it has been the policy of the American military to forbid surgeons to close wounds incurred in wartime. When some tried to experiment with primary closure, the incidence of complications grew exponentially.

In peacetime, military surgeons in the United States, led originally by Ernst Dehne, demonstrated excellent results from the use of Trueta's method and reported on thousands of open fractures treated in that manner. I personally had the privilege of seeing his work and subsequently enjoyed the opportunity of working with two of his students, Paul Brown and William Burkhalter, who joined the full-time faculty of the University of Miami during my chairmanship of the department in the 1970's.

The situation, here illustrated, eloquently demonstrates the fact that coverage of exposed bony structures is not always necessary. This young man sustained a severe open fracture of his tibia and fibula when a fast moving automobile struck him. He was initially treated at a local hospital in Puerto

Rico where the wound was minimally debrided and the bone stabilized with metallic pins above and below the fracture. He was then transferred to Jackson Memorial Hospital, in Miami, where we assumed his care. Under anaesthesia we carried out further debridment of the wound and excised a large free bony fragment that protruded in the wound

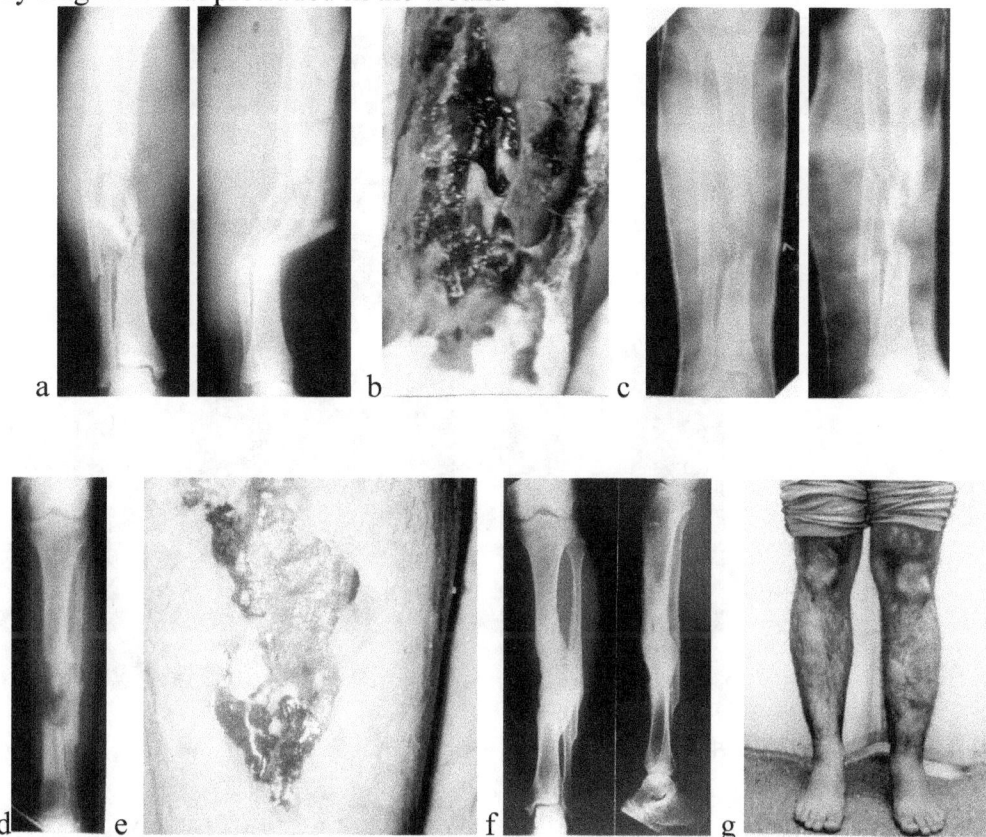

Fig. a through g. Open fracture treated with debridement of the wound, the subsequent application of a functional brace and active ambulation. The fractured bone and soft tissues healed spontaneously.

Without making any attempts to close the skin or cover the defect with a skin graft, a minimally padded below-the knee functional cast was applied. Within four weeks the bone was visible only over a small area. The cast was discontinued and replaced with a below-the-knee functional brace that permitted free and unencumbered motion of all joints. The fracture healed without complications and the skin grew over the previously exposed bone.

Since the bony and soft tissues were being subjected to intermittent stresses throughout the entire healing process, the callus that bridged the fragments was strong and the skin did not adhere against the underlying bone. Skin adherence to the bone is a common complication following the treatment of open fractures with the Trueta's method. However, such a problem can be significantly reduced and even eliminated in many instances, if activity, muscle function and weight bearing are introduced early

There are still, and probably always will be, regions of the world where the infrastructure of the area precludes the implementation of procedures and techniques which are safely utilized in more affluent societies. War or war-like condition will continue to exist until the end of time, and under those circumstances it is wise to remember that there are old, effective ways to manage open fractures. A victim of an open fracture in an area of the world where the necessary requirements for modern care are not available is more likely to heal without complications if treated by debridement and cast immobilization than with internal fixation and skin closure[158]. (Fig. 47 a, b, c.).

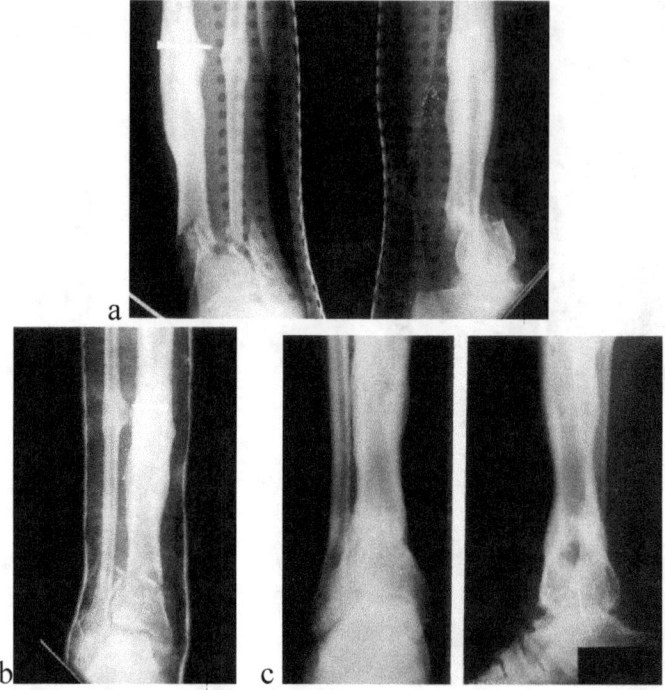

Fig. a, b and c. Open fracture treated with debridement and functional casting.

In the early 1980's I participated in a symposium on Fractures, where in addition to presenting scientific material I chaired a panel on open fractures. The other participants were Harald Tscherne, from Germany, Emile Letournel, from France and John Webb, from Great Britain. I asked the panelists to tell us the incidence of deep infection in their respective institutions. Tscherne, who had just illustrated the superb transportation system in his city of Hanover, where patients injured on the road received medical care within minutes of the accident, responded that the figure was approximately 4%. Webb, from Nothingham, England, commented that their transportation system was inferior to that of his German colleague; that his patients had to wait a longer time to have surgery, but his infection rate was similar. The figures from Letournel were almost identical. I then recalled that at our institution, the Los Angeles County Hospital, the infection rate in open fractures was also 4%. This despite the fact that at the LA Hospital, the average time between time arrival to the Emergency Room and reaching the Operating room was 26b hours.

I am sure that the figures given us at that meeting presented the average of all combined open fractures, but I suspect that if the question had been limited to type II and III fractures, those associated with severe soft tissue damage, Tscherne's figure would have still been the lowest. In my opinion, the sophistication of his program has not been matched by anyone else, in either Europe or America.

I had to surmise from the information presented at the symposium, indicating that if the infection rate was so similar in the four countries, it was because in all four situations antibiotics were administered immediately after arrival to the hospital. This conclusion dismisses the argument often given by younger orthopaedists, that today they carry out better surgical debridement. It is a silly argument. Good debridement has been practiced for a very long time. Better antibiotics explain the lower incidence of infection in open fractures and surgery of all types.

I made the mistake of sharing my experience at that meeting with the chief of General Surgery at our hospital. He was responsible for the allocation of operating time to the various surgical departments. I had quarreled with him many times over the issue of insufficient time being given to orthopaedics and had claimed that the long waiting time for surgery was creating more infections and other complications. He was thinking faster than I was and commented that I had just given him support for his system of operating room allocations. Because of my "big mouth" I certainly deserved to lose that battle.

SECTION I - TRAUMA

OSTEOMYELITIS - CHRONIC

Hematogenous osteomyelitis, a condition that a few decades ago killed countless numbers of children even in the most developed nation of the world, is now a rare condition. As a sequella of surgery or as a surgical complication, it is also a not very frequent problem. The use of antibiotics should get the credit for such an improvement. However, the specter of increasingly strains of antibiotic resistant antibiotics looms on the horizon. We must assume some responsibility because we have abused the use of the available ones to extreme degrees

Chronic osteomyelitis following open fractures is more easily managed today with debridement and powerful antibiotics. On occasion the problem cannot be overcome rapidly, and several surgical procedures are necessary.

I have treated several patients with chronic osteomyelitis of the tibia with a method I learned from Austin Moore during my residency days. Later, when I became involved in the use of isolative extremity perfusion in the management of this condition, I performed several such procedures. The procedure consists of debridement of the infected bone, followed by the filling of the defect with cancellous bone that had been made into a paste. The paste is similar to the one used today with the Bone Impaction method for acetabuli and femoral defects.

I do not recall our success rate, even though our results with Isolated Extremity Perfusion were reported at a meeting of the American Medical Association, for which we received an award. The success rate must have been low since the perfusion was abandoned. I suspect the merit of the graft-impaction technique still survives.

The following illustrations document the use of the Graft-Impaction technique in the case of a man who had suffered from chronic osteomyelitis for many years and had had multiple surgical procedures. After debridement of the infected bone and the impaction of the graft the wound was closed. Healing took place uneventfully.

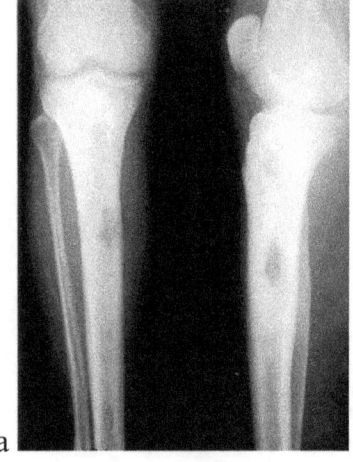
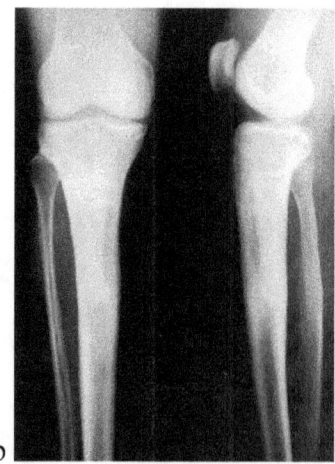

Fig. a and b. Chronic osteomyelitis (a) treated with debridement, compression allograph and primary closure of the skin. The sepsis was eliminated (b).

SECTION I - TRAUMA

P

PATELLA (Fractures)

The most popular method of treatment of patellar fractures during the past few decades has been open reduction and internal fixation. The perception exists that anatomical reapproximation of the fractured fragments ensures the best results. The perception is logical but ignores some factual points. 1) Anatomical reapproximation is not always possible. Incongruous surfaces are often left behind and we do not know much about the patellar cartilage's ability to remodel. It is the thickest in the body and therefore, perhaps, the one least likely to repair itself well. 2) Since many patellar fractures are the result of direct blows it is very likely that permanent, irreversible damage to the articular cartilage takes place at the time of the injury. The damaged articular cartilage could easily set the stage for subsequent generalized degenerative arthritis as the opposing femoral surface undergoes similar pathological changes.

The removal of a major fragment is often recommended for moderately comminuted fractures. Though, probably a good therapeutic approach, it is beset with possible adverse sequella. The complicated anatomy of the patella-femoral joint with six articulating facets on its surface is permanently altered when a major fragment is excised. This alteration and the possible initial and irreparable damage to the articular cartilage may be responsible for the late degenerative changes often found in the joint.

The initial post-injury clinical and radiograph examinations are helpful in assessing the degree of injury sustained by the patellar retinaculum. Major separation between the patellar fragments usually indicates major damage to the patellar retinaculum. This is more likely to occur when the injury occurs with the knee flexed and/or is associated with a significant contraction of the quadriceps. The identification of this separation is not always reliable but it is helpful.

Patellectomy, in my opinion, can be, and should be the treatment of choice in many instances. The results from a properly perform patellectomy, followed by proper post-operative management, are good in most instances. The residual weakness that allegedly accompanies patellectomy is, for the most part, a myth. Though, it does exist if measured very critically, in clinical terms it is inconsequential in most instances. I have seen patellectomized people function normally; they are able to climb and descend stairs without difficulty and in a few instances participate in track and field exercises.

Once, at a meeting of the American Academy of Orthopedic Surgeons, in the days when the meetings were smaller and the discussions were more animated, a surgeon, at the end of a panel discussing patellectomy ran down the isle and up the steps to the stage. He squatted down in rapid succession and then jumped on the desk where he repeated the motions. He then jumped down to the ground and landed on his feet with the knees flexed.

SECTION I - TRAUMA

As he began to walk away from the podium, he grabbed the microphone and said, "I had my right patella removed when I served in the military two decade ago".

I suspect that the bad name that patellectomy has at this time is not due to proven inefficacy. The old American and foreign literature is rich with reports demonstrating the fact that a high percentage of patellectomized knees resulted in very acceptable functional results. Furthermore, there are not, to the best of my knowledge, long term results of comparable patellar fractures treated surgically. I would not be surprised at all if an objective comparison of results between patellectomy and internal fixation of comminuted fractures conclude that the patellectomized patients did better than the ones treated with internal fixation. The incidence of late arthritic changes could be higher in the latter group.

Austin Moore said, "Patellectomy is the most gratifying operation an orthopaedist can do." He was not a fool, quite the contrary a very good surgeon, a great thinker and a visionary. Numerous time I saw him remove the patella of college athletes if during the routine treatment of internal derangement of the knee, he identified associated chondromalacia of the patella. He justified his actions by saying, with great conviction, that he was preventing later degeneration of the knee joint. I saw many of his long-term follow-ups and must admit that I was very positively impressed with the results.

I do not think Austin Moore's radical approach to the issue was totally correct. He probably went too far. His overly enthusiastic excesses should not minimize or obliterate the merit of his observations and his forward thinking. Internal fixation of fractures has improved significantly over the years and total knee replacement was not available in his days. Though I am not a total knee surgeon, I am reluctant to accept without questioning the popular belief that all patellectomized patients do poorly following total knee replacement. I have seen a few patients who have done very well under those circumstances.

The presence of a patella is not indispensable for walking, climbing or running. Some of the fastest quadrupeds, such as the cheetah have relatively small patellae in relation to their size. The ostrich, a bipedal and also an extremely fast animal, has a relatively small patella. Some of the slower animals have large patellae.

The post–operative management of the patellectomized patient is of great importance. Immobilization of the joint should be avoided and patients should allowed to ambulate as soon as possible with aid of crutches until strength has returned to the quadriceps, in order to prevent dehiscence of the repaired extension mechanism.

Even the most benign injury to the knee joint is followed by atrophy of the quadriceps. As a matter of fact, quadriceps atrophy occurs following conditions that have nothing to do with the knee joint. For example, the arthritic hip seems to be always associated with quadriceps atrophy; and some patients who have their arthritic hips replaced with prostheses find it very difficult to overcome the atrophy even after a prolonged period of active, resistive exercises. This suggests that great quadriceps strength is not required for the normal conduct of daily activities and even many lower athletic endeavors.

SECTION I - TRAUMA

PERIOSTEUM IN FRACTURE HEALING. (See FRACTURE HEALING)

===

PERIPHERAL NERVE INJURIES

Have the magnifying loops and microscope improved the prognosis of surgically repaired peripheral nerves? I doubt it. I have not been able to find solid evidence that the more accurate re-approximation of nerve endings has made a difference. In my opinion the surgical procedure has been made easier and more convenient to the surgeon. Also third party payers reimburse him at a higher rate. I suspect the clinical results obtained from surgical procedures perform today do not differ from those of yesteryears.

My introduction to orthopaedics came through peripheral nerve injuries. As an orthopaedic intern at the Military Hospital in Bogota, Colombia in the early 1950's, I assisted Guillermo Vargas, a surgeon who was deeply interested in the subject. He had a wealth of clinical material, since the Korean War was raging and a large number of soldiers were returning home with a variety of peripheral nerve injuries. That surgical material and Doctor Vargas's enthusiasm helped me write my graduating thesis on *The Prognosis of Surgically Repaired Peripheral Nerves*. My interest in such injuries lasted into my residency years but waned when I became "distracted from distraction by distraction."

Fifteen years ago, I was particularly fascinated by a presentation made by a Swedish surgeon. He had conducted laboratory studies in primates and was able to demonstrate spectacular spontaneous healing of severed nerves. I recall that he isolated the severed ends of the nerves and left a gap between the two ends. The gap was rapidly filled by new nerve tissue. More interesting was the fact that when he severed the nerve and displaced the ends in a lateral fashion, healing still took place. The growing nerve tissue found its mate anyway.

His results have not been duplicated in humans. Neither electrical nor chemical stimulation has approached the results obtained in primates.

I think peripheral nerve injuries remain a challenge. Good results are frequently obtained from the repair of lacerated "pure" nerves, such as the radial nerve and smaller nerves in the fingers. However, major, "mixed" nerves such as the sciatic nerve and brachial trunks continue to render less than ideal results. I wonder where the answer lies.

SECTION I - TRAUMA

PERONEAL TENDONS – DISLOCATION

While assisting a resident perform a surgical procedure aimed at preventing further dislocation of the peroneal tendons, it occurred to me that the rather complicated procedure we were about to perform was not necessary. We had planned to carry out the well-described bony procedure that would elevate a segment of the fibula and create a deeper groove for the tendons. At that time I noticed, at the bottom of the wound, the fibula-calcaneal ligament. I then speculated that an effective way to stabilize the ligaments would be to re-route them underneath the ligament. Their further dislocation would be permanently prevented.

We proceeded to sever the ligament, place the tendons under the divided fragments and then re-approximate and suture the ligament. We moved the ankle and sub-talar joint passively in all directions and found the tendons easily gliding under the repaired ligament.

We protected the suture in a cast for three week and then allowed unassisted ambulation. The patient did well. Further dislocations did not occur and all other symptoms of irritation subsided. We followed the patient for five years and confirmed a successful outcome.

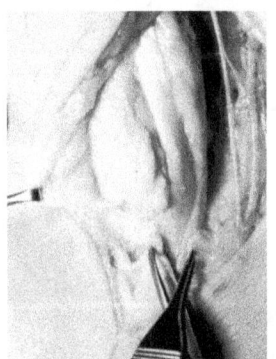 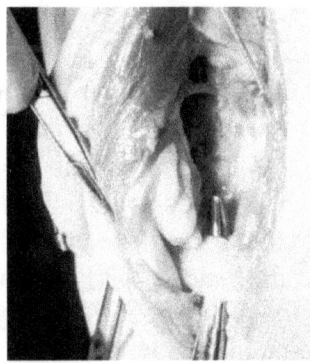 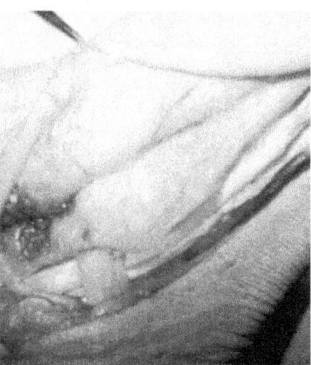

Fig. a b and c. The calcaneo-fibular ligament (a) is sectioned in a transverse manner and the peroneal tendons are placed under the sectioned ligament (b). Then the ligament is repaired (c).

After performing the operation, we reviewed the English literature and were unable to find any evidence that the procedure had been previously reported. As the manuscript (case report) was being prepared, we discovered that the procedure we had considered original had been described in the German literature many years earlier. Our article acknowledged such a finding when it was published in the JBJS. [110].

I had an opportunity to perform the procedure in two more instances. However, I modified it in order to avoid the possibility of rupturing the suture ligature and the formation of adhesions between the repaired ligament and the tendons. The modification consisted of severing the two tendons at different levels, re-routing them under the intact ligament and then suturing the ends together. Rather than immobilizing the ankle in a cast we stabilized it in a heavy soft dressing that kept the joint from significant motion and encouraged active exercises soon after surgery. Both patients did well since re-dislocations did not occur and adhesion between the tendons did not occur.

Several surgeons have performed the procedure, and according to some their results have been satisfactory. I have not seen, however, any reports in the literature, making me wonder if further experiences prompted other surgeons to abandon the technique. I have not been able to think of a possible adverse sequella and suspect that the ligament, subjected to new stresses, probably adapts itself to them without causing damage to the underlying tendons.

PLAFOND FRACTURES: TIBIA

These fractures are frequently managed by means of open reduction and internal fixation. The obsession with the idea that anatomical approximation of intra-articular fragments is essential has led to this practice. There are indeed many plafond fractures that are best treated surgically. There are, however, many which are best treated by nonsurgical means. They are the ones that demonstrate minimal displacement or have a degree of comminution that is beyond adequate surgical reapproximation of the fragments; the condition of the surrounding tissues is precarious; or the patient suffers from brittle diabetes or severe peripheral vascular disease.

Attempts to achieve anatomical reduction in severely comminuted fractures are often an exercise in futility, even in the most skillful hands. Anatomical congruity is not always attained. In the process of carrying out the open reduction, small fragments are de-vascularized and further damaged. Furthermore, since many of these fractures are the result of impaction forces, permanent damage to the cartilage is likely to take place at the time of the injury regardless of the accuracy of the reduction. Post-operative infection is always a probability. At our own institution in the Los Angeles County/USC Medical Center, Don Wiss reported a high incidence of complications not previously acknowledged by others. This type of surgery should not be taken lightly. It is best, sometimes, to accept a shattered joint and fuse it at a later date, than to attempt surgical reconstruction shortly after the initial insult.

The additional immobilization of the ankle joint, which is frequently recommended in the form of external fixation that bridges the tibia with the os calcis, is likely to be detrimental. Articular cartilage needs motion and compression in order to maintain its viability. The fixator prevents those essential ingredients from taking place. Synovial fluid, the nourishment of articular cartilage, does not form in immobilized joints.

Good results have been reported by James Hudson, from the University of Miami, with the use of minimal percutaneous fixation of major fragments, supplemented with the Ilizarof External Fixator. Not enough time has elapsed to tell whether the traumatized cartilage will remain normal.

SECTION I - TRAUMA

It is interesting that in one of Wiss' studies, where a large number of ankle fusions were reviewed, none of the patients came to a fusion because osteoarthritic changes developed following and extra-articular diaphyseal fracture of the tibia that healed with malalignment. (See INCONGRUITY).

Osteoarthritis, as a sequella of these fractures, is frequent but impossible to predict with accuracy. I suspect many patients, sooner or later develop symptoms. The ultimate arthrodesis of the arthritic joint (since prosthetic replacement at this time is not as yet good alternative) is more likely to be successful when the ankle joint was not subjected to previous surgery that required he use of plates and screws. The infection rate, in the latter instance is much higher.

Arthrodesis is currently performed through the arthroscope, by reaming the articular cartilage and creating bleeding subchondral surfaces. Then, screws are driven across the destroyed joint. A good idea. Gallie, the famed Canadian surgeon of half a century ago, reported on successful ankle fusions, where screws were placed across he joint without previous destruction of the articular cartilage. He felt that the immobilization of the join was enough to create arthrodesis. I recently saw a patient on whom I had performed an ankle arthrodesis according to Gallie's teachings. Forty years after surgery, his ankle was solidly fused and asymptomatic.

Infection following open treatment of plafond fractures can be, and usually is, a major complication that frequently requires a long period of time to resolve and often leaves the foot with deformities and ankylosis of the adjacent joints. Amputation surgery, not infrequently becomes the most logical and practical approach to this dreadful complication.

PLICA

Painful symptoms in the knee joint are being explained with increasing frequency on hypertrophy of the plica and a subsequent inflammatory response. Though the plica can be found hypertrophied in some instances, and is probably responsible for the presence of unexplained symptoms, it is my opinion that a great deal of unnecessary surgery dealing with the plica is performed. It is an easy and profitable way out.

Peter Vierhout, from Holland, who performed arthroscopy in patients with so-called bilateral plica syndrome, confirmed my unsupported view. He elected to section the plica in only one knee; while the plica on the other side was left intact. An equal degree of relief of symptoms was obtained in both sides. This observation led him to belief that the distension of the capsule produced by the injectable fluid was sufficient to bring about a resolution of whatever pathology was producing the pain.

A surgeon in our community brags about the fact that in the course of a given short period of time he performs arthroscopic release of painful plica over one hundred times. He must be tired from his frequent trips to the bank!

SECTION I - TRAUMA

I suspect the hypertrophied plica of today is what the hypermobile meniscus or the hypertrophied fat pad was forty years ago. A myth, that is.

R

RADIAL HEAD FRACTURES

The development of smaller plates and screws has made it possible to surgically stabilize many radial head fractures. It would be difficult to argue that excision of the fragments is preferable to anatomical restoration of anatomy. Anatomical reduction is also a more attractive concept. However, open reduction and internal fixation do not always give the anticipated good results. The blood supply of the radial head is precarious and therefore it may be permanently damaged at the time of the initial insult. It can be made worse during the exposure of the fragments and the soft tissue stripping that inevitably must take place. This probable explains the incidence of non-union following internal fixation, which is in the vicinity of 25 per cent.

The mechanism of injury that leads to the fracture is of prognostic significance. In Monteggia fractures, where the ulna shaft and radial head are fractured, the pathology precludes a good result from surgical excision of the head. In this instance, the interosseous membrane is damaged and, therefore, unable to maintain the length of the radius following surgery. Shortening of the radius and the resulting associated distal radio-ulnar sub-luxation often develop. Under these conditions, excision of the radial head should be accompanied with prosthetic replacement of the missing bone.

The complications are even greater when the ulna fracture is at the level of the olecranon or slightly lower, particularly if the ulnar fracture was treated by surgical means. Synostosis is a likely complication. Their surgical correction is seldom a rewarding operation.

Excision of the radial head, either in the care of acute fractures without dislocation, or for the care of localized osteoarthritis is often a gratifying procedure. Under these circumstances radial shortening does not occur, and if it occurs it is usually minimal and inconsequential. Prolonged immobilization of the elbow following surgery is unnecessary (See CAPITELLUM FRACTURES).

SECTION I - TRAUMA

RADIAL NERVE PALSY

Humeral shaft fractures are frequently associated with radial nerve palsy. In our own series we reported a rate of 11%. [116, 131, 155, 157] I believe that radial palsy that appears immediately after a closed fracture of the humeral diaphysis has a good prognosis. Almost without exception, the nerve deficit improves without treatment. However, radial palsy that appears a few days after the injury carries a guarded prognosis. This latter palsy suggests that the nerve has been entrapped within the forming callus. Surgical exploration in this instance is often necessary even though this complication is extremely rare.

William Burkhalter, with whom I worked at the University of Miami in the early 1970's, conducted a most interesting animal laboratory experiment that sheds light into problems related to peripheral nerve injuries, while at the same time provoking additional questions. Using experimental dogs he created fractures of the humeral shaft and made a tunnel in the bone into which he located the intact radial nerve. He then fastened the bony fragments together.

After the fracture healed he exposed the nerve and found it intact and functional. However, if he contused the nerve prior to placing it in the tunnel, recovery did not take place. The nerve was incorporated into the healing bone.

This experiment probably explain the phenomenon of late paralysis but raises the question of why most nerves, which are contused at the time of the injury, and demonstrate deficit from the outset, do not become incorporated into the healing callus. The prognosis is serious if the radial nerve palsy results from a penetrating injury. These injuries are probably best treated with early surgical exploration and repair.

It is customary to fit patients with radial nerve injuries with cock-up appliances that hold the wrist in dorsiflexion and the metacarpal-phalangeal joints in slight flexion, in a effort to prevent permanent flexion contractures. I have learned from experiences with functional bracing of humeral fractures that there is no need to protect the wrist and fingers from possible contractures. The humeral brace allows the patient to extend the elbow, usually within the first two weeks after the injury. In this manner the partially paralyzed wrist that deforms into flexion when the arm is supported in a sling, extends to the neutral attitude and spontaneously corrects the flexion position of the joint. This does not help the thumb, which has a tendency to develop an adduction contracture. The patient, encouraged to use his hand, takes care of preventing such deformity.

SECTION I - TRAUMA

RADIO-ULNAR JOINT: Distal

The integrity of this joint is the key to understanding the behavior of fractures of the distal radius. In most instances a non-comminuted Colles' fractures, not associated with distal radio-ulnar pathology, can be reduced by manipulation and the reduction maintained. If comminution is present or the geometry of the fracture permits proximal sliding of small fragment the reduction may be lost (Fig. 48). This occurs because the surrounding muscles contract, particularly the brachio-radialis. (SEE COLLES FRACTURES).

However, the single most important factor responsible for the stability of these fractures is the condition of the distal radio-ulnar joint. Recurrence of deformity almost always develops when the triangular ligament is ruptured. This is the site of chronic pain in the vast majority of healed distal radius fractures in patients who continue to experience disability. Rarely, is chronic pain found over the distal radius.

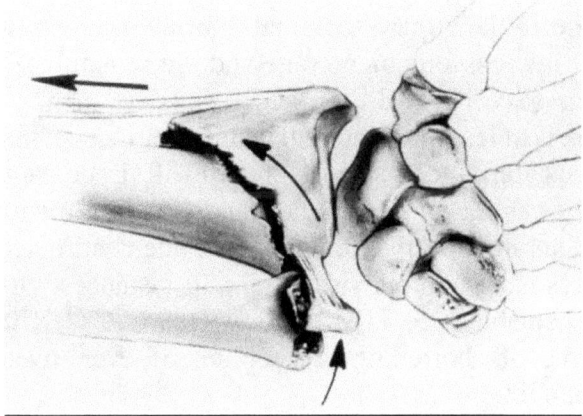

Fig. The oblique extra-articular fracture of the distal radius with an associated fracture of the styloid process readily displaces in a radial direction form the pull of muscles, particularly the brachio-radialis.

SECTION I - TRAUMA

S

SHORTENING IN FRACTURES

The orthopaedic community had always accepted that some shortening was inconsequential following a fracture. If it does not exceed one to one and one-half centimeter it does not produce a limp or late adverse sequella. However, at this time mild shortening is no longer considered an irrelevant mild deviation from the normal, but a "complication"; a complication that cannot be accepted. Since the technology exists to restore normal length to a fractured extremity or correct any angular or rotary changes, it is assumed by many that the technology must be used. So much for good science and common sense.

We have amply documented the fact that closed fractures of the tibia and forearm experience at the time of the initial injury the final shortening. This occurs through a mechanism controlled by the interosseous membrane and the remaining intact soft tissues surrounding the fracture bones. (See TIBIA FRACTURES). (Fig.   ) The shortening in the case of the closed tibia fracture is of less than one-half centimeter in most instances. Fractures of the tibia shorten to a degree determined by the degree of soft tissue damage Having been involved in the care of fractures and have treated thousands of tibial fractures and carefully reporting our findings in the literature, I am convinced that one centimeter of shortening in the treatment of tibial fractures is acceptable virtually in all instances. Oftentimes one and one half centimeter is also acceptable (See TIBIAL SHAFT FRACTURES). Most people, short or tall, with that degree of shortening are seldom, if ever, aware of the length discrepancy and walk without a limp.

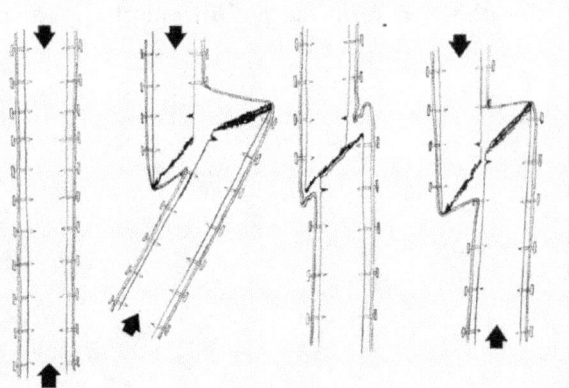

Fig.. Schematic drawing of the likely mechanism responsible for the prevention of shortening Above that experiences initially. Attempts to regain length by means of traction in the case of axially unstable tibial fractures results in recurrence of shortening to its initial degree.

SECTION I - TRAUMA

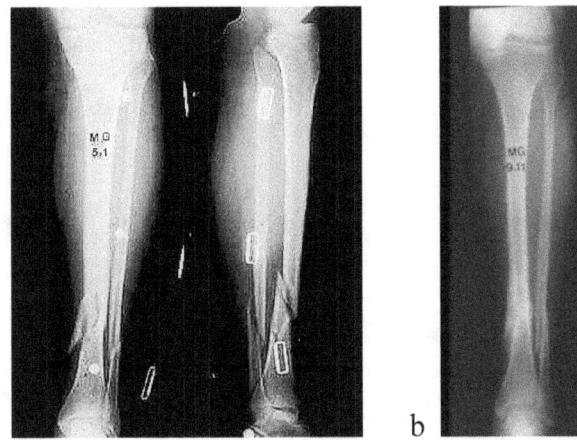

Fig. a and b. Comminuted fracture of he tibia with an associated oblique fracture of the fibula. Shortening did not increase.

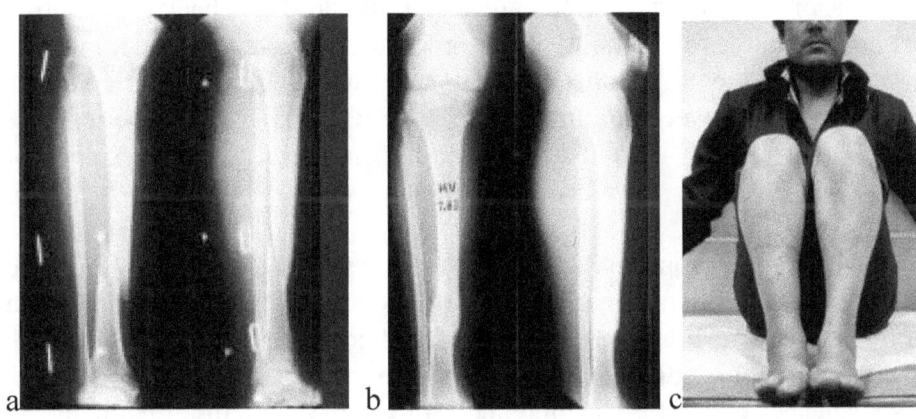

Fig. a, b and c. Closed, oblique fractures of the tibial and fibula. The inconsequential shortening did not increase with graduated weight bearing.

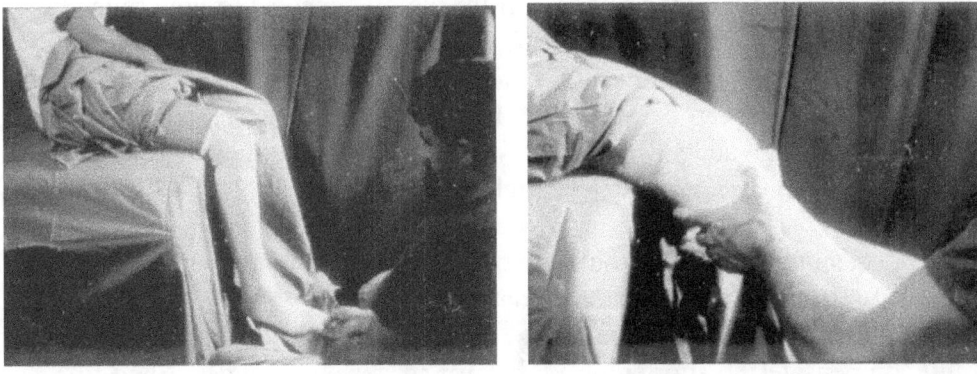

Fig. a and b. During the application of he functional cast the hip and knee should be at 90 degrees (a)..During molding the proximal tibial and patellar tendon the patient's heel should rest on the surgeon's thigh and the quadriceps totally relaxed. The patient's knee should be at 45 degrees (b).

SECTION I - TRAUMA

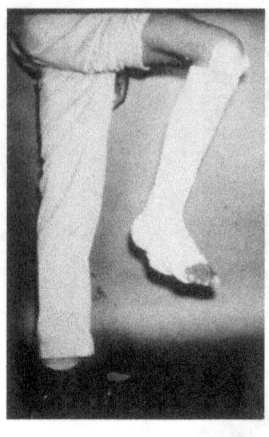 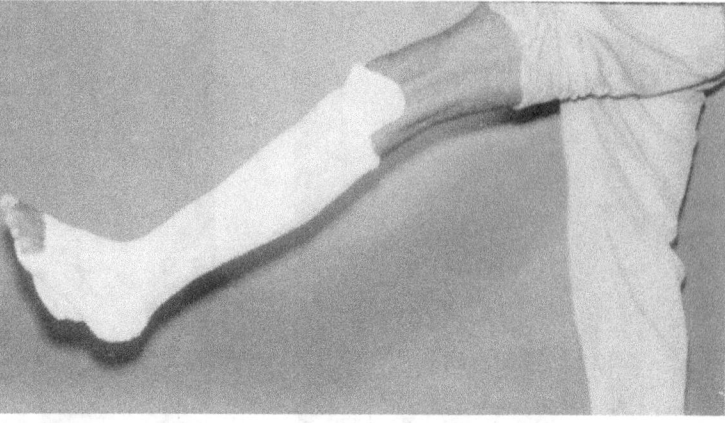

Fig. a and b. The functional cast should permit full flexion and extension of the knee. The cast should extend over the patella and far posteriorly.

The idea that shortening of the degree I am describing produces back pain is absolute nonsense that has no reasonable foundations. That some patients have reported improvement of low-back symptoms with the use of a lift does not prove anything. Even patients without length discrepancies in their lower extremities who have back pain, can experience relief after using a lift. The mechanics involved in low-back pain are very complex and poorly understood.

Ian McNaab, from Toronto, Canada, one of the great thinkers in modern orthopaedics, was not only a brilliant clinician but also a most gifted researcher and educator. For several years, the two of us presented an instructional course at annual meetings of the American Academy of Orthopaedics dealing with the treatment of tibial fractures. He discussed the basic sciences of fracture healing and I took care of fracture treatment. Since my topic centered primarily on the use of braces as the method of treatment, I had to acknowledge that a high percentage of patients treated in that manner heal their fractures with some shortening.

Such a statement always provoked the question from the audience as to how much shortening was acceptable. McNaab, who was humorous and of short stature, upon hearing the question, stood up, faced the audience and said: "For God's sake I am tired of hearing people ask Gus how much shortening can be accepted. I am telling you shortening is not important". He rolled up his pants and added," Look at my legs. They are congenitally short and have never given me a problem". The audience laughed.

When, on another occasion, I was asked the same question, but did not have McNaab to bail me out, I responded, "In my sixteen years old daughter's case I would accept one centimeter; in my elderly mother's situation, I would not hesitate to accept as much as two centimeters, and would compensate the shortening with a lift in her shoe; and if I had to render a verdict in the case of my mother-in-law, I would plate her tibia."

SECTION I - TRAUMA

SHOULDER DISLOCATION

I have vivid recollection of the number of surgical procedures for recurrent anterior dislocation of the shoulder we had to learn when I entered orthopaedics. All were aimed at restricting external rotation of the gleno-humeral joint, and a debate ranged as to the most appropriate method of treatment for the first dislocation. The most popular recommendation was immobilization of the shoulder in a Velpeau sling for a period of six weeks.

Six weeks seems to be, even today, the magic number that all injured tissues require for their repair. I wondered how we arrived at that figure. Where is the evidence that in six weeks collagen fibers or osteons in a fractured bone align themselves in a mature enough way to tolerate the stresses of motion and activity? I have never seen that evidence. It is more likely that by six weeks the painful symptoms that follow any injury subside. The absence of pain suggests that the tissues have healed. The fact remains that at six weeks the strength of the callus in a diaphyseal fracture is minimal, and a re-fracture can be produced with relatively minor force. However, that does not mean that prolonged immobilization is necessary in most instances. Quite the contrary, early subjection of tissues to stresses accelerates the maturation of collagen fibers.

Is six weeks of immobilization sufficient to allow spontaneous healing of the damaged tissues of the dislocated shoulder or is a much shorter time more desirable? I suspect the latter is correct. Furthermore, it is likely that the shoulder can be ranged through a significant degree of motion before it can dislocate again and without placing undesirable tensile stresses on the capsular and ligamentous structures. Can we safely say that immobilization is not necessary at all? That if the pathology experienced at the time of the initial injury does not involve the labrum, a recurrence of the dislocation will not take place regardless as to when the shoulder is actively mobilized again? That the dye is cast at the time of the initial insult and that no matter how long or how short the period of immobilization is, some shoulders (those with labrum damage) will dislocate again; and those free of labrum damage will do well?

Today a popular treatment for recurrent anterior dislocation of the shoulder is thermal capsulorraphy. The possibility exists that it may prove to be an effective method of treatment. Without having any clear understanding of the technique, I am somewhat skeptical about its long lasting benefits. I envision thermal capsulorraphy creating tissues with the physical and characteristics of burned skin: friable, inelastic and thin, which readily ruptures when subjected to tensile stresses.

Perhaps it could be said that the good results from the procedure are obtained when given to people who did not need the treatment in the first place.

SECTION I - TRAUMA

SHOULDER SUB-LUXATION

We do not quite understand why the humeral head frequently experiences sub-luxation following fractures, particularly those located in the proximal humerus. It has been said that perhaps it is due to injury to the axillary nerve. This is unlikely because the phenomenon is often seen in fractures that occur at great distance from the nerve. Furthermore, I have not seen an associated sensory deficit over the territory of the axillary nerve.

Another explanation often advanced is that of a relaxation of the capsule and inhibition of the rotator cuff, which normally assists in maintaining the close contact of the humeral head against the glenoid fossa. There is no evidence that this mechanism really exists.

Spontaneous relocation of the humeral head usually takes place over a relatively short period of time. It has been suggested that abduction exercises should be encouraged in anticipation that a functional deltoid will bring the head into position.

Though, this argument is reasonable it is impractical and at times even detrimental. A patient with a non-rigidly fixed fractured humerus cannot and should not carry out early active abduction exercises. The exercises are not only painful during the early stages of healing, but capable of creating undesirable varus angular deformity.

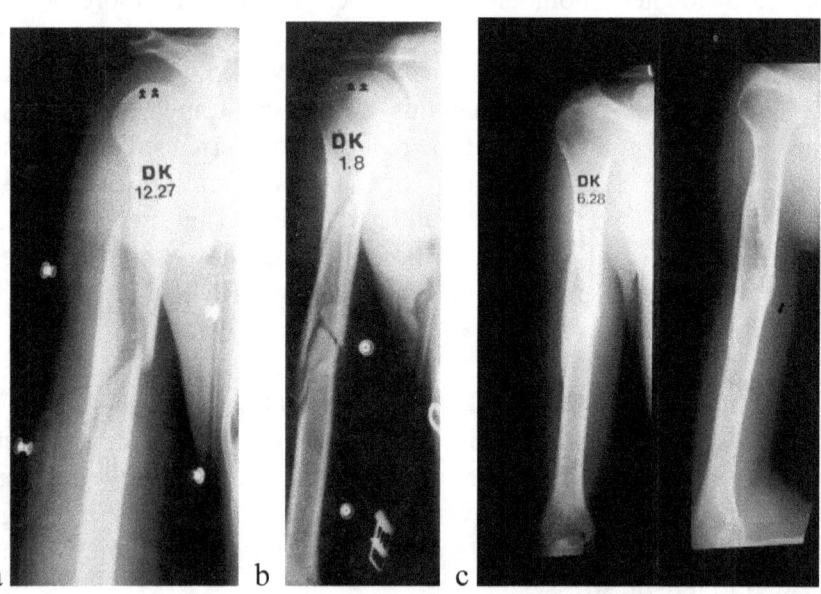

SECTION I - TRAUMA

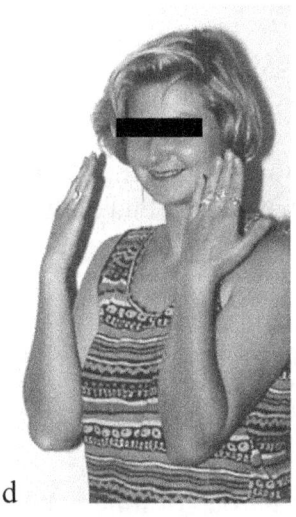 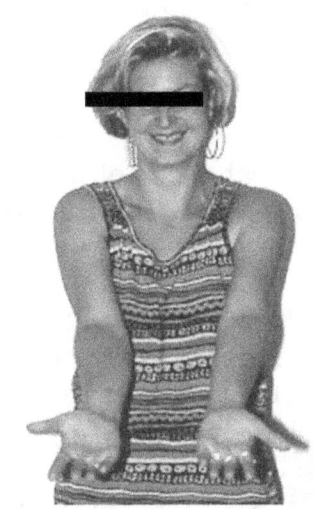

d e

Fig. a, b, c d, e. Shoulder subluxation accompanying a comminuted fracture of the humeral diaphysis. The subluxation promptly improves following the introduction of active flexion and extension of the elbow.

My experiences with the management of hundreds of patients with humeral diaphyseal fractures treated with functional braces have indicated to me that active isometric contraction of the flexors and extensors of the elbow brings about a rapid reduction of the subluxated shoulder (Fig. 49 a, b.). Both groups of muscles have attachments on the scapula and the humeral diaphysis. Their contraction forces the proximal fragment to ride upwards and in that manner eliminate the pathology [150, 151, 155]

SPINAL CORD INJURIES

"Things have changed a great deal since the days when you ran the Rehabilitation Center in Miami", a member of the rehabilitation team at Jackson Memorial Hospital told me recently. "Now we train our paraplegics to walk," he added. "Oh really?" I responded, "Tell me what is it that you do now that we were not capable of doing twenty years ago". "Now we brace them and give them lots of physical therapy". So what else is new? They have gone full circle and are doing the very same things we stopped doing when we found out they did not work. What became obvious to me from listening to my naïve and optimistic friend was that spinal cord rehabilitation programs have become big businesses. In order to promote them, managers of the programs, in order to get the lay community to assist them financially, all kinds of false claims are made. I am sure that the paraplegics he was referring to were young people with very low lesions of the corda equina. The limited injury preserved important muscles necessary for ambulation. Those patients are not paraplegics.

It irritates me a great deal to see movie stars and sports figures suffering from spinal cord lesions being exploited by those who give false and unreasonable hopes for unrealizable outcomes. Not that I do not see the need and the potential benefits of research in this important area. It is even conceivable today to imagine the day when by means of molecular biology a transected spinal cord will be successfully repaired.

SECTION I - TRAUMA

In the mid-sixties, if I am not mistaken, we were excited when we learned the news that a distinguished neurosurgery professor from the University of Toronto had successfully repaired the severed cord of a young man. On the "the evening news" we saw the young man walking while assisted with the aid of crutches. A few days later the truth was revealed. The famed surgeon had not repaired the contused cord. That was the end of the breakthrough as well as the academic career of the professor.

I readily recalled the experience I had with a former classmate of mine, who at 22 became paraplegic following a car accident. He was an in-patient at the Military Hospital in Bogota, Colombia, when I began my surgical internship. One day, as I walked in front of a dark room I heard someone calling me by my first name. Calling out to me was a bearded young man with an ashen face and sunken eyes. Upon recognizing him he gave me details of his ordeal. He had had surgery a few weeks earlier by a group of itinerant French neurosurgeons traveling through Latin America and promising miraculous cures.

The room had that terrible smell that the combination of sweat, urine, feces and pus produces. His back was rotten with decubiti that went down to his pelvis and legs. It was a pathetic scene, and every day for the next fourteen months, until I left Colombia for the United States, I prayed that the next morning he would be found dead and free from his miserable existence.

I became interested in spinal cord injuries after listening to Howard Rusk, from New York, give a talk on the subject at a meeting of the Dade County Medical Society in 1963. The results he was showing and the photographs of paraplegics ambulating with aid of crutches and braces impressed me. Up to that time I had felt that there was nothing that could be done for this unfortunate group of people.

Howard Rusk's talk was a shocking revelation to me. The day after I listened to his presentation, I approached the chief of neurosurgery and asked him his opinion about the most appropriate way to treat paraplegia. He responded by saying that there was nothing to be done, "Those poor bastards develop kidney infections and septicemia and die within a short time." When I mentioned to him the experience with Rusk the previous night he grinned sarcastically. Obviously he did not believe him.

At that time I was having difficulty finding a niche in orthopaedics at the medical school. Previous efforts to devote special attention to specific areas were blocked by my chief with whom I was not getting along well. It occurred to me then to approach the professor and ask him for his support in establishing a rehabilitation program at Jackson Memorial Hospital, where the only token of service was one non-registered physical therapist and two orderlies. They gave massage, applied diathermy and other physical modalities to patients with neurological disabilities and to a variety of orthopaedic, post-traumatic conditions.

The professor agreed with my suggestion and promised to leave me alone. This was the beginning of what I have always considered the most exciting and productive years in

SECTION I - TRAUMA

my entire academic career. Soon I was on a plane to visit Howard Rusk and his famed Institute in Manhattan. There, for the first time in my life I saw the "team approach" to rehabilitation: physical and occupational therapists working in concert with recreational therapists, psychologists, social workers and vocational rehabilitation personnel. The physiatrist was the captain of the team and highly regarded by all. Establishing a similar program in Miami became an obsession from that moment on.

When I returned to Miami I approached the medical director of the hospital and asked him for an area within the hospital where we could begin our program. I was told that there was no space available and that the hospital budget had been cutback in recent months. Such a response did not mean the end of my dream, it only made it stronger. I found a vacant ward in a recently condemned area in the "colored hospital", where termites and lack of air conditioning had prompted the closure of the ward. The very next afternoon I asked one of the physical therapy orderlies to accompany me at the end of the day to visit nursing homes looking for paraplegics. They were not difficult to find since every home had at least one or two. I offered the young paraplegics the opportunity to be admitted to the hospital in the hope that something could be done for them. Readily, they agreed.

With the help of Leroy Collier, the PT orderly, I picked up the first young paraplegic and put him in the front seat of my car after placing newspapers on the vinyl to protect it from the odorous secretions coming from his pressure sores. We transferred him to the hospital emergency room where we had arranged with the orthopaedic resident on call to have him admitted with a diagnosis of an acute fracture of the femur. We repeated the visits to the local nursing homes until we had six paraplegics in the orthopaedic ward.

The second visit to the medical director took place shortly afterwards. His response was no different than the one he had given me a few weeks earlier. My retort, however, was different. I said, "Doctor Gates, I do not care if the empty ward in the "colored hospital" has no air conditioning and the walls are riddled with termites. The six patients we have in the orthopaedic ward come from nursing homes where they did not have air conditioning either. True, they had no termites but lived among cockroaches they saw crawling up and down their paralyzed limbs. Let me have the space and give me a minimum of support personnel to take care of their needs. It is an embarrassment that our hospital, a university hospital, does not have even one registered physical therapist". Doctor Gates acquiesced and within a short time we had the six paraplegics and a number of amputees and stroke victims receiving some type of rehabilitation for the first time.

Little by little we succeeded in obtaining several physical and occupational therapists as well as recreational therapists, social workers, psychologists and vocational counselors. Our protocol with the paraplegic called for fitting their limbs with braces and to teach them how to walk with the aide of crutches. Time, however, taught me many practical lessons. I admit that some young low paraplegics, indeed learned to take a few steps in areas without obstacles of any kind, and for very short distances. However, the overwhelming majority of them never used the braces once they returned home. We decided to discontinue the routine prescription of braces. On occasion, and usually because of a serious request from a paraplegic sincerely convinced that he could master ambulation, we prescribed braces.

SECTION I - TRAUMA

Otherwise, our job consisted of convincing the patients of the futility of the ambulation effort and to maximize their overall rehabilitation potentials.

Their other problems related to sexual activities, bladder and bowel control and psychological needs were managed in the most realistic manner possible.

Practicing that logic we succeeded in building what I considered a first -class Rehabilitation Center, where a pragmatic and serious approach to major musculoskeletal disabilities was the order of the day. Orthopedic residents, as well as residents from urology, family medicine, neurology and neurosurgery had an opportunity to appreciate, if nothing else, what is like to be severely incapacitated and still survive in a hostile environment.

The president of the Paraplegic Association visited us and I explained our philosophy to him. He seemed to be very interested in my remarks but remained quiet during my entire presentation. When I got through I expected some king of complimentary comment, but he wheeled himself out of the room and as he slammed the door said loudly, "I was the worst doctor he had ever met"

His shocking remark made me think and to carefully reassess my philosophy. I must admit that the experience did nothing but stiffen my resolve. I began to explain more clearly to all people in the Center and to all rotating students and residents the rationale of our actions. Even I understood it better and to this day I hold strong feelings on the issue of rehabilitation of spinal cord patients as well as many other physical disabilities. Rehabilitation is one of the most abused medical services in our country and it is a major source of financial profit to many in today's managed care environment. [26, 88, 100, 158] (See REHABILITATION).

SYNOSTOSIS

Synostosis is either produced by the transfixion screw used to repair a syndesmosis or develops spontaneously following a surgically or non-surgically treated fracture of the distal tibia or fibula. It is more likely to occur in surgically treated patients.

The motion that takes place at the distal tibio-talar-fibula joint is complex. Up and down motion is obvious and so are rotary and antero-posterior displacement between the three bones. How necessary are those motions? Can their absence adversely affect the tibio-talar joint? Is the proximal tibio-fibular joint able to compensate for the resulting pathologic change in the distal end of the fibula?

If the presence of synostosis is inconsequential there is no need to worry about it. However, if it is potentially harmful, how does that harm manifests itself? Through arthritic changes at the ankle joint at the proximal tibio-fibular joint? It is commonly recommended that syndesmotic screws be removed as soon as the soft tissues have healed, because if left in place for a long time they break from fatigue of the metal. This is true in some instances, but not necessarily in all instances. It is more likely that the hole, into which the screw is

SECTION I - TRAUMA

placed, enlarges with time and all stresses on the screw are eliminated. That being the case, should we always remove the screws?

Similar questions can be raised in regards to the proximal tibio-fibular synostosis. Residual pain is not uncommon following unreduced subluxations of the proximal tibio-fibular joint, and arthritic changes are frequently seen. The abnormal motion between the unstable components is much greater than that present in the distal fibula-talus-tibia joint. The insertion of the lateral collateral ligament and the biceps tendon on the head of the fibula, in addition of the muscle pull from the several dorsiflexors and plantar flexors of the ankle, render this joint more vulnerable to chronic degenerative disease.

Is fusion of the proximal tibio-fibular joint a procedure free of complications? Can it be performed with impunity in the athlete that places great demands on his or her legs? We have recently learned that patients who have a large segment of the fibula used as a vascularized bone graft for the treatment of avascular necrosis of the femoral head are prone to develop chronic ankle pain. Is it because of loss of normal motions at that level or the addition of new demands on the complex joint?

It is interesting that my personal experiences with fibular ostectomies performed in the treatment of tibial non-unions have indicated that some of the most gratifying results were obtained in those instances where a permanent non-union developed at the ostectomy site. (See NON-UNIONS).

T

TALUS FRACTURES

Talus fractures are, in my opinion, one of the most challenging fractures. The complication rate is high and avascular necrosis is still a common sequella. There is a great deal of information in the orthopaedic literature regarding diagnostic techniques available to classify the various types of fractures; the prognostic findings, such as the Hawkins sign for avascular necrosis, and techniques for internal fixation.

In spite of the many advances in imaging technology, surgical instrumentation and sophisticated surgical approaches the prognosis for these fractures remains poor.

There is something contradictory about the manner in which we reason our approach to issues related to possible avascular necrosis and the protection against excessive weight bearing on the injured bone. Since the stresses on the talus are very high during ambulation it is recommended that weight bearing be curtailed as much as possible until the fracture is healed. That makes sense. However, it the fractured talus is vascular, the time required for the fracture to heal is only a few weeks. If the bone is avascular the time required for its revascularization- if revascularization is to occur – could be many, many months. Therefore, in the latter situation avoidance of weight bearing would be mandatory during the entire period of time required by the revascularization process

Initially, the avascular necrotic bone retains its mechanical properties, as do all dead bones. Its collapse is not likely to occur as long at it remains avascular. Collapse takes place only when revascularization begins since it is then that the bone gets soft. ! However, the common practice is to curtail weight bearing during the early stages of the condition while the bone is not collapsible, but to permit weight bearing when the bone is getting soft from increased revascularization!

The whole approach is totally unphysiological. However, I do not know a solution to the dilemma. After all, who is going to remain non-weight bearing for a year or two, which may the time required for the bone to revascularize and regain its mechanical properties? Perhaps, a device such as a brace that unloads the fractured talus could conceivably be used. But such a brace or cast does not exist. To believe that a so-called PTB cast would do the job runs contrary to popular belief. I designed the first such cast and soon learned that it unloads the fractured tibia only minimally. Certainly, not enough to make a difference. (See TIBIA SHAFT FRACTURE).

It is not uncommon to see patients who have experienced talus fractures, treated either surgically or non-surgically, who after months of apparent success find themselves disabled from osteoarthritic changes. Fusions of various types are then performed with mixed results. By the time the arthrodesis procedures are contemplated, it is difficult to tell which joints are responsible for the painful symptoms since the tibio-talar, subtalar and the talo-navicular joints may be compromised.

In view of the discouraging picture presented by the fractured talus one cannot help but wonder if more aggressive measures should be taken early. Is it logical to suggest that, in those instances when it seems obvious that revascularization is impossible, a resection of the body of the talus and fusion of the tibia to the distal talar fragment may be a viable option. This type of fusion, first described by Blair a number of years ago, has been known to function quite well in many instances. It preserves the height of the hind foot while permitting subtalar and talo-navicular motion.

Another possibility would be an early, but not immediate, triple arthrodesis. This approach sounds too radical. However, it may be a conservative one if one realizes that the arthrodesis will eventually be, in many instances, the ultimate treatment, after everything else has failed.

SECTION I - TRAUMA

TIBIAL CONDYLAR FRACTURES

Refined instrumentation has made surgical stabilization of tibial condylar fractures a good treatment. It is, however, not a panacea. These fractures are often the result of major trauma and elderly patients, particularly those suffering from either atherosclerosis and or diabetes are very likely to develop complications such as infection and or skin necrosis. These can be major complications that may even lead to amputation. Obviously, in the younger individual the results are usually better.

All condylar fractures, in the absence of associated plateau depression do not necessarily require surgery. The knee joint tolerates incongruity to degrees not generally known. Lansinger, from Sweden, Christensen, from Denmark, and Dietz, from Iowa, among many others have reported on long term follow-up of incongruous tibial condyles with most impressive clinical results. Lansinger, for example, states that he documented excellent results, as long as thirty years after injury, in patients who had as much a one centimeter of step-off deformity at the fracture site. Though my experience is limited, I was able to produce similar findings following the treatment of condylar fractures using articulated functional braces [19].

We conducted laboratory studies using cadaver specimens that led to some very interesting observations. In human cadavers we produced non-displaced osteotomies of the condyles that simulated the variety of fractures encountered in clinical practice: isolated fractures of the lateral condyle, isolated fractures of the medial condyle and fractures of both condyles. With each of these fractures we studied the role of the fibula in the behavior of the tibial condylar fractures.

The laboratory specimens were subjected to vertical loading and the produced changes in the relationships of the fragments were monitored with cineradiography and photographs. We concluded that the changes seen in the laboratory corresponded very well with those observed in clinical situations: 1) Medial condylar fractures readily collapse into varus under vertical loading. (Fig. 50). 2) Lateral condylar fractures with intact fibulae did not collapse into valgus. It appears that the intact fibula, supporting the lateral condyle, prevents the collapse. (Fig. 51). 3). Fractures of the lateral condyle with an associated fibula fractures readily collapsed into valgus. (Fig. 52). 4). Fractures of both condyles with intact fibulae collapsed into varus (fig. 53) and, 5) Fractures of both condyles with an associated fibula fractures were depressed evenly but without varus or valgus deformity (Fig. 54). If the force applied had been increased it is logical to assume that major depression would have been noticed. (Fig. 55) that internal fixation of non-displaced or minimally displaced condylar fractures is not always necessary and that the treatment must also be based on the type of fracture and the condition of the fibula. In our clinical study we had assumed that ligamentous and meniscal injuries had been ruled out in our patients, before initiating the closed functional treatment. This work was done prior to the invention of the MRI, which I suspect would have revealed pathology we could not identify through simple clinical examination. The lessons learned from the project, however, should not be too quickly dismissed.

SECTION I - TRAUMA

Years later, still suspecting that incongruity does not necessarily lead to late osteoarthritis, we conducted laboratory studies using adult rabbits to determine the effects of step-off deformities in the knee joint, with and without associated instability. (See INCONGRUITY).

It is very likely that patients who become osteoarthritics do so either because the incongruity was too severe; irreparable damage to the articular cartilage took place at the time of the original insult; or unrecognized associated ligamentous instability, or meniscal tears was present. I suspect also that when surgery is performed to reapproximate fractured fragments, particularly in comminuted fractures, major damage to the blood supply of the small fragments can be done [38, 41].

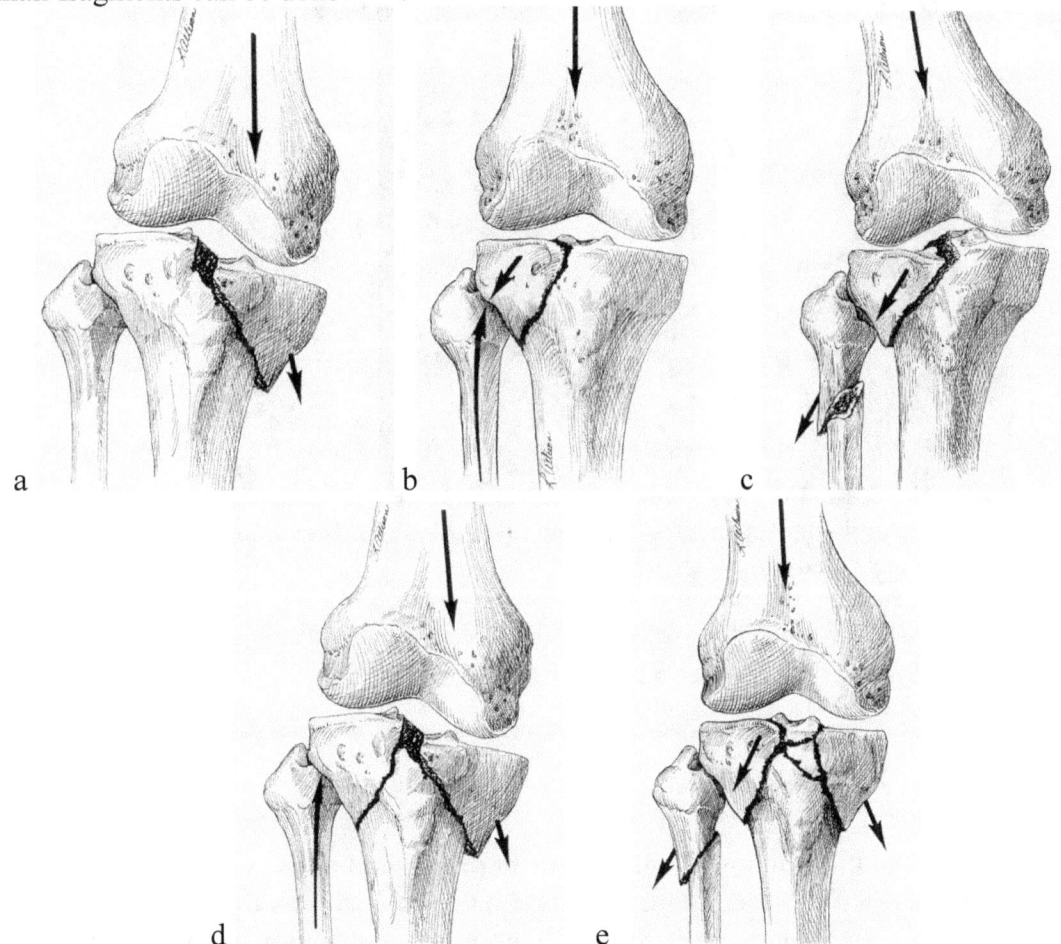

Fig. a through e   Oblique fracture of the medial condyle readily displaces distally creating a varus deformity (a). Oblique fracture of the lateral condyle with an intact fibula does not displace further (b). Oblique fracture of the lateral condyle with an associated fracture of the fibula displaces distally creating a valgus deformity (c). Oblique fractures of both condyles with an intact fibula deform into a varus deformity (d). Oblique fractures of both condyles, with associated fibular fracture depress evenly (e).

SECTION I - TRAUMA

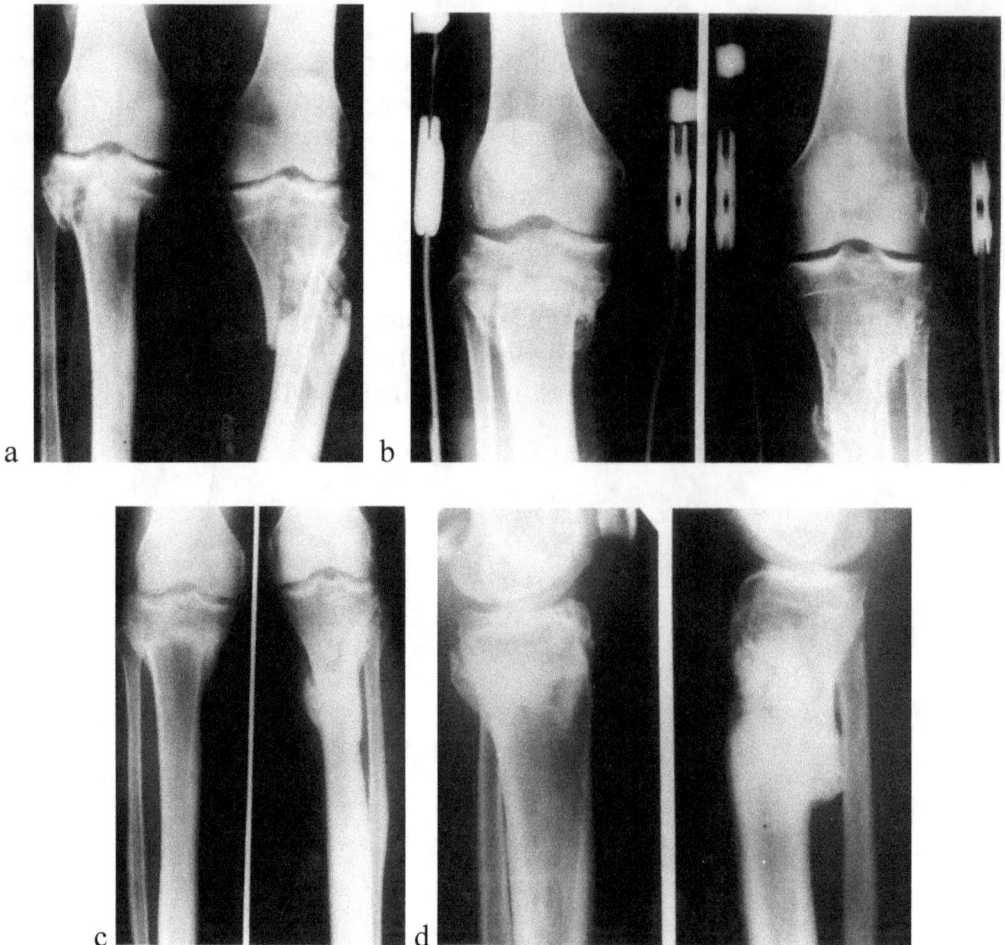

Fig. a through d. Fractures of the tibial condyles ® and proximal tibia (L). Thee transverse nature of the medial tibial condyle prevented a varus angular deformity.

TIBIAL PLAFOND FRACTURES (See Plafond Fractures)

TIBIAL SHAFT FRACTURES

There is no such a thing at this time as a single treatment that should be used consistently in the management of tibial shaft fractures. Good results are reported with a variety of surgical and non-surgical approaches, be it plating, external fixation, intramedullary nailing, casting or bracing. External fixation is still the preferred mode of treatment of fractures with severe bone and soft tissue damage in spite of the fact that several reports have indicated good results with intramedullary nailing. The peripheral de-vascularization of the bone diaphysis, produced by the injury is compounded by the damage to the endosteal circulation during the reaming and introduction of a nail. This trauma to the circulation of the bone may explain the reported instances of massive necrosis of the entire bone.

Since plating is predicated on the mistaken belief that rigid immobilization is good for fracture healing, the use of plates has fallen into disrepute in recent years. It took a long

SECTION I - TRAUMA

time for the orthopaedic community to recognize how unphysiological the method is. Rigid immobilization delays healing. Also the callus that ultimately bridges the fragments is of poor quality. [38, 78, 15, 122]

I suspect that the day might come when, as in the case of femoral fractures, intramedullary nailing will become the universal treatment of choice. I have felt this way for several years as I see progressive improvements made particularly in imaging technology. This observation prompted me in the late 1980's to suggest and participate in the design of the first Titanium intramedullary nails for the tibia and femur. (See INTRAMEDULLARY NAILS). I felt that there were many tibial fractures where intramedullary fixation should be the preferred method of treatment.

This might surprise those who have identified my name with functional bracing of fractures and my long advocacy of non-surgical treatment of many long bone fractures. Common sense dictated to me that it would be foolish to ignore the progress made in the field of fracture stabilization with the use of intramedullary nails.

Having said the above I still claim that the non-surgical treatment is the best choice in the management of many closed tibial fractures, particularly for those produced by low energy injuries. Intramedullary nailing of those fractures does not constitute and improvement over functional bracing. I base this statement on my personal experience with the over 3000 tibial fractures I have treated personally. (Fig. 56 a, b, c.).

The study of tibial fractures dominated my academic career for over forty years. I reviewed and/ or participated in the analysis of data, and was involved in a large number of laboratory investigations that led to the publication of dozens of peer-reviewed scientific papers .[92, 93, 101, 103, 109, 119, 123, 125, 130, 147, 150, 151, 152, 172] For our work on fracture healing and behavior, Loren Latta and I received the most coveted research award in America, the Kappa Delta Award. For the work I conducted on Functional Bracing I also became the recipient of the Nicholas Andre Award from the Association of Bone and Joint Surgeons.

At this point in time it is not appropriate to create a strong analogy between the femur and the tibia in regard to the place and value of intramedullary fixation. In the case of the femur there is no doubt that the surgical approach has many advantages over skeletal traction: hospitalization and its cost is significantly reduced; the adverse sequela from prolonged bed rest are eliminated; rehabilitation is short and minimal; nonunion is low; and problems related to deformities are significantly less. (See INTRAMEDULALLARY NAILING OF TIBIAL FEMORAL FRACTURES).

In the case of the closed tibial fracture, those advantages do not always exist. Quite the contrary, at this time, the complications from intramedullary nailing are relatively high. Closed functional bracing does not require hospitalization in the overwhelming majority of instances. Patients with low energy produced fractures are treated in the emergency room of hospitals where the initial stabilization in a cast is carried out. They return home where they continue to walk with aide of crutches. Within one to three weeks (depending on the degree of swelling and discomfort) patients have the above-the-knee cast removed and replaced with an adjustable and removable brace that allows them to mobilize all joints in the injured limb and to ambulate in a manner that encourages progressive weight bearing. (Fig. 57 a, b, c., 58 a, b., 59 a,b,c., 60 a,b,c., 61 a,b,c. 62 a,b,c,d,e,f., 63, a,b,c,d,, 64 a,b,c. and 65 a,b,c,).

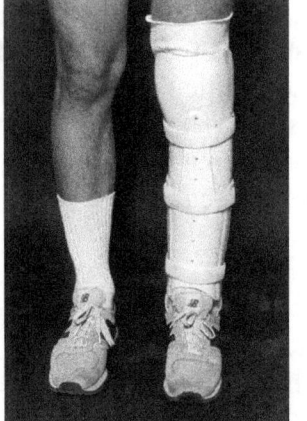
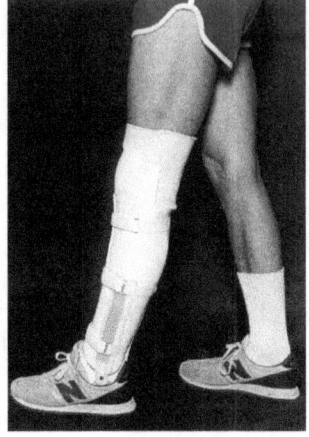

Fig. a and b. Prefabricated brace used in the treatment of tibial fractures.

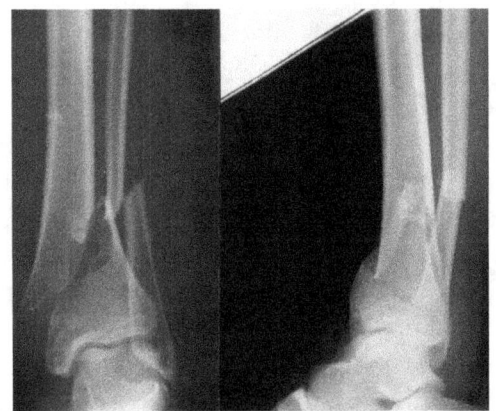
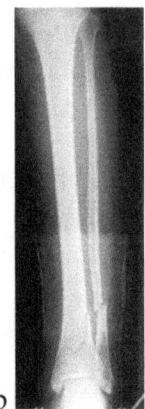
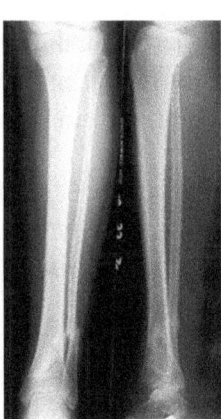

Fig. a and b. Oblique fracture with associated fibula fracture treated with a functional brace.

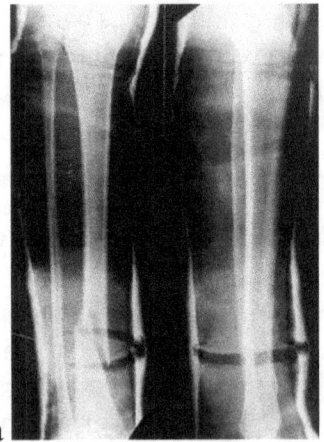
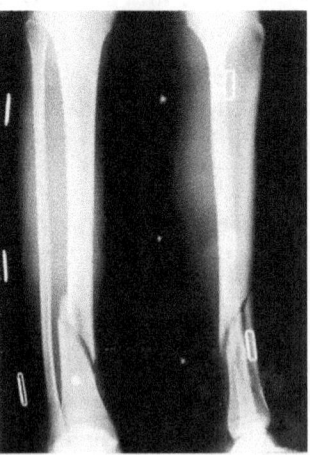

Fig. a and b. Oblique fracture without the desirable associated fibular fracture. These fractures should not be braced since the varus deformity cannot be manually corrected.

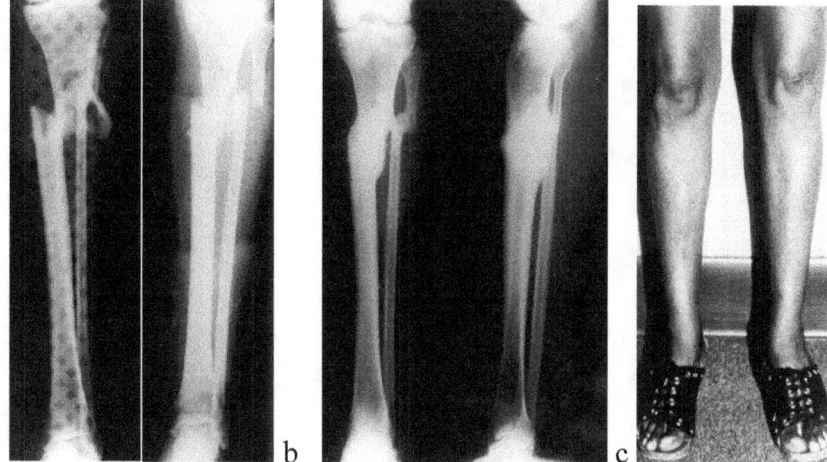

Fig. a, b and c. Comminuted fracture with associated fracture of the fibula treated with a functional brace. The translatory deformity was corrected manually

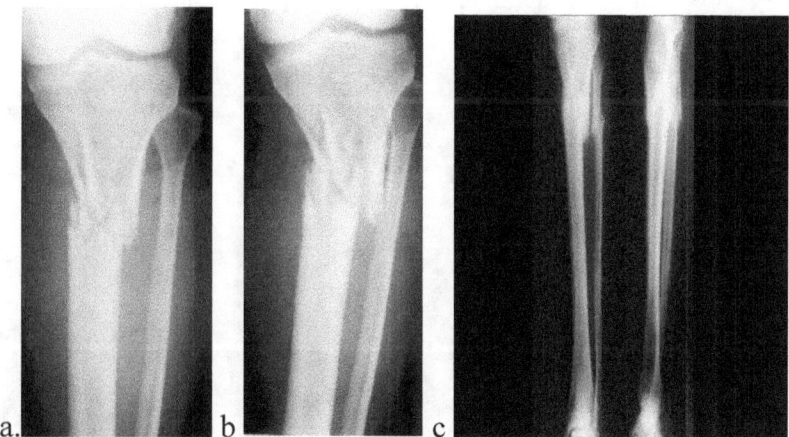

Fig. a, b and c. Comminuted fracture of the proximal tibia without an associated fracture of the fibula. These fractures readily angulate into varus. The deformity was treated with an osteotomy of the fibula, followed by the application of a functional brace.

SECTION I - TRAUMA

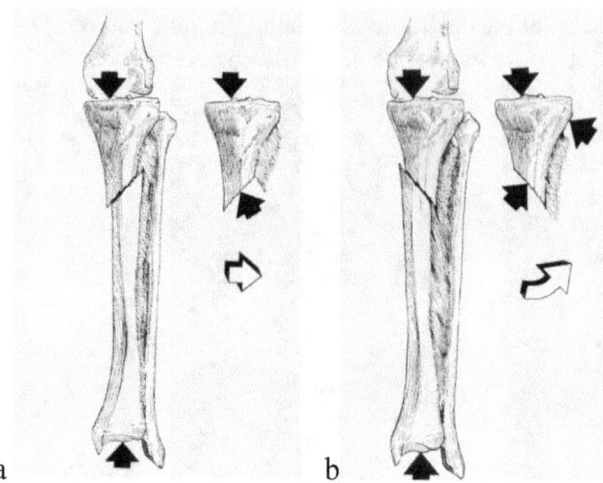

Fig. a and b. In the case of the fractured tibia with an intact fibula, the direction of the fracture determines whether or not a varus deformity is likely to occur. It an oblique fracture runs from proximal to distal and from lateral to medial, the tendency of the proximal fragment to drift into varus is partially or completely prevented by the abutment between the two fragments.

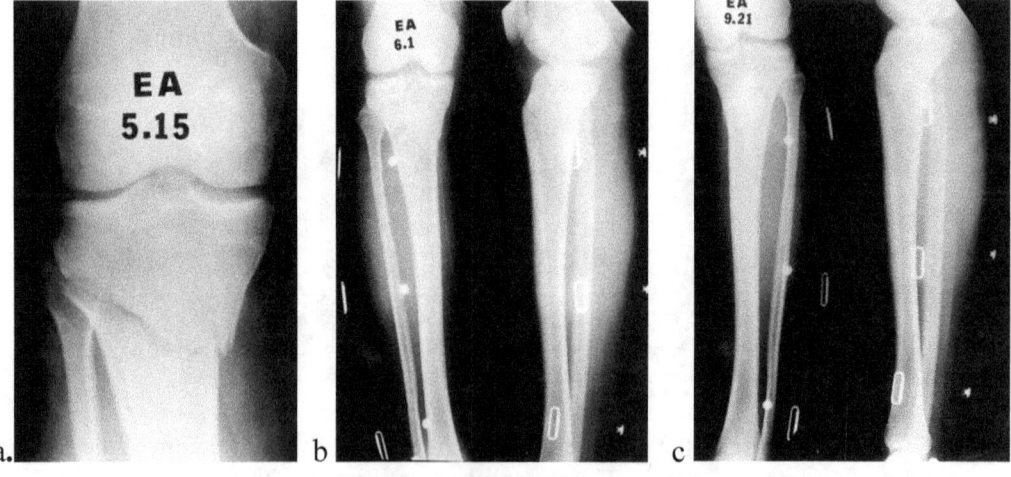

Fig. a b, and c. Fracture of the proximal tibia with intact fibula. Notice the direction of the fracture.

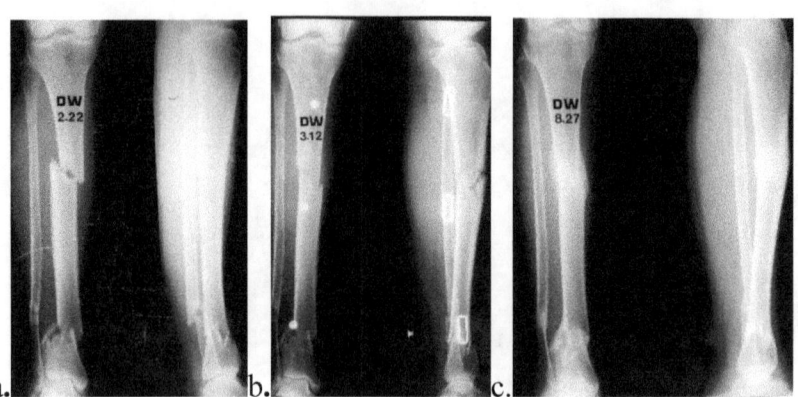

SECTION I - TRAUMA

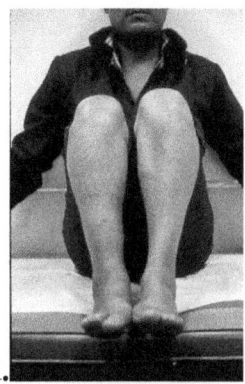
Fig. a, b, c and d. Segmental fracture treated with a functional brace.

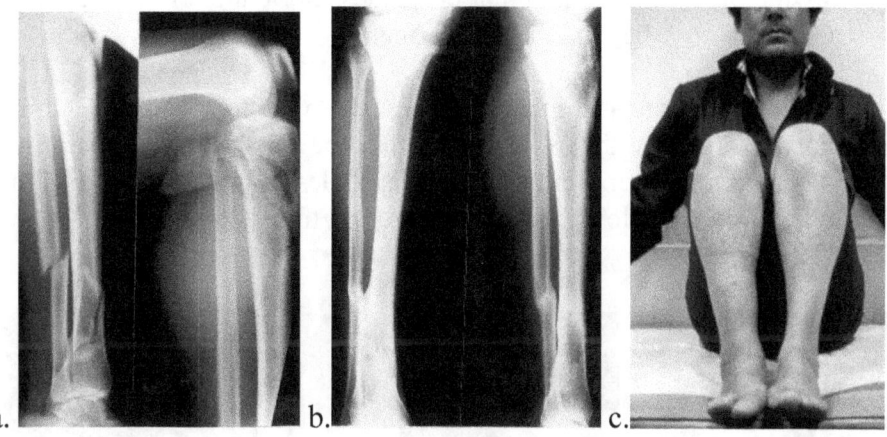
Fig. a, b and c. Segmental fracture of the tibia and fibula treated with a functional brace.

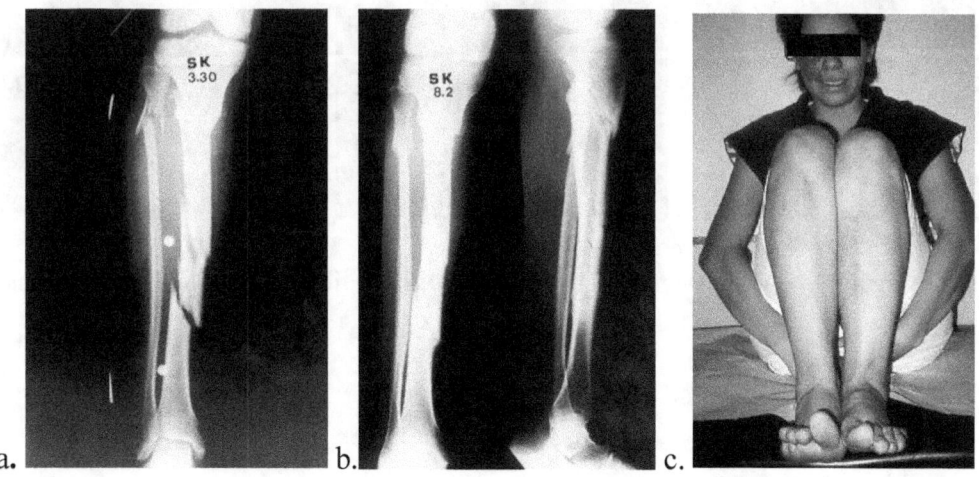
Fig. a, b and c. Closed double segmental fracture treated with a functional brace.

SECTION I - TRAUMA

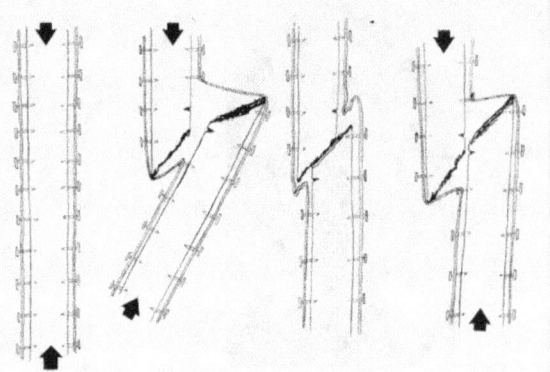

Fig.. Schematic drawing of the mechanism that precludes shortening of closed fractures beyond the initial one.

It is not appropriate to create a strong analogy between the femur and the tibia in regard to intramedullary fixation. In the case of the femur the sur and minimal; non-union is low; and problems related to deformities are significantly less gical approach has many advantages: the complication rate is low; and hospitalization time is reduced.

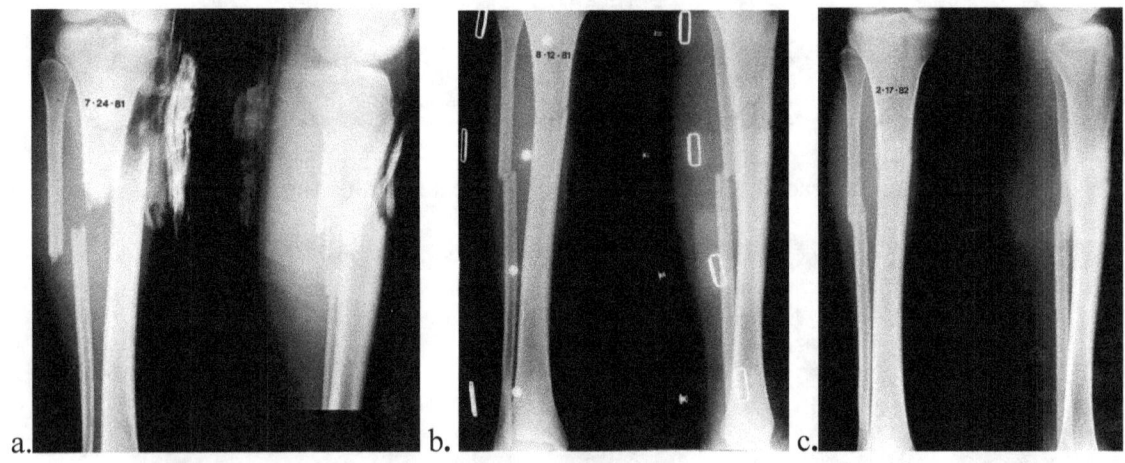

Fig. a b and c. Low-grade open, transverse fracture of the tibia and fibula treated with a functional brace.

SECTION I - TRAUMA

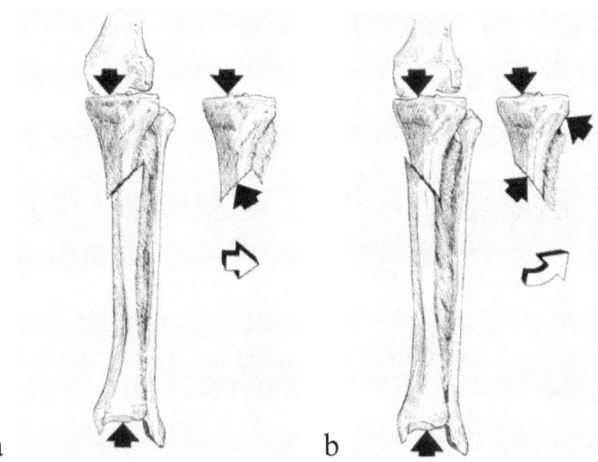

Fig. a and b. If the fractured tibia with an intact fibula runs from lateral to medial and from proximal to distal a marked varus deformity is prevented by the opposing distal tibial fragment (a). If the fracture runs form medial to lateral and from proximal to distal a marked varus deformity may occur since the proximal fragments is unopposed by the distal fragment (b).

Some has criticized functional bracing on the grounds that shortening cannot be prevented and that angular deformities can occur. Braces cannot prevent shortening. This is why functional bracing should not be used in anticipation of preventing shortening. The final shortening of closed fractured tibias is determined at the time of the injury; it does not change with the introduction of graduated weight bearing ambulation. The initial degree of soft tissue pathology determines the shortening. This shortening does not change unless additional damage to the tissues is inflicted.

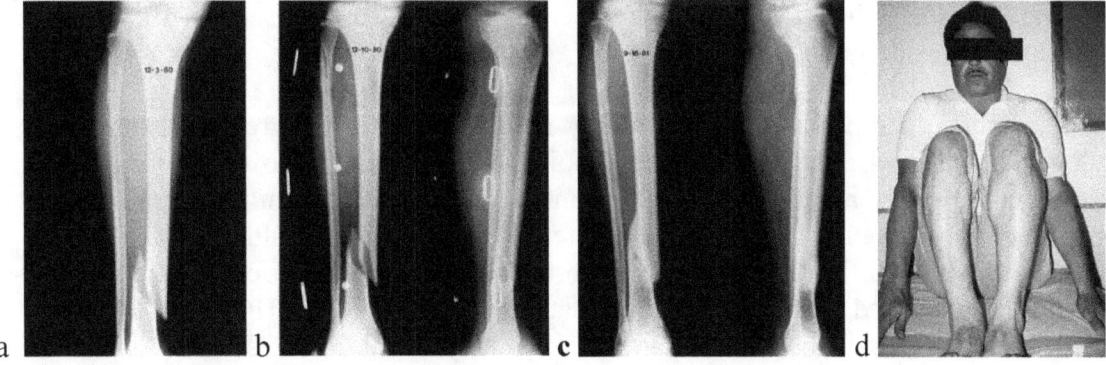

Fig. a b, c and d. Closed oblique fracture of the tibia with associated proximal fibula fracture successfully treated with a functional brace. Notice the mild shortening ot the fractured leg.

Only axially unstable tibial fractures that have initially acceptable shortening should be treated with functional braces in anticipation that the shortening will not increase. If the axially unstable fracture is subjected to traction in order to correct unacceptable shortening, the regained length is lost upon the initiation of ambulation.

Intramedullary nailing of the tibia is still beset with major technical difficulties when used in the management of fractures of the proximal third of the bone. Residual angular deformities are frequent. Infection from closed intramedullary nailing is low but it has been reported in virtually all series.

The incidence of nonunion from IM nailing is higher than from functional bracing. Our latest reported series of one thousand closed diaphyseal tibial fractures indicated a non-union rate of 1.1%. A nonunion rate that very few series of surgically treated fractures have been able to achieve [129, 138, 156].

In several instances massive necrosis of the tibial cortex has been reported in the literature. A major complication. The same is true for the major complication of iatrogenic Muscle Compartment Syndrome (See COMPARTMENT SYNDROMES).

It is well known that intramedullary nailing is very frequently associated with residual knee pain brought about by the trauma created by the insertion of the nail either through the patellar tendon or adjacent to it. This pain is particularly disabling for people whose occupation requires kneeling. Removal of the nail for reasons of knee pain is estimated to be necessary in over fifty percent of all patients. What makes matter worse is that the removal of the nail often fails to eliminate the pain. According to some orthopaedists, a high percentage of patients continue to have painful knees for many months or years.

Breakage of the interlocking screws is common and has been reported as being as high as 15%. Bending of the nail is also a likely complication, particularly when used in comminuted fractures or in heavy people with small medullary canals. The removal of broken screws is not always necessary, but when required the surgical procedure can be a rather complex and difficult one. Removing a bent nail that also shows broken screws becomes a mammoth undertaking.

One argument in support of intramedullary nailing has been the greater assurance that length can be restored. It is indeed a good point. This argument, however, must be objectively assessed. We have been able to document that the overwhelming majority of closed tibial fractures shorten less than one centimeter at the time of the insult. We have also been able to accurately confirm that the initial shortening does not increase following the initiation of early, graduated weight bearing ambulation. (Fig. 66). (See SHORTENING) . Therefore, it can be safely said that if most patients with closed tibial fractures have less than one centimeter of initial shortening, the same number will have less than one centimeter of shortening upon completion of healing. This degree of shortening is inconsequential since it does not produce a limp and it is not associated with any adverse sequella. (Fig. 67)

I strongly support the use of intramedullary nailing for axially unstable fractures of the tibial diaphysis – i.e. oblique, comminuted or spiral- that experience initially more than one and one half centimeter of shortening. Not because a few millimeters of additional shortening beyond that necessarily create a problem, but because many people can display a limp when the shortening approaches 2 centimeters. Obviously, the surgeon, in concert with the patient must determine whether surgery or a lift in the shoe constitutes the safest and most appropriate treatment. Transverse fractures can be manipulated, reduced and made axially stable. They should heal without shortening.

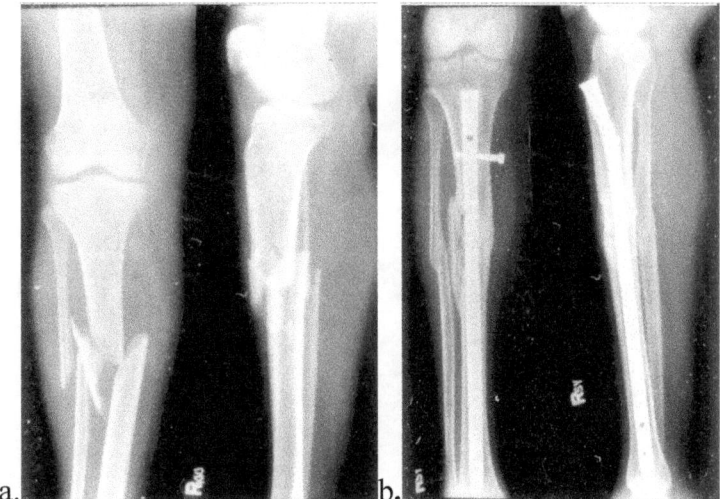

Fig. a and b.   Shortened closed fracture of the proximal third of the tibia and fibula (a) successfully treated with an intramedullary nail (b).

Another argument in favor of intramedullary nailing is that it guarantees maintenance of alignment. In actuality, nailing does not "guarantee" perfect alignment of the fractured bone, but it does indeed offer a greater chance of providing better anatomical alignment. As I indicated early, fractures located in the proximal third of the tibia, are treated with intramedullary nails, frequently leave a residual angular deformity. The same is true, though to a lesser extent, with fractures of the distal third of the bone.

Our data has indicated that functional bracing of closed tibial diaphyseal fractures can render acceptable results in regards to angular deformities. Ninety-five of those fractures healed with less than 8 degrees of varus angulation; and 90% with less than 6 degrees [138, 156]. Those degrees of angulation – the most common angular deformity – are cosmetically acceptable. I have shown residents in training many patients with varus angular deformities of 5 to 10 degrees, where they were unable to tell which leg had the deformity.

In general, patients with tibial fractures treated with intramedullary nails do not return to unprotected ambulation and function without discomfort sooner than those with comparable fractures treated with functional braces. The fact that some patients are able to walk in that manner at approximately six weeks following nailing does not negate the fact that some patients treated with functional braces can do likewise.

To argue that a nail should be used in order to preclude the presence of inconsequential deviations from the normal, more specifically a shortening that does not produce a limp and an angular deformity that is aesthetically acceptable, is difficult to justify. Addressing surgically non-existing problems is not, in my opinion, a logical and sound approach.

SECTION I - TRAUMA

It would be wrong to leave the subject of tibial fractures without touching on the ill effects of angular deformities regarding the possibility of late osteoarthritic changes developing in the adjacent knee and ankle joints. There is no evidence to demonstrate that a few degrees of angulation in a tibial fracture leads to subsequent arthritic changes (See ANGULATION)

U

ULNAR FRACTURES

Watson Jones, the British surgeon whose influence in orthopaedics in the 1949's and 1950's extended throughout the world, made the statement that even though he was a firm believer in the non-surgical treatment of fractures, the isolated ulnar fracture was one he thought it should be treated surgically. He justified his remark by saying that a long arm cast did not "immobilize" the fragments well enough to permit uneventful healing. Based on my experiences with the close functional treatment of many different fractures, I am comfortable stating that if isolated ulnar fractures do not always do well when "stabilized" in above-the-elbow casts is not because the cast does not immobilize enough but because it immobilizes too much. [92, 112, 114, 142]

I have spoken a number of times to orthopaedists from poor regions in Africa, Asia and Latin America, and asked them how ulnar fractures are treated in their respective areas of the world. Most respond such injuries are seldom brought to their attention; that the local "healer" splints the broken arms for a short while. The physicians are aware that the fractures occurred because of the residual lump on the arm.

Our success rate in the management of isolated ulnar fractures treated with braces that extend from below the elbow to just above the wrist, is due to the fact that physiological motion at the fracture site takes place, creating a most desirable environment for uneventful healing (Fig. 66). Our non-union rate in a group of 444 fractures treated with braces was 1% [142]. The group included a very large percentage of open fractures (Fig. 69)

Our data indicated that the level of the fracture does not influence the final outcome. However, others have suggested that fractures located in the proximal third are associated with a greater loss of limitation of motion. To some extent they are correct.

Upon conclusion of healing the permanent limitation of motion is minimal. The degree of angulation that normally takes place in isolated ulnar fractures is usually mild. The mechanism of injury is, in most instances, a direct blow over the bone and the displacement of the fragments is mild because the intact radius prevents major displacement and the strong interosseous membrane further tethers the fragment into position. The final displacement rarely exceeds 5 degrees; a deformity associated with none or minimal permanent limitation of prono-supination. (Fig. 70 a, b, c. and 71 a, b, c, d.)

SECTION I - TRAUMA

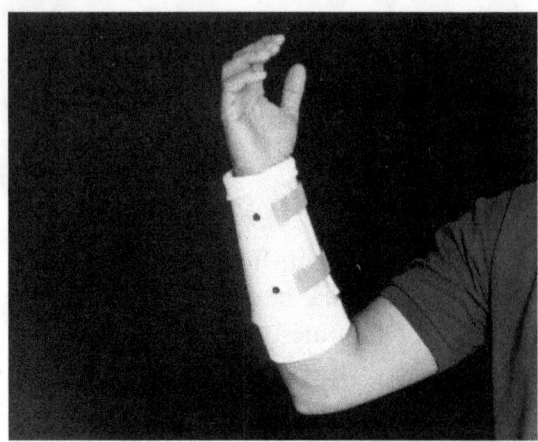

Fig.. Prefabricated ulna fracture brace, which usually applied a few days after the initial insult.

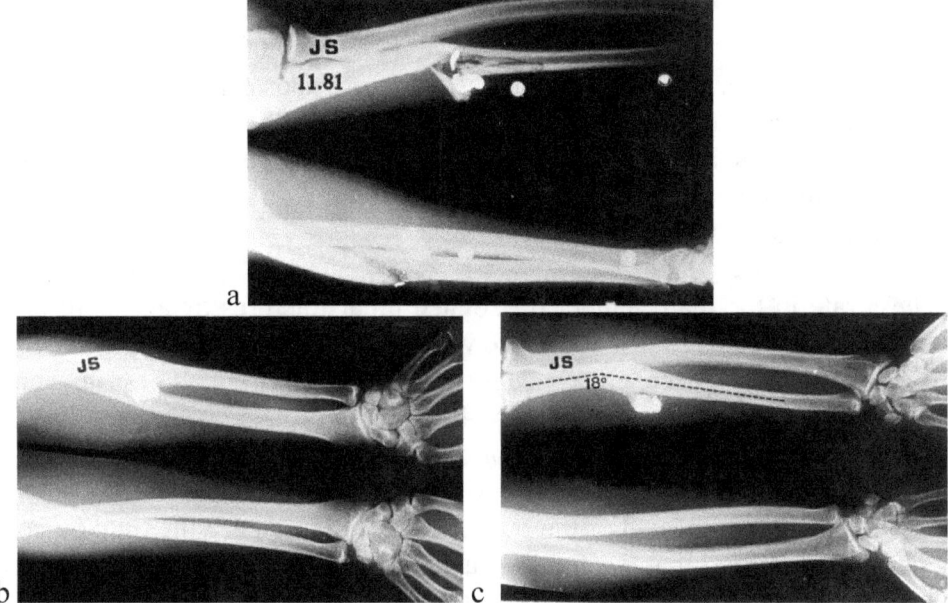

Fig. a, b and c. Fracture of the proximal third of the ulna produced by a low-velocity projectile (a). Pronation and supination views of the forearm (b and c)

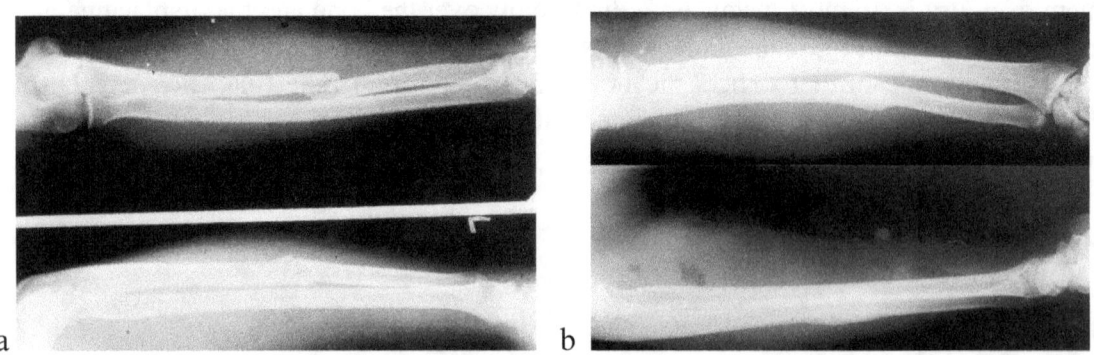

SECTION I - TRAUMA

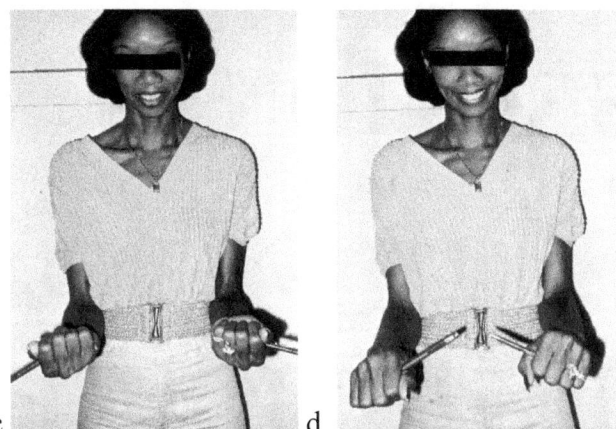

Fig. a, b c, and d. Isolated fracture of the proximal third of the ulna (a) treated with a functional brace. The fracture healed uneventfully (b) The patient experienced a mild permanent limitation of pronation, which was inconspicuously compensated with shoulder rotation.

I believe that the injured forearm is best stabilized in a long arm cast for a few days until the acuteness subsides. It should be stabilized in a relaxed position of supination. Since most activities of daily living require pronation of the forearm the patient is forced to pronate the forearm on a very frequent basis, helping to restore that important motion. A permanent limitation of supination is more disabling than a comparable loss of supination. The patient that loses pronation compensates very readily by inconspicuous flexion, abduction and internal rotation of the shoulder; a compensatory motion that amputees use when fitted with prosthetic appliances that do not permit prono-supination of the forearm. There is no comparable inconspicuous compensatory shoulder motion for the lack of supination.

SECTION II

THE HIP JOINT

FRACTURES AND RECONSTRUCTIVE SURGERY

SECTION II – THE HIP JOINT

A

ACETABULAR FRACTURES

New technology has made possible the surgical treatment of many acetabular fractures in ways not dreamt possible a few years ago. This new opportunity, however, has resulted in an exaggerated emphasis on the technological aspects of treatment and given many the impression that all acetabular fractures must be treated by surgical means in order to restore absolute anatomical reduction of the fracture. Any incongruity, is said, is unacceptable because it inevitable leads to late degenerative changes

To accept the concept that intraarticular fractures inevitable lead to arthritic changes is wrong. It cannot be true. Thousands, if not millions, of people who sustained acetabular fractures in the past and did not have anatomical repositioning of the fragments, never developed arthritic changes, and among those who developed them, many never became sufficiently symptomatic to require surgery. This statement is made not to suggest that congruity of articular cartilage fractures is not desirable, but to emphasize that other factors must be included in the decision to perform surgery under all circumstances.

The effects of incongruity of articular cartilage is a subject, which we are just now beginning to understand. Nature spontaneously repairs small step-off defects without leading to arthritic changes. The works of Lansinger, in Sweden, Kristensen, in Denmark and Dietz and Marsh, in Iowa and our own in the United States are convincing, even though they do not deal with the hip but with the knee and ankle joints. Some of these investigators have demonstrated in long-term follow-up studies that most fractures of the tibial condyles that healed with residual significant incongruity did not develop arthritic changes some thirty years later. Our own laboratory work and clinical experience support their findings. I have long suspected it is more likely that instability is more important than incongruity as we recently documented in laboratory animals [3, 8, 41, 119].

It must be remembered that since many of these fractures are the result of violent impaction of the head of the femur against the acetabulum, the articular cartilage may be irreparable damaged from that moment on. Repositioning the displaced fragments under those circumstances does not change the pathological situation and osteoarthritic changes may ensue.

Senior surgeons have recently reported that long-term follow-up of their patients indicated that those who had open reduction and internal fixation developed painful arthritis and required total joint replacement sooner that those whose fractures were treated nonsurgically. One must assess these experiences very carefully. Lumping all fractures into a single package, may lead to wrong conclusions. There are fractures that are definitely best managed by surgical means.

Surgically exposing severely comminuted acetabular fractures requires additional stripping of soft tissue attachment to those fragments, bringing about associated risk of devascularizing them even further, and setting the stage for the development of heterotopic bone. In addition, even in the best of hands, anatomical reduction is not always attained. Gaps between the many fragments frequently remain. Plate and screws left behind require major additional surgery at a later date when arthritic changes call for prosthetic replacement. Total hip replacement under those circumstances is more traumatic to perform, as it often requires the removal of the fixation devices. The greater the stripping of tissues, the greater the likelihood of heterotopic bone formation.

Despite some reports to the contrary, consideration must also be given to the nature of the original injury and the degree of initial displacement of the fragments. I suspect that a fracture produced through a high-energy mechanism behaves differently that one sustained from a fall to the ground after slipping on wet pavement.

I believe that certain acetabular fractures, particularly in the elderly, can be treated by non-surgical means in anticipation that if arthritic changes occur, the situation could be remedied with an electively performed total hip replacement. Primary total hip replacement can be on occasion the treatment of choice. I have performed such a procedure a few times. However, I believe that under this circumstance heterotopic bone is more likely to form. This also is true for acute fractures of the femoral neck treated primarily with total hip implants.

In the case of younger patients, I suspect that surgery is not necessary in many instances. Comminuted fractures that show minimal incongruity and very mild step-off deformity are likely to lead to good results following non-operative treatment (FIG. 1a, b). Fractures located over the less important weight bearing area of the dome fall in that category

Protection from significant weight bearing for a few weeks (a period probably no longer than the one recommended after surgery) often restores the patient to a very acceptable degree of independence. With surgery or with conservative treatment, patients with these major fractures do not return to normal overnight. Pain lingers for some time.

Regardless of the type or location of the fracture, the presence of floating fragments in the join (easily documented with CT scans) constitutes an ominous sign. If left in place degenerative changes are almost always inevitable.

In the case of the surgically managed patient, the surgeon must worry about infection, sciatic nerve injury, vascular injury and heterotopic bone formation.

SECTION II – THE HIP JOINT

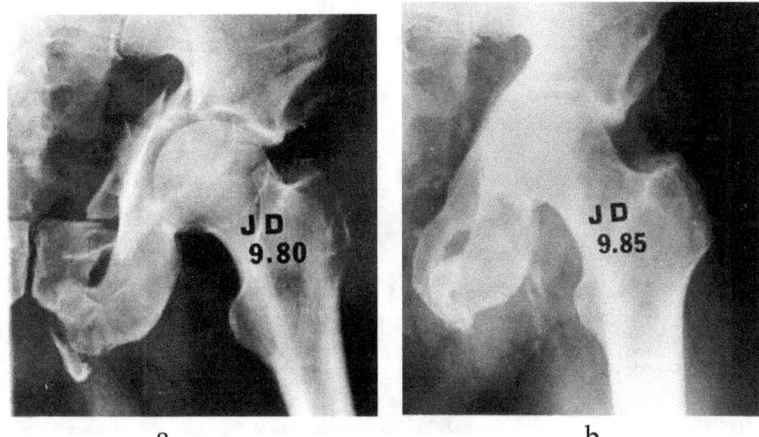

Fig. a and b. Five-year follow-up of non-surgically treated comminuted acetabular fracture. Notice the well-preserved joint space.

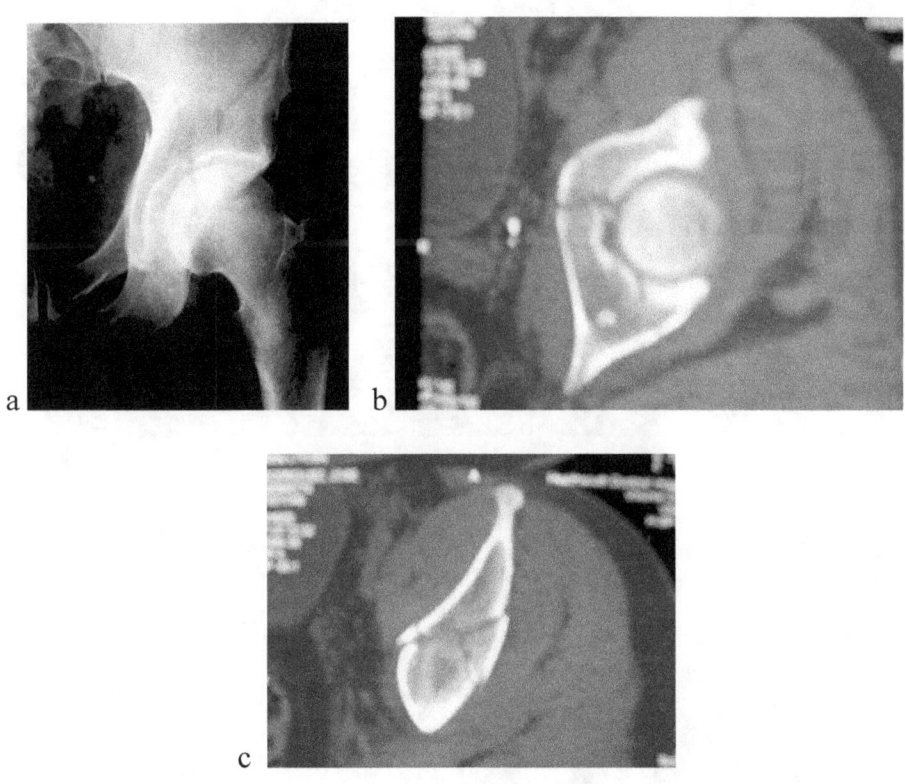

SECTION II – THE HIP JOINT

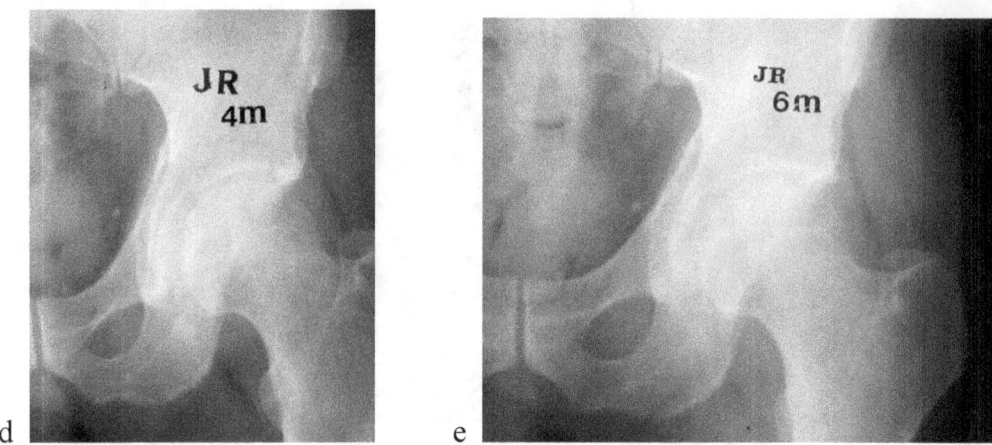

Fig. Minimally displaced, unstable acetabular fracture in a 45-year old man. The fracture was treated with bed rest and passive exercises for four weeks. X-Rays taken 6 months later showed no evidence of displacement.

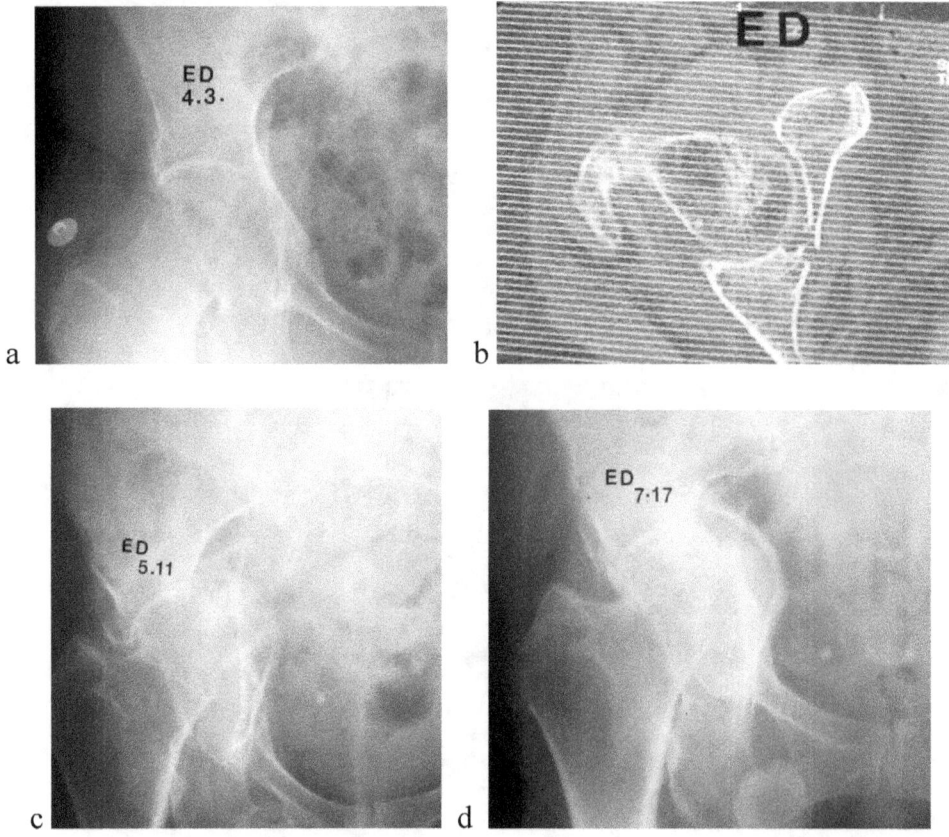

Fig. a, b, c and d. unstable acetabular fracture in an eighty four year old woman. The fracture was treated symptomatically. The head migrated into the pelvis within a few days. Three months later patient was minimally symptomatic but ambulatory with the aid of a walker.

Heterotopic bone develops in the overwhelming majority of instances only on the outer table of the iliac bone, even though stripping of periosteum and muscles is done on both tables. I have speculated that the relative absence of heterotopic bone on the inner table is due to the effect of pulsatile peristalsis from the adjacent intestines. A mechanism that resembles destruction of vertebrae adjacent to an aortic aneurysm. The same reason as to why vessels are rarely obliterated in the callus of healing fractures.

ACETABULUM ORIENTATION (Total hips)

We have long believed that the acetabular cup of a total hip arthroplasty should always be placed with a few degrees of anteversion and at forty-five degrees of inclination in the coronal plane. There is no evidence to refute that premise, however, every surgeon who has performed a large number of total hip replacements would admit that, on occasion, the cup ends up in greater or lower inclination that he or she thought was present at the completion of the surgical procedure.

The question that I have asked myself, upon realizing that numerous times I had inadvertently placed the cup in too much valgus, was "what happens to those hips after a period of time?" From memory I could not recall a higher incidence of dislocations, loosening or excessive wear. We reviewed their moderately long follow up performance and found out that the perceptions I had originally drawn were correct. Wear, in spite of an intuitive knee jerk reaction, was not higher and neither was the dislocation rate. On the other hand the rate of wear and the development of bone-cement radiolucent lines was higher with cups placed in a significantly transverse position [132].

During our review of the orientation of the cups, we also looked at the importance of bony coverage of the implant by pelvic bone. We did this because we realized that in several instances exaggerated valgus placement of the socket had occurred when I was dealing with shallow acetabuli I could not make any deeper, forcing me to tilt the implant into valgus in order to have it fully covered with bone.

The conclusion we drew from this study was that, at least during the period of follow up of our patients, a valgus attitude of the acetabular cup of as much as 50 degrees does not lead to the above mentioned complications and that coverage of the implant is more important than its vertical orientation.

Unable to state scientifically the reasons for the findings I extrapolated that the higher radiological loosening of the transverse cups was the possible titter-totter change in the stresses to which the cup is subjected in this position. Abduction versus adduction of the leg probably brings about those changes. The more vertically placed cup is probably likely to experience mechanical changes of a lesser degree. Needless to say, longer follow-up may prove that our earlier findings did not withstand the test of time.

ACETABULAR OSTEOTOMY

Acetabular osteotomy in the treatment of early osteoartritis, secondary to coingenital hip dysplasia has gained significant popularity in recent years. It is likely that lack of enthusiasm for this procedure is due to the somewhat disappointing results from femoral osteotomies. I suspect these bad experiences suggesting to some surgeons that comparable results would follow procedures carried out in the acetabular side. In addition, the procedure is more difficult to perform appropriately when dealing with the acetabulum.

Currently, the acetabular osteotomy that appears to provide the best results is the one developed and popularized by Reinhold Ganz, from Switzerland. It is, however, an operation that requires special surgical skill and precision in its performance. In the United Sates, Joel Matta, from Los Angeles, has refined the intervention and has reported very good results. I practice my profession in the same office with Doctor Matta for nearly fifteen years and had the opportunity to observe him in the operating room a number of times. I believe his results cannot be easily duplicated by most surgeons who are likely to lack his superior surgical skills.

It has become evident that this operation does not yield good results when the arthritic process is advanced. It is the patient with early symptoms whose x-rays demonstrate only minimal degenerative changes, and the range of motion of the hip is very good who benefits the most. Nonunion of the pubic osteotomy is not an uncommon complication. It appears, however, that such a finding has little if any clinical importance. Also, many patients react adversely to finding that the operated leg is longer the normal one. Since the discrepancy is usually of less than one centimeter, the resulting limp improves and even disappears within a relatively short time.

I have noticed that in some instances there is a residual limitation of internal rotation that may or not be important. I have learned over the years that any procedure that abruptly limits motion of a joint is prone to develop late arthritic changes. Since my experience with acetabular osteotomy is totally vicarious, any of the comments I have made I cannot support; they are anecdotal and should be assessed in that light.

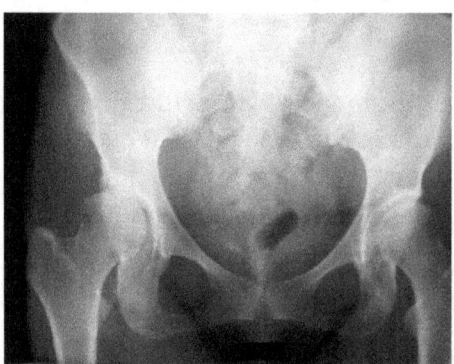 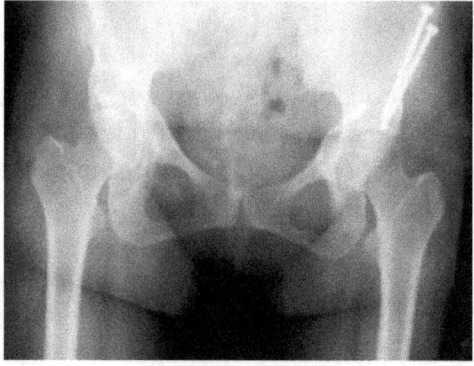

Fig.. Shallow acetabuli with early arthritic pain and minimal limitation of motion of the hips treated with bilateral acetabular osteotomy. Pain disappeared and normal motion and function were restored. (Courtesy of Doctor Joel Matta)

AGE IN TOTAL HIP SURGERY

It is generally believed that the age of the patient has much to do with the way in which the implant and surrounding bone perform over a long period of time. Instinctively, we all share that view. However, experiences have not always supported that perception. I have seen patients with cemented total hip implants who had surgery in their late thirties or early forties, who after 30 years after surgery, showed no clinical or radiological changes to suggest impending failure. Some of those implants looked as good as they did the day after surgery. On a number of occasions these patients le very active lives and were heavy and tall (Fig. 73 a,b,c). Other older patients, light in weight and who lived rather sedentary lives demonstrated signs of failure in a short period of time.

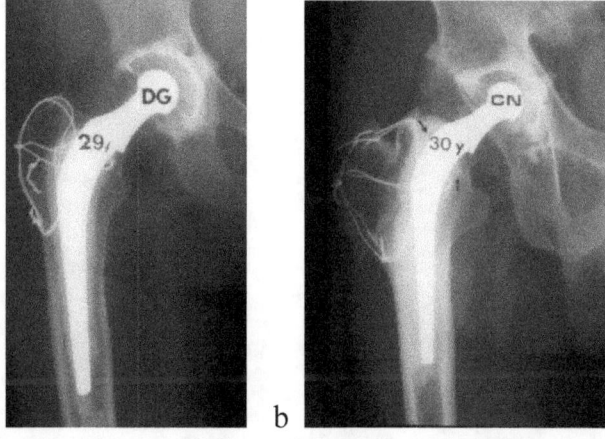

Fiig. a and b. Twenty-nine year follow of Charnley arthroplasty in a 48- year old male (a). Thirty-year follow-up of Charnley arthroplasty in a 35-year old man, six-foot, four- inches tall (b).

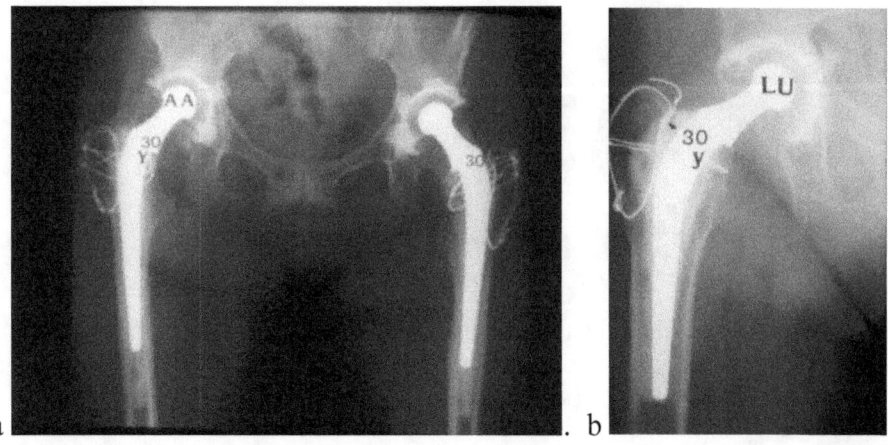

Fig. a and b. Radiographs of two patients who underwent prosthetic replacement in their late thirties.

What is the explanation for such apparently inconsistent results? Much speculation has surrounded the issue and no clear-cut conclusions have been reached. Many of my best total hip arthroplasties, among the thousands I have performed over the years, were cemented Charnley replacements performed with the crude thumb-packed cementing techniques of the early 1970's. Those implants were cemented on both sides of the joint; no metal-backed acetabula were used; no irrigation, pressurization or plugging of the canal was done; the polyethylene material was probably of a better quality, and the sterilization process less damaging to the plastic material.

We have reviewed out clinical material several times over the past years and have carefully looked at the issue of age in relation to success or failure of total hip prostheses. We found that, in general, older patients experience a lower number of radiological changes with the passage of time. Women had a higher incidence of bone-cement radiolucent lines on the acetabular side. We identified that age, per se, was not the reason for the difference between the two groups. The disease for which the operation had been performed was the most important finding. Patients with avascular necrosis had the worst radiological results. It happens, however, that most patients with avascular necrosis are younger. If the group of patients with avascular necrosis is removed from our entire series the difference in performance between the young and the old disappears. [126, 133, 135, 141] (Fig. 74a, b, c)

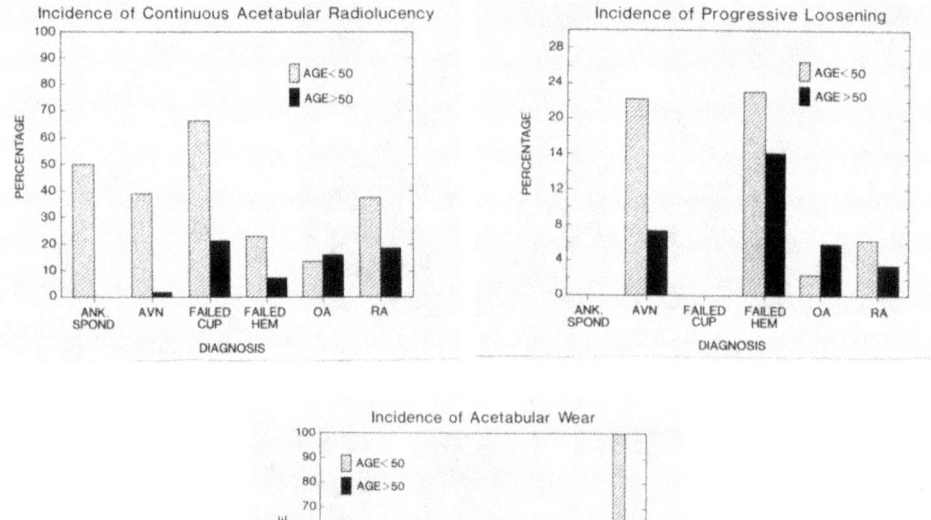

Fig. a, b and c. If the patients who undergo prosthetic replacement for the care of AVN are deleted, the performance of the implants becomes very similar. Surgery for AVN seems to render the worst results.

On the other hand, it is only fair to admit that this is true only if the two groups are followed for the same period of time. It is likely that young people with total hip implants, if they live to an old age, will have a higher incidence of complications. John Charnley, who rarely made a wrong observation or prediction, categorically stated that no total hip implant would last thirty years in an active individual. I guess that to some extent he was wrong but his warning should be remembered as our enthusiasm with the operation increases. He was thinking at that time that wear would be the ultimate problem that made total hip implants fail. Perhaps, the problem of wear will someday soon be solved. If and when that happens we will be able to finally say that prosthetic replacement of the hip is truly a long lasting procedure.

AVASCULAR NECROSIS- (FEMORAL HEAD)

One of the yet to be conquered frontiers in orthopaedics is Avascular Necrosis. After many years of feverish attempts to find answers about its true etiology and management we are still puzzled by its elusive nature. Reports abound of promising solutions, be it core decompression, osteotomies or grafting of various types. The fact remains that there is not as yet a method of treatment that consistently renders good results. To complicate matters, we have now learned that there is a previously unrecognized condition called "transient osteoporosis" that gives similar clinical and imaging changes. Such a revelation makes one wonder how many of the reported successful procedures performed for the care of avascular necrosis were carried-out in patients with "transient osteoporosis", not with avascular necrosis.

I have personally become skeptical about the true value of the many surgical approaches in vogue. This in spite the fact that I am familiar with the various reports. I have seen very satisfactory short-term results from vascular zed fibula grafts performed in patients with Grades I and II disease but I have lingering doubts concerning the lack of consistency. In grade III, the procedure is very likely to fail.

The more core decompression procedures I see, the greater my lack of enthusiasm with this approach becomes. In too many instances a second and more definitive procedure becomes necessary. The decompression seems to be very effective in patients who do not need the procedure.

I participated in an effort to duplicate the results reported by Sugioka using his osteotomy. I have heard him illustrate his wonderful results on several occasions. Our attempts resulted in failure. We either did not know how to carry out the procedure appropriately or the osteotomy was performed for the wrong reasons and in the wrong patients.

We all seem to believe that a well-established AVN if left alone eventually demonstrates the classical collapse of the femoral head. Particularly if a "crescent sign" has already appeared on the lateral x-ray of the hip. I have seen probably four or five patients with "obvious" AVN, who without treatment of any kind never demonstrated progression of the disease or collapse of the femoral head.

I remember the case of an alcoholic man I presented at an Academy meeting in Miami Beach in the early 70's to a panel of gurus of hip surgery in those days. Upon looking at the projected x-rays, there was unanimous consensus that the pathology causing the radiological signs was characteristic of AVN. Someone even said that there was evidence of an early "crescent sign". When asked about their preference for treatment some of the panelists agreed that prosthetic replacement was the treatment of choice. One panelist suggested mold arthroplasty; another one mentioned osteotomy and a third one thought that fusion was probably a good option. He backed-down as the discussion continued and he was reminded that the incidence of bilateral disease was as high as sixty percent. Doctor Lazansky, from New York, an early disciple of Charnley, recommended total hip replacement. Most of the panelists were barely familiar with the new procedure.

After listening to the various recommendations I informed the experts that the x-rays they had reviewed had been taken five years earlier. I then summoned the patient to the stage. I suspect he had imbibed a few drinks on the way to the hotel, which helped make his performance all the more entertaining. He ran the distance and once there he proceeded to squat down a few times, spread his legs apart and run down the steps. He denied any pain. I then proceeded to flash on the screen recent films that showed no progression of the disease process and a perfectly round head. I followed him for several years until he disappeared.

I have another patient, a bartender, who in the late 1960's presented himself with pain in both hips. A diagnosis of bilateral AVN was made, which I proceeded to treat with an endo-prosthetic replacement of his most painful joint. Histological sections of the femoral specimen showed large necrotic areas and the sub-chondral "fracture". Over the ensuing months the non-operated hip showed spontaneous clinical improvement, so much so that we decided to postpone surgery on that side. Three years later the Austin More replacement became painful and bored into the pelvis. The painful condition was approached by replacing the endo-prosthesis with a Charnley total hip arthroplasty, which within a relatively short time showed signs of loosening, fracture of the cement and distal migration of the femoral stem. The symptoms ranged from minimal to non-existing at times. Twenty-two years later he died. X-rays had been taken a few months before his death. The "failed" arthroplasty had become stable many years earlier and never showed any evidence of mechanical loosening or lysis. The opposite hip, the non-operated one, never collapsed and maintained the mild loss of sphericity that appeared on the original radiographs. These, and other experiences have convinced me that there is much we do not know about the subject and that it will be a long time before the final word is written.

I would not be surprised if total hip arthroplasty becomes the universal treatment for all patients with avascular necrosis. For practical purposes, that is the case today. If the results from this operation continue to improve there is no reason to doubt that the procedure will ultimately displace all others [128, 135, 141]. The road to such destination is, however, rough and full of obstacles.

During a panel discussion at an Academy annual meeting just a few years ago, the four panelists agreed that the incidence of lysis in their respective patients with avascular necrosis, who had been treated with cement less total hip arthroplasty, was twenty five percent at the end of the fifth post-operative year. When I pursued the discussion and asked them if they felt that lysis was progressive in nature, they all agreed it was. That meant that the chances were that most of the young patients reported in their series would eventually require additional surgery.

I took advantage of the agreement between the panelists so I, as moderator, could try to get them to share their views on related issues. I remarked that they had agreed that lysis occurs in 25 percent of the patients with cement less prostheses at five years after surgery.

Therefore, what bizarre logic could justify the use of such implants when the incidence of lytic changes with cemented prostheses was so much lower? Without giving them a chance to answer the question I added, "Why use non-cemented implants in these younger patients realizing that sooner or later they will have to have secondary surgery which oftentimes is likely to be very difficult to perform and requires major bone reconstruction?"

I suspect that I was not quite as candid as I should have been. I personally have no answers to the problem and find it very difficult to decide what is best for these patients. For a few years I performed hybrid arthroplasty in most instances (a cemented femoral component and a non-cemented acetabular cup). In more recent years I have been using uncemented implants in most instances, based on reported evidence that the "new" implants have solved many of the previous problems.

In regards to the behavior of avascular necrosis, there is not much solid information up to this time. Most of what the "experts" say is based, to a great extent, on hypothesis and speculations. I have remained attracted for many years to the ideas on the mechanism of progression of AVN described by Glimcher, from Boston, in the 1960's. He, I believe, stated that a dead, avascular femoral head does not collapse as long as it is dead. He jokingly remarked that the "avascular" bone the dog plays with in the backyard of the house never collapses. It is only when vessels succeed in restoring blood supply to the dead structure that the, now softer, bone collapses under the weight of the body. This hypothesis probably explains the situation of my previously above mentioned patients who never showed bony collapse. It can be safely suspected that revascularization never took place and the dead head remained dead and therefore, like the dog's toy, hard and strong.

Some have tried to fill the curetted femoral head with bone graft, but with disappointing results; others have packed the "empty" head with acrylic cement with similarly poor outcomes. I personally worked in the laboratory dealing with the subject of acute fractures of the femoral neck. I was hoping to develop a method that would allow us to remove all bone from the femoral head and placing the remaining cartilaginous shell over a metallic prosthesis. We were unable to find a mechanism that would firmly stabilize the two structures. More recently, packing of the curetted head with bone marrow has been reported. Though the concept is sound, I doubt it will become successful. I anticipate that similar efforts will be made using a combination of bone marrow, BMP and varieties of gels and pastes containing bone induction properties. My pessimism extends also to those "new" approaches.

At this time I seldom recommend core decompression or grafting procedures and prefer to treat patients symptomatically until clinically and radiographically the situation calls for prosthetic replacement. The very young is an exception. The grafting is an alternative. The possibility of a chronically painful ankle following the fibular resection has been made. I was surprised to hear about this complication, because my experiences with ostectomies of the fibula in the treatment of tibial non-unions had not shown ankle pain as a serious problem [150]. The few patients, who had pain, eventually, and within a relatively short time, rid themselves of the discomfort. Perhaps the same is true for those who had their fibula transplanted (See NONUNION) (See BIPOLAR PROSTHESES)

SECTION II – THE HIP JOINT

B

BILATERAL TOTAL HIPS

The temptation to perform bilateral simultaneous total hip arthroplasty is great when we seek solutions for the severely incapacitated individual. There are very good arguments to justify the approach, but the potential risks must be carefully weighed. Replacing both hips during a single surgical procedure is rather traumatic to a patient who may have other major medical problems. The blood loss, time under anesthesia and post-operative discomfort are greater than with unilateral procedures. However, there are circumstances when simultaneously performed bilateral arthroplasty is clearly indicated.

Doctor K.D.Goswami, a fellow in our department in Los Angeles, reviewed my own experiences and presented the results at a meeting of the American Academy of Orthopaedic Surgeons and has submitted for publication the manuscript detailing the experience. The paper compares the results obtained between our two different groups. One group consisted of patients who had bilateral simultaneous replacements and the other of patients who had the two joints replaced within a period of six weeks. In all respects those in the former group demonstrated fewer complications and a number of practical benefits. Simultaneous replacements were associated with fewer episodes of thrombo-embolic disease and required less blood replacement and shorter hospitalization. The incidence of dislocation was the same, very low in both instances.

The performance of bilateral simultaneous hip arthroplasty should not be undertaken unless the surgeon has had considerable experience with the replacement procedure and is capable of performing it expeditiously. The time of surgery in our group was of two and half hours, which included the time necessary to dress the wound from the first operation and the preparation of the opposite side since the procedures were performed through a posterior approach. In other words each replacement took approximately one hour [30].

Ambulation was started the day after surgery. When the operation is carried out with or without the use of cement on both sides of the joint and without trochanteric osteotomy there is no concern about possible damage due to early weight bearing. When non-cemented implants are used for both the femur and acetabulum some have expressed concern about early weight bearing. Since my experience with bilateral simultaneous arthroplasty using non-cemented components is relatively limited, I am reluctant to voice an opinion. Many of my patients received hybrid implants and the results have not suggested that early, protected weight bearing is contraindicated.

There is no question that the tasks of transferring from the bed to chair and initiating ambulation when both hips are replaced simultaneously are more difficult since the patient does not initially have the power to lift himself or herself with ease from the prono position. The overall hospital stay therefore is slightly longer. On the average, however, it did not exceed 10 days.

SECTION II – THE HIP JOINT

I have often wondered why is it that we consider so important the initiation of ambulation on the first post-operative day. What is the magic of it? Do we really believe that standing up 12 or 24 hours sooner makes a difference? Does the standing position influence the development of thromboembolic disease? Through what mechanism? I suspect that active use of the musculature and active and passive exercises of joints are more important than assuming the erect position. And those activities can be carried out in bed and without pain or apprehension. If one waits an additional 24 hours before beginning ambulation, patients are more comfortable and less apprehensive about walking.

The recent infatuation with mini-incisions in total hip surgery, with its claims that patients have less pain, their wound heal faster, and hospitalization is shorter, has fueled interest on immediate ambulation. Have we given sufficient thought to the issue? Are we begging for more government and insurance companies' regulations and mandates, which in the long run we will resent?

Following the example set by Medicare, many HMO have refused to authorize bilateral simultaneous replacements and have made it clear that if carried out the hospital and physicians are reimbursed for only one arthroplasty. My latest experience had to do with a 22 years old rheumatoid girl who met the criteria for simultaneous procedures. She was in very good general condition, had severe bilateral flexion-adduction contractures of the hips and considerable pain. The replacement of only one hip, even if successful, would have carried out the problems associated with sitting. The non-operated hip, still with a flexion-adduction contracture, continues to dictate to the operated hip, free of the deformity, how much to flex. Therefore, complete correction of the disabling contracture is not gained until the second hip is replaced.

SECTION II – THE HIP JOINT

BIODEGRADABLE MATERIALS

With increasing frequency degradable materials are being used in the treatment of fractures. The concept, needless to say, is very attractive. Not having to remove the implants upon healing makes sense.

In the early 1980's I had the opportunity to investigate the use of polylactates for that purpose [39]. We designed plates and screws and after extensive mechanical testing we implanted them in experimental animals. We encountered considerable difficulties and obstacles. First of all, we never succeeded in making the biodegradable screws strong enough to resist the strong torque often necessary to hold them against either a plate or a bone. I am certain that if we had continued the study, stronger materials would have resolved the problem. However, the main reason for abandoning the project was the fact that when the experimental animals were sacrificed we discovered that, even though the material had grossly disappeared after a period of time, the disappearance from the body was never complete. In the case of the screws the cavity where the screw once rested remained filled with "gunk". Bone never filled the gap, at least during our relatively long period of observation. Plates did grossly disappear but the surface of the underlying bone never seemed normal. It remained covered with the same "gunky" material we had noticed filling the screw holes.

It may be extrapolated that the defect in the bone could be a permanent stress raiser. That concerned us.

The new biodegradable materials now being investigated are, hopefully, free from the problems we encountered. If successful, the opportunities for their use will be many. Malleolar fractures, tibial condylar fractures as well as many upper extremity fractures and anchoring prosthetic screws will provide fertile material for beneficial usage.

BIPOLAR HIP PROSTHESES

Bipolar prostheses have been popular for at least 30 years and have been used primarily in the treatment of sub-capital fractures of the femoral neck and avascular necrosis in the younger age patient. Some have reported on their successful experiences with the implant in cases of osteoarthritis and for the salvage of failed total hip arthroplasty. My experiences have been mixed. In general, however, I have grown dissatisfied with many of the results. I have seen some of the most aggressive cases of osteolysis, particularly in young patients (FIG. 76 a,b,c,d). This is not difficult to understand since the amount of polyethylene debris is higher than from the traditional polyethylene-metal total hip arthroplasty.

Microscopic examination of the debris found in failed bipolar prostheses almost consistently demonstrates polyethylene debris, usually in great amounts. The diagnosis of polyethylene debris-induced failure can often be recognized by the development of a large radiolucent space between the metallic cup and the bone rather than the narrowing of the joint space seen in non-bipolar implants. The fact that on occasion metal debris is also found in combination with plastic debris gives credence to my belief that endoprostheses often fail from biological damage to the bony acetabulum and medullary canal created by metal debris.

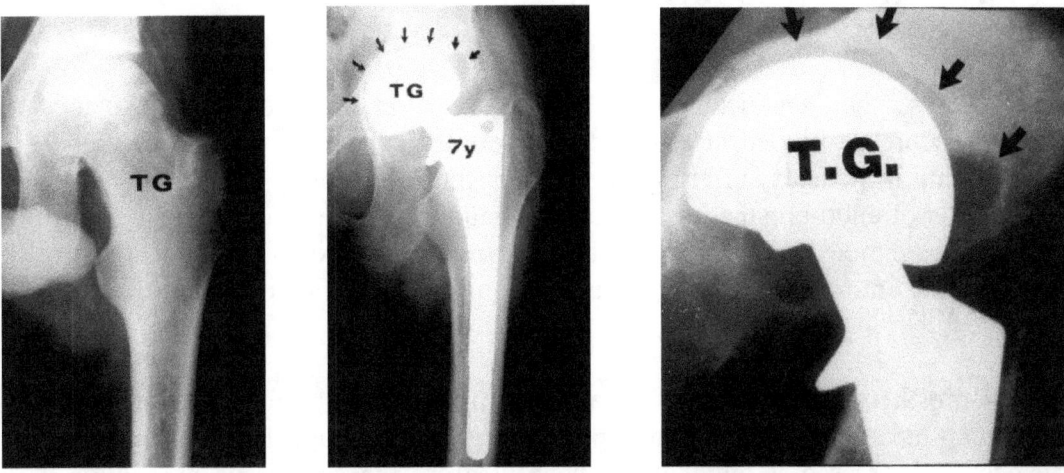

Fig. a, b and c. Idiopathic Avascular Necrosis (a) treated with a bipolar cement less arthroplasty (b) Aggressive lysis from polyethylene debris was recognized three-years post-operatively.

C

CAPSULECTOMY IN HIP OSTEO-ARTHRITIS

In the late 1960's, when American orthopaedists had not yet embraced the new total hip replacement procedure developed in England, I experimented with synovectomy and capsulectomy of the hip in patients suffering from osteoarthritis. Prior to that time I had been a strong supporter of endo-prosthetic replacement using the Austin Moore prosthesis. My results, however, were mixed and therefore not totally satisfactory: relief of pain was not always complete; boring into the acetabulum was common; and so was loosening of the medullary stem [37, 82, 85, 87, 104, 117].

During endoprosthetic replacement of the arthritic hip, I usually performed posterior synovectomy and capsulectomy to the greatest possible extent. Though I knew that the chances of dislocation increased, I felt that the benefits from the soft tissue procedure outweighed the potential disadvantages. For a long time I thought that the synovectomy and capsulectomy improved the results.

In 13 patients with osteo-arthritis and in one patient with rheumatoid arthritis I performed synovectomy and capsulectomy without replacement of the joint. Following surgery I placed the patients in balanced suspension for a few days and initiated early passive motion of the hip joint. After one week in traction, patients began to ambulate on crutches and gradually, over a period of four weeks I allowed them to ambulate with one cane.

At first the results were gratifying since the pre-operative pain diminished significantly. However, within months or years the pain returned. One patient remained minimally symptomatic for 12 years before I performed a total hip replacement.

The major lesson I learned from this limited experience was that none of the 13 osteoarthritic patients developed avascular necrosis despite the fact that at the time of surgery I not only performed the soft tissue procedure but also completely dislocated the hip posteriorly (Fig. 10). I had been afraid that during surgery I might have severed the retinacular vessels and rendered the head of the femur avascular.

CARBON COMPOSITES IN TOTAL HIPS

Several years ago at our laboratory at the Orthopaedic Hospital of Los Angeles, then a joint venture between the Hospital and the University of Southern California, I became involved in experimental work with carbon-composite materials, in anticipation of eventually developing total joint implants made of that material. The concept was extremely attractive at the time. The inertness of the product and the ability to regulate its modulus of elasticity at different places within the implant prompted our enthusiasm.

Working with the support of a major industrial concern, we conducted extensive mechanical and animal studies [4]. At first we felt the results were encouraging. Animal bone responded very well to the implanted material. Under pressure from the sponsoring industry to move into the clinical application of carbon-composite prostheses, we designed a hip implant which theoretically would distribute weight bearing stresses through the femur in the most desirable physiological way.

Just prior to authorization from the hospital's research committee to proceed with the clinical component of the experiment, I grew suspicious of the strength of the data accumulated from the animal work. When I requested it be repeated at another institution in order to validate our findings and to add credibility to our laboratory, the request was denied. The industrial sponsors argued that they were satisfied with the information obtained thus far and further emphasized the great cost that repeating the experiment would represent.

I decided to hold fast to my demands, which were nonetheless rejected. The project was then taken away from us and the sponsoring industry sold the area of carbon composites to another firm, which allegedly was interested in the project. The transfer took place and it is my understanding that within a short time further studies were discontinued. To this day the idea of carbon composites for hip implants remains dormant. The observations we had made about the release of carbon fibers into the systemic circulation and their lodging in organs far from the operated bone must have convinced the new owners of the dangers involved in their clinical use. Our unhappy experience was similar to the one with carbon composite cruciate ligaments conducted by others.

D

DISLOCATION

The introduction of CT scans and MRIs in orthopaedic diagnosis, has had incalculable benefits. I am convinced, however, that CT scans and MRI are often requested unnecessarily.

Long before such sophisticated machines became popular, I had the opportunity to work with Herman Epstein, from Los Angeles, for early thirteen years. He was a most intellectually honest and generous individual. He conducted long term follow-up of many indigent patients at the USC-Los Angeles County Hospital, often at his own expense. This made it possible for him to make observations of great importance. He came to the conclusion that all traumatic dislocations should be surgically managed because he found out that, in many instances, small free pieces of bone and cartilage were floating in the joint, eventually producing late degenerative arthritis. He compared the clinical and radiographic results between those patients who had closed reduction and those ones who had their hips surgically treated. He found that the surgically treated patients did better. The introduction of the CT scan has obviated the need for routine surgical exploration. However, his findings and observations deserve recognition.

It used to be customary to prevent early weight bearing following reduction of traumatic hip dislocations. The reasons for such a practice never made any sense. First of all, re-dislocation is very unlikely in the absence of associated acetabular pathology. Secondly, the intact articular surfaces do not require precautions against weight bearing. Thirdly, curtailing weight bearing should not have any influence on the condition of the important vessels, which if initially severed, would lead to avascular necrosis.

This was my reasoning, even during my residency training, when traction in bed for a period of six weeks was the recommended method of treatment. My approach to the issue has not been modified with time; however, I have seen patients develop osteoarthritis at a later date, without avascular necrosis. Is it possible that the initial injury crushed the articular cartilage and damaged it irreparably at that time? Methods to determine the condition of the cartilage with the use of MRI is pretty much in its infancy. In the near future, I hope such a technique will be available and my question will be answered.

DISLOCATION IN TOTAL HIPS

Although we would like to be free of dislocations in total hip surgery, it appears that we will be confronting them from time to time, particularly in the case of revision surgery. Much has been said about its etiology, prevention and treatment but no last word has been written on the subject.

I don't think it serves any purpose to rehash what has been said many times before about the importance of proper orientation of the acetabulum. In my opinion, malposition of the acetabulum is not a common cause. For a dislocation to occur, the malposition must be significant since the hip may be stable even in the presence of a socket anchored without anteversion. A socket in a few degrees of retroversion does not always necessarily result in dislocation when the surgery was performed through a posterior approach. We demonstrated this quite well using an artificially created hip that allowed us to study various attitudes of the acetabulum [7, 8]. (See ACETABULAR ORIENTATION)

I suspect that most dislocations are the product of soft tissue imbalance. A prosthetic replacement that shortens the extremity too much, leaves major soft tissue instability. This does not mean that all total hip replacements that end-up with a shorter leg eventually dislocate since scaring down of the tissues can provide the necessary tethering that insures stability. The clicking that some patients complain of during the first few weeks following surgery and its eventual disappearance testifies to that effect.

I worry about the role that making a leg too long plays in the etiology of dislocation. This is particularly true in patients with tight hamstrings. I discovered this while performing surgery in an individual with significantly tight hamstrings. I deliberately inserted a temporary implant with an excessively long neck. When the hip was reduced and the hip ranged, the stability of the joint was good as long as the knee was kept in flexion. However, when I flexed the hip to approximately 80 degrees and then extended that knee the hip dislocated posteriorly. The tight, inelastic hamstring created the pathological situation. Applying a brace post-operatively under those circumstances is likely to result in subsequent dislocations particularly if a commonly, ill-conceived brace that limits flexion, is applied.

It is a common practice to "shuck" the hip joint prior to selecting the best possible femoral neck length. Though I do pay attention to the findings from such maneuver, I do not rely too heavily on my findings. Often one is able to obtain significance separation between the prosthetic head and the artificial socket in the presence of the desired length of the extremity, due to unusually high degree of elasticity of the capsular tissues. Other times the same phenomenon can be seen because of the degree of stripping of soft tissues from the surrounding bony structures: the greater the degree of soft tissue detachment the greater the "shucking".

Since I prefer wide exposure of the joint, and usually detach the insertion of the gluteus maximus from the shaft of the femur, as well as generous resection of the posterior capsule, almost always I detect a separation between the articulating surfaces when I apply traction to the extremity. If I were to totally eliminate shucking I would be inserting prostheses with necks excessively long and making many patients extremely unhappy because of the longer legs that the surgery gave them. Laxity of a minor degree is overcome by the inevitable scarring of the soft tissues

Hip dislocation braces that limit flexion of the hip do, in my opinion, more harm than good. When a patient, fit with a brace that limits flexion beyond 75 degrees, sits down, the normal hip, which easily reaches 90 degrees of flexion, forces the operated hip to dislocate posteriorly. Hip dislocation braces should not limit flexion of the hip; simply adduction and internal rotation. Failure to adhere to this design explains why so many surgeons have grown dissatisfied with the use of braces for the prevention of recurrent dislocation of artificial hips.

Braces to prevent dislocation that cover too much of the pelvis and thigh are not necessary. All the hip-dislocation brace needs to do is to ensure that the hip cannot be adducted and internally rotated. That can be accomplished with a very light appliance that simply needs a thin pelvic band and a small, adjustable thigh band. The brace I have used in the recent past creates those limitations very effectively. It is designed to permit normal ambulation with an economic narrow gait but forces the hip to abduct as the patient assumes the sitting position. (Fig. 77 a, b, c).

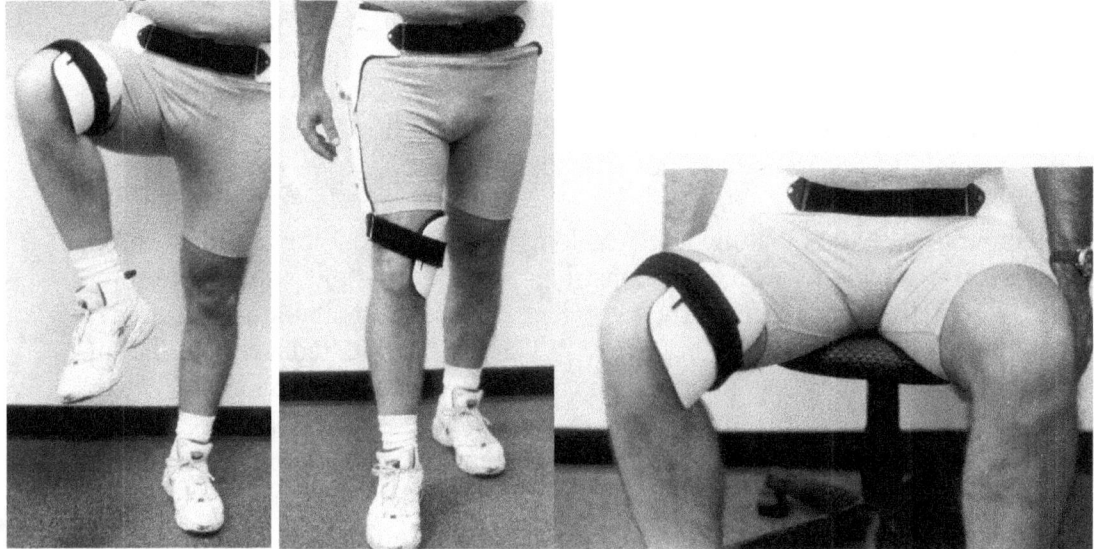

Fig. Dislocation prevention brace. The pelvic joint is constructed in such a manner that during ambulation the leg swings in a normal fashion, however, during flexion of the hip, the hip abducts and externally rotates.

Frequent dislocations of total hip prostheses end-up needing surgery. Many times the procedure is helpful and the dislocations stop because the hip is "tightened" and the newly stripped soft tissues have a new chance to scar down in a tighter fashion. Self-constrained sockets that retain the head in place and prevent dislocations are in vogue at this time and early results seem satisfactory. We should remember, however, that Letournel, in the 1970's developed a similar socket only to find at a later date that the rate of polyethylene wear was too high.

The range of motion of the hip of patients with total hip replacement changes with the passage of time. I have noticed that flexion increases as patients grow older. This is not

SECTION II – THE HIP JOINT

true for internal rotation, which frequently decreases with age. This phenomenon I have also observed in able-body people whose hips were never replaced. Patients with very thin or muscular thighs are more prone to dislocate their total hips. In a couple of instances I have seen patients who twenty five years after surgery dislocated a total hip implant while carrying out activities that they had regularly performed over the years without any problem. The only detectable finding was a significant loss of weight that was clearly visible on their thinner thighs. Wear of the polyethylene was not a factor in these particular cases.

E

ENDO-PROSTHESES

Austin Moore's initial experiences with his endoprosthesis were limited to degenerative and neoplastic conditions. As a matter of fact, the first procedure he performed with Harold Bohlman, from Baltimore, was for the management of a malignant giant cell tumor. It was not until later that Moore began to use the prosthesis for the care of unstable femoral neck fractures.

He believed, and rightly so, that the technique for inserting a prosthesis had to be precise and he did not believe in short cuts. The fit of the ball in the acetabulum had to be as perfect as possible. He said, however, that a tight fit was better than a loose one. I wonder how he would feel about that today, when we claim to have so much more knowledge about cartilage's response to friction and pressure. Perhaps his views would have been reinforced. The stem had to fit tightly into the canal, and the collar of the prosthesis rest squarely on the medial cortex of the femur.

I was his senior resident when he realized how important the contact of the prosthesis against the cortical wall of the femur. He then went to work on the design of his new implant. He determined the various prosthetic sizes by using cadaver specimens in the morgue and filling the femoral medullary canals with "putty". We split the femur and the rubbery "prostheses" were removed, packed and sent to the Austenal Company in New York. Austenal later became Howmedica.

It has been said that the window in the Austin More prosthesis is there because there was no manufacturing capability to avoid it. This is not true. Austin Moore conceived the idea of the fenestrations as part of his conviction that the new bony bridge, made possible by the window in the metal, would make the implant "part of the living body". Many years later I personally studied the quality of the bone that forms in the fenestration and was disappointed to find out that the fenestration, though usually filled with bone, very often has a rather thick membrane separating the bone from the metal. The thickness of the membrane reached several millimeters in some instances, making the removal of the implant very difficult; often more difficult than removal of an implant where a thick and hard bony bridge has formed. Only on a very few occasions have I seen the fenestration filled completely with bone.

I also noticed after examining a large number of post-operative specimens that motion between the prosthesis and the bone takes place primarily in a rotary plane [104]. Antero-superior and medial-lateral forces do not always demonstrate motion unless the loosening of the implant is gross. A similar mode of failure has been identified in total hip implants.

Boring of the prosthesis into the acetabulum is commonly seen and it is claimed to be cause of failure in many instances. We have assumed that such a phenomenon is due to the difference in the hardness of the acetabulum and that of the prosthesis. This mechanical explanation may be accurate but only to some extent. If the mechanical differences, as pronounced as they are, are the simple and universal explanation for the boring of the implant, then we should see all endoprostheses fail through that mechanism. This is, however, not the case. Many implants have lasted many years without radiological changes on the acetabular side.

I recently reviewed some of my remaining slides of successful endoprostheses and found evidence of large amounts of metal on the surface of the acetabulum (Fig. 78). I suspect that some of the unusual cases of femoral lysis in the medullary canal are due to metal debris (Fig. 79). Metal debris without secondary polyethylene debris may be a cause of lysis. I have come to realize that our explanation for the failure of many endoprostheses was too cavalier; and that we too quickly concluded that mechanical conditions would easily explain the failures. Now that we have a much better understanding of the modes of failure of total hip implants, a fresh look at the failure of endoprostheses is desirable.

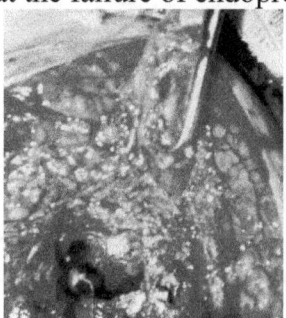

Fig... Metal debris in the acetabulum found during revision of a failed endoprosthesis.

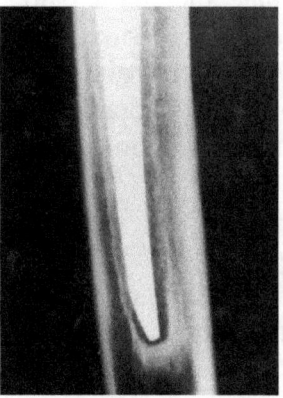

Fig. Loose non-cemented endoprosthesis. Large amount of metal debris was recovered from the area of lysis.

A decrease in the width of the joint space takes place usually in a gradual manner. If the decrease occurs within a short period of time and the patient complains of groin pain, the chances are that there is an infection. If groin pain, rather rapid narrowing of the joint space and heterotopic bone are seen, the diagnosis of a deep infection can be made with almost with complete certainty.

SECTION II – THE HIP JOINT

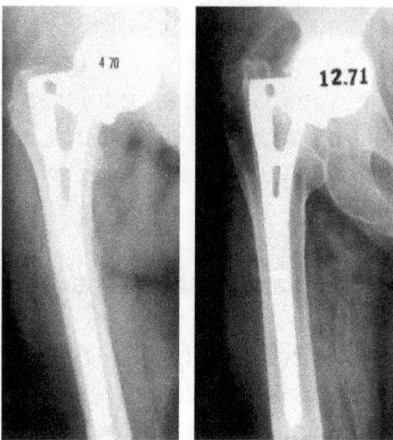

Fig. Rapid boring, associated with pain in the groin is suggestive of low-grade infection.

I have reviewed my personal experiences with endo-prosthesis in the management of acute fractures as well as in various arthritis [85, 87, 104, 117]. My reviews were conducted in my younger days without the critical, detailed information required in contemporary medical literature. In general, I believe that the procedure is a good one in the treatment of displaced fractures, particularly in the elderly. It is, however, far from being a panacea. Pain does not always disappear and radiological signs of failure are not uncommon. Many "failed" implants are not revised into total hip arthroplasty either because the patients get used to the imperfect joint or we, the surgeons, do not consider them to be suitable candidates for major surgery.

Younger patients treated with endoprostheses often require a long period of time before being able to completely eliminate the thigh pain. Sometimes the pain never disappears and total hip replacement becomes necessary. I have seen, however, a number of patients who after six to nine months of persistent pain spontaneously find themselves free of pain. Therefore, my practice is not to rush into total hip surgery until the patient has had a relatively long period of observation and protection from full weight bearing with the aid of crutches.

Today, I am inclined to perform primary total hip replacement in some patients with displaced, high femoral neck fractures. Further incursion into this area must be done carefully and abuse of the procedure must be prevented if at all possible. (See FEMORAL NECK FRACTURES)

Patients, who receive endoprostheses for the treatment of arthritis or avascular necrosis, an approach common before the advent of total hip arthroplasty, did not do well in many instances. Osteoarthritics did better than rheumatoid arthritics or those suffering from avascular necrosis. [82, 104] A difference that has been identified with total hip treated patients as well [23, 25, 37, 141] (See AGE IN TOTAL HIP SURGERY)

F

FEMORAL HEAD FRACTURES

Fractures of the femoral head are not very common. A busy trauma center may see no more than a couple every year. Trauma to the hip is more likely to produce a fracture of the neck or metaphysis of the femur, dislocate the joint or fracture the acetabulum or pelvis. When a fracture of the head occurs the prognosis is guarded. The possibility of avascular necrosis becomes very real. With more sophisticated diagnostic imaging tools we will soon be able to determine immediately whether the head is viable or not. At this time we are still obligated to institute some type of treatment,

Pipkin described the various types of femoral fractures and clearly demonstrated that his Type 4, the one that has the smaller fragments, carries the worst prognosis. Currently, many surgeons consider primary prosthetic replacement the treatment of choice. I agree there are many situations when such an approach is the most rational. However, treating the young in that manner may expose them to the complications that frequently accompany endo-prosthetic arthroplasty. The use of a bipolar prosthesis in preference to a traditional prosthesis is not the answer. As a matter of fact, I think, the bipolar prosthesis is more likely to produce more serious complications. Polyethylene debris from this implant can produce very serious and extensive lysis in the surrounding bony structures. (See BI-POLAR PROSTHESES).

Many years ago I had an opportunity to treat a patient with a Pipkin 4 fracture-dislocation of the femoral head. My attempts to obtain a closed reduction of the dislocated head were unsuccessful. I found it necessary to do an open reduction. Rather than performing a prosthetic replacement I elected to carry out an anatomical reduction of the fragments and to maintain the reduction with metallic screws. I temporarily removed the proximal fragment and created a "trap-door"- like defect on the articular surface of the free articular fragment, as far as I could from the superior dome, into which I threaded a screw. I placed another screw at the insertion site of the excised ligamentum teres. This was done under direct vision while the free fragment was on the Mayo table. I then reduced the fracture anatomically and placed the screws deep into the femoral head [107].

The patient did very well for eight years when arthritic changes developed necessitating replacement arthroplasty. It is interesting to note that microscopic examination of the removed femoral head specimen did not show evidence of avascular necrosis. The changes observed were those of osteoarthritis (Fig.81 a,b,c). A phenomenon similar to what I observed following synovectomy and partial capsulectomy in osteoarthritic hips (See CAPSULECTOMY).

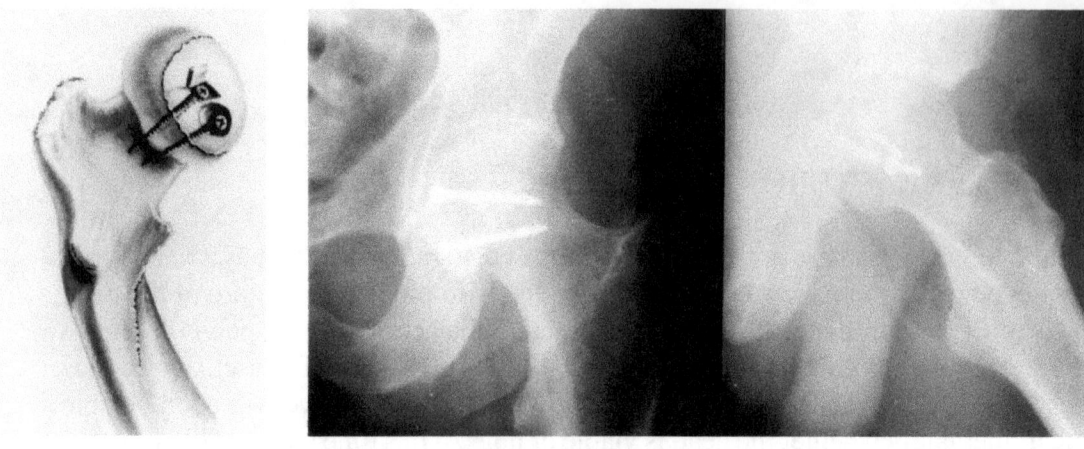

Fig. Fracture of the femoral head (Pipkin 4) treated with open reduction and screw fixation. Eight years later prosthetic replacement became necessary.

FEMORAL NECK FRACTURES

Progress in the understanding and care of femoral neck fractures has moved at a snail pace. I wonder if there is anyone who seriously believes that today we have a clearer understanding of the factors that may lead to non-union or avascular necrosis than we did thirty years ago. This in spite of the enormous progress made in imaging technology and other fields. We still use either Pauwels' or Gardner's criteria for their classification and have accepted the fact that the greater the displacement of the fragments and the more vertical the fracture the worse the prognosis. Then, we debate whether the fracture should be nailed or the head of the femur be replaced with an endoprosthesis, a bipolar prosthesis or a total hip arthroplasty.

In the past some believed that all fractures of the neck of the femur should be nailed. In very persuasive terms they stated, "Reduce them well, fix them well and they get well". No one believes that any longer, in spite of the strong evidence presented by the zealous advocates of internal fixation. We have learned that obtaining anatomical reduction of the fracture by closed methods is difficult to achieve and often unsuccessful. That open reduction does not yield better results and that no matter how perfect the reduction is, avascular necrosis frequently takes place. Reduction in valgus, a technique made popular in the 1960's, eventually lost favor in the orthopaedic community. In addition, the need to protect the fracture from full-weight bearing is almost impossible in the older age group. These patients are either incapable of walking without bearing full weight on the extremity. or their memory span is too short to remember the prescribed precautions [72, 75].

It is commonly believed that avascular necrosis is the result of the sudden severance of the retinacular vessels at the time of the injury. There is some evidence to suggest that tearing of those important vessels does not always occur. Bach, from Germany, demonstrated in experimental animals, that the vessels are simply kinked as the femoral shaft displaces superiorly, and in that manner the blood supply of the femoral head fragment is eventually rendered avascular. If this theory is valid it should be logical to extrapolate that a displaced fracture of the femoral neck should be reduced as soon as possible to restore circulation through the critical vessels. Others, like Smith, from Oregon, have said that it is the rotation of the fragments that produces the stoppage of circulation. Others insist that tamponade, brought about by the intracapsular bleeding is the culprit.

All these hypotheses indicate that if vascular complications are to be avoided, early reduction of the fracture, and its fixation and aspiration are the important steps to be taken. However, there is no data to strongly support them. Perhaps it is out of frustration that most orthopaedists prefer to use endoprosthetic replacement as the initial method of treatment. This treatment, although very effective in many instances, is not a panacea. Many patients never regain the ability to ambulate without pain in spite of satisfactory x-ray pictures. Loosening of the implant and boring of the femoral prosthesis into the acetabulum are common complications. (See ENDOPROSTHESES).

In the case of the non-displaced femoral neck fracture, it is also commonly accepted that nailing should be done in order to prevent subsequent displacement. Though there is merit in this argument, I suspect that such a practice is not always necessary. I have seen a number of patients, including my own mother, who recovered well without surgery, after been told to use crutches or a walker for a few weeks.

I have come to believe that in the management of non-displaced, impacted femoral neck fractures, the severity of pain and its progression can help in determining the need for surgery in. If the pain seems to decrease in a few days, chances are that the fragments will not displace. If the amount of pain increases, displacement is likely to occur. In this latter instance, nailing should be done early. Some still believe that the contraction of the abductor muscles is the force primarily responsible for the varus deformity usually seen in patients with hip fractures; a deformity that is recognized immediately after the fracture occurs. I was able to demonstrate that the adductors, rather than the abductors, are the muscles mainly responsible for the varus deformity. (See VARUS DEFORMITY IN HIP FRACTURE).

I am not sure that there are any advantages for the use of the bipolar prosthesis over the traditional mono-polar Austin Moore prosthesis. I have no strong feelings either about whether these implants should be cemented. Relatively very few elderly patients end-up requiring revision to total hip arthroplasty; either because they do not live very long after the initial surgery or the symptoms are not severe enough to justify surgery. We must be cognizant of the fact that the one-year mortality following femoral neck fractures is very high. In the younger patient with displaced femoral neck fractures, I believe, internal fixation is the treatment of choice. I prefer multiple pins to a single screw. The multiple pins must be placed peripherally in order to attain the greatest degree of rotary stability.

The residual pain that many patients experience following either cemented or non-cemented endoprosthetic replacement may be of short duration (See ENDOPROSTHESES).

SECTION II – THE HIP JOINT

I admit that I have performed several primary total hip arthroplasties in the care of acute femoral neck fractures. I am very reluctant at this time to suggest that this treatment should be implemented in all displaced femoral neck fractures, even though the results have been, for the most part, very gratifying. My reluctance comes from fear that many surgeons will treat all these fractures in that manner, ignoring the fact that many subcapital fractures do very well with nailing techniques. There is usually no comparison between a healed fracture and a hip arthroplasty. I reserve the primary total hip replacement for those people with severe displacement of high vertical fractures who, though no longer young, are still very active and whose remaining life expectancy I suspect to be moderately long.

FUSION

Hip fusions are rarely performed at this time, since total hip replacement seems to have replaced virtually all other procedures used in the past. The same applies to osteotomies, muscle release and others. Fusion, however, is a procedure that still has a place in the armamentarium of the orthopaedic surgeon. The fact that it is not frequently performed does not mean that it should be totally dismissed.

There are situations when a fusion is the only viable alternative. A child or adolescent suffering from certain posttraumatic or septic conditions is the appropriate subject for the procedure. Very active young adults with conditions such as active infection may also be candidates for arthrodesis. Though I would had made this argument with strong conviction a few years ago, I find myself wondering if such an attitude is logical at this time. Infections are being managed successfully with increasing frequency. In addition, the undesirable sequella of hip fusion are many and the results from total hip replacement are becoming increasingly better. Back pain, and particularly secondary knee osteoarthritis, is found in too many people who underwent arthrodesis of the hip joint earlier in life.

Therefore, I find it increasingly difficult to recommend fusion for young people even though I am keenly aware that most of them are not capable of protecting an artificial joint sufficiently enough to make it last for a long period of time. When a young person suffering from an arthritic disease of the hip, he or she, will usually request a total replacement. They have heard that some professional athletes have had the operation. What they do not know is how quickly they found themselves in surgery again having the replacement revised. Attempts to educate them are usually an exercise in futility.

The fact that there are orthopaedists who openly recommend total hip replacement for the very young has made that education virtually impossible. More recently, the enthusiasm for "new" techniques and materials has given increased expectations to those seeking an answer to their painful conditions. I anticipate that adolescents and young adults experiencing the limitations that healed Perthes and slipped capital femoral epiphysis often produce will be subjected to total hip replacement surgery. The fact that most patients afflicted with those conditions do not develop symptoms until late in life should not be ignored.

SECTION II – THE HIP JOINT

Recently I was asked to render an opinion concerning a nine-year-old child whose congenital dysplastic hip was producing pain and disability. A few years earlier he had been subjected to reconstructive surgery. The physician and the patient's family wanted to know if a total hip replacement could be done. I have the uncomfortable feeling they found someone who satisfied their wishes.

When hip fusions are performed it is not unusual to find that in the process the gluteus mediums is denervated. If such a fusion is "taken down" at a later date, and a total hip is performed a significant limp can be expected. On one occasion a very attractive lady in her mid-forties came to me asking to have her fused hip replaced with a total hip arthroplasty. My examination revealed a complete absence of the abductor mechanism, which in my opinion contraindicated the procedure. Not satisfied with my answer she sought advice elsewhere. She ended-up having a total hip arthroplasty performed. The gait she subsequently displayed was grotesque and a series of recurrent dislocations made her life miserable. The ipsilateral knee soon developed instability and pain.

I have "taken down" a few fused hips because of progressively incapacitating osteoarthritis of the knee and or lumbosacral spine. The procedures were performed without trochanteric osteotomy (Fig. 82 a.b). It usually takes these patients a longer period of time to regain motion and to develop strong abductor power to walk without a limp. The abductor muscles have been minimally functional for a long time and therefore severely atrophied.

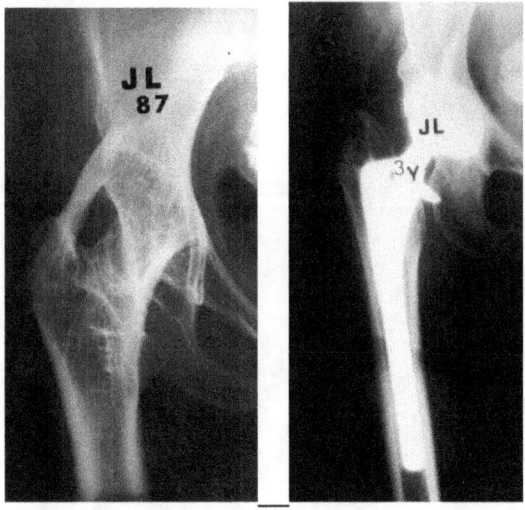

Fig. Surgically fused tuberculous joint was replaced because of knee and back pain.

SECTION II – THE HIP JOINT

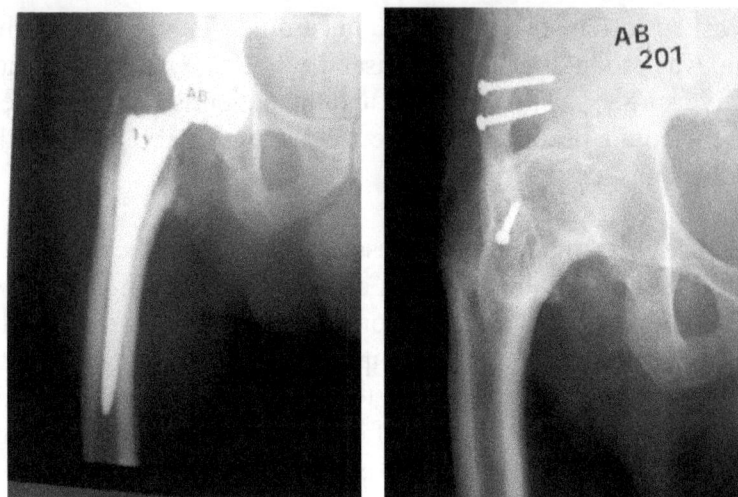

Fig. Surgically fused hip 30 years earlier. Following total hip surgery function, back and knee pain significantly improved.

G

GRAFT (Acetabulum-Total hip)

There are those who believe that bone grafting of the shallow acetabulum is frequently necessary. I do not think so. This does not mean that the shallow acetabulum should never be grafted, for indeed there are times when the grafting is absolutely necessary. In most instances is possible, however, to obtain good containment of the artificial acetabular component without resorting to grafting.

I have come to the realization that in many instances, when a graft is used, only a very small portion of the graft provided support to the artificial socket (FIG. 83 a, b,c.). Obviously, a socket that does not have complete coverage is vulnerable. Mild lack of coverage, however, is not harmful. This statement gains greater credence when non-cemented porous sockets are used. If bone ingrowth is obtained over the medial/superior surface of the cup, the fixation obtained may be sufficient.

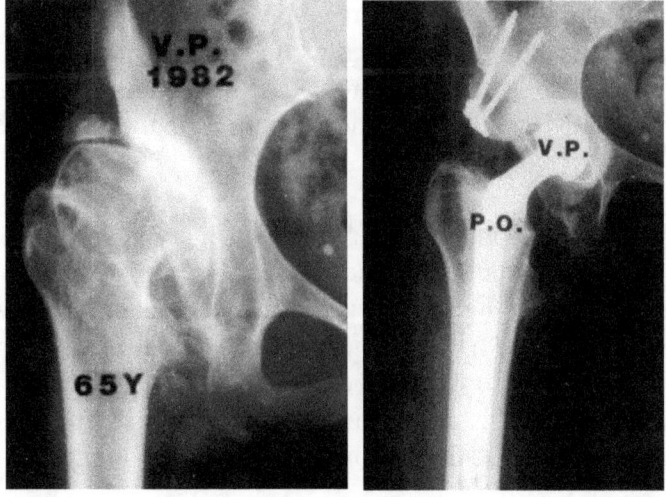

Fig. Advanced osteoarthritis secondary to hip dysplasia. Notice the shallow acetabulum. Once the acetabulum is deepened the graft no longer provides additional support.

SECTION II – THE HIP JOINT

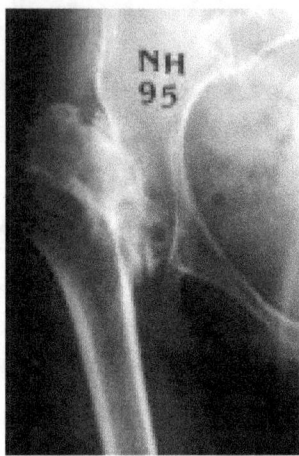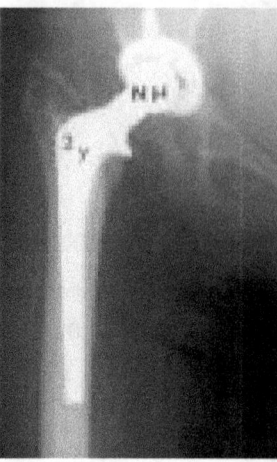

Fig. A sequela of a congenitally dislocated hip. It is possible in many instances to perform total hip arthroplasty without the need for trochanteric osteotomy or acetabular grafting.

Militating against bone grafting of the acetabulum is the fact that large grafts may undergo late resorption or collapse. Progressive revascularization and remodeling of the dead bone may prompt the late collapse, since the new bone does not yet have the mechanical properties necessary to withstand the powerful forces to which the acetabulum is subjected. If no revascularization occurs, the cumulative stresses on the non-viable bone may result in its collapse. There are those, like Rene Marti, from the Netherlands, who holds opposite views and has reported very convincingly full incorporation of the graft eventually takes place. (Fig. 84 a, b.)

The placement of cancellous bone to fill large defects has been proven to be effective when used with the technique of "impaction" developed by professor Sloof in Holland. However, I am rather skeptical about the routine use of cancellous graft whenever a defect is found. I doubt the value of adding a second interface to the system. When using this technique porous surfaces should not be used. To expect the "dead" bone graft to grow into the porosity of the metallic cup is wishful thinking. The remaining normal bone on the deficient acetabulum is more likely to achieve growth into the porous surface.

Grafts placed medially to fill defects in the acetabulum are not always necessary. The porous fixation obtained throughout the rest of the structure is usually sufficient to ensure long lasting fixation. (Fig. 85 a, b, c) I have seen several grafts placed in that region undergo resorption. The reasons for that phenomenon are not fully understood by me.

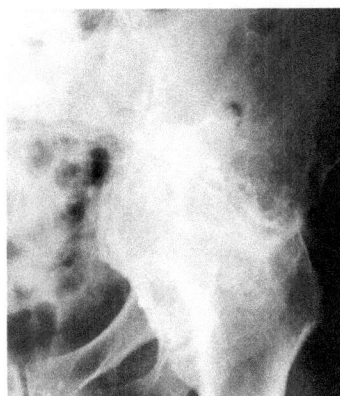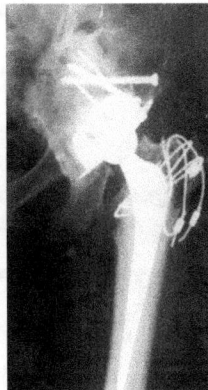

Fig. Central dislocation of the hip. The femoral head was used as an acetabular graft.

I have found that large medial defects such as those encountered following an ununited fracture of the medial wall of the pelvis can be managed well by transfixing the femoral head to the surrounding pelvic bone. Under those circumstances the acetabular cup should be cemented. (Fig. 86 a,b.). Once I elected to leave in place a well-fixed cemented acetabular component and simply replaced the femoral component. The polyethylene socket was in a protrusion situation. I cemented a new plastic socket on top of the old, one after drilling several holes into the polyethylene cup and packing more cement (Fig.)

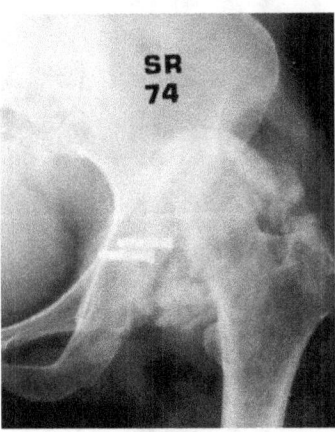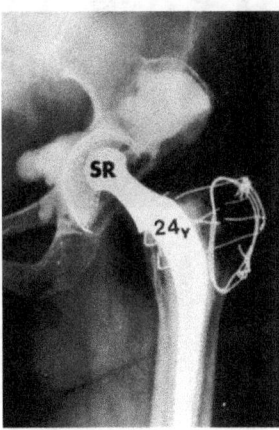

Fig. Old dislocated hip. Charnley prosthesis inserted after filling the acetabuloar defect with acrylic cement.

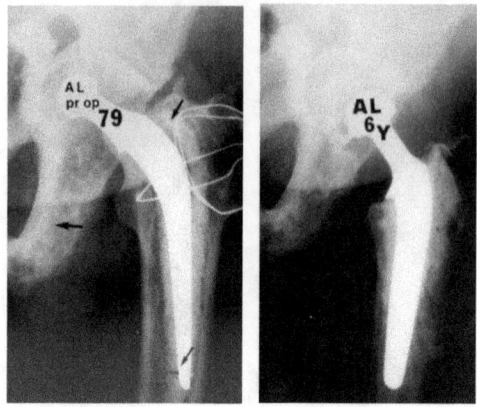

Fig. Failed cemented femoral component on a patient with Paget's disease. The acetabulum was left in place. A new plastic acetabular implant was cemented over the old one; and the femoral component was revised.

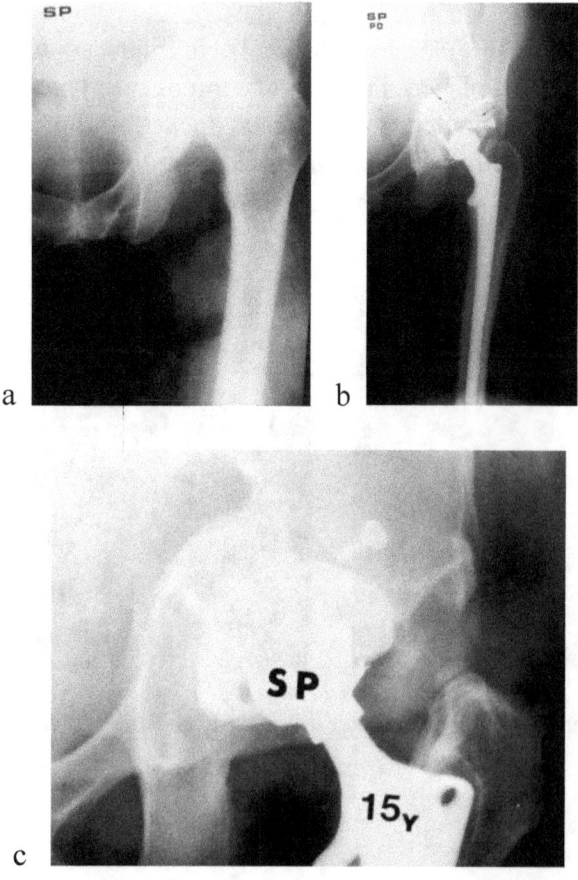

Fig. a, b and c. Post-traumatic osteoarthritis treated with an Isoelastic acetabulum cemented over the sectioned femoral head. The Isoelastic socket failed. The graft-head had incorporated into the pelvic bone.

SECTION II – THE HIP JOINT

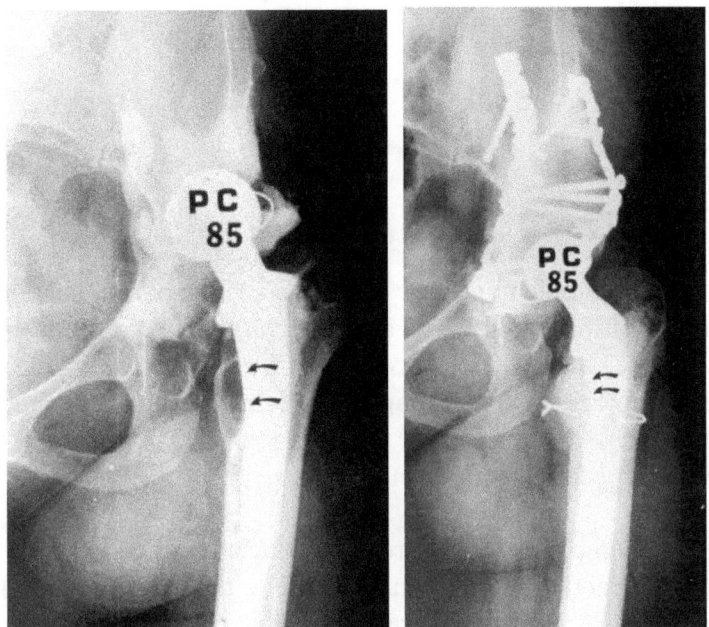

Fig. a and b. Failed cemented total hip replacement treated with femoral autograph, reinforced with metallic plates.

SECTION II – THE HIP JOINT

H

HETEROTOPIC BONE

It is well know that heterotopic bone may form in a variety of clinical conditions. Its etiology is not clear. It is seen following burns and often at a distance from the site of the burn. It is not uncommon to see those with burns around the hand develop heterotopic bone about the elbow that may even fuse the joint completely. Its presence is even more common following head injuries. The possibility of some type of metabolic or chemical abnormality triggering the phenomenon has been widely discussed.

Heterotopic bone is a complication that frequently occurs following total hip surgery and open reduction of pelvic fractures. I personally believe that the clinical consequences of such a development have been greatly exaggerated, and that in most instances the presence of some new bone in the area is inconsequential. The degree of limitation of motion of the hip is oftentimes minimal. However, it can be severe enough to create serious problems and also predispose to dislocation. I find the frequent use of radiation difficult to justify unless there is a history of previous heterotopic bone formation. Indocin seems to be as effective as more radical measures.

I suspect that in the case of the total hip, a possible cause for the heterotopic bone is the degree of trauma inflicted to the soft tissues during the surgical procedure. Surgery that is performed through a small incision and requires forceful retraction cannot be performed without traumatizing tissues and creating the physiological environment that leads to the formation of new bone. The traumatized tissues are temporarily rendered partially avascular. This brings about changes in the pH of the local medium and therefore the deposition of calcium. A phenomenon probably similar to the one observed around torn conoid and trapezoid ligaments of the shoulder following acromio-clavicular dislocations. This explanation may not suffice since the "bone" seen there is calcification, not ossification.

We should not panic prematurely when we see heterotopic bone form around a total hip replacement. Oftentimes the initial limitation of motion improves spontaneously. The illustrated clinical case proves the point (Fig. 90 a,b,c.)

If the limitation of motion is major, it is also a good idea to wait until the active process has been completed. Early attempts to remove the new bone are followed by early recurrence of the pathological process. A cold bone scan is a reliable method to determine when to intervene surgically. Douglas Garland, from California, who has seriously studied the problems associated with heterotopic bone over the years, has said to me that in the case of the head injured patient, the bone scan activity is not as important as the degree of spasticity at the time of surgery. The spastic patient is more likely to develop new bone following its resection.

It has been my experience that the presence of bony spurs on the ischial tuberosities prior to surgery is not a reliable predictor of post-operative heterotopic bone. Nor is the disease for which the operation is performed. I have not found, for example, that patients suffering from ankylosing spondylitis are more prone to develop the complication.

What I have noticed is that many of the patients who developed massive amounts of new bone experienced a disproportional degree of pain in the immediate post-operative period. (Fig. 91 a,b.)

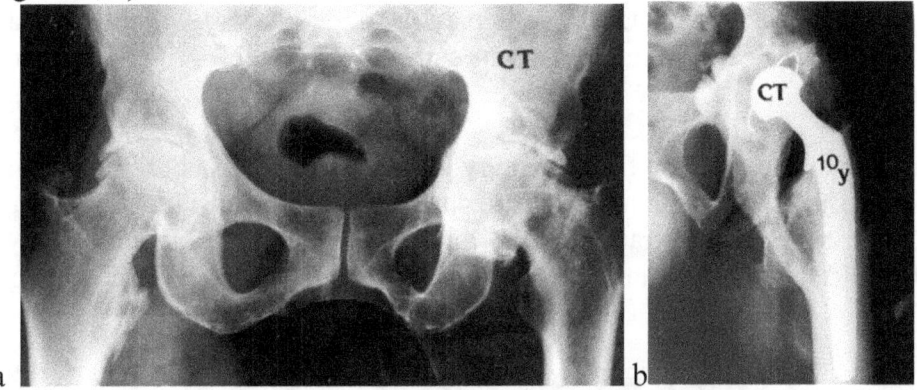

Fig. a and b. Osteoarthritis treated with cemented total hip arthroplasty. Spontaneous ankylosis rapidly developed.

In the case of open reduction of fractures of the pelvis it is interesting to note that the heterotopic bone almost always forms over the outer surface of the pelvic bone, even though the soft tissues are stripped from bone on both tables. I suspect that the reason for this phenomenon is that intestinal peristalsis and its resulting pulsatile nature, prevents the new bone formation. In the same manner that the intermittent expansion of an aortic aneurysm dissolves adjacent vertebral bodies.

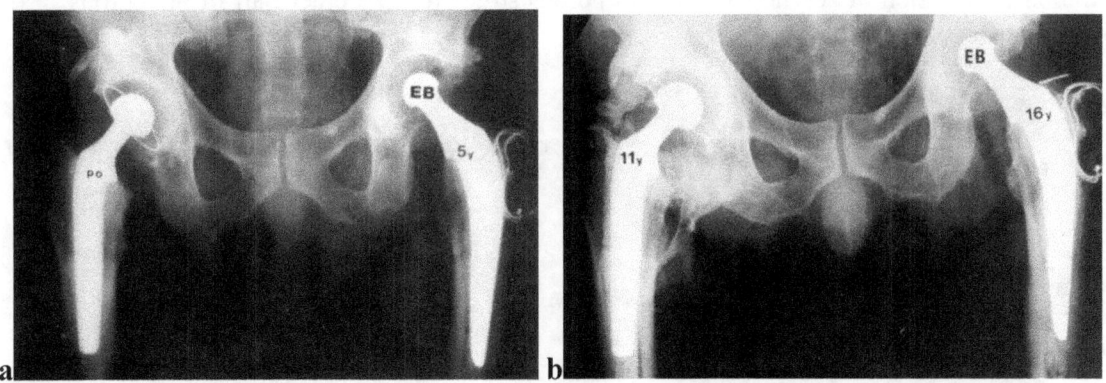

Fig. A and b. Heterotopic bone formed when the second implant was performed. Despite the massive amount of new bone the range of motion of the hips was almost identical in both hips.

HYBRID TOTAL HIPS

When the orthopaedic community began to have concerns about the value of porous, non-cemented total hips I thought a simple method could be developed that would take advantage of porous ingrowth while retaining the known efficacy of acrylic cement. I developed a simple system where one-centimeter "cubes" of porous metal were driven tightly into the cancellous bone of the acetabulum and proximal femur, until their outer surface was flush with the floor of the socket and the endosteal surface of the femur. At this point the acetabulum was firmly packed with acrylic cement in the traditional way. I anticipated that bone would grow into the deep wire mesh, and the cement would stabilize the plastic socket in a better way.

We had tested the concept in the laboratory prior to using the "cubes" in the human. We learned that pressurizing cement into a square porous "cube" –placed inside a container- would allow the material to penetrate half the thickness of the metallic structure. The remaining half would remain in contact with cancellous bone, into which bone could grow. (Fig. 92).

Fig.. Illustration of intrusion of acrylic cement into porous structure. The other half of the porous material is in contact with bone.

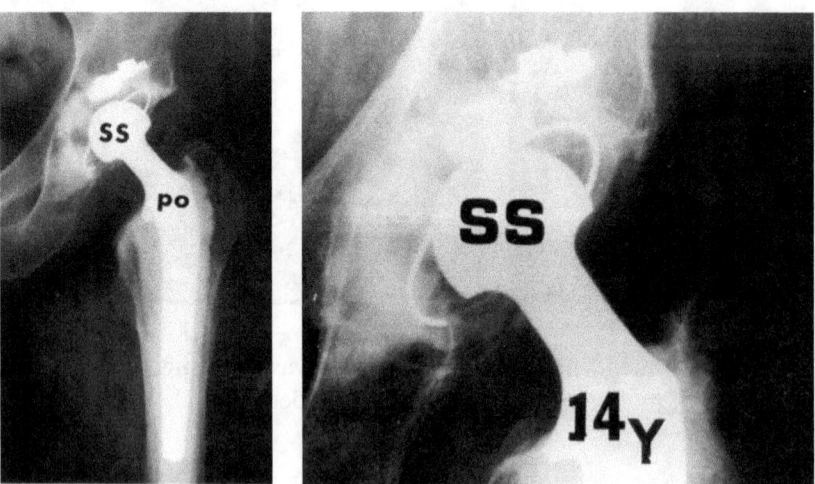

Fig. Fourteen-year follow-up of cemented fixation of porous "cube" to ensure bone ingrowth.

We used this technique in thirty-five patients. Originally, only in the acetabulum but later in both components. After a while, using well designed instruments, the insertion of the plugs became an easy task. Under the microscope, we saw evidence of bone having grown into the mesh. Sometimes, however, the porous material was filled with soft fibrous connective tissue. Though we later reviewed the experiences and found them satisfactory, I began to wonder if the totally porous metallic cup was not easier to insert and associated with an even higher degree of success. Therefore, we abandoned the use of this "hybrid" method of prosthetic fixation. (Fig. 93 a,.b.).

The concept of total hip prostheses performed using cement on the femoral side of the hip joint and a non-cemented acetabulum, gained popularity in the mid-1980's. By that time orthopaedists had concluded that non-cemented components were performing well in the acetabulum but not as well on the femoral side of non-cemented implants. The combination of the two systems was most appealing. Whether or not the procedure proves to be significantly superior to totally cemented or totally non-cemented techniques is not yet known.

We have carefully reviewed our experiences with the current hybrid method and have compared it with the experiences we had with totally cemented implants. We selected patients from the two groups and tried to match them according to age, sex and underlying disease. All patients had had cemented Titanium alloy, mono-block femoral components with heads of 28 millimeters. One group had non-cemented acetabular components of the Harris- Galante type. We evaluated the traditional elements of cement thickness, prosthesis orientation, canal-stem ratio and acetabular orientation and coverage. Post-operatively various changes were recorded, such as revision, the presence of bone-cement and metal-cement radiolucent lines, fractures of the cement, wear and lysis.

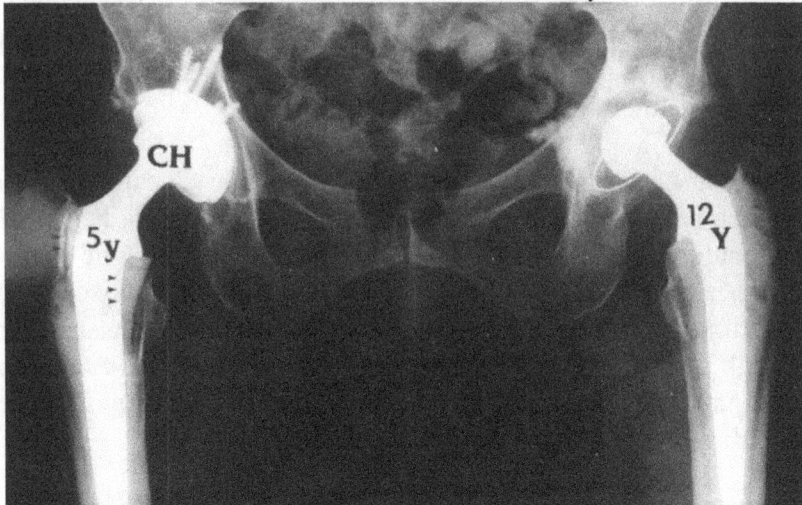

Fig. Illustration of bone-cement radiolucent lines on the Hybrid side.

We found that all major adverse changes took place in larger numbers in the hybrid group. Wear, for example, was twice as great in the hybrid group. The incidence of calcar resorption, cement-metal and bone-cement radiolucent lines was also higher in the hybrid group. On the other hand, the complication rate on the acetabular side was lower in the hybrid group. The findings supported the concept that the non-cemented acetabulum performs better. However, the pathological changes on the femoral side increase under those circumstances. (Fig. 94 and 95 a, b.).

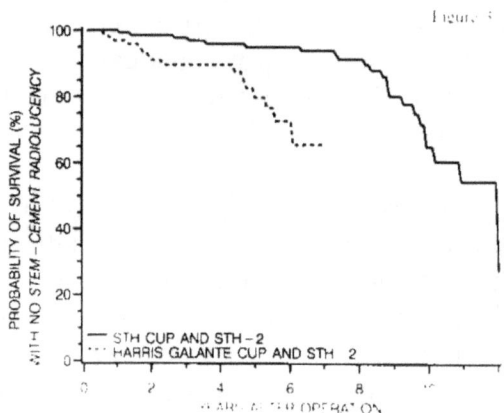

Fig.. A comparative study of totally cemented and hybrid total hips indicated a higher incidence of stem-cement radiolucency in the hybrid group. The same was true for the degree of wear and bone-cement radiolucency.

We had previously measured the wear of our Titanium alloy femoral prosthesis and had compared it with that of stainless steel implants. The Titanium alloy implants had shown measurable wear slightly higher than stainless steel. However, the wear was lower when compared with other surgeons' reports using stainless steel and cobalt chrome alloys. We also knew from previous experiments and clinical observations that cemented titanium alloy femoral components performed poorly when used in combination with cemented metal-backed acetabuli (See METAL BACKED ACETABULUM). We had concluded that in this environment, fragmented particles of cement and metal from the acetabular side travel into the joint space and initiate a dangerous third-body wear process [62, 67, 71, 141].

This observations and extrapolations have made me very suspicious that non-cemented total hips, which have been reported to be associated with a higher incidence of lytic changes in the acetabulum and femoral canal, may be developing the lytic changes from loose particles of metal, generated in some instances from toggling that may occur between the stem and the surrounding bone. Since many total hips cemented prostheses are made of a Titanium alloy, the high rate of lysis can be explained. This forces me to conclude that Titanium alloy implants, unless significantly improved, should be abandoned in preference to cobalt-chrome or stainless steel implants.

I

INFECTION IN TOTAL HIPS

One of the most dreadful complications associated with total hip replacement is infection. Over the years this problem has become less frequent and today we have assumed a rather cavalier attitude that one day we might regret. Our heavy reliance on the power of antibiotics is responsible for that attitude.

As far as I know, most, if not all surgeons use prophylactic antibiotics in different ways and amounts. There seems to be ample evidence to indicate that intravenous antibiotics must be given immediately preceding surgery in order for them to be truly effective. Also, that one day of antibiotic prophylaxis is all that is needed. In spite of that evidence, I have not been able to discontinue the routine I have used for nearly three decades: I expose the joint and observe the synovial fluid. If surgery of any kind had been performed earlier, I obtain a sample for gram-stain studies and request a permanent culture. I do not administer antibiotics prior to obtaining the sample fluid. I am afraid that the prior administration of antibiotics might give a false reading. I also profusely irrigate the wound with an antibiotic solution throughout the entire surgical procedure.

If the synovial fluid is clear and the patient had no previous surgery, I proceed to request the IV injection of antibiotics. For the past few years I have used one gram of Ancef, which I give for three additional days, four times a day.

It is possible that the amount of antibiotics I give is unnecessary high. I continue to do it based on reasons that may not be scientific or logical. I do it because I think that the prolonged administration might be good in preventing possible infection associated with the epidural and Foley catheters. I used to leave the epidural catheter for two or three days and the Foley for twenty-four hours. The fact that my infection rate has been low with this protocol has, in my opinion, justified its continued use. I, no longer leave the epidural catheter in place longer than 24 hours. I gave up the old practice upon noticing a high incidence of hypotensive episodes upon initiation of ambulation on the first post-operative day.

We have submitted for publication a manuscript summarizing my personal experiences with infection in over two thousand total hip arthroplasty. Doctor Goswami, from the United Kingdom, who served as a reconstruction surgery fellow in our department in Los Angeles ten years ago, conducted the study [31].

When he first showed me his preliminary findings indicating that the number of infected primary hips was very low, I reacted by saying that, to the best of recollection, I have had more infections that the small number he had presented to me. I mentioned by name several patients I could readily remember. It turned out that most of those patients had

had secondary rather than primary surgery. A previous procedure such as nailing of a fracture, an osteotomy or partial joint replacement had been performed earlier.

Doctor Goswami divided the data into three categories: a) primary arthroplasties, made of the truly "virgin hips"; b) secondary arthroplasties, consisting of patients who had previous surgeries, excluding total hip replacements; and c) revision surgery that included only those patients who had had a previous total hip arthroplasty.

The results were very interesting: the deep infection rate for the first group (group a) was 0.8%; for the secondary group (group b) was 1.5%; and for the revision group (group c) 2.5%. The findings suggested that if the protocol described above is carefully followed the infection rate in total hip surgery could be very low.

It is interesting to note that Sir John Charnley, who reported a very low incidence of infections, never used prophylactic local intra-operative irrigation or systemic antibiotics of any kind. He argued that such a practice was a mistake and I heard him say, referring to the use of antibiotics, that "eventually the chickens will come home to roost". He anticipated a high incidence of late infections under those circumstances. He was absolutely convinced that infections were exogenous in nature and, therefore, the best way to prevent them was by taking isolation precautions in the operating room. His believe on the effectiveness of the vertical laminar airflow was unshakable.

I have been pleasantly surprised to see the success rate recently obtained with antibiotic management of infected total hips. In earlier years I saw a number of infected total hips, which in spite of removal of all foreign material and thorough debridement of the area, continued to drain. Oftentimes, a second or third debridement was necessary. At this time, prolonged IV antibiotic therapy following thorough debridement has made the prognosis much better [84].

A couple of years ago I was asked to care for a rheumatoid woman in her early sixties who had an infected total hip prosthesis that drained profusely. Staph aureous. coagulase positive was the identified organism. She refused my recommendation to remove the implant.

Because of her adamant plea for the preservation of the implant, I acquiesced. I opened the hip widely and debrided as much as I could. The cemented metallic and plastic components were bathed in pus and the quality of the soft tissues was poor, as is often the case in patients with sub-acute chronic infections, particularly in the rheumatoid patient. I closed the skin loosely and asked the infectious disease specialist to prescribe the appropriate antibiotics. She received intravenous antibiotics for six weeks. The wound never drained again and the hip became asymptomatic. Two years later she suffered a major stroke that left her operated side markedly spastic. The prosthesis dislocated but her treating physician did not recognize the dislocation for nearly two months.

Under the new painful circumstances she agreed to the removal of the implant. No signs of infection were found, and all cultures taken at the time of surgery were negative. I think such success was made possible by better antibiotics.

INTERTROCHANTERIC FRACTURES

There is no doubt that closed intramedullary nailing has earned a place in the armamentarium of the orthopaedic surgeon. However, the system is not a panacea and many have reported complications. Its success in the very comminuted, unstable intertrochanteric fracture is limited, leaving room for the traditional nail/plate combination.

There are factors that are important in determining the efficacy of any intramedullary nail. In the absence of fracture stability, achieved by contact between the proximal and distal fragments, weight-bearing stresses are taken by the metallic appliance. Much the same as in the case of the comminuted diaphyseal fractures of the tibia or femoral diaphysis. In addition, in the case of the diaphyseal fracture the forces are primarily of an impaction nature, where in the intertrochanteric fracture the forces are also of a bending nature. The tendency of the nail to cut superiorly is offset mainly by the cancellous bone of the proximal metaphysis and epiphysis of the femur.

Success with interlocking nailing of intertrochanteric fractures is predicated on obtaining contact of cortical surfaces (something that is impossible with comminuted fractures or in those with an extremely vertical geometry).

These observations come from personal clinical and laboratory experiences. I published studies on the behavior of intertrochanteric fractures using retrieved proximal femur from patients that had expired within a few days after surgery. Using very crude methods of investigation, we placed the entire proximal femurs under a hydraulic vise and applied vertical loading. The changes that took place in the relationship between the bone and the nail were recorded by means of photography and sequential radiographs [83, 94].

It became obvious that oblique intertrochanteric fractures, where anatomical contact between the cortical walls of the proximal and distal fragments had been obtained at the time of surgery, tolerated vertical forces greater than the yield point of the appliance itself. If the vertical pressure continued the nail eventually bent. This meant that the bone itself was taking most of the weight and that the nail was only providing stability against a varus deformity. When contact between the medial surfaces of the two major fragments was not achieved, the nails cut out of the neck superiorly in a rapid manner.

When we compared the efficacy of 135 and 150-degree nails under similar mechanical conditions, we documented that the 150 degrees nail tolerated much higher forces. These findings gave me the necessary support to pursue studies with two different angle nails, which eventually led to the development of an I-Beam nail. We elected this design as we confirmed that its strength and rotation-prevention characteristics were superior the then popular tri-flanged Jewett nail.

Subsequently, we modified the I-Beam design when we realized that the geometry of the proximal nail made its initial penetration into hard femoral head difficult at times. The modification resulted in a nail-plate that had its tip end shaped like a T-Beam. The cutting power of the nail was improved.

My clinical experiences were gratifying for the most part. In moderately oblique fractures where reduction of a large surface of the two major fragments was achieved in surgery (even if the lesser trochanter was avulsed and left unreduced) we allowed patients to bear weight before leaving the hospital. In many instances, the protocol called for graduation to a cane prior to discharge (Fig. 36 a,b.)

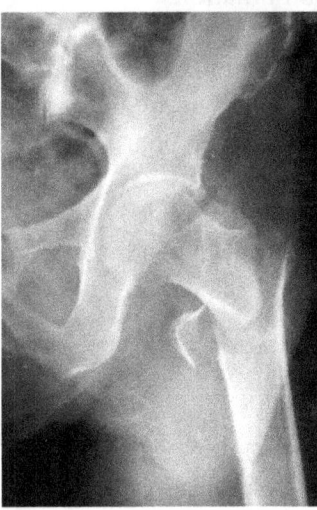 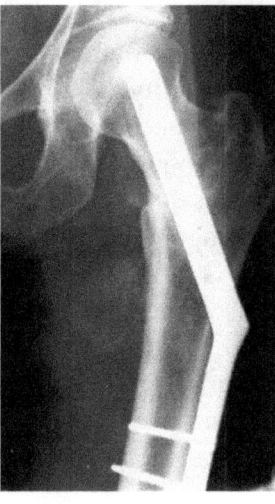

Fig. a and b. Stable intertrochanteric fractured treated with 150 degree I-Beam nail that permitted immediate weight bearing ambulation.

Richards Manufacturing Company introduced the sliding nail to the orthopaedic community shortly afterwards. The concept had been conceived by Kay Clawson, then professor and chairman of orthopaedics at Washington University in Seattle. This nail constituted a major advance in hip surgery and readily eclipsed our one-unit I-Beam nail. The sliding properties of the Richards nail reduced the incidence of superior migration of the nail. Stable fractures, however, do not need sliding nails because cortical surfaces prevent such sliding. The bone itself, as I indicated earlier, absorbs weight-bearing stresses.

More vertical fractures, even if anatomically reduced, cannot be subjected to major weight bearing because of the likely possibility that shearing stresses would permit the fragments to displace and the nail to move in an upward direction, eventually cutting through the articular cartilage. This observation prompted me to describe a valgus osteotomy, which for a number of years we used with some success in a large percentage of instances. The valgus osteotomy made possible the achievement of contact between the medial cortex of the two main fragments now oriented in a less acute angle (Fig.37 a,b,c,d. and 38 a, b. and 39 a,b,c,d,e). [102, 106].

SECTION II – THE HIP JOINT

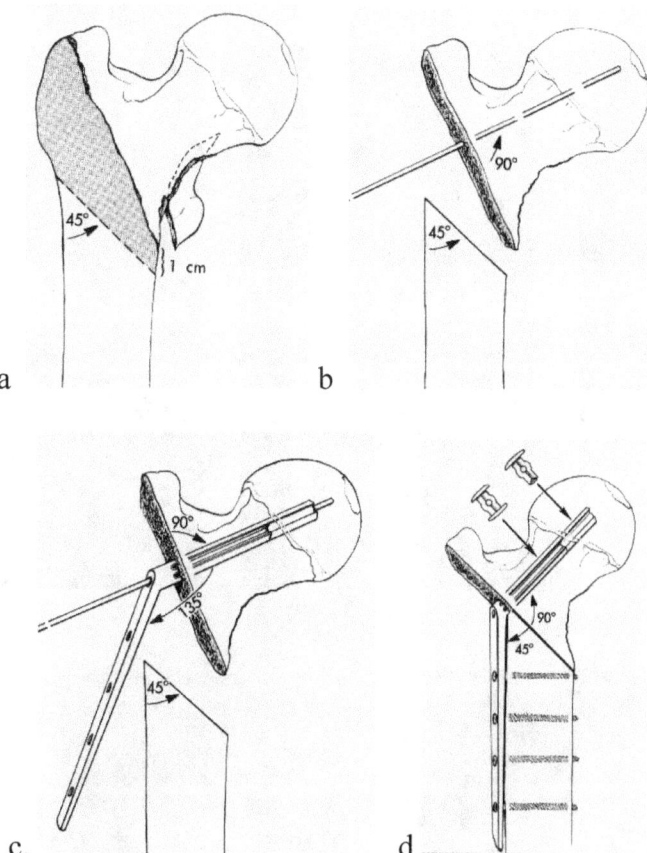

Fig. a, b, c and d. The femur is sectioned at a 45 degree angle with its apex determining one centimeter below the end of the proximal fragment. This one-centimeter prevents making the leg too long (a). The bony segment is excised or displaced and the 13 degree-angle is driven into the head of the femur at a 90-degree angle (b). Then the fracture is reduced. Contact between intact, more horizontal surfaces is achieved (d).

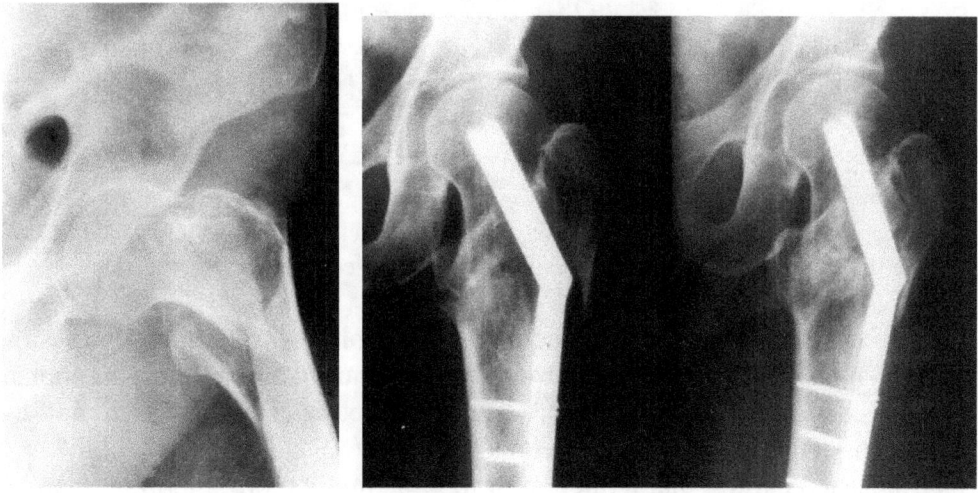

Fig. a and b. Unstable vertical intertrochanteric fracture (a) treated with a valgus osteotomy. Notice the contact between the now more horizontal cortical surfaces (b).

SECTION II – THE HIP JOINT

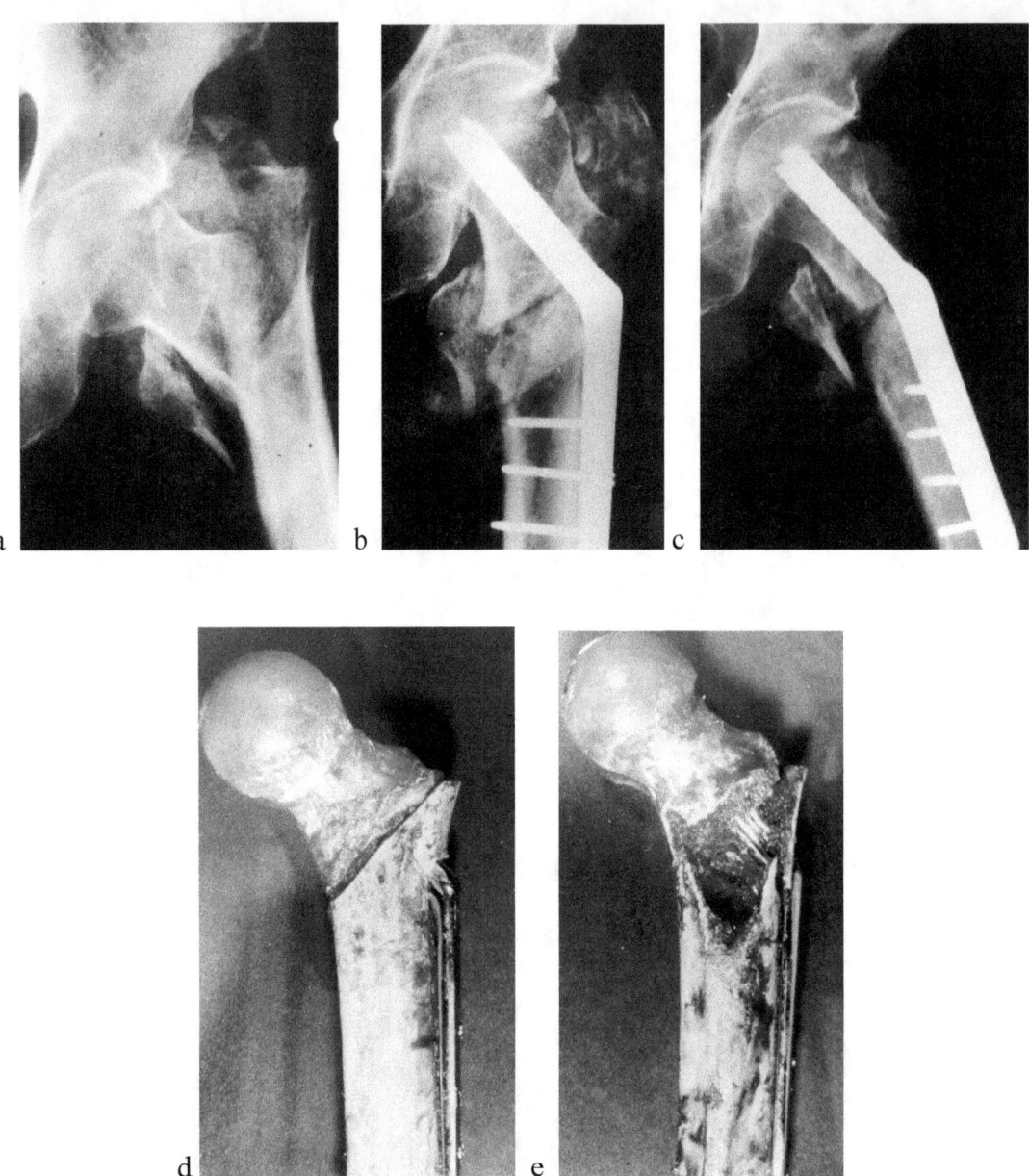

Fig. a, b, c, d and e. Radiographs obtained in surgery following the performance of a valgus osteotomy (a, b and c). The patient expired a few days later and the proximal femur was dissected and analyzed. Notice the stable reduction of the medial and anterior cortices (d and e).

During the process of studying hip fractures I was able to make some interesting observations. For example, I recognized that absent weight bearing and contrary to popular belief, the main varus deforming force in intertrochanteric fractures is he contraction of the adductor muscles rather than the abductor mechanism (See VARUS DEFORMITIES). I also learned, as I indicated earlier, that reduction of the fracture is more important than the design or shape of the nail. That the best position of the nail in the femoral neck, contrary to still popular belief, is not posterior, but anterior. I suspect that we have been told that the nail should be placed posteriorly because when it cuts out of the head it is almost always in an anterior direction. The conclusion was that the nail should be placed posteriorly to increase the opposing mass of bone and make longer the traveling distance of the displacing nail.

Though, the argument is attractive, it cannot be supported with evidence. Quite the contrary, common sense suggests the opposite. A good way to illustrate my argument that the nail, at the level of the fracture itself, should be against the anterior wall of the femur is with the following analogy. The force of a heavy wind will throw an unstable object, sitting on the ground, against the nearest wall. If the object initially leans against the wall, rather than away from it before the storms arrive, it has no place to go.

In the case of the reduced intertrochanteric fracture, the forces acting on the proximal femur are of an external rotation nature, as depicted by the fact that the leg has a tendency to rotate externally, rather than internally. The external rotation means that the nail is forced to move anteriorly and eventually cut out of the head in an anterior direction. If the nail leans against the anterior wall of both fragments, external rotation forces simply press the nail against the "wall" of the bone and it cannot cut out in that manner. [83, 94] (Fig. 40 a, b and 41 a, b).

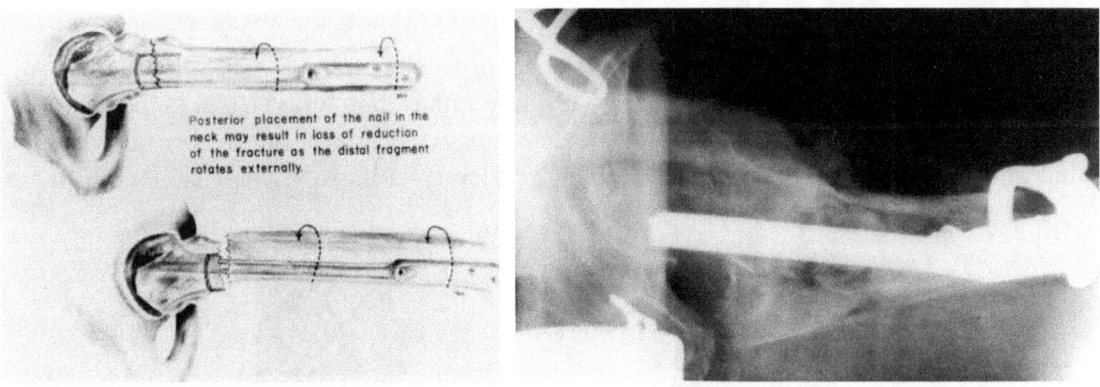

Fig. The nail close to the posterior wall, at the level of the fracture provides less stability When the leg rotates externally.

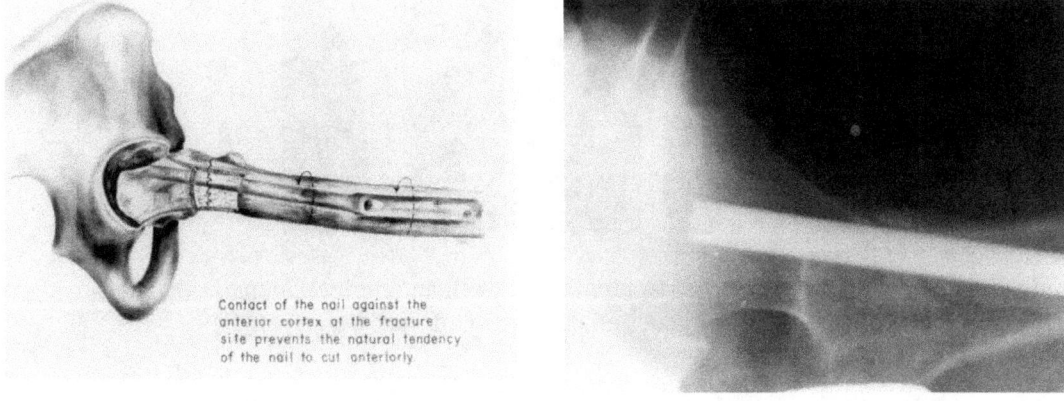

Fig.. The placement of the nail close to the anterior cortex of the femoral, at the level of the fracture provides additional stability against anterior cutting of the nail.

SECTION II – THE HIP JOINT

My premise about the desirable position of the nail against the anterior corteces of the bone, as shown on a lateral x-ray, does not negate that perhaps its proximal end should be slightly posterior in the femoral head. I say, perhaps, because I suspect that since the femoral head is equally dense throughout, it should make no difference where in its surface should the nail be. Furthermore, since the femoral neck has a few degrees of anteversion, a nail that is placed parallel to the ground and anteriorly at the level of the fracture, ends-up in the center of the head.

In more recent times intramdedullary nail has become a frequently preferred method of internal fixation for intertrochanteric fractures. The method is not new; Kuntscher, in Germany used in the 1940s. However, image intensification in the operating room in the United States did reach wide usage until a few decades later. There is little doubt today that IM, interlocking nailing is a very good technical approach. It requires, as it is true for many other techniques, a clear understanding of its rational, indications and contraindications.

A high degree of intrinsic stability of the fracture must be obtained in order to achieve healing without collapse of the fractures and either penetration of the nail into the pelvis or into the soft tissues above the femur. The ideal fracture to be treated with an interlocking nail is the one where the medial corteces of the two major fragments of the fracture are approximated. This reduction permits the concentration of forces on the bone rather than on the nail. Therefore the fracture that is moderately oblique rather than too vertical is the most likely to withstand maintenance of reduction (Fig.   ). A vertical fracture, or one very comminuted and therefore not intrinsically stable, frequently collapses when subjected to weight bearing stresses (Fig   ).

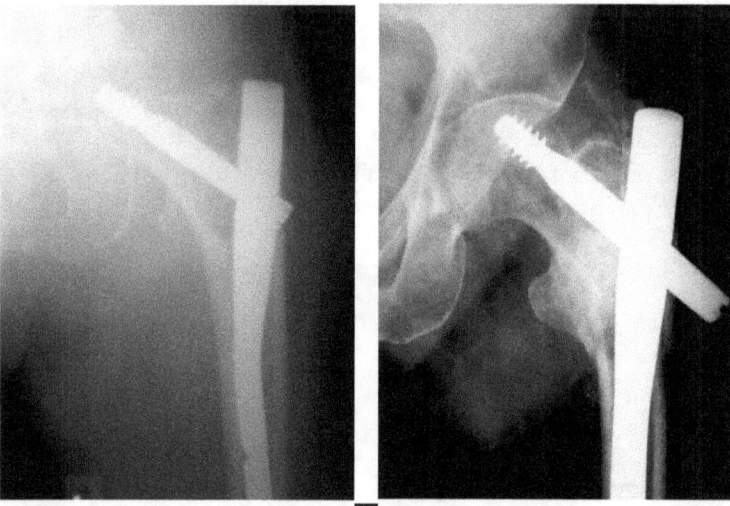

Fig. Anatomically reduced intertrochanteric fracture treated with an interlocking nail (a). The fracture healed while maintaining reduction. (Courtesy of Jack Cooper, MD)

SECTION II – THE HIP JOINT

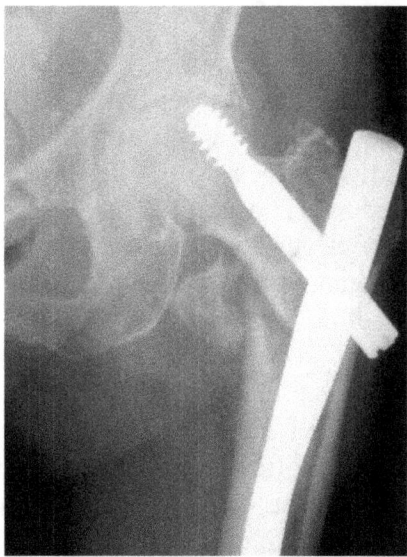

Fig.. Stable intertrochanteric fracture treated with an interlocking nail. Despite adequate contact of the major fragments the fracture displaced into varus. It is possible that the fracture was more unstable than initially suspected. (Courtesy of Jack Cooper, MD.

ISOELASTIC TOTAL HIP PROSTHESES

In the early 1980s, when the non-cemented total hip prosthesis was first introduced on the market, an isoelastic prosthesis was strongly heralded as the answer to the alleged problems arising from the "cement disease" I joined the crowd and began to look for the best non-cemented implant. Different ones became available within a few months. Somewhat skeptical at that time about porous implants, I took advantage of a trip to Europe to visit some of the individuals heavily involved in the development and use of the new implants.

Erwin Morscher, from Basle, Switzerland, advanced the concept of isoelastic prosthesis. The idea made a lot of sense to me. He had proposed an implant that had mechanical properties closer to those of bone and made of a material with a low modulus of elasticity. Loosening, therefore, should be lower. I visited with Morscher, learned about his technique and philosophy and observed him perform the procedure. I was very impressed with his early results. Then I went to Italy, where I visited with Renato Bombeli. He had a wealth of experience with the method and had capitalized on the huge northern Italian population suffering from osteoarthritis secondary to congenital hip dysplasia.

It was during my visit to northern Italy that I learned about the frequency of congenital hip disease in that part of the world. A high frequency shared by the southern Germans, particularly those from Bavaria. I later learned that there are only three other racial groups in the world with an even higher incidence of congenital hip disease: the Eskimos, Navajos and the Indians of Ecuador. The theory frequently expressed that congenital hip dislocation is due to the practice of wrapping the infants in a mummy-like garments that hold the legs in adduction loses credibility. Neither the Germans nor the Italians dress their infants in that manner. The Eskimos and Ecuadorian Indians do.

SECTION II – THE HIP JOINT

Bombelli gave me the opportunity to see him perform surgery in a large number of patients and allowed me to look at the pre and post-operative x-rays of all of his patients. The European experience with the two surgeons, who later were to become good personal friends, convinced me that the Isoelastic prosthesis was "the way to go". Upon my return to America, I began to perform the procedure. The early results were most gratifying clinically and radiographically. I must admit, however, that I never used the femoral component of the Isoelastic implant, only the acetabulum. I had been using a Titanium alloy implant with a low modulus of elasticity and therefore I did not see to change he isoelastic femoral component.

Shortly afterwards Morscher himself came to Los Angeles as my guest for a post-graduate course on total hip surgery. I performed surgery and he assisted me. I wanted to be sure that I was performing the procedure well. A couple of years later I received a telephone call from him informing me that his most recent review of his isoelastic prostheses had indicated an unexpected high incidence of complication. Loosening and lysis were seen with disturbing frequency. I argued with him that my experiences did not support his; that my better results could be explained by the fact that I had not used the isoelastic femoral component.

I began to look more carefully at the x-rays of my patients. Lo and behold, in a short time I identified the same problems Morscher had seen. Within the very short follow-up of seven years I saw more than 70 per cent of my patients developing sufficient pathology to require revision surgery. At the time of the revision surgery we demonstrated massive amount of plastic debris separating the plastic cup from the underlying bone. (Fig. 96 a, b. and 97 a, b.) We undertook the task of carefully analyzing the material and studying the microscopic findings.

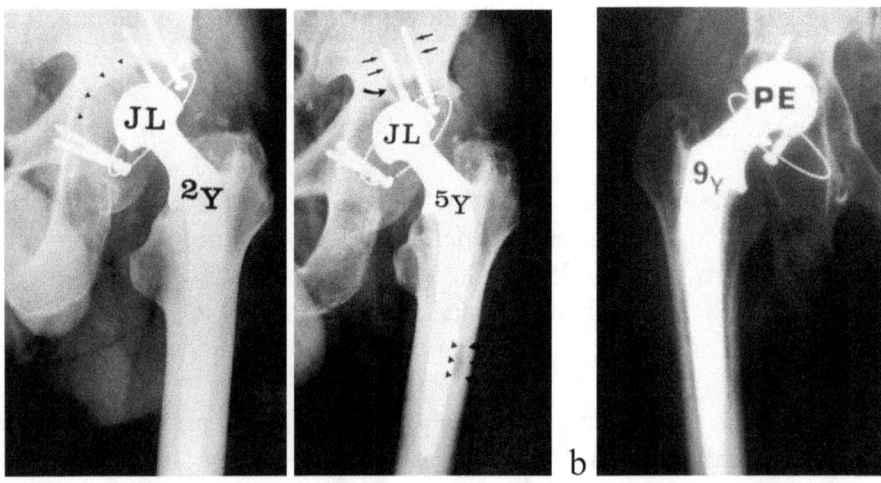

Fig. a,b. Isoelastic acetabulum demonstrating at two years the desirable sclerotic line at the bone-plastic interface (a); three years later the line has disappeared and lytic lesions developed at the level of the calcar and on zone 2-3 of the femur (b). Fig. 118. An Isoelastic acetabulum nine years after implantation. Extensive wear resulted in penetration of the prosthetic head through the plastic material.

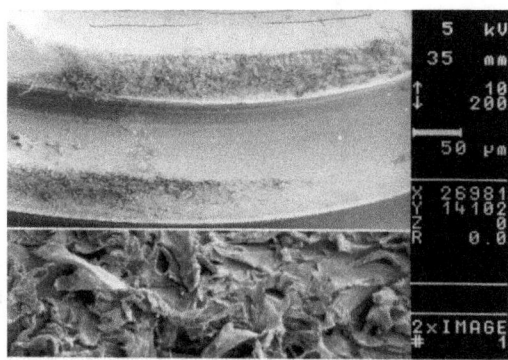

Fig. Under high magnification this unused Isoelastic acetabulum component shows serious manufacturing defects, which probably result in the rapid production of debris.

We discovered a very interesting feature: brand-new, unused isoelastic cups were often found to have manufacturing defects consisting of rough, unpolished surfaces that under repeated motion could fragment and break off (Fig. 98). We surmised that such a defect was one of the reasons for the high failure. Obviously, micro or macro-motion between the cup and the acetabular bone was producing the harmful plastic debris. The findings were published at a later date. [40]

I have always admired the intellectual honesty Morscher displayed when he called to inform me of the problems he was having with his prosthesis, and to advise me to abandon its use. Not very many people do that. This is depicted by the fact that a number of prostheses have disappeared from the market because of failure, but without the developers or manufacturing letting the orthopaedic community know about the failure and the reasons for discontinuing their usage. Worse than that, several of those implants continue to be marketed and sold. I was not surprised when I found out that some implants that have been discredited in the United States were being heavily marketed in Latin America. I surmise that the distributors of the implants were hoping to get rid of whatever inventory still existed. A very dishonest practice.

SECTION II – THE HIP JOINT

L

LABRUM   (ACETABULUM)

Very little attention was given in the past to the role of the acetabular labrum in regards to its integrity and possible role in the development of degenerative osteoarthritis. Only a few papers had appeared in the literature dealing with the subject

Having followed the recent interest in the subject during the ast ten to fifteen years I have become increasingly convinced that in many instances osteoarthritis is preceded by an acute or chronic damage to the labrum either in the form of a tear or a dislocation. Many patients who experience pain in the groin which is aggravated by flexion and rotation of the hip but who do not show radiological evidence of arthritis, eventually develop radiological changes.

I have referred for arthroscopy a few patients with painful flexion of the hip on whom a diagnosis of a damaged labrum was conformed. They all experienced significant relief but the several of them eventually developed the classical radiological and clinical picture of osteoarthritis. It appears that if the arthroscopic procedure does not reveal articular cartilage damage the prognosis following surgery is good. However, if the cartilage is damaged the procedure fails to provide long-term relief of symptoms.

As it is true with so many new techniques, arthroscopy of the hip is being abuse by some. I know of an orthopaedists who within a period of a couple of years has arthroscopically treated hundreds of patients "suffering from diseased acetabular labrum." The possibility exists that he is correct in his aggressive approach and that he may be blazing beneficial trails. I need to see some solid data before I cease to suspect that greed and hunger for fame are major reasons for his unorthodox practice.

R. Ganz, from Switzerland has presented some very interesting and convincing evidence regarding the etiology of labrum pathology. Ganz has suggested that the labrum is damaged when the neck of the femur abuts against the labrum in extreme positions of flexion. I am not comfortable with his theory. It does fit with the fact that valgus femoral necks, by virtue of their increased length, permit the hip a greater degree of motion and therefore diminishes any possible contact of the neck against the acetabular labrum. These are the patients who most frequently demonstrate labrum pathology, and the ones who show narrowing of the joint space superiorly. On the contrary, patients with varus hips are the ones who should experience abutment of of the neck of the femur against the pelvic bone sooner. They usually show arthritic changes that are either of the protrusion type or with narrowing of the joint space throughout

SECTION II – THE HIP JOINT

LAMINAR AIR FLOW SYSTEMS

Despite the fact that there is still controversy about their value, I do my total hip surgery in an operating room equipped with laminar airflow. I have chosen to take sides with John Charnley, who started the trend, because there is nothing to suggest it does any harm. Furthermore, there is plenty of data to suggest that it is beneficial. How can anyone argue against a system that reduces air contamination, a possible source of infection?

John Charnley's contributions to orthopaedics were many. Needless to say, the one that first comes to mind is his Total Hip Arthroplasty. However, I suspect his work on infection was equally as important. Charnley conducted his pioneer work in Wrightington, England in a facility, which by modern standards was inferior. Originally, it was a place for the treatment of tuberculosis and designed with open spaces and large patients wards. When converted to a hospital, the rate of postoperative infection was high, which led him to study the etiology of infections and to seek a solution.

He looked at the effect of traffic in the operating theater by measuring the number of bacteria that deposit on Petrie plates scattered throughout the room. He found out that the number of bacteria grows in direct proportion to the number of times people enters or leave the theater. Also that the bacteria count is greater when the number of people in the room is higher.

The attire of the surgeons and nursing personnel was also revealing. Female nurses "bellowed" a much greater number of bacteria when wearing skirts than when wearing long pants with ankle cuffs. Conversation also had an impact. The more talking in surgery took place the greater the degree of contamination.

Charnley then proceeded to develop the vertical laminar air system that is now used throughout the world. The air that the surgical team breathes is taken out of the operating room, making conversation safer and reducing the shedding of bacteria from the operating team.

Charnley concluded that a vertical airflow was superior to a horizontal one since the latter can create turbulence as it strikes solid objects such as the surgeon's body. He was so convinced that infections in surgery had an exogenous origin that he would not hesitate to carry out replacement arthroplasty on patients who had an active infection in another joint or bone in the body. He believed that bacteria from the infected site were not likely to lodge on the fresh wound. I personally accepted his premise and was able to successfully perform a few arthroplasties in patients with long standing sepsis elsewhere. It should be noted that Charnley never used irrigation in surgery and did not use prophylactic antibiotics. Commenting on the practice of some orthopaedists of using antibiotic prophylaxis, he said, "sooner or later the chickens will come home to roost".

To support his thesis he demonstrated that normal people experience transient bacteremia during activities such as defecating or having sexual intercourse. Such a bacteremia does not result in infection. However, the deposition of new organisms in the open wound could result in infection.

From my point of view the laminar airflow, requiring a helmet and an exhaust system, forces the surgeon and surgical personal into a discipline likely to be ignored in their absence. In other words we behave better when the inconvenience of the system is present.

My own personal experiences have indicated a lower infection rate in the group of patients who had the surgery performed under the cleaner environment provided by the laminar airflow system [65]. However, I am reluctant to insist that the entire credit goes to the protection provided by the laminar flow. There are other important factors to be considered. A greater awareness of the possibility of pre-operative infection in the case of revision surgery or in cases of previous surgery has made us take precautions. In addition, I have used prophylactic antibiotics routinely and profusely irrigate the surgical wound.

A major problem that surrounds the issue of laminar airflow is that the true purpose of the system is not universally clear. I have seen many operating rooms, where the laminar airflow is installed and the surgeon and other scrubbed personnel wear helmets and exhaust systems. The circulating nurses, anesthesiologists and the ubiquitous "reps" do not. They carryout animated conversations during the surgical procedures; walk in and out of the room with great frequency; wave their arms; and "throw "supplies on top of the instrument table, such as sutures and other materials. The vendor points with his finger at the instrument to be used next and loudly instruct the surgeon on the various steps of the procedure. This is more common during **revision** surgery when appliances manufactured by other companies are being replaced with ones made by others.

Since they do not wear protective devices it implies that they must think that the uncomfortable equipment is used by the surgeons to protect them from being contaminated by the patient and not the other way around.

SECTION II – THE HIP JOINT

LENGTH DISCREPANCY (Total Hip Surgery)

Finding out upon completion of an uncomplicated total hip arthroplasty that the operated extremity is longer than the normal one, is a disappointment that can become a nightmare. For reasons I do not clearly understand, patients who have this experience are, often, deeply concerned over the limp the sudden discrepancy produces. The same reaction is not usually seen when shortening of a similar degree is noticed.

Discrepancies that do not exceed one centimeter are rarely a problem, as far as the patient is concerned. If the leg is made shorter than prior to surgery, the patient might notice the difference, but within a very short time the "problems" is forgotten. However, if the leg is made longer than the other one, it is very likely that the patient will complain for a longer periods of time. It is unfortunate that there are surgeons who contribute to making the situation of a "longer leg" a problem, and in doing so provoke litigation against the surgeon who performed the operation.

A number of suggestions have been advanced regarding the most effective means to ensure that at the end of surgery both lower extremities are of the same length. The simplest and most commonly used one is the placement of two Steinmen pins as reference points: one on the iliac crest and the other on the proximal femur. The distance between them is recorded, and the figure used while trying the various neck lengths, prior to select the most appropriate one. This simple method works well in most instances. However, to rely entirely on it may lead to unexpected disappointments. Sometimes, a flexion contracture may go unrecognized, resulting in increasing unnecessarily the length of the operated extremity.

One should not always rely entirely on the figures obtained from measuring the distance between two points the pelvis and the femur. The history of a fracture of the tibia or femur during the growing years may have left the extremity longer than the other. In this instance, the two-point measurement does not recognize the actual length discrepancy. The same applies to a shorter or longer length due to a congenital variant.

When an adduction contracture is present and its presence has not been of a very long standing nature, is not unlikely to see a spontaneous correction of the deformity over the ensuing months. Some adduction deformities, secondary to trauma that affected the sacro-iliac joints never improve. This fact must be kept in mind at the time of surgery.

Patients who have associated structural scoliosis often hope that their gait will be improved following replacement of their arthritic hips. Though often some benefit is achieved in this regard, there is no reliable method to predict its effectiveness.

Many surgeons pay a great of attention to the "shucking" that manual traction on the extremity produces during the selection of the appropriate neck length. I also use the method but pay relatively little attention to the findings. Not that I completely ignore them because major separation between the socket and the prosthetic head, but because it is influenced by several factors. A common one is the significant difference in the elasticity of the collagen tissues surrounding the hip joint. A patient with very elastic capsular tissues shows, under a given traction, major displacement between the components, even if the appropriate length of the neck had been chosen. A patient with less elastic tissues, subjected to even stronger traction, will show no separation between the acetabular and femoral components.

Another factor that heavily influences the separation between the acetabulum and prosthetic head is the extent of soft tissue striping carried out by the surgeon. Those who like to perform the surgery through a small incision are less like to see major "shucking". Others, including myself, who prefer a wide exposure of the hip joint and surgical severance of the insertion of the gluteus maximus from the shaft of the femur, as well as posterior capsulectomy, observe a greater "shucking" during traction. If we were to strive in all instances for a minimal shucking, we would be creating a legion of patients complaining of "disabling" length discrepancies.

LYSIS

Today when we hear the word lysis, we assume it is in reference to total hip replacement. It is the "disease" that replaced the "cement disease", which attracted so much attention in the 1970's and 80's.

John Charnley recognized and dealt with lysis during his unhappy experience with Teflon, the material he used to replace the acetabulum of his newly developed total hip prosthesis. Until the end of his career, he insisted that polyethylene wear was the greatest challenge facing hip replacement surgery. It is unfortunate that for too long we ignored his warnings and chose to devote our efforts toward the design of new prostheses of different shapes and lengths. based on the presumed belief that all failures could be explained on that type of mechanical grounds.

Now lysis is with us even though attempts were made to eliminate the acrylic cement, which had been mistakenly identified as the culprit. I say mistakenly, because the cement is rarely responsible for lysis. As a matter of fact the use of non-cemented prostheses has significantly increased the incidence of lysis. Lysis is, in most instances, produced by wear debris shed by the polyethylene acetabular component. This seems to be universally agreed and most research nowadays is devoted to finding materials with better wear characteristics, be it new polyethylene, ceramic or metal on metal.

The pathophysiology of lysis has been extensively covered in the literature. It should suffice to say that its prevention probably rests primarily on elimination of debris from the articulating surfaces. The debris may be polyethylene or metal. Offensive debris may come from metal corrosion at the Morse taper of the modular prosthetic neck [69], other modular components in either the socket or the femoral stem, the interface between the metal cup and the plastic acetabulum, the screws used to reinforce the fixation of the acetabular shell, the porous surface of the stem and acetabulum or the stem itself.

Since there is general consensus that polyethylene debris from the concavity of the polyethylene cup is the most likely etiology of lysis of the femur, it should be logical that preventing the entry of debris through the top of the femur would significantly reduce the complication. Some have designed non-cemented prostheses that attempt to provide a "lid" at the level of the calcar. Though the concept is sound, I have long questioned the effectiveness of the system on the grounds that the very small size of the debris particles, floating in synovial fluid, find their way into the medullary canal through the space that inevitable remains between the porous implant and the cortical bone.

This assumption prompted me to conceive a method that could more effectively seal the "mouth" of the femur, preventing therefore the entrance of debris into the bone-cement interface. I accomplished this by packing bone graft over the exposed and still viscous acrylic cement around the prosthetic stem. Once the cement becomes hard, the bone chips are solidly fixed against it, but also in contact with the cortex of the femoral neck (Fig. 99a).

Though at this point I do not know the ultimate fate of the "graft", since I have not had the opportunity to explore any of the 50 operated hips, I have some evidence to suggest that the bone graft heals against the wall of the femoral cortex and remains viable. The suggestive evidence comes from CT scans that have shown bone surrounding the implant. In addition I have several patients on whom I had reattached windows I had performed on the femur, while performing revision of failed cemented arthroplasties. Rather than using wires or other sutures to replace the window, I had chosen to place the bone fragment over the still viscous cement. Upon completion of the polymerization process the window was firmly held in place by the cement. In all instances the bone healed and incorporated into the body of the femur (Fig. 99b).

One could question the appropriateness of the method based on the experiences with femoral windows, since in the case of the femoral window the bone fragment receives blood supply, not only from the surrounding soft but also from the viable femoral cortex. Similar degree of nutrition may not be available in the femoral neck, where the graft is deprived of surrounding soft tissues and it is bathed in synovial fluid. A maximum follow-up has failed to demonstrate complications that could be related to the grafting procedure. .

I am convinced that a seldom-recognized source of offensive debris comes from the femoral stem rubbing against the rough surface of the femoral cortex. This belief is supported by the fact that lysis became a household word only after the non-cemented prosthesis came onto the scene. Prior to that time, lysis was seen usually in small degrees and rarely manifested in the form of large cavities, as we currently see with non-cemented implants. Lysis is more likely to occur with Titanium implants since this material is "softer" than other popularly used metals and alloys, such as Chrome-Cobalt or Stainless Steel (See TITANIUM PROSTHESES). Lysis produced by metal debris without any evidence of polyethylene is rare, but I have seen it in several instances (Fig. 100a, b.). Though it is logical to assume that the greater the wear of polyethylene the greater it should be the degree of lysis, there are many situations where such correlation is not found (Fig. 101a, b.)

SECTION II – THE HIP JOINT

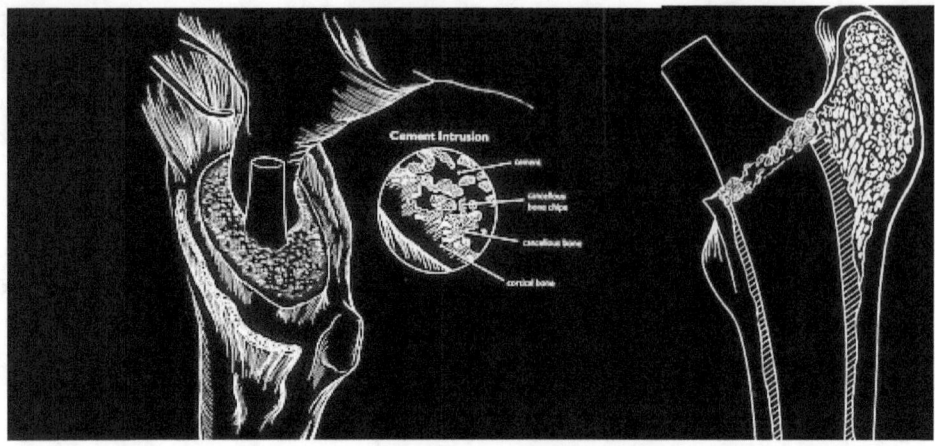

Fig. a and b. The bone chips are pressed over the still-doughey cement. The fully polymerized cement holds the grat in place. The graft must be in close contact with the cortical bone of the femur.

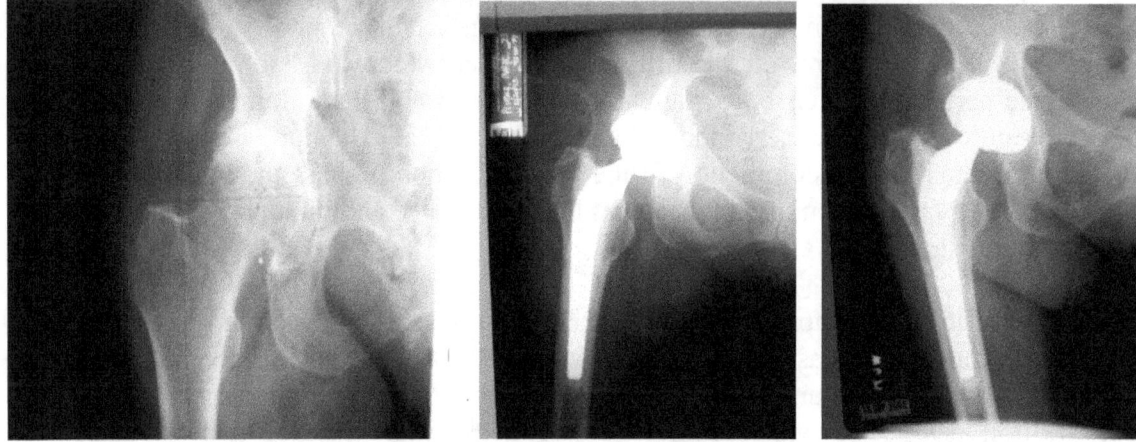

Fig. a, b and c.   Eleven-year follow-up of bone/cement lid over the mouth of the femur.

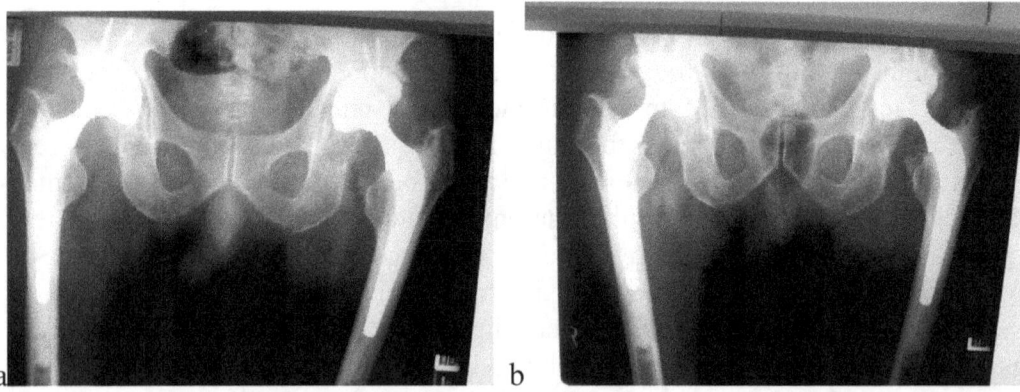

Fig. a and b.   Simultaneously performed total hip replacements. The grafting procedure was performed only on he left hip (a). Notice the bone mild bone resorption in the nongrafted side. (b)

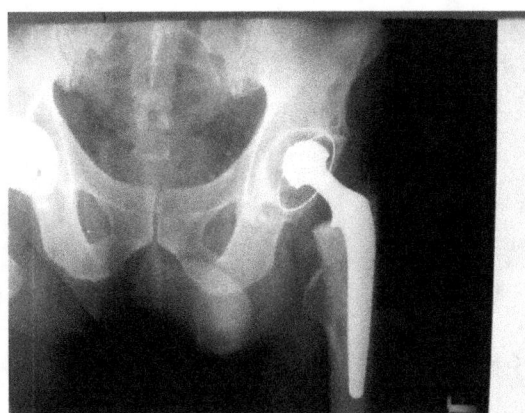

Fig. Severe wear of polyethylene associated with relatively mild bone lysis.

I have seen a few instances of metallosis associated with noncemented Moore endoprosthesis. This phenomenon is so rare, that we dismissed it cavalierly. I discovered the metallosis during revision surgery. Lytic lesions had formed, which I mistakenly suspected as being expressions of infection. However, infection was not found, only lysis. Up to that time I had not known that endoprostheses could produce metallosis. (See ENDOPROSTHESES).

New polyethylenes are being frantically investigated and have been released to the public. If the alleged improved wear properties of the materials prove to be superior, a major break-through in hip and knee surgery will occur. Perhaps the most common source of complications will then be eliminated.

I remain cautious about the project, since products and concepts that had been heralded as panaceas have disappointed often us. I am particularly interested in seeing good results because the polyethylene developed by Harry McKellop and associates was conceived and processed in our laboratories at the Orthopaedic Hospital during my tenure at the University of Southern California [15, 19, 24, 27, 46, 54, 56, 57, 59, 60, 67]

Progress will be made in the future and it is very likely that lysis will be eliminated from the scene. However, better polyethylene may not be the total answer. I suspect that more serious attention will have to be paid to the metal used for the implant since it is metal release that damages the polyethylene, which in turn creates the harmful debris.

Frequently, questions have been raised regarding when to intervene surgically in the presence of lytic lesions in the acetabulum or femur. There are those who say that early intervention is best; first because lysis is always progressive, and secondly because the condition of the bone is better. If these two premises were always true, I would agree. However, I have seen many instances where the size of the lytic defects remained unchanged for many years. It is true that the condition of the bone is better when surgery is done early, but do we have any evidence that the surgical results are better when the size of lytic lesions differ only in minimal degrees? Is one lesion that measures two centimeters in length and three millimeters in width a more difficult one to approach surgically than one that measures a couple millimeters more in both planes?

SECTION II – THE HIP JOINT

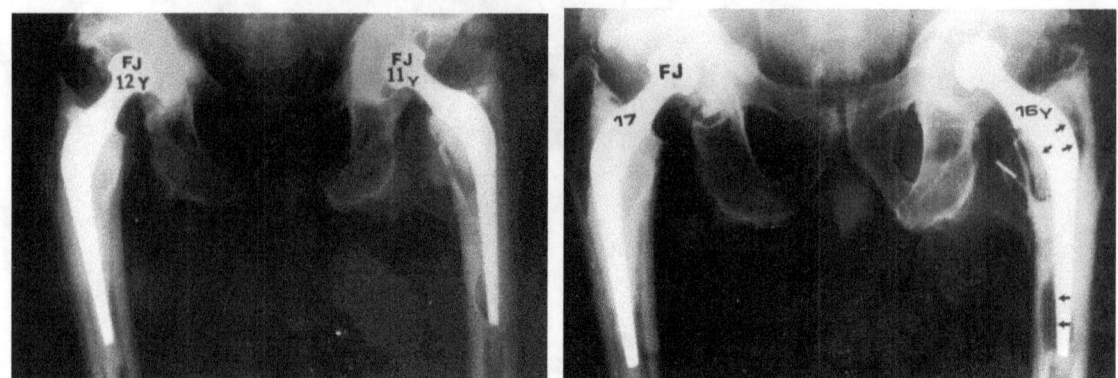

Fig. a and b. Bilateral cemented total hip arthroplasty. Though a lytic process developed on the right hip, its progression was gradual. A chronic medical condition precluded revision surgery. The hips, however, remained asymptomatic for twenty years.

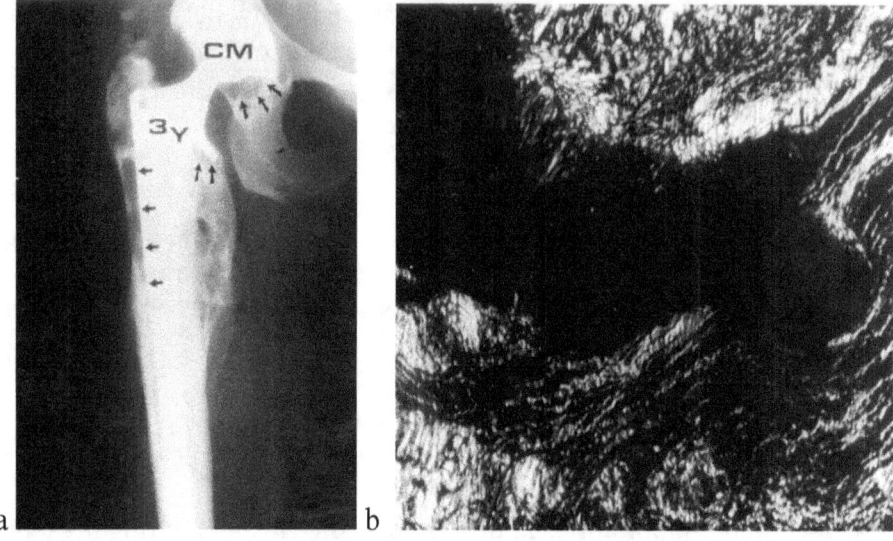

Fig. a and b. Lytic lesion involving the proximal femur and acetabulum. No polyethylene was seeing under the microscope, only metal debris.

M

METAL-ACKED ACETABULUM IN TOTAL HIPS

As a result of finite element analysis, which quite cleverly illustrated stress distributions on the acetabular floor in total hip replacements, the concept of reinforcing cemented polyethylene sockets was born. It was surmised that the addition of a metallic shell behind the cemented cup would bring about a reduction of loosening of the component.

Time has shown that the appearance of radiolucent lines between the acetabular bone and the column of cement is not necessarily the product of abnormal distribution of mechanical stresses but more likely the presence of debris, and the resulting chemical and histological changes. In any event, the concept of the metal-backed cemented acetabulum gained immediate acceptance in the surgical community in the late 1970's and early 1980's.

I became suspicious of the value of the innovation and of possible harmful effects of the reinforced cup when we found that a large number of implanted femoral cemented Titanium prostheses with metal-backed components experienced early failure accompanied with significant metallosis. We found no evidence of metallosis in seventeen consecutive acetabular components that we had retrieved from patients who had Titanium cemented femoral replacements. These prostheses had been inserted without metal-backed acetabula. However, when the same Titanium prosthesis was used with metal-back acetabula metallosis and early failures were frequently demonstrated (Fig. 103 a,b.).

Careful analysis of the removed specimens was conducted in our laboratories at the Orthopedic Hospital of Los Angeles. We demonstrated that the cement around the polyethylene socket fragmented and generated debris that also carried metal from the plasma-sprayed cup. The fall of those fragments in the plastic-metal articulation produced a third-body wear phenomenon [62].

The finding of this phenomenon with Titanium prostheses can be explained on the grounds that Titanium is a relatively softer material when compared with harder ones, such as stainless steel or cobalt-chrome alloys. However, the problem is not exclusive to Titanium implants and other investigators have also documented a higher incidence of acetabular loosening with the use of reinforced acetabula.

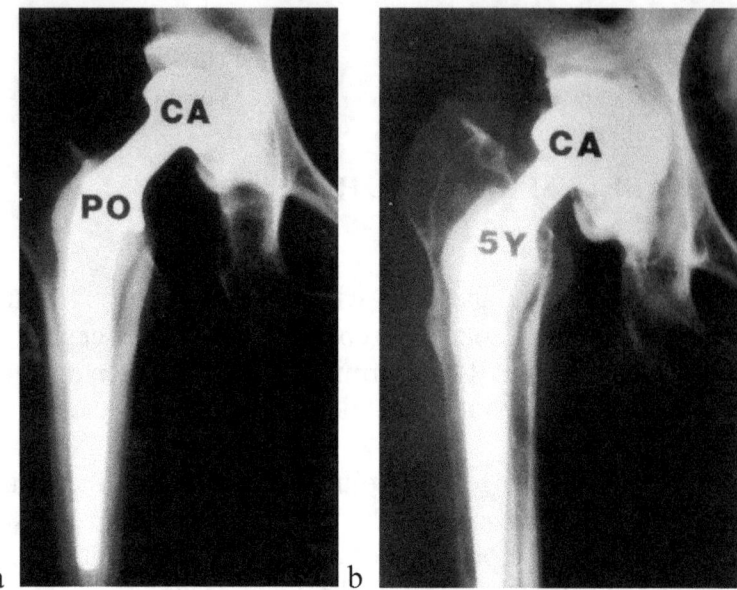

Fig. a and b. Monoblock Titanium prosthesis with a metal-backed cemented acetabulum. The prosthesis failed rapidly. Notice the loose acetabulum, the subsidence of the femoral component and the lysis throughout.

METAL ON METAL TOTAL HIPS

Will they work or will they prove to have been another "flash in the pan" and disappearance from the scene? It is hard to tell. The concept is not new. Marshall Urist, from California, reported in the 1950's, his experiences with a metallic endoprosthesis used in combination with a Smith Petersen-like acetabular metallic cup. The procedure never gained wide acceptance and I surmised it was because of unsatisfactory results. A few years later, and after the introduction of acrylic cement, MacKey and Farrar, in England described their metal-on-metal total hip arthroplasty. Their prosthesis was widely used throughout the world with mixed results. The Charnley approach to total hip arthroplasty won the day and it became the preferred method eclipsing the contribution of the other two British surgeons.

Contributing to the demise of the McKee-Farrar arthroplasty was the presence of an annoying increased friction between the components, and the finding of severe metallosis in a number of instances. In spite of that, many McKee-Farrar arthroplasties did very well and currently some still exist in patients who are functioning perfectly well thirty years after implantation. At this time, I personally follow several such implants where surgery was performed between thirty and thirty three years ago.

Webber, from Switzerland, an honest reporter, has been the strongest proponent of metal-on-metal arthroplasty. His results are most encouraging and suggest that a successful return to the concept may be around the corner. He, as well as others, claims that the McKee-Farrar implants failed because of poor matching of the two components and a poor design of the contact areas. They may be right. Unfortunately, as it is frequently the case, some promoters eager to gain overnight fame and fortune, have marketed the procedure by all possible means before adequate follow-up can be produced.

There are, however, other serious considerations that should not be ignored. Though there is laboratory data to indicate that friction between metal surfaces is less than that present between metal against polyethylene, wear still takes place. Therefore, metallic debris is inevitable. Will this debris be harmful? Can it be a source of malignant changes?

Of greater concern, in my opinion, should be the recently reported finding of chromosomal abnormalities around areas of metallosis in patients with hip implants. Professor Patrick Case, from Bristol, England has illustrated his findings in a very serious manner. The degree of chromosomal abnormalities in these instances is higher than that found in the normal population. Other like Black, in Philadelphia, Jacobs, in Chicago, and the group at McGill University in Montreal, have shed further light into the issue.

This latter finding makes one have second thoughts as to whether metallic implants likely to generate debris should be used in women during their reproductive years or in young people with an anticipated long residual life span. I predict metal-on metal will soon disappear from the scene.

The fact that metal on metal prostheses are more expensive and new and hopefully better polyethylene sockets have been introduced in the market, casts doubts on the future of the more expensive metallic implants [56, 57]. Ceramics have been used for a number of years with varying results. More recent reports appear encouraging. I suspect they will become increasingly popular, and hope long term follow up will be equally as encouraging.

It is deeply disturbing that surgeons, promoters of the system, have chosen to use the media to market their product and to claim the method to be the ultimate solution to the problems surrounding total hip replacement. This in spite of the fact that their own clinical data is based on a few years of follow-up. They are acting as unprofessionally as those who claim. Also in the absence of any clinical data, that new polyethylene's justify the performance of total hip surgery on patients of any age. The manufactures of the implants are equally as guilty of unprofessional conduct by advertising implants as "guaranteed for life".

MINIMALLY INVASIVE TOTAL HIP REPLACEMNT

In surgery, a s it is true in many other walks of life, we love changing fashions. They fascinate our collective mind and we assume that each new fashion means progress. In the business world, entrepreneurs welcome and encourage new fashions with enthusiasm. The manufactures of clothing cannot wait for the release of short skirts to replace longer ones and for the shorter ones be replaced with mini-skirts a bit later. The next year the cycle begins anew. Money is made in that manner. In orthopaedics we have been burned too many times by blindly accept changes. Not every change is good and unintended consequences always lurk around the corner.

SECTION II – THE HIP JOINT

The most recent "new" fashion is the performance of total hip surgery through a mini-incision. I underline "new" because there is nothing new about it. Maurice Muller did his arthroplasties through an incision no longer than the width of his hand. Nearly 20 years ago I also witnessed nearly twenty years ago the performance of total hip replacement through a very small incision by Garcia, a Buenos Aires surgeon. He gave me a tape he had taken describing the procedure.

I came back home and performed the surgery according to his technique. Surgery was completed satisfactorily, however, it made me ask which the advantage of a smaller incision were. True, the blood loss may have been less, and it took a couple minutes less to close the soft tissues. The retraction of the soft tissues had to be forceful and traumatic and the exposure of the various bony structures acceptable but not as good as it was when the surgery was performed with a longer incision.

The patient had pain and I could not tell if it was more or less than the one experienced by others who had the surgery performed through a conventional longer incision. With PCA the patient controlled the pain, and I did not pay attention to whether the number of "injections" he received had been fewer or greater than my other patients had received, on whom I had made a longer incision. I was keenly aware that pain varies a great deal from patient to patient. What difference would have made it the amount of analgesic or narcotics was greater or lesser? The physical therapist got the patient out of bed the next day according to the prescribed "ritual" and the patient left the hospital a few days later independent with the aid of crutches. By the time of discharge from the hospital all analgesics and narcotics had been discontinued, as it was the case with all other patients..

It is obvious that surgery can be performed through a smaller incision in many instances. However, there are many times when a very long incision is required in order to obtain the necessary exposure of all bony and soft tissue structures. For example, an osteoarthritic hip, secondary to slipped femoral epiphysis, usually accompanied with a fixed external rotation, requires a wide skin incision. There are many other similar situations. Performing the surgery through a small incision for the sole purpose of "proving" that it can be done in that manner is sophomoric and possibly even dangerous.

The foolishness of thinking that small incisions are always better is exemplified by the surgeon who spends an inordinate amount of time repairing a torn rotator cuff, or threading an intramedullary nail into a canal difficult to "hit" with the aid of imaging technology. The thought of making an incision and exposing the elusive medullary canal is tantamount to the acceptance of defeat. What is wrong about direct exposure of the bone when difficulties are encountered? Millions of femoral nailing's were performed in the past before interlocking nails and image intensifiers were invented. These "proud" and "macho" surgeons should read a report by William Stryker in the 1960s, dealing with over 100 (if I am not mistaken) open nailing of femoral fractures that were performed without a single infection.

There is hidden problem we might be creating by the recommendation that smaller incisions are better, because they reduce hospitalization and complications. The powers that be, the government and insurance companies, which often dictate policies we strongly recent because they infringe on our exercise of "judgment" in the care of patients, will soon reduce the number of "approved" hospital-days even further. Our ability to determine the length of hospital stay will be compromised.

MODULAR COMPONENTS

Modularity has become a well-accepted concept in total joint surgery, and more recently has gained acceptance in trauma implants. I have serious reservations about its long-term future unless significant improvements in metallurgy and implant design are made.

Metal debris can be generated from the porous mesh or beads when toggling or gross motion between the metal and the bone takes place. The additional modularity in the femoral component is also likely to produce debris.

We identified a cause of lysis for a number of failed Titanium prostheses when metal backed acetabular shells were used to reinforce the cemented cup [62]. It is possible the fragmented cement carried with it small particles of metal that eventually fell in the joint initiating a third party body wear process? (See METAL BACKED ACETABULUM)

I conceived a modular femoral stem that through a mechanism of antero-posterior wedges would ensure rotary stability to the non-cemented implant. Long after we had conducted lengthy and detailed studies at the Orthopaedic Hospital in Los Angeles to determine the efficacy of the product, I found out that someone in Italy had already produced a similar product. The American company working on our project came to the conclusion that the release of the new prosthesis should be cancelled. They were concerned about the possibility of motion between the wedges and the body of the implant and its possible complications.

Although at first I was disappointed with their decision, I promptly appreciated the wisdom of their judgement. The engineer that had represented the company during the studies at our institution left the organization and moved to another one. He took with him the data we had gathered and gave it to his new employer. They produced the prosthesis and a former resident of ours, who became an unofficial peddler of the product claiming it was his idea. The implant is no longer manufactured suggesting to me that complications must have developed. However, since there are so few willing to report on failures, we will never know.

Now that modularity has been introduced in trauma products such as interlocking nails, early reports of lytic changes are appearing in the literature. Nails broken at the site of modularity have shown extensive corrosion. I am certain that if blood and urine tests were conducted in these patients, the presence of metal would be identified. This may not be of great concern at this time but it could eventually become a problem particularly in light of the fact that most victims of trauma are young people in their reproductive years. (See Lysis).

SECTION II – THE HIP JOINT

Fig. Corrosion at Morse taper surface in the neck of the prosthesis.

O

OSTEOARTHRITIS

John Charnley was my visiting professor at the University of Miami in 1974. While he was at the podium answering questions from the audience, I asked him to give us his views on whether or not someday arthritis would be prevented, or if a non-surgical cure could be developed. Without the slightest hesitation he responded, "never, never will there be an effective preventive measure for osteoarthritis. Osteoarthritis has been in our genes for many a millennia and it will be with us forever". He added that the same was not true for rheumatoid arthritis and that a cure for it was around the corner.

Five years later he, once again, served as my visiting professor at the University of Southern California, where I had an opportunity to ask him the same question I had asked him in Miami. His response was the same. It would have been wonderful to have the opportunity to ask him those questions today, when rumors of the identification of the gene that causes osteoarthritis are rampant and new medications claiming "cures" are inundating the market. Charley was right in an incredible number of issues he addressed. Perhaps this is one where he was mistaken by underestimating the forces of molecular biology and genetic engineering.

Trueta, from Oxford, in my opinion, conducted very elegant and persuasive work dealing with the circulation of the femoral head and made impressive observations. The one which has been indelibly stereotyped in my mind is his observation that the narrowing of the joint space of the hip in osteoarthritis is not in all instances the result of wear of the articular cartilage, rather its replacement with bone growing from the sub-chondral region. This bony substitution gives the radiological appearance of cartilage erosion from wear against the opposing acetabular surface.

Our obsession with mechanics and our desire to explain everything on mechanical bases has blinded us on more than one occasion. This is true for most areas of orthopaedics be it in fracture care, prosthetic replacement, spine surgery and many others. Hopefully, the day will come when orthopaedists will reason with greater emphasis on biological basis.

There should be no question at this time that our understanding of the etiology of osteoarthritis is limited. However, there are certain obvious factors that in themselves carry a great deal of weight. In the case of the hip, a shallow acetabulum predisposes to the disease. This is difficult to refute. Nonetheless, how do we explain the fact that very often one hip develops arthritic changes when the shallowness of the acetabulum is equal in both hips. A mechanical explanation in this instance does not suffice.

Reinhold Ganz, from Switzerland, recently proposed that the most common cause of arthritis is "chronic" impingement of the neck of the femur against the labrum during flexion of the hip. (See LABRUM)

SECTION II – THE HIP JOINT

Now that total joint replacement has been proven to be an effective means to restore relief to the osteoarthritic hip and knee, many have benefited from the surgical intervention. Questions remain, however, as to when to replace an osteoarthritic joint. I have struggled hundreds of times making recommendations to osteoarthritic patients regarding the most appropriate course of action. The struggle comes from the fact that we cannot predict with certainty the course of the non-surgically treated disease. There are exceptions to this deficit and that is the case of the patient suffering from congenital hip dislocation. I am convinced that in the absence of a radiologically "perfect" femoral head following closed or open reduction, with or without additional reconstructive surgery, arthritic changes develop at a later date.

The division of orthopaedic care into sub-specialty areas has precluded the study of the sequella of congenital hip disease, as well as other diseases suffered by children. The pediatric orthopaedist stops seeing his patients when they reach the arbitrary age of 16 or 21 years of age. In general, they are not aware of late complications and they find themselves often reporting unrealistically good results. Children frequently manage to function normally and be asymptomatic during childhood and adolescence, despite the presence of deformities of the hip and other joints. It is not until they reach late adulthood that symptoms develop. I am of the opinion that if the pediatric orthopaedist were better aware of the late sequella, a different approach to many musculoskeletal conditions in children would be structured.

I suspect that a better system must be developed. The Shriners Hospital system is coming closer to finding a possible solution, by virtue of the fact that, to the best of my knowledge, there are no rigid age limitations. Orthopaedic investigators at the University of Iowa, where a large percentage of the patient population is local and rather stable, has been able to conduct long term studies of congenital and developmental diseases. It would be great if other institutions were to follow suit. Valentin Malagon, a most distinguished professor of orthopaedics in Colombia, internationally recognized as an authority in congenital hip disease, will soon publish a book where he deals with the disease "from the cradle to old age". His book should become a major contribution to the field.

John Charnley used to say that when a patient presented complaining of mild pain in the groin and the x-rays showed early narrowing of the joint, within five years the condition would deteriorate to the point of requiring arthroplasty. I have subsequently made the same observation. I have often tried to reason, however, that if deterioration of the joint is inevitable and predictable, why not perform the operation earlier and spare the patient pain and inconveniences during the next five years?

I have tempered this temptation to operate on many occasions by remembering that there are exceptions to the rule and that not everyone with mild osteoarthritis of the hip requires surgery five years later. I have seen patients who have gone a lot longer without aggravation of symptoms. Patients with bilateral osteoarthritis, who had one hip replaced and obtained good clinical results, often find themselves complaining very little about pain on the opposite arthritic hip. I wonder if there is some chemical factor that explains this

SECTION II – THE HIP JOINT

phenomenon. I have made the same observation while dealing with rheumatoid patients [1,2,164].

Another reason for not performing the prosthetic replacement early is that we cannot guarantee a good clinical result, despite the relative predictability of the operation. Complications following surgery can and do occur in a percentage of instances. If one adds to the very low incidence of infection nerve palsy, dislocation, heterotopic bone, thromboembolic disease in its various manifestations, early loosening, subsequent revisions and other problems, one must conclude that replacement arthroplasty should not be taken lightly.

OSTEOARTHRITIS (DESTRUCTIVE)

I had the opportunity to see and treat a few patients suffering with the "destructive" type of osteoarthritis of the hip. Most of them were older females. The symptoms were severe and the deterioration of the bone took place in a very short period of time.

Radiologically, the joint initially resembles rheumatoid or septic arthritis. Gouty arthritis can also give the same x-ray picture. The joint space disappears rapidly and the femoral heads seems to melt before your eyes (Fig. 104a,b.) On two occasions at the time of surgery I encountered a large collection of purulent-looking fluid upon entering the joint. In one instance there were large loose cartilaginous fragments that resembled tuberculosis. All cultures were negative for infection and laboratory and clinical tests ruled out rheumatoid arthritis.

I wonder what causes this bizarre type of arthritis, and suspect that its classification as "osteoarthritis" is probably inappropriate.

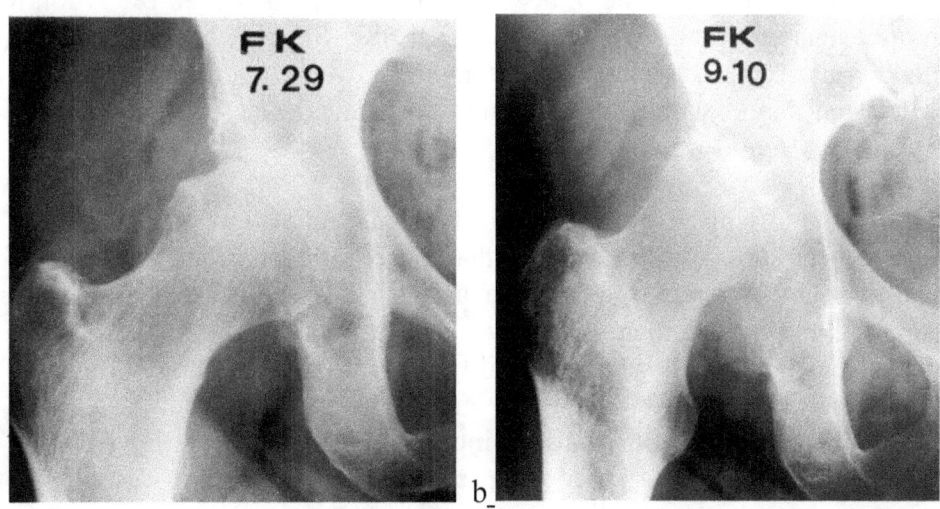

Fig. a and b. Destructive type of osteoarthritis demonstrating rapid lysis of the femoral heads and acetabulum. There was no evidence of rheumatoid arthritis or avascular necrosis.

P

PLUGGING THE MEDULLARY CANAL (Total Hip. Cementing)

What are the biological reasons for plugging the medullary canal during total hip arthroplasty? I cannot think of any. The plugging is done for mechanical reasons, which may not even be desirable. It is done, to a great extent because it is cosmetically pleasant. It avoids the presence of cement beyond the tip end of the prosthetic stem. True, if revision is necessary at a later date, the removal of the distal column of cement makes the procedure more difficult to perform. Is this reason sufficiently strong to offset the possible biological disadvantages? I do not know.

If we look carefully at the long term follow-up results of Charnley arthroplasties, we cannot help but be amazed by the high number of "pristine" x-rays in spite of the fact that the cement extended far below the prosthetic tip or did not reach the end of the prosthetic stem. What explanations can we offer for those experiences? Much has been said about the value of "new and improved" cementing techniques. In most of those reports, other things in addition to the different method of cement injection, took place. Different stems, different prosthetic designs, different acetabular cups, different cement manufactures and other important factors come into the picture and we do not know the effect they may have had in explaining the different results.

Allegedly, plugging of the canal distally permits better pressurization of the cement. Let's assume this to be the case. But, is pressurization really important? From what point of view? Biologically or mechanically? It is possible that pressurized cement might do some damage to the underlying cortical bone in a way similar to that observed by us following pressurization of cement into cancellous bone (See PRESSURIZATION). Some may argue back that the additional damage is inconsequential, since even without pressurization and plugging the endosteal blood supply of the femur is damaged but spontaneous recovery eventually takes place. A good argument.

I am still uncomfortable with reaming of the canal until all vestiges of medullary blood supply have been destroyed. I believe that extreme rasping and brushing of the medullary canal is bound to render the cortex avascular. The additional thermic changes generated by the polymerizing cement probably make matters worse. If the harm is not obvious it is because nature has the uncanny ability to overcome the hurdles we, so often, throw in its path. The recovery of blood supply and the formation of new osteocytes are comparable to the phenomenon seen following intramedullary nailing of long bones. The relatively dormant peripheral blood supply experiences a sudden surge of activity that provokes the formation of peripheral callus.

Charnley was opposed to plugging of the canal and pressurization of the cement. He firmly believed that thumb packing was sufficient to obtain the desirable fixation. He did not rasp vigorously, as he wanted to preserve some cancellous bone into which the cement would interdigitate. He explained the relationship between the cancellous bone and the cement as being similar to that of the bristles of a brush moving back and forth without breaking at the base. An analogy, which can be biologically supported as we realize that such microscopic motion, should result in hypertrophy of the stressed bone.

PRE-COATED TOTAL HIP IMPLANTS

For a short while the concept of pre-coated prosthetic stems gained the attention of the orthopaedic community and became quite popular. However, the idea of preventing separation between the cement and the metallic stem by impregnating the stem with a layer of cement concerned me. Instinctively, I suspected that such a fixation would transfer stresses to the cement-bone interface and lead to possible prosthetic loosening, a trade off not worth making.

Several former associates of mine at the Orthopedic Hospital/University of Southern California Laboratory have conducted interesting studies concerning the bonding of cement and stems which supported my initial concerns [9, 1, 12, 14, 16, 18, 19, 24, 27, 32, 54, 58, 62, 64, 71, 74]. The clinical and laboratory experiences reported by Ling and his colleagues in Bristol, England, have eloquently demonstrated that smooth, polished cemented stems perform better that those with rougher, matte surfaces. The sinking of the metallic stem inside the cement mantle makes it possible for the smooth stem to maintain a permanent close contact between the two structures. Unsatisfactory experiences with pre-coated stems reported by several orthopaedist have settled the issue once and for all. I suspect that insufficient experimentation and reasonable clinical follow up prior to the introduction of the concept to the public led to the bad clinical results.

Much harm has been done by the premature release of orthopaedic implants to the orthopaedic community. Most disappointing is the fact that manufacturers and developers of these inferior products often insist on their continued sale. Apparently they feel no responsibility for the harm that is done. Implants that have been discontinued in the United States because of an associated high incidence of complications, are later sold in Latin American countries without any attempt made to inform the new customers that the product had proven to be poor and is no longer used in the States. I assume the prostheses are sold until the inventory is exhausted.

A certain number of these total hip non-cemented prosthesis failed in my hands. When I submitted a manuscript to a journal reporting the bad results, I was told that the paper was rejected because, among other things, the prosthesis we had used was no longer on the market and, therefore, it was of no interest to the readers. Model II was now in use. I then question the journal's editor as what response he will give to the surgeon, who ten years later submitted a paper demonstrating that model II was as bad as Model I. Would he reply that Model II was no longer used and that Model III was the popular one?

SECTION II – THE HIP JOINT

PRESS-FIT IMPLANTS-NONCEMENTED PROSTHESES

For a variety of reasons the orthopaedic community seems to be fascinated with intramedullary nails and prostheses that fit as tightly as possible in the medullary canal. It matters not that in the process we must destroy the endosteal circulation of the bone. Since such deprivation of circulation does not seem to have obvious adverse consequences we continue to carry out such mutilation of the blood supply. It has been well documented in the literature that several patients who had their tibia reamed developed necrosis of their entire diaphysis. Another point that is not considered is that the tight fit of a nail is not sustained indefinitely. The force required to remove a nail, tightly fit in the bone immediately after its insertion, is much greater than that necessary force to remove it a few days later. The bone against which the nail rests is "dead" and remains dead for a period of time until it undergoes remodeling and revascularization. In addition it is very likely that cold flow develops after the forceful insertion of the flexible nail, resulting in a loss of the original tightness of fit [18, 19, 54, 60, 65, 74, 169, 170, 171, 175].

I have been told that when the technique of intramedullary nailing was popularized by Kuntscher, in Germany, and his compatriots began to use it, he received several desperate calls from surgeons in the operating room who had found themselves in the predicament of not being able to either drive the nail beyond a certain point or remove it. It is said that Kuntscher suggested that the surgeon desist in trying to solve the problem and proceed to leave the wound open, pack it with sterile dressings and send the patient to his hospital. Upon the patient's arrival to his institution, he did not rush him to the operating room but let him stay in bed for a few days. He then took him to the operating room where with a firm blow he either drove the nail further or removed it. The nail was no longer as tight as it was during the original intervention.

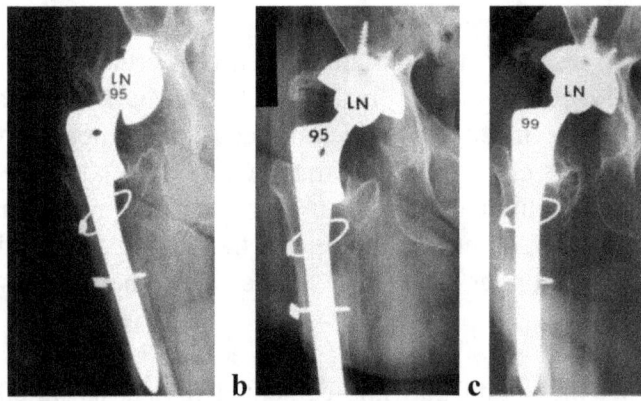

Fig. a, b and c. totally porous prosthetic stem demonstrating severe demineralization of a progressive nature.

PRESSURIZATION OF CEMENT

The concept of pressurization of cement was readily accepted after it was suggested in the late 1970's. It was and remains an attractive idea. At first glance the concept is sound from the mechanical point of view. However, this may not be the case from the biological point of view, particularly in the acetabulum where cement is in contact not with cortical bone but with cancellous structures. Replacing bone with cement is unphysiological, but this biological disadvantage may not be important. Long-term clinical experiences have not demonstrated unsavory consequences.

When the concept of pressurization of cement into the cancellous bone of the acetabulum was introduced, I felt uncomfortable because of the possible damage that the deep penetration of cement into cancellous bone might have. I speculated that though it is obvious that the deeper the penetration of the cement into the cancellous bone would provide better mechanical fixation, a greater amount of cancellous bone would be immobilized by the stiffer cement. That degree of unphysiological immobilization could result in eventual atrophy of the now non-stressed cancellous bone.

We took the idea to the laboratory where we injected cement deep into the greater trochanter and in the distal femoral condyles of rabbits. The animals were sacrificed at regular intervals and the injected areas were studied microscopically. We found that at first there was a burst of capillary reaction suggesting an inflammatory response. We also noticed that with the passage of time the capillary activity decreased, the osseous walls of the cancellous bone got thinner and the viability of the remaining bone was significantly lost (Fig. 105a,b).

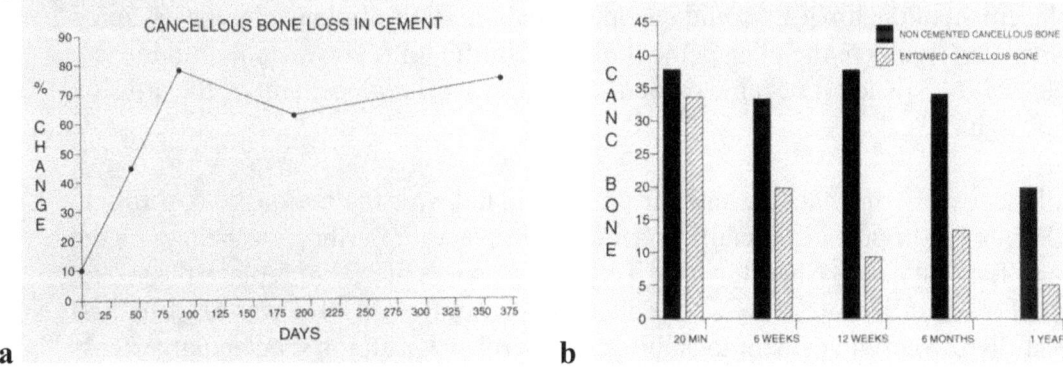

Fig. a and b. Cement that penetrates deep into cancellous bone produces a larger area of bone death, probably due to the immobilization of bone created by the foreign material.

The length of the study was limited to one year. We have no idea what the biological changes in the area would have been if the animals had been followed for a longer period of time. We concluded, however, that the deeper the penetration of cement into the bone, the greater the degree of bony atrophy and death of bone. We speculated that the weak mechanical area present at the junction between normal and damaged bone was capable of partially explaining the late loosening of cemented acetabular components [3, 162, 163].

I am not suggesting that this is the only mode of failure of cemented acetabular cups. To conclude this is the only cause of loosening would be foolish, since we know that other mechanical and biological phenomena may also play a role. Our findings however, should not be dismissed too quickly.

It is well known that as we age the medullary canal of our bones expands at the expense of the cortical bone. The inner diameter of the canal increases and the cortex gets thinner. This normal phenomenon suggests that over the years all cemented implants should get loose as the inner diameter of the cortex increases. However, this does not seem to be the case. It is possible that the reduced bending, tensile and compressive forces on the cortical bone are compensated by previously non-existing hoop stresses.

PROGRESS IN TOTAL HIP SURGERY

There is no question that total joint arthroplasty represents one of the most important and impressive technological developments in the history of orthopaedics. Orthopaedists had tried to replace the hip joint for nearly one hundred years with nothing more than an occasional clinical success. With the advent of anaesthesia and later more sophisticated metallurgical advances, progress began to take place. The encouraging results obtained with use of a Vitallium cup, designed by Smith Peterson; the acrylic cement prosthesis of Judet and similar ventures into the field, early in the twentieth century, gave impetus to further experimentation.

Austin Moore and Fred Thompson's endo-prostheses in the 1940's suggested that effective replacement of the hip joint could become a reality. Their implants, however, failed to provide consistent results in the management of the arthritic joint. It was not until the late 1950's and early 1960's when it became evident that successful replacement of the arthritic hip was within sight.

The pioneer work of MacKee and Farrar, in England, was the major break-through. McKee and Farrar used opposing metallic surfaces to replace the arthritic cartilage of the acetabulum and femoral head. Charnley used Teflon, a plastic material to replace the socket and a metal ball made of Stainless Steel to replace the femoral head. He was also the first one to successfully use acrylic cement to stabilize the parts. Charnley's spectacular success with Teflon was short lived. The massive bone lysis around the prosthetic components that developed in virtually all of his patients necessitated the removal of the prostheses, leaving the patients with flail, disabling joints. The Teflon material, underweight bearing conditions, underwent massive wear. The particles of debris traveled into the medullary canal and all areas around the femur and acetabulum and created havoc.

Charnley readily recognized that Teflon, though heralded as the ideal material to tolerate weight-bearing stresses, did not do well in the human body. Undeterred by the major tragedy and professional failure, he proceeded to search for a better material. He found it: high-density polyethylene. A material that thirty years later may still be the best one available to oppose the metallic head. Recent work with improved metallic designs and ceramics has raised questions regarding the permanent acceptance of polyethylene as the preferred bearing surface. Within the next few years we should have an answer.

As soon as the word got out that Charnley's results with the new material were very good, the world's orthopaedic community embraced the concept. People from all over the world traveled to England to learn about the new procedure. I personally made my pilgrimage to John Charnley's Mecca and spent nearly three months observing his operation and learning about his overall philosophy of hip disease.

Some orthopaedists, blinded by the sight of possible overnight fame, modified the design of Charnley's implant even before they had an opportunity to learn and appreciate Charnley's teachings. It is well known that a California surgeon spent three days in Wrightington, England, at Charnley's hospital, and on his return flight he designed his own prosthesis. He made minor modifications to the original design and attached his name to the new implant. He, however, chose the wrong material and his implant was promptly discredited, but not before he swelled his pockets with royalties from the sale of the ill-conceived product.

Industry saw also enormous market opportunities and began, with the aid of physicians, to further modify the Charnley's prosthesis, since his design was protected with a patent. By the mid-seventies there were dozens of different total hip prostheses available on the market. They differed in length, width, shape, texture and every conceivable geometric variety. Some had groves, others notches; some were longer, others shorter. Larger and smaller collars were designed and some prostheses not even had a mark where the old collars once existed. Some advocated matted surfaces while others claimed that polished surfaces were better. Some implants had larger heads in millimeters increments. The sockets were also modified. Some were reinforced with metal-backed shells or had projections to better make the column of cement equal in thickness. Modularity was introduced in order to best accomplish gains during leg length equalization.

At a meeting of the Academy of Orthopaedics, where a huge number of commercial products are displayed, I heard the president of the Australian Orthopaedic Association make the comment that the spectacle of hundreds of different hip implants was "obscene." Today there are over 350 different total hip prostheses on the market.

A variety of innovations were made in the technique of cement injection: plugging, water picking, rasping and pressurizing. These variations became known as the second generation of cementing techniques. The cement itself was then offered with different speeds of polymerization. Some were more viscous than others.

The osteotomy of the trochanter, essential components of Charnley's original operation, began to lose popularity and within a few years virtually disappeared from the scene. I, for one, referred to it as an unnecessary "masochistic ritual".

New materials were introduced and efforts were made to discredit Stainless Steel, after occasional stem fractures were reported. Cobalt-Chrome alloys replaced Stainless Steel implants. I personally became involved in the frenzy of improvement and thought that a material with a lower modulus of elasticity would eliminate the stress shielding of the proximal femur that the stiffer Stainless Steel and Cobalt-Chrome alloys seemed to have created. I designed the first Titanium prosthesis in the United States, anticipating improvement in the radiological and clinical results. My expectation was not fulfilled in spite of initial encouraging results. (See TITANIUM PROSTHESES).

In the early 1980's, after thousands of orthopaedic surgeons throughout the world had performed millions of hip arthroplasties, reports of complications with the operation began to flood the medical journals. Loosening of the components was the main problem. Acrylic cement was blamed for those complications and "cement disease" became a familiar term among orthopaedic surgeons.

Efforts made to eliminate the "evil cement" from the surgical procedure gave birth to the non-cemented prosthesis. With alacrity and without waiting for good documentation of the superior qualities of the non-cements implant, the new technique became an epidemic. It was heralded as the answer to all the problems created by the cement. The non-cemented prostheses had porous surfaces into which the bone, following instructions dictated by the surgeons, would grow!

It didn't take very long, however, for the orthopaedic community to find itself disappointed by the lack of consistent good results. Thigh pain appeared to be a very frequent sequella that either could not be spontaneously cured or persisted for a long period of time. Furthermore, and more disturbing was the appearance of a high incidence of lysis, both in the pelvis as well as in the femur.

Post-mortem examinations demonstrated that bone ingrowth did not occur in all instances or throughout the entire porous surface. Even in patients who had remained asymptomatic during their lives, only small areas of bone ingrowth were found. Femoral osteopenia around the implant, some times of worrisome degrees, was encountered in some instances.

Hoping to eliminate the unexpected complications, the extent of porosity on the surface of the metallic components was modified. Arguments were advanced in favor and against the degree to which the stem should be covered with porous material and soon we witnessed the manufacture of prostheses with porous surfaces throughout their entire length; others only to mid-level or proximal third and even just over a small area below the collar of the femoral implant.

Surgeons found themselves having serious difficulties removing porous implants which though well fixed in the medullary canal or acetabulum needed to be revised for a variety of reasons such as recurrent dislocation, disabling pain, infection, fractures of the components or of the femur. Bone had grown into the pores making their removal difficult if not impossible.

Wear of the polyethylene socket also became a concern with both cemented and uncemented arthroplasties. Wear was found to be higher with the uncemented ones for reasons, which are not yet clear. I believe that one reason for the higher wear observed with uncemented implants is the increased number of foreign body elements arising either from motion between the stem and the surrounding bone; from the outer surface of the acetabular cup; the plastic-metal articulation; the Morse taper head fixation or from other modular components. These phenomena occur more frequently with Titanium implants because the material is softer and therefore has a propensity to scratching.

SECTION II – THE HIP JOINT

The results from newer cementless prostheses have indicated that most of the problems seen with their use are decreasing. The initial increasing dissatisfaction with the cementless implants prompted a solution: the use of a non-cemented acetabulum and a cemented femoral component. This modification was allegedly inspired by the finding that cementless acetabuli had experienced a very low failure rate, while the femur had not performed as well. This "hybrid" model is the most popular one at this point. However, I have doubts about its future. I have personally documented a higher incidence of radiological complications in patients who had "hybrid" Titanium prostheses than comparable cohorts of totally cemented Titanium arthroplasties. (See HYBRID PROSTHESES).

Experiences with implants that have ceramic heads rather than polyethylene ones are very encouraging. The success is explained on the reduced wear of the material as documented in laboratory conditions and in relatively short term clinical series. The same is being said about metal-to-metal articulations. Whether or not these materials will replace polyethylene has yet to be decided. A number of Ceramic heads have fractured, and metal on metal prostheses are beginning to show, in small numbers, metallosis. This development has produced concerned, in light of the finding of chromosomal abnormalities at the site of metallosis, as reported by Professor Case, from Bristol.

While the new approaches to weight bearing surfaces are being evaluated, significant improvements on the wear performance of new polyethylene are being revealed at this time. It will be a while before the issue is resolved.

Thirty years after the introduction of total hip surgery in America I find it difficult to see a great deal of progress having been made [141]. Some progress has been made but its degree does not seem to be proportional to the efforts made to improve results and the costs of those efforts. I a convinced that the results obtained from the initial Charnley arthroplasty have not been surpassed by any other implant. There is ample evidence to support the validity of that statement. The results reported by several surgeons testify to that effect [126, 128, 141].

I suspect that the slow progress is because orthopaedists relinquished many of their responsibilities to Industry. Industry controls, to a great degree, the trends and future of total joint design, to the point that I have been able to state on numerous occasions that "the education of the orthopaedist at this time is structured to satisfy the marketing needs of Industry". The same can be said about Research.

Had we retained control of our destiny it is possible that we would have been in a better position to identify important issues and set aside ones which have only marketing value. John Charnley himself warned us that wear was the biggest problem looming on the horizon and suggested that a concerted effort should be made in that direction. We ignored his words and today we find ourselves confronting problems that should have been solved long ago.

PULMONARY EMBOLISM (See Thrombo-embolism, Section III, MISCELLANEOUS)

R

REHABILITATION OF TOTAL HIP PATIENTS (See REHABILITATION, Section III)

REVISION SURGERY WITHOUT TROCHANTERIC OSTEOTOMY

It was not until recently that most surgeons began to realize that revision surgery for failed total hip prostheses could be safely performed without trochanteric osteotomy. For a number of years, even those who used the posterior approach in primary arthroplasty felt that in revision surgery the trochanter had to be osteotomized in order to obtain adequate exposure of the acetabulum. This is not necessarily true. Very good exposure of the proximal femur and acetabulum can be achieved without trochanteric osteotomy.

By this time we all have recognized that failure of union of the reattached greater trochanter in revision surgery is very high. In revision surgery one is likely to find the greater trochanter very osteoporotic. Bringing it down against the femoral shaft and holding it with wires very often result in fracture of the wires, displacement of the trochanter, nonunion of the fragment and an increase in the degree of rotation of the hip joint, which predisposes to dislocation. If filliform cables are used the seriousness of the problem is magnifies manifold. (See BROKEN WIRES).

Revision of one component without revision of the other is possible without osteotomy of the greater trochanter in most instances. The secret behind the success is sufficient dissection of soft tissues from the bone, particularly from the proximal femur. Severance of the insertion of the iliopsoas muscle is a necessary step in instances when a significant amount of shortening of the extremity needs to be overcome. This also applies to primary surgery, such as arthroplasty performed for congenital dislocation of the hip with major shortening of the leg.

Detachment of the insertion of the gluteus maximus from the proximal femur is essential for good exposure. On the other hand, severance of the gluteus medius and minimus is, in my opinion, unnecessary. It is better to osteotomize the trochanter than to section the muscles and then repair them. Under this latter circumstance the repair that takes place under tension frequently breaks lose. Lengthening of these muscle can be best achieved by stripping their insertion on the wing of the ilium. Care, however, must be exercised to avoid injury to major vessels and the inferior gluteal nerve.

Attempts to remove a failed femoral component without trochanteric osteotomy may result in fracture of the trochanter. Therefore it is important to expose well the proximal-lateral aspect of the femur. If the failed implant was cemented, the proximal/lateral cement mantle must the removed prior to any attempts to "hammer" the implant out of the canal, and the medial wall of the greater trochanter thoroughly rasped. Otherwise as the broader section of the proximal prosthesis exists from the canal it can easily break the osteoporotic trochanter (Fig. 106).

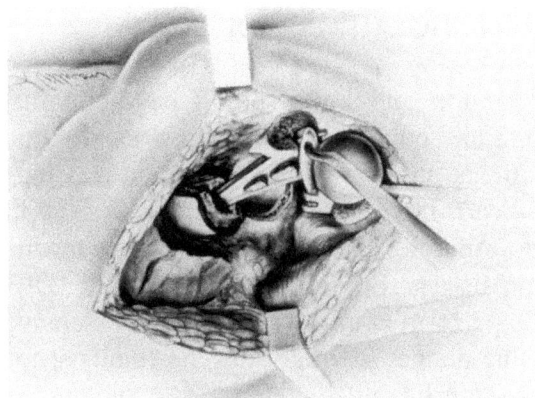

Fig. Removal of cemented or uncemented prostheses without trochanteric osteotomy may produce a fracture of the greater trochanter unless great care is exercised

Upon completion of the procedure the severed insertion of the gluteus maximus on the shaft of the femur should be repaired. For a number of years I considered this step unnecessary until I realized that some patients had a deformity of the buttock as a result of the superior displacement of muscle belly as well as mild weakness of the muscle. In order to successfully perform revision surgery without trochanteric osteotomy the incision must be a generous one. Small incisions make the procedure more difficult; require forceful compression of the soft tissue and provide inadequate exposure of the important areas of the femur and acetabulum (Fig. 107 and 108a,b.).

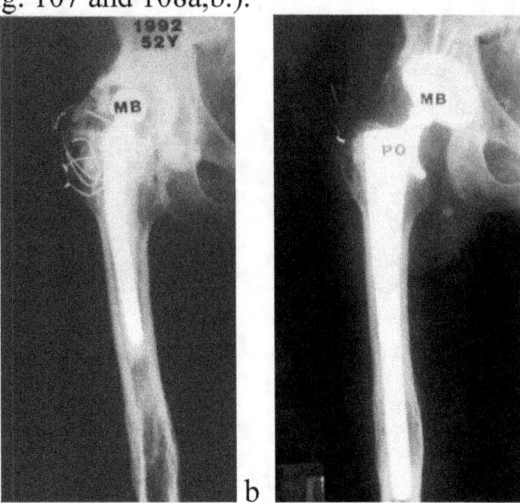

Fig. Failed Charnley arthroplasty (a) revised without the need for trochanteric osteotomy (b).
It is a common mistake to hold the hip in flexion and internal rotation during the exposure and preparation of the acetabulum. Such positioning does nothing but make the surgery more difficult. The hip should be held in a neutral position or only in a few degrees of flexion. The knee is also held in extension.

SECTION II – THE HIP JOINT

The extended position of the hip and knee not only facilitates exposure, but also precludes possible damage to the major vessels of the leg. Damage that probably sets the stage for the development of thromboembolic disease because of the kinking of the vessels at the time of surgery. (See THROMBOEMBOLIC DISEASE)

Significant flexion of the hip and knee should be maintained only during the preparation of the proximal femur and only for the shortest possible time. There is no need for the assistant to hold the leg in that position while the cement is being mixed. This period of waiting should be utilized by carrying out passive exercises of the hip, knee and ankle. Exercises, I suspect, are more valuable than any chemical or mechanical prophylactic measure against thromboembolic disease (See THROBOEMBOLIC DISEASE).

When revision surgery is performed in instances where extensive lysis of the lateral aspect of the femur is present, the danger of fracturing the femur at that level, during the flexion position of the femur, are significant. As the hip is flexed and internally rotated the greater trochanter may abut against the pelvis producing forces that can easily fracture the weakened bone. In order to prevent fracture it is often best to perform the splitting procedure of Wagner, which consists of separating the entire lateral wall of the femur, including the greater trochanter, and retracting it until completion of the work that needs to be done on the femur. Then the bony wall can be reattached to the main femoral shaft.

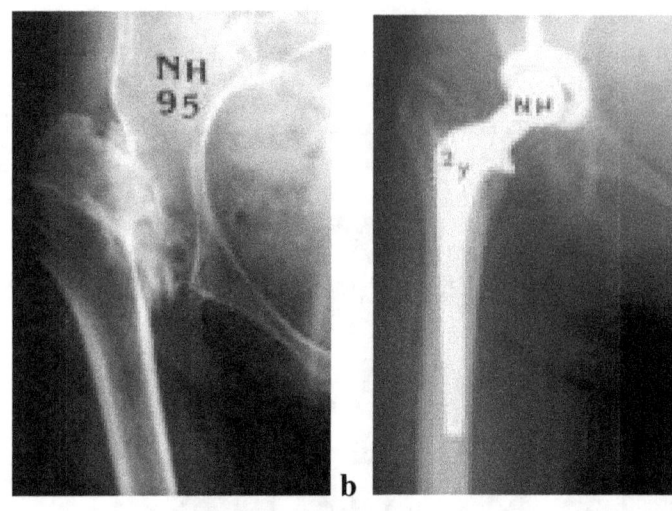

Fig. a and b. congenially dislocated hip. Arthroplasty performed without trochateric osteotomy.

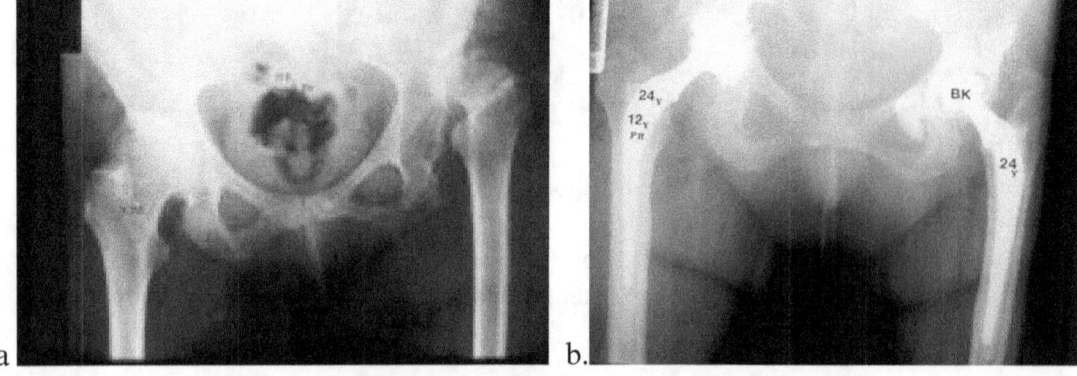

Fig. a and b. Twenty-four year follow-up of total hip arthrroplsties. Right hip required revision twelve years after the initial surgery.

SECTION II – THE HIP JOINT

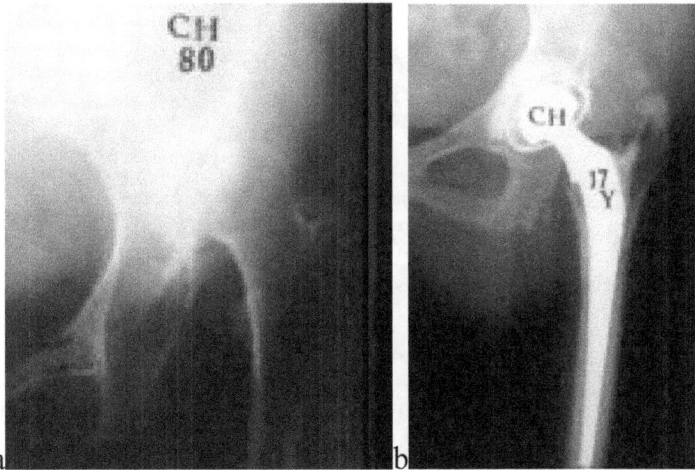

Fig. a and b. Untreated dislocation that occurred in childhood treated with total hip arthroplasty without trochanteic osteotomy. It is likely that a partial avulsion of the greater trochanter took place shortly after surgery.

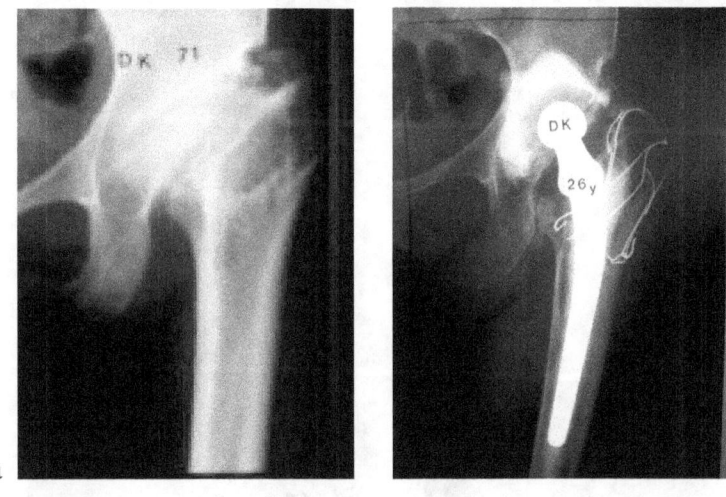

Fig. a and b. Sequela of congenital hip dysplasia (a). A 24 year follow-up of the Charnley arthroplasty (b)..

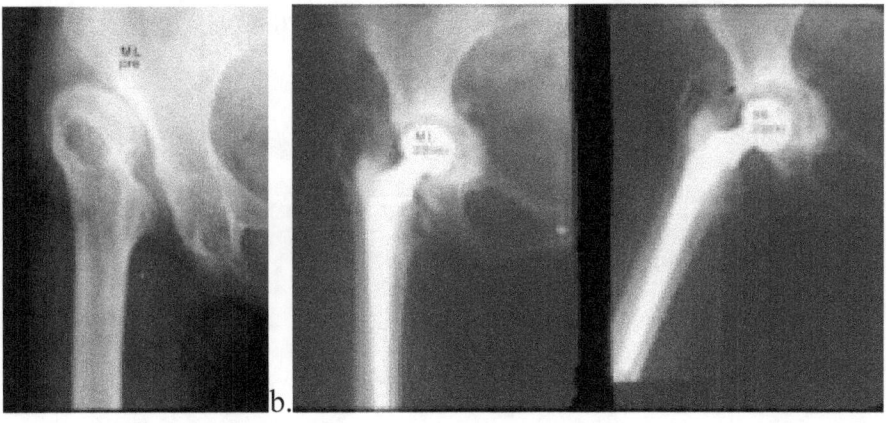

SECTION II – THE HIP JOINT

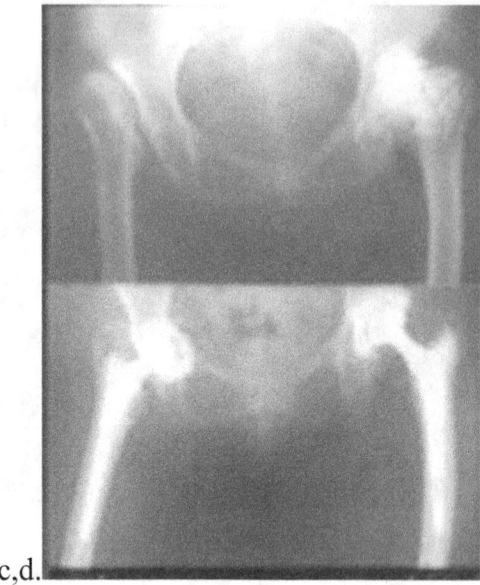

Fig. a, b, c and d. Bilateral congenital hip dysplasia.treated with total hip arthroplasties performed without trochanteric osteotomy.

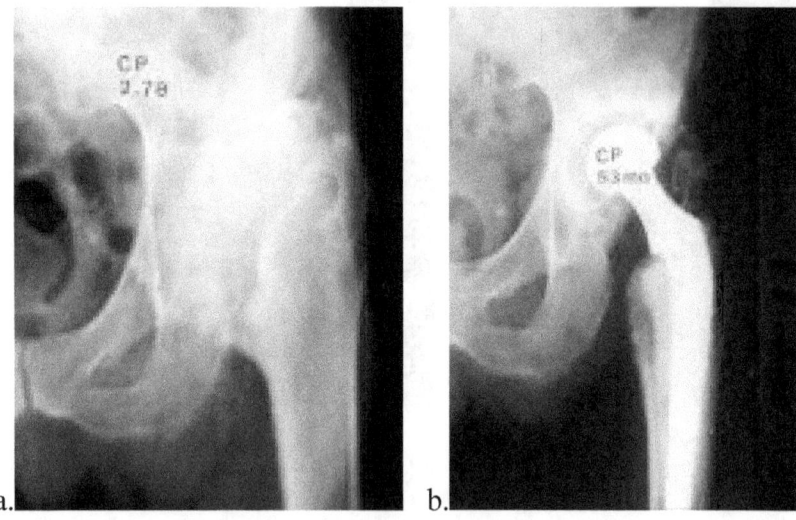

Fig. a and b. partially ankylosed hip treated with cemented arthroplasty performed without trochateric osteotomy.

T

THROMBOEMBOLIC DISEASE

Infection used to be the complication surgeons who performed total hip arthroplasty feared the most. More effective prophylactic antibiotics have made the procedure much safer. Thromboembolic disease following hip surgery became the number one problem. So much so that it is virtually impossible to find a surgeon who does not use some type of prophylactic agent whenever he or she performs any major surgery around the hip or knee joint. Others extend the prophylaxis method to fractures and other conditions of the musculoskeletal system. In Germany, I am told, it is almost mandatory to administer low molecular Heparin to all patients with fractures.

Is the danger of thromboembolic disease as great as we have been led to believe? Is chemical prophylaxis the most effective way to prevent it? I doubt both premises. No one denies the fact that pulmonary emboli and/ or thrombophlebitis can complicate major hip surgery but, in my opinion, their incidence has been greatly exaggerated and interested pharmaceutical companies have unduly promoted its chemical prophylaxis.

I doubt the popularity of prophylactic anticoagulants has had a positive influence in the incidence of thromboembolic disease. As far as I am concerned we have made a mountain out of a mole and have allowed the pharmaceutical industry skillfully manipulate the issue.

Doctor Lorraine Day, during her tenure as chief of orthopaedics at the San Francisco General Hospital in the 1980's reported on 1000 patients who underwent nailing of intertrochanteric fractures, and who did not receive chemical prophylactic anti-coagulation of any kind. None of the patients died from pulmonary embolism, though she acknowledged that at the time of autopsy a few of them had demonstrated pulmonary emboli. They had died with blood clots in their lungs but not from them.

I was very intrigued by her remarks when I first heard them. It prompted me to look more carefully into the issue. Today, based on careful analysis of my own data [34, 153] and the review of the world literature, I am convinced that the problem, though a potential one, is being approached by most people without solid scientific support.

In the case of total hip arthroplasty it is very likely that vascular damage, caused at the time of surgery, eventually leads to the formation of clots and their possible dislodgment into the systemic circulation. This observation was first made by surgeons in New Zealand, whose names unfortunately I do not recall. Others in this country have repeated the New Zealanders' studies and some have claimed originality. The initial studies were performed using venography during surgery. It indicated that the femoral vessels experience severe kinking during extreme degrees of flexion and rotation of the hip. This kinking is significant enough to injure the vessels. They also demonstrated that the degree of kinking was greater when the surgical procedure was performed through an anterior approach that called for flexion and external rotation of the hip. The kinking was less when the posterior approach, requiring flexion and internal rotation was used. Our clinical experiences have supported this view, since the incidence of thromboembolic complications was higher when the anterior approach is used.

This lesson prompted me to begin an intraoperative protocol consisting of avoidance of extreme rotation and flexion of the hip and knee, and the frequent passive mobilization of the hip, knee and ankle during the surgical procedure. Since it is necessary during surgery to hold the hip joint in flexion and internal rotation during the preparation of the femoral side, when the posterior approach is used, the length of such position should be shortened as much as possible. There is really no need to hold the knee in full flexion and internal rotation of the hip for more than the few seconds necessary to obtain the proper orientation.

I am also convinced that physical exercise is the most effective means of prophylaxis, better than any chemical or physical method. In my practice I insist that patients begin active isometric and isotonic exercises of their gluteus maximus, the quadriceps and ankle and toes muscles as soon as possible. I also recommend deep breathing and trunk and abdominal exercises.

When I first visited Sir John Charnley's Hip Center in England in 1970, I heard him discuss the problem of thromboembolic disease in total hip surgery. At that time he kept his patients in bed for a much longer time, following surgery. He had tried various methods with ambivalent results. At that particular time he was experimenting with ReoMacrodex. When I returned to the States I used it in a large number of patients. I was disappointed by the high incidence of extensive swelling of the extremity that accompanied its use. I then proceeded to use aspirin as prophylaxis. For nearly twenty-five years it has been my preferred chemical agent. The results have been satisfactory, however, I suspect that it is not the aspirin that led to those results but the program of intraoperative and postoperative exercises [43, 153].

Doctor A. K. Goswami, a former fellow in our department in Los Angeles and now a surgeon in the United Kingdom, reviewed all my total hip arthroplasties and made some very interesting observation. For example, the incidence of fatal pulmonary embolism in nearly 1500 patients was 0.4%. There was no difference in results in relation to gender or age of the patients; the same was true for the type of stockings used, compressive elastic or intermittent compression devices. There was also no difference in the rate of complications between those patients who had the surgery performed on the East and West coasts of the United States. Epidural anaesthesia, however, was associated with a lower incidence of complications as well as the posterior approach when compared with the lateral, trans-trochanteric one.

The American literature is virtually empty of reports where no chemical prophylaxis was used. The British literature has seriously addressed the issue and some have claimed that prophylaxis is not needed. I am inclined to believe they are right. It is not likely that similar reports will be forthcoming from surgeons in the United States. The fear of litigation in the event of a fatality scares all of us. The power of the pharmaceutical industry in this regard is awesome and a number of orthopaedists are under their direct or indirect payroll.

Their testimony against anyone who fails to administer their product is likely to bring about the guilty verdict of malpractice.

There is a pharmaceutical firm that offered $800 per patient to orthopaedic surgeons who were willing to use their product and complete forms indicating demographic information and post-surgical data. Several of them have become popular speakers across the country, whose expenses and honoraria are taken care by the sponsoring organization [158].

Obviously, aspirin and exercise is not the only effective protocol against thromboembolic disease. Good results have been reported using other methods such as Coumadin. However, this method is complicated. The incidence of associated bleeding is relatively high and its use requires daily laboratory tests, which increase the cost of care. However, the cost is not nearly as high as it is with the use of low–molecular heparin where the hospital charge for each of the two daily injections is close to $100. The need to continue the daily injections for either twenty or thirty days further raises the ultimate cost. Low-molecular heparin precludes the use of spinal and epidural anesthesia because of the reported danger of spinal bleeding. Instances of paraplegia secondary to the administration of heparin have appeared in the literature.

TITANIUM IN TOTAL HIPS

I hold the dubious distinction of having designed and used the first Titanium Total Hip Prosthesis in the United States. At the time I was unaware that Pierre Boutin, from Pau, France had just began to use an implant made of the same Titanium alloy (Aluminum 10, Venadium 4). He, however, used ceramic heads rather than the monoblock implants we used.

The idea of using Titanium occurred to me when I saw a couple of my patients experienced fractures of Stainless Steel Charnley prostheses I had inserted a few years earlier. Similar complications were being reported in the literature in various parts of the world.

By that time I had some knowledge about the mechanical properties of Titanium because of my interest in fracture healing. We had documented through clinical and laboratory studies that diaphyseal fractures managed without immobilization, other than a cast or brace, healed faster than those treated with rigid fixation. We speculated that motion at the fracture site brought about stresses at the fracture site that encouraged osteogenesis.

My own experiences, as well as those of others, indicated that resorption of bone at the level of the calcar in Charley arthroplasties was a common phenomenon [120]. We suspected that such resorption was due exclusively to stress shielding in the area due to the stiff nature of the metallic component. We had learned that the stiffer the metal the greater the transfer of weight bearing stresses to the distal bone which explained the frequently associated distal cortical hypertrophy [3, 6, 11, 12, 14, 27, 46, 64, 175]. We were not aware at that time that resorption of the proximal-medial cortex of the proximal femur could also be caused by lysis, secondary to plastic debris. We learned that much later.

SECTION II – THE HIP JOINT

It occurred to me then that using a metal less stiff than Stainless Steel could eliminate the resorption of the cortex or Cobalt/Chrome alloys. With those thoughts in mind I approached engineers at Zimmer, the largest manufacturer of orthopaedic implants. They had toyed earlier with the idea of making Titanium alloy intramedullary nails. I used a few of those nails but the company soon abandoned the idea of marketing the new nails, allegedly because of the increased price.

Working with Zimmer's engineers we designed a total hip Titanium prosthesis that resembled the Charnley implant. The size of the head was 28 millimeters in diameter. The Charnley, 22 millimeters. The offset of the Titanium implant was also 4 degrees lower than the Charnley prosthesis. Extensive laboratory studies were conducted regarding the mechanical and wear properties of the new implant and were found to be very good. Indeed, the Titanium prosthesis transferred stresses in a more desirable manner throughout the entire proximal femur and its wear against polyethylene appeared to be even superior to Stainless Steel and Cobalt Chrome alloys [1, 12, 14, 23, 126, 149, 128].

Rostoker, a distinguished engineer from Chicago, did indicate, however, that even though the wear properties of the material were good under laboratory conditions, its wear behavior was unpredictable. In the early 1970's the engineers could not explain this phenomenon and decided to ignore it. Years later Rostoker's observation proved to be prophetic.

We consulted with others in the United States, such as Patrick Laing, from Pittsburgh, who had published his work on Titanium alloys earlier. To the best of my knowledge he had not worked with total hip prostheses.

Our initial clinical experiences with the new implant that the manufactures had elected to call the STH Prosthesis were very encouraging. Simultaneously I had abandoned the use of the lateral approach to the hip along with Charnley's recommended trochanteric osteotomy.

Grateful to Charnley for his teachings and friendship I contacted him and informed him that I was no longer using his implant, osteotomizing the greater trochanter or using the lateral approach. That I had moved to a Titanium implant and was approaching the joint through a posterior approach.

My letter prompted a very interesting response. After thanking me for providing him with information about my change in philosophy and technique, he proceeded to say that I had never really learned how to perform his operation correctly; that using a "flexible" metal was a big mistake; and ventured to add that I had missed my call. He wrote, "You do not have the mentality of a surgeon but that of a gynecologist". My approaching the hip from behind would have proved his point.

Our relationship was slightly strained. Obviously, he resented my leaving his fold. After all we had developed a very good personal relationship and I had invited him on several occasions to lecture at various meetings sponsored by the Academy and the University of Miami.

A few years later when I reported my results with the STH prosthesis before the International Hip Society in Bern, Switzerland I titled my presentation " A Gynecologists approach to Total Hip Surgery" and dedicated the presentation to Charnley who was in the audience. We both had been founding members of the Society, which at that time had only twenty members. The audience, after learning the genesis if the title of my talk, enjoyed the levity. My relationship with Charnley went back to normal. A couple years later the Queen of England knighted him.

Our original publication relating to the first six years of follow-up with the new implant indicated that the overall behavior of the Titanium prosthesis was comparable, if not slightly better, than the Charnley Stainless Steel implant. Unfortunately, subsequent longer follow-up began to reveal a higher incidence of radiological changes with the STH prostheses. The revision rate was also higher. Eventually, I abandoned its use all together. The fact remains that many mono-block Titanium prostheses have performed extremely well over a relatively long period of time. A very active acromegalic has performed without any clinical problems for over 27 years. His x-rays have shown a thin metal-cement radiolucent line on zone 1 for over five years without signs of progression (Fig. 109 a,b).

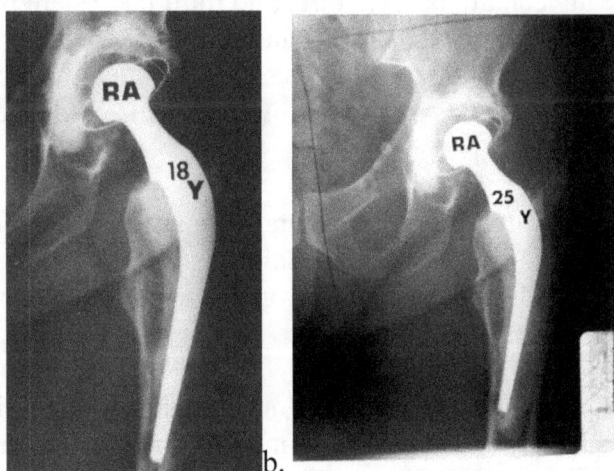

Fig. a and b. Titanium nonoblock total hip prosthesis 18 and 25 years post-operatively performed in an extremely tall acromegalic. A metal-cement line and a luytic l;esion have appeared, but have progressed very slowly

.

SECTION II – THE HIP JOINT

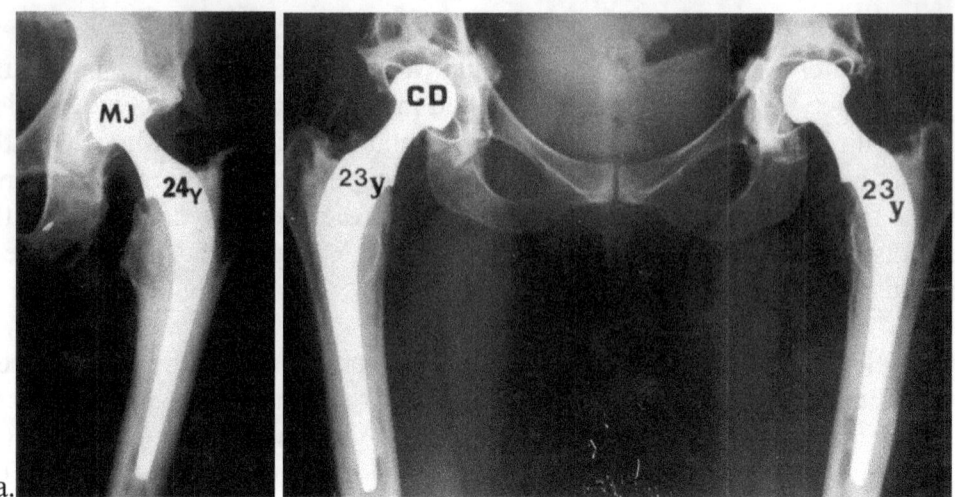

Fig. a and b. Monoblock Titanium prostheses demonstrating no evidence of wear, signs or loosening or lysis 24 and 23 years respectively after implantation.

It appears that Titanium, as an articulated surface against polyethylene sockets is very good but only under "clean" conditions. That is, if no third bodies are present between the metallic head and the plastic acetabulum. Any material capable of scratching the relatively "soft" alloy, if interposed between the two surfaces can initiate a third body wear process. In our laboratories at Orthopaedic Hospital of Los Angeles, this point was clearly proven [15, 56, 62, 64].

I first became aware of the problems others were having with Titanium prostheses from reading of anecdotal reports of massive metallosis encountered in isolated instances. Claims were immediately made that the wear properties of Titanium were poor and the original work of Rostoker was cited.

The Hospital for Special Surgery, in New York, had developed a Titanium alloy Total Hip Prosthesis that was strongly marketed by Zimmer. Sometime in the late 1980's I was informed by the director of research at Zimmer that the surgeons at that hospital were seeing early failures with their Titanium implant, associated with severe metallosis. Accompanied by him we traveled to New York where we had an opportunity to confirm the findings of serious early failures and the associated presence of metal debris. This took place in the presence of the local surgeons and pathologists.

I was flabbergasted at the magnitude of their failures and returned home puzzled by them. I could not explain them. Their implant was made by the same manufacture, using the same material. The geometry was the only difference between theirs prosthesis and ours. It was hard to believe that mild geometrical differences in the stem would explain the problem.

I was particularly troubled because at that very same moment we were in the process of submitting for publication a manuscript reporting on 17 surgically retrieved STH prostheses that had not shown any evidence of metallosis, either under the naked eye or under the microscope. Trying to explain the differences became extremely difficult. We then elected to withhold submission of the paper awaiting a local review of our findings.

The new review did not indicate anything contrary to the original findings. It was at the moment that I recalled that the x-rays of the failed implants I had seen in New York had their acetabular components cemented with metal-backed polyethylene cups. Ours did not. It dawn on us then that this could be an explanatory factor. Simultaneously, a local Los Angeles orthopaedist who had used a few STH prostheses informed me of his bad experiences with the implant and the presence of metallosis recognized at the time of revision surgery. His failed implants had been stabilized with metal-backed acetabuli.

We obtained his removed specimens and studied them in the laboratory. Harry McKellop did the work and reported the strong probability that very small pieces of metal and cement may have fallen from the cemented metal-backed sockets into the joint, precipitating a rapid and aggressive third body wear process. I had personally never used the metal-backed acetabular cups and had never seen metallosis.

Once when I was about to cement the acetabular cup I noticed that the implant the nurse was handing me was a metal-backed one. She proceeded to inform me that the vendor of the implants had generously replaced the "old cups" with newer ones, which were "much better". It was the only metal-backed cup I ever used. Within a couple of years it failed and at surgery we demonstrated metallosis. (See METAL BACKED ACETABULAR CUPS)

The dilemma was trying to explain why in our own series the failure rate with non-metal-backed acetabuli was higher than with the Charnley implants. I could not blame the metal-backed socket. We had previously remarked about the dulling noticed on the surface of failed Titanium implants. We observed, measured and correlated the degree of dulling of the heads with burnishing of the stem and concluded that there was a direct correlation between the degree of burnishing of the stem- a reflection of motion between the stem and the cement- and the dulling of the heads- a proof of wear. There was no direct correlation, however, in regards to the length of implantation. Failed prosthesis that had been in place for long periods of time often demonstrated less dulling and burnishing, that in more recently implanted components. This indicated the possibility of a late, sudden presence of a third body capable of initiating the wear process. It probably came from the stem as it moved against the column of acrylic cement [57, 59, 60, 62, 67, 71, 74].

The fact that the surface of the metallic heads of retrieved failed implants that had been removed with an intact mantle of cement, and where the failure had obviously taken place at the bone-cement interface, did not show dulling of the head, further supported the initial hypothesis.

These observations concerning laboratory investigations, plus a 27 year follow up of nearly 600 hundred cemented total hip Titanium prostheses, has given me sufficient information to speculate that Titanium is not the best material to use in total hip replacements regardless whether cemented or non-cemented implants are used.

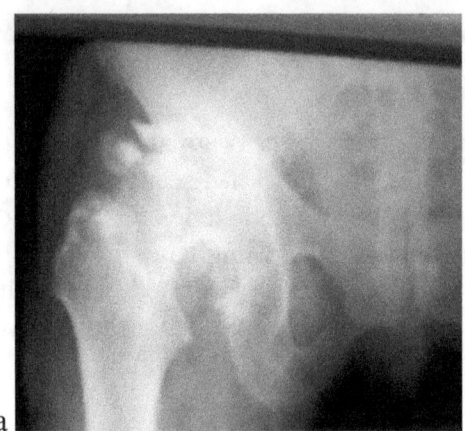 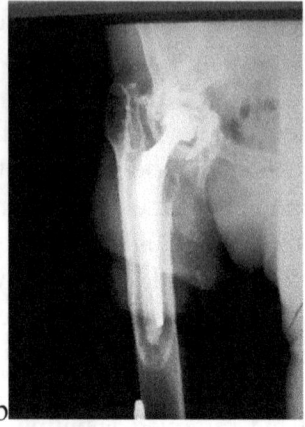

Fig. a, b and c.   Neuropathic (Charco) joint (a). The condition was treated with a monoblock Titanium implant. Within a short time severe lytic changes were seen throughout. Th ejoint remained only minimally symptomatic.

Though our studies have dealt exclusively with cemented implants I think it is appropriate to extrapolate that a comparable mechanism might explain the failure of non-cemented prostheses. It is well known that the incidence of lysis in non-cemented hip prostheses is higher than in cemented implants. A variety of explanations have been offered. The most commonly accepted one at this time is that polyethylene debris arises from the plastic socket and accumulates at the interface between the metal and/or cement and surrounding bone. (Fig. 110, 111)

Corrosion from modular components, motion between the plastic liner and the metal cup, and poor wear properties of the polyethylene are the most popular explanations. Regardless as to what theory is eventually proven most accurate, the fact remains that motion between the metallic stem and the cortical bone of the femur might be sufficient to generate metal debris. If it travels to the joint in sufficient amounts it may initiate polyethylene wear and the resulting lysis. The metal debris could also produce lysis. I have seen instances where the histological evidence indicated lysis produced by metal and complete absence of polyethylene debris (See LYSIS).

For those reasons I believe at this point that "harder" metals should be used in total hip replacements in preference to Titanium, which is softer and therefore more sensitive to "scratching".

It is of great interest to not that in a small number of cases I found myself replacing only the acetabular component. For as long as an additional 18 years we have not seen additional measurable wear of the new polyethylene socket. Harry McKellop conducted an experimental study comparing the wear of polyethylene articulating against retrieved Titanium femoral heads and new ones. The difference between the two was insignificant. It appears that the prosthetic head polished itself during the years of usage and improved its properties. It suggests that exchange of both components because of fear of increased damage to the head cannot be justified.

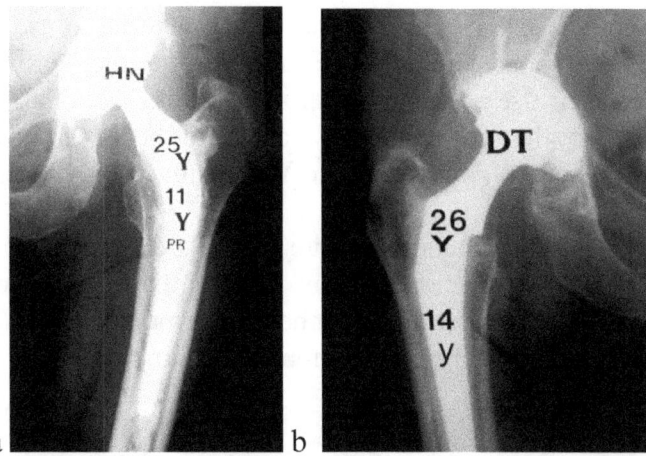

Fig. a and b. Titanium monoblock prostheses 25 and 26-years post implantation. The acetabular components had been revised 11 and 14 years respectively. Notice the absence of measurable wear.

TOTAL HIP SURGERY: (CEMENTED) Factors predictive of success

A great deal has been written about total hip replacement. If we were to believe everything we read, we would be utterly confused. Everybody has wonderful results according to the thousands of publications. Every new prosthesis is marketed as "new and improved"- as in the case of toothpaste or soap– and as the product of extensive research. If that were true, one could choose any of the nearly 400 different prostheses in the market and count on having perfect results.

The fact remains that complications occur with any and all implants and that very little research goes into the design of many of the new modifications. In actuality the difference between various implants is minimal and represents only minor changes in shape, length, width, angle, texture, you name it.

New implants appear in the market on a frequent basis simply because the competition between the manufacturers is fierce. Each company has to protect its turf to keep ahead of the pack. The president of a major manufacturing company told me once that as soon as they released a new implant they are already working on its modification which would be released the following year. This pattern has been tempered somewhat in recent years after Industry realized it was too expensive.

I do not intent to go into a lengthy discussion regarding the many factors that influence the behavior of total hip implants. I will limit my comments to cemented arthroplasty based on a review of my own experiences [22, 25, 37, 126, 128, 132, 133, 141]. My results are supported by the reports of others. I will not discuss non-cemented implants because I have not critically reviewed my own experiences with them. I believe that their long term success has not matched the success of the Charnley cemented prosthesis. I admit that the possibility exists that one day the opposite may be true. Recent reports are beginning to suggest that with certain non-cemented prostheses the results are most impressive.

SECTION II – THE HIP JOINT

1. The metal of the prosthesis: Titanium is the wrong material to use and Stainless Steel or Cobalt Chrome is better. This statement does not preclude the possibility that one day we may have to abandon their use as we discover undesirable sequella resulting from the release of harmful debris. Not that Titanium alloys are better because this material also has powerful toxic components such as Aluminum and Vanadium.

2. The type of socket remains debatable in spite of early results indicating that non-cemented sockets are better. My own experiences comparing totally uncemented prostheses with Hybrid ones indicated a better performance of the non-cemented ones (as far as the acetabular side was concerned) but inferior when the femoral component was observed [141]. (See HYBRID TOTAL HIPS)

3. The attitude of the acetabular cup has been traditionally believed to be ideal when it measures 45 degrees of inclination. This did not prove to be true in our own series. Cups that were inadvertently cemented with a higher degree of inclination behaved as well as the more transversely placed ones. Furthermore, we suspect that the more vertical cup has an advantage over the more transverse one, as it seems to be subjected to lesser "teeter totters" weight bearing stresses [132]. See ACETABULAR ORIENTATION.

4. The socket should be fully covered with bone. Coverage is more important than vertical orientation. It is better to place a socket in 55 degrees of orientation and have it completely covered with bone than place it in a 45 degree tilt but leave a portion of the implant uncovered [132].

5. A few degrees of anteversion have always been recommended. This stands to reason, but a neutral attitude is not always bad. It is difficult to dislocate a hip prosthesis that has a socket in neutral. Dislocation has many etiologies, many of which are far more important than the lack of full anteversion (See DISLOCATION OF HIP PROSTHESES) .

6. The orientation of the femoral component is relatively important. The best attitude of the implant is in few degrees of valgus. Varus renders a higher incidence of radiological complications [22, 23, 25, 141]. However, I am convinced that varus per se is not bad; it is bad because it might decrease excessively the thickness of the medial column of cement. If the canal is wide, a few degrees of varus still permit the presence of a wide medial column of cement (Fig. 110).

SECTION II – THE HIP JOINT

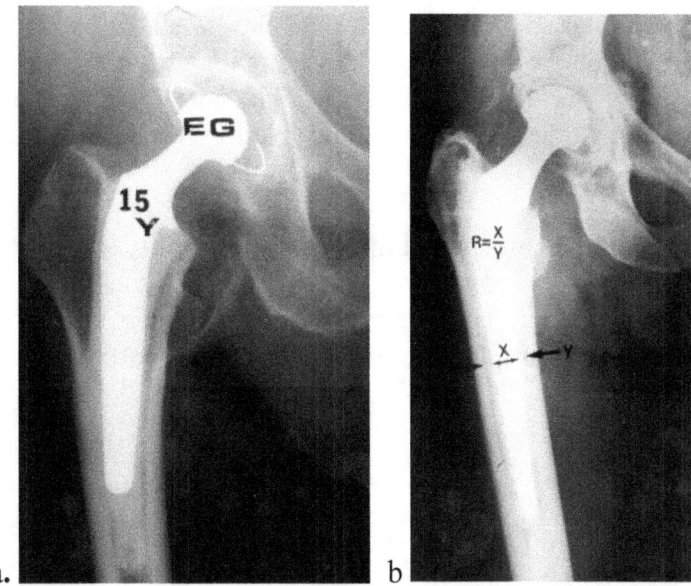

Fig. a and b. Cemented prosthesis inserted in a varus position. A thick column of cement at the level of the calcar seems to ensure long-term stability (a). Ideally, the stem should fill more than 50% of the canal at seven centimeters below the calcar (b).

7. The thickness of the cement at the "calcar" level is best if it is not less than 2 millimeters or greater than 5 millimeters. Too little cement probably fragments and initiate the production of harmful debris. A column of cement greater than 10 millimeters also appears to be associated with a higher incidence of radiological complications.

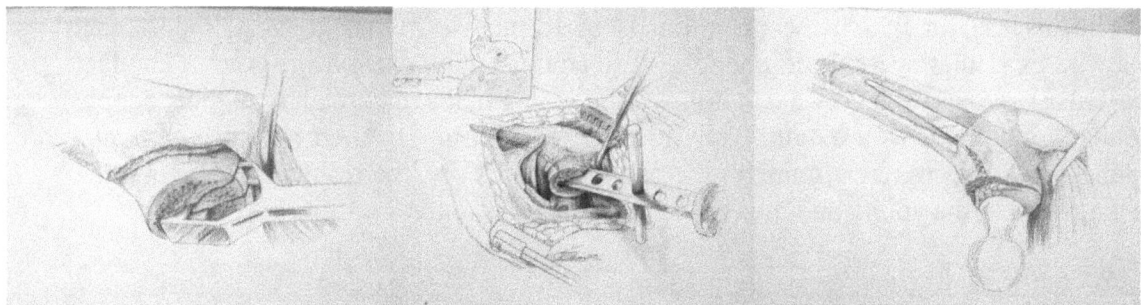

Fig. a, b, and c. In order to obtain a thick column of cement medially, at the level of the calcar, the lateral aspect of the femur must be forcefully rasped..

8. The diameter of the stem should not be either too large or too small. It appears that at seven centimeters below the calcar more than 50% of the canal should be filled with the stem. (Fig.)

9. A distal plug may be desirable. I say, "May be desirable" because I am not convinced it makes biological sense. It is rather naïve to claim that pressurization of the cement is not possible without a plug. It may not be as great without it but there is no data to suggest that maximum pressurization is ideal (See PRESSURIZATION). Some of my best results were obtained with the original Charnley prostheses when the cement was driven into the canal

under thumb pressure. I admit that aesthetically the plug canal "looks better" and that revision surgery is easier when the cement mass does not extent too far below the tip of the prosthesis. The possibility exists that polyethylene debris may pool above the plug and create lysis of the bone. Without the plug it should be able to seep beyond that point and be free of compressing stresses.

10. The age of the patient, up to this point, is important. Younger patients are more likely to experience complications [25, 133, 141]. However, our data showed that the risk of the femoral component loosening was similar in young and old patients. The risk of socket loosening is higher in younger patients and the risk of acetabular loosening is higher in female patients.

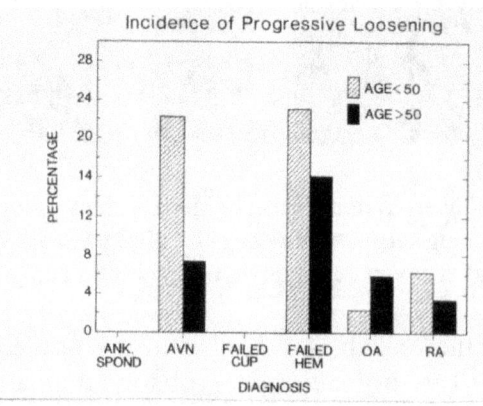

Fig. Progressive loosening in relation to the patient's age.

11. The disease for which the operation is performed is of the greatest importance. Patients with avascular necrosis do not do as well as those with osteoarthritis [133]. The fact that avascular necrosis is usually a condition of the young helps to explain why most people believe that young patients are more likely to experience failure of their total hip implants. If from the overall series one eliminates the patients with AVN, the results indicate that the difference between the young and the old are not as significant.

12.

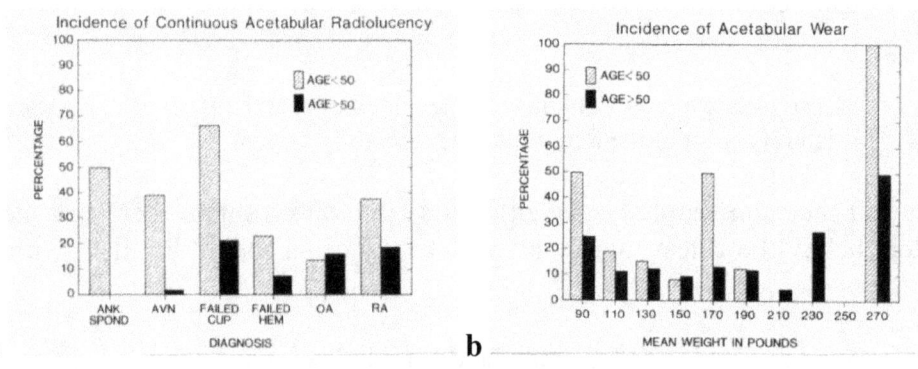

Fig. Acetabular radiolucent lines (a) and acetabular wear according to patients' age.

V

VARUS DEFORMITY IN FRACTURES OF THE PROXIMAL FEMUR

We never see patients with acute, displaced femoral neck fractures of the femur present to us with x-rays demonstrating a valgus deformity. They all have a varus deformity. Muscular forces working on the fragments must cause the deformity. I have always believed the teaching promulgated in textbooks that were popular in my early career, that is, the varus was produced by the contraction of gluteus medius and minimus. The two muscles, attached to the greater trochanter displaced the proximal fragment superiorly without any opposing force.

One day, while observing patients with such fractures, I noticed, as I tried to move the fractured extremity that the motion least painful was that of additional adduction. The most painful one was abduction. I reasoned that if the two gluteal muscles were pulling on the greater trochanter additional adduction would be met with resistance and create more pain. The opposite was the case.

I decided then to carryout electromyographic studies. We placed EMG needles into the adductors, abductors, knee extensors and hamstrings. We did not try to study the iliopsoas muscle, first because it would have been difficult to identity with certainty and secondly because it's possible deforming force was annulled by its frequent separation from the two major fragments of the fracture, as in the case of the intertrochanteric fracture. The EMG studies indicated that contrary to the traditional belief the abductor muscles were silent during the acute stages, but the adductors were in a state of spasticity that lasted until the pain subsided many days later. In essence, we had mistakenly assumed that the gluteal muscles were responsible for the ubiquitous varus deformity. They are innocent bystanders in the production of the deformity [83]. (Fig. 72).

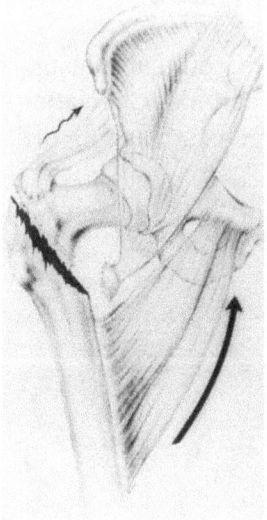

Fig. 149. The varus deformity seen in femoral neck and intertrochanteric fractures is due to contracture of the adductor musculature rather than from the pull of the "unopposed" abductor mechanism.

During the performance of a total hip arthroplasty I had the terrible experience of piercing one of the obturator vessels with a sharp drill bit. I had anticipated surgery would be uneventful since the patient was a slim, fifty five-year-old woman who had osteoarthritis with good skeletal structures. I was performing a hybrid replacement and was finishing the acetabular side. Two screws were already in place. As I drilled the last hole a strong stream of blood exploded and hit me in the face. At first I thought I was dealing with an arterial injury but in retrospect it was a vein. Not knowing what to do under the circumstances I put my index finger over the screw hole to stop the bleeding. I knew I would be encouraging intra-pelvic bleeding, but hoped that tamponade would stop it.

We summoned a vascular surgery which the hospital in Los Angeles did not have on-board. The one they eventually found could not be on the scene until forty-five minutes later. There was nothing I could do but continue to hold my "finger on the dike" and wait, observe the abdomen getting distended and gave blood transfusions.

When the vascular surgeon arrived I removed my finger from the screw hole and found that the bleeding had stopped spontaneously. He opened the abdomen and identified the injured vessel that I had torn by the rotating drill bit. The bleeding had stopped, not from tamponade but from spontaneous homeostasis. The enlarging abdomen was a product of my imagination: a phantom pregnancy of a sort.

Trying to determine how the accident occurred we went to the morgue and reproduced the surgical intervention by filling every hole on the acetabular cup but allowing the drill bit and the corresponding screw to penetrate three quarters of an inch beyond the inner wall of the pelvis. The findings were most revealing: protruding drill bits, through a whipping effect or screws penetrating too deeply can damage important structures such as the sciatic or femoral nerves and major vessels [5].

I also learned from the vascular surgeon that female patients with a history of pelvic inflammatory disease experience scaring and loss of elasticity of tissues on the pelvic floor that makes impossible their retraction from an advancing drill or screw.

W

WEAR

John Charnley was the first surgeon to successfully replace both sides of the hip joint. Unaware of the ultimate complications he used Teflon as he embarked on the development of his original cemented total hip replacement. His original results were disastrous. He soon realized that the plastic material that allegedly had performed so well under laboratory conditions experienced rapid and massive wear in a physiological, weight bearing environment. He found it necessary to revise all his surgeries because of severe lysis of the surrounding acetabulum and femoral bone.

I had an opportunity to see the alleged last patient to have the Teflon socket removed by Sir John Charnley. He came to Wrightington while I was there. The lysis to the pelvis and femur was massive and granulomata had formed in large masses that could be easily seen and palpated under the skin of the thigh and abdomen.

Charnley's courage, integrity and determination are legendary. He readily acknowledged the fact that he had made a mistake by using a product that did not tolerate friction well and proceeded to investigate other materials. He found polyethylene, which proved to have excellent wear properties. It has been used now for over thirty-five years with impressive results. Charnley, however, recognized that wear of the polyethylene would eventually become a problem and called this to the attention of the world community.

Time has proven him right in this score as well as in many others (See PROGRESS IN TOTAL HIP SURGERY). Today wear has become the most talked about problem related to arthroplasty surgery. Mistakenly, when lysis was identified in the 1970's it was felt that it was secondary to a reaction to the acrylic cement. This mistaken perception led to the development of non-cemented prostheses that rather than reducing the incidence of lysis, increased it. The problem was being produced from wear of the polyethylene, most likely as a result of a third-body wear mechanism, either from metallic particles arising from the non-cemented porous surface of the femoral and acetabular components; from the modular Morse taper in the neck of the prosthesis; or from friction between the plastic acetabular liner and the metallic cup. (See LYSIS).

Efforts to improve the wear properties of the polyethylene socked were undertaken by many and it appears at this time that progress is being made. However, the various products developed thus far have not been sufficiently tested clinically.

SECTION II – THE HIP JOINT

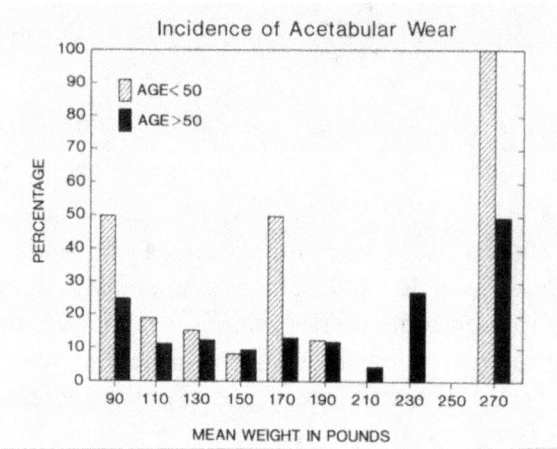

Fig. Bargraph documenting the degree of wear of polyethylene according to age.

My own experiences with polyethylene sockets in the early 1970's were probably the most rewarding. In my own practice I have been able to confirm that the arthroplasties I performed in those days were the best. I have approximately 100 patients with 25 to 32 year follow up whose hips look very good and without evidence of wear or with minimal one. The same is not true for subsequent surgeries. It is possible that the manufacturing and sterilization methods or the intrinsic composition of more recently manufactured cups adversely altered the mechanical and wear properties of the material [15, 56, 57, 59, 62, 67, 71]. It is puzzling to see active patients who after a period of time show significant wear but no evidence of lysis. Contrariwise other patients demonstrate no measurable wear but show significant amount of lysis.

We had an opportunity to study the behavior of monoblock hip arthroplasties where only the acetabular components had failed and therefore revised. New acetabulae were used and followed for a maximum of 15 years. At the time of surgery we had noticed the typical "dulling" of cemented Titanium prosthetic heads. Surprisingly the speed of wear of the new sockets was slower than that observed following the "virgin" surgery. Intrigued by this phenomenon, Harry McKellop, director of our research program, placed old failed Titanium femoral components against new polyethylene cups and subjected them to a wear testing environment. The wear that the study identified was virtually equal to that seeing with "virgin" prostheses and plastic acetabulae. Food for thought.

Wear is perhaps inevitable regardless of the material used. The hope is that it will so minimal that no complications can be detected. It is hoped by some that new polyethylenes, ceramics or improved metals can accomplished this. Reports on the small amount of wear from ceramics are convincing the orthopaedic community that the time has come to use them routinely. I encourage some caution and keep reminding myself that past experiences with ceramic heads were beset with the problem of breakage.

Metal-on-metal hips have been advertised as being the permanent solution to the problem of wear. It is claimed today that the problems that were identified with the original metal-metal total hip MacKey-Farrar prosthesis are not possible with the new metallurgical techniques and design. It could be true in both instances. However, skepticism still surrounds the issue. Reports of initial clinical trials with minimal follow-up cannot justify their usage. I suspect metal-on-metal total hip implants will soon vanish from the armamentarium of the orthopaedic surgeon. See METAL TO METAL.

WIRES (Broken)

Trochanteric osteotomy in the performance of total hip replacement is not done as frequently as it was years ago when the teachings of John Charnley dominated the field. Eventually we learned that in spite of the minimal theoretical value of trochanter transplantation the inconvenience and complications associated with the procedure did not justify its routine performance. (See TROCHANTERIC OSTEOTOMY).

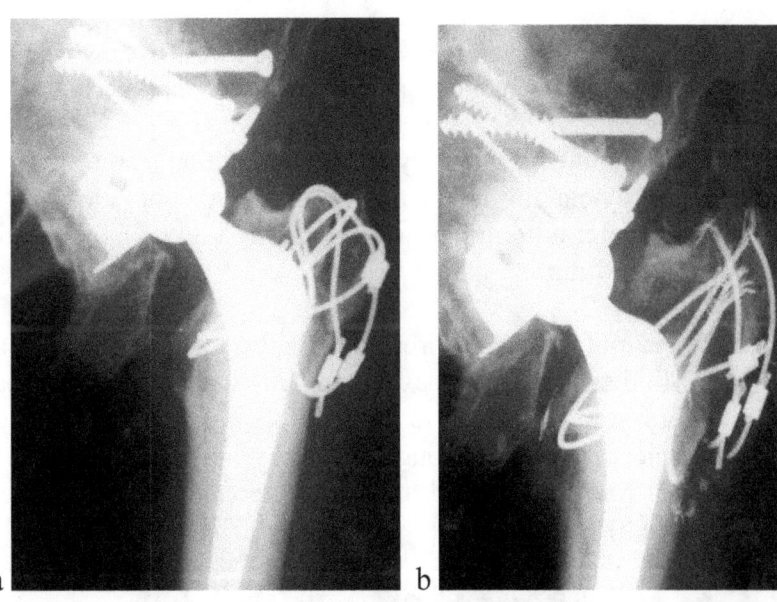

Fig. a and b   Filliform cables used to stabilized the trochanter shortly after surgery (a). The wires broke into smaller pieces, some of which lie closed to the joint (b). Their migration into the metal/plastic interface is possible.

Occasionally, however, the osteotomy is necessary in order to appropriately carryout the surgical procedure. Wiring the osteotomized trochanter is the most common method at this time. Because simple wires fracture frequently, the filliform wire has been recommended and heavily marketed in recent years. Its strength is alleged to be greater and it probably is. However, I have learned that when the wire fatigues, the thin filaments break into small pieces. These small pieces can easily travel to the joint and get caught in the plastic-metal articulation (Fig 112 a,b,c and 113). These are likely to produce aggressive third party wear resulting in lysis of bone in the femur and acetabulum. [141]

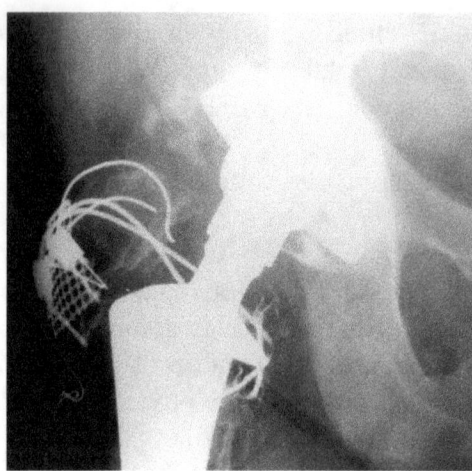

Fig. Filliform wires used to stabilize the greater trochanter. The wires fractured and traveled proximally and distally. They might create a third-body wear process.

The cases here illustrated demonstrate how rapidly the fragmentation of the small filaments can take place and how easily they can fall inside the joint. I have concluded that Filliform wires should not be used near a total hip implant without taking into consideration the high risk of major complications in the future.

Though I strongly condemn filliform wires I also have serious concerns about the role that trochanteric wires of other types may have in the initiation of the third party wear process. Single wires often break and continue to break into smaller pieces due to the fact that the fragments remain subject to fatigue brought about by motion of the soft tissues. I also suspect that lytic changes can be preceded and/or accelerated by debris arising from broken regular wires (Fig. 114a,b).

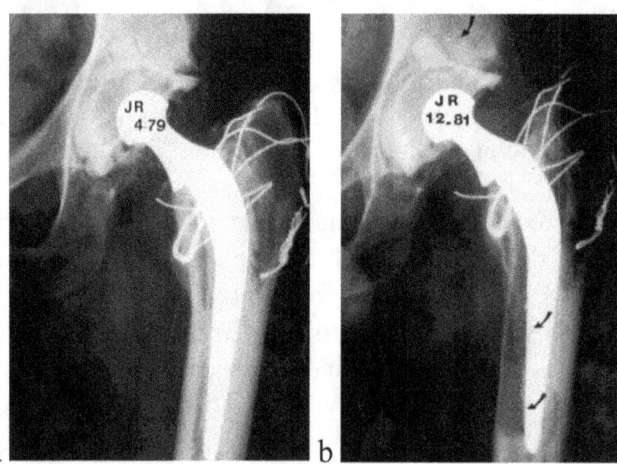

Fig. a and b. Broken wires in a cemented total hip arthroplasty showing minimal signs of early acetabular loosening (a). Two and one half years later severe lysis is present in the acetabulum and femur (b).

WOUND CLOSURE AND DRESSING

Little attention is paid to the manner in which a wound is closed and dressed. We take for granted that any type of closure and dressing is appropriate. I hold a different view and suspect that the way the to close the wound and dress it is important. Based on knowledge I acquired during my residency, I did not suture the subcutaneous layer even of major incisions. I was told that sutures simply strangulated the poorly vascularized adipose tissues and prevented residual blood from draining to the outside. I do not know why I stopped that practice myself, for it makes a lot of sense.

In any event I believe that running sutures strangulate tissues a great deal more than separate sutures. Such a phenomenon might render poorly supplied tissues of the necessary blood supply to heal uneventfully. I am more comfortable removing sutures early if the suturing took place with interrupted stitches.

I find a pressure dressing most valuable, particularly in hip surgery, which is after all the only surgery I have performed for the past thirty years. Hematomas are significantly prevented, as well as local swelling around the surgical wound. I probably spend more time applying the dressing (which stubbornly I do not allow anyone else to apply) than preparing the acetabulum. If properly applied, a pressure dressing does not produce the tape blisters which are so uncomfortable and are more likely to occur in patients with very light skin.

SECTION III

MISCELLANEOUS

SECTION III – MISCELLANEOUS

A

ADVERTISING

Physicians who placed advertisements in newspapers were bitterly criticized in years past, since such an action was considered unprofessional and therefore beneath the dignity of the profession. Though, advertising of physician's services is now seen with increasing frequency, I believe it should not be done. It leaves me with a bad taste in my mouth. Why should an individual who reached a high level in the ladder of our society, lower himself to seeking "customers" by putting his name on magazines, news-papers or before the television cameras? The fact that other "professions" do it does not lessen my criticism.

There seems to be no ending to the extreme degrees that marketing has taken us. It is not uncommon to see the names of physicians on billboards in cities and freeways. Many pay for ads in newspapers and magazines claiming special expertise in a variety of areas. Some contact the media and beg for coverage whenever they do surgery on a well-known athlete or celebrity of some type. Others regularly get their names in the local newspapers, reminding the readers that next door to them they have the best surgeons on the face of the earth. The litanies of the sports teams to which they provide care accompany the tasteless ads. In Miami today, there are a couple of orthopaedic surgeons who claim, through large and attractive ads in the local newspapers, to be the State's experts on cartilage transplant for all types of arthritis. One of them actually gained his alleged expertise during of a short visit to a Scandinavian hospital where he observed a few surgical procedures being performed.

In recent days we have witnessed some of the most egregious and obscene advertising of techniques and products dealing with hip replacement. On one occasion, a surgeon stated that "new and improved" polyethylene liners are so perfect that we can now safely perform total hip replacement in very young people. He makes this statement despite the fact that there is no clinical data to support his claim. Other surgeons are advertising metal-on-metal total hip replacements claiming that athletes can function normally following the surgical intervention. It should go without saying that these surgeons hold major financial interest in the product they so articulately advertise.

I will probably be told that times have changed and that without some type of marketing is impossible to build a practice. This is not true. We used to do it by introducing ourselves to other physicians in the community, attending medical meetings and by "taking call" in emergency rooms. More importantly, we got patients by doing a good job in responding to their needs, by obtaining good results from the treatments we chose to provide and by being courteous to them. Little by little our practices grew. Today, it may not be as simple as it was then because many physicians must apply for membership in HMOs or other organizations. But the basic premises I have outlined above remain unchanged [158].

Society has relaxed its unwritten rules and regulations in many areas. Anything goes. Radio-talk-shows are the most eloquent example of the degree to which the marketing of drugs, foods and all types of gimmicks, that are supposed to cure or prevent all diseases, has reached. Allegations are presented about the "research" that has been done to prove the efficacy of the advertised product. The surprising thing is that those "preachers" of miraculous cures receive attention and manage to amass fortunes in the process.

At the annual meeting of the AMA in the early 1990's, Warren Berger, former Chief Justice of the United States, addressed the fellowship. He talked about ethics in medicine and other related subjects. At one point he stated, "I would not trust the physician who finds it necessary to advertise his services." How wise he was!

During my tenure on the Board of Directors of the Academy I fought (unsuccessfully I might add) against the Academy's involvement in marketing efforts. Those who won the debate argued that marketing to the lay community was needed to make them aware of what orthopaedics is all about. I stated that most people in this country and, I suspect, in any other country, know what orthopaedists do and have known it for a long time. Marketing orthopaedics by negotiating television appearances, was not in keeping with the high standards of the profession; and that the end product would be nothing more than having a hand-full of orthopaedists hope that their appearance on the screen would generate them more referrals.

The proponents of the media blitz argued that others in medicine were doing the same thing and apparently with great success. No one, however, could document how the alleged success had been measured. I further argued that once we began marketing, our competitors would increase their own efforts and do their marketing in ways we still consider inappropriate, unprofessional and even unethical.

The Board of Directors voted on the proposal and approximately $ 750.000 were set aside for that effort. What came of the effort and subsequent similar efforts? I suspect that nothing was gained from it. The venture was probably nothing more than an expensive exercise in futility.

ALTERNATIVE MEDICINE

In the last quarter of the 20th century we in the West witnessed an increasing interest in alternative methods of medical care, many of which with an Oriental flavor. This interest parallels the growing interest in Oriental and Middle Eastern religious and philosophical practices. Islam and Buddhism have spread rapidly in certain parts of the West with large number of new practitioners joining the ranks. Meditation and introspection attracts the many, who a short while back appeared to be enamored with the fast, boisterous pace of American life. Books and seminars dealing with the ancient, ascetic philosophies are quite popular. The Dalai Lama lectures in cities across the land and packs huge auditoriums.

It is not surprising to see this phenomenon taking place in the United States. People seem to have tired of our spiritually empty way of life. The all-encompassing materialistic ethos of the times and the unquenchable thirst for more, no longer satisfies their needs. The obsession with death and the almost pathological desire to reach immortality in this life and the frantic narcissistic move toward preserving indefinitely anything associated with youth, are no longer satisfying pursuits.

The increased popularity of alternative modes of medical treatment is partially due to distrust of the medical profession. This, in spite of the fact that Americans and Europeans are keenly aware that they receive the best medical care in the world. Paradoxically, however, poll after poll has indicated that Americans respect their personal physicians but do not trust the medical profession. They claim that medicine has become a business and that doctors constitute a group of privileged self-serving people who use and abuse their position to extract as much profit as possible from their patients.

It would be ludicrous for me to suggest that all types of non-conventional medical care are useless. Quite the contrary, there is much to say in their favor. Additional time is required before we have sufficient knowledge of the worth of many of the approaches to illness and disease to justify their wide use. We should remind ourselves that in many instances they have a history of use of thousands of years.

Traditional allopathic medicine is being challenged. That challenge may be the catalyst that brings about a reasonable compromise and appreciation for both forms of care.

SECTION III – MISCELLANEOUS

AMERICAN ACADEMY OF ORTHOPEDIC SURGEONS: AAOS

The "Academy", as we refer to in the United States, has been a wonderful educational institution not only for American orthopaedists but also for orthopaedists throughout the world. It has provided leadership in continuing education to all other medical organizations. Its annual meetings, continuing education courses and many other educational activities have been the envy of the academic world.

For me, personally, the Academy has been very important. I joined its fellowship in 1962 and have attended, without exception, every one of its annual meetings. For forty consecutive years I participated in the Scientific Program and/or its Instructional Course Section of the Annual Meeting; very often in several of those various activities in the same year.

I not only participated in those educational ventures, but also served uninterruptedly on one of its committees for a period of thirty-five years. I started as a member of the committee on Prosthetics and Orthotics and from then on to the Committees on Injuries, Rehabilitation, Continuing Education, Educational Programming, the Advisory Council on Education and the Education Committee. I served as chairman of several of those committees. From there I went to the elected position of Member at Large of the Board of Directors and subsequently to the Board in the presidential line. From 1991 to 1992 I was president and for an additional three years I sat on the Board as past-president of the organization.

I have mentioned the above privileges and opportunities simply to emphasize my loyalty to the Academy and to acknowledge the many wonderful benefits it bestowed on me over my entire career.

The Academy has changed a great deal in recent years in ways I find, at times, disturbing. I see it moving in directions that, in my opinion, detract from its primary educational mission. Because of the rather dramatic changes that have taken place in medicine in the United States, a vocal segment of the Academy's fellowship has succeeded in shifting the direction of the organization from being primarily an educational one to also being a business-like organization, concerned with socio-economic matters. They expect the Academy to serve as a political body deeply involved in lobbying politicians and attempting to influence the course of socio-political events in a major way.

I do not deny that the Academy has a responsibility to speak on behalf of its members and their profession in the most effective way and at various levels of state and federal offices. As a matter of fact it has discharged that responsibility very well over the years. Despite recent efforts to emphasize education and communication, the shift toward socio-economic endeavors is obvious.

I have long believed that what the Academy is able to accomplish in influencing the current so-called Health Care Reform is limited. I suspect that organized medicine cannot alter the course of those events since they are of a social nature and beyond the scope of medicine per se. Physicians and organized medicine should limit their involvement to

SECTION III – MISCELLANEOUS

informing and educating the powers that be in matters where we have knowledge. Knowledge that can help them in reaching conclusions. A cooperative relationship rather than a confrontational one, as it has been for many a year, is more likely to produce results.

Still vivid in my mind was the day- eight years ago- when our very capable representative in Washington, reported to the Board of Directors. He commented that it was difficult for him to meet with Congressmen or their staff representatives and argue convincingly that the proposed reduction in reimbursement for orthopaedic services was unfair. Making it difficult was the fact that when he presented the Academy's arguments, his listeners had before them a copy of the latest issue of Medical Economics. That issue stated that the average income of an orthopaedist was $250.000 a year. He was asked, how the Academy could be so adamantly opposed to a mild reduction in reimbursement in light of such large individual income; income higher than that over 98 per cent of the American people, but also higher than that of most other members of the medical community. And what about the continued, ominous escalating cost of medical care? What was the Academy doing to curtail it?

The perception that the Academy was more interested in personal pocket-book issues rather than in the problems created by the cost of medical care existed then and it exists today [143, 159]. (See addenda 7, 8.)

During my tenure on the Board of Directors we discussed issues related to the tax status of the Academy and seriously debated the pros and cons of them. We concluded, every time the discussion took place, that the Academy should maintain the tax status that emphasized its educational agenda, as its most important component while still devoting large amounts of money for political activities. As a Director during those eight years, I anticipated that pressure on the Board to change the tax status to one that permitted almost unlimited expenditures to political activities would one day become enormous. However, I did not anticipate, that the Directors would cave in as quickly as they did. Now the Academy's parallel Association, has a C6 tax status and, therefore, is in a position to devote even greater and greater funding to political matters.

Though the Board continues to claim that the change in tax status and the creation of a parallel organization will not result in a diminution of interest in education, common sense, if nothing else, projects a different picture: the day will come when a huge percentage of the Academy's resources will be allocated to political activities, much to the detriment of its educational mission. I envision the Directors' meetings totally consumed in political-economic issues. The educational agenda will be delegated entirely to committees with minimal input from the Board.

Such was the history of the American Medical Association. Once a powerful educational organization, today it plays a minor role in education and is a paper tiger in the political arena. We, however, chose to ignore history. After all, as Hegel said, "The grand lesson of history is that we do not learn the lessons of history".

SECTION III – MISCELLANEOUS

Another change in the Academy's philosophy that I find most unpleasant is the obvious commitment to make the organization a major financial institution.

Today, the Academy Bulletin carries advertisements of commercial products from which it derives quite a few dollars. Previous Boards had opposed such a practice and wanted to keep its official publications free of commercial involvement. The Academy's own Journal now fills approximately fifty percent of its pages with scientific material; the remaining pages are commercial ads, which have become a major source of revenue.

At the time of this writing, the Academy is negotiating with industry a deal that would make continuing education courses a joint venture. I have already spoken and written in opposition to the idea, as I consider such a practice the equivalent of surrendering to industry. Within a very short time, industry will be dictating in more obvious terms the content of educational programs: "He who pays the piper calls the tune."

The Academy's annual meeting, which I have attended uninterruptedly since 1953, has experienced changes, which I consider ominous. It appears that this event, the educational highlight in the life of most orthopaedists in the United States for several generations, is considered by an increasing number of orthopaedists as no longer being worthy of attendance. To many, it does not seem to be any longer relevant to their practices. Attendance to educational ventures presented by subspecialty societies or by industry receives more attention from the fellowship.

A few years ago I wrote a letter to the president of the Academy and urged him to address in earnest the Annual Meeting. I said to him to count carefully the number of Academy fellows who actually attend its scientific programs, not the number of registrants. I felt that many people who registered for the congress do not attend the meeting. They register in order to be able to "deduct" the expense, but immediately afterwards either leave the building to either enjoy the city or to move on to other vacation sites.

I told the president that I had purposefully stood at the door of various conference rooms and auditoria as the attendees exited them. I saw very few "yellow badges" (the ones given to members of the Academy). Instead, those attending the programs were either newly inducted members of the organization, or foreign visitors and particularly representatives of industry, which incidentally, outnumber orthopaedic fellows.

In my letter to the president, I remarked that during my eight years as member of the Board of Directors I had openly asked the chairman of the Annual Meeting Committee, following his report to the Board, which was the most common complaint he had received concerning the meeting. His response, year after year was that the meeting was too big. The Academy, in his infinite wisdom, responded to the "most common complaint" not by making the next meeting smaller, but by making it bigger. I expressed my opinion that the system in existence encouraged the "new" chairman to outdo his predecessor by making "his meeting" bigger. Instead of addressing the issue as I had expected, the President "passed the buck" to the chairman of the Annual Meeting. This gentleman responded to my concerns, not by acknowledging any deficiencies but by arguing the growing popularity and success of the meeting.

SECTION III – MISCELLANEOUS

During the course of my original letter, I had stated that the upper echelon of the organization should be cautions about relying on the increased number of foreign physicians attending the meeting, and in that manner offsetting the reduced attendance of members. The phenomenon indicated to me that the meeting was ceasing to be relevant to a growing number of American orthopaedists. This was a problem that should not be ignored. Furthermore, I added, that since the growing number of foreign orthopaedists had their expenses paid by industry, the possibility existed that industry could shift their financial support to other meetings. Lo and behold, within less than two years this change took place to the point that at the 2002 Annual Meeting, I have been told, 500 fewer foreign orthopaedists attended the meeting in Dallas.

In spite of my not so well disguised cynicism and my obvious concerns over the course the Academy seems to have chosen to take, I must admit that I could be wrong in my assessment. Nothing would please me more than to discover that rather than losing its compass, the Academy ended up blazing new trails. I doubt it, but will not give up yet.

SECTION III – MISCELLANEOUS

AO: (ASSOCIATION FOR THE INTERNAL FIXATION OF FRACTURES)

The initials AO loosely stand for a Swiss organization "The Association for the Internal Fixation of Fractures". It was founded in Switzerland by a handful of general surgeons and orthopaedists led by Maurice Muller, a man of worldwide reputation. Every orthopaedist in the world is familiar with it. The contribution of the AO to the treatment of fractures was most impressive. It literally changed the way in which fractures were treated.

The AO philosophy of internal fixation of fractures was inspired by the work of Danis, a Belgian surgeon who, allegedly, was the first person to advocate compression of fractured fragments. The AO developed sophisticated fracture instrumentation that replaced rather crude instruments and advocated an organized approach to fracture care.

For nearly four decades in the twentieth century, the AO's concept of rigid immobilization, compression and interfragmentary fixation reigned unchecked and unchallenged. Its precepts became the orthopaedic bible.

My ideas on functional bracing of fractures, which I first described in the early 1960's, collided with the AO philosophy from the very beginning. My philosophy was based on the opposite premise: physiologically induced motion at the fracture site is good for osteogenesis and rigid immobilization is unphysiological. Both philosophies could not be correct. The AO produced an abundance of laboratory documentation to prove their point. And so did I.

The 1971, the Encyclopedia Britannica's supplement discussed the two different approaches to fracture healing and treatment and raised the question as to which of the two would best withstand the test of time. Based on the popularity of the AO views and its dominance throughout the world, it is easy to conclude that that the AO prevailed. Many still believe that rigid immobilization is good for fracture healing. "The stronger the fixation the greater the chances of attaining healing." That is their universal banner.

Time, however, in a softer and slower manner, began to side with me. The AO basic investigators, primarily its guru, Stephan Perren, began to report modifications of their compression plates, first by making them more flexible and later by redesigning them in a manner that their contact with the bone was minimized. He had known for a long time that the bone under the plate underwent atrophic changes that led to the development of a weak callus. (See FRACTURE HEALING).

At a meeting where tibial fractures were being discussed, and both Stephan Perren and I were among the panelists, Perren discussed the merits of his new, limited-contact plate. The moderator asked for my opinion of the modified plate and I responded: "The concept of moving the plate away for the bone is, in my opinion, the best idea Stefan Perren has had in a long time. I thoroughly agree with his new concept and have long believed that plates should be kept far away from the bone. So much so that I do not even have them in the operating room". The levity of my remarks addressed to someone I highly respect, broke the solemnity of the occasion.

SECTION III – MISCELLANEOUS

I consider the use of plates in the management of diaphyseal fractures of long bones an undesirable therapeutic approach and have often said, "Fractures heal not because they are rigidly immobilized but in spite of the immobilization". [115, 122, 150, 151]

At the 1998 meeting of the Orthopedic Trauma Association in Vancouver, Canada, Stefan Perren stated that the AO's philosophy of fracture healing had changed. He stated that he no longer believed that rigid immobilization is good for fracture healing. He then proceeded to explain how some type of theoretically conceived mechanism of elongation of the osteoblasts leads to a better callus. We had documented twenty years earlier the beneficial effects of motion on fracture healing [119, 124].

In spite of the fact that the AO contributed in a meaningful way to an organized approach to fracture care and successfully exported its ideas to the rest of the world, I think that in the process much harm was done. Harm in the sense that it retarded investigations of a biological nature. The approach to fracture healing by the AO was based on mechanics not on biology.

In abandoning many of the ideas that they so passionately espoused for four decades, the AO no longer advocates plating of fractures with a similar fervor. Today it advocates intramedullary nailing in preference to plate fixation. An admission that the rigid immobilization provided by plates is inferior to the motion that intramedullary nails permit.

I realize that those changes in attitude and philosophy will not mean that my ideas on functional bracing of certain fractures will prevail. It is impossible under current circumstances. The AO has the awesome economic power of industry on its side. As a matter of fact, the AO is an integral part of industry. Their resources applied to educational and commercial marketing has been the envy of the world's Orthopaedic/ Industrial complex for many years. Furthermore, as long as surgeons get paid more for treating fractures by surgical means, it is logical that the surgical trend will prevail. That is human nature. Imagine a situation where by edict the payment for treating conservatively distal radial, humeral shaft, and tibial fractures was higher. Overnight the present trend would be reversed.

On several occasions I have been the keynote speaker at meetings sponsored by the AO, because in spite of our profound philosophical differences our mutual respect has remained unscathed. I have never hesitated to disagree with their beliefs and in turn they have disagreed with mine. Once they invited me to spend several days at each of their major centers in Switzerland: Davos, Saint Gallen, Bern and Bassel. Professor Hans Willineger, one of the OA founders and a gentleman per excellence, personally escorted me throughout the entire trip.

My first participation in their meetings took place in Davos, where Loren Latta and I presented our laboratory and clinical findings to a large international audience. I said at the beginning of my presentation, "after three days of listening to very erudite and convincing teachers tell you that that rigid immobilization and interfragmentary fixation is the best way to treat fractures, Doctor Latta and I are going to prove to you that plating is unphysiological. That the fractures they have been showing you healed after plating, not because they were plated but in spite of the plating. That healing had taken place because it is very difficult to cheat nature. Nature can overcome many of the hurdles we place in front of it ".

Maurice Muller once visited our outpatient clinic at the Los Angeles County/ University of Southern California Medical Center. It was a wonderful experience to see this great man, accustomed to the clean environment of the Swiss hospitals, carefully observing the poorly dressed sixty patients, most of them Mexican immigrants, being treated with braces of various types. I suspect that the curiosity he displayed that morning was a clear sign that the method we were using worked and worked well.

My relationship with Maurice Muller has grown stronger with time. In spite of our philosophical differences he invited me to become a Board Member of the Maurice Muller Orthopedic Foundation of North America, a position I held for over fifteen years.

As recently as the fall of 1998, I was the guest speaker of Christopher Colton, then president of the AO, at the annual meeting of the Board of Directors in Davos, where its nearly one hundred and twenty members assembled. I took advantage of the opportunity to comment on the problems our profession was facing as a result of the Health Care Reform sweeping the world. I commented on the dangers associated with an overly exaggerated emphasis on the surgical approach to fracture care and the parallel weakening of its biological foundations. I added that we were rapidly becoming cosmetic surgeons of the skeleton; an undesirable change. I also discussed my concerns about the exportation of expensive, sophisticated technology to regions of the world where neither the infrastructure nor the economic environment of the regions allowed their proper implementation.

ARTHRITIS AND OSTEOPOROSIS PROGRAMS

It is unfair to cast adverse judgement on subjects about which we do not have thorough knowledge. There are situations, however, when first impressions and personal observations allow us to form impressions of some validity. One such a case is the ongoing trend to run Arthritis and/ or Osteoporosis programs, especially at for-profit hospitals.

At first glance the two diseases deserve special attention. They both benefit from the services of individuals possessing expertise. What I have seen, however, in some instances, is the exploitation of patients with resulting enormous profits gained by some hospitals and physicians.

At a hospital in Miami there are special areas dedicated to those conditions. The Arthritis Unit is a ward that accommodates approximately fifteen patients. Every Sunday a group of new patients is admitted to the unit where they remain for seven days. During that time they receive group- therapy consisting of active exercises of their arms and legs. In tandem, they respond to the physical therapist's instructions. Treatments are not individualized. All patients do the same thing. This ritual is repeated twice a day. Once, during the course of the day they march to the pool where they carry out similar exercises. They also play group games, have lunches and outings on the grounds. After a while they return to their rooms.

So far, there seems to be no harm done. As a matter of fact it represents a pleasant recreational activity, which, I am sure, patients appreciate. What I question is the manner in which the program functions. Since Medicare pays for one week of hospitalization per year for arthritic patients, the directors of the Unit recruit patients for admission, regardless of the need for such a luxury. Obviously they get reimbursed for the "services" they provide and the daily visit to the ward. Actually the therapist and the aides do all the work.

The therapist keeps records of the dates of admission to the Unit, and when twelve months have elapsed they are informed that they are ready to return for additional treatment. This is, in my opinion, an abuse of the system and a factor that further contributes to the escalating cost of care. It is inconsistent with the enforced rule of not permitting longer hospitalization for post-surgical patients in need of longer in-hospital care.

On one occasion, a lady in her early sixties saw me in the office complaining of pain in her right hip. She had osteoarthritis and had been admitted to the Arthritis Unit three times in the past. A friend of hers, on whom I had performed a total hip replacement, suggested that she consult me. Subsequently, I replaced her arthritic joint and she got relief of her symptoms. She went back to see her rheumatologist and demonstrated the improvement she had experienced from surgery. A few months later the lady was contacted by her physician reminding her that she was due for readmission to the Arthritis Unit. She informed her doctor that she was asymptomatic. Nonetheless, the next day she received a call from the Unit to emphasize how important it was for her to be admitted again.

Something similar occurs in Osteoporosis Services. Elderly patients line the halls of the consultation area waiting to have the density of their bones measured. It does not matter how old they are or whether or not they are symptomatic. The measurements are indispensable. I suspect that probably without exception every elderly patient is diagnosed with osteoporosis and receives the "appropriate" medications. There is no doubt in my mind that they all return on a regular basis to have the density of their bone measured again and be reassured that progress is being made.

I hate to be so cynic about the inappropriate manner of handling problems of this nature. Some progress has been made in the diagnosis and treatment of osteoporosis but that progress has been minimal. To capitalize on the naiveté of people for the sake of profit is not right[158].

ARTHROSCOPY

Arthroscopy is one of the most significant technological developments in recent times. Its impact on orthopaedic has been enormous as it has made possible the diagnosis and care of conditions which until recently had eluded traditional methods of diagnosis or treatment. However, as it is often true with any new technological development, it has been abused to an obscene degree. [154, 158] Arthroscopic procedures are being performed in large numbers without appropriate indications. Surgeons are generously compensated for its performance. I know of one so-called sports medicine doctor, who limits his practice almost entirely to arthroscopic surgery, who allegedly submitted bills over an eighteen-month period for two and one half million dollars. It does not take the brains of a rocket scientist to know that he is performing a great deal of unnecessary surgery.

The art and science of the physical examination of a painful or injured joint are becoming obsolete. At the sight of a painful knee a MRI and arthroscopy are carried out. Facetiously, it is said that the indications for knee arthroscopy have expanded so much that the presence of a knee, in itself, is now an appropriate indication for the procedure.

During my days of practice in Los Angeles, a secretary in the department asked me to listen in another phone a conversation she was about to have with the office of a well-known group of sports medicine orthopaedists in the area. Pretending that her husband had twisted his knee ten days earlier during a weekend tennis game, she inquired as to the possibility of obtaining an appointment with one of the doctors. The receptionist responded that her husband had two options: either to come to the office for an examination or to go directly to the hospital to have his painful knee arthroscoped. She added that the doctors prefer the second option because the chances were that they would end up recommending arthroscopic surgery, anyway.

My knowledge of arthroscopy is minimal. I have no experience with the procedure. I have simply followed its applications with interest and have observed my colleagues and residents' attitude toward the new technology. I am amazed at the cavalier attitude that seems to permeate the minds of so many orthopaedists. At the slightest sign or symptoms of intraarticular pathology a MRI and arthroscopy are scheduled. All kinds of abnormal findings are identified and "treated". Debridement of any cartilage fibrillation is carried out; the patella is "shaved"; the plica is sectioned or excised and the menisci are trimmed. I suspect that in the process damage to the articular cartilage may be done. I suspect the inadvertent lacerations created by the sharp instruments are not totally harmless.

At the University of Miami investigators published a very interesting paper illustrating the findings obtained from MRI studies conducted in asymptomatic college athletes who had no history of pain or shoulder injury in their past. Most of the MRI's demonstrated some "pathology". One can surmise that if young athletes who sustained injuries and the MRI had demonstrated those "pathological" changes, would have been treated arthroscopically by some surgeons.

This experience is reminiscent of a report from Doctor Lorraine Day a number of years ago, in which she presented to a group of unbiased surgeons the history and plain x-rays of patients with cervical spine injuries. She did not show them the CT scans that she had also obtained. She asked each one of the surgeons for a diagnosis and proposed treatment. It turned out that the diagnoses made and the treatments suggested were exactly the same ones that the treating surgeons had administered after having the CT scans available. Doctor Day was not trying to belittle the role, importance and place that CT scans have in modern medicine. She simply wanted to emphasize their exaggerated use.

This is food for thought. There is data to indicate that the number of CT scan and MRI machines in the whole of Canada is equal to that in a single large city in the United

SECTION III – MISCELLANEOUS

States. The discrepancy between the numbers of those expensive diagnostic tools is even more dramatic in the most sophisticated countries in Europe. They use the technology a lot less frequently than we do in America. There is no evidence to suggest that either the Canadians or the Europeans are worse off than their American counterparts. As a matter of fact when it comes to mortality rates and other indicators of health care standards we do not score very well.

In the mid-nineties I spent nearly a year in Glasgow, Scotland, where the number of CT scans and MRI's is much lower than in any city in the United States of comparable size. I seriously doubt that the Scots in Glasgow are a lot worse off than we are. A very distinguished sports medicine surgeon in the Netherlands said to me that at his institution they had abandoned the routine use of MRI in knees suggesting internal derangement. If pathology was suspected clinically an arthroscopic procedure was carried out.

The perceptions I have discussed are not a sign of blindness on my part. I am keenly aware of the tremendous contributions that these technologies have made to medicine and to our own discipline. What I question is why we do not seem able to appropriately define the true indications for their use. If nothing else, because of the cost of care. I recognize that the time has come when with increasing frequency patients will demand that all new technologies be used in the diagnosis of their ailments. We respond by accommodating them while paying very little attention to the fact that the expense is great and that the need for the use of these technologies is often unnecessary.

I suspect, however, that unless some radical changes take place, soon most traditional methods of clinical examinations will be obsolete. Patients will have MRI, CT scans and whatever new technologies are developed in the interim and will be given a diagnosis without ever having seen a physician. Yearly medical examinations will take place in that manner. Whether our economy can afford such luxury is the big question.

ASSOCIATION FOR THE RATIONAL TREATMENT OF FRACTURES (ARTOF)

I was elected the first president of this organization in 1997. The association was conceived and organized by a group of European surgeons who had become increasingly concerned over what appeared to be an exaggerated and rapid move toward the surgical treatment of fractures. They felt that the biological principles upon which orthopaedics had been built were being relegated to the trash heap of history. They wanted traditional closed methods of fracture care recognized as viable in the armamentarium of the orthopaedic surgeon.

The concept being espoused by the association appealed to me greatly, because it was close to my own personal philosophy. With great enthusiasm I accepted the honor and opportunity to serve the cause. I recruited a large number of distinguished surgeons from several different nations and began a series of educational ventures; ventures, which were designed to emphasize the need to balance the therapeutic approach to fractures between the various modalities.

SECTION III – MISCELLANEOUS

By the time my tour of duty as president came to an end in the spring of 1999 and prior to turning over the reins to my successor, we had presented educational courses in Montevideo, Lima, Budapest, Bologna, Auckland, Vancouver and Berlin and had organized similar courses held in cooperation with EFORT (the European Federation of Orthopaedics and Traumatology Societies) in Barcelona in 1998 and other meetings in Sydney, Australia, during the SICOT biennial congress. We had scheduled courses in Finland, Japan, Singapore and Slovenia in the year 2000.

The success of such educational ventures cannot be determined at this point. It will be a while before we know if the orthopaedic community is willing to come to grips with the concept that the exclusive use of the surgical approach is not logical; it not only converts our profession into a technical trade and makes its practitioners cosmetic surgeons of the skeleton; eliminates the important biological foundations of orthopaedics but provokes a rapid escalation in the cost of fracture care [136, 154, 158]. (See addenda 2, 6, 9).

Debates were held at each meeting during which spokespersons from various schools of thought argued their views. Then attempts were made to find a consensus between them.

The audiences at several symposia seemed to have received with enthusiasm ARTOF's approach to education in the area of fracture management. We were given a warm response. I am personally convinced that it is essential that the goals and methodology of ARTOF be continued and that if the blind and rigid surgical approach to fracture care is not harnessed in the near future, we might be facing regulations imposed on us by insurance companies and governmental offices much to the detriment of all. In addition, orthopaedics will have to cope with the fact that others, outside of the specialty, will continue to erode our traditional territory and will become the leaders when biological methods of fracture repair, i.e. growth factors, reach the clinical level.

The survival of the organization is questionable. For a variety of reasons interest in the philosophy espoused by ARTOF began to whither, most likely because pressure on the surgeons from the "establishment." The enthusiasm of the leaders of the group also suffered. I suspect being outside the trendy surgical practice that permeates the orthopaedic community made it very difficult for some people to sustain the mistaken perception that they were not a part of the elite, modern school. I anticipate that before this book is finally printed ARTOF will be nothing more than a memory.

SECTION III – MISCELLANEOUS

B

BACK PAIN

Early in my career I was deeply interested in painful disorders of the spine. I thought at that time that lumbar spine disease was the most challenging and exciting area of orthopaedics. My three years of orthopaedic residency under Austin T. Moore, in South Carolina, gave me an introduction to this interesting and fascinating subject. I lost interest, however, when total hip surgery and fracture research consumed most of my academic time.

Contrary to popular belief, Austin Moore's forte and main interest was spine surgery rather than hip surgery. He was a pioneer in the understanding of disc disease and its management by conservative as well as by surgical means.

There is little doubt that the distal lumbar spine and the lumbo-sacral spine constitute the most vulnerable segments of the spine when it comes to degenerative disease. The evolutionary demands imposed on that segment of the body and the expectation of motion in all directions can be the primary cause of degenerative changes. Having assumed the erect position, the human frame was forced to develop bending and rotational motions in joints, which previously, as quadrupeds, only required flexion and extension. Such new demands created new stresses on the apophyseal and intervertebral joints.

The size of the spinal foramen decreases as the sacrum is approached, making the foramen between the first and second lumbar vertebra wider than the one between the fifth lumbar vertebra and the sacrum. Paradoxically, however, the nerve root that travels through the higher space is smaller than the one in the lumbo-sacral space. Therefore, minimal narrowing of the lumbo-sacral foramen is likely to impinge on the larger nerve root traveling through it. On the contrary, significantly greater narrowing of the foramen at the first lumbar level is not likely to impinge on the smaller nerve root. This anatomical incongruence readily explains the effect that herniated discs have on the nerve roots: large herniations at higher levels may not produce nerve root symptoms while small ones are likely to significantly irritate or compress the corresponding nerve roots.

Based on these anatomical findings it is logically to assume that in order to reduce impingement on nerve roots at compromised levels, flexion of the spine is of benefit, since flexion enlarges the size of the spinal foramina. The fact that the axis of rotation of the spine is located anterior to the spinal canal makes that possible. Extension, on the other hand, further narrows the spinal canal and spinal foramina.

This explains why most patients with "bulging" discs experience relief of symptoms during flexion of the spine and increased pain during extension. When it comes to spine fusion for degenerative disc disease, it is imperative that the segments be fused in flexion. If fused in extension the chronic nerve root irritation will be maintained even after motion between the vertebrae is eliminated. The vertebral bodies may be rigidly immobilized, but the nerve roots will continue to glide back and forth every time the spine is flexed, perpetuating the irritation of the nerves.

On one occasion I fused one level of the lumbar spine on a young man who had allegedly injured his back at work. Since the myelogram had indicated only a mild protrusion, but not a rupture disc, I did not explore the space and simply fused the two vertebras while spreading the spinous processes with a lamina retractor. I wanted to enlarge he foramina as much as possible. The young man's spinal segment fused well. Nearly a year later I ran into one of the senior orthopaedists in town while he was reviewing some spine films. He called my attention to the fact that he was serving as an expert witness in the Workers Compensation case of the young man I had previously operated upon. He remarked that he was amazed to see how well the patient had done. As I looked at the newly obtained x-rays I noticed that I had mistakenly fused the wrong intervertebral space. I did not say anything about it to the reviewing surgeon at the time, but once the case was settled I informed him of my error. I assume that the fusion in flexion of one segment had resulted also in the enlargement of the adjacent segment and the relief of nerve irritation.

A question still remains regarding the future of the discs adjacent to fused segment or segments of the spine. Are they likely to develop degenerative changes now that they are expected to assume the responsibility of providing motions previously distributed among a greater number of vertebral segments? Such a concern is legitimate particularly at this time when a virtual epidemic of spine fusions is raging as a result of the perceived early success with pedicular screws. To a similar extent, the same can be said about the use of "cages" anchored between vertebral bodies. I suspect that sooner or later "the chickens will come to roost" and a legion of people disabled from the sequella of spine fusion will be seeking relief for the care of recurrent back pain.

Some time ago the secretary of a spine surgeon asked me if I would be willing to see a friend of hers who had had her back operated five times by her "boss". She knew I did not perform back surgery and she did not want anyone know that I had examined the patient. The patient was a young, slender lady in her early forties. I examined the patient and found a completely negative neurological examination. Her complaints were vague and she described her problem as lumbo-sacral pain after prolonged sitting.

I obtained her medical records and found that the last note written by her surgeon was a short and pithy one: "Pain continues. Will fuse again. Back and front. Diagnosis: Flat back". Nothing was said about the condition of the fused back; whether a non-union was present or the reasons and expectations from the performance of a sixth surgical intervention.

I was not really surprised by what I had discovered. I was familiar with the unreasonable amount of unnecessary back surgery performed in the community. As far as I am concerned the epidemic of surgery will continue unabated. Some very profound change in the reimbursement for surgery will have to take place before those unethical individuals can be brought under control. In the process the ethical surgeons will be penalized.

SECTION III – MISCELLANEOUS

BONE GRAFTS

I have always found difficult to justify the routine use of bone grafting following surgery performed in patients with acute fractures of bones such as the forearm, tibia, and humerus. I seriously question the benefits to be derived from it, particularly when plating is the method of fixation used. Though, I am convinced that plating, which accomplishes rigid fixation and interfragmentary compression, delays healing. [35, 36, 47, 48, 115, 122, 167] the addition of pieces of dead bone is probably of no benefit. Bone, in order to mature, requires it be stressed. Dead bone, and that is what a graft is, leaning against the fractured bone, is incapable of drawing the capillary invasion that stress brings about. Often we see bone grafts of that nature remain avascular.

There is much we do not know or understand about the behavior of bone grafts of various kinds.

Currently there is a growing interest in the use of bone substitutes and often I find myself in the operating room being told that I should squirt some type of gel that miraculously will make bone grow and bridge all kinds of bone defects. To this day I remain rather skeptic about the true value of growth factors in the care of acute fractures. Molecular biology will play a prominent role in the management of many musculoskeletal conditions, but its time has not yet come.

I do not doubt that the day will come when the benefits of bone growth factors will be clearly documented. It is a promising field. Bone Morphogenic Protein (BMP) was discovered over thirty years ago by Marshall Urist, but despite his excellent work and occasional bursts of enthusiasm in the orthopaedic community, clinical applications for the product have failed. The same thing is happening to TGF Beta in its many types. Some ten years ago we celebrated their discovery and expressed amazement over the beautiful photographs showing large masses of bone forming at the site of their injection over the shaft of a normal bone. Subsequent experiences and attempts to use the substances in clinical situations have not, in my opinion, met the expectations. This does not mean that someday, after addition laboratory and clinical work, a place for bone growth factors will be found to be effective at the clinical level.

Premature claims of success will do more harm than good to such new and promising techniques. They will be used for the wrong reasons and improper indications and by people who have no idea of the manner in which they work. I picture an epidemic of bone growth factors injections into all kinds of pathological skeletal situations with highly disappointing results. If we were to be careful in their use and subject those to critical analysis before releasing them for public use much progress could be achieved. The failure of electrical stimulation as a practical tool in orthopaedics can be explained on those grounds. No one would dare question that piezo electricity is a proven phenomenon and that it must play a role in fracture repair. However, the rush toward achieving quick financial profit led to the release of the various products to the general medical public and to the abuse of the system. Industry, I am certain, pushed for the wide sale of the products before they were ready for their appropriate use. The failure of the pioneers to conduct and report on prospective, randomized studies has temporarily driven nails into the coffin of a very worthwhile therapeutic approach.

I anticipate that if and when solid clinical applications for the local application of bone growth factors have been demonstrated, a large number of people from a multitude of disciplines will be injecting the substance into fractures, non-unions, osteoporosis, etc., etc. The orthopaedist will only be one of them. Emergency room specialists will do it as part of the management of patients with acute fractures. Family physicians, podiatrists, chiropractors, physician assistants, physical therapists and many others will join the feast. Anybody capable of applying a cast over a fractured limb will feel qualified to use the products.

I suspect that bone growth factors in acute fractures will not expedite healing. Improving upon the "grand design" is not likely to become a reality. We will probably see larger masses of callus but their maturation to an effective mechanical level will not be shortened. We will see what happens! The same probably applies to other popular methodologists such as ultrasound stimulation.

Some twenty years ago I participated in experimental studies dealing with bone forming substances in the management of artificially created fractures in small animals. A committed and talented resident in our program developed a technique where by intra-medullary methods a paste of hydroxi-apatite could be injected into the fracture site [28]. The technique was easily standardized. Radiographs demonstrated the formation of bone at the fracture site within a short period of time. However, when the animals were sacrificed, we found out that the newly formed bone had adhered to one end of the fracture but not to the other end. It is unfortunate that once this resident left the program the study was discontinued. Perhaps the fate of the technique would have been disappointing any way.

I had an opportunity to observe and participate in the use of demineralized bone grafts during my days at the University of Southern California, cooperating with Doctor El Gendler at the Orthopedic Hospital of Los Angeles [165, 166]. His laboratory findings were very impressive and for a while I was convinced that the osteo-inductive properties of the material were so superior to other types of bone graft that soon it would replace all other methods of grafting. Now I am not convinced of the superiority of the demineralized bone graft. They all seem to work equally as well or equally as poorly.

In the 1960's I was deeply interested in bone and joint infections. I delved in isolated extremity perfusion with antibiotics with mixed results. I concluded that perfusion, using the heart-lung machine; by itself was not a satisfactory approach to chronic infections. A good debridement was more efficacious. The experiences with the method were nonetheless rewarding and resulted in a research award from the American Medical Association. Subsequently, I experimented with bone grafting of osteomyelitis defects. On several occasions I carried out thorough debridement of the infected area and tightly packed the defect with morselized cancellous bone. Today, the technique would be called "impaction allograft." A number of patients with long standing chronic osteomyelitis responded to the treatment (Fig. 13a,b).

SECTION III – MISCELLANEOUS

I have, on a number of occasions, used slabs of bone allograph to reinforce bone damaged from lysis that occurred around failed total hip prostheses. I have noticed that it takes a long period of time to obtain incorporation of the graft into the living femoral shaft. On two occasions I found myself performing surgery in patients on whom I had used the long cortical grafts. I was removing wires that I had used to fasten the grafts to the main bone that were causing local discomfort. More than a year had elapsed since the initial surgery and x-rays had suggested that full incorporation had taken place. Much to my surprise I discovered that I could lift the grafts away from the bone with only minimal difficulty. These two experiences do not negate the fact that eventually most such grafts become part of the living shafts.

C

CARTILAGE TRANSPLANT

It has been a long-term dream of scientists to bring about a cure for cartilage lesions not only of a traumatic origin but also with a degenerative etiology. However, the enthusiasm with the newly marketed techniques of cartilage transplants for the care of intraarticular defects could very easily come to a screeching halt in the near future. Not because the experimental effort does not deserve attention, for indeed it does. The technique was released to the public prematurely and it is being abused and improperly used. To many it has become simply a gimmick to generate additional income.

I am certain that in some instances cartilage transplant using cultured cells will bring about good results. There is good scientific data to indicate that the size of the lesion is important in predicting good outcomes; that the locations of the defect and its depth are also important considerations. This has been known since the 1950's when Pap, a Hungarian surgeon, conducted investigations on the subject.

Furthermore it is important to recognize that the etiology of cartilage defects varies a great deal. The defect from osteochondritis dissecans is quite different from that produced by idiopathic degenerative arthritis. In the latter case very often the articular cartilage becomes thinner, not from "wear and tear" but from its replacement with bone arising from sub-chondral structures. It is foolish to believe that this generalized type of articular damage can be overcome with transplanted cells.

Much discussion has taken place over the years regarding the possibility of preserving the articular cartilage of avascular necrotic femoral heads. William Enneking, from Florida reported in the 1960's on his unsuccessful attempts to excise the entire necrotic bone and replacing it with cancellous bone graft. Melvin Glimcher, from Boston, carried out a similar procedure and filled the defect with acrylic cement. The procedures failed through a possible combination of biological and mechanical reasons. In the case of Glimcher's operation, it is likely that the acrylic cement created an unphysiological hard bed to the softer articular cartilage. In our laboratories at Orthopaedic Hospital of Los Angeles, we unsuccessfully attempted to improve upon Glimcher's project by using endoprostheses deliberately smaller than the excised femoral head and covering the metallic head with the shell of articular cartilage of the femoral head. We had in mind the possibility of using the system in the treatment of those acute fractures of he femoral neck, which are usually treated with primary endoprosthetic replacement. Though it is likely that the project would have failed regardless of any improvement in the technique, we found it impossible to anchor the cartilage shell to the underlying metal.

SECTION III – MISCELLANEOUS

CERTIFICATES OF ADDITIONAL QUALIFICATIONS: CAQ's

Approximately fifteen years ago there was great interest in some segments of the orthopaedic community over the idea of creating new mechanisms to ensure better documentation of competence among members of sub-specialty groups. One such mechanism was called Certificate of Additional Competency (CAQs).

It is difficult to argue against attempts to improve the knowledge that we should possess to provide the best care to patients. In an attempt to document such knowledge, organized medicine has used the system of Certification and more recently that of re-certification. That being the case why should I be opposed to extending the method to sub-specialists? [137].

Though I recognize that sub-specialization in medicine was inevitable and to a great extent good for the profession and patients alike, some harm has also been done. I think that in orthopaedics it has gone too far, and in the process weakened the glue that made our discipline so strong. Within a relatively short period of time a plethora of sub-specialties surfaced with the parallel structuring of sub-specialty societies. Now there are at least 20 different sub-specialty societies identified with major bone and joints in the body and a number of surgical techniques.

The issuing of Certificates of Additional Competency, in my opinion, encourages excessive fragmentation, leading to the loss of cohesiveness and strength. And since the fragmentation has been almost exclusively along technical developments, not biological ones, others have begun to question the right that orthopaedist claim to have over the care of many musculoskeletal disorders. They seem to have surmised that all it takes to treat musculoskeletal disorders is the ability to perform a limited number of surgical procedures; something that can be done by virtually anyone who possesses a modicum of surgical skills, without the need to understand the complex biological foundations of orthopaedics.

I have also felt that such certificates are discriminatory. There are many orthopaedists who though competent to provide good care of patients afflicted with conditions within a certain sub-specialty, do not meet the requirements of the given society, such as completion of one-year post-graduate fellowship, or do not wish to devote the required percentage of time to the specific area and prefer a broader scope for their clinical endeavors.

The Hand Society was the first sub-specialty society in orthopaedics that achieved high reputation for its organization and the quality of its educational programs. The Hand Society was also the first society to develop Certificates of Additional Competency. Currently it requires the possession of such a certificate for membership in the organization. Why they came to the conclusion that such a certificate was desirable is not clear to anyone. We do not know if the certificates came about as the result of perceived or documented evidence of weakness within its members. I doubt it. I suspect the Hand Society elected to begin the issuing of certificates as a response to the challenges and competition the orthopaedic hand surgeons were getting from the growing number of general and plastic surgeons who were also sub-specializing in hand surgery.

SECTION III – MISCELLANEOUS

Now that CAQs have been issued for over a decade, I wonder if there is anyone in the upper echelon of the Hand Society in a position to tell what effect the Certificates have had in the quality of care given to hand injuries and diseases. Have they made a difference? Or have they simply legitimized the performance of unnecessary surgery in the eyes of unscrupulous surgeons?

At the time of the writing of these comments there is a strong move afoot to get approval for CAQs to sports medical specialists. I am afraid the Sports Society will be successful in making mandatory the possession of these certificates. However, I anticipate that very adverse consequences will become apparent one day. I see no good reason for the move, which I suspect is the result of a selfish concern among some insecure "leaders" over their territory being shared with others within and outside the orthopaedic discipline. I think they are trying to protect their fellowship system, which gives them cheap labor and a great deal of assistance in the management of their patients.

CHONDROMALACIA

We do not really know why chondromalacia is so much more common in the patella than in other bones in the body. Perhaps because the patella is subjected to impact trauma more often than most other joints. Also, another possible explanation is that the patella has an articular cartilage thicker than that of any other joint in the body. This increased thickness makes the cartilage more vulnerable to permanent injury and difficult recovery. However, there are many people, particularly women, who suffer from this condition who had lived a sedentary life and were rarely exposed to trauma. Men, who at least until recently engaged in sports to a greater extent, experience the symptoms of chondromalacia less frequently.

I doubt the theory that shallow femoral condyles predispose to the condition. The femoropatellar joint is not a congruous one and the shape and depth of the six facets vary from one person to the next.

Chondromalacia may represent the first stage of generalized knee osteoarthritis. It may be speculated that strands of fibrillated cartilage fall into the joint, initiating a synovial reaction that can be severe enough to become detrimental to the normal cartilage of the tibia and femoral articulating surfaces. Many people have patellae that under direct inspection demonstrate evidence of chondromalacia but who never experience any symptoms and do not develop osteoarthritis of the knee.

It is well known that chondromalacia of the patella produces a "mirror image" defect on the opposite surface of the femoral condyle. DePalma, in the 1050's spoke of this phenomenon. I had an opportunity to perform a patellectomy in my younger days on a patient who had painful chondromalacia. I observed at the time of surgery the "mirror image" defect on the femoral condyle and photographed it. A few years later the patient returned with a dislocated patellar tendon. She was then 60 pounds heavier and the valgus of her knees more obvious. I explored the knee joint during the performance of a medial transfer of her tibial tuberosity to find that the femoral defect had disappeared as if the extensor mechanism had polished it. I speculated at that time that if the patella had not been removed originally, the degeneration of the femoral condyle would have gotten worse. Who knows? There is so much we do not understand about the mechanism of joint degeneration.

The management of chondromalacia has been debated for a very long time, and even now there is no clear consensus on the issue. The introduction of the arthroscope in the treatment of intraarticular conditions has prompted many to believe that "shaving" of the damaged cartilage is the treatment of choice. I performed a number of patella "shavings" long before the arthroscope was invented, and oftentimes I witnessed significant temporary improvement. I do not think, however, that I cured any of them.

Surgical procedures, such as the Maquet elevation of the patellar tendon by lifting the tibial tuberosity have been criticized by many, and consider this treatment most inadvisable. Transfer of the tibial tuberosity to a more medial position has also been performed, especially when a valgus attitude of the knee is recognized. None of these procedures have proven to be consistently successful. Patellectomy was the treatment of choice in yesteryears, and I still believe it should be in many instances the treatment of choice.

To mention patellectomy for the treatment of chondromalacia at this time is to many something akin to heresy. Preservation of the patella at all times has become an unshakable dogma not to be challenged. I question the rigidity of this position for it ignores the fact that patellectomy is not necessarily a bad procedure. It has improved the condition of many patients without adverse sequella (See PATELLA FRACTURES).

The British orthopaedic literature of the 1950's and 1960's was rich with evidence to support that patellectomy had a place in the armamentarium of the orthopaedic surgeon. To dismiss the value of the operation in radical terms is probably a mistake.

There is a reasonable argument against patellectomy in the management of chondromalacia or fractures of the patella: the possible difficulties that the absence of the bone may create if and when a total knee replacement becomes necessary.

COMPLICATIONS IN SURGERY

There is not a surgeon who has not had complications of one type or another. Those who deny it either have not done enough surgery or are liars. Complications occur in spite of good judgment and proper execution of surgical procedures. Other surgeons have complications because they cut corners or do not carry out the procedure appropriately. However, all of us, at one time or another, cavalierly perform new procedures only to discover in the middle of surgery that we were not sufficiently knowledgeable to safely undertake the task.

Regardless of the reasons and causes for the complications, I feel that the best thing to do is to acknowledge to the patient that a mistake was made or that an unexpected complication occurred. Trying to hide it does not pay. Too often patients wonder whether the doctor has really told the whole truth about the entire affair. In our litigious society it is not likely that we can get away with false information. Giving the patient honest information

SECTION III – MISCELLANEOUS

as soon as the problem occurs is the best strategy. It reinforces the necessary rapport between physician and patient. The injured patient usually appreciates candor and honesty.

I have vivid recollection of the first surgical procedure I performed after completing my residency: it was the internal fixation of a non-united fracture of the navicular bone. I had carefully exposed the fracture and approximated the two fragments with a minimum of dissection of the surrounding soft tissues. Once in close proximity, I held the fragments together with two towel clamps that were firmly held by the assisting resident. With the two fragments held in that position I placed two staples across the gap. I then moved the wrist in various directions and confirmed the stability of the metallic fixation. I closed the skin and applied a cast, which I had planned to keep in place for a few weeks. Rather than taking an x-ray in surgery I requested that one be obtained in the recovery room.

That night, prior to my going home, I stopped by the x-ray department to look at the post-operative films. To my dismay I discovered that in my attempts to minimize soft tissue dissection I had mistakenly placed the staples, not connecting the two fractured fragments, but between the distal pole of the navicular and the body of the greater mort angular.

What was I to do? What was I going to tell the patient? All kind of thoughts crossed my mind. Should I remain silent about it and never tell the patient that I had stapled the wrong bones together? Destroy the x-rays that the radiologist had not yet read? Wait to see how symptomatic the patient became and then when the pain failed to disappear tell the patient that unfortunately the operation had been unsuccessful and another one was needed? Go home and think further about what to do or confront the patient at that very moment, tell the truth and face the consequences? I chose to go directly to the patient's room where I informed him, "I made a mistake and inadvertently I misplaced the staples. I have to take you back to surgery tomorrow." Needless to say he was upset and made it very clear to me.

The next morning we went back to surgery, where I removed the staples and carried out a distal radial styloidectomy. For some unknown reason the patient did very well. The pre-operative pain disappeared. The young man, the parent of two children, left town and moved to Louisiana. For three consecutive years I received a friendly Christmas card from him. The correspondence stopped either because the distance blurred the memories or because the pain returned. I will never know. However, the lesson I learned from that episode guided my future behavior. I have no regrets. It would be argued by many that such an approach would be unwise today, because litigation would be the immediate response of the patient. I doubt it. Things have changed a great deal since the episode took place, but the value of honesty is still high in the mind of most people.

Much too often I have witnessed situations where the physician had invented the strangest and most bizarre stories in an attempt to cover his mistakes. Silly claims that the failure of fixation of an implant was the fault of the patient himself because he did not follow instructions; or that the nurses did not move the patient correctly, or the physical therapist failed to provide the patients with the appropriate instructions. I have heard those excuses dozens of times, even when it was obvious that the cause of failure was the improper performance of the surgical procedure.

SECTION III – MISCELLANEOUS

COMPRESSION AND RIGID FIXATION (See Fracture Healing, Section I)

CRITICIZING COLLEAGUES

It is very distasteful to see physicians criticize other physicians in front of patients. "Oh, my God, who operated on you?" How many times have we heard that remark? There is no more effective way to discredit a colleague, to poison patients' mind and to encourage litigation. This is often done in an effort to impress the patient of the critic's superior knowledge, hoping to become the one to perform the surgery that will offset the other physician's error. A terrible practice.

On the other hand, I believe the physician has a responsibility to his colleagues to see that high standards of care are held in the community. Though it is difficult to do it and friendships can be irreparable damaged, I think that when a physician recognizes that a mistake was made by one of his colleagues he should contact the culprit doctor and inform him that he has found out that something was probably not done correctly. It hurts to hear that, but in so doing the likelihood of litigation may be assuaged and if the receiver of the call recognizes the honest intentions of the caller everyone benefits.

The same is true in cases of malpractice litigation. There is nothing more disgusting than to see physicians making a living out of testifying against other physicians. They make fortunes in the process, prostitute themselves and damage the image of the medical profession. However, malpractice in medicine occurs and it should be fought. To deny its existence is counterproductive. The public is served by having the recourse of malpractice litigation against someone who committed malpractice. The problem is, as it is true for just about everything else in life, that some people abuse their privileges. Unfair litigation takes place every day of the week. In the process careers are destroyed, reputations ruined and an enormous of unnecessary mental suffering is placed on innocent, honest physicians.

The question is how a physician should behave when called to testify against another physician accused of having committed malpractice. Should he refuse "to get involved" even it is obvious that his colleague has committee mal-practice or testify that his colleague is innocent of wrongdoing? Or should he follow the dictates of his conscience and tell the truth?

I must admit that I have always avoided as much as possible any involvement in litigation matters. However, a few times I have agreed to do so, sometimes because the accused physician was a friend or an acquaintance of mine or because the description of the "case" indicated a serious situation. After reviewing the material I have, without any hesitation, picked up the phone and told the accused orthopaedists that, in my opinion, the charges against him were legitimate and that trying to prove his innocence was futile. Then I would suggest a settlement of the case if at all possible. In that manner my colleague would avoid the painful experience of court appearances and a final verdict of guilt.

SECTION III – MISCELLANEOUS

E

EROSION OF ORTHOPAEDICS

Even though it is well known that considerable progress has been made in orthopaedics due primarily to technical advances, others in medicine have eroded into the traditional orthopaedic territory. The orthopaedist is no longer the professional who is universally recognized as the one solely responsible for the care of most musculoskeletal conditions. Others are now considered to be experts in this area.

Neurosurgeons, with increasing frequency perform surgical procedures in the spine that until recently were under the exclusive jurisdiction of the orthopaedic surgeon. Spinal instrumentation was a procedure the orthopaedist had taken for granted no one else would attempt to perform. That is no longer the case. In many medical schools and hospitals, neurosurgeons are responsible for the care of spine fractures and their sequella. It is no secret that until recently the neurosurgical resident did not receive any training in that area. I suppose financial considerations prompted the organized neurosurgical community to seek advice from the manufacturers of orthopaedic implants regarding the use of the necessary instrumentation. I also suspect that little thought was given to the need to possess knowledge in related matters such as the biologic understanding of osteogenesis, osteoporosis , post-operative infections, metal failure, non-unions etc.

Similarly, podiatrists who as recently as one generation ago limited their work to the care of simple foot problems, such as ingrown toenails and calluses, now perform major orthopaedic procedures such as fusions, osteotomies, arthroscopy, and internal fixation of fractures of the foot, ankle and leg and total ankle replacement. I would not be surprised if one day podiatry claims jurisdiction over the entire leg as well as the hand (See PODIATRY).

The list of areas that orthopaedists have lost to others gets larger every day. Though it is easy to venture simple explanations for this phenomenon, it is likely that many factors brought it about. I believe that a major reason was the perception that orthopaedics was no longer a clearly identified body of knowledge, gained through a long and arduous period of training; it was simply a series of surgical procedures that anyone, with a modicum of knowledge and surgical skill could perform[136, 140, 143] (See addenda 1,2,7,9)

The orthopaedic community lost interest in the nonsurgical care of musculoskeletal conditions and concentrated almost exclusively on their operative management. This trend opened opportunities to others, who saw a chance to invade the orthopaedic territory.

At this time the American Academy of Orthopaedic Surgeons is attempting to stem the tide and is making plans to reverse the trend by "suggesting" to the orthopaedic community to become involved in the non-operative approach to musculoskeletal diseases. I personally believe this to be a commendable plan but question the sincerity of the effort and the outcome of the venture. Without a radical revamping of education, beginning at the

SECTION III – MISCELLANEOUS

residency level, the project will be nothing more than an exercise in futility. I do not believe the heads of residency programs will be willing to accept major changes. I picture many of them claiming that the time has come for us to realize that the orthopaedist is a surgeon who should limits his work to the surgical care of musculoskeletal conditions and let others assume the responsibility of providing nonsurgical care [143, 159]

I anticipate they will be successful in their opposition to change. Their success, however, will further destroy our discipline as a scientific profession and will forever identify its members as surgical technicians.

ETHICS IN MEDICINE

Medicine is a microcosm of society and as such is influenced by society's moral values and ethics. Any observer of contemporary society would readily admit that our hedonistic attitudes focused almost exclusively on material matters and consumed with the obsession of profit, have created a similar ethos in medicine.

A society that selects its values according to personal convenience and appears to say that "everything is OK", sends the message that "nothing is morally wrong". This relativistic attitude permeates through the medical profession with increasing ease, particularly as we witness the growth of managed care in the daily life of the physician.

The loss of autonomy experienced by the physician and his greater dependency on the whims and wishes of entrepreneurial businessmen, has done nothing but aggravate the condition. In order to compensate for the rapid diminution in income, the medical man finds himself resorting to a variety of moves in order to maintain the economic status to which he grew accustomed. Some of these moves often compromise professionalism and ethical behavior [127, 146, 148, 154, 158].

Actions that the medical profession had long considered inappropriate or outright unethical are being practiced by an increasing number of members of the medical profession. Advertising and marketing of services via the printed media and radio and television and the Internet, seem to be common practices today. Many are doing the acceptance of gifts from Industry for the use of medications or surgical products. Handsome kickbacks for the utilization of prosthetic devices or other implants have become a routine practice in other countries. Such a pattern is gaining increasing acceptance in our own land. Just a few years ago a physician would have been ostracized for indulging in those activities [148, 158]

Perhaps as a result of socio-economic changes sweeping through the field of health care delivery, we have witnessed an increased complacency with the performance of unnecessary surgery and the utilization of diagnostic tests not essential to the practice of medicine. For example, many in unprecedented degrees have abused arthroscopy a most revolutionary diagnostic and therapeutic modality. (See ARTHROSCOPY)

Total joint replacement, a procedure still in evolution, is being performed in the presence of the slightest symptoms. Patients with mild symptoms of arthritis of the hip are

SECTION III – MISCELLANEOUS

subjected to total hip arthroplasty even though the pain was easily controlled with medications.

The obsession with the need to increase revenues by hook or by crook has driven our representative organizations to engage in educating physicians in ways to maximize their income. Oftentimes that education is nothing but instructions on how to "game the system "and find out means to outsmart those trying to set rules and regulations.

It saddens me to see many of our representative organizations devoting a great deal of time, money and effort to this endeavor. Radical changes in the delivery and financing of medical care will soon take place as we are running out ot time for gradual change. The government will be taking Draconian measures to curtail the increasing costs of medical care in manners that will further intrude into the autonomy that allowed medicine to grow to the degree it is today. One cannot help but wonder if our struggle against the system is simply making matters worse. The overall issue of health care and cost is a social matter that the medical profession will not be able to control; the political powers that be see this as their responsibility and will prevail, no matter how much opposition physicians will demonstrate.

My feelings along this line should not be misconstrued as a suggestion to surrender the control of our destiny to others; simply an effort to emphasize the need to be realistic about our degree of power and jurisdiction as well as awareness of the fact that the socio-economic nature of the problems we confront will eventually must be in the hands of governmental bodies. Our role should be that of demonstrating to them our commitment to serve the public through our expertise and professionalism.

SECTION III – MISCELLANEOUS

F

FELLOWSHIPS IN ORTHOPAEDICS

What is the value of post-residency fellowships in orthopaedic sub-specialties? Who should take them and what should a fellowship entail? I raise those questions because the answers are not obvious. For several years, during my tenure as professor and chairman of orthopaedics at the University of Southern California, I witnessed several times the twelve graduating residents apply for and obtain fellowship positions throughout the country.

I did not like the trend; first because I anticipated a glut of fellows flooding the country and finding themselves unable to practice in the area they had chosen to spend an additional year of their lives. Secondly, because I could not see fellowships for everybody as a logical or rational move. When I asked residents, ready to apply for fellowship positions, to tell me their individual reasons for the decision to take them, I received different answers. Seldom were the answers the product of well thought analysis of their needs. It was apparent to me that the main reason was their perception that without fellowships their chances of obtaining a "good" practice opportunity were markedly reduced. That with a fellowship came more lucrative job offers. Others took fellowships simply because other residents were taking them: "monkey see monkey do". I made my concerns known to the residents. I told them that only those who felt insecure in any given area of orthopaedics, in which they anticipated being involved, should take fellowship positions. Also those who had plans to enter academic medicine and devote a good portion of their time to teaching and research in a specific area, and those who had been told that a position would be available to them in the private sector providing that a fellowship in a clearly designed area had been completed.

When medical students applying for residency position are interviewed, it is not surprising to hear almost all of them say that upon graduation from residency they will pursue a fellowship. The most common one at this time is Sports Medicine. They do not have the foggiest idea what sports medicine is all about but are keenly aware of the "sexy" nature of the sub-specialty. If today sports medicine is the darling of orthopaedics and one of the most profitable of all sub-specialties, it is likely that its popularity may diminish and another sub-specialty will take its place. Some years ago hand surgery was the most sought after sub-specialty. Then came total joint replacement to be followed by spine surgery. Who knows what will be next [136, 137, 140, 158]. (See INTERVIEWING PROSPECTIVE RESIDENTS).

I had spoken to residents in that way because I was also convinced that those who graduated from our program had received an adequate general education and practical exposure to all segments of the profession. They were ready and capable of being good orthopaedists anywhere in the country. Some took my advice and a few years later only half of the graduating residents took sub-specialty fellowships.

I have long believed that residents should not jump directly from residency to fellowship, unless some very powerful reasons exist. The resident is better off if he goes into general orthopaedic practice and gains additional practical experience in the whole of orthopaedics. Trauma, I believe, is the most important for it provides the foundations for a better understanding of all other sub-divisions. After a while in the practice of general orthopaedics the orthopaedist can begin to zero-in on a few areas or in only one area. As a sub-specialist he is in a better position to excel if his background is more eclectic.

I have been amazed a number of times by the appalling ignorance of some orthopaedists who went directly into a small sub-specialty and by-passed general orthopaedics. They do a good job only in their limited area of expertise but fail to grasp the meaning and importance of other areas.

I have the distinct feeling that the obsession with fellowships still persists. The number of available fellowships staggers one's imagination. It is my understanding that there are 250 fellowships in Sports Medicine in the United States. Any surgeon who has a large practice based on arthroscopic surgery announces his accredited fellowship and applicants flood his office.

I am not at all sure that the body that governs fellowships has done a very good job monitoring the various programs. The quality of some fellowships is poor and the fellows receive very little "education". Many of them are simply assisting hands to the busy surgeon. They create time for the director to indulge in profitable financial activities. The fellow closes wounds; oftentimes perform surgical procedures in private patients without supervision; makes daily rounds; changes dressings; removes sutures; dictates operative reports; takes care of patients' telephone calls; and covers the emergency room. In some programs the fellows bill as assistant surgeons and the revenues go to the director of the program. Academic instruction is often minimal. Research, if it is done, consists of chart reviews and the preparation of manuscripts for possible publication.

There are, however, very good fellowships where the students learn a great deal and where their time is balanced between academic lectures, surgical experience, patient contact, and research endeavors.

The health care reform now sweeping the country is emphasizing the importance of the generalist and discouraging the use of super-specialists. Therefore, the surgeon who tries to obtain a place in HMOs and announces himself as a highly specialized individual who takes care of only one segment of the body or one joint or bone, is not likely to get the position. I, personally, experienced that problem upon my return to Miami in 1994, at the time when HMOs were rapidly expanding in Dade County. Since I had performed only total hip replacements for the previous 25 years, I had to inform the HMOs I had applied to the limited scope of my practice. I had little success. They did not want a super-specialist but someone to whom they could refer as many different conditions as possible.

I resent the practice of some orthopaedists who announced themselves to HMOs as being general orthopaedists when in fact they are not. Their practices are limited to specific areas. Most of the patients referred to them suffering from conditions the surgeons do not handle, are nonetheless seen by them in their offices. They are examined and subjected to whatever tests, x-rays, CT scans and MRI seem appropriate. Then they inform the patients that they need to see a specialist. They practice in that manner because they know that they are paid for seeing those patients in "consultation" and reap financial benefits from some of the tests they request. To make matters worse the "specialist" oftentimes repeats the tests the original orthopaedist had already obtained.

FOR-PROFIT HOSPITALS

For-profit hospitals exploded during the battle the federal government and the medical establishments were fighting regarding the provision of medical care to an increasingly large number of Americans who did not have medical insurance. Medicare had addressed the issue of the elderly and Medicaid was finalizing coverage of the child and the indigent. Not much progress was being made. Some hoped that the impasse was an indication that the government would give up on its attempts to solve the dilemma. Others kept on fighting, hoping to win the battle and preserve intact the autonomy of the medical profession.

Almost overnight the private sector stepped into the arena and with the speed of light took over the situation. HMOs (Health Maintenance Organizations) and other similar systems were developed. Within a short time their numbers increased dramatically and a large percentage of the population joined them. HMOs promised a solution to all problems ranging from the curtailment of costs to ideal and comprehensive medical care to all.

Time has shown that the promises were not fulfilled, and at this time the disappointment with HMOs is rapidly reaching the naïve and optimistic public. The speed of the unhappiness with the system has been relatively slow, probably because most people enrolled in HMOs are healthy individuals, who have not had the unfortunate experience of needing medical attention. It is not until they find themselves in need of medical care that they discover that their HMO does not provide the services they were told they would receive in the event of injury or illness.

The growth of for-profit hospitals took place simultaneous to the explosion of HMOs. Entrepreneurs saw opportunities for offsetting the anticipated reduction of financial reimbursement for services rendered, while making huge profit. The success of the for-profit hospital was spectacular. Acquisitions and mergers began to take place at a fast pace. Before long some hospital chains were formed and the gross wealth of some reached into the billions of dollars. CEOs of major hospital chains began to earn enormous amounts of money. In the early 1990s, The Los Angeles Times published a report on the annual income of CEO's of major industries in California, which identified the CEO of NME (National Medical Enterprises, a large chain of for for-profit hospitals and other health care facilities) as having earned the previous year 34 million dollars. Two other members of the organization also appeared on the list of the highest paid CEOs in California. NME was the organization that financed the construction and managed the University of Southern California Hospital.

For-profit hospitals bought physician practices and offered them opportunities for greater revenues. Special deals were made with the manufacturers of hospital equipment and supplies. Enthusiasm for the new idea of for-profit institutions appeared to be inexhaustible. Soon, however, trouble developed in paradise. Fraud became rampant. Officers of several such organizations were prosecuted. Large suits were issued. For example, within a few months after the opening of the University of Southern California Hospital, NME was prosecuted for major fraud in some of its hospitals. Rehabilitation facilities and psychiatric hospital were identified as the main culprits. Settlements in the order of hundreds of millions of dollars were made.

Similar problems have been identified around the country. Columbia, the largest chain of for-profit hospitals in the United States, was found to have committed fraud on a major scale. Its CEO, who had already amassed billions of dollars, was fired and the investigation is still on going. More recently HealthSouth, the largest chain of rehabilitation facilities in the country is confronting the accusations of fraud on an unprecedented major scale. Its CEO will likely be indicted and sent to jail. He is a former filling station attendant who rose through the ranks and eventually claimed to be worth billions of dollars. "The bigger the hubris the harder the fall."

In order to maximize revenues, for-profit hospitals engage in a plethora of activities that oftentimes are inappropriate, lower the level of medical care, are conducive to abuse or are outright unethical. They establish programs of no medical value in order to attract patients and reduce to a minimum the number of needed ancillary personnel, while expecting that the remaining employees will still maintain a façade of good care. (See ARTHRITIS AND OSTEOPOROSIS PROGRAMS)

I do not wish to come down with strong criticism of for-profit hospitals based primarily on vicarious information. I suspect that there are for-profit hospitals where good care is provided and where greed is not the ethos of the institution. I think, however, that the idea of making medical care entirely a business, and where there is no end to the level of profit that must be made, is not good for society. It is difficult to conceive a situation where the altruistic goals of medicine can be reconciled with the material interests of business ventures. A return to exclusively non-for profit hospitals is very unlikely. However, it is difficult to predict what is in store in the future.

The problem of providing medical care to all Americans is rapidly becoming a moral imperative that soon will call for a resolution. Most economically advanced nations in the world have, in various degrees, addressed the issue and have met with significant success. There is no reason to suspect that the United States will be incapable of solving its problem without compromising the integrity and foundation of medicine.

I am convinced that within a few years this matter will be resolved. I hope organized medicine will have the wisdom and courage to shed the increasingly discredited image of a profession motivated so greatly by self-serving interests, and, in doing so, gain a seat at the table where the ultimate decisions will be made [158]. (See addenda 7,9)

SECTION III – MISCELLANEOUS

FRAGMENTATION OF ORTHOPAEDICS

The rapid changes in the orthopaedic profession gave rise to sub-specialization. The perception developed that the new knowledge was so overwhelming that no one individual was any longer capable of appropriately master the entire field. I suspect this is not true. A careful review of the scope of orthopaedics should indicate that it is not a lot greater than it was 20 years ago. It is more likely that new knowledge has simply replaced old knowledge. I think that we have responded the way we have out of panic. It is logical that once we become accustomed to doing things in a particular way, the thought of having to change scares us. We intuitively imagine that the new technology that replaces the old is very difficult to master[135, 136, 137, 143].

Examples abound. Let us look at arthroscopic surgery and joint replacement. ``For someone who for a long period of time had been managing internal derangement of the knee with open surgery may see arthroscopic surgery as an extremely difficult procedure and beyond his skills. However, after a bit of practice with the new methodology he learns that, after all, is not that complicated. Given time he tells himself that he can do better surgery through the arthroscope.

The same applies to total joint replacement. For many years I approached the hip joint through a posterior approach. I used that approach in thousands of instances and reached the conclusion that there was, probably, no surgical intervention in the hip joint that could not be done through that incision. After visiting Charnley I began to approach the hip through an antero-lateral approach. At first I was literally confused. I could not get oriented in space. It took a while to appreciate the simplicity of the approach.

Years later, after having performed nearly one thousand Charnley arthroplasties via the anterior approach, I began to question the need for trochanteric osteotomy. I tried the posterior approach that I had once considered a panacea. The first few total hip arthroplasties I performed through the posterior approach were difficult. Once again I was lost and found it difficult to get oriented. A few weeks later I was comfortable with the posterior approach.

Another good example is closed intramedullary nailing of long bone fractures. At first, those who had practiced open nailing of fractures for many years, asked themselves why they should use the closed technique which is, after all, more difficult to carry out and sometimes takes longer to complete. Those who fear that threading a nail through non-exposed fragments must be very difficult found the change undesirable. As in the case of arthroscopy and total joint replacement, experience made the initial fear disappear.

I venture to say that it is easier for an orthopaedist to practice general orthopaedists today than it was for his counterpart 30 years ago. Fewer different surgical procedures are performed today than in the past. For example, in the case of arthritis of the hip, total joint arthroplasty has replaced the multitude of surgical and non-surgical modalities that the earlier orthopaedists had to understand and carry out.

The fragmentation of orthopaedics has been, in most instances, almost exclusively, along surgical procedures. That explains why at meetings of sub-specialty societies virtually

SECTION III – MISCELLANEOUS

all discussions deal with the surgical aspects of a well-defined, limited number of conditions. In their open meetings, the Hip and Knee societies address nothing but total hip and knee arthroplasty. The trauma society discusses exclusively internal fixation of fractures. Some societies do not even bother to claim interest in anything but the technical aspects of management of a few conditions. The arthroscopy society is a good example.

It is futile for me to pretend to know what the long-term effects of fragmentation in orthopaedics will be. It is possible that the trend will continue and that one day there will not be general orthopaedics as we have known them for some time: everybody will be a specialist in a small area of the body or on a given surgical procedure. I personally doubt this possibility will be a viable one. Economics will dictate otherwise. It is more likely that others, outside of orthopaedics, will continue to involve themselves, in greater degrees, in the management of patients with disorders of the musculoskeletal system, which until recently the orthopaedist had taken for granted as being under his exclusive domain (See EROSION OF ORTHOPAEDICS and SUBSPECIALTIES).

SECTION III – MISCELLANEOUS

G

GAIT ANALYSIS

Beginning with Duchenne and followed in modern times by the likes of Vernon Inman, John Paul, Jacqueline Perry and others, the subject of gait analysis has attracted academicians to the point that it is difficult to find an orthopaedic or rehabilitation program that does not have a Gait Laboratory. I have visited dozens of such facilities and have discussed their contributions with the investigators.

In spite of the fact that our knowledge of gait is better today than it was some years ago, I continue to experience a feeling of frustration as I see major efforts, time and money spent in this area with very modest, meaningful clinical outcome. I recognize that there are exceptions such as amputations and prosthetics.

Most of the research dealing with gait disorders has focused on hemiplegia, spinal cord injuries and spastic congenital disabilities. In the past I was involved in these areas but today I am skeptical about the progress that has been allegedly made. Attempts to make the ambulation of the paraplegic possible, for example, have failed completely (See SPINAL CORD INJURIES).

The some extent, the same is true regarding the hemiplegic patient. Though bracing of the affected lower extremities has benefited many, the same cannot be said about bracing of the flaccid or spastic upper extremities. I believe that rehabilitation of the stroke patient should be concentrated mainly on the use of the unimpaired opposite limb. I do not know what information has been gathered from analysis of hemiplegic patients' gait during the past twenty-five years that has made a difference in their function. (See HEMIPLEGIA).

The gait of children with spastic or athetoid cerebral palsy has been studied for several decades. A number of surgical procedures and functional braces have been designed and used for their benefit. I wonder, however, how many of those operative procedures were conceived from information obtained from sophisticated gait analysis. I suspect that simple observation of those children and a good dose of common sense would have brought about the same results.

I feel uneasy when I see some children with terrible congenital or developmental conditions being subjected to an unending number of operations aimed at making them more functional. Uneasy because I see the futility of many of those efforts and realize that the treating surgeons must be aware of that. If all those measures are taken for the sole purpose of demonstrating a commitment "to do something" and in doing so satisfy the desires, hope and dreams of parents, I think such a practice is wrong.

On one occasion I served as visiting professor at a major medical school in the Orient. During the "case presentation" ritual I was shown a child, probably fifteen-year-old, who suffered from the severe sequella of poliomyelitis. She was brought into the conference room in a wheel chair. She was curdled like a pretzel and had the saddest look on her face. I learned she had never walked and that the muscle paralysis had also seriously compromised her spine: pronounced scoliosis had deformed her body and affected her respiratory capacity.

The young lady had had numerous surgical procedures and on that particular day the discussion centered on what the next one should be regarding her scoliotic deformity. Her vital capacity was minimal and the attending consultants had expressed their opinion that surgery could be fatal. The group of physicians attending the meeting discussed various surgical options. One of them suggested that at the time of the spine surgery the dislocated hips should be surgically treated.

When I was asked for an opinion I stated that I was far from being an expert on spinal deformities, but my suggestion was, "To replace her worn-out wheelchair with a new one; buy her a large television set; some books, find ways to entertain her in her miserable existence; to keep her away from surgery; to give her love and allow her to die in peace". I do not know how the surgery went, since I suspect it was performed a few days later.

GRAND-ROUNDS

The gathering of faculty, residents and medical students on a weekly basis to listen to formal presentations delivered by local or visiting lecturers, residents and others, has been a long standing tradition in academic circles. Attendance to the weekly ritual was compulsory to faculty, residents and medical students and became a good learning experience and a platform for young physicians to learn and practice their public speaking skills.

Over the years changes have taken place that deserve attention. In many institutions, Grand Rounds are failing to be the wonderful learning opportunity that once was. I vividly recall that during my years as chairman of the department of Orthopaedics and Rehabilitation at the University of Miami in the 1970's, we filled a very large auditorium with a variety of people. In the audience we had the entire full-time faculty and resident body, rotating medical students, physical and occupational therapists, prosthetists and orthotists and a large group of voluntary faculty.

The meetings were animated and made interesting by the involvement of many in the ensuing discussions. In order to ascertain that the attendance was not poor when the topic of discussion was not a highly interesting and popular one, we did not announce in advance who the speaker or topic of the day. We promised the audience a good meeting and encouraged them to attend. They were supposed to have a "treat" every week.

Obviously, that was not the case every time, but we tried to do well consistently. Had we announced the topic of the week in advance, I am certain that many would have chosen not to attend when the subject was of no interest to them. Imagine if a physical therapist was speaking on rehabilitation of the hemiplegic. Many would have slept one hour longer before heading toward the operating room or office. The system worked well because the speakers knew that a great deal was expected from them.

SECTION III – MISCELLANEOUS

However, eventually it became difficult to keep the subject or speaker a secret from the full-time faculty. Some of them began to skip Grand Rounds when the subject was not attractive to them and occasionally retained with them their respective residents. Though this evolving pattern disturbed the educational program, it was obvious to me that the rationale behind the absences from Rounds had some validity if I were to accept its logic. The full-time faculty had become, or were becoming, sub-specialists. They were soon convinced that listening to scientific presentations outside of their limited territory was a waste of their time. The spine surgeon, for example, could not understand what he was to gain from listening to a lecture dealing with traumatic conditions of the foot. In turn the foot surgeon reasoned that lectures on topics such as the shoulder, the spine and many others were of no benefit to him.

Now administrators or "scientists" who are full-time employees of pharmaceutical houses frequently serve as guest speakers or "visiting professors" at Grand Rounds. They offer their "services" at no charge, and make "small" contributions to the department's educational efforts.

When orthopaedists are the speakers at the meetings, much too often they are there to represent industry. They are usually surgeons who have developed their own implants. When they enter the auditorium a group of vendors accompany him. They are there to follow through with sales pitches after the visiting dignitary leaves the room.

Untill recently most of the industry-sponsored speakers were surgeons marketing implants, now it is not uncommon to hear physicians marketing anti-cuagulants, non-inflammatory medications, bone glues and similar products.

We seem to have accepted this accepted this demeaning practice and no longer frown before it. Hopefully one day soon we will awake to the dangers that the control of education have created and will do something about it.

GREED

While discussing the many problems besetting medical care, someone said that what was needed was greed reform. Though not an entirely accurate prescription it has a kernel of truth. There is no doubt in my mind that rampant, exaggerated greed underscores many of the problems that our society now confronts.

It is the underlying greed that so easily creeps in all of us that diminishes the enormous pluses of capitalism. The greed that has also engulfed medicine is responsible for many of our problems. No one seems to be exempt from it. We see it manifested in our educational institutions, our hospitals, our insurance companies, the medical-industrial complex, and our colleagues and in all of us [135, 158]

It is greed that has made it possible for universities and medical schools to lower their standards by accepting 'endowed chairs' whose appointees are named by "donors"; no longer to the best qualified individual. In increasing numbers we are seeing orthopadic chairs diagnosis or the required treatment. Some physicians use these technologies on anybody who walks into their offices. In the case of the injured or painful knee, an arthroscopic procedure becomes and indispensable second step, following which prolonged supervised physical therapy is prescribed.

Some physicians, for no other reason that it generates more profit abuse surgery. Many conditions of the musculoskeletal system are surgically approached despite the fact that conservative measures can provide equally as effective results. Fractures that can be treated with a splint or cast are taken to surgery and then sent to rehabilitation facilities for a long period of time.

Such a behavior, which is becoming increasingly common in our midst benefits not only the physician, the hospital and the rehabilitation facility, but also the manufactures of surgical implants. That being the case, why should anyone interested in making greater profit be interested in changing the system? They are only interested in seeing additional financial opportunities, and therefore many spend their energy lobbying and complaining over every measure that challenges the status quo.

The possibility of litigation is often used as a reason for the use and abuse of technology and surgery. Though litigation against physicians has reached and obscene degree, it cannot excuse the abuses committed by some physicians. It is a fact that some physicians commit medical malpractice; therefore a legal system that protects the public is necessary. However, tort reform is urgently needed, if nothing else in order to assist in the reduction of medical care costs.

To expect the National or States Legislatures to address this topic has been until now an exercise in futility. The legislators are not interested in doing anything that might impact on the profit that their colleagues derive form medical litigation. Realizing that neither the medical profession, nor the hospitals, insurance companies, rehabilitation facilities, attorneys and many others are not willing or capable to accept the required changes, why should one be optimistic about a resolution of the alleged "health care crisis"?

I suspect that sooner, rather than later, the Government will impose Draconian measures to a crumbling system. A National Health Insurance of some type will be implemented. This potential development in itself will not be necessarily ominous; quite the contrary it may be a salutary event, which will bring new vitality into a profession facing dark clouds on its horizon. I, for one, will welcome its arrival.

HEMIPLEGIA

The orthopaedist of today knows very little about the care of the hemiplegic patient. We relegated that responsibility to others, when we found ourselves enjoying the more exciting and lucrative surgery for arthritic joints, the spine and arthroscopy. We did not want to be bothered with chronic diseases that do not respond to surgery in dramatic ways. It was for the same reasons that we stopped amputating limbs and rehabilitating amputees, taking care

SECTION III – MISCELLANEOUS

H

HEALTH CARE REFORM

Virtually all economically advanced nations of the world have been deeply concerned over the past few decades over the escalating growth of medical care, and the resulting financial burden in their economies. The situation in the United States seems to be the grave.. Concern over the situation has riveted the citizenry to a daily debate, if nothing else because health care cost is the highest in the world and occupies the largest percentage of the national budget, when compared with that of other countries.

I have lost faith in the possibility of a solution to the "crisis" in the foreseeable future. A solution cannot come from the use of "hot compresses" and mild compromises. Only a very radical change will effect results. Organized medicine has been very vocal in its opposition to the increased reduction in the income of its members and the encroachment of the government and third party payer in their professional lives.

These two issues fill the agenda of virtually every medical organization. Even educational organizations, whose primary mission is not the financial welfare of its members, find themselves totally consumed in protestations against the situation, which in their eyes appears to deteriorate on a daily basis. The neglect of their educational mission has inevitably adversely affected this important aspect of medicine, and has encouraged industry to assume a large and unhealthy role in physician education.

I stated that that I have lost faith in a prompt solution to the "crisis", because I do not see the possibility of basic changes in the attitude of the medical community and others involved in medical care. It is not in the best interest of the insurance companies, the pharmaceutical industry, the for-profit hospitals, the physicians themselves, the litigation attorneys, and many others, if major changes are made.

To many physicians, the profession has become a business. Since physicians still have a major role in determining the costs of medical care, that privilege is often abused for personal financial reasons. The more third party payers reduce the reimbursement for services rendered by physicians, the more "treatment" is given to a higher number of patients. The number of tests is increased, though many of them are unnecessary; more surgery is performed for conditions which readily respond to conservative methods; more conditions are treated with expensive methods, which are also frequently unnecessary. Extensive and expensive rehabilitation is given to patients who do not need it, and for unnecessarily long periods of time. Consultations from other physicians are requested for the sole purpose of being in turn called to consult in their patients. All this, not only benefits the physicians but also increases the costs of medical care.

The abuses are often flagrant. The CT and MRI have replaced the physical examination of many patients. In increasingly large numbers, physicians requests those tests even though they know that whatever information they obtain form them will not alter the

SECTION III – MISCELLANEOUS

Was it ignorance that prompted the surgeon to perform surgery in this very old and sick man? Did he really believe that surgery would help? In my opinion neither answer is correct. He knew that surgery would not solve any problem. He performed the surgery because he knew that he would get paid several thousand dollars for it. Greed. Pure and unadulterated greed.

The second example took place only a few weeks later, when an 87-year-old man, afflicted with a rapidly progressive peripheral neuropathy had sustained an acute fracture of the elbow and femoral neck six months earlier. The hip fracture had been treated with an endo-prosthesis. Prior to the fall that produced the fracture he was already barely able to take a few steps with the aid of a walker. The surgery apparently had weakened him even further.

He was brought into my office in a wheelchair. His hip was painless but he was unable to take more than three or four steps, while holding on to the walker and with the additional help of his young son. The son, an attorney, spoke on his behalf. He wanted additional rehabilitation for his father so "he could not only walk independently but also be able to drive his automobile." I had to look at the young man twice because I could not believe that any reasonable person could expect such a miracle.

After a lengthy conversation with the son, I finally convinced him that it was in his father's best interest not to pursue rehabilitation aimed at restoring his ambulatory faculties. I suggested to concentrate on improving his transfer activities and to continue giving the old man the affection of his family and friends. Apparently I succeeded in getting my message across. However, as they were about to leave the office, the son asked me if I would write a prescription for "some" therapy while waiting for the surgery that his father was to have on his elbow two weeks later.

It turned out that surgery, in the form of a total elbow replacement, had been scheduled by one of the local "hand surgeons". The old man's elbow was asymptomatic but lacked some motion. The lack of extension did no preclude his ability to use the walker for the short walks he had been told "were good for him." The forearm had moderate functional pronation and supination, so much so that he was able to carry out most of the activities of daily living required by a wheelchair ridden individual.

I raise questions about the motives of the surgeon who recommended the total elbow replacement. Was it ignorance or a sincere belief that surgery would bring major benefits to a man who by all reasonable measurements was to die within a relatively short period of time? I do not believe that any of the two alternatives influenced his decision. Greed was the reason for the surgery. Surgery would put money in his pocket.

funded by industry. To avoid the embarrassment that the acceptance of such "gifts" probably affects respectable university representatives, the name of the donating industry is not acknowledged, simply the name of some physician who serves as a peddler for the commercial venture.

It is greed that makes for-profit hospitals indulge in all types of shady deals and practices for the sole purpose of enriching the coffers of officers and stockholders. The same is true for the loss of professionalism in our ranks, when we calmly tolerate the practice of many physicians indulging in inappropriate medical related business in order to benefit financially.

The explosion of programs with no medical value, designed only to help organizations or a few individuals, fits into the category of greed-driven ventures. The abuse of so-called rehabilitation facilities; the unnecessary production of pharmaceuticals and surgical products; the unbundling of charges; the rampant medical fraud; the unnecessary prescription of treatments and the equally unnecessary performance of surgery, are clear expressions of how greed has infiltrated our profession.

Pages, if not volumes, can be filled with examples of greed among members of the medical profession. In Miami, the medical-fraud capital of the United States, I have had the opportunity to observe in a relatively short period of time the most egregious displays of greed. Let a couple of examples illustrate my point.

Once, I was called in consultation to see an old patient of mine who was being treated by a Family Physician. Twenty-five years earlier, I had performed bilateral total hip replacements for the treatment of osteoarthritis. He was now 90 years of age. He had had a multitude of surgical procedures for a variety of neurosurgical, intestinal and cardiovascular conditions. His ambulation had been limited to taking the couple steps required for the transfer from bed to a wheel chair.

During the course of some type of abdominal study, it was discovered that one of his total hips was dislocated. His wife estimated that it had probably taken place several months earlier. In any event, the patient occasionally complained of discomfort in the groin.

It did not take me long to conclude that the dislocated hip should be left alone since it was not giving him pain and it was not in any way responsible for his inability to ambulate. I discussed my recommendation with the patient and his wife, who readily agreed with it. I then proceeded to write my report on the patient's chart. Within a few hours, the referring physician was on the phone, virtually demanding that the dislocated hip prosthesis be reduced. He indicated that the patient was in excellent condition and capable of withstanding the necessary surgery. I argued against such an approached and refused to perform surgery. I then suggested that another orthopaedist be called to assume care of the elderly gentleman.

As I anticipated, an orthopaedist was summoned, and the next day the patient had surgery. Not only was the hip reduced but also one of its components were revised. Within a few days the hip dislocated again and a brace was prescribed. The patient died some time later.

SECTION III – MISCELLANEOUS

of spinal cord injured patients and providing non-surgical care to patients suffering from degenerative diseases of the spine.

Now that the so-called health care reform has affected our pocket books in a threatening way, we are lamenting the losses. Attempts to regain the lost territory are likely to be unsuccessful. Those who took our "land" do not want to give it up, and we, orthopaedists, particularly those in academic circles, who are comfortable with the well-established sources of patient referrals, are not anxious to shift directions. They do not want to recruit faculty capable of discharging the required new duties and provide teaching to students and orthopaedic residents. Time will tell what the future of our discipline will be when we find ourselves functioning solely as technicians, cosmetic surgeons of the musculoskeletal system. A time when people outside of orthopaedics will provide the care of a large percentage of those conditions; even by people without medical degrees.

As in the case of the spinal cord injured patient, to whom, at one time we gave intensive physical and occupational therapy in anticipation of achieving a major improvement in function, I learned from experience that efforts to improve upper extremity function in the hemiplegic are, for the most part, an exercise in futility. Most hemiplegics start out with a flaccid paralysis, which, fortunately, becomes spastic within a few days or weeks. Therapy aimed at making the patient able to use the spastic upper extremity is met with disappointment. The return of function in such extremities is frequently minimal and not practical enough to make the limb functional. Therapy to the impaired upper extremity should be minimal and that the major rehabilitation efforts should be concentrated in maximizing usage of the non-affected upper extremity and in ambulating with external devices for the ankle and foot.

Subjecting the paralyzed arm of the hemiplegic patients to months of therapy is not only expensive but also frustrating to the already frustrated patients. I am convinced that most disabled patients prefer to learn the true facts and prognoses of their diseases rather than be subjected to exercises that lead to nowhere. Deceiving patients for the sake of sustaining false hopes or to exploit them financially is contrary to their best interests[51, 88, 158]

SECTION III – MISCELLANEOUS

I

INDUSTRY AND ORTHOPAEDICS

Without the contributions made by Industry to orthopaedics, our patients would not have been able to enjoy many of the improvements that have taken place in recent years. A continued relationship between the two groups is essential for future progress.

I believe, however, that this relationship has gotten out of hand, much to the detriment of the orthopaedic profession. It is no longer a balanced relationship. It is a lop-sided one where Industry has the upper hand and the orthopaedic profession serves and responds to Industry. It is a master/employee relationship, where the wealthier of the two parties has the ultimate control. And since Industry is the richer partner, the old adage, "He who pays the piper call the tune", readily applies.

I have devoted many years of my life to the study of this issue [127, 135, 136, 140, 143, 146, 148, 154, 158]. My statements are therefore not the result of impulsive, emotional reactions. They are based on close observation of the evolution of the relationship and its consequences.

Industry controls today, to a great degree, the practice of orthopaedics. It does so in education as well as in research. Neither one of these activities are possible today without strong support from Industry. Not that support for the success of those endeavors is wrong. The contrary is true: support is welcomed. The issue, however, is that Industry dictates the scope and direction of education and research.

Without the financial support of Industry the continuing education of the orthopedists is thought to be impossible. Virtually every educational meeting addressed to an orthopaedic audience is held with Industry support. Industry in many instances, directly or indirectly, dictates the content of the educational venture by appointing or suggesting the speakers.

Currently, the American Academy of Orthopaedic Surgeons is negotiating a deal with Industry, which will create a co-sponsorship in the production of continuing educational courses. I have expressed my deep concern over such a development, as I realize that Industry, within a very short time, will have full control of orthopaedic education. The "leadership" of the Academy responds by saying that they will not tolerate such a scenario. How naïve can they be? Don't they realize that their tenure in office is very brief, and that once the door is open to Industry no one will be able to close it? Have they forgotten the old saying, "He who pays the piper calls the tune?

Over the years I have chaired nearly one hundred continuing educational courses for orthopaedic surgeons as well as for allied health professionals. As chairman of educational committees of the Academy, I presided over hundreds of similar courses. In those days the Academy's dependency on Industry's support was minimal. If profit for the Academy was minimal or non-existent, no one panicked. Education was the name of the game.

SECTION III – MISCELLANEOUS

In the late 1980's I organized an international course dealing with Total Hip and Knee Arthroplasty. The large faculty was composed of some of the most distinguished surgeons in Europe and America. I approached Industry and offered them the opportunity to display their products in the exhibit hall of the hotel. A fee was charged to them for the purpose of subsidizing the expenses incurred in transportation and lodging of the faculty.

Without exception, every one of the invited industrial concerns accepted the invitation. However, three of the accepting companies asked how many of the speakers were they entitled to select. My response was "none", and made it clear to them that the venture was an educational one not a business convention.

I realized then that some successful courses being held around the country are not only subsidized by industry, but also controlled by Industry. The topics discussed inevitably accommodate Industry's desires.

Two of the most popular courses now held regularly in the United States are bazaars where vendors, disguised as orthopaedists, gather to peddle their respective products. One needs only to close one's eyes during some of the scientific presentations made at those meetings and listen to the words. It is often impossible to tell whether the speaker is a surgeon or a vendor of industrial nails, plates, prostheses or other instruments and gimmicks. The Academy has tried to curtail this practice by requiring speakers to acknowledge their industrial involvement. That has become a joke. It punishes those who professionally and ethically have sought involvement with Industry in order to advance their research efforts, but rewards the professional peddlers who wear the asterisks with the pride of highly decorated Russian generals displaying metals on their lapels.

Hundreds if not thousands of "educational" courses and workshops held every year are sponsored by Industry. Most times all expenses are paid by Industry regardless of the location of the meeting. Winter or summer resort areas are the most popular. The meetings consist of practical demonstrations of the "latest" products, where the students have the opportunity to rehearse the surgical procedures in plastic or cadaver bones. Very little if any information is provided regarding the biological considerations behind the surgical procedure. Sometimes a perfunctory lecture dealing with biology is given to avoid criticism.

I have come to the conclusion that the orthopaedic community of the United States would be better served if a number of continuing education courses, rather than structured to teach surgical techniques, were devoted to educate physicians on the appropriate indications for surgery. I reached that conclusions, while observing the types of complications referred to our hospital from other institutions. Though sometimes the complications were the result of improperly performed surgery, in most instances the problem had been created by the performance of surgery for the wrong reasons and under the wrong circumstances.

Research dealing with disorders of the musculoskeletal system is heavily subsidized by Industry. This in itself is commendable as much as is the subsidy of continuing education. However, as in the case of the latter, what should concern our discipline is that the profession finds itself determining its research priorities along lines designed by Industry. Much of the support from Industry to educational institutions for the purpose of conducting research is tied to product-oriented research.

Organized orthopaedics needs to address in earnest its relationship with Industry if it is to regain its autonomy. Further erosion of our professional values and acceptance of the values and ethics of Industry will profoundly affect our future.

INTERVIEWING PROSPECTIVE RESIDENTS

For nearly forty years I was involved in the process of interviewing medical students applying for residency positions. Though, for twenty consecutive years it was my responsibility to organize the interviews and actively participate as an interviewer, I never truly enjoyed the experience. I found it, much too often, a very artificial exercise. It is difficult to form a valid opinion of an applicant on the basis of a few minute chat.

Applicants for residency appointments no longer come to an interview unprepared. Now they take courses on how to respond to questions and which ones to ask themselves. The applicants dress alike in three-piece suits, which I am sure are never worn again. Candor is difficult to bring forward.

I stopped asking medical questions long ago, because I had concluded that by the time the medical student has completed his schooling and is ready to enter residency training, he is very knowledgeable in medical matters. Why then waste time confirming the obvious. I chose to use the brief interview time to asking questions that could shed some light into the inner makeup of the applicant. Questions that relate to the student's feelings about issues unrelated to medicine. For example, I frequently asked about their views on capital punishment, societal changes, or their involvement in civic or church activities. Frequently, I asked about their relationship with parents, grandparents, siblings and friends, as well as the type of sporting activities they enjoyed the most.

Rightly or wrongly, I felt that their answers to those questions were more likely to shed information about them. When I moved to Los Angeles to serve as professor and chief of orthopaedics at the University of Southern California, I encountered an established system of interviewing centered on the applicants potential abilities to function under stressful physical and emotional conditions. The Los Angeles County-USC Medical Center was the institution where the residents spent most of their time during their five years of residency training. The hospital was extremely busy and the residents were expected to work long and arduous hours, with very little attending support. The residents had to assume major responsibilities.

There was a special emphasis on finding out if they felt capable of functioning physically and mentally after 30 hours of interrupted work. The LAC/USC residency program seemed to be designed only for the toughest people. "Machismo" was key for their acceptance. Female applicants were subjected to similar questions and their responses had to match those of their athletic masochistic male counterparts.

SECTION III – MISCELLANEOUS

I never thought such an approach to residency evaluation was conducive to the selection of the best applicants. I tried to change the system but I doubt I had an impact.

One of my favorite questions was, "Describe your strengths to justify your being selected over the five hundred other applicants competing for the 12 positions available". Every applicant had carefully memorized his or her answers, particularly after word got out to expect this question. They all proceeded to recite a litany of virtues such as being in fatigable and committed workers, compassionate, honest, sincere and wonderful team players.

When I asked them to mention their weaknesses, the responses did not usually come out quickly. I understood that. No one really wants to disclose weaknesses during an interview because they fear being ruled out on account of honest answers. On one occasion the fourteen or sixteen people who composed the interview committee interviewed a young lady. When I asked her to mention her assets she responded, "I don't think I have very many. I am pretty much a run of the mill person. My grades in school were far from being the best and in sports I never did well". I anxiously awaited her response to my next question regarding her weaknesses. She said, "Many, and I am not sure you want to find out about all of them. Basically, I lack the aggressiveness that many others possess; I don't have the wit and intellectual speed some of my classmates display; my concentration is not as good as I would like it to be. You would have to ask others that question, because I am sure I am not giving you a complete answer".

I was fascinated by the young woman's candor and preceded to probe further into her life and personal backgrounds. I concluded that she was a first class applicant and hoped the other interviewers would cast, along with me, a favorable vote. That was not the case, however. They concluded she would not make a good resident. Wrong, I said. She would have been not only a good resident but also a very good doctor and a wonderful human being. I don't know if she ever found a residency position in orthopaedics. I doubt it.

Whenever an applicant presents himself, or herself, with a strong record of research activities, the interviewers do their best to convince the student that their program is the ideal one for them and strongly try to recruit the candidate. It took me a long time to realize that participation in research was not always done because of a sincere interest in investigation.

A few years ago one such applicant went through our interview process. He had written several papers while in medical school; spent a great deal of time conducting research and had obtained the most enthusiastic letters from his mentors in the lab. His grades were also very high. He accepted our offer. Just before he was to begin his fourth year of residency he had not done any research. When I approached him and said, "We took you in anticipation that later you will pursue an academic career. What happened to you?" He responded, "Doctor Sarmiento, I spent many days and many nights in the lab during my college and medical school days. I hated every bit of it. I did it because I knew that such a background would enhance my chances of getting into a good residency program. Now that I am in one of them I never, never again want to see the inside of another laboratory for as long as I live". I was floored by his response, which, nonetheless I appreciated very much. It made me open my eyes to reality.

SECTION III – MISCELLANEOUS

Program chiefs take a great deal of pride in having residents that have graduated from the most prestigious medical schools and with the highest grades; those who have conducted research studies and co-authored scientific papers. I must admit that I also strived for a long time to have that type of residents. Eventually I came to the conclusion I was wrong: the medical students with the best grades do not necessarily make the best orthopaedists; high IQ's are not necessary to be a good doctor. Performing research at the undergraduate level does not ensure a future academic career. Our need is for honest, empathetic individuals who are motivated to be professional. Those, who according to the definition of "professionals" would place the interest of the people they serve ahead of their own.

Everyone has long known that those in the medical profession earn high incomes. In the past, applicants for medical school did not, to the best of my knowledge, sought a medical career primarily because of potential financial opportunities. I am sure that there were always exceptions to the rule, but the overwhelming majority of medical students entered the profession motivated with altruistic ideas. The commercialization of medicine that began in earnest in the 1960's brought about a new crop of medical students. Some of them seem to be primarily interested in the profession because of its anticipated economic advantages. As physicians experience daily reduction in their incomes, brought about by health care reform, the new crop of medical students may be returning to the traditions of the past. Furthermore the greater percentage of women graduating from medical school could easily swing the pendulum even faster. I suspect their personality is more conducive to an unselfish view of patient care.

SYNOVIAL CHONDROMATOSIS AND INTRA-ARTICULAR OSTEO-CHONDROMAS:

Loose intra-articular cartilaginous bodies are uncommon. Most times they are clinically inconsequential, but occasionally may create clinical problems. I have had a few patients who had moderately severe symptoms associated with multiple loose bodies in the hip joint. When the involved hips were opened, I found a huge number of loose cartilaginous bodies. Since the x-rays had not shown as many fragments as I found in surgery indicates that many of the bodies were made entirely of cartilage and others were osteochondroma. The latter were the radio-opaque ones. It is logical to assume that the pure cartilaginous ones were the product of synovial metaplasia and the osteochondromas were fragments of initially blood-supplied osteochondromas that became separated from the initial "tumor". I did not realize this until I treated an older man with a giant intraarticular osteochondroma of the knee that had assumed the shape of the underlying condyles of the femur (Fig. 66 a,b,c,d,e.). It was connected to the synovium through a vascular pedicle through which blood supply was carried making ossification possible. Mistakenly I had believed that such growths could form without blood supply [113]. In the few instances of multiple enchondromatosis of the hip the removal of the lose bodies failed to produce a permanent relief of symptoms. Eventually clear radiological and clinical signs and symptoms of osteoarthritis developed. The few patients who had synovial chondromatosis of the hip had the loose bodies removed. However, all of them experienced recurrence of the condition and equired total joint replacement at a later date. One of the showed recurrence within two years and most of the loose bodies had formed a mass that at first glance suggested malignant degeneration.

SECTION III – MISCELLANEOUS

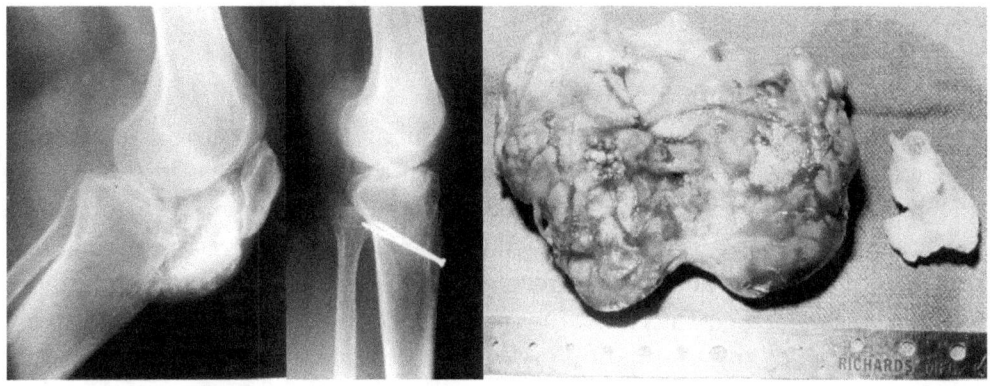

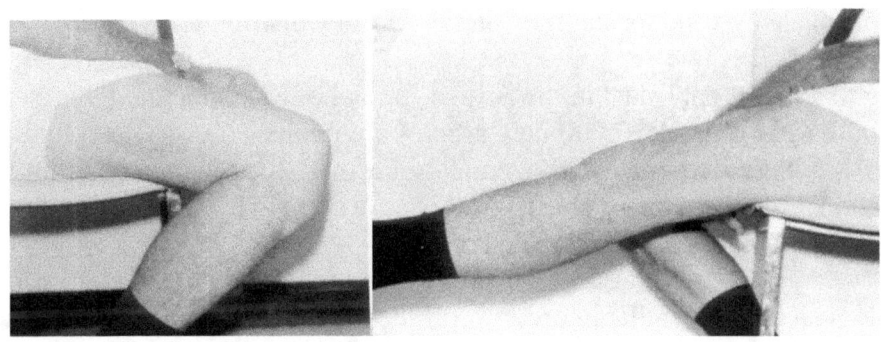

Fig. Giant intraarticular osteochondroma treated with its excision, followed by patellectoy because of advanced degenerative disease and debilitating pain.

SECTION III – MISCELLANEOUS

JOURNALS AND OTHER PUBLICATIONS

The proliferation of medical journals in the recent past is amazing and somewhat difficult to understand. Difficult for me because I am convinced that the orthopaedist of today reads less than he did a few decades ago. Today a good portion of the education of the orthopaedist is gained from attending seminars, continuing education courses and local, State and national meetings. They are also receiving additional information through the Internet. Furthermore, the plethora of through-away magazines that crowd our desks seems unending. Regrettably, the orthopaedist's dependency on information given to him by the vendors of implants and other industrial products has become the main source of information for many practitioners of the art. There are many orthopaedists who change from one appliance to another, simply based on comments made by vendors and the "literature" they distribute.

According to a report published in the British Journal of Medicine in 1996, there are 30,000 medical journals worldwide; 3,000 new articles are published every day; and 1,000 new articles enter Medline. I wish I could accurately estimate the number of orthopaedic journals in circulation throughout the world. In America we seem to have a journal identified with every other conceivable musculoskeletal disorder.

It is only logical to suspect that in order to fill the pages of the monthly publications a large numbers of useless and superfluous papers are published. What is the editor going to do if the time to roll the presses is around the corner and there are not enough "good" papers to print? Publish garbage. Therefore a lot of second-class articles are published every day of the week. I have often wondered what percentage of the papers published in so-called peer-review journals could really survive close scrutiny. Not long ago the editor of one of our most prestigious journals wrote an editorial indicating that the board of editors had decided that the chief editor could request from the authors the raw data upon which the papers were based. It is my understanding that within a few weeks a number of submissions were withdrawn. It tells you something!

Do we need so many journals? Should every subspecialty in orthopaedics have its own journal? Would it not be better if several journals were merged and jointly produce better products? My answer is that there is no need for most of the Journals now published. Ideally, there should be only one, but such a wish is not realistic. Several subspecialty journals have been around for a very long time and there are therefore deeply entrenched. I don't see them willing to compromise at this time. The merging of several journals into a few would be a salutary event. And that is doable.

To support the point that orthopaedists read today a lot less than in the past, I have several times "played a game" with the residents in our program. Without previous notice I asked them from the podium during grand-rounds if they had read the most recent issue of the Bone and Joint Journal. Most nodded to indicate that they had done so. I then chose a hand-full of them and asked them to come to the podium, where I produced the latest copy of the publication. By that time I could see some of the residents blushing and squirming in anticipation of disaster.

SECTION III – MISCELLANEOUS

One by one I read the title of several articles published in that issue and quizzed them on their content. To make a long story short, most of the residents I had questioned had not read any of the articles published in that issue and I suspect of many other issues. At most, some had read a few abstracts.

Shall we blame them for not reading the Journal regularly and for preferring to read the through-away magazines that report almost exclusively on presentations made at various meetings and summaries of presentations selected because of their emotional appeal, as well as papers that report on data not yet subjected to peer review and almost always are based on studies describing a new operation or technique? Tabloid orthopaedics had won the day.

I do not know how to respond to my own concerns, because it is difficult for anyone to read every journal published every month. The JBJS, which some years ago constituted the only source of written information for the orthopaedist, chose, and rightly so, to remain the premier publication upholding the highest levels of sophistication. In the process, however, it ended up publishing many articles that often were difficult to read. The topics were frequently extremely esoteric and indulged in minutia, which most orthopaedists found irrelevant. This practice should not be criticized because, after all, at least one journal had to serve as model to others. History will also recognize the service it did to the profession.

Not that I find every policy of the journal reasonable. Having submitted many papers for publication and having had my share of rejections, I have at times been irritated by some of the excessive "nit-picking" of some of the reviewers. I must admit, however, that after putting up with the nit picking and the large number of revisions the ultimate publications looked good. As a matter of fact a lot better that my original submissions.

In the not too distal past I wondered if JBJS had lost sight of its mission: to educate the orthopaedic community. I suspect the Journal is succeeding in reversing the trend. It recently made changes, which are making the Journal a very attractive publication. These changes will soon result in a return of its previously unchallenged popularity. If people were not reading it as much as they should have, was because they were not getting from it what they thought they needed. They ended up seeking that information elsewhere. By combining esoteric topics with relevant clinical subjects the JBJS is "having the cake and eating it too."

I also believe JBJS missed the opportunity to provide a platform from which issues of importance to the orthopaedic profession can be addressed. There is no such platform anywhere in this country. Throwaway magazines are beginning to fill that void by devoting, on occasion, the editorial page to those issues. That responsibility should rest on the shoulders of a journal with the required moral authority. JBJS is beginning to respond to such a need.

The JBJS has given me a few times the opportunity to write editorials and "commentaries" on issues of the nature I am referring to. I am grateful for that. I know, however, that several reviewers remain reluctant to use the publication for that purpose in a major way. Their pusillanimous attitude is based on concern with involvement in

SECTION III – MISCELLANEOUS

"controversial" issues. That I cannot understand. What is wrong with controversy? What harm can come to the Journal for becoming the vehicle for the expression of ideas that are not always "politically correct? Quite to the contrary, it would enhance its prestige and influence; and in the process reinforce the values upon which the American system of journalism has managed to remain the envy of the world.

Not very long ago I suggested to the editor of one of the most popular "tabloid orthopaedics" the publications of an address I had delivered at a major meeting, where I discussed the orthopaedic relationship with industry. He responded that the message I was sending out was "extremely" sound and that he thoroughly agreed with it. He promised to print portions of the address. However, time passed without reaching the printed stage. Later I received an e-mail from the editor indicating that my critical comments had been found too "risky" by the publishers. They had mentioned the major subsidy they received from industry, and were therefore afraid to antagonize the "hand that was feeding them." This episode speaks volumes about our exaggerated dependency on industry and our loss of autonomy

L

LITIGATION

Litigation against orthopaedic surgeons has reached an intolerable degree, and represents a major source of unhappiness for thousands of orthopaedists throughout the land. The resulting extravagant cost of malpractice insurance is forcing many to practice without such protection. State Legislatures address the ever-increasing problem, but tort reform remains elusive.

The issue is complex and to make it a simple one is ludicrous. Menken once said, "For every major problem there is always a simple answer, which is always wrong". His comment applies to medical malpractice. Whether we want admit it or not, the public needs protection against medical malpractice, and at this time the legal system is the only body structured to determine the most fair and just system.

Needless to say, the problem comes from the rampant dishonesty that a large percentage of attorneys display and which the legal profession seems to have accepted as being appropriate. In order to satisfy the economic thirst of the ridiculous number of attorneys in this country, nuisance litigation is pursued. Enormous amounts of money are demanded in order to compensate for the "suffering" and "pain" experienced by anyone who does not have a perfect result from whatever treatment the orthopaedist carried out. Attorneys drag their "cases" for as long as possible, hoping to better justify their work and get a larger settlement. At the last minutes most cases are settled out of court. The attorneys on both sides of the issue benefit.

The only hope for reasonable tort reform may come soon, as the legislators confront a serious situation, which will affect the public. Until now the public has not expressed any interest in taking sides with the medical profession. This silence speaks volumes, as it sends a message that should disturb us. I suspect the public welcomes the costs of malpractice insurance, because they have come to the conclusion that the medical profession is composed of people who are more interested in making fortunes, rather than providing compassionate care to those in need. If they had felt differently, I am sure we would have heard from them long ago.

That perception on the part of the public will not be reversed unless we openly display the tenets of professionalism they expect from us. The public learns from the media of the frequent prosecutions of physicians because of Medicare and Medicare fraud. We hear of wrong-side surgery, erroneous diagnoses, unnecessary performance of surgery and consultations with other physicians, and the prescription of useless tests and treatments. They are aware of the high income of physicians and expect them to devote more time to them and be treated with greater empathy. They only see the dark side of medicine, which makes them forget the many benefits they receive from their doctors. They assume that the

SECTION III – MISCELLANEOUS

medical profession is heavily contaminated and that with the possible exception of their individual doctors, all others are money-hungry businessmen.

We need to do much to assist in the solution of the problem. To insist that we are "lily white" and the "others" are the only culprits, will not take us anywhere. We must get our house in orders and realize that we often encourage the perpetuation of litigation against us.

Examples to illustrate our fault abound. Currently, the most common cause of malpractice against orthopaedists in South Florida has to do with failure to operate on wrist fractures. We have not had the courage to stand up and be counted by stating unequivocally that mild anatomical deviations are not complications. Rather we follow the surgically trend because "monkey see, monkey do" and it gives us a higher reimbursement. This is happening in many other areas. It appears that a "bad result" from surgery is understandable. In the case of fracture care, if a complication occurs or the result is not perfect, "The doctor did every possible thing to obtain a perfect result." If a problem follows the nonsurgical treatment of the same condition, "The doctor failed to operate and therefore practice the modern standards of care."

We perform too much surgery and that trend has increased the changes of litigation. We perform too many unnecessary laminectomies and spine fusions; too many arthroplasties; too many open reductions of fractures; too many arthroscopic procedures; too many carpal tunnel releases; too many surgical procedures in the hand and foot. We use the excuse that such surgeries are necessary and represent the state of the art. I agree, but only if they are performed with moderation and logic. The idea that surgery is always the preferred treatment because best helps to offset reduced reimbursements is wrong and unethical.

We prescribe expensive MRIs and CT scans for conditions that do not need them. We claim that employers and insurance companies require them. Wrong. We should stand up and make it clear that we do not agree with such an irrational request. If the findings from those studies are "suggestive" of some abnormality, we immediately institute expensive surgical treatments without admitting that very simple nonsurgical approaches can provide a resolution to the "problem." Some argue that if those tests are nor performed they will be accused of not doing the right thing. Often, this is an excuse used to legitimize the financial gains they have from this practice.

Finding orthopaedist to testify against their colleagues is no longer a problem. There are many unscrupulous surgeons who make living traveling around the country making court appearance doing just that. On the other hand, recruiting hones physicians to objectively testify in support of others is beset with difficulties. Somehow they seem to be afraid of "being embarrassed" by the "other" attorney."

Academia has also contributed to the aggravation of the problem. Recently I heard a professor of orthopaedics state publicly that an orthopaedist commits medical malpractice if he fails to prescribe Vancomycin following the implantation of metal in the body. When I pressured him to justify what I thought was a wrong practice, he responded that such was "the standard of care in the community." Nothing could be further form truth. No

SECTION III – MISCELLANEOUS

orthopaedist in the area agreed with professor's statement. Unwittingly, the professor was encouraging litigation. (COMLICATIOS AND LITIGATION)

We also add coals to the fire by the manner in which we publish in the medical literature. Traditionally, our publications are organized in such a manner that the case material and methodology are first described, followed by results, complications and then a discussion. In the case of fractures, for example, we present as complications infections, nounions, nerve injuries and other legitimate problems. They are without any boubt complications. However, we also list as complications angular changes and shortening. These findings are sometimes "real" complications. But should any shortening or angulation be considered a complication? Can we call minimal shortening of the tibia or femur a complication when we know that such shortening does not produce a limp, is not noticed by anyone and is not accompanied with late adverse sequella? The same applies to minimal residual angulation at the fracture site.

We seem to have forgotten that attorneys also have access to the Internet. They read our publications and realize that we, orthopaedic surgeons, call those changes "complications", even though they are often recognized only through radiological examinations. The attorneys then argue that if those "deviations from the normal" the experts call complications, their clients should be compensated.

SECTION III – MISCELLANEOUS

M

MAGNETIC RESONANCE IMAGING - MRI

What a spectacular development the MRI has been! It is difficult to think of any other technical innovation in the diagnostic field that can equal the impact that the MRI has had in orthopaedics. It has literally revolutionized the profession. However, like any new technology, it is struggling to find its appropriate niche. At this time we continue to "stretch the envelope" in the hope of being able to determine its true value and the proper indications for its usage.

At this time the technique is being abused to a major degree and is rapidly replacing physical examination. At the suspicion of any intra-articular pathology and before a careful physical examination is conducted, a MRI is requested. Often if it shows any deviation from the normal, a diagnosis of surgically treatable pathology is established.

I do not find it difficult to believe that one day MRI studies will conducted in virtually all conditions of the musculoskeletal. They provide information that plain x-rays do not. The question that will be increasingly asked is "how does that information affect treatment?" If it does, then the MRI should be used? If it does not, the expense cannot be justified. I have been involved in numerous discussion regarding the value of MRI studies in intra-articular fractures. There is no doubt that the MRI provides additional data but many times that data does not, in any way, influence the treatment. The MRI, in those instances, provides data but not useful information.

At the University of Miami a large number of students involved in athletics were entered into a study. They were chosen because they denied any history of shoulder problems. Their shoulder were examined via the MRI. A very high percentage of them had "positive" MRIs, which if found in patients with symptoms would have had arthroscopic examinations.

There are dangers in allowing the technique to run unbridled. Though it is true that the MRI has facilitated tremendously the diagnosis of pathology previously difficult to recognize, it has also allowed the pervasive pattern of relying too heavily on the findings depicted in the impressive visual evidence. Oftentimes, what the MRI shows as abnormal has no clinical significance. Often, however, some type of treatment is instituted. Arthroscopy is usually the next step since in a "knee jerk" reaction any abnormal MRI findings are immediately subjected to the procedure. The cost of this practice has escalated exponentially and I see nothing on the horizon to suggest that moderation is about to set in.

At the slightest symptoms of back pain, even in the absence of neurological findings MRI's are ordered indiscriminately. I suspect that any person older than fifty and without history of back pain shows some changes either in the intervertebral discs, the spinal foramina or some other structure. This, in my opinion, explains the obscene epidemic of

SECTION III – MISCELLANEOUS

spine surgery that now sweeps the land. The legal problems that our profession faced a few months ago regarding the "pedicle screw" can be partially explained by the abuse of an operation which when performed for the appropriate indications is a very sound procedure.

Unscrupulous members of the legal profession have taken full advantage of the new MRI technology by obtaining an MRI on their customers (through equally unscrupulous physicians) claiming an injury either at work or in situations likely to be amenable to litigation. Since today MRI's are done in facilities that are open to the public, virtually anyone can request a MRI and claims of abnormalities or legitimate pathology can be readily documented.

The dilemma presented by use of MRI is that every day we find more and more legitimate indications for its use. Attempts to regulate its use before we determine its appropriate boundaries would be a mistake. On the other hand, hoping that honesty will suddenly creep into the entire medical and legal professions, is an exercise in futility. Perhaps local monitoring systems in hospitals might have some tempering beneficial effect. I still doubt it.

SECTION III – MISCELLANEOUS

N

NURSING HOMES

There is nothing that older people fear more than ending up in a nursing home. To them it is the end of independence and the surrender of all human autonomy. They have seen pictures or have visited friends or relatives in such facilities. The thought of becoming one of "them" is frightening.

The fear, as far as I am concerned, is legitimate. Too many nursing homes are dumping grounds where every bit of dignity is lost and where care is non-existent. They are profitable business ventures, and if one knows how to manipulate the system, handsome profits can be made.

Now that Medicare and Medicaid pay for a number of weeks of rehabilitation care in hospital Skill Nursing Units, in nursing homes and in rehabilitation centers, the business of taking care of the elderly has become a bonanza. It is commendable to see such programs made available to the elderly, but the abuses being committed in its name are appalling. Fraud is reported on a daily basis throughout the country. Miami, the medical- fraud capital of the United States, gives you a good education on the subject.

A couple of years ago, a small hospital in Miami was sold to a group of entrepreneurs. A large for-profit health-care corporation had owned that hospital. The bed occupancy had been low for a period of time. Five days after the new owners took over, the bed occupancy went up dramatically. Their "secret' for the success quickly became public knowledge: a large number of patients were transferred from nursing homes to the hospital under a variety of different diagnoses. Not a difficult thing to do, since old people under custodial care are bound to suffer from chronic conditions such as hypertension, diabetes, heart disease, arthritis, pressure sores, etc. etc.

Once in the hospital all types of tests were requested. Everyone had a chest x-ray, blood count and urine analysis. Consultants from various specialties were summoned. They, in turn, requested additional tests and prescribed the "appropriate" medications. Of course "rehabilitation" was mandatory. The twenty one day Medicare-paid arrangement was sufficient. At a later date, if still alive, those same patients would be once again readmitted for the same round of "medical services".

More recently I learned that there are Nursing Homes where the medical director is empowered to request whatever in-patient tests, medications or consultations he deems appropriate. Anything goes!

I have often wondered how I would like to spend the last years of my life if I live to a ripe old age with my marbles still somewhat preserved. Would I like to be left alone, to vegetate and die peacefully at home, or to be dumped in a Nursing Home with people around telling me to do things I have no desire to do? To have some well-intentioned do-gooder call

SECTION III – MISCELLANEOUS

me "honey" and send me to the :treatment area to participate in the useless ritual of physical therapy, where in tandem with others in the same or worse shape than I am go through the motions of lifting my arms and legs up and down for a few minutes every day?

That is what goes on in many Skilled Nursing Units and Rehabilitation Centers around the country. Once the period of Medicare-approved rehabilitation is finished, the "need" for addition therapy seems to come to an end. Is it possible that the government in its infinite wisdom guessed that in precisely 21 days everybody would get maximum improvement from rehabilitation? Or that greed dictates that when the approved period of time has come to an end it is time to stop? (See REHABILITATION).

O

OBJECTIVITY

See Addendum #

===

OSTEOARTHRITIS (See OSTEOARTHRITIS Section II, THE HIP JOINT)

===

OUTCOME STUDIES

Analysis of clinical results based on retrospective studies are being criticized at this time on the grounds that conclusions drawn from such reviews are flawed because they lack the benefits that prospective, double blind, placebo-controlled studies have to offer. There is little doubt that the argument is sound. I think, however, that the proponents of the new method have gone too far in their enthusiasm and seem to have concluded that traditional methods of reporting clinical results are unreliable and not worthy of publication. They have forgotten that we are where we are today, that is in a very advanced degree of sophistication, thanks to studies which in most instances were not prospective, double blind and non-placebo controlled. I do not think the way to advance new ideas is by condemning old ones, much less before having proved the superiority of the new ones.

Some orthopaedic outcome studies conducted in the manner now being proposed are expensive to carry out. They call for the hiring of additional personal that most physicians and many academic departments or medical offices cannot afford. Consistency in documenting extensive data is often poor. The "verifiable questionnaires" to which investigators must adhere in order to make their reports "worthy of publication" are awkward, complicated and full of irrelevant questions. When the project is multi-institutional the problems are compounded manifold. (See STATISTICS).

This criticism cannot be extended to all ongoing Outcome Studies. That would be a mistake. Many of the pioneers of the method are very knowledgeable and committed individuals. My criticism is intended to be constructive and I simply wish to avoid hurtles that impede progress.

I participated in the American Academy of Orthopedic Surgeons' original attempts to develop outcome studies dealing with total hip arthroplasty. It was an uncomfortable experience and I predicted that as proposed the project was condemned to failure.

For example, a questionnaire that the participating patients were expected to complete had no relevance to the project under study. Elderly patients, (most total hip

SECTION III – MISCELLANEOUS

arthroplasty patients are elderly) who are experiencing or have already experienced deterioration of their physical and mental abilities, are expected to state whether they can walk one block, two blocks, ten blocks or more; climb one flight, two flights or three flights of steps. Silly and meaningless questions because most elderly people do not walk more than short distances. Let's assume, however, that the question has merit. What do you do with the information? Report that 15% of the patients can walk one block and another 15% three blocks? What does that mean and what do we learn from it?

Another question was whether the patients held on to the rail when walking down stairs. What meaningful information can be obtained from this question? Holding on to the rail is something that many do for reasons that have nothing to do with the operated hip. They did it routinely long before their hips became painful. Once again, let us assume that the information is important. Then what do you do with it? What do you do with the information in view of the fact that a large number of elderly people never walk stairs because there are none in the house or nursing home where they live? Once again, what do we gain from knowing that a certain percentage of elderly patients, whose hip were replaced, held on to the rail? What do you do with the data? Nothing. If that is the case, then why then ask those silly questions.

Obtaining long term responses from older people about the condition of their operated joints is extremely difficult. I personally prepared a simple questionnaire for my total hip patients scattered throughout the country. I send it to them every year accompanied with a form letter to which I always add a hand-written friendly comment. The questionnaire simply asks questions about the presence or absence of pain and the degree of external assistance needed for walking. The questions on pain are limited to whether the hip is totally painless, painful only upon getting up, the hip is painful and the pain is either tolerable or intolerable. The form has space for checking whatever category is most appropriate. A number of elderly patients do not understand those simple instructions and check all categories. In the space provided for comments they often write a note indicating that the pain they have is intolerable. However, after contacting them on the phone I have found out a number of times that the hips are painless but their spines, feet or knees are giving them pain. A sample of the unreliability of questionnaires when dealing with older patients.

It is necessary in most instances to establish an end-point to determine the outcome of a given procedure. In the case of cancer, death is the end-point. Most have used "revision" as the endpoint for total hip replacements. This end-point is very misleading. For example, the x-ray of a total hip shows continuous radiolucent lines both in the acetabulum and femur; the components have migrated; the cement is fractured; and even lysis in various locations is recognizable. Even in the presence of such radiological changes, the hip can still be painless. If painful, the patient may not want to have additional surgery. That hip is not revised and therefore, according to the criterion for failure, this patient is not classified as a "failure". In other instances we, the surgeons, do not recommend surgery for an obviously failed arthroplasty because of the patient's age or compromised general condition that preclude a surgical intervention. Once again, this "failed" joint is not considered "failed "because it was not revised.

SECTION III – MISCELLANEOUS

I suspect that many reports in the literature that indicate very high degrees of success are based on data obtained in this erroneous manner. It is because of this that one must be careful in interpreting reports that claim a very low incidence of "failures".

Recently, I read a paper on closed tibial fractures written by experts in the field of outcome studies. The authors claimed to have reviewed several thousand articles dealing with the subject. I wonder if one of the authors read them all or the task was divided among all the authors! It must have taken a lot of time even if we assume they did nothing else during that time. In any event, they concluded that they could not find any articles that met the requisites of a good review paper. From the over two thousand papers, they discovered a few that came close to meeting the requirements. One of these chosen papers was one I had published some thirty years ago, in which I described my initial experiences with the treatment of tibial fractures using a below-the-knee cast in one hundred patients. They totally ignored the fact (which was known to them) that several of my original recommendations I had modified or recanted in subsequent papers in which I reported on seven hundred patients, and a more recent one on one thousand patients. The latter two articles addressed a multitude of factors that had not been identified previously.

Another flaw of outcome studies is that the prejudices of the authors often play a major role in the preparation of the study. For example, they compare two different procedures and leave out others, which the investigators do not use, but others prefer. The conclusions, however, are that the "best treatment" for a given condition is the one that in the comparative study between their two chosen methods provided the best results.

Health Care Reform has brought many problems to the delivery of medical care, created many hurdles and a multitude of difficulties for those interested in conducting clinical research. Long term follow-up of patients is forbidden by most, if not all, health plans. There is no possible way to study the long-term effects of many medical conditions. Trauma has suffered the most. Once the patient receives initial care, his follow-up is frequently approved only in another facility. The initial treating physician never sees him again. Therefore, many outcome studies become meaningless. I hope and trust that this "plague" of for-profit managed care will soon be eradicated.

My criticism is not of outcome studies per se. I recognize their worth, so much that during my Academy presidential tenure I persuaded the Board of Directors to establish a Center for Research within the walls of the Academy. The first activities of the Center were to be the preparation of Outcome Studies projects.

Outcome studies are currently financed by major governmental organizations and they are expensive. I am concerned that one of these days the funding agencies will be asking, " what has come out of the project?" If the answer is that nothing concrete has been produced; that compliance has been difficult to achieve; that the medical community has not been able to see the superior value of the method; and its cost precludes the practitioner of medicine from getting involved, then the projects will die.

P

PHYSICAL THERAPY

When I was offered the chairmanship of the department of orthopaedics at the University of Miami in 1970, I indicated to the dean of the School of Medicine that I would like to name the new department the Department of Orthopaedics and Rehabilitation. He agreed and we became the first such department in the country. Within a few years others followed suit and renamed their departments in the same manner.

The idea of having a department of Orthopaedics and Rehabilitation was based on my strong conviction that rehabilitation was an integral part of orthopaedics and that by neglecting it we were losing important territory. Territory that because of our comprehensive training we needed to preserve. Physical and Occupational Therapy, therefore, became very important to me. Their role in the management of the neuro-muscular-skeletally impaired was essential. A respectful cooperation between orthopaedics and Physical and Occupational was developed and our educational programs blossomed.

I pursued the concept of giving the therapists a great deal of latitude and authority in the management of patients. A sharing of information and joint educational programs fully justified such an approach. It worked well for us during the time I remained in Miami. Now, as I look at the relationship between orthopaedics and physical and occupational therapy, I wonder if our thoughts in the sixties and seventies were sound. That relationship has vanished. The two professions have drifted apart and there is virtually no contact between the two. Physical and Occupational Therapy are now fully independent professions who take care of their own destiny.

Was this development good for patient care or simply one that satisfied the ego of the therapists and nothing else? Are patients better off today because of the absent relationship between the two disciplines? I have serious doubts and continue to believe that we could have worked a mutually beneficial compromise that would have allowed the perpetuation of a meaningful and respectful relationship. No point worrying about it now, since such a solution is out of the question. The "horse is out of the barn."

When I moved from the University of Miami to the University of Southern California in 1978, I was appalled by the lack of physical therapy resources at the Los Angeles County-University of Southern California Medical Center, the main teaching hospital of the Medical School. In Miami we had a large number of therapists covering all services and the program was under our jurisdiction. The outpatient clinics were always attended by physical and/or occupational therapists who became involved in the care of patients from the very beginning. In the Los Angeles County Hospital, the number of therapist was very small. One and one half therapist covered the orthopaedic service which had nearly two hundred in-patients. I don't believe I ever saw a therapist in any of our clinics in fifteen years. Never once did we hold a conference where therapists were in attendance. In Miami all the occupational and

SECTION III – MISCELLANEOUS

physical therapists in the department attended our weekly Grand Rounds and actively participated in that activity.

In Los Angeles I personally ran a Fracture Brace Clinic where we saw approximately sixty or seventy patients a week. No therapist ever came to those clinics. I expected that the clinical results in California would be inferior to those we had in Miami. Surprisingly, there was no difference. Patients were instructed by the residents on what to do to regain function and to progress in their recovery. Soon I got used to the system just as we get used to about everything in life.

Medicine, much to our displeasure has become more a business than a profession. The recent "health care crisis" has done nothing but aggravate the situation. This is also true for Physical and Occupational Therapy. When professions become businesses, patients suffer. The abuses committed on behalf of Physical and Occupational Therapy are rampant. It appears that anybody with any medical or surgical condition needs physical therapy; and lots of it. Money, big money can be made from it.

There is now a rule that forbids Physical Therapists to take care of the rehabilitation needs of the upper extremity. Several times I have been requested by Physical Therapists to order occupational therapy for total hip patients of mine. On one occasion, when I asked he reason for the request, I was informed that the patient's upper extremities "were weak". When I probed further, I was told that the elderly lady was recovering fast from the hip surgery but a program of "intensive" occupational therapy should be very helpful. Helpful to whom? Obviously not to the patient who lived at home alone and who prior to being admitted to the hospital for the hip surgery procedure had managed to carry out all daily activities without difficulty. The "intensive" occupational therapy was good only for the hospital business. Medicare would pay for the "services" without any questions being asked..

I have limited my surgical practice to total hip surgery exclusively for the past thirty years and have developed opinions regarding the role that physical therapy should play in the management of these patients. Their role is important but should not be exaggerated. Therapists are the best qualified people to instruct patients in transfer and ambulation activities, to emphasize measure that prevent dislocation and thromboembolic disease and to reassure them and to provide comfort. But as far as I am concerned, that should be the extent of their involvement. With the exception of active abduction, range of motion exercises of the lower extremities may be unnecessary and even harmful. Following surgery one wants the soft tissues to scar down so dislocation does not occur. Trying to regain full range of motion early may preclude the desirable tightness of the tissues. Mother Nature will spontaneously restores the "necessary" motion after the patient returns to normal activities.

Based on that philosophy, only on rare occasions do I order any post-discharge supervised therapy for my total hip patients? During the five to seven days in the hospital they learn to transfer from bed to chair, how to climb steps, get in and out of a car and how to ambulate with the aid of crutches or a walker. Very rarely is subsequent supervised home physical therapy ordered.

What is the point of sending a therapist to visit patients at home, at a high cost, to see them do the same things they can do several times a day without supervision? However, since home therapy is good business, social workers and therapists encourage patients while still in the hospital to request home therapy. They make it sound as an indispensable step in their recovery. In addition, they argue, the patients are entitled to it since Medicare pays for it. I have lost several patients I had planned to operate upon, when they found out that I did not routinely prescribe therapy after discharge from the hospital.

I had the opportunity to see the protocols used at a hospital for the administration of Physical and Occupational therapy. It was a shocking experience. They had no scientific or empirical foundations to justify many of the procedures. Six months of post-surgery therapy was not all unusual, even for some simple orthopaedic conditions. Often, for situations that required no more than simple instructions for patient to follow at home without supervision. I do not understand why Medicare officials and third party payers companies have failed to recognize the great waste of money providing unnecessary rehabilitation services [158].

PODIATRY

The growth and expansion of the scope of podiatry over the past thirty years disturbs orthopaedists who see their territory eroded in a major way. The orthopaedist completed his training convinced that his qualifications to take care of disorders of the foot were unquestioned. They saw the podiatrist as a practitioner whose expertise was limited to the care of ingrown toenails, the prescription of arch supports and the trimming of callosities.

Suddenly the podiatrist became competition. At first this was dismissed. It was assumed that the was no way that organized orthopaedics would allow the podiatrists to carry out surgical procedures that had been traditionally performed by orthopaedists! It was inconceivable that someone without medical school and residency training would attempt to challenge the system.

The orthopaedic profession experienced a rude awakening when its members realized that organized medicine was powerless in preventing podiatry's intrusion into traditional orthopaedics. Almost overnight, they saw hospital credentialing committees open the hospitals' doors to podiatrists, who effectively claimed expertise in the medical and surgical management of all disorders of the foot. At first it was the foot, then the ankle and later the leg. Insurance companies also gave opportunities to the podiatrists to compete with the orthopaedists, assuming that their services were cheaper and probably as effective.

How did all this happen and so rapidly? Mainly due to complacency on the part of orthopaedic surgeons. We took for granted that if allowed to perform major surgery, the podiatrists would soon find themselves in trouble with litigation and high malpractice settlements and premiums. That, however, did not take place. Quite the contrary, the scope of podiatry grew larger by the day.

The orthopaedist was then satisfied carrying out the new and glamorous surgical procedures that arthroscopy, total joint replacement and spinal instrumentation had created

SECTION III – MISCELLANEOUS

for them. The had concluded that taking care of the mundane and "dirty work" of taking care of sores, calluses and ingrown toenails was to be done by others with less education. Those services could not be obtained from orthopaedists when requested from other practitioners of medicine. The podiatrist, on the other hand was their beck and call, ready to render those menial services. Consequently, we lost the support of our colleagues. Diabetic clinics soon became staffed only by podiatrists.

While we slept podiatry began to lobby state legislatures and bombarded them with daily requests. The practitioners of podiatry were voluntarily taxed by their representative organizations for the purpose of lobbying. At one time every podiatrist in the country paid $400.00 a year to their Academy for that purpose. I do not know what the amount is today. In any event the measure paid handsomely. State legislatures, one after another approved their requests for expanded privileges. When applications for privileges were discussed at hospitals' credentialing committees, the fear of litigation forced those committees to relax their rules and accommodate the new practitioners.

Today in many States podiatrists have privileges to perform all kinds of minor and major surgical procedures on the foot and ankle. In most Sates the podiatrists treat fractures of the foot and ankle as well as of the leg. Soon, I anticipate, they will be doing surgery on the knee and hand. They will claim (as a matter of fact they are already claiming) that many disorders of foot have their origin in the knee and hip joints and therefore they should be the ones best qualified to handle those problems. I suspect they will also successfully claim that the hand, being anatomically so similar to thee foot, should also be part of their territory. The current political environment favors the expansion, since quality of care is remote in the minds of those now controlling health care delivery. To them profit is the only thing that matters.

During my tenure as professor and chief of orthopaedics at the University of Miami in the 1970s, I found myself embroiled in a major controversy with a podiatrist who applied for surgical privileges at Jackson Memorial Hospital, the main teaching hospital for the University of Miami Medical School. It was my responsibility to prepare the hospital's delineation of privileges for podiatry. They ended up being very restrictive and limited the podiatrists to carrying out procedures that did not go below the skin.

The podiatrist in question turned out to be a committed individual who apparently told himself that by hook or by crook he would win his battle. I suspect that he was being used by his national organization in an effort to break the status quo. Not willing to accept the Board of Trustees' privileges, he requested and received approval to present his case before the Board. To his first appearance he brought along his own attorney. That made the Trustees quite nervous and they asked me to compromise. I promptly rejected the idea.

On a monthly basis for nearly six months, the Trustees met the podiatrist and his attorney. During that first meeting, he provided his extensive curriculum vitae, a list of the various honors he had received over the years, and copies of the operative reports of the 500 different surgical procedures he had performed the previous year.

SECTION III – MISCELLANEOUS

He argued that the care of the foot of the indigent population at the Hospital was badly neglected by the orthopaedic service. He flashed statistics indicating that during the course of the previous year, and while he performed 500 surgical procedures, the department of orthopaedics had performed only approximately 100 procedures. This in spite of the fact that the department had ten orthopaedic surgeons on his full-time faculty, an additional 30 voluntary faculty and 00 orthopaedic residents.

I responded that if we had used the same lax criteria for the performance of surgery, we would have performed several thousand operations during the same time. I added that, in my opinion, greed was the reason for his large number of surgeries. The hospital attorney, sitting next to me, kicked me under the table and pleaded with me not to make remarks of that nature. I was well aware of the political incorrectness of my remarks, but wanted to set the stage for future discussions.

Having failed again, he proceeded to request that he be examined by a group of appointed individuals from various medical and surgical departments within the hospital. I warned the trustees against such a request and made it clear that they were being set up. They ignored my concern and proceeded with the appointment of a group composed of internists, general surgeons, anesthesiologists and a pathologist.

The podiatrist performed exceptionally well during the interrogation. He had all the right answers. He knew how to diagnose medical complications and how to treat them, be it a diabetic coma, an allergic reaction or an infection. However, at the end of every response he added that the answers he was giving were predicated on his being alone with the patient at the time of the emergency, and without the services of others with greater expertise in the respective areas. Then he said, "I do exactly what doctor Sarmiento does under similar circumstances: provide emergency care while waiting for someone else to follow through with definitive care". He was right. Since I was not permitted to participate in this session I had to remain silent.

At an earlier meeting, I made reference to the fact that organized medicine had been denied access to schools of podiatry to assess their quality and that their practitioners were not subjected to board certification of any kind. Two months later the podiatrist in this story made the announcement that he had successfully past his Board Certification examinations. I assume his profession got busy in a hurry and established some type of Board to accommodate the situation at hand.

Pretending to be desperate with the lack of progress in his negotiations with the trustees, the podiatrist walked into the meeting one day and announced that he had dismissed his attorney and was willing to put his fate in my hands. He stated, "Doctor Sarmiento is an honorable man and I propose that he scrub with me in surgery and observe my performance. He can do it one time, ten times or a hundred times. If after that time he still feels that I am not qualified to do surgery, I will leave and none of you will ever hear from me again".

I sensed a sigh of relief on the part of the trustees, who anticipated that I would accept his proposal. I responded that I had been an educator of medical students and orthopaedic residents for quite some time and had paid relatively little attention to the surgical skills of

SECTION III – MISCELLANEOUS

the students. That I had assumed that if they lacked such skills, they themselves would have chosen a non-surgical discipline. "For me", I said "there are other things more important than surgical skills, such as empathy for patients, concern for their plights, integrity and honesty. Those who had not met those requirements were let go. In the case of the doctor concerned, I cannot in all honesty say that he meets those requirements. He has told us how much surgery he does, which in my opinion is excessive. From that I have surmised that financial profit is the most important consideration in his professional life."

The meetings with the Trustees were over. He then went the route of the Courts. There he fought the battle without an attorney as he chose to represent himself. After a lengthy trial, a verdict was rendered in our favor. He had sued the various parties for 50 million dollars, an amount unheard of in the mid-seventies.

I had already left Miami for Los Angeles when the litigation was over. I received a telephone call from our attorneys while celebrating the victory at a noisy bar. He said that they had just toasted, "Doctor Sarmiento's stubborn commitment to do the right things". It made me feel good.

If had to face a similar situation today I would not follow the same rout. Things have changed and podiatry is in a more secure position at this time. I, for example, could not argued that podiatrists have no training in surgical matters. We, the orthopaedist took care of correcting that deficiency. We invited them to attend our own continuing education courses dealing with surgery of the foot. A very well-known and distinguished orthopaedist said to me when I questioned the wisdom of inviting podiatrists to attend his bio-skill courses that, "he was educating them on the seriousness of major surgery so they would not attempt it in their practices." What naïve logic. What made him think that anyone would be willing to spend several hundred dollars in tuition, plus all the expenses that go along with traveling and accommodations, plus the loss of income for several days, and then not practice what he had learned during those days?

In addition, podiatrists needed only to call the manufactures of surgical implants to find out how to use them. Industry readily responded to their request as they saw new and lucrative marketing opportunities. This is exactly what neurosurgeons did a few years later, when they decided to perform spine fusions and carry surgical correction of spinal deformities.

During my tenure as president of the American Academy of Orthopaedics in 1991-92, I received an invitation from the president of the Academy of Podiatry for a personal meeting. He wanted to discuss the possibility of joining forces to develop joined ventures between the two Academies. He argued that health care reform was going to affect both groups equally and therefore joining forces would be in everybody's best interest. No doubt he was right in saying that the politics of reimbursement was going to hit everybody in medicine.

We held a very cordial meeting. I told him that before I could take his message to our Board of Directors, I needed to know two things. First, was his profession willing to have its educational programs open for scrutiny from others outside podiatry? Secondly, how did podiatry define its scope, so we could understand the rapid changes taking place in his discipline? I illustrated my point by the fact that the previous year a referendum had taken place at his annual Academy meeting to determine whether or not the field of podiatry should be extended to the knee or remain at the level of the ankle. I said that I had learned that those in favor of staying at the level of the ankle had the higher number of votes. "Do you determine your field of expertise by vote?", I asked. He responded by saying that we should not pay attention to such a referendum, since some mavericks within the Academy brought it about. I rebutted his explanation by saying, "They may have been mavericks but, I submit to you, they were powerful enough to receive approval to hold the referendum. Let's assume that another referendum is called next year and the majority votes in favor extending the scope of podiatry to the knee. Does that agreement become official and from then on the entire podiatry profession can claim competency in the care of disorders of the knee? " Our conversation came to an end shortly afterwards without any concrete resolution of issues.

It is a fact of life that podiatry is here to stay. IT will continue to play an ever expanding role in the delivery of health care, much the same that others such as chiropractors, nurses, physician's assistants and others on the fringes of medicine have already accomplished. The current economic environment favors their ambitions since third party payers, for-profit hospitals, and managed care organizations see competition as being good for them. Not for the patients but for them.

On one occasion I was part of group of orthopaedists who visited the offices of the Trade Commission in Washington to inquire about the possibilities of them curtailing the growth of bogus boards in questionable disciplines. The response we received was clear and pithy: the government was not interested in interfering in such a problem. As a matter of fact the competition that unregulated boards creates should help in the reduction of the escalating growth in the health care delivery. So much for concern about quality.

PROFESSIONALISM

In spite of the many problems facing the medical profession I can't think of one more deserving of attention than that of loss of professionalism in our ranks. I first brought this to the attention of my peers during my vice-presidential address to the American Academy of Orthopaedics in 1991 (Addendum No. 1).

A professional has been defined as an individual who, as possessor of especial knowledge within a specified realm, places the interest of those he serves before his own. That is exactly what the physician, as a professional, is supposed to do. This has never meant that the medical doctor is expected to provide services free of charge and therefore not benefit financially from caring for the ill and injured. Quite the contrary, it has always been agreed throughout the centuries that charging for medical services rendered is a legitimate practice. Even the medical missionary working in dark corners of Africa or in other less economically fortunate parts of the world, must receive something in return for his services, be it in the form of food or materials needed for his existence.

SECTION III – MISCELLANEOUS

When medicine becomes primarily a business; when making more and more profit at the expense of patients is the name of the game, we lose professionalism. This is what patients resent about our profession, because much too often such "hunger for more" is obvious to them. It does not have to be only when the physician unfairly and directly charges too much for his services. It is equally as wrong when he takes advantage of third party payers and orders unnecessary tests, performs borderline surgery and prescribes medicines or therapies of various types in order to increase his income.

Greed has crept into our profession to a very undesirable degree. To a great extent, whether we want to admit it or not, greed in the medical profession, para-professionals and in the medical/industrial complex, helps to explain the draconian cuts in the reimbursement for services provided that we have witnessed in the last few years. Hospitals, particularly the for-profit ones, have abused the system in high degrees. The provision of quality care seems to be the furthest consideration in their activities. If the stock value of the organization drops a few points, panic sets in. The corporate elite then responds by reducing even further important medical services. Those organizations have no heart. Adam Smith, the alleged father of Capitalism must be turning in his grave seeing how much his theory of profit with "compassion" has been so badly abused [136, 158].

A clear sign of loss of professionalism in medicine is the way many physicians now advertise themselves by a number of available means. They use newspaper and magazines, the radio and television and more recently the Internet, to market their alleged superior expertise and qualifications. Not long ago, such practices were frown upon and were considered inappropriate and demeaning. It should have remained so. We cheapen ourselves when we indulge in actions of that nature. (See ADVERTISING).

When the physician accepts money for the inclusion of his patients in alleged new drug studies he lowers himself and invites patients' loss of trust. When he becomes a tool of industry for the marketing of products, he not only discredits the profession but harms the progress of his discipline.

SECTION III – MISCELLANEOUS

R

REGISTRIES

The sophistication brought about by revolutionary advances in communication and computer sciences has given impetus to the establishments of Registries for a number of medical conditions. It makes sense to take advantage of such progress in an effort to obtain more reliable information and therefore advance the state of the art.

During my tenure as president of the Hip Society in the late 1970s, I made the establishment of a Total Hip Registry an important focus of my administration. There were at that time less than 30 members in the Society, compared to the nearly 200 it has today, and several members felt that the time was ripe for such a venture. The number of different total hip implants on the market was also very small. I obtained the services of a physician, known for is knowledge of the subject and very familiar with computer technology. He met on two different occasions with the entire fellowship of the Society and made clear to them the feasibility of the project.

The effort failed, not because anyone felt it was not a good idea, but because egos, huge egos got on the way, and tripping on them became the name of the game. The biggest egos dreaded the thought that their systems of documentation would be threatened, despite assurance that nothing of the sort could possibly happen. The Registry would allow them to continue to use their individual methods; all they had to do was to agree to a common core of items to be included in their forms.

A few years later, Clement Sledge, from Boston was elected president of the Hip Society and devoted a great deal of time and effort to establish the Registry. He also failed. Now, some twenty years later, a renewed effort to create a Registry in underway. Interest on the idea has been fueled by the alleged success of a Swedish Total Hip Registry.

I suspect the project will fail. We are not ready for it. The Swedish registry may have been a success, however, analogies with the European success cannot be made. Sweden is a small, homogeneous, highly disciplined country, quite different from ours. They recorded information and drew conclusions on he basis of a few different implants. In North America there are hundreds of different implants. According to a report from Harvard University, a few years ago, there are nearly 350 different total hip prostheses on the market.

That being the case, will all 350 different prostheses be included in the Registry? And what about the new ones, which without any doubt will be marketed every so often? If not all implants are to be included, then which ones will be chosen? Will the manufactures of implants accept a verdict rendered by a group of self-appointed individuals? How do the managers of the Registry plan to handle surgeons who have their own prostheses and use them in institutions, heavily supported by Industry, to maintain an assembly-line operation? Have they given thought to the "influential" orthopaedic surgeons who have their own manufacturing companies?

SECTION III – MISCELLANEOUS

In addition, I suspect that a number of participating surgeons, aware of the fact that the Registry will be including information on their own results, and that such result will be common knowledge, will distort the data they provide to the central computer. The idea that somebody else's results are better that theirs will be a totally unacceptable option.

As Chairman of the Committee on Injuries for the American Academy of Orthopaedics, also in the 1970s I proposed to the organization the creation of a Fracture registry. The project was funded as a pilot study. Even though fractures of the femur were the only fractures to be included in the study, and only a hand-full of institutions were to participate in the effort, success eluded us. The supply of information was incomplete, and when obtained, it was also obvious that certain people were "making up" their information. The project was aborted.

REHABILITATION

"Orthopaedics is Rehabilitation" was the title of a scientific exhibit we displayed at an annual meeting the Academy in the mid 1960's. We were concerned about the growing lack of interests among our orthopaedic colleagues in the rehabilitation aspects of musculoskeletal conditions. The preference for the more glamorous surgical approaches to those conditions was permeating our discipline. We were also witnessing the erosion of orthopaedics by physicians from other disciplines. At that time our concern was almost entirely limited to the relatively new discipline of Physical Medicine and Rehabilitation, which very aggressively was developing expertise in the care of conditions such as hemiplegia, spinal cord injuries and similar neuromuscular disabilities. The federal government had thrown its support to the fledgling branch of medicine and was encouraging medical students to choose it as a career.

I sensed the danger of a continued pattern of erosion and decided to do something about it: I established the first rehabilitation facilities at Jackson Memorial Hospital, the main teaching hospital of the University of Miami. I expressed concern to the hospital administration over the lack of care for spinal cord injured patients in the area, and was given a few beds in a condemned floor of the hospital, then called the "colored hospital". It lacked air conditioning and was riddled with termites. We were authorized to recruit the first certified physical therapist. Within a week, we had a handful of spinal cord injured patient transferred from various nursing homes in the community.

Since I knew virtually nothing about the management of spinal cord injuries, I decided to spend a few days at the Howard Rusk Rehabilitation Institute in New York, which at that time had the most advanced rehabilitation programs in the country. My brief experience there convinced me that with effort and tenacity we would be able to develop something comparable at the University of Miami.

In a short period of time we succeeded in establishing rehabilitation programs for patients suffering from amputations, hemiplegia, spinal cord injuries, head injuries, cerebral palsy, fractures and several other related conditions [51, 87, 88, 100].

SECTION III – MISCELLANEOUS

When I became chairman of the department of Orthopaedics at the University in 1970, I was able to persuade the dean of the medical school to name the new department the Department of Orthopaedics and Rehabilitation. Soon other orthopaedic departments adopted our department name.

I am convinced that our orthopaedic residents benefited greatly from their intense exposure to non-surgical conditions of the neuro-musculoskeletal system. Not that the residents looked forward with much enthusiasm to the compulsory rotation through rehabilitation, because there would be very few surgical opportunities. I told them, and I am certain I was right in saying it, that by the time they completed the rehabilitation rotations, they would be better doctors and more importantly, better men. They had a chance to see the truly physically disabled at close range and observe what major disability is all about, not only from the physical but from the emotional point of view.

By the time I left the University of Miami to assume a comparable academic position at the University of Southern California, we had moved to new and larger quarters and had broken grounds for the construction of a new building. The number of hospitalized paraplegics and quadriplegics on that day exceeded thirty five. The others beds were occupied by amputees, arthritics, hemiplegics and the like.

Interest in rehabilitation on the part of orthopaedics has dwindled over the years not only at the University of Miami but throughout the entire country. Though a few departments of Orthopaedics and Rehabilitation still exist, the comprehensive involvement of the orthopaedist in the educational and research areas is minimal. Those responsibilities have been transferred to others. Even amputee rehabilitation programs are now run by physiatrists who also manage spinal cord units.

Some of the most exciting years in my academic career were spend building and dealing with rehabilitation matters. Time has given me a more objective view of the place and role of rehabilitation in the care of the musculoskeletal impaired individual. Overall, rehabilitation has been abused enormously. The abuse is contrived at times and other times simply the result of adherence to traditional practices that go unchallenged and acquire the odor of sanctity that precludes debate. My specific views on rehabilitation of spinal cord injured patients, hemiplegics and amputees I discuss under the respective sections (See SPINAL CORD INJURIES and HEMIPLEGIA).

In general, the blatant commercialization of medicine and allied medical professions that has swept this country, has moved rehabilitation away from being a medical art or a pseudo-science to a business enterprise. Gadgetry and its use now dominate the field. Physical Therapy facilities have sprouted all over the land and many are filled with dozens of different machines and gimmicks that often do nothing more than to entertain patients.

Quackery is probably the best word to describe many of the ritualistic modalities to which patients are subjected. It is no longer the "heating, baking and ultraviolating" that Vernon Nickel, from Rancho Los Amigos Rehabilitation Center in Los Angeles, strongly criticized in the 1970's, but the plethora of exercise machines, electrical appliances and

SECTION III – MISCELLANEOUS

voodoo-like rituals that now dominate the spectrum of rehabilitation. The treatments are expensive to administer and are often rendered for unreasonably long periods of time.

Fortunately, the government and third party payers are finally responding to the abuse and have begun to curtail the unbridled avalanche. In doing so, however, we are seeing the danger that always comes when somebody from outside of medicine gets involved on issues they do not understand. Some patients who need an extended period of rehabilitation are denied those services.

The proliferation of for-profit hospitals and other health care facilities has aggravated the problems resulting from abuse of the system. For them rehabilitation has been a gold mine to be exploited until the last minute. In-hospital rehabilitation areas are structured and named "skilled nursing units", "arthritis units" or sub-acute medical services. Patients are admitted to these units for several days in order to take advantage of the Medicare plan that subsidizes such admissions [158] (See ARTHRITIS and OSTEOPOROSIS PROGRAMS).

SECTION III – MISCELLANEOUS

RESEARCH

In many areas of orthopaedics, the care we provide today is profoundly better to the one we gave as recently as ten or fifteen years ago. Most of the advances have taken place through improved technology that made possible, for example, the surgical stabilization of the scoliotic or arthritic spine, the internal fixation of fractures, the successful replacement of joints, the endoscopic evaluation and treatment of internal derangement of various joints, and many others. More recently sophisticated advances in intra-operative imaging technology and the invention of the CT scan and MRI further revolutionized the practice of orthopaedics.

However, many of the major changes in orthopaedics came as a result of contributions made by others outside of our profession. The discovery of the polio vaccine and antibiotics had a profound impact in our profession. Prior to the development of the polio vaccine and the introduction of antibiotics, the orthopaedist devoted a good portion of his time to the care of infections, tuberculosis and the sequella of poliomyelitis. While some or all of these developments were evolving, progress in the biological arena was significantly delayed. Not only was support for research from governmental agencies not proportional to the needs of the musculoskeletal system, but interest in basic research dwindled among orthopaedic surgeons. The mechanical approach to disease treatment dominated the imagination of the surgeons. The power of the manufacturing industry grew exponentially and became a major provider of financial support for research. Most departments of orthopaedics, soon came to depend almost entirely on support from Industry for the conduct of their research endeavors.

Orthopaedics took a backseat to other disciplines during its negotiations with NIH, the major funding agency of research in the United States. Rheumatologists, virologists and more recently molecular biologists, gained the lion-share of NIH funding. (See addendum # THOUGHTS ON THE ROLE OF ORTHOPAEDICS IN BASIC RESEAC)

Recently, following a suddenly renewed interest in the biological approach to tissue repair, we have seen an upsurge of research activities in this area. A most welcome development! However, it is very likely that progress in this promising area will encounter a multitude of hurdles that will delay the sound implementation of the newly acquired knowledge. The premature introduction into the marked of products that have shown early encouraging results might give the promising technology a major blow. It has happened before and it could happen again. (See ELECTRICAL STIMULATION).

There has been an epidemic of so-called new biological techniques for fracture healing. Along with exploration of worthwhile ideas we have also seen a myriad of gadgets and gimmicks of questionable benefit invade the orthopaedic territory. Many such gimmicks might prove to be good and I will regret having called them a part of the interminable list of quackery items. Listening to or reading about the many new techniques is reminiscent of the days when copper bracelets, leaches and other similar therapeutic modalities dominated the market.

SECTION III – MISCELLANEOUS

Currently, we are witnessing a popular swing toward "magnetism". I recently heard a presentation dealing with the effect of mattresses containing magnets. The study had been well conducted in experimental dogs. Arthritis had been produced in the dogs' knees by severing the cruciate ligaments. A group of animals was placed in cages where they slept on mattresses with magnets. The other group slept on regular mattresses. Upon sacrifice, it was found that dogs that slept on the magnetic mattresses showed minimal osteoarthritic changes when compared with the control group.

Various explanations were offered to indicate that the cells of the arthritic cartilage responded in a positive form to the magnetic forces. Since not only the operated knee of the dog was exposed to the magnetic field, but the entire body, one can surmise that if the dog had arthritic changes in the spine or others joints in the body, the disseminated arthritic process would have benefited in a similar manner. I asked the investigator what effect the magnetism had upon other tissues: the brain, the intestines, and the prostate.

Can we anticipate that during the next few months we will see advertisements indicating that magnetic mattresses cure not only osteoarthritis but rheumatoid arthritis as well? Why not? In Roman day's people with diarrhea, headaches, arthritis and melancholy were exposed to electric fish to rid themselves of their various illnesses. Along with quackery from antiquity we might get to see the rebirth of the spectacle of gladiators fighting hungry lions and tigers. A healthy break from sitcoms and murders!

It is hard to believe all reports dealing with results obtained from research investigations, since many of those studies are flawed from the very outset. Many are sponsored by Industry, which obviously is interested in large financial profit and in a big hurry to release the new product for clinical use. In the process, corners are cut and dishonesty creeps into the picture.

Recently, I witnessed an investigator break the approved protocol for the investigation of a gadget designed to expedite the cure of multitude of soft and bony conditions. The protocol had made it very clear that the only clinical subjects to be included in the study would be patients who had suffered for several months from the various conditions, and had failed to achieve relief from other conventional medical and or surgical treatments.

The investigator, however, used the experimental device in many instances as the first and only modality of treatment. In addition he served as the individual responsible for the selection of patients as well as the administrator of the technique, the evaluator and recorder of the findings and the reporter of the findings. In other words he was jury, judge and executioner. Obviously any research findings from studies conducted in this manner are not believable. The Food a Drug Administration (FDA) nonetheless approved the technique for general use.

Recently, the media has uncovered and reported on practices that touch on the ethical relationship between Medicine and Industry regarding payments to physicians, based on the number of patients they can include in the research study. Obviously, such a practice entices the dishonest person to include as many patients as possible into the study, even patients who the physician knew in advance were not appropriate candidates for inclusion.

A pharmaceutical company approached an associate of mine and offered him 800 dollars for every total hip and knee patient he would include in the testing of a prophylactic anticoagulant. The physician was to fill out several prepared forms and return them to the sponsoring organization. A number of physicians became involved in the project and some of them have been generously recompensed. Some of them are now official spokesmen for the company and their names are frequently seen as "visiting professors" and keynote speakers at a variety of so-called scientific meetings. Through academic prostitution they became overnight celebrities.

We discuss at meetings of academicians the need to encourage medical students and orthopaedic residents to get involved in research. Some departmental chiefs advocate exposing residents to research endeavors by having them spend a year in the research laboratory being directly involved in basic investigation. Unfortunately, I do not think this methods has produced the anticipated results. The number of basis researchers and academicians that have come out of those programs has been much too small.

ROYALTIES

It is customary and appropriate for industrial concerns to give royalties to the investigators who propose the development of specific appliances. It is a logical expectation. It also encourages the innovative surgeon to think about making improvements in areas where improvement is desired.

As it is true in most situations where financial incentives enter into the picture, the awarding of royalties has its downside, particularly if the revenues being generated are significant. The thought of losing the steady stream of income prompts many to deny actual or potential complications from the product from which they are benefiting financially. They continue to promote the product until it has been thoroughly discredited by the orthopaedic community and the industrial company is forced to withdraw it from the marked. Needless to say many patients are harmed unnecessarily in the process.

Another downside of royalties is that many "innovations", motivated by profit, do not deserve to be disseminated for general use. One gets the impression that inferior products are manufactured without appropriate research being conducted. This is done with greater frequency when the name of a popular surgeon is involved. Industry must assume that if the medical community knows who the individual behind the "new" development, its commercial success is guaranteed.

Since a number of industrial concerns are involved in the manufacture of orthopaedic products, the competition is fierce. Luring physicians to associate themselves with a company, and particularly with a specific product, is an ongoing effort. The professional boundaries are often ignored.

SECTION III – MISCELLANEOUS

I was once approached by the vice-president of a major manufacturing company who presented me with a brand new total hip prosthesis. The implant had been allegedly designed "according to my philosophy and in recognition of the many contributions I had made to orthopaedics". It is interesting to note I had no idea I had an identifiable philosophy of hip surgery and I wondered how they had managed to discover something I had not recognized myself. He indicated that they wanted to name the implant the "Sarmiento total hip prosthesis". He then handed me a check in the amount of $250,000 and suggested that royalties were negotiable.

When I indicated to him that I would not allow my name to be attached to an implant I had had nothing to do with, he apologized. Two months later a picture of the new prosthesis was prominently displayed on the pages of orthopaedic journals. When I asked the vendor who the orthopaedist behind its development was he gave me the name of a fairly well know surgeon from a prestigious medical school.

I have suggested a number of times that industrial concerns should consider giving the monies, which until now had been allocated as royalties to surgeons, to the Orthopaedic Research and Education Foundation. This Society could then distribute the funds among organized academic orthopaedic research programs throughout the land. (See Addendum THE ROLE OF ORTHOPAEDICS IN BASIC RESEARCH)

SECTION III – MISCELLANEOUS

RUNNING AND EXERCISING

Physical exercises of various forms have become popular rituals in America's Narcissistic Society. Jogging and running are part of the effort to maintain health and to prevent aging. Often, this enthusiasm becomes an obsession. Some people give the impression that exercise is the whole reason for living. They run or jog until they seem to be ready to collapse. They are in pain, but tell us that the pain makes them "feel good". When others ask me why I do not run and then feel better, I respond, "If I felt better I could not stand it."

Parallel to the exercise regiment is a fanatic concern for appropriate diet. Gaining one pound of weight becomes a tragedy. Those people weigh themselves several times a day, drink bottles of water and dream about exercising again.

I can't help but wonder what the long term impact of these trends will be. Is it possible that heavily exercised joints will sooner or later break-down and develop degenerative osteoarthritis? Are those people asking for trouble and instead of earning a better quality of life in later years, will they be victims of a greater number of painful disabling conditions? They seem to believe that exercise will forever preclude muscular atrophy and that when they become older their muscle mass will remain unchanged. I have news for them!

Drinking bottled water might bring about a new generation of people who, as in the past, lose their teeth early in life, from a lack of Fluoride that must be ingested. The Fluoride in toothpaste may have a local effect in the prevention of carries, but does not satisfy the systemic needs, unless we choose to swallow the foam.

SECTION III – MISCELLANEOUS

S

SETTING LIMITS

Daniel Callahan, a philosopher and brilliant American scholar, has written a number of books dealing with death and aging in America. He has been one of the strongest and most articulate voices warning about the consequences of medicine's efforts to prolong, at any cost the life of the elderly suffering from terminal conditions. Through a combination of theoretical and practical arguments, he has advanced his concept that society must address in earnest the issues of death and dying.

One of Callahan's earlier books was titled *Setting Limits* in which he suggests that heroic measures to prolonged life in people over the age of sixty-five are not, in general, justified. He argued that people who reach that age have lived a full life; have begun to experience the inevitable decay of body and mind; and sooner, rather than later, death would be at their door-steps. That the prolongation of life through expensive and uncomfortable artificial methods had little meaning. He emphasized the financial implications of universal efforts to extent life under those circumstances, and spoke of the increasingly lopsided number of young versus old people. He discussed the increasing burden being placed on the shoulders of the young, responsible for subsidizing the needs of the older generation.

Regarding health care financing, he discusses the drain of dollars from other important sectors of society. He said something to the effect that cities could become huge hospitals and nursing homes while their infrastructure would suffer tremendously.

One does not have to agree completely with Callahan's views. However, it would be very foolish to dismiss lightly his prophetic views. I, for one, find myself in agreement with virtually everything he has written on the subject.

Our society is obsessed with immortality in this life, and seems to believe that with continuous technological advances the life span will double within the next few decades. Such a change is not necessarily impossible. However, it will not be the Fountain of Youth, where ageing is arrested. Quite the contrary, the increased longevity will be accompanied by a parallel decline and eventual collapse of the human frame.

The Greeks of antiquity, during their Golden Age, found appropriate examples of virtually every possibility affecting the human condition. They dealt with the three Kantian priorities, immortality, God and liberty in unsurpassed degrees. According to them their Gods were immortal and remained forever young. Others were condemned to die eventually. On a specific occasion, a mortal asked the gods to give him immortality. The request was granted but the body and the mind of the new immortal human continued to age.

This is probably what will happen when new techniques will make possible a further prolongation of life in this planed. The specter of a nation made of increasingly older people will overwhelm society, setting the stage for a Malthusian-like catastrophe of unpredictable consequences. It is questionable that discoveries in the field of neurosciences will alter the predicted picture.

The orthopaedic community and medicine in general have been very cavalier about the cost of medical care. This attitude invited the government to step into the arena. It soon began to infringe in the traditional autonomy of the medical profession. I suspect that those in charge of the financing of medical care came to the conclusion that the medical profession was not interested in addressing the consequences of the escalating cost of medical care; that the financial impact of new and expensive technology to the economy of the nation was being ignored by the medical profession.

The initial reaction of the government resulted in an unanticipated involvement of the private sector and its eventual control of physicians' actions. HMOs and a variety of managed care organizations are dealing a final blow to the autonomy of the medical profession.

SPONDYLOLISTHESIS

I have often wondered if spondylolisthesis has been with us from the beginning of time or constitutes a rather recent phenomenon (thinking in terms of tens of thousands of years). What made me think of spondilolesthesis as an evolutionary change was the recollection that someone said at one time that asymmetrical inter-vertebral facets represent changes that gradually occurred when quadrupeds began to assume the bipedal position. Quadrupeds, as far as I know, do not have asymmetrical facets since the motion of their distal lumbar vertebrae occurs in one plane. The bipedal human, with distal lumbar vertebrae designed originally to move in only one direction, now must be expected to function as universal joints that move in all directions. They must provide not only flexion and extension but also bending and rotation. The introduction of these demands may have resulted in the gradual reorientation of the facets and, therefore, the appearance of transitional, asymmetrical facets.

I have extrapolated that a similar mechanism might explain the development of spondylolisthesis, which represents a further step in the evolution of asymmetrical facets. . All I need is an anthropologist to demonstrate how wrong I am, by showing me that spondylolesthesis is older than asymmetrical facets and constitutes a variation more common than asymmetrical facets. To save myself that embarrassment of being wrong, I should have consulted with one of the local anthropologists before putting my thoughts in writings.

SECTION III – MISCELLANEOUS

SPORTS MEDICINE

What is Sports Medicine? After all these years I have not been able to understand why this concept has been perpetuated for so long and continues to fascinate young trainees. I have been told there are over two hundred and fifty Sports Medicine fellowship positions filled in the United States. During interviews with medical students applying for residency positions, a large number of them volunteer the information that once they complete their residency they will take a fellowship in Sports Medicine.

What is the difference between general orthopaedics and sports medicine? None. Both do the same things. The arthroscope, which is the tool most used by sports medicine surgeons is not their exclusive domain. Most general orthopaedists use the arthroscope with frequency. Both rely and prescribe physical and occupational therapy with the same enthusiasm.

No one could deny that a great deal of progress has been made in the area of sports injuries, and that such progress has often come from individuals whose practices include athletes. However, the offices of those individuals are full of patients of all ages. The elderly lady, suffering from severe osteoporosis, who falls and sustains a fracture of the humeral head is there in the waiting room expecting the same care the professional athlete receives. These doctors manage all kind of fractures, dislocations, sprains and injuries, perform total joint replacements ad do spine surgery. So where is the difference with the general orthopaedists?

What sports medicine orthopaedists have done is to convince themselves that the treatment they give to the high-demand athlete should also be given to everybody else. I think, this is wrong, for it ignores the fact that many conditions which are best treated aggressively in the athlete respond very well to simpler methods in others, particularly in the elderly. And with fewer complications.

I have seen non-displaced malleolar fractures in professional athletes treated with internal fixation devices. Fractures, which within a few weeks would have healed uneventfully. We are told that the surgery is performed in order to permit that person to play an important game two weeks later. There may be some merit to that argument. However, to use the same approach in the care of similar fractures when dealing with older people does not, in my opinion, make sense.

Such a scenario, though theoretically possible, needs to be thought out carefully. We must not forget the lessons learned from the AO experience. When the AO perfected the technique of plate fixation of fractures, we sincerely believed that the close treatment of fractures had become obsolete. It did not take long for the orthopaedic community to realize that open surgery was not a panacea. Many fractures that had been treated with plate fixation failed to unite or the healing was retarded; infection developed in some instances; and cast immobilization following the surgical procedure was often required.

Eventually plating fell into disrepute for the management of diaphyseal fractures, and currently is used with decreasing frequency. Very few femoral or tibial fractures are currently plated. Intramedullary nailing has become the treatment of choice.

Another more disturbing phenomenon, equally if not greater than the abuse of technology, is the outrageous abuse of physical therapy. The amount of unnecessary and extremely expensive therapy given to patients is inexcusable. It has become so pervasive, that now all patients demand it. Conditions which require a minimum of therapy are prescribed months of a variety of "Mickey mouse" modalities, many of which are borderline, if not actual quackery. The cost of that abuse is costing millions of dollars to the economy of this country.

SUB-SPECIALTIES IN ORTHOPAEDICS

Alexis de Tocqueville, the famous Frenchmen who visited America in the mid-nineteen century and wrote the most profound and unsurpassed analysis of the people of the United States, remarked about the deeply rooted desire among Americans to join societies and associations. That trait has not changed in the one hundred and fifty years since Tocqueville made that statement. Quite to the contrary, it has become a way of life for millions of people.

I do not know what makes us so eager to form such groups. Is it an innate desire to be with people who hold views, opinions or interests similar to ours? Or some strange fascination with the idea that membership in some society or association separates us from the rest of the people and places us at a higher level? Perhaps a combination of the two. I know colleagues of mine whose curriculum vitae is filled with pages listing the many societies and association they belong to. I understand it. There was a time in my life when I thought that I needed to belong to as many societies as possible. Time cured me of the fallacy and immaturity of such a perception.

Sub-specialization in orthopaedics and probably in other branches of medicine as well, has multiplied like rabbits. Currently, there are sub-specialty societies for virtually every bone and joint in the body and for many surgical procedures or regions of the musculoskeletal system. We have the Hand Society, the Foot and Ankle Society, The Knee, the Hip, the Hip and Knee, the Lumbar Spine, the Cervical Spine, the Scoliosis, the Shoulder and Elbow (this one will probably split soon), the Arthroscopy, the Trauma, Sports Medicine, etc. etc. Approximately twenty different orthopaedic sub-specialties societies form COMMS, the Council of Orthopedic Muscular-Skeletal Societies, and new society's spring up on a regular basis. Groups identified with other subjects such as the Pelvis and Acetabulum are planning to become Societies. The same is true for those who have study groups dealing with the sacro-iliac joint, the cruciate ligaments, and only God knows what else. Perhaps the plica Society and the medial malleolus society will soon be announced as COMMS' new members.

COMMS was the product of a very legitimate concern on the part of the Board of Directors of the Academy. They realized that sub-specialization in orthopaedics was inevitable. The Hand Society had already become a prestigious organization and was

SECTION III – MISCELLANEOUS

holding its well-attended annual meeting on the days preceding the Academy's own annual meeting. It had also began to hold separate continuing education courses. The Board of Directors feared that the example set by the Hand Society would be followed by some of the other societies, resulting in a loss of attendance to the Academy's meetings. Soon, there would be independent meetings of a number of societies with a proportional decrease of participation by a large segment of the fellowship in the activities of the Academy.

In order to "keep the family together", as Charles Rockwood, president of the Academy in the early nineteen seventies, stated in his vice-presidential address, COMSS was structured to give balanced opportunities to subspecialties. Administrative support was offered at no charge. Ultimately one entire day during the Academy's annual meeting was devoted to the sub-specialty societies, which were allowed to keep the revenues generated by their meetings. It was an unexpected bonanza for them. The Specialty Day became extremely successful.

If being a member of a sub-specialty society was a highly desired status for many, and being an officer in such organizations a major ambition for some, it was only natural that new societies would sprout. Membership in the nobility created by some subspecialty societies was made available to virtually anyone who expressed a desire to join it. A certain society was formed by a group of friends who arranged the presidential succession in such a manner that each one of the founding members would eventually become president of the organization.

Several of the new societies began to organize their own separate educational meetings, heavily subsidized by Industry, and accompanied by the display of scientific and commercial exhibits. Other groups established lobbying offices in Washington, claiming that their collective views were not being appropriately represented by the Academy. A move difficult to understand since orthopaedics as a whole represents only 3% of the medical population in the United States. Even a large sub-specialty society represents only a fraction of a percentage. To think that the small group would receive more attention from the legislators is rather naïve and counterproductive. We all should know by now that power comes from numbers and money. If you have any doubt ask leaders of labor unions, bankers or industrialists. (See FRAGMENTATION)

Sub-specialization is here to stay. It has done much good and many important contributions have come from sub-specialize d people. There is nothing wrong about anyone wishing to limit his or her practice to one limited area of the discipline. I did it myself. For the past 30 years I have limited my surgical practice to total hip replacement and have kept a strong interest in the study of fracture healing and the use of closed functional methods of treatment of certain fractures. I have enjoyed the experience and suspect that because of that, voluntarily imposed limitation I was able to make a small contribution to my profession.

The questions that need to be answered are whether sub-specialization should be recommended for every orthopaedist. Is that good for the discipline of orthopaedics? What are the possible good and bad consequences of that move; and what it does to the future of our own organized profession?

Based on the many points I have tried to make, I must conclude that the trend toward wide-spread sub-specialization should be harnessed. If not, orthopaedics will cease to be. The education of the orthopaedist should be modified. Otherwise, it would be very difficult to justify, academically and financially, requiring four years of medical school and five years of residency for an individual who at the completion of training would limit his practice to the performance of a hand full of surgical procedures in separate segments of the body.. Procedures that can be mastered in a short period of time.

The total number of sub-specialists would have to be reduced, because there would not be enough clinical material to satisfy their economic needs unless their reimbursement is increased in a dramatic way.

Others, outside of orthopaedics will take over the general care of patients with disorders of the musculoskeletal system. The problems they cannot handle, they will refer to the sub-specialists. Surgeons in other disciplines such as neurosurgeons, general surgeons, plastic surgeons and podiatrists will, in increasing numbers, perform the surgery themselves.

If and when growth factors become a therapeutic reality, the orthopaedist will not be able to claim to be the best professional to apply the new method. Which one of the orthopaedic sub-specialists will have better qualifications to carry out the procedure? Many others in medicine, surgery or on the fringes of medicine will claim the same qualifications. Why should we then forbid physician assistants from being the ones to inject a dose of bone growth factor into a fracture or non-union and then apply a brace? He, after all, can reduce a fracture and apply a brace better than the traumatologists whose expertise is limited to surgical stabilization of fractures.

Even though it may be too late to change course, I firmly believe the entire orthopaedic profession should address the many issues concerning excessive sub specialization. It might fail in finding a solution, but nonetheless the effort should be made. On the other hand, we could just as well let events go unchecked and let future generations live according to the new systems. History has taught us many lessons along those lines.

SECTION III – MISCELLANEOUS

T

TEACHING

I think that by making residents get accustomed to asking questions, they benefit the most. It is said that we all need well-established principles in order to be able to advance. There is much to be said in favor of that argument. However, while discussing medical issues with mature individuals we must recognize that many of the concepts we consider principles are nothing but opinions and preconceived notions; opinions that lack scientific support. Opinions that become principles and acquire an odor of sanctity because of sheer longevity. Despite that reality

Because of the commercialization of medicine and the exaggerated emphasis on the surgical approach to the care of musculoskeletal conditions, role models in orthopaedics are becoming a thing of the past. The traditional bedside rounds are being replaced with the rapid presentation of "cases" and discussion of patients whose faces the educator never sees. The contact that many teachers have with residents is primarily in the operating room, where for obvious reasons, if any teaching is done, it relates to technical matters.

The need for fulltime faculty in medical schools to generate funds for their own support and for their departments, has taken many educators out of indigent clinics, the environment where the best source of teaching material is. In many training programs only members of the voluntary faculty are found there today. To complicate matters, the fulltime academicians are often led to believe that members of the voluntary faculty are individuals who lack their competency. They are, in the opinion of the "professors", not versed in the latest advances in medicine. That view filters to the residents who then view the attending voluntary faculty as a nuisance rather than an asset.

TENDON TRANSFERS

Perhaps the most common surgical procedures performed by residents some thirty years ago were a tendon transplant. Patients suffering from the sequella of poliomyelitis were the surgical subjects. With the discovery of the polio vaccine and its effective use in most affluent countries, the procedure vanished from the daily armamentarium of the orthopaedic surgeon. Arthroscopic surgery, internal fixation of fractures and arthroplasty replaced them.

I learned many lessons from the experiences I had with such procedures. The most important, perhaps, is that, particularly in the lower extremity, long lasting good clinical results are rare. I saw hamstrings transferred to the patella in order to provide active knee extension. Though at first the transplanted muscles seemed to work well, over a period of time they lost their efficiency. The same was true for transplants of the peroneal muscles to the os calcis to provide plantar flexion. The results were consistently poor. Almost within the same category was the transplanted posterior tibial tendon, through the interosseous membrane, to the dorsum of the foot. This latter procedure had the added disadvantage, which at first we did not recognized, of creating a "flat foot" deformity.

In the upper extremity the experiences were more rewarding. However, on many occasions the clinical results did not meet expectations. This was the case in polio patients, but more obvious when dealing with patients suffering from spastic conditions. Though transplants for the care of peripheral nerve injuries have withstood the test of time a bit better, oftentimes we see them stretch and lose their efficacy. We have a long way to go before we see consistent long-term good results from this type of surgery.

TRAUMATOLOGY

I am not familiar with the history of the separation between orthopaedics and traumatology in Europe, where the discipline was first born. It is my understanding that the "orthopaedist" initially took care only of children's congenital, developmental and infectious diseases in the growing child. I suspect, he also provided care to adults suffering from the sequela of these conditions.

Fractures were the responsibility of general surgeons. This was the case in the United States as well, a practice that lasted till only recently. However, over the years, as the orthopaedic community became better organized, orthopaedists assumed the care of all patients with all types of musculoskeletal conditions, including fractures.

In the 1960's a trend began in Central Europe that lead to the establishment of a separate discipline dealing exclusively with trauma. The "traumatologists" became experts in all aspects of traumatic conditions. They were very well trained to handle trauma, not only of musculoskeletal structures, but also of the chest, vessels, nerves and abdomen. They organized themselves and soon advanced the specialty in a dramatic way. Trauma Centers in the Germanic countries became the envy of the world. Under the leadership of Harald Tscherne, from Hanover, Germany, the specialty gained worldwide acclaim. Patients with any major trauma were rapidly transported to trauma centers where treatment was instituted immediately.

However, over the years the traumatologists began to treat degenerative conditions as well as traumatic ones. At first they limited their involvement outside of acute injuries, to post-traumatic conditions, but within a short time expanded their scope to many other chronic conditions. Currently, in many trauma centers in Central Europe the traumatologists perform surgery for osteoarthritis, rheumatoid arthritis and avascular necrosis of the hip. They perform arthroscopy, fuse spines, correct hallux valgus etc. etc.

As their territory expanded at one end, it became more limited at the other end. They began to depend on urologists, general surgeons, cardio-vascular surgeons and others for the care of chest, abdominal and genito-urinary injuries. In other words they began to resemble the orthopaedic surgeons of the more Western Europe, North America and the rest of the world.

SECTION III – MISCELLANEOUS

In America there is a small group of orthopaedics who would like to see the establishment of the sub-specialty of "traumatology" outside of orthopaedics. They anticipate that the traditional orthopaedist will refer to them all trauma cases in need of surgery, and will keep retain only those traumatic conditions amenable to non-surgical management.

I personally believe this approach to be most unwise. The traumatologists will see themselves undergoing the same evolution that the European traumatologists experienced, and realizing that the orthopaedists, responsible for the nonsurgical care of fractures, will soon dictate what fractures are to be surgically treated. The third party payers, mistakenly believing that the nonsurgical treatment of fractures is always cheaper, will deprive many patients of the benefit of surgical care, which oftentimes is the treatment of choice. Economic considerations in the United States, will also prevent the success of the effort, unless radical changes in the reimbursement for services render occurs in the near future.

I suspect, based on observation of the sweeping changes in health care reform throughout the world, that in Central Europe the disciplines of Orthopaedics and Traumatology will join forces and rid themselves of the artificial differences that now separates them. Such a move should benefit all parties.

TUBERCULOSIS

It is fortunate that tuberculosis no longer affects a large number of people. In the United States as well as in many other affluent countries, however, there has been an increase in its incidence, perhaps due to the large immigration of people from regions of the world were the condition is endemic.

Numerous reports have indicated that skeletal tuberculosis is no longer an extremely rare occurrence. Even though my practice directly does not call for exposure to patients with the disease I have had the opportunity to see, as head of two large orthopaedic departments, a relatively large number of patients suffering from the deadly disease. During my residency days in South Carolina, there was an entire ward in the hospital dedicated to them.

The fact that the young faculty and today's residents have not had experience with the condition may result in diagnostic errors. Spinal disc narrowing associated with sub-chondral changes often suggests tuberculo, however, other bacterial infections might demonstrate simila changes prompting the initiation of antibiotic therapy with medications to which the tuberculous bacilli is not sensitive. It is not until failure to observe improvement is seen that additional laboratory test are conducted and the appropriate diagnosis is made.

The perception that joint tuberculosis is always an insidious process, and never an acute one, means that oftentimes it is not considered during initial examinations during the care of patients having had acute onset of symptoms. I have seen a hand-full of patients who presented themselves in the emergency room because of sudden excruciating pain in the groin. The x-rays failed to demonstrate evidence of significant pathology but the symptoms indicated joint disease. Upon surgical exploration a large amount of purulent material was evacuated. The pathological findings and other test diagnosed tuberculosis. The infections seemed to have developed in the joint through the hematogenous route and did not appear to have arisen from a tuberculous psoas abscess. The final diagnosis, however, was tuberculosis.

Several elderly patients were referred to our institution because of a spontaneous compression fracture of the spine, thought to be secondary to osteoporosis. Review of the x-ray films showed the soft tissue "white abscess", oftentimes before bony abnormalities were detected. At that time, prior to the invention of the MRI, we were keenly aware that many times, the soft tissue findings were the first ones to appear.

The debate then hinged around the subject of spine fusion. Some people felt that once the abscess was surgically drained, there was no need to fuse. Others advocated early fusion. I suspect that the "fusers" won the day, because by intervening early they prevented severe collapse of the vertebra and the development of kyphosis.

Nearly thirty years ago, while visiting the city of Lima, Peru, Roberto Temple, then professor of orthopaedics at the University of San Marcos (the oldest university in the Western Hemisphere), took me to the out-patient clinic where I saw an enormous amount of muscular-skeletal pathology and observed at first glance the incredible obstacles that orthopaedists in such parts of the world must overcome. Several children, being seen for the first time, were complaining of back pain. With the naked eye one could see the kyphus deformity either very mild or already well established. Without even a single x-ray, the diagnosis of tuberculosis was made; a bottle full of "pills" was given to the child's mother, and both mother and child were then sent back to their far-away home with instructions to return when they ran out of pills. I was told that in most instances the original visit was the last one. Once in the farm, miles away from the city, all treatment ceased.

This experience exemplifies the terrible care the less fortunate receive in poor regions of the world, aggravating my long-standing anger over the often unheard, and until now unresolved plight of the poor. A social injustice that has existed since time immemorial and gets worse as time goes by. I am one of those romantic people who fears the globalization efforts sweeping the world, will make matters worse for the already disadvantaged.

At the hospital in Peru, back in the 1960s, I saw patients sharing beds while awaiting surgery or recovering from whatever conditions afflicted them. I did surgery there. I wish I had not done it because the surgical experience turned into a near-nightmare. I was to perform an endo-prosthetic replacement of an arthritic hip joint. The patient was a local Indian girl of small stature. I had been led to believe that there were Austin Moore prostheses of various sizes. Upon removal of the arthritic head, I realized I was staring at a very narrow medullary canal into which I was going to implant a prosthesis. After literally three quarters of an hour of rasping, in order to enlarge the canal, I finally succeeded in tightly fitting the smallest prosthesis available.

SECTION III – MISCELLANEOUS

ADDENDA

ADDENDA

Addendum # 1

STAYING THE COURSE

I accept the presidency of this Academy with great pride and thank you for the immense honor. Aware of the difficult times ahead, I embark on this journey confident that the fellowship will assist me in setting and staying the course. I ask God to favor me with the gifts of vision and leadership as well as the courage to stand behind my convictions.

As we prepare to embark on this journey together, I believe you have both the right and need to know my position on several issues of importance to the future of our profession and this Academy.

Most of these issues are not new, but they do deserve our renewed attention. In my thirty years as clinician, researcher, educator, and participant in Academy affairs, I have seen us struggle again and again with most, if not all, of the issues. It is my hope that your Board of Directors and I can count upon your continuing support as we deal with the difficult issues which confront our profession.

Recertification

By the end of this century, nearly ten thousand members of this Academy will be holders of time-limited certificates. This organization has the obligation and responsibility to assist those who will be going through the ten-year cycle of recertification. To that end we have, as the fellowship has directed, continued our dialogue with the American Board of Orthopaedic Surgery in an attempt to best identify The Academy's supportive educational role in the recertification process.

The American Board of Orthopaedic Surgery has assured the orthopaedic community that it will develop pathways to recertification which will be practical, tailored to individual needs, and as inexpensive and convenient as possible. I believe they are honoring that commitment.

I will continue to recommend that the ABOS give serious consideration to the establishment of a pathway, which is based on continuing education and periodic open-book, self-administered home or office-based examinations. The fellowship should support the establishment of such a pathway. Educators tell us that repeated educational experiences are superior to single ones held at widely spaced intervals. Open-book, non-proctored examinations have already proved to be as effective as supervised ones. This alternative also eliminates the natural fear that supervised examinations inevitably portend.

The real issue for us today is not what pathways to select for recertification, but rather, the need for the fellowship to rally in support of the Board's efforts to implement the recertification process. The occasional strident opposition of a few does nothing but create unnecessary disruption and ill feelings. Our profession does not need such dissension, particularly when so many other major issues fill our agenda. Recertification must be supported not only because it has been mandated by the only recognized national certifying body in our specialty, but also because it is in our own best interest. It provides the assurance that we, as professionals, are responsibly maintaining and upgrading our knowledge in a rapidly changing specialty field, and it allows us to demonstrate, in a meaningful way, our accountability to society.

The Fragmentation of Orthopaedics

In 1984, Dr. Charles Rockwood spoke of the need to keep "the orthopaedic family" together because he recognized the growing fragmentation of our specialty and warned us of its dangers. Today, in spite of the establishment of the Council of Musculoskeletal Societies and the resulting closer ties between The Academy and the various subspecialties, I believe the dangers that Dr. Rockwood addressed are still present and growing.

To date, certificates of added qualifications have been granted to only one subspecialty in orthopaedics, and other subspecialty societies have, wisely I believe, tabled their own requests for such certificates. It should be noted, however, that some groups are making plans to issue certificates of proficiency in certain surgical techniques. I believe no additional certificates of added qualifications or any certificates of proficiency in surgical techniques should be issued to anyone until the matter has been carefully studied and the impact of these extra credentials on the entire fellowship is thoroughly explored. This has not been done.

Adverse repercussions from a proliferation of certificates that suggest the possession of special qualifications are quite possible and should not be minimized by the fellowship. The possibility exists that, just as some hospitals now require fellowship training for the granting of surgical privileges, and the Hand Society requires the holding of a certificate of added qualifications to be a condition of future membership, all hospitals and specialty societies will adopt the same requirements. We should not even be surprised if those carriers who reimburse us for our surgical services predicate future payment for those services on the holding of such certificates of added competence.

Another disturbing trend that needs to be addressed is the interest expressed by industry in credentialing orthopaedists in the use of surgical equipment. The Academy has already spoken against this, and we, as members of the orthopaedic community, should be cognizant of the adverse implications that such a practice, if widespread, could have on orthopaedic surgery. Through our hospital medical staffs, board certification, and continuing medical education, we have adequate mechanisms to develop skills and knowledge and should retain the right to determine what equipment we should use to provide appropriate treatment. Industry should not dictate our options.

The Academy and the specialty societies together have a responsibility to continue to study and closely monitor these and other related issues that threaten to further divide and fragment the enveloping specialty of orthopaedics which is the glue that binds us all together.

An increasing number of specialty societies can be taken as a healthy sign of our eagerness to better ourselves and our desire to share new information with others. However, the formation of a new society just for the sake of having one is not in the best interests of orthopaedics. Many such societies are simply restricted-membership clubs, which leads to

ADDENDA

resentment on the part of those excluded and tends to foster the formation of even more superfluous societies.

The rapid proliferation of self-designated specialty boards which do not have the approval of the American Board of Medical Specialties is another disturbing trend. I suspect that in some instances these boards are the result of frustration and resentment on the part of those not belonging to established societies, but in other instances, they may well represent an effort to seek recognition and prestige by whatever means are available.

Regardless of personal motive for being involved in these irregular activities, I do not believe these trends are healthy for our specialty as a whole. We often complain bitterly about the intrusion of other specialties and paraprofessional groups into what we claim to be our jurisdictional territory, without realizing that our greatest dangers may come from within our own ranks. We must be alert to the implication of our own actions and behavior and avoid selfish parochialism which, in the long run, can only prove harmful to all of us.

Research

I believe the next two decades will prove to be the most revolutionary period in the history of medical science. Spectacular changes will occur, driven by advances in molecular biology, genetic engineering, imaging, immunology, and other disciplines. The possibility exists, however, that orthopaedics may find itself playing only a minor role in this scientific revolution which has already begun, because, up to this time, we have not devoted much of our attention to basic research. For the most part, our research efforts have related to the technical orientation of our specialty and have dealt with methods and techniques applicable to the surgical treatment of orthopaedic conditions.

Aware of the need for our specialty to seek greater involvement in research, I proposed to the Board of Directors of The Academy the establishment of a Center for Research within our organizational framework. The proposal was accepted, and the Center is being structured and organized. I anticipate this Center will become the vehicle that will appropriately identify the research needs of orthopaedics and improve our image in the eyes of federal and private funding agencies.

In addition, the Center will foster a cooperative relationship with the Orthopaedic Research Society and the Orthopaedic Research and Education Foundation, a relationship that can only result in strengthening the effectiveness of each organization.

Many bright medical students who have excellent basic-science backgrounds and research potential make a career choice for orthopaedics, but we have been unable to retain many of them to make use of their research talent after they complete their residencies. Our new Center for Research will attempt to develop mechanisms to allow a larger cadre of orthopaedic surgeons to combine the pursuit of research interests and clinical orthopaedics without major economic sacrifice. This Center will also assist in the development of fellowship skills in the areas of clinical research and outcome studies. In addition, it will assist orthopaedic investigators in coordinating their research activities and in preparing and analyzing research protocols and data.

ADDENDA

The emphasis that the federal government is now giving to outcome research should not be underestimated. Because of its socioeconomic implications, we must recognize and accept that research into the outcomes of our clinical treatments will dominate most future research agendas. On a positive note, however, the conclusions derived from our outcome studies should further facilitate the establishment of sound and practical clinical policies, developed by us and not be outsiders. It is my hope that our clinical policies will have a major educational value, will help to reduce the cost of medical care without compromising quality, and will allow us to define quality, not on the basis of providing everything possible to patients, but on the basis of providing what is appropriate and beneficial for them.

I plan to recommend to the various Councils of The Academy that the subject of aging be identified as a major focus for orthopaedic study. I trust this recommendation will generate the enthusiasm and energy necessary to make it a successful project, because aging is a subject offering enormous opportunities to us for coordinated basic, clinical, and outcome research.

Ethics in Medicine

The world is experiencing difficulties and turmoil, not necessarily of unprecedented proportions, but of great magnitude. Their outcome and their implications are impossible to predict at this time. There are those who agree with Oswald Spengler that the future of our civilization is doomed and that the "Decline of the West" is inevitable. President Havel of Czechoslovakia, in an eloquent address to a joint session of the United States Congress a year ago, stated that "without a global revolution in the sphere of human consciousness, nothing will change for the better, and the catastrophe toward which the world is headed will be unavoidable."

I do not necessarily belong to the growing legion of pessimists, but I would be remiss if I were to deny that deep inside me I have the nagging suspicion that the pessimists may be right. Not a day goes by when we do not hear complaints about the need to re-establish ethics in government, in banking, in industry, in education, in research, in family relationship, and in medicine. These concerns portend a very important message to which we all must pay close attention.

We are all aware that medicine is under attack and believe that we are being blamed for problems which we did not create. The public no longer holds our profession in high esteem, and medical doctors are frequently harassed by the media, by the politicians, and by the public at large. The escalating cost of health services that continues to deprive a larger and larger number of people of appropriate medical care is, in the opinion of many, the fault of the medical profession. The press exploits those feelings and adds to further discrediting of the image of organized medicine. As a profession, we seem to be paralyzed and incapable of stopping this onslaught but, hopefully, this sense of paralysis is only temporary. Winston Churchill is reported to have said, "You can always count on the Americans coming out with the right answers; but only after they have given all the wrong ones first."

ADDENDA

Why is there such a strong resentment against us? Why is it that a profession which, almost from its beginning, was considered the most noble of them all now finds itself in this dilemma? Have we done wrong and are we now being forced to pay for previous wrongdoing? We should not be reluctant to ask those questions, even if the answers find us guilty as charged. I personally believe that we are guilty to a great extent and that we have brought on ourselves some of the resentment and criticism now voiced against us. However, I also believe that many opportunities exist for us to modify and even reverse these critical perceptions about us.

Too often we have responded to these criticisms defensively rather than in a proactive manner. That approach has not worked well in the past and will not work well for us in the future. Our responses are often perceived as being knee-jerk reactions aimed at protecting our higher economic well-being. If we are to prevail as an intact profession in this confrontation, we must develop a posture in which we consistently respond constructively, objectively, and as unselfishly as possible.

Efforts to reduce the income of physicians are underway. Those with the power to do so are apparently convinced that our fees are outrageous and that entrepreneurial activities which are permissible to others are devious in our hands. Rulings along those lines have already begun, and it would be naive to believe that we will not see more of them. The worst is yet to come.

I do not believe that the American people, in articulating their criticism of us, accuse us of incompetence, although some degree of incompetence does exist in a small segment of our profession. The American people know that the best medical care in the world is provided in this country by the best physicians, equipped with the most effective diagnostic and therapeutic tools at their disposal.

Recertification, although potentially of value to us, will do little to improve the image of our profession, because the public does not complain of our incompetence but of our insensitivity and lack of compassion. They accuse us of prescribing unnecessary tests and treatments, of performing too much surgery, of unbundling fees, and of charging too much for our services simply for greater revenues for ourselves. In short, they accuse us of greed and view us as materialistic and insensitive business people who have an unquenchable thirst for money.

Are they wrong, or has the public identified our Achilles heel? Are we guilty of those charges? I believe that to some extent the public is correct, but the real question for us is to what extent.

I suspect that the greed of which we are being accused is the same greed that corrodes our culture and permeates throughout our society. But that does not and cannot excuse us.

It is often said that unnecessary surgery is being performed in this country. This argument is frequently raised by politicians and third-party payors. I personally support those who want to have documentation of the validity of those charges. I venture to say, however, that deep inside our own consciences we know and feel that in orthopaedics, and I suspect that in all our branches of surgery as well, unnecessary surgery is being performed. It is not difficult to detect a pervasive attitude among the attending staffs and residents in training programs throughout the country. Residents, and often the attending faculty as well, seem to react instinctively to the sight of an x-ray depicting some pathological process not with the question of "what is best for this patient?", but with the question of what operation does this problem need?"

Major advances in orthopaedic technology over the past few decades have made the results of our treatments a great deal more successful than they have been before. However, abuses in our use of this new technology exist, sometimes motivated by logical desires to test the limits of its benefits, but other times motivated by financial reasons. I also suspect that continued growth of for-profit hospitals and similar health-care systems will contribute further to the inappropriate and excessive use of orthopaedic technology. We all need to continually call to mind the point made by Daniel Callahan when he said, "Not all so-called progress has really bettered the human condition. Maximizing choice does not necessarily maximize wisdom."

Certain surgical techniques, such as arthroscopy, which carry great potential benefits for our patients, are overutilized and abused by some of our practitioners. Leaders in the field of arthroscopy are pleading for careful monitoring of its use before limitations are placed on its use by others, whose only concern is the effect overutilization has on the escalating cost of medical care. The epidemic-like increase in the number of surgical carpal-tunnel releases or procedures for internal fixation of simple, uncomplicated fractures defies any logic. Financial benefits that physicians can derive from overutilization of physical-therapy services have been recognized and have prompted a negative government response. More government regulations will not cure greed in those physicians so afflicted, orthopaedists included. Orthopaedists who overuse our technology bring dishonor to us all, and we must all unite in discouraging such behavior. In the final analysis, such behavior is not conducive to progress, further damages the image of our profession, and contaminates the minds and attitudes of our residents, who, in louder and louder terms, are already being accused of becoming technicians rather than surgeons.

Over the years, orthopaedics has developed a relationship with industry which has been beneficial to both parties. On numerous occasions, industry has contributed significantly to our research efforts, and we would be remiss not to acknowledge that without such a relationship we would not have been able to reach the level of technical sophistication we now possess. However, concerns about this relationship exist that we must recognize and address. Continuing education of the orthopaedist has traditionally been the responsibility of The Academy and other educational groups and organizations. Recently, however, we have seen industry move to play a larger role in this educational arena, not only by their direct presentation of courses, but also by their subsidy of and involvement in educational courses held under the aegis of other organizations. What creates the problem and the concern with this development is that some of the orthopaedics involved do not speak as impartial educators, but rather, as salespeople for industry. Under the guise of presenting course material, they are, in fact, advertising products in which they have a financial interest.

Some business and entrepreneurial activity does not violate our code of professionalism, but we all must keep in mind that the ethos of trade is quite different from the ethos cherished by the medical profession. Admittedly, this is an area with unclear boundaries, but no one can doubt that we have a legitimate concern when profit, not education, becomes the overriding consideration for such activities. Such orthopaedists may become peddlers of products and may cease to be professionals able to subordinate their interests to the needs of their patients. It is difficult even for the most honest and well intentioned entrepreneurial orthopaedist not to lose sight of the fact that failure to promote and advertise his or her product could result in the reduction or total loss of handsome revenues.

The cost of orthopaedic technology is high, and it must be recognized that this cost is passed on to patients. Implants, particularly total joint prostheses, have a very short marketing life-span before they are declared obsolete and are replaced with newer models. This practice, frequently prompted by competitive financial considerations, simply increases the cost of the implant to patients. All of us should question the validity of the argument that these newer prostheses are greatly superior to the older ones and it is that greater superiority that justifies charging higher prices for them. I believe the difference between many of these widely advertised prosthesis is non-existent, or minimal at best, when measured against clinical outcomes and benefits derived by patients. How much longer will this and other practices that I have mentioned continue? Can we justify condoning them when health-care rationing is being discussed, supposedly because our country's financial resources are scarce?

We should all work together to identify areas in which we might be able to suggest intelligent answers to help to control the cost of our technology. If we, the providers of care, do not do it, the third-party payers will. If we do not get involved in this arena, we may well be forced to admit, one day, that we lacked the wisdom to control technology and that this failure cost us dearly. I would like to paraphrase President Eisenhower and say that the orthopaedic-industrial complex needs to be carefully monitored and appropriately harnessed.

We have recently incorporated into the charges of many of The Academy's committees the responsibility to study the financial and medical impact that new technologies will have on the health of our patients. This action should heighten the awareness among some of the fellowship of the need to assess, in an objective fashion, the cost/benefit ratio of orthopaedic technology.

I have discussed situations and behaviors that some of our fellowship do not consider unethical, but rather, claim are representative of the ethos of the times. Those who hold this view feel that efforts to change this behavior are futile, because they believe human behavior cannot be modified. Still others say that ethics is a personal matter and that values are a matter of taste. I respond to those views with a resounding objection. Ethics is not an individual choice. Ethics is a well-defined branch of philosophy that deals with universal, not individual, principles of conduct.

If we are serious about preserving the traditional values that made medicine great, we must make every effort possible to restore professionalism to our ranks. We must turn our backs on the beliefs and behaviors that suggest to others that we are businesspeople and, rather, embrace again those professional values we once held so dear, because it is only as professionals that we can succeed. Medicine will have a far different future if it becomes regarded as a business or trade union instead of as a profession. Our own Academy will become irrelevant.

The decisions that we make on these matters over the next few years will have long-term effects. We cannot continue to pretend that we can maintain the status quo. Major changes in the way that medicine is going to be practiced are inevitable in the near future, but these changes need not be ominous. Like the mythological phoenix, medicine can rise again from the ashes of change, stronger than ever before and free of whatever guilt it now carries on its shoulders.

Let us set and stay a new course together as we pursue new solutions for the problems that lie ahead. The seemingly easy solutions we found for the problems of yesteryear may not be applicable, in our shrinking, highly technical world, for the problems of today and tomorrow. Our country is going through difficult times, and additional difficulties loom on the horizon. Our economy is strained, the budget deficit climbs, and the international competition that our products face is fierce. The Persian Gulf War will bring an additional financial burden to an already overburdened society. Our health-care system, as a result of all these burdens and difficulties, will undoubtedly continue to suffer to a degree not yet clearly apparent. However, in addressing the critical issues of health-care delivery, we should not rush into hasty solutions prompted by pressures to "do something about it". A sound dialogue with many other segments of government and society is essential.

These problems call for new and innovative solutions, some of which may be painful for all of us. Unless we are willing to accept the inevitability of change and the need for us to change, we will continue on a course Barbara Tuchman has described as a "March of Folly".

As your President, I stand ready to accept the challenges associated with change and the need for new solutions. As we begin this journey together, I invite you, the fellowship, to join with me in setting and staying this new course.

Thank you for your attention.

References
1. CALLAHAN, DANIEL: Health Care Reform: How Deep, How Wide? J. Med. Assn. Georgia, 79:817-818, 1990.
2. ROCKWOOD, C. A. JR.: Keep the Family Together, First Vice-President's Address. J. Bone and Joint Surg., 66-A: 800-805, June 1984.
3. SPENGLER, OSWALD: The Decline of the West, New York, Knopf, 1926.
4. TUCHMAN, B. W.: The March of Folly: From Troy to Vietnam. New York, Knopf, 1984. J. Bone and Joint Surgery, 73-A:479-483.

ADDENDA

Addendum # 2

ORTHOPAEDICS AT A CROSSROADS

Orthopaedics stands at a crossroads. As the year 2000 approaches, the direction that we take may well determine whether the over-all field of orthopaedics survives into the next century or disappears as a medical specialty.

Three related developments have converged to bring us to this point. They include the fragmentation of orthopaedics, a troubled relationship between industry and our profession, and the crisis of health-care financing.

Orthopaedics has become fragmented, with subspecialties drifting in the direction of independent entities, divorced from a coherent body of medicine. If this process is allowed to continue, I am convinced that not only will orthopaedics disappear as a distinct branch of medicine, but that the new breed of specialists will often resemble skilled technicians more than medical professionals. Eventually, financial remuneration will drop to match the new status.

In searching for ways to arrest and reverse this fragmentation, we must first examine how it developed. For twenty years, I served as Director of Residency Programs at two institutions. I, along with many others, became infatuated with the idea that a first-class department must be composed entirely of subspecialists. Accordingly, we encouraged faculty members to restrict their work to a single area. This, in turn, set the stage for a proliferation of fellowships. Residents training in this new environment were led to believe that, in order to be ensured of findings a job, they must pick a specialty and complete a post-residency fellowship.

However, many fellowship-trained young orthopaedists have discovered that, in the real world, their professional activities do not correspond to the specialized training that they had received. Most have found themselves unable to devote a large portion of their time to the area that they had spent a year of their lives studying.

The newly narrowed focus has spawned a multitude of subspecialty societies. No one can doubt that some of those organizations have made outstanding contributions. However, while some are based on well-defined bodies of knowledge and a sound scientific foundation, others border on the frivolous. A few are little more than exclusive clubs. If things continue in their current direction, we will see newer societies based on just one bone or joint in the body or devoted to one disease, one operation, or one gadget. Subspecialization is beginning to give rise to an exclusionary and elitist culture, one that looks down on the mere orthopaedist. Resentment will breed among those locked outside. This state of affairs is undesirable, distasteful, and out of step with the actual practice of orthopaedics today and the strategic needs of our profession.

The Hand Society now demands that applicants for membership hold a certificate of additional qualifications (CAQ). While no other orthopaedic society has yet adopted a similar requirement, we should anticipate that at least some will follow the example of the Hand Society. The potential consequences, although unintended, are fraught with danger.

A young orthopaedist who had just graduated from a respected residency program wrote to inform me that a hospital in the community where he had set up practice granted him all of the surgical privileges that he had requested, save one, hand surgery. The reason for this exception was that he had not taken a fellowship in hand surgery. We must consider what the consequences will be if this hospital's policy spreads and if the medical staffs of other hospitals retaliate by granting privileges to surgeons holding CAQs only in the areas covered by their CAQs. The resulting pandemonium could spell the end of orthopaedics as a discipline.

Fragmentation from within orthopaedics has lent momentum to erosion from without. The restructuring of orthopaedics around discrete operative procedures has opened the gate for others to move into territory once considered solely our own. Plastic surgeons are performing many of these procedures. Neurosurgeons have staked out the spine, claiming expertise in stabilization, osteosynthesis, and other operative procedures. The American College of Surgeons developed a proposal – on hold for the time being – for a trauma fellowship that would quality its holders to provide "fracture stabilization." It appears that if physicians lack training in orthopaedic procedures, industry is more than willing to step into the breach, organizing how-to courses and signing up prospective customers for gadgets and hardware.

In 1978, paraphrasing President Eisenhower's famous warning, I called attention to the ominous growth of an orthopaedic-industrial complex. In the years since, the situation has become no less ominous. It is widely recognized that, without the close relationship between industry and orthopaedics, the technical sophistication that we have achieved would have been possible. At the same time, the unhealthy side of this relationship needs to be recognized.

Industry has assumed the role of a major financial underwriter of graduate and post-graduate orthopaedic education. Its subsidies, both direct and indirect, underpin programs at all levels: residency programs, local and regional organizations, and national and international scientific meetings. Much of the education of the orthopaedist seems to be structured to satisfy the marketing needs of industry.

We must recognize that industry has come to play an inordinate role in the shaping of the education of the orthopaedist and that it bears major responsibility for the excessively technical orientation of orthopaedics.

Courses in bioskills, which have become increasingly popular, are said to reduce the number of poorly performed operations. Two or three hours of manual training, however, is of little use to someone lacking basic knowledge of the subject and the required operative skills. In fact, some individuals may go on to try their hand at procedures that they remain unqualified to perform. It is more likely that the greater problem will be unnecessary operations rather than poor technique. We need more courses on operative indications and fewer on how to operate. We also need to reorient orthopaedic education toward an understanding of the basic sciences and the foundations of musculoskeletal diseases. Only in that way can we prepare ourselves to become major participants in the ongoing revolution created by the explosion of knowledge in molecular biology, genetic engineering, immunology, and other areas.

To some, it appears that the release of each new gadget, instrument, or operative procedure calls for its own bioskills course, but we must ask how many of these courses are truly warranted. We need criteria for deciding which innovations actually necessitate parallel education. The responsibility for determining these criteria belongs to organizations such as The American Academy of Orthopaedic Surgeons and not to industry, which is encumbered by its economic interest.

Frequently, when an industrial concern directly or indirectly subsidizes a scientific meeting, it expects the opportunity to select speakers, thereby guaranteeing the presence at the podium of someone who will advertise its products. Often, speakers are orthopaedic surgeons who have a financial stake in the marketing of that company's products. Some speakers on the lecture circuit become outright peddlers for industry. Personal financial reward takes precedence over all else. Product failures and complications associated with use of products are either minimized or not widely publicized. Frequent modifications of devices, supported by no or minimum research, are announced solely to keep up with or to beat the competition.

While it is not unethical for surgeons to involve themselves in the development of products that will improve the care of their patients, there is no excuse for a surgeon participating in unscrupulous marketing ventures or allowing financial considerations to supersede professional responsibilities.

Industry and organized orthopaedics need to come together to address common concerns. Both would benefit from an educational system that is untainted by commercial considerations and through which industry can effectively disseminate information about new technology.

Some implications of the growth of medicine for profit demand careful scrutiny. We must ask whether medicine is just one more commodity, no different than others – that is, whether provision of medical services is the same as the selling of soap or cereal. We must consider the ethical foundation that has set medicine apart from the world of business and ask ourselves if, in our relationship with industry, we simply play by their rules.

Loss of professionalism and the commercialization of medicine are, in my opinion, the most critical issues facing physicians today. Without correction of those problems, the healthcare dilemmas facing this nation cannot be resolved. Also, our position at the negotiating table will remain forever weak.

As a step toward the elimination of harmful conflicts of interest, I have proposed that industry consider turning over most royalties that are now allocated to orthopaedic surgeons to the Orthopaedic Research and Education Foundation, the organization that currently represents the research funding arm of the profession. These donations would be partially earmarked for outcome studies designed to determine the cost-benefit ratio for therapies involving technological innovations as well as for other forms of patient care.

Board certification and recertification represent attempts by our profession to answer society's demand that physicians have the expertise that they claim to have. Recently, however, some industrial concerns have taken the initiative to credential surgeons independently in technical proficiency. This is a mistake. I understand that, in our litigious society, industry may fear potential liability if its products are used improperly. Nonetheless, credentialing must remain in the hands of the medical profession. We have mechanisms for determining who is qualified to perform operations and to use certain devices. More importantly, we have the ability to assess not only technical proficiency, but also ethical and professional factors as well as judgment and interpersonal skills.

While there are many reasons why medical care in the United States has become so expensive, technology is a major element. Contributing to rising costs is the pervasive belief, nurtured during residency training, that most orthopaedic conditions are best treated with operative intervention. The glamour of surgery and its greater financial rewards perpetuate this trend. Physicians and hospitals should continue to work on outcome studies and the parallel clinical policies as means for defining appropriate care. The cooperation of industry would expedite this process.

We are living in difficult times. Everyone is worried about the economic crisis that we face. The cyclical nature of capitalism leads me to expect a new period of prosperity. However, it is widely accepted that profound changes in the nature of health-care delivery are inescapable. Orthopaedists must ask how we can affect the nature of these changes.

The medical profession is but one voice in this discussion, and the field of orthopaedics represents only 3 percent of medicine as a whole. Our ongoing fragmentation threatens to diminish our already weak voice. The fact that new orthopaedic subspecialties have or will open lobbying offices in Washington as a way to influence independently the course of the debate is likely to further compound our difficulties.

Several bills before Congress, if approved, would dramatically alter the subsidization of graduate orthopaedic education. Some in Congress think that those who wish to become surgical specialists should finance their training themselves, much as they financed their medical schooling. It appears that a move to limit the subsidy of specialty training in orthopaedics to three years is well under way. I firmly believe that we have not yet had an opportunity to present our case to the government. First of all, we need to persuade the government that the education of the orthopaedic surgeon – the traditional expert in the diagnosis and care of disorders of the musculoskeletal system – requires five years of graduate education and that drastic reduction in the duration of that training is unwise, if not outright harmful, as it would substantially affect the quality of care without reducing cost.

Precipitous reaction to these possibilities on our part may be harmful. If we fail to convince the government of the value of our argument, we should prepare ourselves to respond to the new realities, avoiding, however, the permanent emasculation of our discipline. I am certain that adjustments and compromises can be made to ensure the survival of orthopaedics as a clear and distinct branch of medicine.

The government is, to a great extent, correct in stating that five years of postgraduate education cannot be justified for surgeons who eventually limit their practice to the performance of one or a handful of procedures. Pointing to the example of podiatry, the government has asked if it is necessary to bear the expense of four years of college, four years of medical school, five years of residency training, and additional time in a fellowship if podiatrists can do the same sort of thing with far less training.

This line of reasoning demonstrates how – in the context of the government's desperate search for ways to cut health-care costs – the fragmentation that we have allowed can lead to the dismantling of the distinct field of orthopaedics. It also underscores the need to balance extreme sub specialization with all-encompassing training and practices of orthopaedic surgery.

We must make sure that the specialty of orthopaedics has a seat at the table when the fundamental decisions on health-care financing are made. For our views to get a serious hearing, we must make clear that our primary concern is the welfare of patients who have musculoskeletal disorders. If reasonable ways are not found for controlling costs – including the enormous expenses brought about by technological innovations – the solution that is eventually imposed will be much worse than anything that we are now contemplating.

George Lundberg, M.D., Editor-in-Chief of The Journal of the American Medical Association, who served as my Presidential Guest Speaker at the 1992 meeting of The American Academy of Orthopaedic Surgeons in Washington, D.C., warned that, in the absence of radical changes in the near future, the meltdown point of the health-care crisis in America could take place in 1996. He predicted that, in a worst-case scenario, Congress would panic and nationalize the entire health-care system, including the pharmaceutical and medical-device industries. Doctors, nurses, and pharmacists would be conscripted into government employment.

We cannot dismiss Dr. Lundberg's forecast as fear-mongering because he is a knowledgeable and well informed person. Unless workable solutions come out of current discussions and we get our house in order, such an eventuality cannot be excluded.

We need to be aware of the seriousness of the situation and of the consequences of our actions if we are to continue to be the providers of care to those who have musculoskeletal problems.

Journal of Bone and Joint Surgery
Vol. 75-A, No. 2: 159-161.

Addendum # 3

ADDENDA

CERTIFICATES OF ADDED QUALIFICATIONS IN ORTHOPAEDIC SURGERY

During the previous decade, there has been considerable debate within the orthopaedic community regarding the issuing of Certificates of Added Qualifications to subspecialists. These Certificates are awarded following documentation of the applicant's major commitment to a particular branch of orthopaedic surgery and the successful completion of a test designed to demonstrate superior knowledge in that area.

Until now, only the American Society for Surgery of the Hand has issued Certificates of Added Qualifications. Recently, it made the possession of a Certificate of Added Qualifications a prerequisite for membership. Other specialties within orthopaedics seem to have shared the views of the general membership and have not made any attempts to develop similar certificates for their respective groups. Recently, however, The American Orthopaedic Society of Sports Medicine has expressed interest in developing its own Certificates of Added Qualifications, allegedly as a result of concerns brought about by the fact that other disciplines, outside of orthopaedics, are issuing Certificates of Added Qualifications in Sports Medicine to their members. Several subspecialties in medicine, also outside of orthopaedics, have obtained approval for Certificates of Added Qualifications for their members, but there has not been a swell enthusiasm for them within the medical profession. The controversy persists as to whether or not they are desirable.

Approval for subspecialty societies to issue Certificates of Added Qualifications is currently under the jurisdiction of the American Board of Medical Specialties. The process for such approval is lengthy, thorough, and complicated. This slow process may have contributed to the fact that other subspecialties have not attempted to develop their own Certificates of Added Qualifications.

I do not believe that Certificates of Added Qualifications in orthopaedic subspecialties should be awarded at this time. I think that they should be withheld until the issue has been studied more carefully, the current health-care debate has been settled, and the benefits to those who have had them for some time have been confirmed.

My argument is not against subspecialty societies that wish to develop means to enhance and document the qualifications of their members. Such an argument would be ludicrous. My position against the issuance of Certificates of Added Qualifications is based on concerns about the harmful effects that they might have on the over-all cohesiveness of our discipline during these turbulent and changing times.

During my Vice-Presidential Address to The American Academy of Orthopaedic Surgeons, "Staying the Course," and in a previous Editorial published in "The Journal of Bone and Joint Surgery, "Orthopaedics at a Crossroads," I expressed concern over the growing fragmentation of orthopaedics and stated that if it was not carefully checked, it could lead to irreparable damage to the point that orthopaedics as a clearly defined body of knowledge would be in danger of ceasing to exist. Observation of the fragmentation trend and the increased erosion of orthopaedics by other disciplines suggests that the awarding of

ADDENDA

Certificates of Added Qualifications to orthopaedic subspecialties could compound this fragmentation. I believe that Certificates of Added Qualifications can be divisive and can further weaken the glue that holds our profession together.

At this time, there is no evidence to suggest that there is a need to extend Certificates of Added Qualifications to any subspecialty group within orthopaedics. I know of no serious efforts by regulatory agencies to bring about such a practice, and a clamor for the Certificates from the public in general has not been heard. Furthermore, I am not aware that the introduction of Certificates of Added Qualifications in Hand Surgery was the result of documented evidence of need, outside pressure, or a sound perception of growing deficiencies spreading throughout the hand surgery community.

If evidence of a problem is lacking or the perception of a problem looming on the horizon is not clear, then there seems to be no reason to create cumbersome, time-consuming, and expensive requirements at a time when medicine is under fire and already over-regulated and when the income of the orthopaedist is decreasing and will, most likely, continue to decrease. It makes little sense to get involved with Certificates of Added Qualifications so soon after the American Board of Orthopaedic Surgery mandated recertification examinations – the value of which has not yet been established.

Certificates of Added Qualifications are potentially divisive because their true meaning can be erroneously interpreted. It is very likely that the possession of a Certificate of Added Qualifications will be used, in a court of law, to enhance or demean the qualifications of physicians according to the circumstances. There is also the possibility that payment for services rendered could be based on the possession of a Certificate without regard for the fact that the quality of care rendered by physicians is not necessarily predicated on those grounds.

In my previous Editorial, I made reference to the fact that during my tenure as President of The American Academy of Orthopaedic Surgeons, I had been contacted by a young orthopaedist who had just finished his residency training and had been awarded by the local hospital all of his requested operative privileges except for those related to hand surgery. The reason given for the denial was that he had not completed a hand fellowship and did not have a Certificate of Added Qualifications. Shortly after this episode, I learned that medical staffs in different states were considering the granting of operative privileges only in the area covered by the Certificate of Added Qualifications held by the surgeon. The retaliation that this action implies could have major undesirable consequences. It could split the orthopaedic community to an irreparable degree.

If Certificates of Added Qualifications are issued for two subspecialties within orthopaedics, it will be very difficult to prevent other groups from wanting to develop their own Certificates of Added Qualifications. That could be associated with problems that I suspect have not been carefully addressed.

The fear that groups outside of our discipline have or are in the process of developing their own Certificates of Added Qualifications is not a sound reason for the issuing of Certificates of Added Qualifications to subspecialties within orthopaedics. It implies a lack of confidence in our ability to maintain our position as the best qualified physicians to provide medical care to patients with disorders of the musculoskeletal system. The issuing of Certificates of Added Qualifications within orthopaedics will do nothing but prompt others whom we perceive as competitors to develop their own such Certificates and to figure our mechanisms for making them more attractive than ours. Some might advertise their allegedly better qualifications by means that we, fortunately, have found unprofessional and unethical. Legally, there will be no mechanism for us to suggest that our Certificates of Added Qualifications are the ones to be recognized. Both theirs and ours will be deemed equal by the courts and the public. No one will benefit from such Pyrrhic battles.

The claim that Certificates of Added Qualifications ensure quality of patient care is questionable. Although it is logical to assume that greater didactic knowledge is likely to lead to better care, the possession of a Certificate of Added Qualifications does not guarantee quality and implies that those without one do not provide the same high level of care. The fact remains that there are individuals who do not qualify for these Certificates simply because they do not devote the required percentage of time to the particular discipline. They might be very competent and deliver high-quality care, but remain general orthopaedists with special interest in one or several areas. They might also behave in a most professional and ethical manner. The reverse scenario is also likely: among the possessors of Certificates of Added Qualifications, there could be unethical and unprofessional physicians.

The more people who have Certificates of Added Qualifications in orthopaedic subspecialties, the more operations will be performed at a time when we are already being accused of indulging in too many expensive operative procedures and, in doing so, aggravating the health-care financial "crisis". It has been argued that specialty care saves money. Although we should attempt to document the validity of that perception, I remain skeptical and worry about the outcome of such an argument. We should continue to emphasize, without belittling the important role that primary care physicians play, that specialty care is often desirable because it is provided by people who have special training, not because it is cheaper.

I have suggested on a number of occasions that the Council of Orthopaedic Musculoskeletal Specialty Societies should be replaced by a more effective mechanism – a mechanism that truly discourages fragmentation – for I suspect that, in trying to "keep the family together," which was the rationale behind the establishment of the Council, the Council has unwittingly condoned fragmentation. New subspecialty societies have sprung up, not necessarily because they were needed, but partially because the Council made sub specialization more attractive. It identified a nobility within orthopaedics, a privileged class to which many wanted to belong. This explains why polls conducted by The American Academy of Orthopaedic Surgeons concerning the type of orthopaedics practiced by its Fellows indicated that a large percentage of orthopaedists claim sub specialization. I believe that many of them are actually general orthopaedists who often have a special interest in one or two particular areas and who wish to continue to practice in that manner.

It is ironic that the threat of major health-care reform is helping to bring orthopaedists closer together and, in doing so, is slowing the proliferation of subspecialty trends. It appears that residents are no longer applying for subspecialty fellowships as they did, in a robot-like fashion, until very recently. They are beginning to realize that the practice of general orthopaedics is more to their liking and also more beneficial to them under the anticipated health-care scenario. This trend will not stop sub specialization, because sub specialization is desirable, but it might help to place it in a better and sounder perspective.

We do not need Certificates of Added Qualifications at this time. They address problems that do not exist. The lack of Certificates of Added Qualifications does not threaten our ability to excel and to practice the best possible medicine. They are inconsequential to the integrity and survival of orthopaedics, and they constitute an expense to those who must obtain them because of organizational requirements. As orthopaedic surgeons, we already have additional qualifications that identify us and separate us clearly from others in medicine. We gain those special qualifications by completing well monitored educational programs and by meeting stringent criteria before successfully completing examinations to document our knowledge and expertise in the broad field of musculoskeletal diseases. Those prerequisites have allowed us to practice our discipline within a very well defined body of knowledge. It is the preservation of that distinction and of that territory that is very important to us, particularly at this time of change and uncertainty. Any distraction from that issue is not in our best interest, and Certificates of Added Qualifications probably are a harmful distraction.

In addition, by putting Certificates of Added Qualifications at the forefront of our agenda, we are placing ourselves at risk of financially disenfranchising some in our profession by placing a large number of patients in the hands of a few surgeons.

There are issues of greater importance to orthopaedic surgeons than Certificates of Added Qualifications. We are, for example, facing the possibility that the number of trainees and the duration of orthopaedic residency will be challenged, allegedly because there are too many surgical specialists and their education is too expensive. The government is arguing that it is difficult to justify subsidization of the education of individuals who, after many years of training, find themselves practicing within a very small technical sphere and developing technical expertise that could have been obtained within a shorter period of time and at a lower cost. There is a great deal of truth in that criticism. I personally believe that we should respond to the government's threat of reducing the subsidy to orthopaedic residency education in a positive fashion. We should insist and document that the entire body of orthopaedics cannot be taught adequately in less than the traditional five-year time period and that the reduction of that time will make it impossible for the discipline to continue to make the valuable contribution to society that it has made over the years. If we let the government know that we are making plans to shorten the training program because of its threats and without putting up a good fight, history will not treat our generation of leaders very kindly.

Rather than waste time creating Certificates of Added Qualifications or other types of certificates of competency, we, the educators, should concentrate on teaching better, on developing new and inexpensive means of education, on keeping the specialty together and preventing its further fragmentation, and on instilling in the minds of our students and colleagues the values that have sustained our profession over the years; honesty and good patient care, based on respect for those whose medical care is placed in our hands. If we

ADDENDA

enlarge the ranks of truly professional orthopaedists, we will not need any additional examinations and certificates.

Journal of Bone and Joint Surgery
Nov. 1994.

ADDENDA

Addendum No. 4

REFLECTIONS ON A 25 YEAR EXPERIENCE WITH TOTAL HIP REPLACEMENT

Reflection on past experience is a dangerous endeavor since biases and prejudice easily creep in, clouding, perhaps inadvertently, one's mind.

I am willing to take the risk and begin by stating that with regard to total hip replacement, relatively little progress has been made since the days of John Charnley in the early 1970s.

I suspect that the reason for the lack of truly meaningful progress is that to some extent we misused and squandered our resources and possibilities in an unwise fashion.

Had we displayed an organized and unselfish approach to total hip surgery, I am certain that today we would be much further along the road. Had we concentrated almost exclusively on improving the weight bearing surfaces of the implants, as Charnley recommended, we would have made a great deal of progress and eschewed many of the complications we have witnessed over the years.

I do not propose to underestimate the natural desire of the Orthopaedic Community to improve upon the original Charnley operation, for there were some obvious flaws in his system which needed to be addressed, such as, the imperfect qualities of the original stainless steel material and the performance of a trochanteric osteotomy.

The less than ideal material was quickly improved by replacing it with stronger alloys; and the masochistic ritual of trochanteric osteotomy was virtually eliminated from the surgical procedure within a relatively short time.

Outside of these two issues, other changes made to the operation or to the implant have had limited benefits and to a great extent have represented nothing more than exercises in futility.

What explanation can we offer for the lack of significant progress? I believe that it was due primarily to our rush to gain fame and to be acknowledged as contributors to this fascinating new venture. We tripped on our own egos and made the terrible mistake of permitting Industry to play an overwhelmingly important role in determining the destiny of total hip replacement. Industry, almost from the very beginning, gained control of total hip surgery and the education of the orthopaedist in this area.

We should have known better. We should have known that once Industry gained control of the situation, things would be done differently. In order to meet the competition and to maximize profit, the manufacturers modified their implants on a frequent basis. Therefore, the modifications were not always made because of clearly identified needs, but because changes were financially profitable.

ADDENDA

Loosening of the cemented implants was being recorded with increasing frequency leading eventually to the description of a condition called "the cement disease". This "disease" seemed to be found with any of the nearly 300 different prostheses in use, regardless of the size of the head, the shape of the neck, cementing technique used, or their modularity.

When we eventually discovered that there were other, more likely causes for the observed changes and not necessarily a reaction to acrylic cement, we realized that we had made a wrong diagnosis by calling the problem "the cement disease".

The era of cement was declared dead with the same certainty with which Nietzsche had announced the death of God nearly a Century earlier.

Then the non-cemented prosthesis entered the scene. The idea of implanting prostheses without cement and eventually having them become part of the living body was most appealing. With great enthusiasm, with pomp and circumstance a new era was born.

However, the new dream did not last long. It was short lived and we awoke to discover that we had replaced "the cement disease" with a worse one: bone lysis, the "non-cement disease", which now rests at the top of the list of concerns facing total hip surgery.

In typical fashion, a large number of different explanations were issued and assurances were given that the causes that had led to the new "disease" had been identified and removed. The "new and improved implants" would not be associated with that complication; much like the marketing ads we have heard repeatedly over the years about the "new and improved" toothpastes which according to their alleged merits should have eliminated the still ubiquitous dental cavities from the face of the earth.

The pathologic changes that occur around some non-cemented implants, such as osteopenia, have been cavalierly dismissed and we have been told they are of no consequence. However, those statements do not assuage our concerns as we do not know what the fate of those femora will be when patients become older and burdened with generalized osteoporosis.

Current reports in the literature speak of progressive lysis approaching 40% with some types of non-cemented prostheses after five to seven years following implantation.

When I learned about this nearly four years ago, I raised the question, and I raise it again: if a 25 or 30 or 40% incidence of progressive lysis is not disturbing enough, then what is the magic number which is going to prompt the Orthopaedic Community to declare a moratorium on the widespread use of those implants? I have also asked and I will ask again today, what bizarre logic has lead us to recommend the use of implants associated with such a high incidence of progressive lysis primarily for the young, who according to actuarial tables will be condemned in a high number to revision of their failed implants?

Also, how can we justify the use of prostheses which if they need to be removed will require surgery of enormous magnitude that sacrifices bony and soft tissue structures to a high and dangerous degree.

ADDENDA

When the popularity of non-cemented prostheses began to wither following the recognition of the problem, a new actor appeared on the scene: the hybrid prosthesis, where the acetabulum would remain uncemented, but the femoral component is cemented. This new approach was heralded as the solution to all the evils that the cemented and non-cemented prostheses had been identified with.

Will that be the case? I doubt it. I personally have had experiences that suggest that wear of polyethylene and the development of pathological changes at the bone-cement, metal-cement and metal-bone junctions in the femoral canal and/or acetabulum are greater with hybrid implants than with totally cemented ones. Our findings have also been noticed by others and I anticipate that hybrid prosthesis as we know it today will not be the answer to the vulnerability of mechanical hip implants in the long run.

Metal to metal articulations continue to be marketed with increasing fervor. However, we are still lacking sufficient data, even though efforts to find a niche for these resurrected concepts have been made for over 10 years. I hope the fate of these new fads will not parallel that of its predecessors. I am afraid it will. We will wait and see.

Obviously, my personal, as well as the vicariously developed perceptions about total hip surgery are an uncomfortable mix. I wish I had a crystal ball so that I could look into the future. All I know is that the good results which were obtained and continue to be obtained by those who use the original Charnley prosthesis have not been duplicated by anyone. Therefore, a return to the original basic precepts espoused by John Charnley, coupled with the greater knowledge that we now possess about polyethylene sterilization and related matters should be seriously encouraged.

I insist that the approach that we have taken over the last 30 years in the development of total hip implants was to a great extent flawed. Allowing Industry and its operatives to control hip surgery with its obvious profit motives did not do much good. If we do not regain control of our destiny – and there is a very likely possibility we will not – we will continue to waste precious time and postpone, perhaps indefinitely, the day when total hip replacement will be carried out with a consistent success rate.

International Hip Society Meeting,   Amsterdam, August 1996
Total Hip Arthroplasty Outcomes
G. Finerman, et al. Churchill Livingston, 1998.

ADDENDA

Addendum # 5

THE WILL TO ACTION

It is believed by many that medicine is going through a serious crisis. That because of changes we are witnessing today, the practice of medicine, as we have known it, is experiencing the pangs of a slow death.

Almost daily we hear older physicians remark that "I would not recommend a medical career to my children because medicine has become a constant hassle; that we have lost our autonomy and cannot make any money practicing medicine. That we work harder than ever, but our earnings shrink."

Some of these complaints are justified. However, I disagree with the conclusions and do not share the Cassandric predictions about the future of the practice of medicine.

In the great scheme of things, the so-called crisis of today will be nothing more than a footnote in the annals of history, and medicine will continue to be one of the most gratifying and exciting professions.

I am not overly concerned, and you should not be either, about the rapidly unfolding events or the magnitude of the dilemma we are confronting in regards to health care reform. We need to put the entire matter in proper perspective. We are not witnessing a crisis in medicine, but simply, a socioeconomic political upheaval.

Not a crisis in medicine, because medicine is vibrant and in excellent shape, particularly in our country where we have attained a level of medical sophistication, which is probably second to none. Progress will continue to be made. New frontiers will be conquered. Quantum leaps forward will take place at an unprecedented pace and the human condition will further improve. After all, that is medicine's raison d'etre.

The erosion of our control over the care of patients has reached disturbing degrees as a result of government decrees or the actions of the newly empowered private sector and business entrepreneurs. It makes one wonder whether the quality of care will be seriously compromised.

I suspect that no matter how bad things have gotten or how much worse they might get in the future, eventually the problem will be resolved. The American people will not tolerate second class medical care and will demand the quality of care to which they have grown accustomed and are entitled to receive. I think that such an outcome is inevitable and suspect that a reasonable compromise where quality care is provided and cost is contained will be reached in the foreseeable future.

It is necessary, however, that we, as members of the medical profession, recognize the role we played in the genesis of the problem that the government and others have found necessary

ADDENDA

or convenient to address. That is, the unsustainable, escalating cost of the delivery of health care.

We need to admit that organized medicine failed to respond unselfishly and objectively when the problem first loomed on the horizon. It elected to ignore the gathering clouds and posited that the thundering was inconsequential.

It is not wrong for us to acknowledge our mistakes. Quite to the contrary, it enhances our credibility and puts us in a better position to negotiate. To err and, sometimes, to fail are part of the human condition.

My generation took many things for granted as we witnessed the ease and speed with which our medical and economic power grew. Now you have to pay the price of our hubris and our lack of humility and vision.

There are those who believe that with financial restructuring, the Academy will be capable of doing much to solve the problems facing medicine today. I submit to you that the Academy cannot do that. Its power is limited. No matter how much money we allocate toward that end, the affect that the Academy has in the final socioeconomic political decisions will be very small.

The Academy's ability to provide advice to those who are in control of the situation should be preserved. However, this should not be done at the risk of losing the strength of our commitment to education, for it is in education where the Academy should continue to excel. Because it is in the area of education where our greatest needs lie.

When all is said and done; when this so-called health care crisis is over, we need the Academy, the premier orthopaedic continuing education body in the world, to remain the pillar upon which the cohesiveness and strength of our profession rest.

Any action that might move the Academy in the direction of a trade union would be a gross mistake. Such an outcome would have extreme and undesirable consequences. The Academy would then suffer the same fate that the AMA and other medical groups suffered and which made their educational roles almost irrelevant.

We should avoid greater politicization of the Academy. I urge you to get involved in its affairs and to discourage such a trend for it is not in your best interest. I give you this advice based on my long association with the organization, and particularly, from my experience as a member of its Board of Directors for eight consecutive years. Over several generations, the Board has done an exemplary job. Look at where we stand today. Look at the excellence of the Annual Meeting which is the envy of organized medicine throughout the world; the CME courses and publications; the innovative educational methodologies and its activities in the health care delivery arena.

The greater participation recently given to the Fellowship in the election of the Nominating Committee increased the opportunity for a more careful and representative selection of the

ADDENDA

Academy officers. I am confident that the committee will, sometime in the future, be charged with the duty of selecting all members of the Board. Not some, but all.

If the proposed resolution to make resolutions of other groups binding on the Academy's Board is passed during this meeting, the effectiveness of our Board will be severely eroded. It would be a regrettable mistake that would, in effect, cripple the organization. The Academy will be converted into a political playground where special interest groups will have the final say.

I am candidly discussing with you issues germane to the Academy. However, these issues and their implications are also important to our profession as a whole and to its long term viability.

You have come to the Academy at a time when Orthopaedics is fragmented, but not critically so. Extreme fragmentation would be dangerous and should be prevented at all costs. It would dissolve the glue that holds our profession together. Excessive sub specialization trivializes orthopaedics and generates unhealthy divisive forces.

The current fragmentation of Orthopaedics was, to a great extent, the result of the rapid expansion of technology and the logical desire of people to assemble with others holding similar interests. However, some superfluous societies came into existence to the point where today there is virtually a society for every bone, joint, anatomical area of the bone, disease and surgical technique in existence.

The growth of sub specialization has increased the cost of training its practitioners and has resulted in the appropriate, as well as the inappropriate utilization of expensive technology and the performance of unnecessary surgery.

Those in control of financing health care are stating in unequivocal terms that they are not going to cater to subspecialists as they perceive them to be the real culprits in the escalating cost of health care. Therefore, the valuable contribution that specialty medicine makes is seriously threatened. We must continue our efforts to develop viable and logical approaches to this dilemma. As orthopaedists, we must present a united, not a divided front.

We have turned technology into a religion to fulfill all of our expectations. This is a very naive and simplistic response for it is known that in the process of solving problems, technology often creates new ones.

The abuse of technology has become Orthopaedic's Achilles heel and has contributed greatly to the position that we find ourselves in today. It has made it difficult for us to expose and criticize those who control an ever larger segment of the health care delivery system.

A number of musculoskeletal conditions which can be successfully and inexpensively diagnosed and treated by non-surgical means are frequently subjected to a variety of tests and surgical procedures of questionable value. Many gadgets and surgical implants proven to be marginally or outright ineffective are successfully marketed, often with the help of orthopaedists who function as agents of Industry. These so-called new, improved and always more expensive products replace recently introduced ones without sufficient documentation of their value.

In no area has the Orthopaedic-Industrial Complex been able to extend its powerful tentacles into the practice of medicine more than in the education of the orthopaedist. I have been a committed student of this phenomenon for the past two decades and there is no doubt in my mind that today the continuing education of the orthopaedist is structured, consciously or unconsciously, to satisfy the marketing needs of Industry.

This is happening in our residency programs where the sources of funding for research and education have dwindled; in the activities of a myriad of orthopaedic societies and even in our own Academy where its economic dependency on Industry continues to grow at a rapid pace. You must remain vigilant and weight the consequences of such an increased dependency.

It is no secret that with increasing frequency others in medicine are rendering care to patients with disorders of the musculoskeletal system which until recently had been treated exclusively by us. The erosion of orthopaedics has not yet ended. Make no mistake, third party payers are watching these developments with pleasure as they assume that in this manner the cost of care will be reduced and their profit increased.

We must be keenly aware of these phenomena and do whatever is necessary to demonstrate that orthopaedic surgeons are the ones best trained and qualified to provide surgical, as well as non-surgical treatment for conditions of the musculoskeletal system.

Our actions to date suggest that we are more interested in treating conditions by surgical means than otherwise. If that perception continues to spread, the scope and strength of our profession will be seriously compromised.

Several of the developments and problems that I have addressed today are largely the result of a decay in our professional and societal values. The real crises in medicine are the declining professionalism of its practitioners; the lowering and anesthetizing of ethical standards and the belief that everything is okay, which eliminates the possibility of being morally wrong.
Success in Western Societies, particularly in the last decades, has been defined in terms of financial profit and virtually without consideration for the substance of one's achievements. We judge success in life primarily on the degree of material wealth, demeaning and undermining the spirit and foundation of our advanced civilization. Profit, the God that modern society has enshrined, dictates the ethos of the times.

We live in a time when a small, but vocal and influential segment of our society claims that the values of yesteryear are irrelevant today. I hope that you appreciate how wrong and damaging such a message has been. Look at the unraveling of our society.

No one has been able to articulate this crisis better than Havel, the president of the Czech Republic, who said that "we seem incapable of appreciating the ever increasing degree of spiritual, political, and moral degradation that has permeated throughout the West" and that, "if the current philosophy prevails, the Western culture will eventually collapse."

You, the fledgling generation of American orthopaedists, come onto the scene, not in bad times, but in challenging times. You arrive at a time when we are losing our inheritance. Nonetheless, you can regain it. It requires only your Will to Action. It is your mandate to be active and committed participants in the renaissance of high values and professionalism in our ranks.

In order to be effective contributors to the solution of the current dilemma, you must be prepared to articulate a coherent set of values and transfer it from your generation to the next because the values that made our society so worthy have become dim. I trust that you will conclude that without moral, political and religious convictions, your message will be an empty one.

Since it is very difficult to modify human behavior, you will not see the results of your commitment overnight. However, in times of crisis, it is easier to rally support for worthy causes.

Do not be discouraged by the magnitude of the task or the fact that the history of mankind is heavy with unrealized possibilities. With Promethean tenacity, other generations succeeded in changing trends and philosophies that appeared unchangeable at the time. You need not follow the path, blaze a trail.

I would suggest that you, the future leaders of orthopaedics, adopt the following lines from Henley's poem as your motto.

It matters not how strait the gate,
How charged with punishments the scroll,
I am the Master of my fate,
I am the Captain of my soul.

On behalf of the Academy Fellowship, I wish you well and welcome your Will to Action as you venture into the uncharted waters of the next millennium.

AAOS Annual Meeting Address to Incoming Class. February, 1996

ADDENDA

Addendum # 6

THE DEVIL IS IN THE DETAILS

I am not going to waste time indulging in platitudes about the progress that has been made in the treatment of fractures in recent years. Only a fool would dare question the fact that people in developed nations receive better fracture care today than they did a few decades ago.

What I propose to question is whether or not the changes we have witnessed have been entirely beneficial or, in some ways, harmful to our discipline and, if so, why.

I believe we have paid a high price to get to where we are today, and unintentionally we have seriously compromised the future of our profession. Though I will limit my remarks, for the most part, to fracture care, I believe many other segments of orthopaedics share the blame.

Since orthopaedics is a technically driven discipline, it is logical that the changes we have seen have been almost entirely of a technical nature. Only to a minimal extent have changes occurred in the biological arena.

It is no secret at this time that many orthopaedic residents complete their training and go on to practice without knowing much about the biological foundations of our profession, much less displaying interest in it. Those biological foundations, which we long considered essential, appear to have little or no significance today.

This was driven home to me, loudly and clearly, a few years ago, when a resident of ours said that he was not interested in knowing how fractures heal, but simply how to fix them. His remark, though shocking at first, prompted me to think about it. Eventually, I came to the conclusion that his response was logical. He was responding to the education he had received, to the example of his mentors, and to his perception of what his contemporaries were thinking and doing. He spoke, contrary to my initial reaction, on behalf of his generation and expressed the ethos of the time.

Orthopaedic residents, to a greater and greater degree, complete their training not knowing how to treat fractures and many other conditions of the musculoskeletal system by non-surgical means. Many do not know the natural history of a fracture treated conservatively. They have no conception of the functional and cosmetic alterations that might result from the acceptance of mild deviations from the normal. They have been taught, and they have learned, that anatomical restoration of fractured bones is an absolute necessity; that any shortening, angulation, rotation, or joint incongruity is a complication that cannot and should not be tolerated because, without correction, all kinds' of late harmful sequelae will inevitably follow. They believe that if the technology to restore normal anatomy exists, it must be used in all instances. Surgery, in other words, is the answer for all fractures. One must conclude, therefore, that we are not educating physician/surgeons, but cosmetic surgeons of the skeleton. Skeletal cosmetologists, as I prefer to say.

Industry eagerly accommodated their desires as they saw an opportunity to expand their markets. I suspect that these surgical disciplines came to the conclusion that orthopaedics was no longer a specialty based on a solid body of knowledge, but rather a series of surgical procedures that anyone with a modicum of surgical skill could perform equally as well.

In North America today, there are some who suggest that orthopaedists should relegate the nonsurgical care of fractures to nonsurgical disciplines or that the profession be divided into two clearly identified branches: one composed of the traditional orthopaedists who are trained to perform surgery, and the other of orthopaedists who will deal only with non-surgically treated conditions. This second group would refer surgical candidates to their surgically trained colleagues.

I find fault in both suggestions. The referral of nonsurgical patients to other nonsurgical disciplines is a naive approach to a problem. Once other groups are empowered to treat fractures by nonsurgical means, they will soon dictate which ones should be treated surgically. Splitting orthopaedists into surgeons and nonsurgeons will do nothing but bring about the prompt demise of our profession. Internecine conflicts would take place within a very short time, with obvious disastrous consequences. Friction, jealousy, and competition within the profession would inevitably result much to the detriment of all.

We should learn from the central European experience where traumatology split away from orthopaedics and became the dominant force in trauma care. Within a few years the traumatologists, however, expanded their territory so much that at this time they perform arthroscopic surgery, elective total joint replacement, and reconstructive surgery for degenerative and developmental conditions of the spine and upper and lower extremities. A professional relationship between orthopaedists and traumatologists is virtually nonexistent. I suspect that economic and sociopolitical events will bring the two groups together again in the not too distant future.

The breakdown of orthopaedics in our country will be accompanied with problems similar to those observed in central Europe. In addition, either proposal will provoke the same response from third-party payers. They will assume that the care of fractures without surgery is cheaper and will do everything they can to see that as many fractures as possible are treated without surgery. The entrepreneurs who have gained control of the so-called managed care programs will see unexpected revenues for their already swollen personal coffers. In the process, patients will be harmed since many who should have their fractures treated by surgical means will be managed conservatively.

The last few years have demonstrated that organized medicine has not done a very good job at preventing problems. Only time will tell whether or not our profession will be wise enough to realize the fallacy of such proposals and nip them in the bud.

I do not question that today surgical treatment is the gold standard for the management of many fractures. It is the one standard against which other treatments must be measured. I also admit that the day might come when all fractures will be best treated by surgical means. Improved surgical materials and imaging technology could make that scenario possible.

ADDENDA

If we accept that eventually surgical treatment will be applicable to all fractures, there are important factors to consider. The first is that is fracture care consists simply of fixing them without the need for a biological background on the part of treating physicians, it is ludicrous to require the long training period we have this time; a shorter one should suffice. Also, others will treat fractures and they will be main users of growth factors when the new technology reaches the clinical level.

Today, even though in the most technically advanced nations many fractures are still treated by nonsurgical means, we are witnessing a rapid reduction in health care budget allocations. One can only imagine what the cuts will be when all fractures are treated surgically, when every patient will have surgery, not just once but twice, since removal of the fixation devices will be necessary in many instances. The cost of fracture care will escalate dramatically and the quality of care will inevitably deteriorate.

In our country and in other nations where some type of fee for service still exists, the reimbursement to physicians has plummeted. If we have an increase in the number of surgical procedures, the reduction will be even greater. It will be so low that surgeons often will choose the nonsurgical approach. Their technicians will do the casting and bracing while the surgeons devote their time and effort to performing the more lucrative arthroscopy, the reconstructive surgery of arthritic joints and the surgical correction of extremities disabled from the improper use of nonsurgical treatment of fractures that should have been treated surgically.

There are reasons for the epidemic of surgery which are not openly acknowledged. In many instances, the surgical fixation of fractures is preferred because it is easier to carry out and more convenient for the surgeon, not because it has proven superior. Surgery is also more prestigious in the eyes of society and definitely more rewarding financially. Also, the role the ubiquitous and powerful industry plays in this regard cannot be underestimated.

In many less economically developed countries, the mathematics of reimbursement is quite simple. Payment for surgery is usually ten times the payment for nonsurgical treatment. For a fractured humerus in some Latin American countries, the physician receives $80.00 for non-surgical care and $800.00 for surgery. It is also well known that when surgery is performed, very often the vendor of the surgical implant gives the surgeon, under the table, an amount of money greater than that paid to him by either the government or private insurance.

In the case of more expensive implants, such as total joint prostheses, the kickback is even more egregious. In some countries, the surgeon is given as much as $1,000.00 for every hip prosthesis he uses. The patient, who pays the vendor for the implant, is overcharged to facilitate the dishonorable transaction. In addition, if the surgeon is a regular customer of a specific vendor or company, all his traveling and lodging expenses at major orthopaedic meetings are paid. To some extent, these practices also take place in the United States and other highly developed countries.

ADDENDA

One could suspect that reimbursement to the orthopaedist is lowered by government or private agencies because they realize that the loss of revenue will be offset by industry or by the entrepreneurial organizations that have lured, with a measure of success, many into accepting financial recompense for ordering MRI and CT scans from their privately operated facilities. These arrangements satisfy those who have agreed to participate in such unethical schemes but profoundly affect the ethical physicians who find them inappropriate. It becomes increasingly difficult to resist the lure of such attractive financial temptations.

The unacknowledged engine that drives the unreasonable abuse of surgery sweeping the world is greed, the insatiable hunger for profit. Both industry and the medical profession have cheapened themselves by such practices. It is a sign of the low self-esteem to which our respective professions have allowed themselves to sink.

Some will accuse me of living in the past and will argue that such is the contemporary nature of business and, therefore, appropriate. I do not agree with that premise. Medicine is not a business, it is a profession. Its members, since the days of Hippocrates, have sworn to place the interest of their patients before their own. If our profession has come to the conclusion that such a philosophy and values are outdated, then, I submit to you, we are in serious trouble.

I am currently President of ARTOF, the Association for the Rational Treatment of Fractures. ARTOF is not an organization promoting the nonsurgical treatment of fractures. Quite to the contrary, it recognizes that the surgical treatment is, in many instances, the gold standard against which other treatments must be measured. It recognizes that there are a number of treatment modalities which have clear indications for their usage and seeks to reach a consensus among the orthopaedic community as to the most appropriate treatment under the circumstances. ARTOF is committed to the preservation of the biological foundations of our profession and wishes to put economic considerations in proper perspective.

ARTOF objects to any attempts by self-anointed individuals or groups to arbitrarily call themselves sole possessors of the truth and declare that they define what constitutes high standards of fracture care. Such intellectual hubris has no place in sophisticated societies.

ARTOF encourages the orthopaedic community to develop treatment protocols independent from third-party payers whose main concern appears to be reduction of health care costs or from industry with its profit driven agenda.

I am not sending a call to arms for a war between the old and the new. I am simply asking for a reason at a time when circumstances call for objectivity and practical solutions. Neither am I suggesting a move against industry, for in a confrontation our profession would be the ultimate loser. Our relationship with industry must be nurtured, but with the clear understanding that preservation of our own values is essential and in the best interest of both parties.

I urge and challenge the Orthopaedic Trauma Association, the Academic Orthopedic Society, the American Board of Orthopedic Surgery, the American Academy of Orthopaedic Surgeons, and the orthopaedic community in general to take a serious look at our profession

ADDENDA

in light of unfolding events, at the way we teach our students and practicing colleagues, at the role and place of subspecialties within our discipline, at the steady erosion of orthopaedics, at our relationship with industry, and at the image we project to the medical community.

Medicine is undergoing profound changes, not only in regards to its scientific scope and opportunities, but in its relationship with society and the national and world economies. A return to the past is impossible and undesirable. We must adjust to and participate in those changes. However, noxious and dangerous trends and even improper and unethical practices are permeating and undermining the essential basic tenets and foundations of our profession. No doubt is easier for all of us to remain silent, but that is not the right thing to do.

If we do not make a serious effort to correct the wrongs, matters will get worse and our heirs will find themselves in a profession whose ethical foundations and values we allowed to collapse.

Jour. Orthop. Trauma, Vol.7, No1: 66-78, 1999

ADDENDA

Addendum # 7

RESPONDING TO CHANGE

The orthopaedic community is deeply concerned about the changes brought about by health-care reform. The primary concerns seem to be centered around the increasing loss of autonomy, the reduction in reimbursement for services provided, the overwhelming number of regulations that border on the irrational, and the perception that there are too many orthopaedists. The entire scenario almost seems to be designed to break the spirit of the medical profession in the hope that physicians, in frustration, eventually will accept a system of controlled National Health Insurance in which they are salaried employees.

While I do not question the legitimacy of those concerns, I believe that efforts to offset the real or perceived trends will be futile unless we acknowledge that we are, to some extent, willingly or unwillingly responsible for many of the problems that we now confront. I suspect that, unless we make a major effort to modify a number of deeply rooted attitudes and practices, we will lose the battle and, in the not-too-distant future, the discipline of orthopaedics will cease to exist.

Economic considerations prompted the government to initiate health-care reform. Organized medicine responded not by officially agreeing that the escalating cost of medical care was a problem that needed to be addressed, but by bemoaning the possible personal financial implications of the proposed plans. We assumed that our fortress was impenetrable and that the discipline was too well entrenched for anything of a draconian nature to happen to us. We refused to acknowledge that we may have played a role in the creation of the escalating cost of medical care, and we continued to indulge in practices that any observer could readily identify as contributing to the problem.

In clear and loud terms, we were told that specialty medicine was too expensive, that specialists relied too heavily on technology, and that too many operations were being performed. Rather than initiating a process to determine whether the charges were valid, we proceeded to indulge in an orgy of technology, to create more subspecialties within our profession, and to treat a greater number of conditions with more ex- pensive operative means. All of these actions contributed to the problems that others were trying to address. Our actions did not go unnoticed. When the fees for services were reduced, we responded by complaining about it and increasing the volume of our services. Many conditions that previously had been treated successfully with simple non-operative means began to be treated operatively instead. This pattern reached the educational institutions, and, within a very short time, new graduates from orthopaedic residency programs were completing their training with only a modicum of understanding and respect for non-operative approaches to diseases and injuries of the musculoskeletal system. Today, the diagnosis and treatment of musculoskeletal conditions nearly always involve the use of expensive technology. For example, tendinitis and bursitis demand not just a physical examination but magnetic resonance imaging as well. A sprained joint is thought to require, in addition to magnetic resonance imaging, an arthroscopic procedure followed by expensive and prolonged physical therapy. Low-back pain, even in the absence of a neurological deficit, is approached with a battery of costly tests followed, once again, by prolonged physical therapy. Although many graduates finish their residency seeming to know little about how to reduce a fracture and immobilize it in a cast, they do know how to insert an intramedullary nail, secure a plate, and apply an external fixator. In fact, I believe that many orthopaedic residents are being trained to be skeletal cosmetologists rather than physicians. An unjustified and unreasonable obsession with perfect anatomical restoration recently has dominated the minds of many, particularly in the field of fracture care. Inconsequential abnormalities are considered to be indications for operative treatment because of the fear of undocumented undesirable sequelae.

Some individuals in academic medicine suggest that orthopaedists should treat only fractures that necessitate an operation and leave the closed treatment of fractures to others. This, I believe, would be professional suicide. Once others become responsible for the non-operative care of fractures, they will instruct the orthopaedist as to which fractures are to be treated with operative means, rather than the other way around.

The emphasis on cost containment has given those outside our profession an opportunity to extend the scope of their disciplines. Today, the neurosurgeon not only performs stabilization procedures on the spine but is often the one who is identified by the medical profession and the public at large as the expert in that area. Similarly, the plastic surgeon is considered by many to be the true hand surgeon, and his or her presence in the orthopaedic operating room is thought to be essential for the care of patients who have a fracture associated with soft-tissue damage. Pediatricians and family physicians treat so-called simple fractures with increasing frequency. Podiatrists now consider the operative treatment of tibial fractures to be part of their armamentarium. Third-party payers welcome the involvement of non-orthopaedists because of the perception that it generally reduces the cost of care.

Thus, the field of orthopaedics has become an attractive prey; it has been easy for others to move in and capture a large portion of our territory. I suspect that other practitioners no longer view orthopaedics as a comprehensive body of knowledge that requires long and rigorous training but rather consider it simply as a series of operative procedures that anyone with surgical skills can readily master. Having reasoned in that manner, these other practitioners only needed to re- quest instructions on how to use the instrumentation from the orthopaedic manufacturing companies. Indus- try saw a new market opportunity and readily accommodated their desires.

To complicate matters, orthopaedists became infatuated with sub specialization and the prestige that sub- specialty societies offered. New and often superfluous societies were established for many specific bones and joints as well as for several operative techniques and diseases. I believe that the large number of operations required for membership in some societies can be an inducement to perform unnecessary procedures. Many of these societies publish their own journals and hold educational meetings in isolation from the rest of the profession. They also established lobbying offices in Washington in the hope of gaining a direct and more effective voice in the halls of Congress. In doing so, they have weakened the cohesiveness of our profession.

ADDENDA

Some twenty-five years ago, academicians began, with the best of intentions, to structure orthopaedic departments to fit the subspecialty trend. Educational institutions recruited faculty who limited their practices to smaller and smaller areas of the body. As the faculty had to be accommodated with residents, rotations through the various sections became shorter and shorter. Soon thereafter, fellowships began to receive greater emphasis, and it did not take long for them to become status symbols. Most residents completed a fellowship, regardless of whether or not they needed additional education. However, in the current health-care environment, many physicians never have the opportunity to practice in the area in which they have received additional training. Managed care and government regulations now discourage rather than encourage referrals to specialists.

To identify problems without offering answers is unwise. Therefore, I will present some possible solutions. I recognize that most will be difficult to implement because of existing practices and long-held beliefs, inherent conflicts of interest, and the natural inclination to accept the status quo.

I suggest that the current system of resident rotations through every subspecialty be replaced with a system that encourages greater exposure to general orthopaedics throughout the entire training program. In that manner, the resident would feel comfortable managing the operative and non-operative aspects of orthopaedics on the completion of training. The frustration and insecurity that short rotations generate would be assuaged. Rotations that are limited to one specific area, such as pediatric orthopaedics, could be preserved, whereas those that focus on more esoteric and highly specialized areas, such as scoliosis and oncology, could be deemphasized.

One could argue that a structured exposure to sub- specialties is imperative because of the explosion of knowledge and technology during the last few decades. My answer to this argument is that, to a large extent, the body of knowledge in orthopaedics is not necessarily greater. Instead, new knowledge has replaced old knowledge. Other professions and trades have clearly demonstrated that point. I also suggest that orthopaedic postgraduate fellowships be deemphasized. Such fellowships should be offered only to those who truly need additional education, either because of deficiencies in the program that they completed or because they have a clear interest, and hope to carry out future research, in one particular sub- discipline. Additional criteria could be established as well. In my opinion, there is little doubt that five years of training in a well-balanced program provides the orthopaedic resident with sufficient education to practice good orthopaedics in the operative and non-operative arenas,

The Council of Musculoskeletal Specialty Societies (COMSS) could help to accomplish these goals by re- structuring itself in a manner that would preserve the existence of groups that focus on specific areas of orthopaedics while eliminating the perceived elitist nature of the system as it is today. The existing barriers to membership in subspecialty societies should be lowered, and unreasonably restrictive criteria should be eliminated. It is not necessary to issue certificates of membership or certificates of additional competency. The field of orthopaedics has a well-structured mechanism to ensure that its members are competent to practice in all areas of the discipline. The rigorous and extensive period of education along with board certification and recertification should suffice. There is no evidence that the addition of new, artificial barriers has enhanced the quality of care.

The composition of the Board of Directors of The American Academy of Orthopaedic Surgeons also should reflect the proposed new philosophy. This goal can be achieved by having all Board members elected by the fellowship. At this time, there are a number of appointed representatives on the Board. Such preferential treatment sends a message to the orthopaedic community that there are some individuals who, for reasons of sub specialization or positions held in certain societies, belong to a higher level in the hierarchy of the profession. This unhealthy perception should be dispelled.

The American Academy of Orthopaedic Surgeons could set a good example by changing its name to The American Academy of Orthopaedics. Such a move would deemphasize the operative aspect of the discipline and would indicate to the public that members of The Academy have been educated to provide the best non-operative as well as the best operative treatment of conditions of the musculoskeletal system. To my knowledge, no one has ever questioned the competence of urologists, ophthalmologists, and others regarding their operative and non-operative expertise. The names of their Academies do not include the word surgeons. Ours should not either.

A major step in paving the way to success would be for the body of orthopaedists to carefully assess its relationship with industry. Our organizations must make it clear that the postgraduate education of orthopaedists should be determined and controlled by the profession itself. This can and should be done without belittling the important role that industry has played, and should continue to play, in the development of the specialty.

We must agree that the cost of orthopaedic care is high and reject the argument that, because this country is very wealthy, it does not matter whether the health- care component of the national budget is 8, 10, or 20 per cent. The medical profession is an important component of society, and it is obligated to use its privileges and to discharge its responsibilities in the most prudent manner. To claim that we should be free to spend as much as we want is not a good argument. We should be al- lowed to spend as much as is necessary, provided that the approach is unselfish, reasonable, and objective. Society cannot, and should not, tolerate abuse simply because there is money to pay for it.

I sincerely believe that these issues should greatly concern us and suspect that, unless current trends are tempered or modified, our specialty will be in serious danger of ceasing to exist.

I will accept criticism for this commentary if criticism is to come. My ideas on these issues are the product of the careful observation and study of my profession during my long tenure in the practice of orthopaedics, in education as well as in research and medical administration.

Commentary. Journal of Bone and Joint Surgery. Vol. 80A, No. 4, April, 1998: 601-603.

ADDENDA

Addendum # 8

EDUCATION IS KEY TO NON-OPERATIVE CARE

It was reassuring to hear Doctor D'Ambrosia's First Vice Presidential address to the Academy (1999 Annual Meeting) emphasizing how important it is for the orthopaedist to seek Involvement in the nonsurgical care of patients with musculoskeletal problems. He eloquently echoed statements made previously by his predecessor, James Heckman, M.D. To see continuity of purpose in the hierarchy of the Academy is indeed a welcome development.

Placing emphasis on our broader involvement in nonoperative orthopaedics is music to my ears. For many years, I tried to champion that concept, both as an academician, as well as an officer of the Academy. During my eight years on its Board of Directors and as its President in 1991-1992, I strived to increase the awareness among my colleagues of the dangers of our exaggerated glorification and promotion of surgical sub specialization in our discipline. I also did my very best to warn all concerned parties of the erosion of our profession and the likely consequences of the steady loss of territory to others in medicine and surgery.

Earlier in my career, I suspected that those trends which began in the 1960's needed attention. As a newly-appointed chairman of the department of orthopaedics at the University of Miami, I persuaded the dean of the medical school to change the name of the department to "orthopaedics and rehabilitation". He acquiesced and ours became the first such department in the country. Several other departments of orthopaedics across the land followed suit and became departments of orthopaedics and rehabilitation.

Having a department with enlarged educational and patient care opportunities made it possible for us to maintain control of a large segment of musculoskeletal territory which was slowly being taken away by others. I think we succeeded in attaining our goals. Residents became exposed in a major way to musculoskeletal conditions where surgery is not a major component, but where the orthopaedist's understanding of their pathophysiology best qualifies us to be the primary providers of care. Victims of hemiplegia, amputees and spinal cord injured patients constituted a large segment of the teaching material. This happened without neglecting the traditional traumatic, congenital, developmental and degenerative diseases.

Unfortunately, the explosion of surgically related technology and the advent of total joint replacement and arthroscopic surgery in the early 1970s rapidly diminished the fledgling interest in rehabilitation while enhancing a parallel growth in the surgical management of orthopaedic conditions. Now, we are witnessing developments that concern all of us. For example, neurosurgeons, plastic surgeons, podiatrists, chiropractors, general practitioners, rheumatologists and others have become responsible for the care of an increasing larger number of patients with conditions of the musculoskeletal system which previously were managed entirely by the orthopaedist.

ADDENDA

As I reflect on the possible outcome of the Academy's efforts to stem the tide and encourage the orthopaedist to assume once again the care of those patients, I worry over the best way to accomplish that goal. It is not an easy task, but a tall order. Words and good intentions will not do any good. Action is essential. We must realize that effective change cannot take place unless a rather evolutionary joint effort of multiple segments within our profession can be orchestrated.

Without major restructuring of residency education, nothing will ever be accomplished. If future generations of orthopaedists are not appropriately trained in the surgical and nonsurgical management of musculoskeletal conditions, nothing will change. Assuming that such a reorganization takes place, the question of who in academic medicine will do the teaching must be answered. For the most part, orthopaedists knowledgeable in the nonsurgical management of musculoskeletal conditions are not found in the full-time faculty of medical schools. Department chairmen and deans encourage the recruitment of orthopaedists whose private surgical practices are guaranteed to be financially successful. Those on the faculty who do not contribute generously to the department coffers and have to support themselves oftentimes find their positions discontinued. It is well known that deans involved with for-profit hospitals excuse the major revenue producing surgeons of any educational responsibilities with nonpaying indigent patients so their time in the operating room, taking care of the insured, is not infringed upon.

Will deans and department chairmen be willing to subsidize the salary of the faculty who devote a major portion of their time to teaching students and residents the nonoperative aspects of patient care and who by the nature of their work are not major earners? I seriously doubt it. Even if that eventuality were to take place, where are the candidates for those positions unless the chairmen and deans are willing to accept orthopaedists who in earlier years learned the nonsurgical aspects of orthopaedics. This, because those who graduated in the recent past never learned that segment of the profession.

The next question that needs to be addressed is whether or not the Academy will provide major support to the effort and assist financially in its development and implementation. Based on my perception of the direction in which the organization has elected to move, I doubt it. In spite of the reassuring words we have heard in recent months that the establishment of the parallel (c) (6) organization will not diminish the Academy's major commitment to education, I suspect that the move toward a trade union organization is inevitable and education might take a back-seat to lobbying the political establishment. Not only could the money available to educational endeavors decrease, but the interest in education might diminish.

We have observed with some discomfort the Academy's recent exaggerated emphasis on business affairs, and I suspect that the amassing of greater and greater profit has become a major obsession in the minds of the hierarchy of the organization. Its commercialization has become rampant. Its financial independence is virtually nonexistence as it depends more and more on industrial subsidies to support its many educational activities. The Annual Meeting is a show where the tail wags the dog and commercial exhibits are a major source of revenue for the Academy. The Academy's significant and successful involvement in

ADDENDA

publishing medical journals and textbooks, the filling of half the Journal of the American Academy of Orthopaedic Surgeons and the Bulletin pages with paid advertisement of commercial products, and more recently the use of the Annual Meeting's printed program for the marketing of drugs and orthopaedic gadgets are clear indicators of the direction in which the organization is moving. At the most recent Annual Meeting in Anaheim, we witnessed, for the first time, the sale of syllabuses, prepared by the various speakers participating in the symposia.

Some probably believe sincerely that such moves are appropriate and they might be in concert with of the ethos of the times. However, I consider them ominous warnings that the Academy's major commitment to education may be dwindling in favor of one directed toward business. I wish President D'Ambrosia success in his position in the Academy's hierarchy and offer him my unconditional support. I know that many in the fellowship feel the same way.

AAOS Bulletin, Letter to the Editor, 1999

ADDENDA

Addendum # 9

MEDICINE AND INDUSTRY:

The Payor, the Piper and the Tune

During my internship, rotating through orthopaedics, I first heard of Doctor Gallie. His name stuck with me because shortly afterwards I was told that his ideas about a number of subjects ran contrary to the practices of the day.

In particular, I remember his writings on the effects of immobilization on cartilage behavior where he combined original scientific concepts with typical Canadian pragmatism. When I later developed a keen interest in fracture healing, his teachings became inspirational to me.

Serving today as the Gallie Lecturer for this most distinguished Royal College of Physicians and Surgeons of Canada is indeed an immense honor. I will treasure your invitation, and this day, forever.

The sub-title of my address, "The Payor, the Piper and the Tune," reflects realization that the relationship between medicine and industry can be summarized with the remark from the old German children's story: "He who pays the piper calls the tune." That, in essence, sums up the issue. The economic power and the resulting awesome influence of industry are at the core of any conversation on the subject.

Absent the pharmaceutical and medical/surgical manufacturing companies, our respective countries would not have attained the degree of medical excellence they now possess. There is no need to recite the litany of advances in patient care that industry's contributions have made possible. They are well known to all of us. It is necessary, however, to look at those advances and to consider whether or not our profession has paid an unreasonably high price for them. I believe we have paid a very high price, indeed.

Until relatively recently, it was not difficult to view industry and medicine as two different entities. To the medical profession, industry meant the drug and medical appliance manufacturing companies. Pure and simple. There was no question Medicine was a profession and industry a business. Medicine had patients and industry had customers.

Industry had its own set of rules. Its practices were all aimed at generating profit. Medicine, being a profession, adhered to the principle that professionals are individuals with a particular expertise and an ideology of service who place the interests of those they serve ahead of their own.

ADDENDA

We had developed our own code of Ethics, though we knew that Ethics, as a distinct branch of philosophy, dealt with universal principles of conduct. Our principles were not items to be purchased to satisfy individual needs.

The values and principles of conduct for many physicians and industry representatives now seem indistinguishable. The line differentiating them is blurred and barely visible. Sadly, industry has not chosen to adopt our code of ethics. Rather, medicine has allowed industry to impose its values on members of the medical profession.

This is why many now consider medicine a business. The definition of a profession is ignored or has been forgotten. Increasingly, we are forced to consider medicine as simply another industry: the medical Industry. And a number of medicine-related areas such as medical education, research, hospitals, sub-specialties, rehabilitation, investor- owned managed care and others, have become little more than branches of the Medical Industrial Complex [1].

I do not wish to indulge in exploring the genesis of the transformation. It is too complicated for me to fully comprehend, let alone discuss. I am simply a concerned observer of the events that have shaped and continue to shape our profession. I am aware of the major role played by the multitude of social and economic developments as well as the spectacular success of medical technology in the creation of the current dilemma.

Medicine's increasing reliance on technology has resulted in a significant neglect of the biological foundations of our profession. In orthopaedics, perhaps because of its highly technical nature, technology is rapidly eliminating the need for the clinical acumen previously required in the diagnosis and treatment of a large number of conditions of the musculoskeletal system. The care of fractures, the replacement of joints and many other therapeutic modalities have become almost totally a series of technical exercises.

In orthopaedics, we call those changes progress and indeed, they are. It would be difficult to deny that our patients, at least in developed nations, are better off today because of them. In the long run, time will tell whether they truly benefited mankind.

Daniel Callahan, one of the leading ethicists in modern America stated, "There is no necessary correlation between the kind of innovation generated by the market and the kind of technology needed to improve overall health. On the contrary, innovative medical technology is designed to appeal to manufactures' desires for profit and consumers' demands for constant medical improvements. Improved health may be a desired and foreseeable outcome, but profit is the initiating motive." He added, "The market is likely to see its greatest profits, and its greatest public lure, in just those techniques".[2]

On a number of occasions I have made reference to an experience with an orthopaedic resident who sat in the back of the room reading a newspaper while I was giving a lecture on the effects of the environment on bone healing. When confronted by me, he responded, with amazing candor, that he was not interested in knowing how fractures heal. He simply wanted to know how to fix them. He was expressing comfort with the fact that in some segments of the discipline the orthopaedist was less a physician and more a cosmetic surgeon of the skeleton.

That experience had a profound impact on my thinking regarding the future of medicine. At first, I thought the young resident was an aberration and that others reasoned differently. After probing further into the matter, I concluded that he was, in effect, speaking on behalf of many of his contemporaries and expressing, quite accurately, the ethos of the times.

After all, his education had taken place in an environment that emphasized technique over the biological sciences. The lectures he listened to were, for the most part, related to the technical aspects of treatment modalities. "What operation does this fracture need?" was the question the sight of an x-ray depicting a fracture instinctively provoked. It had replaced the traditional, "What is best for this patient."

The commercial throwaway magazines, tabloid medical journals that frequently report on untested new products and operations had become his most common source of information. For the most part, he had relegated the peer review journals to a secondary level of importance.

Several of the "visiting professors" who enriched his educational experience and some of the popular speakers he heard addressing medical meetings were, unbeknownst to him, agents of industry. Peddlers who travel and lecture at medical schools, medical societies, continuing education courses and seminars to market products in which they often have a vested financial interest.

He had attended several continuing education courses, some in resort areas where "new and improved" prostheses and implants were demonstrated. The local industrial representative, very generously, had paid his expenses. I am sure this student did not pause to consider that the claims of superiority of the new products had not been documented and that the research preceding their release was probably non-existent. If he had given thought to the alleged improvements, he may have wondered how this was possible when between the years of 1976 and 1995 the Food and Drug Administration had approved over 700 new applications concerning total hip prostheses [3].

I should have enlightened the young doctor by telling him about a continuing education course in Los Angeles dealing with joint arthroplasty, for which I had assembled a distinguished international faculty. I had also invited orthopaedic manufacturing companies to display their products in the exhibit hall of the hotel. I had asked them, in return, to make a financial contribution to defray the cost of the meeting.

They accepted the arrangement. Among the many manufacturers represented, several of them wrote letters inquiring how many speakers they were entitled to appoint. Industry was anxious to partake in the financing of the course but also expected to be able to select the faculty.

I should have also told the fledgling orthopaedist that only a few weeks earlier I had been visited by the vice-president of a major manufacturing company who presented me with a box containing a brand-new hip prosthesis his engineers had allegedly developed "according to my philosophy." He stated his company wanted to name the implant the "Sarmiento Total Hip Prosthesis." Before I had a chance to tell him that I was not aware I had a unique philosophy, he presented me with a check in the amount of $250.000 dollars. Royalties were to be discussed next. I rejected the offer. A few months later the prosthesis was advertised in major journals. A well-known orthopaedist was given credit for the implant's unique features.

The resident may have also benefited from knowing that on another occasion I had been offered a "very good deal" from a major distributor of surgical implants. He promised to give me $200 for every prosthesis of his we used at the five University of Southern California affiliated hospitals. Pretending to be interested in the attractive financial venture, I asked if the figure was negotiable and suggested $250 dollars.

His immediate response was, "That's a deal." When I asked the gentleman what made him think I would accept such a dishonest proposal, he became visibly embarrassed and apologized profusely. However, just before leaving, he said, "But Doctor, we do this all the time."

These few anecdotal experiences, which many others in orthopaedics and in different branches of medicine have shared, exemplify quite well some aspects of the current relationship between medicine and industry. The relationship should be balanced but it is not. The balance has been replaced by the dominance of one party: Industry now pays the piper and calls the tune.

At the root of the overall issue is one incontrovertible fact: in its dealing with industry, medicine has compromised professionalism in order to reap financial benefits. We have sold our birthright for a pot of porridge.

Are my remarks exaggerations? Am I blinded by a few unsavory personal experiences?

Let me attempt to illustrate several areas in order to support my views.

ADVERTISING

Physicians long considered that advertising and marketing themselves was inappropriate and demeaning. The practice was acceptable for others outside the medical profession. Today, an increasingly large number of physicians freely use all available media to market themselves without shame or sanction.

I suspect this trend was aggravated when industry took it upon itself to identify physicians who were willing to cooperate with them in the marketing of their products. They showered them with attractive financial opportunities and the likelihood of instant fame.

It is no secret that industry has very successfully capitalized on the endorsement of those individuals. When the name of a well-known physician or institution is identified with a product the response from the public and the medical community is more favorable. It works for selling medications and medical appliances just like it works for basketball shoes. Why not? What's the difference?

The drug manufacturing companies had, until recently, limited their open-media marketing techniques to over the counter drugs: analgesics, laxatives, vitamins and like-products. Today, in the United States prescription drugs are also marketed on TV and radio and in newspapers and magazines. And more recently through the Internet. Obviously, this is being done in an effort to persuade the lay audience to pressure their physicians to prescribe such products for them. And it's working.

EDUCATION

There is no doubt in my mind that the continuing education of the American physician is structured largely to satisfy the marketing needs of industry.

Industry is currently responsible for a very large percentage of all continuing educational activities in my country. Probably, a thousand CME courses a year are held under its direct or indirect control. Directly, when it is officially announced as part of its marketing effort. Indirectly, when the educational courses are offered in "cooperation" with universities, hospitals or medical societies. In such a manner industry legitimizes its marketing practices and gives a semblance of impartiality to the event.

It is not easy to detect the role industry plays in many of the activities we regularly attend and upon which we depend for our continuing education. From glancing at the scientific content of the program, one does not suspect the machinations that took place in the preparation of the course. In orthopaedics, some of the most successful and best-attended courses dealing with total joint replacement and trauma have become little more than bazaars. Manufacturing companies display their products and well-known orthopaedists preach from the podium on the greatness of their respective implants.

I do not want to criticize the innovators. We owe them a great deal. I only question the subservient role they play to those who market the innovations in ways that subvert medicine and subordinate patient care to corporate interests.

Most educational organizations have welcomed industrial support of their activities because it covers the costs associated with invited guests and other matters. But they have purchased that support at far too high a price.

Dinners, banquets and a multitude of amenities held during medical society meetings are officially acknowledged as being funded by various industrial concerns. The revenues generated from industry have allowed our large medical academies to hold the elaborate and extravagant meetings we attend today.

The endowment of chairs to universities and other educational institutions by industrial concerns, often carefully disguised as private foundations, is becoming more frequent. A condition imposed by the generous donors that the recipient of the chair be selected by the grantor makes it obvious that something is expected in return. Industry and the university administration are the only winners.

We are prisoners in a gilded cage that we ourselves have built.

INVESTOR OWNED MANAGED CARE

While the government, employers and insurance companies struggled with the relentless escalation of medical costs, investor-owned managed care appeared on the scene. Its arrival was welcomed by many, particularly those who favored having the private sector assume full responsibility for the control of health related matters. The government would be out of the picture. Initially, the public found the benefits offered by the HMO's to be very attractive. With the speed of lightning, the new industry spread throughout the land and for a while it was taken for granted it would soon replace all other methods. It did not take long for dissatisfaction to grow. The medical profession realized its autonomy was being destroyed. Physicians, who had finally admitted that curtailment of costs was essential watched the success of the new managed care system with some enthusiasm. They assumed the government would be kept out of their affairs.

Then they saw reimbursement for their services reduced dramatically. They lost their traditional role in determining whether or not admissions to the hospital were necessary. Even their choice of treatment modalities was monitored and subjected to the veto power of non-medical personnel. They had become little more than corporate functionaries, whose every decision was subject to review.

The lay community was mesmerized into delusional thinking that the new system would answer all their needs. They happily followed the fad and joined HMOs while healthy. When illness struck, they discovered that they had lost the freedom to choose a physician, and then learned about the denial of many services requested by their doctors.

It is very likely that investor-owned managed care will not last much longer. Arnold Relman, who has critically followed the health care crisis over the years, wrote that this industry has "already seen its best days" [4]. He is probably right. The profit making philosophy that governs the system is incompatible with good medical care. In the long run, it is even incompatible with cost containment since all savings in the cost of medical care will be consumed by stockholder dividends and executive salaries. Entrepreneurs will benefit. Physicians and patients will pay.

FOR-PROFIT HOSPITALS

The growth of the for-profit hospitals a couple of decades ago was received with enthusiasm in some quarters. It was heralded as the answer to escalating costs and declining quality of patient care. That, too, has turned out to be a naïve assumption. In general, for-profit hospitals have neither reduced cost nor improved quality. Too often, they have produced the opposite result.

For-profit hospital chains have become giant business corporations. Their CEO's and other top executives have become multi-millionaires overnight, while nursing staffs and other essential personnel were cut to a bare minimum. Support for financially profitable though medically questionable programs has been expanded. On a number of occasions, for-profit hospitals became sources of egregious dishonesty, abuse and outright fraud.

The transformation of American hospitals from community institutions to businesses is now almost complete. Profit margin and stock price are the banners guiding the performance and mission of many for-profit hospitals. Traditional quality measures are now virtually ignored since patient care is rarely if ever a priority.

AMBULATORY CARE INDUSTRY:

We learned long ago that the explosion of medical technology was creating a major additional cost to the economy. Costs had to be curtailed. We, in medicine, ignored the warnings and failed to do something about it. Rather than moderating its use, we used even more. Some in the profession saw opportunities to benefit and embarked in commercial ventures of various types.

Freestanding MRI and CT scan facilities appeared throughout the country. Equipment purchased by entrepreneur's lured physicians into the profitable ventures. The Physicians-Partners sought opportunities to increase their income by referring their patients to certain facilities.

It was reported at one time that in the State of Florida, forty per cent of medical doctors had some type of involvement in medical commercial business such as MRI or CT scan facilities, physical therapy programs, or many others. The government, finally intervened and forbade such activities.

Freestanding medical and surgical facilities also came into the picture. Monitoring of quality of care at these low-capital cost, high-income facilities soon proved difficult. It is now possible to perform a larger number of surgical procedures outside the traditional in-hospital operating room. Therefore, many surgical interventions are performed in the isolation and privacy of freestanding ambulatory surgery facilities and in doctors' offices.

Some physicians—a growing minority who seem to view their profession exclusively as means to maximize revenues—have abused this new opportunity. In the absence of the rigorous peer and administrative oversight inherent in a hospital environment, they can deviate from normal ethical and professional boundaries without the fear of exposure and sanction. We can rightly call this new venture the Ambulatory Care Industry.

ADDENDA

SUBSPECIALIZATION

We, in medicine, were told that excessive sub-specialization was contributing to the increased cost of care. We responded simply by admitting that charges submitted by specialists are usually higher than those from non-specialists. We argued that such added fees were customary, usual, proper, and produced better patient care.

Rather than reducing the number of sub-specialists, we increased it. In the United States, there are nearly 30 different sub-specialty societies in orthopaedics alone. One gets the impression there is a society for every bone and joint in the body, as well as for a number of specific surgical techniques and several pathological conditions.

Joseph Califano, former Secretary of Health in the United States wrote, "The specialization of practice, however necessary to keep up with the constant spin of the medical merry-go-round of innovation and newly found knowledge all too often encourages the drift between a doctor's interest and a patient's needs."

Califano goes on to say that a "cease-fire is needed in this struggle, which has accelerated the medical equipment arms race with cost far beyond benefits to most Americans."[5] He quotes Robert Reischhauer, former director of the Congressional Budget Office as having said, "In the health care world, innovation is the mother of necessity. Once we discover something we decide we need it."

When reimbursement for medical services was reduced, the volume of services was increased. An epidemic of surgery followed. In my specialty, we are witnessing the widespread abuse of many types of surgery, such as spine instrumentation, arthroscopy and internal fixation of fractures. There is nothing on the horizon to suggest that a voluntary end of this abuse is in sight [6].

To complicate matters, the musculoskeletal territory the orthopaedists had controlled for many generations has become the prey of other medical practitioners. With the help of the manufacturing industry, they learned how to use the necessary instrumentation and how to perform a number of specific surgical procedures. The number of their patients who need these procedures seems to be rising just as quickly as these newcomers learn to do them. Obviously, the cost of care went up even further as the volume of services expanded.

For-profit hospitals have welcomed the new practitioners of surgery with open arms as they saw additional admissions and revenues.

THE RESEARCH INDUSTRY

Medicine no longer depends exclusively on grants from governmental agencies and personal donations for the conduct of research. The pharmaceutical and implant manufacturing industry is now a major partner with the universities. It subsidizes a good percentage of the basic and applied research conducted in medical schools, and also carries out its own in-house investigations.

ADDENDA

I do not know to what extent other medical and surgical disciplines are exposed to the research activities of industrial concerns. In orthopaedics, the fierce competition between the many industrial firms has resulted in an avalanche of new products being released to the medical community on a constant basis. For example, it has been estimated there are currently more than three hundred different total hip prostheses on the market.

Many of these new implants are nothing more than inconsequential modifications of existing prostheses. The claim that extensive research preceded the release of all new products is disingenuous at best. The changes are made to lure surgeons into believing that their usage will improve the clinical results. The cost of implants cannot be expected to decrease under those circumstances. Lower costs would come only from reasonable standardization and more economical channels of distribution.

Though it is very likely that most basic research is conducted in a professional and ethical way, there are reasons to question the findings of some firms. Paying physicians for the recruitment of patients for the evaluation of drugs has been loudly criticized in major newspapers in the United States, but the practice continues. The manufacturers of an anti-coagulant that is now widely used paid physicians as much as $800.00 for every patient in its study. Can this be good science?

THE REHABILITATION INDUSTRY

In my early professional years, I devoted a great deal of time and effort to rehabilitation. I was involved in the establishment of a comprehensive rehabilitation center at the University of Miami. It was the first rehab center in the State of Florida and I served as its director for nearly a decade. Those years gave me the opportunity to see at close range the many benefits patients in need of rehabilitation can receive.

Those experiences also made it possible for me to better appreciate the growth and development of another medically related industry which has been a major source of abuse and fraud in the United States: the Rehabilitation Industry.

Legislation was passed several years ago that gave the Medicare population coverage for rehabilitation of chronic and acute conditions. This legislation was needed and well-intended. However, it quickly became a potential bonanza. Tragically, it opened the door for a stampede of entrepreneurial hospitals and independent organizations.

Nobody seems to have escaped the epidemic of rehabilitation. Physicians and surgeons, confront relentless pressure to use the entire period of in-patient rehabilitation allowed by Medicare or private insurance. In many instances, however, care is needed only for a short period. We used to take great pride in minimizing the extent of rehabilitation required by our patients. Yet hospitals often encourage rehabilitation facilities stays to the absolute maximum allowed by the insurers. Overreacting to the abuse, now third party payors often deny the needed period of rehabilitation.

ADDENDA

Rehabilitation is now a major business and it has extended its tentacles in many directions. Every medical condition appears to be appropriate for some type of rehabilitation care. Physical Therapy facilities have sprouted up all over the map. Schools are now graduating too many therapists, yet the over-saturated marketplace continues to produce more need for therapy.

The flood of rehabilitation–related equipment entering the medical marketplace and filling physical therapy units, staggers one's imagination. Separate billing for every modality of treatment is often submitted and paid accordingly.

The new discipline of Sports Medicine has given major impetus to the attractiveness of rehabilitation. Professional and amateur athletes are often subjected to unreasonably long periods of therapy that typically end only when third-party payment is terminated. The growing popularity of physical fitness, wellness, and youth sports programs may or may not eventually produce a healthier population. We will not know that for many years. We do, however, know that it has already produced an extraordinary boom in the construction and management of rehabilitation facilities.

Tragically, even the most severe health catastrophes—medical conditions such as spinal cord injuries—have also given entrepreneurs the opportunity to reap financial benefits. Despite all of the progress that has been made in the understanding of these conditions, the restoration of functional ambulation remains only a hope.

Nonetheless, a handful of alleged successes are widely publicized by the health care industry. Innocent victims of these terrible disabilities are exploited in order to guarantee continued financial support to the marketers of the false dreams. Actors and sports celebrities become poster-boys to further enrich the financial success of the Rehabilitation Industry.

SURGERY

Over and over, medical literature has identified and reported examples of alleged abuse of surgery in many disciplines, be it obstetrics and caesarian sections; otolaryngology and tonsillectomies; spine surgery and laminectomies; orthopaedics and arthroscopy. These abuses have been documented.

There is no question that the surgical treatment is the gold standard for many conditions. Unfortunately, surgery has been abused far too often. Many conditions that can be safely and less expensively managed conservatively, are treated by surgery, representing an increase in cost.

I can only speak with some degree of authority about my own discipline. In orthopaedics, we have been indulging in an orgy of surgery of such unprecedented dimensions that soon we will witness a profound change in the face of the specialty. Orthopaedics faces the possibility of losing its biological foundations, and becoming simply a craft where the possession of manual skills, and nothing else, are the only requirements for membership in the guild.

ADDENDA

During a visit to a major trauma center I was told that every fracture seen there was treated surgically. Sure that there must be exceptions to such an unreasonable rule, I inquired further. I discovered, however, that even the simplest fractures were subjected to surgery. In fact, most patients required two operations: one for the initial care and a second one for the removal of the stabilizing implants.

Still skeptical about the sweeping statement all fractures were surgically managed and expecting to hear a correction, I facetiously asked if fractures of the clavicle were also operated upon. To my surprise, I was told that with greater and greater frequency, surgery was becoming the treatment of choice. The reason for the new trend was that patients no longer tolerated the lump that some healed fractures left behind. Obviously, hypocrisy had replaced the Hippocratic Oath.

I have long believed that oftentimes, the preference for surgery is due largely to the satisfaction the intervention gives the surgeon and the prestige that accompanies its performance. But equally, if not more important, is that surgical treatments pay better.

EXPORTING TECHNOLOGY TO THE UNDERDEVELOPED WORLD

Anyone who has had an opportunity to observe the practice of medicine in less fortunate regions of the world cannot be but disturbed at the sight of the inferior conditions in the hospitals where care is provided to the poor. However, in the same countries where the infrastructure is so deficient, one often observes the use of the most modern western technology.

Ironically, those with means to afford its use, frequently are victims of the circumstances. Though the surgeons applying the technology may have received technical training, the infrastructure of the facility where the treatment is rendered precludes consistent good clinical results. Complications such as infection are common.

Once I visited a hospital in a developing country where the professor and chief of orthopaedics told me that all long-bone fractures were treated surgically at his institution. He had learned the most modern techniques of fracture treatment at a major hospital in Europe.

What he failed to tell me, as I found out a few hours later from one of his assistants, was that the complication rate was staggering. Many patients who had been treated surgically developed osteomyelitis, frequently requiring amputation. One entire ward was devoted to them.

One cannot help but wonder, what is to be gained from exporting certain modern Western technology to those areas? Technology that is usually costly and requires a sophisticated infrastructure that does not exist in most underdeveloped regions of the world.

ADDENDA

I am convinced that often more harm than good is done to those who become the recipients of our expensive products. A number of African surgeons, unable to hide their annoyance, made that comment to me. As in the case of instruments of war, the sale of medical technology to anybody who wants to purchase it is a very lucrative business but has a large number of unfortunate side effects.

Latin American orthopaedists used to express open anger at the growing practice of industry financially rewarding surgeons for the use of their products. Apparently, the pattern is now so widespread it is accepted without loud complaints. Those who object to it have concluded that there is nothing they can do about it. Since competition between the various companies is fierce and perks such as subsidies to attend national and international meetings are added to the initial deal, the hope of stopping the practice has dwindled.

It is widely known that distributors often pay surgeons who use their joint implants in private patients 100 to 1000 dollars per prosthesis, depending on the country where they practice. This is possible because private patients purchase the prosthesis directly from the vendor, who overcharges the patient in order to facilitate the dishonorable transaction.

This practice is no longer limited to developing countries. It just takes a slightly different shape in the United States, as exemplified by the experience I illustrated earlier regarding the local Los Angeles distributor who offered paybacks to me, when I chaired the department of Orthopaedics at USC. A professor at an European university very candidly admitted to me that several of the people he hired to care for his house and garden in town and at his summer home were paid from under-the-table monies he received from manufacturers.

The flagrant arrogance of wealth and power displayed by the industry representatives carrying out such practices is matched only by the lack of dignity and self-respect of the physicians who lower themselves to indulge in such unethical activities. Their behavior runs contrary to the most basic tenets of professional conduct.

CONCLUSIONS

At first glance it might appear that I am overly preoccupied over the picture of a relationship between medicine and industry that seems to have gone amuck. Some might say that I am a cynic, critical of medicine and industry, in its many disguises, without valid foundations to justify a ridiculous, narrow-minded attitude. That all I have are personal anecdotes of no consequence.

Though there may be kernels of truth in those assumptions, it should not take long for anyone to realize the relationship is now crowded with elements even the most naïve among us would have to consider ominous.

If the issue of professionalism in medicine remains unresolved, it will destroy the foundations of this most noble of professions. Eliot Freidson remarked, "Professionalism is both necessary and desirable for a decent society." [7]. I believe loss of professionalism in the

ADDENDA

medical profession is the most serious challenge facing medicine today. Professionalism, not for the sake of power and control, but as a commitment to service.

Professor Richard Creuss, during the delivery of the Gregg Address, here at McGill University, wisely said, "One can make a point that we in medicine have not failed so much as we have as professionals." [8]

Gradually and perhaps unconsciously, physicians have abandoned the shaft of Aesculapius as their symbol, adopting the Caduceus of Hermes, the god of commerce, in its place. The shaft of Aesculapius has but a single serpent. The Caduceus of Hermes has two serpents intertwined around the rod carried by this Greek god of commerce and trade. Is that change a Freudian slip, suggesting that we physicians now think of ourselves as tradesmen?

One way to address the situation is to accept the changes as a reflection of a society that no longer stands behind traditional values and ethics. A society where greed permeates throughout and who's thirst for profit appears to be insatiable. A society, manufactured by Hollywood, which says "everything is OK", indicating, therefore, that nothing is morally wrong.

I believe the majority of physicians in my country are decent, committed and honest individuals. However, the constant economic pressures to which they are being subjected and the fear of a continued loss of income is making it increasingly difficult for them to resist the temptation to indulge in the inappropriate behavior of the minority. Therefore, I do not have great hopes for a prompt resolution to the problems I have referred to.

An appropriate answer calls for fundamental changes in societal attitudes that may be beyond the realm of the possible. The causes of the changes may be so deeply ingrained in the psyche of so many that only generations of evolution could modify them. However, this is no reason to cave in and give up the quest to right the wrong [9].

Professor Creuss, has expressed optimism by saying that we may have a rare opportunity because there appears to be now a confluence between what the profession wants and the public wishes[8].

Anything is possible. Victor Hugo said once "there is nothing more powerful than an idea whose time has come." Maybe the time for ideas regarding a restoration of medical professionalism has arrived.[10] There are reasons to be hopeful. There is more awareness, more concern, more understanding of fundamental issues than at any time in the past. An astute observer of the situation in the United States commented that there was no need for health care reform, only greed reform.

Throughout recorded history, nations and institutions have voiced concerns over impending crises of a political, military, economic or moral nature. Often the concerns proved valid. Other times not. In all walks of life, in the Western World, we have seen profound changes in the last several decades. At times, they are suggestive of a brighter future. Other times they augur impending disaster. Some claim our civilization is just beginning to blossom. Others see signs of decline. President Vaclav Havel, of the Czech Republic, one of the truly

ADDENDA

great thinkers of our time and a living incarnation of Plato's Philosopher King, remarked during an address to a joint session of the United States Congress, that "without a global revolution in the sphere of human consciousness, nothing will change for the better, and the catastrophe toward which the world is headed will be unavoidable."

We might find ourselves, perhaps from ignorance, not in agreement with the playwright-politician and remain complacent about the ultimate triumph of the current system that in so many ways seems to be the way to universal prosperity. I would be remiss, however, if I did not acknowledge doubts about the ultimate success of profit-driven medicine.

It is overwhelmingly obvious we can no longer blame others for the predicaments we now confront. We ourselves are largely responsible for them. Shall we say, according to the popular American cartoon figure Pogo, "We have met the enemy and he is us?"

"The fault, dear Brutus, is not in our stars, but in ourselves" Those were Caesar final words as his traitor-friend stabbed him to death. Those are my words to you today.

For many years, the medical establishment in the United States has attacked the National Health system of Canada. It has argued that that your system represses physician income, prevents innovation and progress, and provides inferior care, and for those reasons some of your physicians move to the United States.

I would like to suggest at this time that the shoe be officially moved to the other foot. It is now your turn to judge the American system. You need not be gentle. We have earned your criticism—royally.

I trust my remarks will be accepted as a sincere desire to identify, without the fear of criticism, dark clouds gathering on the near horizon. Clouds that threaten to engulf not only the United States but also the entire Western world.

Thank you again for inviting me to give this prestigious address.

The Gallie Lecture
Royal College of Physicians and Surgeons of Canada
Montreal, Canada, September 26, 1999

REFERENCES:

1. Relman, A., The New Medical-Industrial Complex. New England Journal of Medicine, Vol.303, No. 17:963-70, 1980.

2. Callahan, D. False Hopes. Simon and Schuster, 1998.

3. Mahomed, N., Sledge, C., Liang, M. Evaluation of FDA's device approval and

ADDENDA

marketing surveillance for Total Hip Implants. American Academy of Orthopaedic Surgeons' Annual Meeting, Paper 21, Page 68, 1999.

4. Relman, A. The Decline and Fall of Managed Care. *Hospitals*, Vol. 727, July 5, 1998.

5. Califano, J. Radical Syrgery. Times Books, 1994.

6. Sarmiento, A. Orthopaedics at a Cross Roads. Journal of Bone and Joint Surgery Vol. 75-A. No. 2: 159-61, February 1993.

7. Freidson, Eliot. Professionalism Reborn. The University of Chicago Press, 1994.

8. Cruess, R. The Gregg Lecture. McGill University, 1998

9. Sarmiento, A. Staying the Course. Journal of Bone and Joint Surgery. Vol. 73-A, No. 4: 479-483, April 1991.

10. Cruess, R., Sylvia Cruess. Teaching Medicine as a Profession on the Service of Healing. Academic Medicine, Vol. 72, No. 11: 941-953, November 1997.

ADDENDA

Addendum No. 10

THOUGHTS ON THE ROLE OF ORTHOPAEDICS IN BASIC RESEARCH

In the June 2001 issue of the *Orthopaedic Research Society Letter*, Gunnar Andersson, immediate past-president of the Orthopaedic Research Society published an address which he titled *The Orthopaedic Surgeon/Investigator*. It dealt with the shortage of orthopaedists in basic research. In his address, Andersson acknowledged me as one of the AAOS presidents "who brought attention and devoted interest to research" [1] Because of that recognition I decided to set aside the concerns I have about rendering opinions on the subject since I am not a trained researcher.

Andersson's desire to solve the shortage of orthopaedic basic researchers is commendable, and his attempts to rally the orthopaedic community behind his efforts a very worthwhile endeavor.

When I assumed the presidency of the American Academy of Orthopaedic Surgeons in 1991, I brought to the attention of the Board of Directors the declining involvement of orthopaedists in basic research and created a Center for Research within the walls of the Academy. I envisioned the Center to become the entity that would clearly demonstrate the Academy's interest in research, assist in the identification of the research needs of our specialty and, when appropriate, speak on behalf of the orthopaedic community [2]. Unfortunately, as it is frequently the case, once I stepped down from office, the Center ceased to exist. Other "more important" issues came to the top the Academy's agenda.

Shortly after the creation of the Center for Research, a workshop was held to address the needs of orthopaedic research. The meeting took place in Washington D.C., and was chaired and skillfully conducted by Joseph Buckwalter, currently Professor and Chairman of Orthopaedics at the University of Iowa [3].

In an attempt to clearly illustrate the serious shortage of orthopaedic researchers, Carl Brighton, then Chairman of Orthopaedics at the University of Pennsylvania, made the comment that if all those attending the workshop were to get onboard the same airplane, and the plane crashed, there will not be a single orthopaedic surgeon serving as principal investigator in an NIH research grant. The lessons I learned upon listening to the orthopaedic scientists discuss the issue, forced me to reassess my views in ways I had not previously anticipated.

On the last day of the meeting, having to address the group, I made up the story that the night before I had a nightmare, during which I saw a group of old men living in a nursing home, terribly distressed over their increasing loss of memory and lack of control of bodily functions. They had called a meeting for the purpose of appointing "study groups" which would eventually make recommendations and find solutions to their problems. Then, I told the group, I had suddenly awakened, only to realize that the old men in the nursing home were the same people participating in the workshop.

My Freudian interpretation of the fictitious dream was that, both the old men and the orthopaedic investigators were addressing problems for which there were no solutions. The problems identified by the senior citizens were part of the inevitable decline of the body and therefore beyond their control. By the same token, the orthopaedic investigators, who had seen the glorious days when they were always the principal investigators in NIH sponsored research, were now concerned over the painful realization that non-orthopaedist investigators in those privileged positions had replaced them. Their desire to regain their previous dominance was as unrealistic as the old men's dream of witnessing once again a return of lost bodily faculties.

My remarks were made half facetiously. Thinking that my pessimistic assessment of the situation might prove to be correct, I added that we should not panic. That if we were to find ourselves without a single orthopaedist serving as a principal investigator in NIH projects, musculoskeletal research would not come to an end. Having orthopaedists serve as principal investigators was not essential for the success of research. The important thing was for orthopaedists to remain active members of the research effort. Musculoskeletal research without strong orthopaedic participation would be the real problem.

It is unfortunate that in an increasingly large number of orthopaedic departments, the research activities in their laboratories are being dictated and conducted by MS and PhDs with minimal or no orthopaedic surgeons input. If this trend continues, Orthopaedics will suffer a major blow as a scientific discipline.

The genesis of the changes I have addressed is complex, and it is very likely that the major involvement of others in musculoskeletal research was inevitable. Orthopaedists do not currently possess the education required for the conduct of basic research, and have not been able to keep up with the avalanche of new research tools and techniques. The involvement of others outside of orthopaedics therefore has had a salutary effect.

I remember a day in the 60s, when during a meeting of the Orthopaedic Research Society Goran Bauer, the professor of Orthopaedics in Lund, Sweden spoke in support of the involvement of non-orthopaedists in the Society, but warned about the potential danger of having the majority of its members be PhD scientists rather than orthopaedists. His warnings were either not heeded, or the inevitable simply took place. Today the majority of members of the Society are not orthopaedic surgeons, but MS or PhDs in a variety of disciplines.

The days when sitting through meetings of the Orthopaedic Research Society, and listening to all presentations was an experience that virtually all orthopaedic academicians could enjoy and benefit from are gone. Today the overall meeting is a Tower of Babel. The sub specialization within the field is s o profound that I doubt there is a single orthopaedist in this country, or any other country, capable of understanding the content and conclusions presented from the one thousand papers delivered at any given meeting. Some sections of the congress look more like elitist clubs where a small group of people present and discuss papers that only they can understand. I venture to say that many of the participants in those small groups are MS or PhD scientists, and probably have never spoken to an orthopaedist. I mention this situation, not as a criticism of the Society, but as a fact of life, which we must accept. In the future, people from other disciplines will be involved in musculoskeletal research. It is the price we must pay for the healthy expansion the basic sciences have experienced

Residents' involvement in clinical research is feasible and desirable. Basic research is another matter. I question the wisdom of requiring every orthopaedic resident to participate during his tenure in basic research activities. This is an impractical requirement, imposed long ago by the Resident Review Committee at a time when it appeared to be an appropriate one. To assume that residents benefit in a meaningful way from such short experience is rather naïve. The experience may even be counterproductive. Some residents, who at one time considered a future involvement in basic research, become discouraged by the frustrations experienced during that short span of time.

In addition, not every orthopaedic department has basic research laboratories sufficiently organized and subsidized to accommodate rotating residents. To expect that every one of them carry out and complete a basic research project is an even greater exercise in futility. The time allotted for this endeavor is almost always too short, and their work frequently interferes with more important activities of the supervising full-time researchers. On the contrary, orthopaedic residents genuinely interested in basic research should be further encouraged in such an involvement, and their interest nurtured.

During my tenure as chairman of orthopaedics at the University of Southern California in the 80s, a fourth year resident, who during his college and medical school education had been involved in a number of research projects had not begun to work on a research project. When I reminded him that he had been accepted to our program, primarily because during the initial interview he had expressed a strong desire to continue his research involvement, and later pursue an academic career, he responded with amazing candor, "Doctor Sarmiento, I spent countless hours doing research while in college and medical school. Believe me, I never, ever again, want to see the inside of a research laboratory. I did research because I was told that a research background would make it easier for me to get a residency position in a good program." His remark speaks volumes.

Andersson proposes that a handful of young orthopaedists interested in basic research be guaranteed financial security, competitive with that of their clinical colleagues. He recognizes that the difference in income between orthopaedic practitioners and researches is significant, and identifies the importance that such difference has the choosing of future careers. I think his proposal is a good and feasible one.

Industry has contributed in a major way to the conduct of research in academic institutions. There is no reason to suspect that such support will diminish. Quite the contrary, Industry will continue to play a major role in musculoskeletal research. It is in its best interest to participate in our organizations' efforts to improve the current deficiencies. Industry's financial support, if properly aimed and channeled, would facilitate the amelioration of the present dilemma and create an environment more conducive to progress.

ADDENDA

The competition between industrial concerns attempting to control orthopaedic education and research throughout the world is fierce. It is regrettable that with increasing frequency research subjects are identified and addressed by industry without meaningful input from orthopaedists, and many investigations are conducted within the walls of industrial facilities. No longer is orthopaedic research conducted exclusively in academic centers.

In order to further ensure the success of Andersson's proposal, I suggest now, as I have suggested several times in the past, that Industry, rather than spreading its financial support for research activities through every residency program, donates those moneys to the Orthopaedic Research and Education Foundation. OREF in turn would distribute the funds to finance the salaries of those full-time career researchers in institutions capable of providing the fertile grounds that serious research requires. In addition, a percentage of the royalties given by Industry to investigators could also be disbursed in the same manner [4].

No one can predict what the future holds for orthopaedic surgeons in basic research. Andersson's proposed plan might find a fertile ground, and generate interest in future generations of orthopaedists. His plan, however, may not grow to fruition and orthopaedics will remain peripheral to basic research. Nonetheless, we should support, in any way we can, efforts made to see that orthopaedics share leadership positions. If that does not prove realizable in a short time, our interest and involvement in basic research must continue.

Such involvement will need the support of medical school deans and chairmen of orthopaedic departments. This support should not be taken for granted because it requires major attitudinal changes, which are often difficult to effect [5]. Full-time faculties in orthopaedic departments must also come to the conclusion that it is their responsibility to partake in the emotional and financial support of their colleagues, whose involvement in research is critical to the success not only of their departments, but to their profession as a whole.

Peripherally related but pertinent to this discussion is the subject of scientific publications. The number of medical publications that fill thousands of shelves in medical libraries is staggering. Information exists that in 1996 there were 30,000 different medical journals worldwide. Three thousand new articles were published every day; and 1000 new articles were added to Medline every day [6].

In light of this information, we should not be surprised to see the huge number of published articles that have no redeeming value whatsoever. They do not contribute to the body of knowledge and remain largely unread. They fill the pages of journals, so the authors can claim credits for their academic survival. A candid look at the "need" for academicians to publish papers in large numbers is long overdue. This requirement has a tendency to discourage potential investigators from pursuing research careers. A more reasonable blueprint can be structured. Whether or not Orthopaedics can accomplish this independently and still receive the support of the academic hierarchy needs to be explored. It is likely that others in various medical school departments share our concerns and might be willing to join us in our quest. It could be a unique opportunity for Orthopaedics to provide leadership in the educational arena.

ADDENDA

REFERENCES:

1. Andersson, Gunnar B.J. The Orthopaedic Surgeon-Investigator: An Endangered Species. *Orthopaedic Research Society Newsletter*; Vol 13, Summer 2001, No. 1: 3-5.
2. Sarmiento, A. Staying the Course. *Journ Bone Joint Surg*, Vol. 73-A, No 4, April 1991: 479-483
3. Building the Future of Orthopaedics. Strengthening Orthopaedic Research. *American Academy of Orthopaedic Surgeons Publication,* 1992
4. Sarmiento, A. Orthopaedics at a crossroads. *Journ Bone Joint Surg*, Vol 75-A, No.2: 159-161, 1993
5. Sarmiento, A. Education is key to nonoperative care. *Academy News*, Vol. 47, No. 2:99-50, 1999
6. Smith, R. What Clinical Information do doctors need? *British Medical Journal.* 313 (7064): 1062-8, 1996

Journal of Bone and Joint Surgery
No. December, 1001, pp

ADDENDA

Addendum #11

ON THE EDUCATION OF THE ORTHOPAEDIC RESIDENT

Despite the many developments in the medical sciences during the past few decades the education of the orthopaedist has retained most of its traditional format. The adaptive changes that it has experienced may not have been as significant as they could or should have been.

The discontinuation of the traditional rotating internship and a year or years of general surgery from the required residency education was the most radical change. Resident exposure of other surgical and medical disciplines was incorporated into the first year of orthopaedic residency. This change may have been justifiable and even helpful to the trainee. The technological explosion that began in the 1960s additionally supported the change.

Another change that occurred in the residency training was the establishment of structured rotations through newly-created orthopaedic subspecialties. Within a few years, the faculty involved in the education of the residents had become subspecialists in various disciplines. Accordingly, residents were assigned to their services for specific periods. As the number of rotations increased, the length of exposure to each subspecialty became progressively shorter.

This phenomenon played a role in the genesis of the subsequent widespread interest in fellowships after residency. The brevity of the rotations must have convinced many residents that additional training was necessary. They no longer felt sufficiently prepared in all areas to enter into the competitive surgical practice.

This view does not represent a negation of the fact that sub specialization in orthopaedics is desirable. Quite the contrary, it has been responsible for much of the progress made in recent years. Residency programs, whether affiliated with medical schools, would find it very difficult to provide good training without the participation of subspecialists.

There is a general perception that it now is virtually impossible for any orthopaedist to competently provide care for all types of musculoskeletal disabilities. Such a perception is to some extent ill founded. The overall body of knowledge required for the practice of orthopaedics today may not be necessarily greater than it was a few decades ago. It is more likely that new knowledge has replaced old knowledge. The number of treatment modalities and the required applicable technologies may have been greater 3 decades ago.

To support my view that the body of knowledge in orthopaedics may not be necessarily greater than it used to be, some examples can be cited. In the past, the treatment of arthritic conditions of the hip required knowledge of various medical and surgical measures, such as several different osteotomies, fusions of various types, neurectomies, forage, mold arthroplasty, soft tissue releases and endoprosthetic replacement. Currently, total hip replacement is the universal answer to virtually all arthritic conditions of the hip in adults. The technology required for its performance is simple and the associated complications are relatively few. The situation is similar with the arthritic knee where arthroplasty addresses virtually all advanced degenerative conditions of this joint.

The same can be said about conditions of the spine where the computed tomography and magnetic resonance imaging have dramatically simplified the diagnosis of many conditions. Spine fusion, aided by sophisticated imaging technology, now seems to be the only answer to many traumatic and degenerative conditions.

Fracture care, which at one time required knowledge of various surgical and nonsurgical techniques, now is done with increasing frequency through surgical operations that are now facilitated greatly by imaging technology. Closed intramedullary nailing, plating, and external fixation are becoming the only methods of treatment. The care of fractures in the eyes of many simply is a technical exercise that does not require understanding of the biologic principles that govern osteogenesis.

The MRI, scan and the arthroscope have radically simplified the diagnosis and treatment of internal derangement of the knee. The vast diagnostic acumen previously required is disappearing rapidly.

Not long ago, orthopaedists were considered the only professionals qualified to diagnose and care for all types of neoplastic diseases of the musculoskeletal system. Benign lesions were treated with surgical excision, bone grafting or both. Malignant tumors were treated by wide resection or by amputation. Some malignant tumors were so aggressive, that only palliative measures were instituted. Today, radiation and chemotherapy ensure the survival of many of these patients.

Orthopaedic surgery has continued to play a role in the care of patients with malignant musculoskeletal tumors, but its involvement now is less. It can be safely anticipated that future advances in chemotherapy, radiation therapy, immunology, and molecular biology will further decrease the role of surgery in the treatment of patients with malignant musculoskeletal neoplasms.

Orthopaedists allowed others to dictate the rehabilitation of patients with musculoskeletal disabilities. In doing so, we probably made a mistake. We lost important territory where our expertise had made possible major contributions to the welfare of many patients. Amputation and prosthetic rehabilitation is an appropriate example. Orthopaedists performed a large percentage of amputations in the past, and were responsible for the education of residents in these subjects. Today, general surgeons do most amputations; physiatrists preside over the rehabilitation of the amputee; and the education of the resident in prosthetics is virtually non-existent. .

Although the origin of modern hand surgery in the United States should be largely credited to Sterling Bunnell, a general surgeon, the orthopaedic community maintained and expanded its involvement in the discipline and soon became the leading force. With time, however, plastic and general surgeons became involved in the care of the hand, first by providing attention to its cosmetic aspects, and later by doing reconstruction of congenital and acquired conditions of soft tissues. Later their role in hand surgery included joints and bones of the hand and wrist. Many orthopaedists even claim the entire upper extremity as their rightful territory. Plastic surgeons have replaced the orthopaedists in the treatment of patients with soft tissue injuries accompanying open fractures in the upper and lower extremities.

Orthopaedists, to a greater and greater extent, are no longer doing myelograms, and their involvement in biopsies of vertebral lesions and discography virtually is nonexistent. Interventional radiologists do those procedures. They currently are injecting cement into osteoporotic spines. They claim greater expertise with imaging techniques and orthopaedists are excluded from this fledging therapeutic modality.

Spinal instrumentation always had been considered the purview of the orthopaedic surgeon. However, neurosurgeons now are in many academic and nonacademic environments the specialists providing surgical care to an increasing percentage of bony conditions of the spinal column. They correct deformities and stabilize segments with vertebral fusions using plates, cages or pedicle screws.

The orthopaedist is no longer the only professional providing surgical care to disorders of the foot. Within less than 3 decades, podiatrists who previously limited the scope of their work to the care of toenail problems and the prescription of shoe modifications became well-known experts in all conditions of the foot. Not only do they now surgically treat hallux valgus, but also do surgery for all conditions in the distal lower extremity. They do arthrodesis, amputations, osteotomies of the os calcis, resection of tumors, internal fixation of foot and ankle fractures, arthroscopy and others procedures. It is likely that soon they will claim expertise in the treatment of conditions of the knee and begin to do diagnostic and therapeutic arthroscopy.

Orthopaedic surgeons are not alone. Similar shifts of territorial jurisdiction have taken place in other fields of medicine. Ophthalmologists and optometrists question the intrusions in their respective arenas. Oral surgeons and surgical oncologists do likewise. Otolaryngologists, general surgeons, and plastic surgeons quarrel over the place and role of each other in the care of several conditions. It is premature to speculate as to effect these shifts will have in the overall care of the patient, and its economic consequences.

Today, medicine seems to operate in an environment where an orderly and well-defined set of rules no longer exists. It is like playing tennis with the net down. The practice is a replica of modern society, where an exaggerated relativist ethos is breaking down the traditional sphere of values, long considered essential for the preservation of a cohesive civilized society.

Orthopaedics is becoming, in the eyes of others, simply a small series of technical and surgical procedures that can be done by anyone possessing basic surgical skills. We can no longer complacently rely on the security that in years past we took for granted.

The above picture of orthopaedics in the overall context of medical and surgical practice suggests that accommodations and reactive changes may be necessary. We must strive to see that the orthopaedist is, once again, universally recognized as the professional best qualified to provide the most appropriate care of musculoskeletal conditions. We cannot prevail unless we can clearly and unequivocally prove to the lay and medical communities that our education entitles us to such a claim.

There are alternative approaches to the situation. We could rationalize that the loss of orthopaedic territory to others should be accepted as a natural evolutionary phenomenon that has not compromised the quality of care. Some will argue that there is no documented evidence that harm has been done.

However, in choosing that option we may be condemning our profession to additional damage. For example, our right to claim that we are the best-qualified people to implement the use of bone and other growth factors, if and when they are proven to be clinically effective, will be compromised. Others will claim that anyone with a modicum of technical skills should be entitled to inject the growth factors into whatever tissues they consider to be in need.

Efforts to solve the perceived problems by means of advertisements via the popular media are expensive, counterproductive, and unlikely to be salutary. Such means simply provoke a reaction from others to use the same media in ways that may depart from the ethical and professional standards to which our profession has long adhered.

To increase the residents' exposure to all orthopaedic conditions and therefore allow them to feel comfortable with their competency in all aspects of the profession, I suggest discontinuing the separate block-time rotations through every subspecialty within orthopaedics. Several of these rotations could be merged. I doubt that separate and short rotations through hand surgery, trauma, foot surgery, hip and knee reconstructive surgery, oncology, sport medicine, or spine surgery are necessary. A resident who throughout the entire 5 years of training participates in those areas would be better off than his counterpart, whose participation in them consists only of either an isolated rotation or widely spread brief encounters.

It serves little meaningful purpose to give residents extensive exposure to subjects such as oncology and scoliosis when in fact they will not be either sufficiently competent to treat patients so affected or be summoned to provide those services. They should, however, be knowledgeable in the diagnosis of the conditions and familiar with the resources available for their treatment. Didactic lectures on the subjects and repeated exposures to those conditions should satisfy the academic and practical needs of the practicing orthopaedist. Those interested in pursuing a career in musculoskeletal oncology or scoliosis will seek fellowships in the respective areas.

Residents should be keenly aware of the existence of the clinical situations that require major, esoteric reconstructive surgery of a type that only a specialized individual should do. In the case of the spine, in my proposed scheme, residents would learn during the 5 years of training, and become sufficiently competent to treat common clinical problems, such as fractured vertebrae, herniated discs, osteoarthritis, spinal stenosis, spondylolesthesis. If the treating orthopaedists consider certain situations to be outside their competency, a referral to another orthopaedists specialized in this area will be, as it always has been, most appropriate.

Through basic sciences lectures, reading, Grand Rounds, visiting professors lectures, bio-skill laboratory experiences, journal clubs, and frequent conferences and case presentations, held under the supervision of subspecialized faculty, residents would receive the necessary education to qualify them to practice their profession without the fear of continued loss of territory to others.

The education of residents in pediatric orthopaedics in separate blocks of time came into being with the perception that residents should be first familiar with the special circumstances that prevail in the immature patient. Once they completed this rotation they moved into the care of the adult. This pattern has endured in slightly modified forms.

Perhaps the concept was valid in yesteryears. I question, however, if such an approach is the best today. Because the care of children in pediatric hospitals ceases on completion of growth, the providers of the initial care do not directly observe the evolution and natural history of many conditions. The late sequella of congenital hip disease, slipped epiphysis, Perthes disease, scoliosis, clubfoot and many other conditions do not appear until late in life. A simultaneous exposure to children and adult orthopaedics may be a more realistic and desirable approach to education. Residents' participation throughout their entire training in clinics, surgery, case presentations, and lectures could be more beneficial to them.

The integration of pediatric orthopaedics with other subspecialties would be, however, difficult because in many programs pediatric orthopaedic care is provided in specialty hospitals located in different parts of the city or in distant communities.

The education of the orthopaedic resident in some areas could be initiated or strengthened. Among them would be amputation surgery and rehabilitation of patients with amputations, soft tissue treatment in open fractures, spinal cord injuries, the nonsurgical treatment of fractures, the comprehensive medical and surgical care of certain rheumatic conditions, osteoporosis, the use of imaging technology in the diagnosis and care of a numerous musculoskeletal conditions, and in emerging techniques for the correction of vertebral deformities secondary to osteoporosis and posttraumatic disabilities. In this manner, the orthopaedic community will be better prepared to participate in new diagnostic and therapeutic approaches made possible as a result of the ongoing scientific revolution.

On entering the practice of the profession, many may not wish to participate in the care of some musculoskeletal conditions, and will limit their involvement to those areas they enjoy most and with which they feel most comfortable. Some will specialize in a simple discipline. This breakdown of involvement in patient care has been in existence for many a generation and has served orthopaedics well.

The overall topic of subspecialty fellowships also should be addressed. Although many benefit from postgraduate fellowships, it is doubtful that all graduating residents need that extended period of education. Residents, who at the completion of training feel lacking sufficient education on a given area, are helped from an additional fellowship. From personal

ADDENDA

observations, I have concluded that fellowship training is not necessary for success in private practice, if the orthopaedist has graduated from a well-balanced residency programs. Insecurity is what drives many into fellowships.

Despite the fact that some educators claim that fellowships do not compromise resident education but rather enhance it, I have ambivalent feelings. Too many times I have seen residents frustrated and deeply annoyed by the fact that fellows do an unduly large percentage of the surgical procedures they think they should do, and that fellows receive greater attention from their mentors.

The implementation of change would not be easy because the roots that support the existing system have grown deep. Many hurdles would have to be overcome. Finding educators with experience in the care of many of the conditions I have listed would be one of them. Departments of orthopaedics, with only a few exceptions, do not have a full-time faculty, either qualified or willing to devote time to endeavors that as a rule do not generate the larger revenues that many major surgical procedures generate. Some deans of medical schools and department chairmen will argue that the economic survival of their respective programs depends on the faculty's ability to generate funds for their own financial support. Some of them are likely to present strong opposition to change in the status quo, because allegiances developed with other departments. In addition, our involvement in areas that we once controlled, but later abandoned to others will bring about resistance from the ones now filling that void.

I am not suggesting turning the clock back and returning to the old system of education. However, we must recognize that no generation has ever had a monopoly on wisdom. There is much we can learn from the lessons of history. My suggestions do not call for a rigid system. Special circumstances would call for special accommodations, such as those dictated by geographic differences, which are likely to exist.

I am keenly aware that our profession has structured within its organization mechanisms to monitor the quality of residency programs, and that as a result of their efforts much progress has been made. The people who constitute those organizations have the know-how and expertise to effect change. However, this should not preclude anyone from offering views that may run contrary to those prevalent in the appointed bodies. I do not make claims that the suggestions I have made constitute a perfect solution to the problems confronting our educational process. I simply offer them as a set of starting points for a dialogue.

Clinical Orthopaedics and Related Research, May 1992.

ADDENDA

Addendum #12

THE RELATIONSHIP BETWEEN ORTHOPAEDICS AND INDUSTRY MUST BE REFORMED

The transformation of medicine into a business seems to be virtually complete. This transition is eloquently illustrated by medicine's tacit acceptance as its official emblem the wooden shaft with two serpents intertwined around it. This emblem is the Caduceus of Hermes, the Greek god of commerce and thieves. The Caduceus of Aesculapius, the patron of medicine, has only one serpent.

Despite the fact that Ethics is the branch of philosophy that deals with universal principles of conduct, medicine and industry have their own distinct codes of ethics. Industry's code is based on the recognition that it has customers, and its *raison d'etre* is to generate profit. Medicine's code of ethics is based on the premise that its mission is to provide medical care. As professionals, physicians are bound by rules that place the interests of their patients before their own. Businessmen are not subjects of similar rules.

The altruistic ethos of professionalism in medicine, the staple of yesteryears, has, in the eyes of many, virtually disappeared. They have accepted with enthusiasm and elan the standards of the business community and seem comfortable relishing the relativism that permeates a society that says, "Everything is OK; therefore there is nothing morally wrong; profit is what matters"

On the front page of the New York Times an article appeared titled, "Justice Department finds success chasing health care fraud", in which a statement was made regarding a "silently common practice of fraudulent billing among many doctors around the country" [5.] Doctor D. T. Lewers, Chairman of the Board of trustees of the American Medical Association responded that his organization "does not condone fraud and will support the new administration's efforts to identify truly fraudulent activities" [6]. He quoted a report from the Health Care Administration stating, "The overwhelming percentage of providers, suppliers and physicians who provide services to Medicare beneficiaries are honest, careful and conscientious".

It is comforting to read the Health Care Administration's general assessment of the medical profession regarding the commission of fraud. The fact remains, however, that there are increasingly common practices among physicians, which though they do not fit into the legal category of fraud, constitute a clear violation of the high standards our profession has held as sacred tenets.

Many of these practices have their genesis in the ever-growing financial dependency of the medical profession on industry [7, 8], which is seriously compromising professionalism in our ranks and undermining the values and ethics of physicians. [11]

The imposed reduction of reimbursement for services rendered by medical doctors, prompted many practitioners of the medical art to look into ways to compensate for the financial loss. Requesting frequent unnecessary office visits, prescribing unnecessary or borderline useful tests, and substituting financially rewarding surgical treatment modalities for less expensive non-surgical ones, became trends.

INDUSTRY AND EDUCATION

In a matter of a few years, industry gained significant control of the education of the orthopaedist. Prior to the 1970s education came under the exclusive domain of academic institutions, and to a lesser degree of medical societies. Today a large percentage of continuing education ventures is stage-arranged and subsidized in various degrees by industrial concerns [8,9]. Visiting professorships and guest lectureships at medical school, local, state or national organizations are frequently masterminded and subsidized by industry. The topics discussed very often deal with commercial products in which the speakers have vested financial interests; and the handsome honoraria they receive and the expenses they incur are paid by the sponsoring industrial organizations. The entrance into the auditorium of these "visiting professors" or "distinguished guest speakers," is often followed or preceded by an entourage of vendors of the products discussed. They are there to pursue business opportunities they hope the lecture will generate.

Industry orchestrates the agenda of the orthopaedists who seem to make a living traveling around the country discussing the latest "new and improved" products. Until recently the topics that the traveling surgeons discussed related almost exclusively to surgical implants; currently others products have been added to the list, such as anticoagulants, osteoporosis prevention medications, as well as recently developed, though not yet fully tested, bone or cartilage inducing pastes or glues.

The elaborate meetings of orthopaedic societies or associations, often held in expensive, esoteric locations are made possible by major contributions from industry. Without such subsidy, invited speakers, banquets, dinner-dances, sporting events and other amenities seem impossible. Young orthopaedists must wonder how was it possible in years past for our medical organizations to hold informative educational meetings, which were subsidized by the reasonable tuition paid by the attendees. "There is no free lunch anywhere." Raising the cost of industrial products offsets the expenses incurred in such marketing practices. A factor that contributes in a very major way to the ever escalating costs of medical care.

Advertising which was long considered below the dignity of the medical profession is no longer frowned upon. Many physicians as single individuals, or as members of groups, clinics or faculties, advertise in manners identical to those utilized by commercial ventures. They use newspapers, pamphlets, letters, the radio, television and the Internet in similar degrees.

At meetings of our orthopaedic organizations, an increasing number of the so-called scientific papers presented, are actually advertisements of commercial products. Listening to some of those presentations without knowing who the speakers are, one can legitimately assume that vendors, rather than physicians are at the microphone. Scheduled heated symposia between orthopaedists discussing their individual results with competitive

ADDENDA

products often resemble Middle Eastern bazaars rather than debates among educated professionals.

Continuing education courses for orthopaedists are advertised as being produced by clinics, institutes, medical societies or departments of orthopaedics in medical schools. Often, however, such identification with educational institutions is a disguise aimed at legitimizing the educational endeavor. In either small or large print, the brochures acknowledge "partial subsidy" from industry. It is not uncommon to see a list of 30 or 40 organizations co-sponsoring the course, clearly indicating that the educational venture is primarily a marketing exercise to generate sales for industry and a financial bonanza for the producers of the courses.

Several years ago I organized an international symposium on total joint surgery in Los Angeles, as part of an ongoing series of continuing education activities. I invited several industrial firms to display their related products at the exhibit hall of the hotel and requested a fee for the opportunity to do so. The invitations were accepted. However, several of them inquired in almost identical words as to how many of the speakers they were "entitled" to appoint to the faculty of the course.

Such a bold and insolent question clearly demonstrates that industry has come to the conclusion that our financial dependency on them gives them the right to dictate the content of our educational activities. They have surmised that, "He who pays the piper calls the tune" The proliferation of industry-orchestrated courses explains why attendance to American Academy of Orthopaedic Surgeons' sponsored courses has so rapidly decreased. Feeling the need to maintain CME activities profitable, the Academy is "exploring the possibility" of making industry a co-sponsor of its courses.[1] This would be a dreadful mistake. It will be a betrayal of its education mission, and the equivalent of driving a strong and irremovable nail into its own coffin.

This development illustrates the consequences of the recent structuring within the Academy a C6 Tax organization, which gradually and perhaps inevitably will shift its priorities from education to the business and political arenas. The next step will probably be to give industry permanent seats on its Board of Directors [12]. our representative organizations seem to be consumed in efforts to seek constantly increasing financial gains; and in the process prostrating themselves before the Golden Calf.

An episode that took place a few years ago made a deep impression on my perception of the profound changes that have taken place in our profession. A resident of ours, responding to my concern over his apparent disregard for interest in learning the basic sciences that explains the process of tissue repair, said to me that he was not interested in knowing how fractures and other structures heal; all he wanted to know was how to fix them. This particular experience sheds light into the impact that education, aimed primarily at technical exercises has had in the current approach to orthopaedic care. The influence that industry has in the education of the orthopaedic resident, through its dominance in continuing education, has helped to instill in the mind of our trainees a disregard for the biological principles that had governed our profession. We are replacing the biologists/physicians with skillful cosmetic surgeons of the skeleton.

ADDENDA

INDUSTRY AND ORTHOPAEDIC RESEARCH

The care of the musculoskeletally impaired has improved dramatically during the last few decades. Much of this progress is the result of research efforts made by many. Industry has contributed to the finance of some of these activities.
However, every outcome from research, which we quickly call "progress", is not. Many products, resulting from research activities have not helped improve the human condition. Quite the contrary, some have caused harm. If such harm were the result of unanticipated complications despite careful planning, if would be unfair to criticize. However, much too often, new products, alleged to be the result of extensive research, are produced simply to neutralize the competition. The hundreds of different total joint prostheses currently on the market are a prime example [3]. Many of these implants are nothing but trivial modifications of existing ones.

Some orthopaedic publications have failed to recognize this flaw and have fallen victim of industry's scheme. A few years ago I submitted a paper to a major journal, reporting on the high rate of complications we had identified with the use of a popular total hip implant. The paper was rejected, primarily on the grounds that the prosthesis we had used was no longer on the market, having been replaced by Model II.

I asked the reviewer how would he respond to a manuscript submitted five years later reporting on a high failure rate with Model II? Will he respond that the paper would not be accepted for publications because Model III had replaced Model II? And how does he react to learning that Model I was still heavily marketed in countries south of the border? Without any evidence that a new appliance is necessary to improve the clinical results of a given condition, new gadgets appear and are effectively advertised. For example, there is no indication that fractures of the clavicle, with relatively few exceptions, require internal fixation. However, a frenzy to treat clavicle fractures with plates or intramedullary nails is sweeping the world. During a visit to a trauma center in a European country I was told that most clavicular fractures coming to the institution were treated with intramedullary fixation. I raised the question as to why such a radical approach in light of the fact that spontaneous healing was the usual course of events. My host surgeon responded that, "times had changed". Patients, according to him, no longer accept the lump produced by the healed fracture. I acknowledged to him my surprise upon the revelation of an incredibly accelerated Darwinian evolution of human behavior.

Colles fractures are another good example. Legitimate reports in the literature indicating improved results from open surgery in the case of certain complicated fractures, soon became a mandate to treat all Colles fractures in that manner. The commercial advertisements of "new and improved" methods of fixation were soon displayed in peer-review journals and in "tabloid" orthopedic publications. Malpractice litigation is now common whenever a residual, though inconsequential angulation persists following the nonsurgical treatment of these fractures. The treating physician is accused of failing to practice his profession according to the most current standards of care. The fact that the surgical approach to this fracture brings about a higher financial reimbursement has helped the rapid popularization of surgical procedures.

ADDENDA

The anticipated clinical application of ongoing investigations in genetic engineering and molecular biology will test our wisdom, as the true value of new projects is evaluated. The marketing of products, the result of such worthwhile research, has already exploded. At times, however, without reasonable evidence of the effectiveness necessary to justify their clinical use.

In earlier days receiving kickbacks from Industry was a well-hidden practice in which very few physicians indulged. Today many accept them and take them for granted. While serving as chairman of the department of Orthopaedics at the University of Southern California, I was offered by a representative from industry money for every total joint implant performed at its five affiliated hospitals. Upon my rejection of the lucrative deal, the industry representative responded that such arrangements "were common and acceptable practices"[10]

In some countries this practice is widespread. Many orthopaedists are given, under the table, large amounts of money for every implant they use. This money often exceeds the payment they receive from the third-party payer covering the procedure. A European professor/surgeon told me that the employees at his home and at his villa on the Mediterranean Coast were paid in cash from funds he received from "special deals" he makes with industry.

On another occasion I was visited by the V.P. of a major manufacturing company, who presented me with a new prosthesis that his engineers had allegedly developed according to my philosophy. The prosthesis was to be called the "Sarmiento Total Hip Prosthesis". Before I had a chance to say that I did not know I had a "unique philosophy" he handed me a check, payable to me in the amount of $250.000. I rejected the offer and found the prosthesis advertised in various journals a few months later. I inquired from the local representative who was the physician behind the concept. He responded that the implant represented the "unique philosophy" of a "very distinguished orthopaedist" from a medical school on the East Coast.

THE REHABILITATION INDUSTRY

The establishment of Sports Medicine as a sub-specialty of orthopaedics, brought about emphasis on prolonged rehabilitation following surgery performed in patients with a variety of musculoskeletal injuries. This emphasis on rehabilitation rapidly extended into other parts of orthopaedics and to medicine in general. Only time will tell how much the extended periods of rehabilitation given today to these patients was really clinically beneficial, and how much of it was an effort to generate greater revenues.

Though orthopaedics as a discipline lost rehabilitation as an integral part of its territory, and physiatrists became known as the experts in the field, many in the orthopaedic community embraced with enthusiasm the practice of offering physical and occupational therapy, whether needed or not, to any and all musculoskeletal conditions.

ADDENDA

The plethora of machines and gimmicks used in the course of therapy staggers one's imagination. Since individual billing for each modality of treatment is a frequent practice, the increase in the cost of therapy has become a major concern. Medicare and other third-party payers "entitle" their covered patients to various periods of post-illness rehabilitation. This "entitlement" is justifiable. However, many patients following a number of surgical procedures become independent within a few days and are in a position to return home. Currently, many of them are encouraged to spend additional time in some type of rehabilitation facility, be it a skilled-nursing unit or a rehabilitation center. It does not matter that the "rehabilitation" they receive consists of their being asked to perform the same exercises they learned and performed during their hospitalization; exercises that can be carried out without supervision. The cost of such "rehabilitation" significantly increases the cost of medical care.

The protocols aimed at the rehabilitation of the spinal cord injured patient also exemplify the extreme degree to which the rehabilitation industry has grown. Despite the fact that ambulation of the complete paraplegic remains only a dream yet to be crystallized, the emphasis on ambulation as the goal of rehabilitation has continued. This approach is unfair to patients, misleading and extremely expensive. Though continued research in spinal cord injuries is worthwhile, an honest and realistic approach to the rehabilitation of this unfortunate group of patients is needed.

SUMMARY

I have titled this article *The relationship between Orthopaedics and Industry must be reformed,* because the relationship is flawed and has created problems we do not like and consider harmful to out profession. I express criticism of my profession as well as of industry, hoping that an earnest effort to address those problems will soon be made. My criticism is an invitation to a serious debate between the two parties, where the traditional platitudes and rhetoric about industry's generosity will be absent from it. A debate where it is candidly acknowledged that orthopaedists, as well as members of industry often egregiously transgress ethical boundaries.

We must recognize that the bedrock of our traditional principles is collapsing; the compass of our moral values is no longer pointing in the right direction; and a number of practices in which both parties frequently indulge, have unequivocal unethical implications [2, 8, 12]. Richard Cruess, from Canada said, "One can make a point that we in medicine have not failed so much as we have as profesionals."[3]

A large segment of the orthopaedic education and research is now in the hands of industry and is structured primarily to satisfy its marketing needs. Industry has used its awesome economic power to develop a subtle and effective stratagem to lull us into the slumber that has kept many of us from realizing the degree to which we have become subservient to them. The many perks and financial help we receive are distractions to allow industry to control our destiny [12]. Industry owns us and dictates the course of education and research, and ultimately the practice of orthopaedics.

ADDENDA

It is deeply disturbing that there are many in our profession who willingly continue to welcome and encourage industry to extend its tentacles into territory that should be exclusively ours [8, 12]. They must be held accountable for the harm being done to present and future generations of orthopaedists.

I suspect that during the last 16 to 24 months, our five physicians' office has received free samples of two popular and expensive non-steroidal analgesics, which in over-the-counter prices would be worth several hundred thousand dollars. This misguided "generosity" is, needless to say, highly responsible for the irresponsibly high cost of drugs in our country.

I now refuse to be the physician in the office who officially accepts the "gift" and have suggested to the industry representatives to donate the samples to "clinics" for indigent patients at the local public hospitals; and if this is not possible, to ship them to countries where poverty and disease are chronic.

I think I am sufficiently realistic to realize that the present trends might be irreversible because, as it is said in the vernacular, "the horse is out of the barn". To prevail in our efforts to right some of the serious wrongs affecting our profession may be beyond the realm of the possible. The leadership of organized medicine in the United States, with very few exceptions, has remained silent about the seriousness of the situation, despite the fact that they have long known that the experiment has not worked. Their silence has precluded an honest inquiry into the matter. They have muffled in equivocation to the point where an open debate is becoming virtually impossible.

Industry is enjoying the incredible huge bonanza that their economic power has made possible for them, and are not interesting in compromising it, let alone terminating it. Industry hears the occasional criticism and ignores it. By not responding, it has been successful in convincing, large segments of the medical profession and of the public at large, that a problem does not exist. However, a problem does exist. If the following information concerning Industry's involvement in physician's educations does not make it obvious even to the most recalcitrant, there is something, verging on the irrational, about how the American people define "problems." The drug company's hosted 314,022 meetings, events and dinners for physicians in 2000, an increase of 11 percent since 1995; a $15 billion-a-year promotion efforts. [13] These figures do not include the likely comparable cost of a multitude of other promotional ventures, such as the ones that disregard all traditional constraints regarding the direct marketing of prescription drugs to the lay public. This marketing approach has been a "successful" one for industry, since it resulted in the lay community exerting pressure on the medical profession to prescribe those drugs.

Despite the enormous difficulties confronting the medical profession, we should remain optimistic, and believe that action can effect change. The salutary changes will take place only if organized medicine musters the courage and the intestinal fortitude to make bold moves, which include a prohibition of industry's intrusions into our autonomy in education and research. This goal can be reached while still maintaining the necessary cooperative relationship between medicine and industry. If industry does not approve of our corrective actions, we should ignore its displeasure and move on [12].

ADDENDA

REFERENCES

1. Academy News. The 2001 Annual Meeting Report. An Interview with William Tipton.

2. Callahan, D. False Hopes. Simon and Schuster, 1998

3. Cruess, R. The Gregg Lecture, McGill University, 1998

4. Mahamed, N., Sledge, C.. Liang, M. Evaluation of FDA"s devices approval and
    i. marketing surveillance for total hip implants. American Academy of Orthopaedic Surgeons Annual Meeting 1999, Paper 21; 68.

5. New York Times. Jan. 23, 2001

6. New York Times. Jan. 27, 2001

7. Relman, A. The new medical-industrial complex. N. Engl. J. Med 303(17):963-7-, 1980

8. Relman, A. Separating continuing medical education from pharmaceutical marketing. JAMA, Vol. 285: 2009-2012, No. 15, April 18, 2001

9. Sarmiento, A. Orthopaedics at a crossroads. J. Bone Joint Surg. (A) 75-(2):159-61, 1993

10. Sarmiento, A. Medicine and Industry: The payer, the piper and the tune. Annals Royal College of Physicians and Surgeon of Canada. Vol. 33, No. 3: 144-149, 2000.

11. Sarmiento, A. The future of our specialty. Orthopaedics and its Trojan Horse. Acta Orthopedica Scandinavica: 71(6): 574-579, 2000.

12. Sarmiento, A. Ethical concerns regarding the orthopaedic relationship with industry. American Orthopaedic Association Annual Meeting, June 16, 2001.

13. Scot-Levin Report. Modern Health Care, July 10, 2001

ADDENDA

Addendum #13

ARE WE LOSING OBJECTIVITY?

Augusto Sarmiento, MD

"Some women are not afraid of dying as much as they are afraid of dying wrinkled"

It is probably safe to say that loss of objectivity seems too often affect us. This human frailty has afflicted society since time immemorial, and has resulted on occasions in the pursuit of unworthy ad even disastrous causes. Our society currently appears to be obsessed with a number of issues, which suggest that we are losing objectivity in regards to important matters. We seem to be fascinated with the pursuit of immortality in this world, though we know it is unattainable. The obsession with profit, perennial youth, physical beauty and the fear of aging is manifested through the widespread emphasis on working longer hours in order to make more money, exercising to exhaustion, voluntary starvation diets and multiple plastic surgery [1]

A personal confrontation with my own lack of objectivity made me delve in earnest over the meaning of many of the things we do in our daily lives. I was visiting my mother, who at the time was celebrating her 97th birthday. Prior to meeting her, a concerned relative complained to me that my mother was not "walking" enough. She suggested that I use persuasion to convince her to change her ways. Without giving any thought to her request I said, "Mother, they tell me that you are not walking enough. You should walk more; it is good for you." "Good for what?" she replied. Embarrassed by my inability to find the right words to respond to her wise and pithy remark, I stuttered, "Well, it is good for you." She smiled mischievously and said, "Son, I have walked for 97 years, and think I have walked enough." She died in her bed two years later, peacefully and without having walked "enough" during her last twenty-four months. The words of Tolstoy in *The Death of Ivan Ilysh,* "For Christ' sake, let me die in peace" have resonated in my ears ever since that unforgettable episode.

Mentally I have used this conversation with my mother as an example with which to compare a number of responses, silent or spoken, we give to a variety of situations dealing with the care we provide to our patients.

One morning, in the days when I presided over the Spinal Cord Injury Center at Jackson Memorial Hospital at the University of Miami, a program I had initiated, the head nurse, agitated over a situation that had arisen on the ward approached me. "Wayne Bowie, the 17 year old quadriplegic who was admitted a couple of weeks ago, is being given "marijuana" by his friends every night. What should we do about it?" Since the level of his spine lesion was very high his friends had to hold the cigarette to his lips. The nurse was shocked when I responded, "Pat, tell Wayne's young friends that if they promise to bring him "pot" every week for three solid months, I will pay for it." To help her recover from my obviously unexpected response I added, "Wayne's friends now feel sorry for him, and that is the reason why they visit him frequently. However, be certain that the visits will become less frequent in the near future, and pretty soon there will be no more. They will soon forget about Wayne and will never return to visit him."

Indeed, Wayne remained in his room, all alone until the day when he was discharged to a Nursing Home where he soon died from infected decubiti and kidney infection. But not before he was taken to surgery to have a tendon on his right hand transferred to a different location. A successful transfer would have hopefully made it possible for him to compress the remote control to the television set. This was his only possible activity for the rest of his days. In the middle of surgery, he experienced cardiac arrest. I watched as the residents performed the routine cardiac resuscitation ritual, and broke his ribs. He survived.

To give this unhappy young man the possibility of gaining some minimal control of his hand was a worthwhile effort. But were the attempts to resuscitate him realistic? Did it make sense to go to extremes to keep Wayne alive? Where and when do we "draw the line"? I strongly believe that the humane, ethical and objective thing that we should have done under the circumstances was to allow Wayne to remain dead. It was also humane, ethical and objective to encourage Wayne's friends to visit him, keep him company and let him enjoy the only pleasure he was to have for the remaining of his days.

It is fashionable nowadays to discuss the successes achieved in the rehabilitation of spinal cord injured patients, and to urge the community to further finance all research efforts along this line. Such worthy projects are commendable. However, much of the publicity has consisted of demonstrations of paraplegics walking thanks to the intensive "rehabilitation" given to them. These demonstrations are misleading because it gives patients false hopes, since no amount of rehabilitation has made it possible for complete paraplegics to walk independently and functionally. Those people whose pictures show them ambulating with crutches and electrically operated braces, walk for a few minutes in front of the camera and with great difficulty. Once the "commercial" is completed they return to their wheel chairs, which they all have discovered to be the most effective, practical and inconspicuous mean of locomotion.

Research in this field, is needed and obviously worthwhile. It should not be used, however, to perpetuate false hopes. Up to now, laboratory research has not found clinical applications. Paraplegics and quadriplegics of today will remain paralyzed, much the same way their counterparts throughout the millennia remained paralyzed till they finally died. We need to regain objectivity, and acknowledge that practical ambulation of the complete paraplegic has not yet been made possible. Retaining objectivity, in the final analysis, is in the best interest of all parties [2]

I frequently walk through the rehabilitation ward of our hospital where I transfer some of my joint replacement patients, and observe victims of hemiplegia. I assume many of them are diabetics and suffer from hypertension. Regardless of their age or degree of disability, they are all "treated" with a variety of psychological, physical and occupational therapy modalities.

How often, however, do we stop to address the issue of rehabilitation of the stroke patient in an objective manner? Why is it that we refuse to be candid about the effectiveness of the treatments we prescribe? Since we now know that the elimination of spasticity or flaccidity and recovery of function are not dependent on the intensity or duration of physical therapy modalities, but on the type and degree of brain damage, why not just simply concentrate on the improvement of the psychological devastation that surrounds the episode, and attempt to make this unfortunate group of people as functional as possible as one handed individuals? If they are fortunate enough to spontaneously regain function in the involved extremities, helping them in their recovery is appropriate. Those who within a relatively short time do not show any signs of improvement, encouraging them to accept the physical impairment and learning how to feed and dress themselves without assistance and to walk with the aid of a below-the-knee brace and a cane, should be the extent of the rehabilitation efforts. Such an approach is possible in most instances without running the risk of depriving them of hope and creating unnecessary depression. Hiding the truth from disabled adults is synonymous to deceiving them and feeding them false hopes, that once recognized bring about anger and frustration [3]

On a recent occasion I was asked by a family to see a patient in consultation, prior to the performance of a surgical procedure a colleague of mine had planned for the following week. It was an elderly lady approaching 90 years of age. She had had several surgical procedures aimed at resolving problems related to a failed total hip arthroplasty. Pain was not a problem; she was feeble and barely able to assist with her transfer to a wheel chair. Her x-rays, however, had demonstrated what appeared to be a nonunion of a fracture of the femur over which a graft had been placed earlier. The nonunion site was spanned by a long cemented prosthetic stem, which seemed to be well fixed.

Why did my colleague find it necessary to treat a non-existing "problem", and fail to realize the additional harm he may have done in the process? What difference does it make if a painless nonunion is seen on the x-rays of a 90 year old non-ambulatory woman, and whose correction is not going to restore the lost youth and vigor necessary for successful return to ambulation? I see similar situations with some frequency. What blinds us to reality? Is it just a lost lack of common sense, or simply greed?

I was once deeply involved in amputation surgery and rehabilitation of the amputee. I enjoyed the experience a great deal, as I found the subject challenging and rewarding. I learned the importance of preserving, if at all possible, the knee joint. Most elderly above-the- knee amputees find it very difficult, if not impossible, to function with an artificial prosthesis. Many of these people are victims of severe peripheral vascular disease, and many of them are diabetics. The usually accompanying neurological deficit makes their mental and physical skills deficient [4]

In the care of the elderly and debilitated above-the-knee amputees, why not just provide them with a sound evaluation; allow them to appreciate what is involved in the process of rehabilitation, and then explain to them that ambulation with a the prosthesis is unrealistic, impractical and frustrating; and that the use of a wheelchair is the best, simplest and most effective means of locomotion. Often an intelligent and candid conversation between the patient, the physician and the prosthetist is sufficient to convince the patient of the reality of his situation. Most patients dealt with in this manner readily accept the advice and go on with their lives with fewer frustrations and less bitterness.

ADDENDA

During one of my visiting professorships I witnessed an episode, which, probably better than most others, exemplifies our frequent lack of objectivity in managing patients with musculoskeletal conditions. In front of a large number of spine surgeons attending a symposium, a girl of approximately 16 years of age was brought to the stage and her condition described. Basically, her problem consisted of severe residuals from poliomyelitis she had suffered while still a very young child. She had been left with profound paralysis of her lower extremities, dislocated hips, marked scoliosis and significantly impaired respiratory function. She sat in an old wheel chair, and her deformities made her look like a pretzel. The expression in her face, if there was an expression at all was that of loneliness and sadness.

The spine experts discussed in her presence the number of surgical procedures that could be performed. The more aggressive ones, concerned over her impaired vital capacity suggested that correction of several of her problems be attempted during one single surgical procedure. Spinal instrumentation to correct the scoliosis should be followed by open reduction of the dislocated hips. I was asked to comment on this subject, which was totally foreign to my areas of expertise. My suggestion was to leave the child alone; to buy her a new wheelchair and a television set; to make her as comfortable as possible; to give her love and attention; and to allow nature to take its course.

I doubt there was anything wrong with my recommendations. Life had been cruel to this pathetic young girl. Why subject her to all kind of radical and heroic surgeries, which at best could minimally improve her vital capacity and extend her life by a brief time, and nothing else? Her miserable existence would be just as miserable as it was before the proposed painful, frightening and debilitating surgery.

Much progress has been made in recent years in the field of limb re-implantation. However, oftentimes re-implantation suggests a lack of objectivity. We hear stories about mangled upper extremity limbs being reattached in situations when the patient has lost a great deal of blood, is comatose and is still bleeding when taken to the operating room. Despite the critical status, which suggests the likely possibility of permanent brain damage, the re-implantation is carried out. Does it make sense to re-implant the limb through a procedure likely to take several hours of additional anesthesia, and therefore increase the changes of brain damage? Is it not more realistic to simply control the bleeding, replace the lost blood as quickly as possible, and complete the amputation? Why not accept the amputation as a small price for being alive and with normal mental capacities? Is it not a loss objectivity to do otherwise?

Visiting a Trauma Center in a European country some years ago, I was told that every patient with a fracture that came to the Emergency Room was treated surgically. Suspecting that the sweeping statement could have been an exaggeration and that some fractures were treated conservatively, I asked if surgery was performed for all Colles fractures, metacarpal and phalangeal fractures. The response was the same: all of them. Still suspicious that some fractures had spared surgery I asked if clavicle fractures were always operated upon, even though the surgeons knew that the vast majority of these fractures heal uneventfully without internal fixation. The affirmative answer called for some editorializing on the part of my young host. He said to me, "Doctor Sarmiento, you don't seem to realize that things have changed. Patients no longer accept the residual lump on the shoulder that those fractures leave behind". There was no need for me to pursue the issue any further: I had just learned of the most accelerated Darwinian evolution of human behavior ever recorded in the history of dear *Homo sapiens.* Is it not a lack of objectivity to perform surgery in all fractures, simply because of the erroneous perception that perfect re-approximation of broken bones is always synonymous with perfection?

Loss of objectivity in the management of fractures has reached a high pitch. No one could question that through new surgical/technological advances the care of fractures has improved dramatically in recent decades. However, one gets he impression that we have surmised that if an effective technique has been developed for the care of certain fractures, the same technique should be used for all other fractures. The example of the clavicle fracture speaks volumes: if intramedullary nailing offers great advantages over nonsurgical treatment of fractures of the femur and tibia, it means that the same modality should be used for clavicle fractures, even though it does not offer clinical advantages over conservative treatments.

Orthopaedist trained during the last two decades have been led to believe that any resulting deviation from the normal is a complication. Therefore no angulation, shortening or rotation of a fractured bone, no matter how insignificant and inconsequential requires a surgical intervention. The same applies to even the mildest incongruity in a traumatized joint. They believe that anatomic restoration is essential for the achievement of "good" results. Though the restoration of congruity is a desirable goal, and if possible should be attempted, such an accomplishment does not guarantee a perfect clinical result. Oftentimes, the acceptance of some incongruity is better than an extensive dissection of tissues and the further damage of comminuted intraarticular fragments. The teachings and beliefs that surgery is always superior to nonsurgical treatments is converting the orthopaedist/scientist of the past into a cosmetic surgeon of the skeleton.

The Colles fracture has received increased close attention in recent years. The availability of small internal fixation devices has resulted in a virtual epidemic of open osteosynthesis of these fractures. This trend has taken place by ignoring a long history of "good" clinical results obtained with conservative treatments. The fact that certain Colles fractures are best treated surgically does not lessen my criticism of the absence of objectivity.

Why is it that we are willing to subject an elderly individual with a simple Colles fracture to a surgical procedure, to be followed by prolonged and expensive rehabilitation therapy, simply because the surgical operation will prevent a painless mild deformity? Or is it because the improved articular surface incongruity will prevent the development of osteoarthritic changes, which are more likely to be of a radiographic nature, rather than clinical? What has prompted us to close our eyes and ears to the fact that asymptomatic radiological arthritic changes and mild angular deformities are not "problems" that justify surgical interventions, which are expensive, require prolonged therapy and are not likely to render better clinical outcomes? The exchange of a frequently unnoticed "lump" for a usually noticeable surgical "scar" may well be a thoughtless trade-off.
Obsession with the need to get away from long surgical incisions, likely to have been fueled by experiences with closed intramedullary nailing and arthroscopic surgery, has gained

momentum. Only time will tell if such efforts eventually proved to have been a meaningful improvement. Recently we learned through the media that total hip replacement can be carried out through a very small incision, rather than through the traditional longer one. It is claimed that the micro-surgical approach makes the recovery faster and more spectacular.

Assuming that this masochistic approach to hip surgery can be done without running the risks of not obtaining adequate exposure of the femur and acetabulum, increasing the likelihood of nerve injury, traumatizing forcefully compressed soft tissues, and other complications; what is the real gain other than the publicity that the "new" operation is likely to generate? That the patients so treated have less pain and are able to function faster sounds like a good argument. However, the pain that necessarily accompanies any surgical procedure, whether performed through a small or large incision, we know how to manage by the administration of appropriate narcotics and analgesics. Patients whose hips are replaced through the tradition surgical approach are taught to walk with a walker or crutches on the first post-operative day. At the end of the third day, most patients are still in the hospital walking with assistance and requiring only a few "pain pills." Two or three days later they return home, independent and rarely necessitating pain medications other than an occasional mild analgesic.

I am sure that the pain that accompanies the surgery performed through a smaller incision lasts just as long as the one produced by a longer incision. But let us assume that "pain" last one day less and that the patient becomes "more comfortable" one day sooner. What difference do those few hours and fewer pain pills make? Can they justify the risks mentioned above?

A few years ago I served as guest speaker at the annual meeting of a small Latin American Orthopaedic Society. A very distinguished "shoulder surgeon" form the United States was the other guest speaker. I spoke about total hip surgery, and he of endo and total joint replacement of the shoulder, emphasizing acute fractures of the humeral head. During one of his very erudite conferences he asked for a "show of hands" regarding the number of such procedures the local orthopaedists had performed. Not a single hand went up. During the discussion period they stated that in their experience, patients treated by traditional close methods improved over a period of time; that their shoulder ended up with some limitation of motion, but were functional and for the most part painless. The high cost of prostheses militated against their usage, and wanted to know if the functional results from prosthetic replacement were superior to their simpler and more primitive approaches. Can we honestly state that the average eventual function and comfort experienced by patients with acute fractures of the humeral head, when treated with prostheses, are greater than in those patients managed by nonsurgical means?

During the coffee break I asked the shoulder surgeon if our presentation of material not practical in countries with deficient infrastructure and major financial limitations made any sense. I have asked myself that question many times under similar circumstances and wondered why we continue to do it. Have we sacrificed objectivity for the sake of ego satisfaction?

ADDENDA

Outcome Studies is now a household word and such a method of recording and reporting clinical results is being suggested as the only and best one. Such statement is probably correct since the system adds credibility to reports dealing with results obtained with different treatments. I have, however, expressed concern over he manner in which some outcome studies are being conducted, and have insisted that the transition from traditional means of reporting data into the new one should be gradual; and that some of the ongoing Outcome Studies were making matters unnecessarily complicated by indulging in meaningless minutia and requiring expensive and time-consuming work for their preparation [5]. I suggest that anyone planning to conduct an outcome study first read Jonathan Swift' *Gulliver Travels,* for the British author did describe in a entertaining way the foolishness of those who spend a lifetime "nit picking" and ignoring what is important in life.

We seem to sincerely believe that orthopaedics will soon be entering the most revolutionary period in history. Developments in molecular biology and the initial completion of the Genome Project augur an inevitable Nirvana. Though such an exciting possibility may become a reality in the future, it is also probable that the road to success will be a lumpy one, and that the anticipated glorious goal was nothing more than a mirage. Which means that the spectacular growth we witnessed in the last few decades were in fact the Golden Days of our profession. Therefore we should regain and maintain objectivity and take advantage of the wealth of knowledge we have inherited from previous generations, and incrementally build upon it.

1. Callahan, D. *What kind of Life. The limits of Medical Progress.*
   Simon and Schuster, 1990

2. Sarmiento, A.
   Orthopaedics and Industry: The piper, the payor and the tune
   Annals Canadian Royal College of Surgeons
   Vol. 33, No. 3:144-149, 2000.

3. Sarmiento, A. and Mc Collough, N.C.
   The Orthopaedist and Rehabilitation.
   Clin. Orthop. & Rel. Res. 41:111-115, 1965.

4. McCollough, N.C., Jennings, J.J. and Sarmiento, A.
   Bilateral Below-the-Knee Amputation in Patients Over Fifty Years of Age.
   J. Bone and Joint Surg. 54A: 6, September, 1972.

5. Sarmiento, A.
   Letter to the Editor Jour of Orthopaedic Trauma.
   (Ref. Christopher Colton discussion of M. Swiontkowski article on Outcome Studies) Jour Orthopaedic Trauma, Vol. 15, no. 6:455-458. Journal of Bone and Joint Surg. 2002

REFERENCES:

1. Sarmiento, A. and Grimes, H.A.
   The Use of the Austin Moore Vitallium Prosthesis in the Treatment of Acute Fractures and Other Diseases of the Hip. Review of 123 Consecutive Cases. Clin. Orthop. & Rel. Res. 28:120-131, 1963.

2. Sarmiento, A.
   Intertrochanteric Fractures of the Femur. 150 Degree Angle Nail Plate Fixation and Early Rehabilitation: A Preliminary Report of 100 Cases. J. Bone and Joint Surg. 45A:706-722, 1963.

3. Sarmiento, A. and Kalbac, J.H.
   Vitallium Austin Moore Prosthesis for Subcapital Fractures of the Femur in the Aged: Experience with 200 Consecutive Cases. J. Western Pacific Assoc. 1:179-188, 1964.

4. Sarmiento, A.
   The Brachioradialis as a Deformity Force in Colles' Fractures.
   Clin. Orthop. & Rel. Res. 38:86-92, 1965.

5. Mann, RJ and Sarmiento, A.
   Two Plate Fixation of the Femoral Shaft. Clin. Orthop. & Rel. Res. 38:93-99, 1965.

6. Sarmiento, A. and Kalbac, J.H.
   The Rehabilitation of The Fractured Hip in the Aged.
   J. South. Med. Assoc. 58:428-431, 1965.

7. Sarmiento, A. and Mc Collough, N.C.
   The Orthopaedist and Rehabilitation.
   Clin. Orthop. & Rel. Res. 41:111-115, 1965.

8. Sarmiento, A., Gilmore, R.E., Jr. and Finneston, A.
   A New Surgical/Prosthetic Approach to the Syme's Amputation:
   A Preliminary Report. Artific. Limbs, April, 1966.

9. Sarmiento, A., Uricchio, J.J. and May, B.J.
   The Patellar Tendon Bearing Prosthesis. Experiences in the Geriatric Amputee.
   Clin. Orthop. & Rel. Res. 50, January, 1967.

10. Sarmiento, A. and Sinclair, W.F.
    Application of Prosthetic/Orthotic Approach to Orthopaedics.

REFERENCES

Artific. Limbs, 1967.

11. Sarmiento, A.
A Functional Below-Knee Cast for Tibial Fractures.
J. Bone and Joint Surg. 59:5, 1967.

12. Sarmiento, A.
Avoidance of Complications of Internal Fixation of Intertrochanteric Fractures: Experiences with 250 Consecutive Cases.
Clin. Orthop. & Rel. Res. 53, July-August, 1967.

13. Sarmiento, A.
Recent Trends in Lower Extremity Amputation: Surgery and Rehabilitation.
Nursing Clinics of North America, 2-3, September, 1967.

14. Sarmiento, A.
Bracing of Fractures.
Fifth Workshop Panel, CPRD, National Academy of Sciences, 16-20, 1968.

15. Sarmiento, A.
Fracture Bracing.
Workshop Fracture Bracing, CPRD, National Academy of Sciences, 1-10, February, 1968.

16. Sarmiento, A., May, B.J. and Sinclair, Wm.F.
Immediate Postoperative Fitting of Below-Knee Amputations.
Physical Therapy, 50:110-18, 1970.

17. Sarmiento, A.
The Geriatric Amputee: Principles of Management.
Contributor. National Academy of Sciences, Washington, D.C., 1971.

18. Sarmiento, A., Infante, J., Jr., and Sinclair, Wm.F.
Development of Refined Fitting Procedures for Lower Extremity Prostheses.
Bulletin of Prosthetics Research, Department of Medicine and Surgery, Veteran's Administration, Washington, D.C., 112-129, Fall, 1971.

19. McCollough, N.C., Shea, J.D., Warren, W.D., Sarmiento, A.
The Dysvascular Amputee.
Current Problems in Surgery, October, 1971.

20. Enis, J.E. and Sarmiento, A.
The Pathophysiology and Management of Pressure Sores.
Orthop. Rev. II:10, 25-34, 1973.

REFERENCES

21. Sarmiento, A.
    Basic Problems in Hip Surgery.
    Orthop. Rev. 6:4,43-45, 1977.

22. Sarmiento, A.
    Reflections on Total Hip Arthroplasty.
    Orthop. Rev. 6:4,83-85, 1977.

23. Clarke, I.C., Gruen, T.A., Tarr, R.R. and Sarmiento, A.
    Finite Element Analyses Studies of Total Hips versus Clinical Reality.
    International Conference in Finite Elements in Biomechanics.
    Vol. II:487-511, 1980.

24. Tarr, R. R. and Sarmiento, A.
    Anatomic Three-Dimensional Finite Element Model of the Proximal Femur with Total Hip Prosthesis.
    International Conference in Finite Elements in Biomechanics. 146:28-36, 1980.

25. Tarr, D., Clarke, I., Gruen, T., Sarmiento, A.,Espiritu, E., Hull, D., McGuire, P., Sew Hoy, A. and McKellop, H.
    Total Hip Femoral Component Design
    Orthopaedic Review, XI, 23-35, 1982.

26. Gruen, T.A. and Sarmiento, A.
    Bone/Biomaterial Interface in Orthopaedic Joint Implants. Key reference in biomaterials
    J. Biomed. Mat. Res. Vol. 18, 577-599. 1984.

27. Sarmiento, A.
    An Agenda for Surgeons and Industry
    Orthopaedic Network News, Vol. 4, No. 1, Jan. 1993.

28. Sarmiento, A.
    Education is key to nonoperative care.
    Academy News, Vol 47, no. 2, April, 1999. March

29. Sarmiento, A.
    Don't shun the non-surgical treatment of Fractures.
    AAOS Bulletin, April, 2000.

30. Sarmiento, A.
    Immobilization of Fractures: Non-surgical Fracture Care
    Orthopaedics Today. Jan. 2000: 15-16.

REFERENCES

31. Sarmiento, A. and Warren, W.D.
    A Reevaluation of Lower Extremity Amputations.
    J. Surg. Gyn. and Obstet. 129:799-802, 1969.

32. Sarmiento, A., McCollough, N.C., III, Williams, E.M. and Sinclair, W.F.
    Immediate Post-surgical Prosthetic Fitting in the Management of the Upper Extremity Amputee.
    Artific. Limbs. 12-1: 14-16, Spring 1968.

33. McCollough, N.C., III., Sarmiento, A. and Williams, E.M.
    Functional Considerations of the Above-Knee Geriatric Amputee.
    Artific. Limbs. 2-2: 28-35, Autumn 1968.

34. Sheplan, L., Lieberman, B. and Sarmiento, A.
    Patellar Tendon Bearing Prosthesis: Value of Routine X-ray Studies.
    South. Med. J. 62:10, 1969.

35. Sarmiento, A.
    Immediate Post-surgical Fitting in the Management of Upper Extremity Amputees.
    Prosthetics International. 3-8, 1969.

36. Marriotti, J.R., Mann, RJ and Sarmiento, A.
    Two Plate Fixation of Fractures of the Femoral Shaft.
    South. Med. J. 62:11, 1969.

37. Sarmiento, A.
    Lower Extremity Amputation: The Impact of Immediate Post-surgical Prosthetic Fitting.
    Clin. Orthop. 68:22-31, 1970.

38. Sarmiento, A.
    A Functional Below-Knee Brace for Tibial Fractures.
    J. Bone and Joint Surg. 52A:2, 295-311, 1970.

39. Sarmiento, A. and Williams, E.M.
    The Unstable Intertrochanteric Fracture: Treatment with a Valgus Osteotomy and I-Beam Nail Plate.
    J. Bone and Joint Surg. 52A:7, 1309-1313, 1970.

40. McCollough, N. C. and Sarmiento, A.
    Functional Prognosis of the Hemiplegic.
    J. Florida Med. Assoc., November, 1970.

REFERENCES

41. Sarmiento, A.
    Functional Bracing of Tibial and Femoral Shaft Fractures.
    Clin. Orthop. & Rel. Res. 82:2-13, 1972.

42. Sarmiento, A.
    Austin Moore Prosthesis in the Arthritic Hip
    Clin. Orthop. & Rel. Res. 82:14-23, 1972

43. Sarmiento, A.
    A Modified Surgical-Prosthetic Approach to the Symes' Amputation.
    Clin. Orthop. & Rel. Res. 85:11-15, 1972.

44. McCollough, N.C., Jennings, J.J. and Sarmiento, A.
    Bilateral Below-the-Knee Amputation in Patients Over Fifty Years of Age.
    J. Bone and Joint Surg. 54A:6, September, 1972.

45. Sarmiento, A.
    Unstable Intertrochanteric Fractures of the Femur.
    Clin. Orthop. & Rel. Res. 92:77-85, 1973.

46. Sarmiento, A. and Laird, A.
    Posterior Fracture-Dislocation of the Femoral Head.
    Clin. Orthop. & Rel. Res. 92:143-146, 1973.

47. Enis, J., Hall, M. and Sarmiento A.
    Methylmethacrylate in Neoplastic bone destruction.
    The Hip Society, Volume 1. Pp.118-138, Mosby, 1983.

48. Sarmiento, A.
    Fracture Bracing.
    Clin. Orthop. & Rel. Res. 102:152, 1974.

49. Sarmiento, A., Latta, L., Zilioli, A. and Sinclair, Wm. F.
    The Role of Soft Tissues in the Stabilization of Tibial Fractures.
    Clin. Orthop. & Rel. Res. 105:116-129, 1974.

50. Sarmiento, A.
    Functional Bracing of Tibial Fractures
    Clin.Orthop. & Rel. Res. 105:202-219

51. Sarmiento, A. and Wolf, M.
    Subluxation of Peroneal Tendons: Case Treated by Re-routing Tendons Under Calcaneo fibular Ligament.
    J. Bone and Joint Surg. 57A:1, 115-116, 1975.

REFERENCES

52. Sarmiento, A., Pratt, G.W., Berry, N.C. and Sinclair, Wm. F.
    Colles' Fractures - Functional Bracing in Supination.
    J. Bone and Joint Surg. 57A:3,311-317, 1975.

53. Sarmiento, A., Cooper, J.S., Sinclair, W.F.
    Forearm Fractures - Early Functional Bracing - A Preliminary Report.
    J. Bone & Joint Surg. 57A:297-304, 1975

54. Sarmiento, A. and Elkins, R.W.
    Giant Intra-Articular Osteochondroma of the Knee.
    J. Bone and Joint Surg. 57A:560-561, 1975.

55. Jennings, J.J., Harris, Wm. H. and Sarmiento, A.
    A Clinical Evaluation of Aspirin Prophylaxis of Thromboembolic Disease after Total Hip Arthroplasty.
    J. Bone and Joint Surg. 57A:7,926-928, 1976.

56. Sarmiento, A., Kinman, P.B., Murphy, R.B. and Phillips, J.G.
    Treatment of Ulnar Fractures by Functional Bracing.
    J. Bone and Joint Surg. 58A:8,1104-1107, 1976.

57. Sarmiento, A., Schaeffer, J.F., Beckerman, L., Latta, L.L. and Enis, J.E.
    Fracture Healing in Rat Femora as Affected by Functional Weight Bearing. J. Bone and Joint Surg. 59A:3,369-375, 1977.

58. Sarmiento, A., Kinman, P.B., Galvin, E.G., Schmitt, R.H. and Phillip P.G.
    Functional Bracing of Fractures of the Shaft of the Humerus.
    J. Bone and Joint Surg. 59A:5, 596-601, 1977.

59. McCollough, N,C., Vinsant, Jr., J.E. and Sarmiento, A.
    Functional Fracture Bracing of Long Bone Fractures of the Lower Extremity in Children.
    J. Bone and Joint Surg. 60A:3,314-319, 1978.

60. Sarmiento, A. and Gerard, F.M.
    Total Hip Arthroplasty for Failed Endoprosthesis.
    Clin. Orthop. & Rel. Res. 137, Nov.-Dec., 1978.

61. Tarr, R., Lewis JL, Jaycox D., Sarmiento, A, Schmidt, J., Latta, L.L.
    Effect of materials, stem geometry, collar-calcar contact on stress distribution on the proximal femur with total hip.
    Trans. Orthop. Research Soc. 4:24, 1079

REFERENCES

62. Tarr, R.R., Clarke, IC, Gruen T., Sarmiento, A.
    Predictions of cement-bone failure criteria. Three-dimensional finite element models versus clinical reality of total hip replacements.
    (Finite Elements in Biomechanics. Simon BR (ed) London, John Wiley and Sons, Ltd. 1981

63. Tarr, RR, Clarke, I, Gruen T, Sarmiento, A, Espiritu, E, Hull, D, McGuire, P., Sew Hoy, A., McKellop, H.
    Total Hip Femoral Component Design. Stem Characterization, Experimental Studies, and Analytical Modeling for Orthopaedic Surgeons. Orthopaedic review.
    Vol. XI, No. 12, December 1982.

64. Sarmiento, A., Zych, G.A., Latta, L.L. and Tarr, R.R.
    Clinical Experiences with a Titanium Alloy Total hip Prosthesis: A Posterior Approach.
    Clin. Orthop. & Rel. Res. 144, October, 1979.

65. Sarmiento, A., Kinman, P.B. and Latta, L.L.
    Fractures of the Proximal Tibia and Tibial Condyles.
    Clin. Orthop. & Rel. Res. 145:136-145, 1979.

66. Sarmiento, A., Turner, T.M., Latta, L.L. and Tarr, R.R.
    Factors Contributing to Lysis of the Femoral Neck in Total Hip Arthroplasty.
    Clin. Orthop. & Rel. Res. 145:208-212, 1979.

67. Sarmiento, A., Zagorski, J.B. and Sinclair, Wm.F.
    Functional Bracing of Colles' Fractures: A Prospective Study of Immobilization in Supination versus Pronation.
    Clin. Orthop. & Rel. Res. 146:175-187, 1980.

68. Latta, L.L., Sarmiento, A. and Tarr, R.R.
    The Rationale of Functional Bracing of Fractures.
    Clin. Orthop. & Rel. Res. 146:28-36, 1980.

69. Sarmiento, A., Latta, L.L..
    Functional Bracing in the management of Tibial Fractures. The intact Fibula.
    AAOS Symposium on Trauma to the Leg and its sequelae.
    Moore T.M. (Ed) The C. Mosby Comp. 1981.

70. Sarmiento, A., Mullis, D.L., Latta, L.L., Tarr, R.R. and Alvarez, R.
    A Quantitative Comparative Analysis of Fracture Bracing Under the Influence of Compression Plating versus Closed Weight Bearing Treatment.
    Clin. Orthop. 149:232-239, 1980.

REFERENCES

71. Clarke, I., Gruen, T., Gustillo, R., Harris L.J., Latta, L., Lynch, M.H., McKellop, H., Ranawat, C., Rostoker, W., Sarmiento,, A.
The use of Titanium alloys in orthopaedic medicine. 1981 Zimmer, pp1- 40

72. Clarke, I., McKellop, H., McGuire, P., Okuda, R., Sarmiento, A.
Wear of Titanium alloys and ultra-high polyethylene combination.
AATM SPT; 706:136-147, 1983

73. Chandler, D.R., Glousman, R., Hull, D.B., McGuire, P., Kim, I.S., Clarke, I.C. and Sarmiento, A.
Prosthetic Hip Range of Motion and Impingement. The Effects of Head and Neck Geometry.
Clin. Orthop. & Rel. Res. 166:284-291, 1982.

74. Clarke, I., McKellop, H., Mcguire, P., Okuda, R. and Sarmiento, A.
Wear of Ti-6Al-4V Implant Alloy and Ultrahigh Molecular Weight Polyethylene Combinations. In: Titanium Alloysin Surgical Implants.
H. Luckey, F. Kubli, Eds., ASTM STP 796, ASTM, Philadelphia, 136-147, 1983 .

75. Chandler, D.R., Tarr, R.R., Gruen, T.A. and Sarmiento, A.
Radiographic Assessment of Acetabular Cup Orientation: A New Design Concept.
Clin. Orthop. 186:60-64, 1984.

76. Sarmiento, A., Sobol, P.A., Sew Hoy, A.L., Racette, W.L. and Tarr, R.R.
Prefabricated Functional Braces for the Treatment of Fractures of the Tibial Diaphysis.
Bone and Joint Surg. 66A:9, 1328-1339, 1984.

77. Tarr, R.R., Garfinkel, A.I. and Sarmiento, A.
The Effects of Angular and Rotational Deformities of Both Bones of the Forearm: An in vitro Study.
J. Bone and Joint Surg. 66A:1,65-70, 1984.

78. Tarr, R.R., Sew Hoy, A.L., Racette, W.L. and Sarmiento, A.
The Evolution and Current Status of Functional Fracture Bracing.
Report of 2800 Tibial, Humeral, Ulnar Fractures.
Orthop. Rev. 13:1, 25-45, 1984.

79. Wagner, K.S., Tarr, R.R., Resnick, C. and Sarmiento, A.
The Effect of Simulated Tibial Deformities on the Ankle Joint During the Gait Cycle.
Foot and Ankle, 5:3:131-141, 1984.

REFERENCES

80. Sarmiento, A. and Gruen, T.A.
Roentgenographic Analysis of 323 STH Total Hip Prostheses with Low Modulus Titanium Alloy Femoral Components: Two to Six Year Follow-up.
J. Bone and Joint Surg. 67A:1, 48-56, 1985.

81. Moore, T.M., Lester, D.K. and Sarmiento, A.
The Stabilizing Effect of Soft Tissue Constraints in Artificial Galeazzi Fractures.
Clin. Orthop. & Rel. Res. 194:189-194, 1985.

82. Tarr, R.R., Resnick, R.T., Wagner, K.W. and Sarmiento, A.
Changes in Tibiotalar Joint Contact Areas Following Experimentally Induced Tibial Angular Deformities.
Clin. Orthop. 199:72-80, 1985.

83. Baumgarten, M., Bloebaum, R.D., Ross, S.D.K., Campbell, P. and Sarmiento, A.
Normal Human Synovial Fluid. Osmality and Exercise -Induced Changes.
J. Bone and Joint Surg. 67A:9, 1336-1339, 1985.

84. Sarmiento, A., Nataranjan, V., Gruen, T.A. and McMahon, M.
Radiographic Performance of Two Different Total Hip Cemented Arthroplasties.
Orthop. Clin. N.A.1-11, 1988.

85. Shanfield, S., Campbell, P., Baumgarten, M., Bloebaum, R., and Sarmiento, A.
Synovial Fluid Osmolality in Osteoarthritis and Rheumatoid Arthritis.
Clin. Orthop. & Rel. Res. 235:289-295, 1988.

86. Gellman, H., Kauffman, D., Lenihan, M., Botte, M.J. and Sarmiento, A.
An in vitro Analysis of Wrist Motion: The Effect of Limited Intercarpal Arthrodesis and the Contributions of the Radiocarpal and Midcarpal Joints.
J. Hand Surg. 13A:3, 278-383, 1988.

87. McKellop, H., Ebramzadeh, E., Fortune, J. and Sarmiento, A.
Stability of Subtrochanteric Femoral Fractures Fixed with Interlocking Intramedullary Rods. In Femoral Intramedullary Rods: Clinical Performance and Related Laboratory Testing. ASTM STP 1008, J.P. Harvey, A.U. Daniels and R.F. Games,
Editors, ASTM, Philadelphia, 1988.

88. Sarmiento, A., Gersten, L.M., Sobol, P.A., Shankwiler, J.A. and Vangsness, C.T.
Tibial Shaft Fractures Treated with Functional Braces.
J. Bone and Joint Surgery. 71(B)4:602-609, 1989.

89. Sarmiento, A., Horowitch, A., Aboulafia, A. and Vangsness, C.T., Jr.
Functional Bracing for Comminuted Extra-Articular Fractures of the Distal Third of the Humerus.

REFERENCES

J. Bone and Joint Surg.,72(B)2:283-287, 1990.

90. McKellop, H.A., Sarmiento, A., Schwinn, C.P. and Ebramzadeh, E.
In Vivo Wear of Titanium Alloy Hip Prosthesis.
J. Bone and Joint Surg., 72(A)4:512-517, 1990.

91. Sarmiento, A., Ebramzadeh, E.,Gogan, W.J. and McKellop, H.A.
Acetabular Cup Containment and Orientation in Cemented Total Hip Arthroplasties.
J. Bone and Joint Surg. 72(B)6:996-1002, 1990.

92. Sarmiento, A., Ebramzadeh, E., Gogan, W.J. and McKellop, H.A.
Total Hip Arthroplasty with Cement: A Long-Term Radiographic Analysis in Patients Who Are Older Than Fifty Years.
J. Bone and Joint Surg., 72(A):1470-1476, 1990.

93. McKellop, H., Ebramzadeh, E., Niederer, P.G. and Sarmiento, A
Comparison of the Stability of Press-Fit Hip Prostheses Using a Synthetic Model Femur
J. Orthop. Res., 9:297-305, 1991.

94. Hoffman, R., McKellop, H.A., Sarmiento, A., Lu,B., and Ebramzadeh.E.
Dreidimensionale Messung von Frakturspaltbewegungen Unfallchirug.
94:395-400, 1991.

95. McKellop, H.A., Sigholm, G., Redfern, F.C., Doyle, B.,Sarmiento, A. and Luck, V.J., Sr.
The Effect of Simulated Fracture-Angulation of the Tibia on Cartilage Pressures in the Knee Joint
J. Bone & Joint Surg. 73-A: 1382-1390, 1991.

96. Llinas, A., Sarmiento, A., Ebramzadah, E., Gogan, W.J. and McKellop, H.A.
Total Hip Replacement after Failed Hemiarthroplasty or Mould Arthroplasty
J. Bone & Joint Surg. Vol. 73-B:912-907, 1991

97. Kuschner, S.H., Orlando, C.A., McKellop, H.A. and Sarmiento, A.
A Comparison of the Healing Properties of Rabbit Achilles Tendon Injuries at Different Levels
Clin. Orthop. & Rel. Res. 272: 268-273, 1991,

98. Brien, W. and Sarmiento, A.
Vascular Injury during Cementless Total Hip Arthroplasty
Orthopaedics, Vol. 15, No. 1: 54-56, 1992.

REFERENCES

99. Sarmiento, A., Ebramazadeh, E., Brys, D. and Tarr, R.
    Angular Deformities and Forearm Function
    J. Ortho. Res. 10-1: 121-133, 1992.

100. Sigholm, G., Gendler, E., McKellop, H., Marshall, G.J., Sarmiento, A..
     Early Healing of Four Different Ethylene Oxide Processed Bone Preparations in Rabbit Ulnar Segmental Defects.
     Acta. Orthop. Scand. 63 (2): 177-182, 1992.

101. Sarmiento, A.
     Staying the Course
     First Vice President's Address, AAOS.
     J. Bone & Joint Surg. 73-A:479-483, 1991.

102. McKellop, H.A., Sarmiento, A., Brien, W. and Park S.
     Interface Corrosion of a Modular Head total Hip Prosthesis.
     J. Arthroplasty. Vol. 7-No. 3:291-294, September 1992.

103. McKellop, H.A., Hoffmann, R., Sarmiento, A., Lu, B. and Ebramzadeh, E.
     Control of Motion of Tibial Fractures with Use of a Functional Brace or an External Fixator.
     J. Bone & Joint Surg. 75A:1019-1025, July 1993.

104. Llinas, A., McKellop, H., Marshall, J., Sharpe, F., Lu, B. Kirchen, M. and Sarmiento, A.
     Healing and Remodeling of Articular Incongruities in a Rabbit Fracture Model.
     J. Bone & Joint Surg. 75-A: N. 10, 1508-1523, October 1993.

105. Sarmiento, A.
     Editorial. Orthopaedics at a Crossroads
     J. Bone & Joint Surg. 75-A, No. 2: 159-161

106. Sarmiento, A.
     Editorial. Certificates of Added Qualifications in Orthopaedics.
     J. Bone & Joint Surg. Nov. 1994. .

107. Schneiderman, G., Meldrum, R.D., Bloebaum, R.D., Tarr, R. and Sarmiento, A.
     The Interosseous Membrane of the Forearm Structure and Its Role Galeazzi Fractures.
     J. Trauma. Vol 35, N.6., December 1993.

108. Ebramzadeh, E., Sarmiento, A., McKellop, H., Llinas, A.and Gogan, W.
     The Cement Mantle in Total Hip Arthroplasty: Analysis of Long Term Radiographic Results.
     J. Bone & Joint Surg. Vol 76-A: N.1, 77-87, January 1994.

REFERENCES

109. McKellop, H.A., Llinas, A., and Sarmiento, A.
Effects of Tibial Malalignment on the Knee and Ankle.
Ortho. Clin. N. Amer., Vol. 25: No. 3, July 1994

110. Ebramzadeh, E., McKellop,H., Dorey, F., Sarmiento, A.
Challenging the Validity of Conclusions Based on p-values Alone: A Critique of contemporary clinical research design and methods. American Academy of Orthopedic Surgeons. Instructional Course Lectures, 1994.

111. McKellop, H., Llinas, A., Sarmiento, A.
Effects of tibial malalignment of the knee and ankle. Orthopaedic Clinics of North America, 25 (3), 415-423, 1994.

112. McKellop, H., Campbell, P., Park, S-H., Schmalzried, T., Grigoris, P., Amstutz, H. and Sarmiento, A.
The Origin of Submicron Polyethylene Wear Debris in Total Hip Arthroplasty.
Clin. Ortho. & Rel. Res., Vol. 311, Feb. 1995.

113. Sarmiento, A., Sharpe, M.D., Ebramzadeh, E., Norman, P. and Shankwiler, J.
Factors Influencing the Outcome of Closed Tibial Fractures Treated with Functional Bracing.
Clin. Ortho. & Rel. Res., No. 315, pp 8-24, 1995.

114. Lovasz, G., Llinas, A., Benya, P., Bodey, B., McKellop, H., Luck, Jr Sarmiento, A.
Effects of Valgus Tibial Angulation on Cartilage Degeneration in the Rabbit Knee.
J. Ortho Res., 13:846-853, 1995

115. Kirchen, M., O'Connor, M., Gruber, H., Sweeney, J., Fras, I., Stover, S., Sarmiento, A. And Marshall G.
Effects of Microgravity on Bone Healing in a Rat Fibular Osteotomy Model.
Clin. Ortho. & Rel. Res., No. 318, pp 231-242, 1995.

116. Park, S-H., Cassim, A., Llinas, A., McKellop, H. and Sarmiento, A.
Technique for Producing Controlled Closed Fractures in a Rabbit Model.
J. Ortho. Res., 12:732-736, 1996

117. Sarmiento, A., McKellop, H., Llinas, A., Park, S-H, Lu, B., Stetson, W.,Rao, R.
Effect of Loading and Fracture Motions on Diaphyseal Tibial Fractures.
J. Ortho. Res., 14:80-84, 1996

118. Lu, Z., Ebramzadeh, E., McKellop, H. and Sarmiento, A.
Stable Partial Debonding of the Cement Interfaces Indicated by a Finite Element Model of a Total Hip Prosthesis.

REFERENCES

J. Ortho. Res., 14:238-244, 1996.

119. Puig, S., Dupuy, D., Sarmiento, A., Boland, G., Grigoris, P. and Greene, R.
Articular Muscle of the Knee: A Muscle Seldom Recognized on MR Imaging.
Am. J. Roent., Vol. 166, No. 5, May 1996.

120. Sarmiento, A. Orthopaedics and Industry. Point counter point.
Orthopaedics. January, 1997.

121. Sarmiento, A. The Orthopaedist and Fracture Care.
Journal of orthopaedic Trauma .
Vol. 11, No.6, pp 389-391, August, 1997

122. Sarmiento. A, Ebramzadeh, E.
The Stainless Steel and Titanium Alloy Femoral Prostheses Total Hip Arthroplasty Outcomes. Finerman at al. 41-53
Churchil Livingston, 1997

123. Sarmiento, A., Latta, L.L. Zych, G., McKeever, P., Zagorsky, J.
Functional Bracing of Isolated Ulnar Fractures. Journal of orthopaedic Trauma, Vol. 12 , No. 6 , pp. 420-424, 1998.

124. Sarmiento, A. Commentary: Responding **to** change.
Journal Bone and Joint Surg. Vol 80A, No. 4, April 1998: 601-603

125. Lovasz, G., Llinal, A. Benya, P. Sarmiento, A., Luck, J.
Cartilage Changes Caused by a Coronal Surface Step off in a rabbit model.
Clinic Orthop. Number 354, pp 224-234, 1998

126. Park, Sang-Hyun, O'Connor, K., McKellop, H. and Sarmiento, A.
The Influence of active Shear or Compressive Motion on Fracture-Healing.
Jour. Bone and Joint Surg. Vol. 80A, No. 6; 868-878, June 1998

127. Sarmiento, A. Latta, L.L.
Functional Fracture Bracing. A review Article.
Journal AAOS. Volume 7, No.1:66-78, 1999.

128. Park, Sang Hyun, O'Connor, K, Sung, R., McKellop, H., Sang-Hyun and Sarmiento A
Comparison of healing Process in Open Osteotomy Model and closed fracture model.
Journal of Orthopedic Trauma, Vol 13, No.2, pp. 114-120, 1999

REFERENCES

129. Sarmiento, A.
 The Devil is in the details
 Journal of Orthopedic Trauma. Vol 13, No. 5, pp 1-5
 June-July, 1999.

130. Llinas, A., Sarmiento, A., Ebramzadeh, E., Park, S.H., McKellop, H., Campbell, P.
 Mechanism of failure with an Uncemented, all polyethylene Socket.
 Clin.Orthop. Rel. Research. #362, pp. 145-155, 1999.

131.
132. Sarmiento, A., Goswami, D.K.
 Thromboembolic Prophylaxis with use of Aspirin,, Exercise and Graded Elastic Stockings or Intermittent Compression Devices in Patients Managed with Total Hip Arthroplasty.
 Journal of Bone and Joint Surgery. Vol.81-A, No. 3, 339-March,1999

133. Sarmiento, A.
 On the Rational Treatment of Fractures.
 Dialogue (AO/ASIF) Vol. 12, Issue II, 21-23. December 1998.

134. Lovasz, G., Park, S, Benya P., Llinas, A., Bellyei, A., Luck, J.V., Sarmiento, A.
 Characteristics of Cartilage Degeneration in an Unstable Joint with a Coronal Surface Step-off. Jour. of Research. (In press)

135. Sarmiento, A.
 Prognostic correlations in Tibial Fractures.
 Journal of Orthopedic Trauma. Vol. 14 # 3 pp: 199-205, 2000

136. Sarmiento, A., Latta, L.L., Zagorski, J., Capps, C., Zych, G.
 Functional Bracing of Humeral Shaft Fractures.
 Journal of Bone and Joint Surgery. Vol. 82-A, No. 4 pp:478-486, 2000.

137. Sarmiento, A.
 Responding to Change.
 Journal of Bone and Joint Surg. Vol. 81-A, No.9, pp1346-48, 1999.

138. Sarmiento, A.
 On the Rational Treatment of Fractures
 Vet. Comp. Orthop. Trauma. 1999; 12: 156-58.

139. Sarmiento, A. Waddell and Latta, L.L.
 Fractures of the Humeral Diaphysis.
 J. Bone and Joint A. An Instructional Course, 2000.

REFERENCES

140. Sarmiento, A.
On the Future of Orthopaedics-I am concerned.
Journal of Orthopaedic Science.(Japan)
5: 425-430, 2000

140 Sarmiento, A., M.D.
Orthopaedics and Industry: The piper, the payor and the tune
Annals Canadian Royal College of Surgeons
Vol. 33, No. 3:144-149, 2000

141 Sarmiento and T. Watson
Functional Bracing of diaphyseal humeral Fractures and Operative Management of Humeral shaft Fractures. FRACTURES Diagnosis and Treatment. McGraw-Hill.
pp: 1225-242, 2000.

142 Sarmiento and Goswami, D.K.
Thromboembolic disease prophylaxis with use of aspirin, exercise and graded elastic stockings or intermittent compression devices in patients managed with total hip arthroplasty.
Bulgarian Journal of Orthopaedics and Traumatology. Vol. 36. 1.2000: 401-413
Reproduced from the J. Bone and Joint Surg. Vol 81A No. 3, March 1999.

143 Sarmiento
Thoughts on the impact of Technology on Orthopaedics
Journal of Bone and Joint Surg. (British, Nov. 2000)

144 Sarmiento.
On the Rational Treatment of Fractures
Veterinary Journal of Orthopaedics Traumatology, 12: 2, 2000.
Reproduced from AO/ASIF DIALOGUE . Vol.12, Issue II: 21-23, Dec. 1998

145 Sarmiento, A.
The future of our specialty.
Acta Orthopedica Scandinavica. 71 (6): 574-579, 2000

146 Sarmiento, A., Latta, L.L.
Functional Bracing in Delayed Union and Nonunion of the Tibia
International Journal of Orthopaedics, November, 2002

147 Martinez, A., Sarmiento, A. Latta, L.L.
Functional Bracing of Closed Fractures of the Proximal Third of the Tibia.
(In Press) Clinical Orthopaedics and related research.

148 Sarmiento, A.
Tibial Fractures
Journal of Orthopaedic trauma. Letters to the editor. (response)

REFERENCES

Vol. 14, No. 7:523-525, 2000.

149 Sarmiento, A.
Respondiendo al Cambio
Revista Colombiana de Orthopedia y Traumatologia.
August, 1999. Translation from JBJS "Responding to Change"

150 Sarmiento, A.
The impact of Technological progress in Orthopaedics
Is it all for the better?
Indian Orthopaedic Society Journal (In press), 2000

151 Sarmiento, A.
Ethics in the Relationship between Orthopaedics and Industry.
Clinical Orthopaedics (in Press). AAOS sponsored.

152 Sarmiento, A,
The challenges facing our Profession.
A tribute to Sir John Charnley. (In Press)

153 Sarmiento, A.
On the Education of the Orthopaedic Resident.
Clinical Orthopaedics. No. 400, pp.259-263, May 2002

154 Lovasz, G., Park, S.H., Ebramzadeh, E., Benya, P., Llinas ,A., Bellyei, A., Luck, J., Sarmiento, A.
Characteristics of degeneration in an unstable knee with a coronal surface step-off.
J. Bone Joint Surg.(Br) 2001; 82-B:428-3

155 McKellop, H., Rostlund T., Ebramzadeh, E., Sarmiento, A.
Wear of titanium 6-4 alloy in laboratory tests and in retrieved human joint replacements.
Titanium in Medicine. D.M. Brunette at al Editors. 748- 770, Springer, 2001.

156 Sarmiento, A.
On the Education of the Orthopaedist.
Letter to the Editor JBJS (A) on Simon's Pres. AOA Address, 2001
JBJS-A Vol. 83-A, No. 9:1427-28

157 Sarmiento, MD.
Antithrombotic Therapy. Letter to the Editor. Journal American College of Surgeons. Vol. 193, No. 4:465-466, Oct. 2001

158 Sarmiento, A.
Is Titanium so bad? Letter to the Editor J. Bone Joint Surg. (B).
Letter to the Editor. 2001

REFERENCES

159   Sarmiento, A.
Thoughts on the role of orthopaedics in basic Research.
Jour Bone and Joint Surg (A) Vol. 83-A:1002-04, 2001

160   Sarmiento, A.
Letter to the Editor Jour of Orthopaedic Trauma.
(Ref. Christopher Colton discussion of M. Swiontkowski article on Outcome Studies) Jour Orthopaedic Trauma, Vol. 15, no. 6:455-458.

161   Sarmiento, A.
Letter to the Editor. Industry and Medicine
JAMA July 18, 2001, Vol.186, No3: 302

162   Sarmiento, A, Latta, L.L
Functional Fracture Bracing. J. of Musculoskeletal diseases. In Press.

163   Sarmiento, A., Waddell, James P., Latta, Loren.
Diaphyseal Humeral Fractures: Treatment Options.
An Instructional Course, AAOS
J Bone and Joint Surg. Vol. 83-A, No. 10: 1566-1579

164   Lovasz, Gyorgy, Park, San Hyun, Nalint, Lehel, Bellyei, Arpad, Luck, J.V., Sarmiento, A.
Regeneration of surface gap within an articular step-off
Jour Bone Joint Surg. (British). In press

165   Sarmiento, A.
Closed Treatment of Distal Radius Fractures.
Techniques in orthopaedics"
15(4):2994-304, Lippincott, Williams and Wilkins, 2001

166   Sarmiento, A
Have we lost Objectivity?
Jour. Bone and Joint Surgery. Vol. 84A, No. 7, July 2002, pp 1254-58

167   Sarmiento, A
Subspecialization. Has it been all for the better?
(Journal of Bone and Joint Surg 85-A. Number 2:369-373, 2003

168   Sarmiento, A.
Ethical Concerns Regarding the Orthopaedic Relationship with Industry.
British Orthopaedic News. (A bridged version of AOA talk, 2001

REFERENCES

169   Sarmiento, A.
The Relationship between Orthopaedic and Industry must be reformed.
Clinic. Orthop Number 412: 38-44, July 2003.

170   Sarmiento, A, Burkhalter, M., Latta, L.L...
Functional Bracing in the treatment of delayed union and nonunion of the Tibia.
International Jour. of Orthopaedics, 27:26-29, 2003.

171   Sarmiento, A.
Letter to the Editor, Is Titanium so bad?
JBJS Vol.84-B, No.6 pp 931, August 2002

172   Sarmiento, A
A Joint Replacement Registry.
A Letter to the Editor of the Academy Bulletin.
May, 2002.

173   Martinez, A., Latta, L.L. Sarmiento, A. Functional Bracing of Fractures of the Proximal Tibia.
Clinical Orthopaedics. (Accepted)

174   Sarmiento, A.
Reflections on Post-graduate Orthopaedic Fellowships.
(Submitted JBJS (B) 2002

175   Sarmiento, A. Waddell, J., Latta, L.L.
Diaphyseal Humeral Fractures.
AAOS Instructional Course Lectures. Vol. 51:257-269, 2002February

176   Sarmiento, A.
Letter to the Editor JBJS-A
Prophylaxis Against Venous Thromboembolic Disease: Cost and Controversy
J Bone Joint Surg. Vol 84-A, No. 12: 2305-06, 2002

177   Sarmiento, A.
Letter to the Editor, J. Of Trauma. Tibial Plateau Fr.
Volume 16, No. 6, pp. 447-448.

178   Sarmiento, A.
Medicine needs more ethics and less business.
Orthopaedics Today. Vol 22, No. 6, pp 4-5

179   Sarmiento, A.
Academy Finances. Letter to the Editor Academy Bulletin,
AAOS Bulletin, February 2003. pp 9

REFERENCES

180 Sarmiento, A
New PhRMA Code. Letter to the Editor AAOS Bulletin
AAOS Bulletin, February 2003, pp 9

181 Sarmiento, A
Mechanism of Injury may affect Outcome after Tibial Shaft Fracture.
Letter to the Editor. J Bone Joint Surg 85-A. no. 3:571-572, 2003

182 Sarmiento, A, Latta, L.L.
Closed fractures of the Distal Third of the Tibia Treated with a Functional Brace.
(Submitted to Clinical Orthopaedics), 2003.

183 Sarmiento, A.
One possible Downside of the Information Revolution.
(Special Interest) J Ort Trauma. Vol. 17, No. 6 p: 466, 2003

184 Sarmiento, A. Latta, L.L
Three to thirty-three year follow-up of 135 Charnley arthroplasties.
(In preparation) J Bone Joint Surg.

185 Sarmiento, Latta, L.L.
A physiological approach to the prevention of femoral lysis in cemented femoral components. (in preparation) J Bone Joint).

186 Goswami, K, Sarmiento, A.
Infection in Total Hip replacement
Clinical Orthopaedics, (Submitted, 2003)

187 Sarmiento, A, Latta, L.L.
A high failure rate in a series of hybrid total hip arthroplasties.
Clinical Orthpopaedics (Submitted 2003)

188 Sarmiento, A.
Bare Bones- The Tale of The Surgeon.
Prometheus, 2003.

Books by the Author

- Closed Functional Treatment of Fractures, English, Japanese, German -1981, Portuguese, Spanish- 2001, Chinese-1984
- External Fixation and Functional Bracing- 1989.
- Function Fracture Bracing: Tibia, Humerus, and Ulna-Manual- 1995.
- Functional Fracture Bracing: A Manual- 2002
- Bare Bones: A Surgeon's Tale, 2003
- Medicine challenged.- 2003
- Passion can win the Day-2005
- Candid Reflections on Medicine and other topics-2005
  Displasia en el desarrollo de la cadera 2006
- Fracture Casting and Bracing (Manual)-2008
- The Nonsurgical Treatment of Fractures in Contemporary Orthopedics- 2012
- Orthopedics: Seeking a Balance- 2012
- Hip Surgery: An Odyssey- 2012
- The Rocky Journey of Modern Medicine- 2014
- Life worth Living - 2016
- Ruminations of an Orthopaedist- In Progress -2017
- The nonsurgical Treatment of Fractures in Contemporary Orthopaedics.-Second edition.-In progress-2017

BIOGRAPHIC SKETCH

Augusto Sarmiento, M.D. is Emeritus Professor and chairman of the departments of Orthopaedics at the Universities of Miami and Southern California. He was a founding member of the Hip Society and the International Hip Society. His productive academic career includes the presidency of the Hip Society and the American Academy of Orthopaedic Surgeons. He has published over a fifteen books, over 400 articles and chapters; lectured in forty different countries and received four of the most coveted orthopaedic awards in the United States: the Elmer Nix Ethics Award of the Clinical Orthopaedic Society, the Kappa Delta Award, the Nicholas Andre Award, and the John Charnley Award.

His research activities involved a number of areas, particularly those of fracture healing and care, and traumatic and degenerative conditions of the hip.